THE CENTURY SOCIAL SCIENCE SERIES

SOCIAL PROBLEMS

BY

JOHN LEWIS GILLIN, Ph.D.

Professor Emeritus of Sociology, University of Wisconsin

CLARENCE G. DITTMER, Ph.D.

Professor Emeritus of Sociology, New York University

ROY J. COLBERT, Ph.D.

Professor of Economics and Sociology, University of Wisconsin

NORMAN M. KASTLER, M.A.

*Assistant Professor of Economics and Sociology,
University of Wisconsin*

THIRD EDITION

D. APPLETON-CENTURY COMPANY
Incorporated
NEW YORK   LONDON

PREFACE

It is in a sober frame of mind that we present this, our third edition. We naturally are gratified with the sustained interest which our book has received through the years. Yet our satisfaction necessarily is overshadowed completely by contemplation of the deathly struggle in which the world is now engaged and of the tremendous problems of reconstruction which are to follow. Indeed, it is likely that the world as our generation has known it will not arise again, that "reconstruction" is hardly the word.

Nevertheless, whatever is to come must be projected inevitably from the institutions and relationships now existing, and students still must be made aware of the elements of the culture in which they live. For these reasons, we have undertaken the third edition of this book at the present time. There has been no attempt to speculate on future problems beyond what the facts of the present reveal. We have confined our effort to analyzing important American social conditions which must be dealt with, perforce, whatever the future may bring.

Most of the materials of the previous editions have been retained, although the arrangement has been changed and some chapters have been combined. Many of the chapters have been extensively rewritten, and all have been brought up to date. Much of the labor of the present edition has devolved upon our fourth collaborator, who joins with the senior authors at this time.

The Authors

CONTENTS

FIGURES

TABLES

SOCIAL PROBLEMS

Chapter 1

THE BACKGROUND OF SOCIAL PROBLEMS

THERE ARE TWO ASPECTS to personality, the *I* and the *We*. It is hardly possible to think of the one without at the same time including the other. Nevertheless, we generally find ourselves viewing life's situations pretty much from the *I* point of view, especially when we are confronted with what seem to us extremely perplexing *personal* problems—the problem of finding the sort of work that satisfies our special aptitudes and interests and pays us a sure and adequate income; the problem of establishing ourselves in a happy relationship with others; the problem of keeping pace with what a constantly changing world exacts of us. But, at the same time, we cannot escape thinking of these problems in terms of *We*. It is the consciousness of our membership in an aspiring and achieving social group, and of the praise and blame of our fellows, that impels us to put forth our best efforts. Even then we have moments when it seems that our utmost powers are inadequate.

Likewise, in the lives of nations and of peoples there come tense times—trying periods of unrest and of great change, periods that call for earnest and far-seeing leaders, for wise decisions, and for sweeping, decisive action. We are to-day living in one of these periods.

Many times, especially during the past two thousand years, the peoples of the Western world have gone through such periods of social upheaval and vast social change. It was one of these periods that crumbled the morally bankrupt Roman Empire and swept civilization into the Dark Ages. It was another of these periods that broke the spell of the Middle Ages and gave rise to the modern state, the Renaissance, and the Reformation. It was such a period that developed the democratic philosophies, established popular government in these United States, crushed monarchy in France, and abolished slavery. The opening of the twentieth century marked the beginning of still another period of major social upheaval, perhaps the most severe and far-reaching ever experienced.[1] The changes of this period not only go to the very foundations of Western civilization, but they are shattering the traditional patterns of human relations in the Orient. As recent war-torn years have

[1] Roscoe Lewis Ashley, *Our Contemporary Civilization* (New York, 1935), pp. 36–45.

3

shown, even the First World War was but an incident in this period
of sweeping change; it was but the beginning of a world-wide struggle
among peoples, nations, and ideas to gain a dominant position in the
new era that is sure to emerge as life becomes adapted to the vast changes
taking place.[2]

Each of these great epochs of history altered the social structure of
nations and, in part at least, transferred from one group to another the
responsibility for directing the affairs of men. In general each epoch
tended to center an increasing amount of authority within reach of the
common people. While these changes in the social structure and in the
source of authority were the more obvious, they were perhaps of less
real significance than the vast changes in the ideas and the ideals of
the people. In fact the *ideas* and the *ideals* changed and gathered strength
and conviction before the old forms and structures gave way to the new.

The review of these great changes in social thought which ushered in
each succeeding epoch is of itself a subject worthy of many volumes
and can scarcely be more than hinted at in our present study.[3] From the
start it is important to remember that with each succeeding period came
increasing consideration of the *general welfare;* little by little, in most
civilized countries, the old idea that the individual citizen existed for
the welfare of the government and the ruling class, gave way to the
idea that the primary function of the government should be the fur-
therance of the general welfare of the people; the *ideal* of equal opportunity and equal justice to all gradually uprooted the ideas of *divine
right,* special privilege, and arbitrary authority.

While the Western world has in the past thus struggled through great
and perplexing problems, never has it been confronted with as vast and
complicated problems as it faces to-day. Furthermore, the experience
of the past offers but slight aid to the understanding and approach to
the solutions of the large-scale problems of to-day. It is little wonder,
therefore, that so many of our thinkers and writers view the present-day
situation with dire apprehension. Some see in the modern trend the
symptoms of moral decay that characterized the declining days of the
Roman Empire and the maddening days of the French Revolution.[4]

[2] *Ibid.,* pp. 46–73; Harold Rugg, *The Great Technology* (New York, 1933).
[3] The student who is interested in this phase of the subject will find the following
books of interest and value: Harry E. Barnes, *Contemporary Social Theory* (1926);
J. P. Lichtenberger, *Development of Social Theory* (1923); Charles Ellwood, *History of Social Philosophy* (1938).
[4] H. G. Wells, *The Salvaging of Civilization;* G. Ferrero, *Ancient Rome and
Modern America;* G. LeBon, *The World in Revolt.*

Some feel that the unprecedented development and expansion on the *material* side of culture has already reached a crisis, and that further progress is hardly possible until the *non-material* culture, especially the *spiritual* forces which form the sound basis of human relations, have had a chance to grow and develop accordingly.[5]

What, then, is the outlook? Is it true that our general culture containing the civilization of which we Americans are so proud is top-heavy with materialism, and is heading for a fall? Are we certain that the strain and stress of our times and the seeming ruthless disregard for the old standards are true symptoms of national decay, or may they be merely the evidence of "growing-pains" and thus a healthy promise of the development of a better social order? Whatever the outlook, we cannot escape the obligation of directing our best thought and our most earnest efforts toward the conservation of progress and the improvement of the common welfare.

Even though the problems of to-day are greater and more complicated than those which faced the generations of the past, we are in a better position to cope with them than were the people of any other period. No other generation has been so well equipped with the social sciences, or had such quick and effective means of communicating their ideas to every man, woman, and child in the population. May we not hope, therefore, that a better understanding of society, and of the great changes that are taking place in it, will help us to understand better our present-day problems and point the way to sound solutions? But, just what is the nature of this thing which we call society? What is its relation to culture? What is the nature of the vast changes which mark this age as being the most baffling age of all history? What is the nature of the difficulties confronting mankind to-day? What is the relation of sociology to the study of social problems? We must have answers to these questions if we are to understand the backgrounds of present-day social problems. To this end it is important that we have a common interpretation of the terms and concepts generally used in sociological studies.

SOCIAL LIFE AND SOCIAL GROUPS

We have already used the word *social* a number of times, but it is so often used loosely that it is necessary to make clear our meaning. Fre-

---

[5] Edward East, *Mankind at the Crossroads* (1923); Graham Wallas, *The Great Society* (1917); Raymond Fosdick, *The Old Savage and the New Civilization* (1927); Roscoe Lewis Ashley, *Our Contemporary Civilization* (1935), pp. 567 ff.

quently it is used in the sense of being separate from and in contradis-
tinction to the *individual* and *personal*. "In its largest sense it denotes
that which pertains to the collective aspect of humanity, to society in
its widest and vaguest meaning. . . . Again, *social* may mean what pertains to immediate intercourse, to the life of conversation and face-to-
face sympathy—sociable in short. . . . In a third sense the word means
conducive to the collective welfare, and thus becomes nearly equivalent
to *moral*, as when we say that crime or sensuality is *unsocial* or *antisocial*." [6] However, in none of these meanings is the term *social* set over
against the terms *individual* and *personal* any more than the *whole* is set
against one of its *parts*. It is this last meaning that comes closest to our
interpretation of the term—"conducive to the collective welfare"—relationships, and products of relationships, that are believed to foster and
promote *group life*, and to insure *group survival*.

Some sort of group life was ever essential to survival, and for this
reason the group has always taken a hand in the shaping and directing
of the life of its individual members. From the very beginning *group
selection* has had an important part in the creating of what we call
human nature—down through the ages the life of the individual has
been circumscribed by an ever-expanding group life, and those individuals whose lives were not in accord with what was believed to be the
best interests of the group were speedily killed, exiled, or shut off from
contact with their fellows. Thus, this constant weeding-out process has
tended to make man increasingly social. If group life could remain static,
if it could cease expanding and cease becoming more and more complex,
we would doubtless soon be rid of those individuals whose propensities
are *antisocial*. However, it is the very nature of healthy group life to
grow; and this growth exacts of the individual an ever-rising standard
of social qualities. Often this growth produces shifts in the standards
and requirements of the group, so that what was once condemned or
disapproved may later be encouraged and rewarded. To-day, because
of the growing complexity of relationships and the increasing interdependence, group selection takes on new and more far-reaching importance.

Simple Group Life. Glancing back over American history we can see
how the society in this country has expanded from the simple group of
the pioneer days to the complex and interwoven nation of to-day. In
those early days the family was held together by the home. The home
was the center of practically all social life, and family loyalties and

[6] C. H. Cooley, *Human Nature and the Social Order* (1902), p. 4.

loyalty to the home were the chief basis of appeals to action in behalf of either the community or the colony. But the dangers and the hardships of pioneer life brought increasing emphasis upon broader coöperation, and soon the people began to think in terms of their settlements and towns. The towns then became the dominant unit of community life, especially in New England. While they were supposed to be under the jurisdiction of the colonial governments, they were, as a matter of fact, practically independent, and were often resentful of, even opposed to, the orders from the colonial governors. Town loyalty became very intense, even to the extent of excluding from the town "strangers" and "foreigners" whose occupations or family connections might be suspected or unwanted. People from other towns and other settlements were treated with much the same suspicion and aloofness that are generally accorded the Oriental or South European immigrant to-day.

These early colonial and pioneer settlements were practically self-sufficient. They raised all their own food, made all their own clothing, and had their own respective brands of religion; each household provided its children with whatever education was felt necessary; the town meetings and the town board of selectmen made the laws and regulations that were imposed upon the inhabitants, affecting even the minutest details of their lives. Those were days when social life was indeed personal. The treatment accorded the poor, the sick, or the orphan depended to a large extent upon how the community regarded the particular individual and his family. If he came from a "good" family and belonged to industrious, pious folk, he might receive the kindly, neighborly consideration that he needed; if, however, he "had no family," or belonged to people known to be "idlers," or if he was careless about attending church or happened to differ in belief from the rest of the community, then the attention given was indeed meager. The treatment accorded the offender and the insane was likewise personal and severe. When whipping-post, stocks, or branding iron seemed too mild, the culprits were "run out of town." Life in these small, self-sufficing communities was simple. There was no complex division of labor; the government was direct and understood by all; there were no experts or specialists, no daily papers or magazines laden with advertising to make people dissatisfied with their drab existence or to lead their interests away from the slow-moving life of the town.

These small, self-sufficing, painfully personal pioneer communities typify what we have called *simple group life*. While these patterns of social life were especially characteristic of pioneer days, they have left an indelible impress upon American culture and to no small extent color and influence our attitudes and conduct even to-day.

Expansion of Group Life. Had it not been for the independence of the colonial groups, and their developing opposition to the dictates of the colonial governors, it is doubtful if the Revolutionary War would ever have taken place. But this common opposition to outside interference in local affairs furnished the stimulus for the expansion of social life. It was the appeals to the local loyalties that brought the colonists together to fight for the cause of liberty. Gradually the local loyalties expanded into State loyalties, and the States began to share with the local communities the obligations and the interests of the people. The emphasis on States' rights clearly indicated that the social mind had not yet grasped the idea of nation, nor did it appreciate the attempts of the Federal Government to share obligations and services with the States.

Then, the different sections of the United States began to absorb the loyalty that for a time had been given to the States. The contrast in social and economic life between the States of the North and those of the South gradually crystallized and became a severe strain on the efforts to create and develop a national life; in the North, because of the more rapid industrial development, localities and States had largely become subordinate to national loyalty; but the South still believed in States' rights, though much sentiment had been transferred to the section. It took the War Between the States, and a long and trying period of reconstruction, to make these United States really conscious of national unity and national interdependence. It is too much to say that this expansion into a solid national life is entirely complete; there is still no little evidence of sectionalism. Nevertheless, there is a growing recognition of the fact that we are living together not as States, but as a nation. Many of the functions that were only a short time ago regarded as belonging exclusively to the States are now being urged upon the Federal Government: regulation of business and trade, uniform labor legislation, adequate provisions for social security, raising the standards of educational opportunity, suppression of crime, meeting the problems of unemployment, promoting conservation of natural resources, insurance of bank deposits—these are but a few examples of this tendency.

Even before nationalism has been fully achieved, there looms upon the horizon another great expansion—*internationalism*. Since industry and commerce depend upon the natural resources which are so unevenly distributed among the nations of the earth, and since communication and travel have thrown the peoples of the world into closer contact with one another, there has been a growing consciousness of the inadequacy and the futility of national isolation. But can we melt down our national loyalties into the common mold of an international society? The melting down of the lesser loyalties was by no means easy. Each expansion was purchased at a great cost; each was entered upon with grave misgiving, with "reservations," and in the face of "irreconcilables." However, these great expansions of social life are now practical realities. May we not, therefore, in spite of the world scene to-day, expect that an international society will some day also be a reality? [7]

Now it should be borne in mind that this expansion of social life not only has a direct causal relation to social problems, but also is a troublesome factor in our achieving sound and timely solutions to those problems. Our thinking has by no means kept pace with the expansion of our social and economic contacts and relationships. Consider the incongruities of our present-day attempts to judge social conduct of this motor age by standards and ideals that were suited to saddle-bag days, or our futile efforts at directing and regulating modern economic life by principles designed to meet conditions of the eighteenth century, or our pathetic attempts to grapple with the menacing problems of international affairs in terms of the cracker-box ideas of "Main Street."

Relation of Expansion to the Functions of Group and Social Life. While each expansion was made at the expense of the smaller cycles of social life, claiming some of the interest, service, and loyalty that formerly were centered exclusively in the smaller cycles, these smaller cycles have not disappeared. They have indeed been modified, but they continue to be of fundamental importance. Each type of group has certain functions that cannot be absorbed or completely transferred to larger groups. Thus, for example, the functions of the family have been greatly modified, as we shall see when we come to study the problems of family life,[8] but nevertheless the family still remains a primary and fundamental group. The neighborhood and the community have also been radically changed, but they too still retain many important functions. No two neighborhoods or communities are alike. Each presents a variety of conditions and circumstances different from all others, making it necessary for the State and the nation to leave much to be done by these smaller groups in order that social life may be better adjusted to the local needs. But just what functions should remain the obligation of the smaller groups, and which functions would be better performed

---

[7] Roscoe Lewis Ashley, *Our Contemporary Civilization* (1935), Ch. XV.
[8] See Chapter 12.

by the larger groups? These questions lie at the bottom of many social problems and constitute an important issue in many of the major social adjustments.[9]

Perhaps nowhere are the effects of expansion of *social* life more dramatically evinced than in the small-town and rural communities of America. Here, more than anywhere else, we see the "minds that were made up" in the "good old days" frantically struggling against the demands of the expanded economic and social life of to-day. Scarcely a generation ago these small towns and villages held practically a monopoly sway over fairly well-defined trade areas; to-day not only are they in competition with the towns and villages of neighboring trade areas, but even more do they feel the competition of the larger cities and of national advertising. It is no longer necessary for people to be satisfied with the meager and inefficient services of Main Street. Likewise, a generation ago the countryside was dotted with the little one-room schools and neighborhood churches designed to serve the less expanded social life of that day. Fortunately these one-room schools are rapidly disappearing and education is moving into well-equipped "consolidated schools" that serve a wider area and more nearly meet the educational needs of expanded social life. But to a large extent the little churches still remain, many of them abandoned or opened for services only now and then. The religious life either finds expression in more distant churches that are better equipped and more "up-to-date," or gives way to the many other absorbing interests that expanded social life affords.[10] Even though the effects of expanded group life in other aspects of national life may be less obvious than in the small-town and rural communities, they are of no less influence.

Relation of the Social Life of Expanding Groups to the Individual. The group, as we have already noted, circumscribes and to a large extent directs and shapes the lives of its members. However, not all aspects of group life exert equal pressure upon the individual; some aspects affect him more directly and more intimately than others. This fact becomes more evident as group life expands and becomes more and more complex.

Even in the family the individual is not the center. He is more concerned with certain family functions than he is with others; some obli-

[9] "Our Cities, Their Role in the National Economy," Report of the National Resources Committee (Washington, D. C., June, 1937).

[10] See Walter Burr, *Small Towns* (1929); Hornell Hart, "Changing Social Attitudes and Interests," Report of Hoover Committee on Recent Social Trends (1933), I: 397 ff.

gations and duties come closer to him and affect him more directly than do others (Fig. 1). Likewise in each cycle of social life the individual cannot escape being somewhat affected by even the most remote factors and conditions. But he is more interested in and more concerned about those matters closest to him, and which he feels most keenly and sees most clearly. Thus, he may not be actively interested in a playground for his neighborhood if his children are already grown. He may not

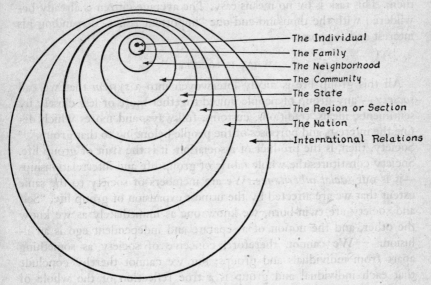

The Individual
The Family
The Neighborhood
The Community
The State
The Region or Section
The Nation
International Relations

FIG. 1.—THE RELATION OF THE INDIVIDUAL TO THE EXPANSION OF GROUP LIFE

like the ugly bill-boards that clutter the vacant lots, but he is not generally much concerned until a bill-board stares into his windows. He may not be much interested in liquor control, being neither a drinker nor the son of a drinker. As owner of an automobile he is strong for good roads. He is interested in the impending coal strike because he would be out of employment if the mill did not receive its regular supply of coal. He is opposed to unrestricted immigration because he is convinced the foreigner would take his place at a lower wage, and he would have to hunt a new job or sell his car. A generation ago his parents came to this country from Germany; he is, therefore, interested in international relations affecting Germany, but he is little interested in what happens in China.

So it goes. No two individuals are affected just alike by the expansion
of social relationships. Matters that one individual feels are incon-
sequential and remote to his interests may be considered of first importance and fundamental to another (Fig. 1). For this reason it is difficult to get the *whole* public behind social reform. The major task of
the reform leader, therefore, consists in presenting the needed changes
in such terms as will bring them as near home as possible to each individual, so that he will feel that he *can* and *must* do something about
them. This task is by no means easy. The average citizen is already be-
wildered with the thousand-and-one "important issues" demanding his
interest and support.

WHAT IS SOCIETY? [11]

All this group life is nicely interwoven into a *system* that we call
society—"any group of people united together more or less closely by
sentiments, ideals, traditions, customs, folkways, and mores which define the interests and purposes of the people belonging to that group." [12]
Society, then, is the product of association; it is the fruit of group life.
Society constitutes the whole fabric of group life and interrelationships
—it is our *social inheritance*. We are members of society to the same
extent that we are affected by the utmost expansion of group life. "Self
and society are twin-born, we know one as immediately as we know
the other, and the notion of a separate and independent ego is an illusion." [13] We cannot, therefore, conceive of society as something
apart from individuals and groups; but we cannot thereby conclude
that each individual and group is a true reflection of the whole of
society. Professor Cooley likens society to a picture that is made up of
so many square inches of painted canvas.[14] Each square inch of canvas

---

[11] The term *society* is often used loosely. Sometimes it is used as a synonym for
the word *mankind* or the word *humanity*. Often it is used to indicate leisure-class
pretenses. It is frequently used instead of the word *association* or the word *organization*, as in The Society for the Friendless, or The Society for the Prevention of
Cruelty to Children. Then, too, it is often used to indicate various groups, as in
American Society, German Society, and New England Society, or to indicate various group aims, as "sympathetic society," "socialistic society," "despotic society,"
and "acquisitive society."

As to the nature of society there are numerous theories—for example, the so-
called "social-contract theory," the "social-organism theory," and the "political-
animal theory." But whatever the theory, no one doubts the existence of society.

[12] J. L. Gillin and F. W. Blackmar, *Outlines of Sociology* (1930, 3rd Edition),
p. 16.

[13] C. H. Cooley, *Social Organization* (1910), p. 5.

[14] C. H. Cooley, *Human Nature and the Social Order* (1902), p. 3.

represents an individual or a group. If we take up and examine these bits of canvas one at a time, we see that each reflects something that is characteristic of the picture; but the whole theme of the painting, its organization and structure, is not thus made apparent. We must view the canvas as a whole, each square in its proper place, to understand fully and appreciate what it is all about. Thus, by centering our attention upon individuals and groups, we cannot get an accurate view of the *system* and *organization* that make up society.

When we view society this large way we see that it is composed of four outstanding and closely interwoven fundamentals: *groups, uniformities, standards,* and *institutions.*[15] The chief difference between the complex society of to-day and the society of the past is to be found in the changes that *time* and *progress* have made in these fundamentals. Furthermore, it is in these fundamentals that the roots of the present-day social problems are embedded. Consequently, if we are to understand fully the nature and scope of the great problems of society to-day, we must study them in relation to these fundamentals of society.

Groups and Their Relation to Society. We have just noted the rôle of group life in human affairs, how American society has developed through the expansion of the simple group life of pioneer days, and where the individual stands with reference to the cycles of expanded group relationships. However, if we are to understand the forces at work in present-day social life, it will be necessary for us to examine more in detail the nature of the groups that compose present-day society.

Broadly speaking, social groups may be divided into two general classes: (1) the *primary* groups, those characterized by intimate face-to-face association and coöperation: the family, religious bodies, friendship circles, neighborhood and play groups—groups that "are fundamental in forming the social nature and ideals of the individual";[16] (2) the *secondary* groups, or those with which the individual becomes identified through his participation and association in the expanded social and economic life—labor organizations, business and industrial associations, civic and welfare bodies, political parties and movements, learned societies, federations of women's clubs, and the thousand-and-one other "organizations," "associations," "clubs," "movements," "federations," "leagues," and "blocs."[17] Many of these secondary groups are channels

[15] E. A. Ross, *Principles of Sociology* (1938, 3rd Edition), Part X.
[16] C. H. Cooley, *Social Organization* (1920), p. 23.
[17] Gillin and Blackmar, *op. cit.* (1930), p. 155.

through which like-minded primary groups find a broader and fuller expression.

The primary groups have an important rôle in present-day social maladjustments. It is through them that the emotional attitudes of individuals are so largely formed, and old customs, traditions, prejudices, and ideals are handed from one generation to the next. Each of these groups is a culture-carrier and strives to perpetuate certain social characteristics. Consequently, each is somewhat different from the others. This difference is often the basis for unhappy and troublesome intra-community situations. Since a community is made up of a number of neighborhoods, it is necessary that all coöperate in order to secure better schools, improved health service, better housing, wholesome recreation, efficient and economical government, and sound plans for future growth. Such coöperation, however, is more the exception than the rule in American communities. Intergroup oppositions, prejudices, and hatreds hamper community development, thwart needed adjustments, and bring about waste of community resources probably more than any other cause. Such oppositions among these lesser groups are by no means of recent development; they have been conspicuously characteristic of American society from the very beginning. However, they take on a deeper significance as social life expands and becomes more complex.[18]

While the primary groups have been to a large extent a *constant* in American life from the beginning, the vast proportion of the secondary groups are of recent origin. The few that are more or less of traditional origin have "swapped saddles," so to speak. Modern labor organizations, for example, are quite different from the craft guilds of earlier times. The Industrial Revolution—the introduction of machinery, the growth of science, modern inventions and discoveries, and improved means of communication and transportation—created an altogether new basis for the organization of society. Instead of royalty and nobility dominating a *stratified* society, we have the financier and the capitalist holding the prestige and power in a *fluid* society. Instead of a population that is fixed to the locality where it was born, we have a mobile population that freely and quickly flows from region to region. Instead of the jack of all trades and the self-sufficing household or self-sufficient community, we have an ever-increasing specialization, in respect to both persons and regions, resulting in an increasing interdependence.

It is this new setting that has recast the old secondary groups and

[18] Walter Burr, *Small Towns* (1929), Ch. III.

given rise to a multitude of new ones. Now it is possible for like-minded individuals and those specializing in a given field to unite and form strong organizations for the protection and advancement of their interests. In fact it is these *interest* groups which matter most to-day.

The personnel of almost every phase of human endeavor—for instance, producers, manufacturers, wholesalers, retailers, artists, doctors, lawyers, bankers, social workers, craftsmen, laborers, and farmers—has organized into a more or less definite interest group. And, to no small extent, the contribution which they are making to society as well as the benefits they receive in turn are in proportion to the effectiveness and strength of their organizations.

It is the expanding and the intensifying of the interest groups that at once furnish us with cause for our highest hopes and our gravest doubts regarding the outcome of the great changes taking place in society to-day. They furnish us with our highest hope, because it is only through group action that progress can be made to-day. They give us cause for apprehension, because group conflict is waged with more devastating weapons than were ever known to the men of any other day.

Uniformities and Standards. Society tends to produce uniformities and standards, *i.e.,* to spread culture and achievement so that its benefits and responsibilities are felt by all its members in varying, yet definite, degrees. Interest groups are the greatest vehicles of this dissemination of uniformities and standards. With each expansion of groups, with each improvement in travel and communication, with each advancement in science and knowledge, the strain to wipe out old cultural differences and attain new standards for all becomes greater. How quickly the benefits of science are disseminated is illustrated by the rapid spread and use of the new discoveries in the field of medicine. A few years ago, two scientists in Toronto discovered insulin, an effective treatment for diabetes, and in less than a year physicians all over the world were relieving thousands of those suffering from that dreaded disease. Inventions, too, spread with amazing rapidity. Witness the swiftness with which the automobile has displaced the horse on our roads; note how, in a score of years, the radio has taken possession and brought concerts and speeches within hearing of even the most isolated!

Now when these facilities and advantages become recognized elements in the culture of a group or a people so that their possession or use is expected of all its members, we say that they have become elements in the *standard of living* of that group or people. What we term *the American standard of living* will vary from group to group in American society. But nowhere is it limited to merely the crude necessities of life; in addition it includes the refinements, advantages, and equipment the possession and use of which can justly be expected of a citizen. When an individual or a family is unable to reach this more or less definite standard he is "hard up," "poor," "in poverty," "needy," "disadvantaged," and calls forth social concern.

In order to appreciate how the great advances in science, invention, discovery, and thought have spread, we need only to compare the *standard of living* of the working-man's family to-day with the standard of living of the same class of working-man's family of but a generation ago. And, as we have indicated, the strain and struggle to maintain and to advance that standard of living become increasingly great. But the aim of democratic society is ever directed to the task of bringing uniform advantages to all. Hence, wherever a family, a neighborhood, or a community is "backward"—not in a position to enjoy these uniform advantages—social agencies are directed to the task of removing the obstacles and developing the resources. This is forcefully illustrated by the manner with which the millions of unemployed and their families were extended public relief throughout the years of the depression. Even on relief they generally enjoyed a higher standard of living than was usually enjoyed by the self-supporting worker of fifty years ago working on a full-time job. This is done in order that "normal life" may be the possession of all. In the old days, when social life was simple, this task was not so difficult; but the complex and expanded social life of to-day makes the task one that calls for the trained specialist. The recognition of this fact has given rise to a new profession, *social work*, which means *scientifically developing and adjusting human relations in a way that will secure normal life to individuals and communities and encourage individual and community progress.*

Institutions. Social institutions represent the more steady and more fixed fundamentals of society. They represent the crystallization of methods of guiding and controlling social relationships. They are more firmly rooted in the past and, unlike science, tend to test conduct and social relations by the dictates of precedent rather than by experimentation. We might say that they are the rigid, bony skeleton about which the flesh of our social system grows. Society could no more function without them than the muscles of our bodies could function without our bones.

There are scores of social institutions, great and small, but in general they group themselves about a few pivotal fields of human relations.[19] Thus marriage, the home, and divorce are some of the most important institutions pertaining to the family and the relations of the sexes; the church is the outstanding institution for instruction and service in the field of religion; around the function of government are clustered numerous institutions, such as the courts, the legislative bodies, and the military; in the realm of education are the schools, the libraries, the museums, the newspapers, and the universities; in the field of economic relations are the institutions of money, banking, stock and produce exchanges, and markets; in the field of health and welfare is an ever-increasing number of institutions, such as hospitals, clinics, health centers, orphanages, homes for the aged, and colonies for the feeble-minded; and in the field of recreation there is also an increasing number of institutions, such as theaters, motion pictures, radio, taverns, and dance-halls.

It is at once apparent that the study of social problems must concern itself to a very large extent with those conditions and changes which affect the social institutions.

Improvement of Society. As we have indicated, it is in the nature of healthy group life to grow and to spread the benefits of civilization as evenly as possible through the entire population. But growth and improvement are not the result of blind drifting. They come from *socializing* the attitudes and aims of individuals and groups in society. By *socialization* we mean the directing of human motives toward giving to "even the least" of the members of the social whole the benefits of cultural development. Socialization is thus practically the opposite to *aloofness, selfishness, greed, exploitation,* and *profiteering*. It causes the individual and the group to *feel* their *oneness* with the social whole. It builds within the individual and group a *sentiment*—a conscience—with respect to sustaining the ideals, standards, institutions, and welfare of society. In brief, what society regards as *moral, i.e.,* good for the whole, becomes the aim of socialized individuals and groups. This being true, the improvement of society rests to a very large extent upon *moral progress*.

Cultural progress is made up of both moral and material progress. In its widest sense it is the development of civilization. "The actual removal of social evils constitutes moral progress; the discovery of principles and the invention of appliances calculated to remove them consti-

[19] C. C. Taylor and B. F. Brown, *Human Relations* (1926).

tutes material progress."[20] This does not mean that the moral growth follows the same principles that characterizes the growth of material progress. Moral progress is a product of *feeling* and *sentiment;* material progress is a product of *thought* and *labor.* Moral progress takes place rhythmically—in spiral cycles, as it were; material progress is a continuous adding of one improvement after another, of one invention or discovery based on the preceding inventions and discoveries. Moral progress is expressed in our attitudes and our behavior toward our fellows; material progress is expressed in our industry and production of commodities. "Moral action aims at the restraint and control of the forces of society, of human desires, prejudices and passion; invention and discovery aim at the control and utilization of physical and mechanical forces."[21]

Moral progress, therefore, always lags behind material progress, and, because it is based on the feelings and sentiments, and concerned with the functions of social control, becomes more or less rigidly fixed in the social institutions. Now and then, when moral progress has got far in the rear of material progress, it has attempted to resist the forward movement of "materialism." There is no little evidence that these attempts are being made to-day. While material progress may thus for a time appear to be checked, it has never been forced backward. "Every age has possessed all the arts of the age that preceded it, and has added something to them."[22]

In every aspect we see society putting forth a continual struggle to improve. Much of this struggle is directed toward harnessing the forces of nature, in order that the struggle for existence may be less harsh, survival more certain, and life more pleasant. But not infrequently the struggle to gain moral progress has been even more devastating and severe. Moral progress has been more a struggle of man with man, and to no small extent it has been a struggle to accommodate social control to the needs of material progress. As a matter of fact, most of the moral progress has come about as an indirect result of material progress. Thus, as we shall presently see, the great progress in invention and discovery has made social life increasingly complex; human interests clash at an ever-increasing number of points, thoughts and feelings travel faster and farther than ever before, and close personal relations give way to the vast and vague impersonal. The moral standard of the small and simple

[20] L. F. Ward, *Glimpses of the Cosmos* (1915), Vol. IV, p. 6.
[21] *Ibid.,* p. 9.
[22] *Ibid.*

community of a generation ago is no longer adequate to guide and control personal conduct. A new and a *deeper* moral growth must possess the man of to-day if he is to live a healthy social life. No longer can one "code" of morals be applied to the man and an entirely different "code" be applied to the woman. The impersonal society in business, commerce, recreation, and travel demands a common standard for each—a "moral sense" deeper and more compelling than was needed by individuals in any other age.

But the struggle to improve has expanded with each expansion of group life. Material progress has already swept across nations, and our industry, commerce, and business extend to "the four corners of the world." But our moral progress seems not great enough to reach beyond national lines. We have made but slight progress in the growth of international morality. There is even a doubt that our national morals have grown to the point of extending as far as the Monroe Doctrine extends! We are hardly ready to do unto other nations that which we would have them do unto us!

The Central Purpose of Society. Civilization has ever presented to society two great inequalities—inequality of knowledge and inequality of material wealth. The central purpose of society, guided by its degree of moral growth, has been directed toward the reduction of these inequalities. It seeks not merely to spread these fruits of civilization so that they will extend to each individual, but it is ever alert to encourage the growth of knowledge and to increase the volume of wealth produced.

In the path of this central purpose, society is confronted with many perplexing problems. And it is with these problems that we are now concerned.

REFERENCES

ASHLEY, Roscoe Lewis, *Our Contemporary Civilization* (New York, 1935), Part I and Ch. XV.

COOLEY, Charles Horton, *Social Organization* (New York, 1910), Chs. III–V.

———, *Human Nature and the Social Order* (New York, 1922, Revised Edition), Chs. I, V, VI.

COOLEY, C. H., ANGELL, R. C., and CARR, L. J., *Introductory Sociology* (New York, 1933), Chs. IV, V, IX, XIV, XXV.

GILLIN, J. L., and BLACKMAR, F. W., *Outlines of Sociology* (New York, 1930, 3rd Edition), Chs. I, V, VIII.

HART, Hornell, *The Science of Human Relations* (New York, 1927), Ch. X.

McMullen, L. W., *Building the World Society* (New York, 1931), Chs. II, III.

Recent Social Trends, Report of the Hoover Research Committee on Recent Social Trends (New York, 1933), Vol. I, Introduction, pp. xxv-xxxiv, Ch. VIII.

Ross, E. A., *Principles of Sociology* (New York, 1938, 3rd Edition), Part X.

Rugg, Harold, *The Great Technology* (New York, 1933), Parts I, II.

Taylor, C. C., and Brown, B. F., *Human Relations* (New York, 1926), Ch. I.

Wallis, Wilson D., *Culture and Progress* (New York, 1930), Chapter X.

QUESTIONS AND EXERCISES

1. Give examples, from your current reading or observation, of serious cultural maladjustment and cultural lag which seem to you to jeopardize the progress of our Western civilization.
2. What reasons have we to be apprehensive lest these conditions prove disastrous? What forces tend to counteract these tendencies?
3. Would Washington, with his eighteenth-century standards, find it easy to stay out of jail, were he to be among us to-morrow morning?
4. Is a "conservative" always wrong, as some people conceive him to be? Is a liberal necessarily right in championing reform movements? Explain.
5. Is there reason to believe we are less moral to-day than were our forefathers? Or is it probable that our moral standards are higher? Give reasons for your answer, and include examples if possible.
6. Make a list of the major interest groups of your community. With what groups are the members of your family affiliated? Do you notice any effect of these affiliations upon their attitudes and views? Discuss.
7. To what extent are you affected by each of the cycles of expanded group life—the family, neighborhood, community, state, national, and international? In this respect how does your situation compare with that of your grandfather's day? What are some of the major differences?
8. Why are the circles representing the various groups surrounding the individual in Fig. 1 (page 11 of the text) drawn eccentrically around the individual, rather than concentrically?
9. Compare the functions of the home in your grandfather's day with those of the home to-day. What new institutions have developed to provide the activities once centered in the home? What effect has this change had on the maintenance of family unity?
10. List several primary and secondary groups toward which you feel a sense of loyalty. Toward which type is your loyalty stronger—the primary or the secondary group? What is the relation between primary and secondary groups?

Chapter 2

SOCIAL CHANGE AND SOCIAL PROBLEMS

WE HAVE NOTED that it is the very nature of healthy social life to expand and that of civilization to grow. But this expansion and growth give rise to vast social changes, and in dynamic times such as we are living in today these vast changes shake the very foundation of our whole social structure. These social changes affect each individual and group in society, and since a large part of the population is unable to change as completely and as rapidly as the times demand, *social maladjustment* results. It is this social maladjustment which gives rise to our major social problems. Hence, if we are to gain an adequate understanding of our present-day social problems, we must study them in the light of the great social changes now taking place.

INDUSTRIAL CHANGES

The Handicrafts. The changes that have furnished most of the causes for social maladjustment are those which have come about in our industrial system. Down to about 1760, industry was still in the handicraft stage. The simple machinery and tools used in manufacturing were driven by hand-power and owned and managed by the craftsmen who used them. Every master craftsman was a capitalist to the extent that he owned his own tools, contracted for and purchased his own raw materials, controlled his own place of employment, set his own pace of work, and controlled the finished product, which he generally sold directly to a patron whom he knew personally. Working along with the master craftsman were perhaps a few journeymen and a few apprentices; but they owned and used their own tools and shared with the master craftsman the same conditions of employment and the same living conditions. There was not much ground for industrial disputes in those days; the relation of the employer to the employee was most intimate and personal. Likewise, the relation between the producer and the consumer was direct and personal, and there was little cause for any public concern about protecting the interests of the consumer. In this stage, *labor* was the dominant factor in production; labor controlled the raw materials, the conditions of employment, the speed of work, and the quality and price of the finished product.

The Beginning of the Industrial Revolution. Starting with the last third of the eighteenth century, mechanical inventions began to work great changes in the industrial system. Steam-power, beginning with the textile industry (1785), took possession of the machines and tools and organized them into our factory system.[1] Generally this last quarter of the eighteenth century is referred to as the period of the Industrial Revolution. But we can hardly say that this period was any more than the beginning; the revolutionary changes are still going on with even greater intensity. In other words, we are now in the midst of the Industrial Revolution. The early stage was characterized by the substitution of the machine for the hand-tool, while the present stage takes the form of the replacement of the simpler machines by the more improved, more complex and elaborate, and more costly machines.

When we examine carefully this great change in our industrial life, we notice that it is in fact a twofold revolution—a revolution of the processes and methods of production on the one side, and a revolution of the nature of ownership and control on the other. On the one hand, we witness the rapid growth and extension of the *factory system*, and on the other hand, we see the transfer of ownership and control to the *corporation* form of business organization. These two gigantic developments have given us most of our great material progress, but they have, at the same time, given rise to our most menacing social problems.

The Factory System. One of the most outstanding features of the factory system is the relation it bears to the worker. It has practically eliminated craftsmanship, and reduced the worker to a mere manipulator and feeder of machines. "The worker of to-day does not make things; he makes only parts of things." [2] He no longer has the stimulus and satisfaction that came to the worker of a century ago, of placing the stamp of his personality on the product of his own hands. He is a mere cog in the wheels, "all his claims being liquidated in the wage he receives for his labor." [3] When he becomes dissatisfied with this, it matters little, since his place might easily be filled by the employment of women and children, or by new and improved machines.

Another feature of the factory system, which further complicates the problems arising out of the minute division of labor and the destruction

---

[1] R. T. Ely, *Studies in the Evolution of Industrial Society* (1913), Ch. II.

[2] John A. Fitch, *The Causes of Industrial Unrest* (1924), Ch. XIX.

[3] E. A. Ross, "The Case for Industrial Dualism," *Quarterly Journal of Economics,* XXXVIII: 385 (May, 1924).

of craftmanship, is the amazing increase in the amount of capital employed per worker.[4] We have noted that before the beginning of the Industrial Revolution labor was the dominant factor in production. The growth of the factory system has placed *capital* in power and control; the owner of the industry holds the power to contract for and control the raw materials, the places of employment, the quality and quantity of production, and the finished product. The question is no longer: What is the speed of the worker? but instead it is asked: How fast will the machine work? How much can the machine turn out in a day? The question is not: How long will the worker last? but instead: How long will the machine last? Is it any wonder, then, that society must concern itself, to an ever increasing extent, with the problems of protecting the welfare of labor? Is it any wonder that labor is restless and ever alert to gain some vantage-point of power where it can wield a more certain control over the means of livelihood?

Furthermore, at no time since the beginning of the Industrial Revolution has the development and installation of machinery been as rapid and as far-reaching in its effects as during the past two decades. The rate of mechanization of American life may be measured with a fair degree of accuracy by the number of patents issued from year to year. From 1790 to 1800 there were but 276 patents granted; for the decade 1851 to 1860 there were 25,087; for the closing decade of the century there were 234,956; for the decade 1926 to 1935 there were 491,076 patents issued—almost half a million.[5] The vast majority of these patents relate to the improvement of machines, making them more efficient either in production or in displacement of labor. During the fifteen years prior to 1931, "the industries of the United States installed about $23.00 worth of machinery each year for each man, woman, and child of our population—a total of some $2,500,000,000 annually. In Great Britain the corresponding per capita figure approximated $10.00, in Germany less

---

[4] "In the manufacture of agricultural implements the capital for each worker has risen from $495 in 1850 to $6,764 in 1920; boots and shoes, from $122 to $2,902; carpeting, from $623 to $5,198; carriages and wagons, from $242 in 1840 to $4,338 in 1920; cotton goods, in the same period, from $708 to $1,979; woolen goods, from $738 to $4,987; paper, from $1,004 to $7,962; tanning and leather goods, from $601 to $9,262; silk goods, from $356 to $4,123; iron and steel, from $669 to $7,082. . . . For American manufacturing as a whole the capital per worker has increased from $328 in 1840 to $4,901 in 1920, that is, about fifteenfold. . . . It is perfectly safe, then, to assume that the invested capital per worker to-day is *at least* ten times as great as it was a century ago." Ross, *op. cit.*, pp. 386-387.

[5] *Statistical Abstract of the United States, 1937* (United States Department of Commerce), p. 794.

than $9.00, in India $0.17, and in China $0.05." [6] The extent to which this revolution in industry has gone in the United States is made more apparent by comparing the per capita production of this country with that of other countries. The United States produces 30 units while China produces 1; British India, 1½; Russia, 2½, Italy, 2¾; Japan, 3½; Poland, 6; Holland, 7; France, 8¼; Austria, 8½; Czechoslovakia, 9½; Germany, 12; Belgium, 16; Great Britain, 18; and Canada, 20.[7]

While this phenomenal development of machine industry has made the United States the wealthiest of nations, it has at the same time created a multitude of serious problems—both national and international. The relation of men to machines as well as the relations of man to man have become more complicated, uncertain, and strained. Furthermore, the marketing and using of the vast output of the increasingly efficient machines give rise to no end of vexing problems, such as "overproduction," the shutting down of plants, and the forcing of thousands of workers into unemployment.[8] Since other leading nations are now industrialized, the struggle for possession of world markets complicates immensely the problems of international relations.

Growth of Corporation Control. Hardly less problematic is the other side of the industrial change—the growth of *corporation* control and management. We noted that during the handicraft period the relation of industry to the employee and to the consumer was direct and personal. But with the growth of corporation control, this personal relationship disappears. Under corporation management the employee is a mere number, much the same as a machine, and the consumer is merely so much impersonal "active demand." The stockholder of the corporation is not interested in, nor concerned about, the conditions under which production is carried on, or the welfare of the workers. Neither is the stockholder concerned about the welfare of the consumer. The only interests that the stockholder has in the industry are (1) the security and safety of his investments, and (2) the dividends that the industry or business produces. He is impelled *solely by the profits motive.* Only to the extent that we are able to put a soul in profits are we able to bestir the stockholders to a consideration of the social consequences of the corporation's conduct.

[6] W. H. Rastall, chief of the Industrial Machinery Division, Bureau of Foreign and Domestic Commerce, United States Department of Commerce, *United States Daily* (Washington, March, 1931).

[7] Thornton Read, of Columbia University, in *Retail Ledger* (December 2, 1929).

[8] Edwin G. Nourse, *America's Capacity to Produce* (Washington, D. C.: Brookings Institution, 1934).

And yet much must be said to the credit of the industrial and business corporation. It has made possible the quick amassing of enormous amounts of capital without which it would hardly have been possible to build our railroads, exploit our vast natural resources, or develop our large-scale industrial and business enterprises. Without these gigantic developments, Americans would have lacked many of the conveniences and commodities that constitute such a large part of the high standard of living so characteristic of American life. Large-scale production and business developed the efficiency and the economy that made it possible to put the fruits of our vast material progress within the reach of all classes in the population.

But these vast economies and efficiency achievements of large-scale industry and big business are gradually destroying the foundation upon which much of our social and economic progress has been made. In most fields, thriving and successful small enterprise is doomed. *Competition,* upon which our national founders depended as a guarantee for equalizing economic opportunity and for securing equality of rights of contract, is gradually fading into thin air. The major lines of manufacturing and business every year witness a decrease in the number and an increase in the size of establishments. Every year sees the consolidation of a large number of corporations into huge mergers for the purpose of effecting more far-reaching economy of management and lessening the field of competition. Thus the control of industry is gradually shifting from the hands of those who are directly concerned with the processes and operations of industry into the hands of investors—into the hands of those who control the banking interests of the nation.[9]

Of the 303,000 corporations filing income tax returns, the 200 largest virtually dominate the nation's economic life. These 200 corporations report 40 per cent of the nation's net income and represent 45 per cent of all the gross assets. Only a few thousand men control and direct these vast "business empires." Such concentration of power over the savings of millions of investors and over the employment opportunity of millions of workers implies a social trust. Many corporations measure up to this high standard of administration. However, accumulated ills and abuses, wholesale fraud and dishonest contrivance, and utter disregard of public interest characterize much of the corporation set-up.[10] The creation of the Securities and Exchange Commission and the many

[9] *American Economic Review,* XXI, No. 1, p. 10 (March, 1931).
[10] I. Maurice Wormser, *Frankenstein, Incorporated* (New York, 1931), Chs. V–VIII.

other efforts of the Federal and State Governments to "put a soul in the corporation" have not been wholly successful.

Social Significance of the Impersonal Relations in Industry. This centralization of the ownership and control of industry and business intensifies the impersonal relations to the worker and to the consumer. But perhaps of even greater social significance is the effect it has upon the *contracting* or *bargaining* power of the worker who must market his labor, of the farmer who must market his produce, and of the consumer whose purchasing power is in the balance. The individual with his guaranteed rights of "liberty of contract" faces the dilemma of bargaining not on equal terms, but on "take-it-or-leave-it" terms. His only way out of this quandary is not to act as an individual, but to lend his will to the will of a strong organization—to organized labor, coöperative marketing, or consumers' leagues and coöperatives. Only such measures as can successfully threaten the assurance of paying dividends can reach the ears of the financiers whose one aim is to keep the business or industry "on a paying basis"—paying profits. This explains why our time has been so characterized by organized groups, and so disturbed with group conflict.

RAPID DEVELOPMENT OF TRAVEL AND TRANSPORTATION FACILITIES

The great industrial and social changes that we have just outlined would not have gone far had it not been for the phenomenal developments of facilities for travel and transportation. We have seen how group life has expanded and we have noted that this expansion has been largely due to the vast improvements in the methods and means of transportation and communication; but we need to see these improvements more in detail to appreciate their significance in our study of social problems.

American Hurry and Haste. It was only a little more than a hundred and fifty years ago that the United States began its career as an independent nation. It started with a population of but little more than three million, mostly farmers and villagers scattered along the Atlantic seaboard and the eastern slopes of the Allegheny Mountains. But this little handful of population laid claim to the vast stretch of untamed wilderness beyond the Alleghenies, and they were determined to people it and to create of it a nation that would reach from the Atlantic to the Pacific. To achieve this great aim they had to *hurry:* they *hurried* pioneers to settle the West—they *hurried* to open up the vast natural resources— they *hurried* to develop their industries—they *hurried* to build cities and they *hurried* to tie the wide-spreading territory into national unity. Thus it was that America became a *hurrying* and *rushing* nation, a quick-moving nation, a nation interested in doing big things in a big way. This hurry and rush became a habit fixed in American culture, and even to-day there is perhaps no characteristic of the American people that is more truly typical of our everyday living. To be sure, "haste makes waste," and not a few of our most baffling social problems must be attributed to our haste in getting things done.

Development of a National Transportation System. To achieve this hasty development, our greatest need was for population—population to settle and hold the vast new territory, to develop our vast natural resources, and to build our industries. There was not enough man-power. Hence we turned to inventing and building machines that would do the work of hundreds of workers. But success of machine industry depends upon ample transportation facilities. So we hurried to build the only transportation facilities then known to us—highways, canals, and river transports. The Federal Government, the States, and the cities all rushed these developments, and by the end of the first third of the nineteenth century, these improvements extended well into the Middle West. Then came the invention of the locomotive and the possibilities of a more adequate means of transportation—the railroads.[11]

No other factor played a more important part in the development of our national maturity than did the railroads. No other phase of our national history so aptly illustrates that dominant American characteristic of *hurry* and *haste*.

The first railroad, the Baltimore and Ohio, was chartered in 1827, but was not completed until 1830. For a time there were many technical handicaps that hampered rapid progress, but by the outbreak of the Civil War these handicaps had been largely overcome and 30,626 miles of railroads were in operation. Table 1 shows the rapidity with which railroad building proceeded. Many of the old settlers are still alive who went West in covered wagons at a speed of from five to fifteen miles a day. To-day one may cross the continent—a distance of over 3,000 miles—in luxurious comfort in less than three days, and at a cost that is well within the means of most of us. This ease and convenience of travel has broken down the *old sectionalism* and has created national unity. But of even greater social significance is the rapid movement of freight, express, and the mail. This has led to specialization of occupation and production and has made each section of the nation inter-

[11] Eliot Jones, *Principles of Railway Transportation* (1924), Ch. III.

TABLE 1

MILAGE OF OPERATING RAILWAY IN THE UNITED STATES, 1830–1940

Census Year	Miles of Operating Railway	Increase
1830	23	
1840	2,818	2,795
1850	9,021	6,203
1860	30,626	21,605
1870	52,922	22,296
1880	93,267	40,345
1890	156,404	63,137
1900	192,556	36,152
1910	240,831	48,275
1920	259,941	19,110
1930	260,440	499
1940	245,740	−14,700

dependent with all other sections. It has destroyed the old, self-sufficing community and made possible the building and feeding of our large industrial cities. Thus many things that we daily use, consume, and enjoy were perhaps only a few days before packed and shipped from the most remote state in the Union.

Development of Ocean Transportation. The same sort of phenomenal progress has been made in ocean travel. The first transatlantic steamship, the *Savannah,* crossed the Atlantic from New York to Liverpool in 1819, in the record-breaking time of twenty-six days. In August, 1936, the Cunard-White Star ship, *Queen Mary,* steamed 3,158 miles from Cherbourg to New York in four days, seven hours, and twelve minutes, an average of 30.01 knots an hour. In 1940 the United States was second only to Great Britain in ocean transportation facilities, the United States having more than 10,000 ships of 100 tons and over with a total capacity of almost 13,500,000 gross tons. In 1939 Great Britain had merchant ships with a total capacity of about 21,000,000 tons. The vast improvement made in American shipping in the last forty years is to be noted in the fact that in 1900 two-thirds of our 3,135 ships of this tonnage were sailing-vessels; in 1935 only 143 of the 10,000 ships were sailing-vessels.[12]

Thus we have brought the world to our very door, and have made ocean travel so cheap and comfortable that even the poorest classes find

[12] *Statistical Abstract of the United States, 1941,* pp. 498–499.

it possible to immigrate to our shores. We have tapped the high-pressure mains of the overcrowded nations, and, as we shall see in a later chapter, our country stands in grave danger of being flooded with immigrants from the lowest economic levels of these overcrowded nations. Through international trade, commerce, and investments the nations of the world have become closer to one another and more interdependent one upon the other than were the various sections of the United States even a half-century ago. In spite of political misgivings, the policy of *national isolation* can no longer be accepted as a sound guide for international relations.

The Automobile. Even more phenomenal than the building of the railroads and the development of ocean travel has been the rapid development of the automobile. Here again we notice the prevalence of that dominant American characteristic of hurry and haste. As early as 1875 we were beginning to look for some means of travel more rapid than the horse.[13] In 1879 a "steam-wagon" was invented that made the trip from Oshkosh to Madison, a distance of about a hundred miles, in three days' "working time," and was awarded the prize provided by the State legislature. But it was not until 1895 that motor transportation gave promise of success. In that year four automobiles were made in the United States.[14] The census of 1900 showed that there were fewer than 4,000 motor vehicles in the United States. Then began the large-scale production that has made this a "motor age." By 1915 the annual production had reached almost a million cars. However, after the First World War production began in earnest, and each year increased rapidly until in 1936 the annual production of cars, trucks, and busses reached 5,621,-

[13] In 1875 the Wisconsin Legislature passed the following law (*Wisconsin Statutes*, 1875, Ch. 134):

"There is hereby appropriated the sum of $10,000 . . . to be paid to any citizen of Wisconsin who shall invent, and after five years' continued trial and use, shall produce a machine propelled by steam or other motive agent, which shall be a cheap and practical substitute for the horse and other animals on the highway and farm; provided that said appropriation shall not be levied or made until a successful award is made. . . .

"Any machine or locomotive entering the list to compete for a prize or bounty, shall perform a journey of at least 200 miles, on a common road or roads, in a continuous line North and South in this state, and propelled by its own internal power, at the average rate of at least five miles per hour, working time.

"The said locomotive must be of such construction and width as to conform with or run in the ordinary track of the common wagon or buggy, now in use, and be able to run backward or turn out of the road to accommodate other vehicles in passing and be able to ascend or descend a grade of at least 200 feet to the mile."

[14] B. G. Backer, *Wisconsin Metal-Working Industries* (bulletin) (Madison: Wisconsin Department of Agriculture, 1924).

715 in the United States alone. As of January 1, 1937, the United States Department of Commerce reported 40,560,167 motor vehicles in use in the 157 nations of the world, approximately one vehicle for every 54 persons. For this same date there were 28,221,291 motor vehicles in use in the United States—seven out of every ten of the world total, and one vehicle for every 4.55 persons in the United States.[15] More than 92 out of every 100 farms of the United States are equipped with a motor car or truck.[16] In other words, there are 4,910,300 cars and 767,200 trucks, or a total of 5,677,500 motor vehicles on farms. In addition, 846,162 farm tractors assisted the cars and trucks in the displacement of over 7,000,000 horses that have disappeared from the farms since the First World War.[17]

In less than the span of a single generation the automobile became a dynamic factor in American culture. It is, as a matter of fact, a recognized essential in the American standard of living. One needed only to visit any of the many state and national parks, or go to any summer resort or winter resort, or take a day off to go fishing, or, better still, try to find a parking space within walking distance of the shopping district, to be fully convinced of this fact.

Hendrik Van Loon aptly expressed this social situation in one of his cartoons. He pictures two old men on Mars, looking down upon the hurrying multitude of cars on the earth.

"What are all those people on Earth doing?" asks one of the ancients.

"Going," is the brief reply of the other.

"Going where?" continues the questioner.

"Nowhere—just going!"

But there was a genuine democracy about this "just going." There was nothing comparable to an old, used car for putting all the youths of the community, rich and poor, on a fraternal footing. The parks, the forests, lakes, and streams belonged to the poor as well as to the rich. The poor might travel in an old "Model T," but they got there; and they paid their share of the gas tax that went to build and maintain their highways. The trailer also became a part of the stream of traffic that was "just going." It is estimated that 50,000 tourist-type trailers were manufactured in 1936—a production which was far below the demand. "Trailer towns" became a problem for many American cities.

Highway Improvement. Along with the development of the automo-

---

[15] *Report of Bureau of Foreign and Domestic Commerce* (November 12, 1937).
[16] *American Research Foundation Bulletin* (Chicago, January, 1931).
[17] Scoville Hamlin, *The Menace of Overproduction* (1930), p. 51.

bile has come the rapid building of good roads, most of which have been built in the past twenty years. Since 1930 the combined appropriations of the local units of government, the States, and the Federal Government, for the building of more good roads, has amounted to more than a billion dollars annually. In 1936 the funds available for highway construction and maintenance amounted to more than a billion and a half dollars.[18] Fig. 2 gives us a fair picture of the extent of the highway system of the United States.

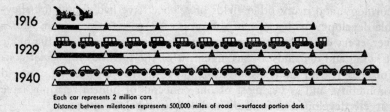

1916
1929
1940

Each car represents 2 million cars
Distance between milestones represents 500,000 miles of road —surfaced portion dark

PICTOGRAPH CORPORATION, FOR PUBLIC AFFAIRS COMMITTEE, INC.

FIG. 2.—DEVELOPMENT OF AUTOMOBILE TRANSPORTATION, 1916–1940

Important as are the other avenues of transportation, the road passing the front door probably touches the lives of people the closest. Roads have widened the range and frequency of human relations, altered trade areas, improved marketing, and broadened the outlook of both the rural dweller and his city cousin. From East to West, from North to South, over most of the United States we may now traverse in half an hour or less the distance that our forefathers considered a good day's journey with the horse and buggy.

Conquest of the Air. We are constantly seeking a more rapid means of travel. A generation ago the possibility of established air-lines of transportation was hooted at. Thirty years ago the airplane began to demonstrate its possible usefulness in carrying mail.[19] The rôle of the airplane in the World War created genuine public interest and confidence in its commercial and military use. The first official air-mail route was established May 15, 1918. In 1940 airplanes flew regularly

[18] *Statistical Abstract of the United States, 1937*, pp. 357–362.

[19] In September, 1911, Earl L. Ovington was appointed the first air-mail carrier, and as a demonstration carried mail from a temporary post office established at the flying field on Long Island at Mineola. During the month he carried 32,415 postcards, 3,993 letters, and 1,062 circulars. The whole experiment was made at no expense to the Government. See *United States Daily* (July 26, 1930).

over 37,940 miles of air-mail routes in the United States alone. The total airplane miles flown with the mail during 1940 was 59,191,000. Besides carrying the mail, airplanes carried over 14,188,000 pounds of freight and express during the year. In 1930 fewer than fifty thousand passengers dared to travel by air; in 1940 there were nearly 3,000,000 passengers carried.[20]

Like the development of the automobile, the progress in air transportation has opened many unexpected opportunities for science and further discovery. Already, photography, surveying and mapping, meteorology, and many other fields of science have had almost unbelievable developments because of the progress in air transportation. Moreover, every advance in transportation ushers in vast changes in the mode of living and demands a rearrangement of the facilities for social control. Progress in air transportation increases the prospect of a world community, and as yet most of our concepts of human relations have scarcely developed beyond the saddle-bag stage!

RAPID DEVELOPMENT OF MEANS OF COMMUNICATION

Hardly less important than the great developments of travel and transportation have been the great improvements in methods of communication. These two great products of science and invention have paralleled one another: the development of telegraphy paralleled that of the railroads and the steamships; the telephone preceded the automobile by but a few years; and the development of the radio has practically paralleled the development of the airplane, though its popularity and installation have been more universal.

The Telegraph and the Cable. The first telegraph-line in the United States was put into operation in 1840, connecting Washington with Baltimore—a distance of forty miles. In 1936 the Department of Commerce reported 2,426,000 miles of telegraph wire, and 96,468 nautical miles of ocean cable, connecting every community of the whole country with the rest of the world.[21] Thus it is that events and transactions over the whole world are so quickly heralded over the whole country. Hence the people of the nation may read the same news and apply their minds to the same issues, all at the same time.

[20] *Statistical Abstract of the United States, 1941,* pp. 425, 492; *Technical Trends and National Policy* (Washington, D. C.: National Resources Committee, June, 1937), pp. 198 ff.
[21] *Statistical Abstract of the United States, 1937,* pp. 342 ff.

The Telephone. While the telegraph was of great social significance, it was not the community-builder that the telephone was destined to become. In 1936 there were 18,433,000 telephones in use in the United States, or almost four telephones for every five families.[22] Over 40 per cent of all the farms in the United States were supplied with telephones.[23] To be sure, the majority of the farm telephones were on "party lines," but this makes it all the more interesting for the women folks, for whom farm life is often lonely and drab. Thus is our population knitted together into closer social and economic life, and months and years are added to our productive life by the time and the steps saved by the increasing use of the telephone.

The Radio. But still another great advancement in communication is ripening in the world of science and invention—the radio. From 1894, when Marconi began his experiments with "wireless," to 1903, when the first wireless message was successfully flashed across the Atlantic, the development of radio was slow. In 1904 steamships began to be equipped with "wireless," and press dispatchers began to use this means of flashing news over the world. In 1915 transoceanic telephony was achieved. The engineers of the Bell Telephone Company telephoned to Paris, France, and Honolulu. During the First World War the value of the radio was thoroughly established, and following the close of the war, the radio art and industry in the United States began its phenomenal development.

During the last fifteen years there have been far-reaching improvements, both technical and in public regulation, making it possible to unite virtually the whole world into one vast system of communication. In 1935 there were 1,367 broadcasting stations in the world. Of this number, 625 were in the United States.[24] Through linking the various stations into chains, we keep in touch with every part of the world and can follow our explorers even to the South Pole!

The swiftness with which the radio has made a place for itself in American culture is amazing. Twenty years ago—so far as the American home is concerned—it was but a crude and imperfect novelty. To-day practically three-fourths of the families in the country are equipped with radios. In January, 1936, there were 22,869,000 sets in use in the United States, almost 40 per cent of the total number of sets in the

[22] *Ibid.*, p. 344.
[23] *Public Service Magazine*, p. 27 (July, 1927). (Estimate based on 1926 figures.)
[24] *World Almanac* (1937), p. 534.

world.[25] Of this number, almost two million sets were in farm homes, approximately one out of every five farm families being equipped with a radio. And, as if to make sure that we do not miss anything anywhere, over three million automobiles have been equipped with radio sets.

At the present time, practically every ship is equipped with both sending and receiving sets. This has been the means of saving thousands of lives, and millions of dollars to American shippers. Most of the passenger airplanes are likewise equipped. During the last few years the police departments of many of our larger cities have installed special radio equipment enabling them to keep in touch with officers in any part of the city and to direct the capture of criminals. As an aid to law enforcement, the radio will undoubtedly become indispensable.

One of the most important uses of the radio—a use having far-reaching possibilities that are not yet fully developed—is in the field of education. It is now extensively used by many universities and governmental agencies. A number of schools have arranged regular courses in a wide variety of subjects, including history, literature, foreign languages, home economics subjects, and physical education; lectures and discussions are given over the radio in much the same manner as in the class-room, and students write out their recitations and mail them to their instructor. Various governmental departments, bureaus, and services also use the radio regularly as an educational medium—especially departments of commerce and agriculture, health services, child welfare bureaus, etc. In connection with the public schools the radio has still further possibilities—in music and in physical education, as well as in many of the regular subjects. Instruction can be given effectively and economically by the ablest specialists, and carefully followed under the guidance of the local teachers in the thousands of school-rooms throughout the country. To facilitate and guide the use of the radio in the public schools, the federal Office of Education has appointed a radio specialist to direct the "school of the air." [26] A number of State departments of education, notably that of Ohio, are coöperating in making use of the radio in their public schools.

Even photographs are now successfully transmitted by radio, so that we are not only able to get directly the news, weather and market re-

[25] The United States Bureau of Foreign and Domestic Commerce reported the world total as 27,500,000 sets—United Kingdom, 3,500,000; Germany, 3,250,000; France, 2,000,000; Russia, 1,000,000; Japan, 713,000; Spain, 550,000; Canada, nearly 500,000.

[26] F. E. Hill, *Listen and Learn* (New York, 1937), pp. 122 ff.

ports, concerts, church services, lectures, and political speeches, but also obtain quickly through the press a detailed picture of events happening over the world. Television still awaits the perfection of certain fundamentals before it can be made practical. There is little question, however, that it will one day make its way into American culture.

The Motion-Picture. Another factor in this phenomenal change in American culture during the last quarter of a century is the motion-picture and sound-films. This industry now represents investments of over $2,000,000,000. Scattered through the cities and towns of the United States in 1940 were 17,541 operating motion-picture theaters with a seating capacity of 10,600,000, attracting a weekly attendance of some 80,000,000 persons.[27] Besides furnishing entertainment, they present happenings throughout the world in a way that makes them more vivid and more real than presentations by either the radio or the daily paper. No more effective medium for spreading propaganda and for aiding education has ever been invented.

During the last few years the educational value of the motion-picture and sound-films has become generally recognized. A large proportion of the public schools throughout the United States now make use of educational films, especially in the teaching of geography, health and hygiene, nature study, biological sciences, and industrial and vocational subjects. Governmental bureaus and agencies, university extension divisions, State departments of education, and many private agencies provide this educational service at nominal cost to the schools and adult-education centers. No facility has ever been devised that was more effective in the diffusion of culture and in furthering understanding.

News and the Press. Augmenting this vast development in communication facilities is a similar development and expansion of the press. Americans, especially, are inveterate readers. There are over 9,100 newspapers and periodicals published in the United States—over 1,875 daily newspapers with an average circulation of over 41,000,000; over 6,200 weekly papers with a circulation of nearly 20,000,000; over 2,500 monthly and quarterly periodicals with a circulation that more than equals the total population of the United States; and numerous other semiweeklies, biweeklies, and pamphlets with huge circulations.[28]

But these newspapers and periodicals do not merely carry news, stories, and education: their chief object is to carry advertising. We are told in a thousand different ways how we should spend our incomes—

[27] *World Almanac* (1942), p. 864.
[28] *Ibid.*, p. 528.

what to eat, what to wear, what cars to ride in, where to spend vacations. Our most private wants are exposed, and we are told in a most intimate and personal way how to supply them. Thus it is that we rush to
spend our incomes and to keep perpetual 40 per cent mortgages on our
future earnings through the "easy credit terms" urged upon us.

Schools, Books, Libraries, Bureaus, and University Extensions. Since
the boyhood days of Abraham Lincoln there has been a phenomenal
development of educational opportunity—opportunities for home education as well as for formal education in our schools and colleges. About
26,000,000 American children are in our public grade and high schools,
and there are more than 1,350,000 students in our American colleges and
universities and professional schools. Now one out of every twenty
school-children finishes college, and one person out of every six between the ages of 18 and 22 is enrolled in college. Much of this phenomenal advancement of education is due to two factors: first, to the
increased health and vitality of school-children; and second, to the improved educational facilities of rural communities, made possible by
consolidation of schools, good roads, and bus transportation of pupils.
And yet, in the poorer rural areas of this country there are more than
half a million children between the ages of seven and thirteen who are
not in school at all.[29]

While schools are the foundation of our cultural advancement, the
opportunities for self-education, for youth and for adult, constitute one
of the greatest advances in our educational progress. In the first place,
there never was a time when information on almost every sort of subject was so readily within the reach of the individual, no matter where
he happens to be located. There never was a time when books were
published in such quantities and on such a wide range of subjects and
as cheaply as they are being published to-day. If the classification of
the books published can be taken as an index of the interests of the reading public, it is evident that Americans are building a broad foundation
for the cultural growth of the future (see Table 2).

But books are not the only sources of information on the vast range
of subjects with which Americans are concerning themselves. There are
thousands of pamphlets, reports, and monographs being published and
distributed annually by bureaus and departments of government and by

[29] *Report of the Advisory Committee on Education* (Washington, D. C., February, 1938), pp. 6–18; *School Life* (Washington, D. C.: Office of Education,
February, 1938).

TABLE 2

AMERICAN BOOK PRODUCTION, 1940 *

International Classification	For 1940	
	New Books	New Editions
Philosophy	99	11
Religion	781	62
Sociology, economics	796	80
Law	141	61
Education (books on)	317	32
Philology	274	45
Science	398	95
Technical books	470	141
Medicine, hygiene	326	146
Agriculture, gardening	108	31
Domestic economy	70	24
Business	344	58
Fine arts	213	9
Music	115	9
Games, sports	156	26
General literature	466	70
Poetry, drama	671	67
Fiction	1,221	515
Juvenile	852	132
History	783	70
Geography, travel	262	46
Biography	569	78
Miscellaneous	83	5
Total	9,515	1,813

* *The World Almanac* (1942), p. 528.

private agencies. No doubt these lesser publications play as important a part in continuous home education as do the books.[30]

Furthermore, it is no longer necessary for the individual to build for himself a large and expensive home library in order to secure these educational opportunities. On every hand are the large public libraries and

[30] Especially notable are the bulletins of the universities and colleges, the federal Children's Bureau, the federal Woman's Bureau, the federal Office of Education, federal and State labor and industrial departments, departments of agriculture, federal and State health services, federal and State commercial and marketing departments, and the departments of public instruction.

library commissions, ready to serve his needs through traveling-library facilities. Further augmenting and systematizing the use of all these sources of information are the university extension divisions that are providing individuals and communities everywhere with counsel and advice, organized reading courses, extension classes, correspondence courses, guided club studies, lectures, educational films, demonstrations, and many other educational services.

In 1938 there were 450 colleges and universities offering extension classes in comparison with 75 twenty years ago. Twenty years ago there were 73 institutions of higher learning offering correspondence-study courses; in 1938 there were 195 such institutions. But of even more importance than the increase in the number of institutions offering this work is the increase in the scope of opportunities offered by them. More than 200 different subjects are offered by correspondence, and instructors are provided by many of the universities where classes of ten or more people are organized. It is estimated that during 1937 more than a million people took extension work.[31]

Rural Free Delivery. Another important means of communication that has been of major importance in the maturing of national life and in spreading intellectual and material advantages to the whole population is the *rural mail service.* Beginning in 1896 with three small experimental routes in West Virginia, the rural mail service now comprises 32,646 routes operating over 1,400,000 miles. Carroll County, Maryland, was the first county to achieve county-wide service, and this was accomplished in December, 1899. To-day there are few counties in the United States that are not penetrated to the utmost corners by daily free delivery of mail. During 1940 the rural mail-carriers traveled more than 424,700,000 miles, and served more than a fifth of the entire population of the nation.[32] Improved highways and the automobile have greatly facilitated this great national achievement.

The rural free delivery has enabled the rural population to keep in touch with the world and has been a major factor in breaking down the evil effects of rural isolation. Now the farm families not only subscribe to the town weekly and the various farm papers, but a large proportion read the daily newspapers as well. Rural mail delivery makes it convenient for them to use the services of the free library commissions, reading-circles, governmental publications, and the many educational advantages offered by their State university extension departments. Fur-

[31] *School Life* (Washington, D. C.: Office of Education, February, 1938), p. 223.
[32] *Statistical Abstract of the United States, 1941,* p. 426.

thermore, much of the marketing of farm produce and the delivery of merchandise used by the farm family is facilitated by rural mail service. The time and energy thus conserved for the rural population through this service has not only encouraged the development of a more uniform culture throughout the United States, but has also done much to create a more adequate social organization of agricultural forces.

SOCIAL SIGNIFICANCE OF IMPROVEMENTS IN TRAVEL AND COMMUNICATION

Perhaps the most outstanding social significance of these wonderful developments in transportation and communication is to be seen in the effect they have had on community life. They have largely destroyed the old community bounds. Until these vast developments set in, the community was, for the most part, limited to the distance that could be comfortably covered by the horse and buggy in a half-day—a distance of fifteen to twenty-five miles, depending upon the condition of the roads. The building of the railroads began a loosening of the bounds of the horse-and-buggy community; but it was the automobile that especially hastened community expansion. With the automobile, a day's pleasure or business trip may extend to two hundred miles from home. The telephone and the automobile have, therefore, widened the social and economic contacts to more than a hundred times those that were possible in the horse-and-buggy days. With the airplane, the radius of social and economic contacts may be still further extended, while the radio enables us to gather entertainment and information not only from the whole nation but also from the world.

While these changes have given the individual a broader social, economic, and intellectual horizon, and raised the standard of living, the machinery for regulating conduct and that for controlling group life have not kept pace. Thus the standards of the family, the church, public opinion, and government remain largely where they were a generation ago.

The effect of these changes on the home life of the nation is profound. While life seems to be enriched by our being able to see and enjoy more, the problem now is one of keeping the family together—of keeping the interests of its members united. Conditions created by these changes of the last quarter-century are largely responsible for the instability of the modern home. The ceremonies, regulations, and ideals that served to guide and control our grandparents are far from adequate for this motor age. New means of regulation and control must be shaped to fit the changed conditions. But just what shall these regulations be, and whence are they to come?

Our grandfathers still talk about the old singing schools and the other home-made amusements that characterized their social life when they were young, but the automobile and the good roads have done away with all these. We have discarded home-made fun, while we pack the theaters and athletic-fields to witness professional artists and entertainers. In the course of only a few years, social life has almost wholly surrendered to commercialized amusements: we have largely ceased to be original producers, and have become a nation of *onlookers* and *listeners*. To be sure, many efforts are now being put forth to combat this tendency and to revive, or rather to reorganize, our communities, so that play may again be a spontaneous expression of community life.

These great changes are rapidly converting America into an *urbanized* nation. The telephone, the automobile, the bus, and rapid transit have spread our cities to proportions hitherto impossible; but more than this, they are bringing to the rural communities the advantages and the problems of suburban life. Thus *urbanization* is taking possession of the whole population—and by urbanization we do not mean merely the shift of the population to the city; it is a social philosophy—"Do as you like to do in a big city, where you are not known"; it is the rule of the impersonal, under which public opinion has little power to control personal conduct.

Our government and laws were not framed to cope with such situations. Our local, State, and Federal Governments were designed to meet the problems of earlier days, when folks rode horseback over unimproved roads. Now most of the problems of government are motorized. Protection of persons and property becomes increasingly difficult under the handicap of antiquated governmental machinery. The open country can no longer be regarded as "too safe to police." If the vice, gambling, and disorderly conduct of the cities and towns are suppressed, we find that we have merely transplanted them into the country, to road-houses, taverns and "inns." If one State undertakes to regulate marriage and divorce, those who would be inconvenienced by such regulations merely motor across the line into another State where such regulations do not exist.[33] In other words, our agencies for regulation and control

[33] For many years Wisconsin has had "eugenic" marriage laws, requiring physical examination and a two-weeks waiting period between application for license and date of marriage. Until Illinois passed similar legislation thousands of Wisconsin couples crossed into Illinois to be married. Iowa border towns became the Gretna Greens for Wisconsin and Illinois couples who wanted quick action.

have not kept pace with the rapid expansion of community life. But how can these adjustments be made? How can these agencies be made to keep pace with the rapid changes produced by the rapid development of the means of transportation and communication?

The church and the religious life of the community have also felt the impact of these vast changes in communication and travel. Most of the religious organizations and churches were designed to serve the old type of community. The little country churches nestled among the pines and the tombstones, as well as many of the small city "missions," offer little attraction to the young folks of to-day. There are dozens of counter-attractions which compete for the interests that once were given unreservedly to the church. Some who still cling to habits of worship and religious devotion motor past the little church to attend the more spectacular service in the more imposing edifice. Others turn the dial of their radio to a favorite station from which comes the rich music, the type of service, and the sort of sermon that to them seem more satisfying than what they would get from the little country church. In either instance there develops an increasing irregularity of worship, and an indifference in regard to church membership. This, to a large extent, explains the decline of the country churches and the decrease in church membership in the rural communities.[34] Likewise the religious life has not kept pace with other aspects of cultural advance. Somehow religious forces also must be reorganized and their methods of reaching and serving recast, if they are to meet the needs of religious life of this changing order.

In matters of community health and education there has been more progress than in most of the other social institutions. Especially since the First World War, education and health have moved forward with great strides—and for the most part they have moved forward together. The "little red school-house" so dear to American traditions is, in most communities, disappearing. Good roads and the automobile have combined to create the consolidated rural schools or to carry the child to the town or city schools. To be sure, the curriculum is still far from adjusted to modern needs, but even here there is a growing recognition that changes must be made The school nurse, medical examination of school children, vaccination, school clinics, dental clinics, special classes for backward children, visiting teachers for crippled children and shut-ins—all these projects indicate that the next generation will start life's

[34] "Our Cities, Their Role in the National Economy," Report of the National Resources Committee (Washington, D. C., June, 1937), p. 23.

work with stronger bodies and a better knowledge of the laws of health than did the children of the past. But with all this, the movement has merely begun and there is a long way yet to go before these advantages are the heritage of the entire child population.

While the improved means of travel have widened our contacts and enriched our social life in many respects, this increase of speed is costing many lives. In 1940 automobile accidents cost 35,000 lives, injuries to 1,320,000 persons, and property damage estimated at more than $1,000,-000,000. Since 1911 (except for the one year, 1932) the annual toll of automobile accidents has steadily increased. While the majority of drivers are competent and careful, reckless driving and speeding, especially by irresponsible youths and persons under the influence of intoxicants, cause a large proportion of the fatal accidents.[35] Irrespective of differences of opinion in regard to the liquor question, there is no denying the fact that the sweeping changes of the last quarter of a century have placed the issue in a vastly different moral setting. In the horse-and-buggy days drunken drivers seldom endangered the lives of other people; but when a person under the influence of liquor occupies the driver's seat of an automobile in the midst of the congested traffic of our present-day highways, then the issue ceases to be a question of "personal liberty" and becomes a *social* problem of the first magnitude. Furthermore, it is a problem that cannot be met by a public policy and a legal machinery designed to meet the needs of an earlier day.

OTHER SOURCES OF SOCIAL PROBLEMS

Changes in the Mode of Living. While the great changes in industrial life and in the means of travel and communication have been major forces affecting our mode of living, there are still other factors of which we should take account. Take, for example, the hundreds of ways in which electricity serves modern life! Now approximately 70 per cent of the dwellings in the United States are using electric power.[36] Not only has electric lighting altered our habits, but also the numerous appliances that lighten housework and conserve energy and health. Thus hours of time have been released from household routine for use in widening social contacts, intellectual advancement, creative arts, and other interests.

In many other respects the standard American home presents a marked change from the home of even a generation ago. Comforts and

---

[35] *World Almanac* (1942), p. 502.
[36] *Recent Social Trends* (New York, 1933), I, p. 668.

conveniences that were then regarded as *luxuries* for the rich are now regarded as *necessities* and *decencies* for all. In both city and country the "modern" dwelling includes running water in the kitchen, inside toilet and bath, screened-in windows, and—especially in the Northern States—furnace heat. These new elements in the American standard of living have already become fixed in our culture, and the American worker and farmer demand an income that will provide these "necessities." Anything that threatens the attainment of these advantages is at once opposed. This explains our increased opposition to immigrants who have a lower standard.

Improvements in refrigeration are another factor that has made far-reaching changes in our mode of living. In the course of a few years this factor has completely modified our diet. At the same time it has reduced by one-fourth the amount (not the price) of foodstuffs required per person. In other words, it has eliminated much of the waste that formerly was unavoidable in transportation and storage. Now fruits, vegetables, and meats can be kept in storage indefinitely and delivered to the consumer the year round in a fresh and wholesome condition. Thus modern refrigeration is not only recasting our habits of consumption, but it is also forcing radical changes in American agriculture and puts the farmer in a very different economic position.

Consumers' Credit. All these "modern improvements"—and many others which, for lack of space, are not mentioned—would not have changed our mode of living so rapidly had it not been for unprecedented development of *consumers' credit.* Instalment buying, as we know it to-day, grew out of the financing of automobile purchases and has now spread to the financing of purchases of almost every sort of property. Now newly-weds start housekeeping with more furniture and equipment than most of their parents were able to obtain after years of skimping and saving. A small payment down and the balance in "easy monthly payments" starts them out with a standard of living that would take years to approach if everything had to be paid for at once. People's solicitude in regard to being in debt is not what it was a generation or two ago. People used to save in order to provide for the future; now they skimp in order to pay the instalments on past purchases. People no longer dread being in debt, but instead they use their credit without stint. In times of prosperity this new *credit culture* produces an almost reckless expansion of our standard of living. But in times of financial depression and industrial shut-down, both debtor and creditor face a difficult situation. People used to look upon bankruptcy as a disgrace;

to-day it is generally regarded as a "business expedient." Unemployment has become a much more serious problem than it was in the days when people generally lived within their incomes. Unemployment relief is no longer regarded as a problem to be met by the local relief agencies; it is now recognized as a national problem and even the Federal Government has to assist.

Thus we see that the huge social and economic changes of the last century and a half have placed a severe strain upon our whole social structure. By virtue of the fact that our social institutions are slow to change, and because of the difficulty confronting such a large part of the population in its efforts to keep pace with the demands of the times, there appear vast and baffling maladjustments. It is with these maladjustments that our study of social problems is concerned.

THE NATURE OF SOCIAL PROBLEMS

We have noticed that social problems are rooted in the social maladjustments caused by social change. But we need to examine these social maladjustments more carefully in order to get an accurate understanding of their nature.

There are hundreds of social problems, big and little. Some are obvious and clamor for remedial measures, and scores of social-work agencies, public and private, have been organized to remedy this one or that of these obvious social ills. Other problems are less obvious, and creep into our community and national life and sap our group vitality without being comprehended. Some problems respond quickly to the proper treatment. Others require a program of treatment extending over a generation or more.

Thus we have the problems of *poverty* and *dependency*, *crime* and *delinquency*, *sickness* and *physical handicap*, *unemployment* and *discontent*, *ignorance* and *inefficiency*, *dissipation* and *wanton waste*, and scores of other social ills that blight and mar the prosperity and progress of society.

Volumes have been written on the "diagnosis" and treatment of each of these social problems. It is now possible to compile an encyclopedia of social reform, similar to the encyclopedia of medicine. Just as medicine has developed its specialized branches of science and service, so social reform has developed its specialized branches of scientific research and service—of finding ways and means of adjusting the elements of social life so that all may enjoy a larger measure of the fruits of civilization. But in certain phases of social life it is not easy to determine the ways and means of social adjustment. In some respects science has blazed no definite trail for us. Progress in some phases of life has led to confusion in other phases. Thus, progress in industry has changed the whole setting of the family and of the social relationship; and progress in communication and travel has rendered our old agencies of social control ineffective and recast the whole outlook of community life.

Primary and Secondary Phases of Change. We cannot achieve progress without social change; but, at the same time, every important social advancement is purchased at the expense of many social maladjustments that become apparent only after a certain degree of progress has been made. Thus, we might say that there are two phases or stages in every important social change, and it is necessary that we recognize these phases in our study of social problems: (1) the *primary phase*, which is directly concerned with the problems of rapid introduction of new inventions and discoveries, the sudden shifts of population as in migration or immigration, or the opening-up and exploitation of new resources and new enterprises, and (2) the *secondary phase*, which has to do with the maladjustments and bad conditions created by the progress achieved in the primary phase. Some illustrations will make these aspects of social change more clear.

A few generations ago our forefathers slowly worked their way, with lumbering oxen and covered wagons, to the homesteads of the "great Northwest." Gradually they cleared away the virgin forests that covered the hillsides and transformed them into wide-spreading fields of waving grain and grassland. More settlers came. Then came the railroads and still more settlers, until finally, by the close of the nineteenth century, the last acre of free land was taken. Towns and thriving small cities sprang up in the centers of prosperous agricultural communities. The clearing of the forests, the building of adequate schools and roads, and the development of marketing facilities constituted the major problems of this *primary phase* of the rapidly growing population of the "New West." Recently, however, we have begun to appreciate the fact that a *secondary* change was quietly taking place. The clearing of the forests left the loose, fertile soil of the hillsides exposed, and each year the farmers found the land more washed, harder to till, and less productive. The wear and wash of the land drove the more progressive farmers to seek better land, or to give up farming and seek their economic opportunities in the city. Their places were taken by less ambitious and less successful tillers and toilers. Thus in many instances the vigorous and thrifty community of farm-owners gradually faded into a drifting, indifferent, and sluggish community of farm tenants. What little fertility was left in the soil was further depleted by the tenant, whose chief aim was to get out of the land as much as he could without putting anything back into it. Many of the communities must now depend upon State aid for the leadership and support of many of their economic and social institutions. Many of the States are even now turning to active programs of reforestation and soil conservation in the hope of rebuilding the fertility that centuries of virgin forests had placed and held there.

Take the progress of modern medicine. In its primary phase we gave our attention to promoting good health and conquering disease. We faced, and still face, some serious problems in reaching every element of our population with efficient and effective public health education and health service. But we are justly proud of the great achievements we have made. We have practically stamped out many diseases; we have literally cut in half the death-rate of a generation ago; we have lengthened the span of life of the average person until it is now sixty-three years; we are now able to save nineteen out of every twenty babies born until they have passed the critical first year of life; we have added months and years to the productive life of the worker by lessening his days of sickness and adding to his vitality the vigor of good health. This is the *primary phase* of the great change that has come with the advancement of modern medicine. But we are beginning to see that all this vast progress in science is not entirely an unmixed good. There are some baffling *secondary* aspects that have crept quietly into changes taking place. In the first place, in our efforts to cut down the death-rate, we are saving thousands who are too weak of mind or body to face the complex and exacting demands of modern life. We have set aside nature's process whereby the fittest survived and the weak and feeble-minded for the most part died young. We are faced, therefore, with an ever-increasing burden of providing care and guidance for these feeble-minded individuals and for those who are otherwise too weak to provide adequately for themselves. Then again, while we rejoice that we are adding so many years to the length of the average life, we are beginning to be dimly aware of the fact that we must make more generous social provisions for the care and treatment of the aged who every year constitute an increasing proportion of the population.

Thus we might multiply our examples to include every sort of the vast multitude of changes taking place in society to-day; but what we have just pointed out should suffice to make clear the necessity of considering the two phases that characterize all social changes. Problems that appear at first glance to be unrelated are often, after more careful examination, found to spring from common causes growing out of the same phase of social change.

It is gradually coming to be recognized that many social ills cannot be considered singly but are merely branches of larger trunks, manifestations of more basic maladjustments. Leaders of social thought realize that effective adjustments cannot be worked out without taking into account the adjustments demanded by these basic social problems out of which so many of the more obvious problems grow. Hence an understanding of the nature and causes of these basic social problems enables us to understand better the surface problems and to interpret more accurately the drift of events. It enables us, also, to take a more effective part in the constructive programs of social reform.

It is with these basic social problems that our study is concerned, and throughout it is important to keep in mind that *the central problem is that of adjusting our social life and our social institutions, so that, as individuals and as communities, we may use and enjoy the largest measure of civilization possible, and promote further progress.*

RELATIONS OF SOCIOLOGY TO THE STUDY OF SOCIAL PROBLEMS

Sociology is the science that deals with society, its origin, development, forms, activities, and functions. The central purpose of sociology is, first, to *understand society;* second, to work out programs and policies which direct this understanding toward social betterment. "Sociology studies man in his social relations, as affecting and as affected by association, together with all the products and processes consequent upon such association." [37] It is closely related to all fields of science, and especially to the social sciences—economics, political science, history, philosophy, psychology, eugenics, euthenics, and education. It is a general social science and is concerned with the broad field of human associations, while these other sciences are concerned only with specialized phases of human relations. Sociology must use and draw generalizations from the data bearing upon social life furnished by the other sciences.

But sociology not only makes use of the generalizations, principles, and laws revealed by the other sciences, but also extends its methods of investigation and observation into fields untouched by them. It espe-

[37] Gillin and Blackmar, *Outlines of Sociology* (New York, 1930), p. 15.

cially investigates the origin, purposes, and results of the social phenomena that have developed out of association. Only to a limited extent is sociology able to carry on experimentation. Social life and its products require long periods of time to develop and ripen and it is not possible to place and hold human beings under especially controlled conditions, like animals, for experimental purposes. Consequently, the major experiments of the sociologist are those which relate to the testing-out of policies and programs that groups or communities may be induced to adopt tentatively.

The principles and the laws that the sociologists are thus able to draw from the mass of data they collect through investigation, observation, and a limited amount of experimentation, furnish the tools with which social progress may be intelligently and purposefully made. Thus it is that social problems furnish the sociologists with opportunity for studying human association under various and changing conditions. At the same time, the principles and laws that they thus discover furnish the understanding and the method which are necessary for working out programs and policies of sound social adjustment.

REFERENCES

EDWARDS, Lyford P., *The Natural History of Revolution* (Chicago, 1927), Chs. I, II.

ELLIOTT, Mabel A., and MERRILL, Francis E., *Social Disorganization* (New York, 1941).

FAULKNER, H. U., *American Economic History* (New York, 1938, 4th Edition), Chs. XIV, XX, XXIII, XXVIII.

FURNAS, C. C., *The Next Hundred Years* (New York, 1936).

GABRIEL, Ralph H., *The Course of American Democratic Thought* (New York, 1940).

GAUS, Christian, *A Primer for Tomorrow* (New York, 1934).

GILLIN, J. L., and BLACKMAR, F. W., *Outlines of Sociology* (New York, 1930, 3rd Edition), Chs. II, III.

HERTZLER, Arthur E., *The Horse and Buggy Doctor* (New York, 1938), Chs. I, XII.

KALLEN, H. M., *The Decline and Rise of the Consumer* (New York, 1936).

Our Cities, Their Role in the National Economy, Report of the National Resources Committee (Washington, D. C., June, 1937).

OVERSTREET, H. A., *We Move in New Directions* (New York, 1933).

Recent Social Trends, Report of the Hoover Research Committee on Recent Social Trends (New York, 1933), I: Chs. III, IV.

Technological Trends and National Policy, Report of the National Resources Committee (Washington, D. C., June, 1937), pp. 24–38.

QUESTIONS AND EXERCISES

1. How has the growth of huge corporations, mergers, and "chains" affected the relations of business and industry to the worker, to the consumer, and to the community? Illustrate.

2. The development of large-scale enterprise has doubtless raised the American standard of living almost immeasurably. How does this new standard express itself in (a) the status of women; (b) the difficulty in establishing a home; (c) increasing our social problems in regard to family life?

3. How has the development of mechanical refrigeration affected the habits and the standard of living of people? Illustrate.

4. Contrast the effect of the railroads and of the automobiles in the spreading of the city population. What was the shape of the city lay-out created by the railroads? How has the automobile affected the direction of city growth and the trend of city planning?

5. How have good roads and the automobile affected: (a) the living of the city worker; (b) the social life of farm folks; (c) the attitude toward local public opinion; (d) the use of spare time?

6. Why is it that the local law-enforcement officers are unable to cope more effectively with offenders? What solution would you suggest?

7. It is estimated that nearly a third of the rural children under 21 years of age do not feel the influence of the churches. What reasons might be cited for this apparent failure of the churches? What are some of the things the churches might do in order to adapt their appeal to the needs of the day?

8. Combined with the influence of the auto, our machine-made and commercialized amusements make us largely a *spectator* people, indulging largely in *passive participation*. How does this influence express itself in other phases of our social life?

9. Is social change *in itself* either good or bad? What is necessary to assure maximum benefits from our new material resources?

10. Is the creative rôle of the individual in cultural change increasing or decreasing? How does he fare as the beneficiary of cultural change? Give reasons for your answers.

11. What are the significant ways in which sociology can contribute to the solution of social problems?

Chapter 3

GROUP CONFLICT

ONE RESULT of rapid changes in any population is conflict. If those changes enhance the prospects of life and of living, population may increase and burst the geographical bounds traditionally acknowledged by its neighbors. Encroachment upon the pastures or hunting-grounds, upon the source of raw materials, or upon the trading areas of neighbors excites hostility and leads to conflict. Rapid changes within a group act as a selective agent in breaking the population into classes. Those who respond to the changes most quickly, and adapt themselves and their habits to the new situation most completely, become set off from the others in interests, attitudes, and culture patterns. Clashes inevitably arise between these divergent groups. Customs become modified. Old relations are strained. Between group and group emotional reactions develop that lead on to conflict.

For the great majority of mankind group struggle is to-day, and so far as history throws any light upon the question always has been, the inevitable accompaniment of contacts between people of different traditions and culture. History is full of the story of wars and battles. The earliest portions of the Hebrew Scriptures picture the struggle between alien groups. The earliest literature of the Greeks presents a picture of individual combat and group wars as making up a very great proportion of life. These great struggles between what we now call national groups still go on.

However, with the growing complexity of human life, with the dividing of people by different interests and occupations into various classes, the group struggles of the present day have been greatly multiplied. In addition to the struggle of ethnic and cultural groups, nationalities, and races, we have the struggle between different classes in the same society. Some of these class struggles are survivals from previous times. For example, the conflict between clergy and laity is a historical survival. So also are the conflicts between peasant and noble, learned and unlearned, and, to a degree, between those who have and those who have not.

Here in the United States the ferment of social change is altering the composition of groups and classes and rearranging their positions in the social structure. However, the change in this country follows a very different pattern from that of the Old World. Class lines in the Old World have been more fixed by traditional arrangements that have existed since the days of feudalism—"once a peasant, always a peasant." There is, therefore, much more of a foundation for class solidarity and disciplines. In America, there are no traditional *closed* classes, except, perhaps the Negro and the "poor whites" of the South, remnants of the stratified structure of slavery days. For the most part, in this country, all classes are *open*, and the individual may readily pass from one class to the other or may even belong to several at the same time. It is, therefore, not easy to secure the class solidarity and permanency that the closed-class pattern makes possible. At least in political theory, the United States is perhaps the closest to being a classless social structure of any in the world. However, in reality it is the economic and occupational differences that create much of the class differentiation in this country. On this basis we observe a marked shift in the composition and function of the classes in American economic life: in industry, the craftsmen no longer can dominate the labor situation; the salaried class has become a larger and stronger element in the population; management has become smaller but more powerful; likewise, agriculture engages a smaller element in the population but is stronger politically and better organized.[1] These are not the only groups that are maneuvering for positions of greater influence and control in the changing social order. But because of the open-class situation, their maneuvers cannot depart far from the *public* interest; they must, as a matter of fact, have support of public opinion in order to attain their objectives. The public, therefore, becomes the umpire in the conflicts between the groups in a democracy. Unless the public is kept informed as to the actual facts that underlie the contentions of the various groups, its attitude is likely to be based on prejudices compounded from the propaganda of the conflict, leading to further instability and uncertainty.

SOME OUTSTANDING GROUP CONFLICTS

To set forth the many group conflicts in our social order would require volumes. Consequently we shall select certain of the more outstanding forms of group conflict and first examine them in an introductory survey before studying them more in detail in later chapters.

Conflict Between Labor and Capital. The economic struggle for advantage between the employers of labor and the laborers themselves is a

---

[1] Louis M. Hacker, and others, *The United States, A Graphic History* (New York, 1937), pp. 167 ff.

development consequent upon the Industrial Revolution. In a former day when the employer and his men worked in the same shop and at the same work there was no division of interests between the two. With the introduction of machinery and the use of large amounts of capital in the productive process, all this is changed. Often the stockholders who furnish the capital are not acquainted even with the manager of the business. There is not that personal touch between employer and employed that once existed. The stockholder is interested chiefly in his dividends; the bondholder in his interest; the manager in satisfying these two groups and at the same time keeping his labor as contented as possible. Labor in many cases does not know anything about the conduct of the business; it knows only what it hears as to the amount of profit that the business pays; it knows what wages it receives and frequently feels that the distribution of the concern's earnings is not fair. Moreover, the conditions under which the laborers work are frequently determined not by conference of employer with employee, but arbitrarily by the employer; and sometimes these conditions are bad for the laborer. Therefore it is easy to see that in the development of our great industrial and commercial civilization the interest of the owners of great industries and the interest of the employees are not always the same. Consequently we have those industrial conflicts which we know as strikes and lockouts. Frequently an industry is for a time paralyzed by a struggle that cannot be settled by agreement between the two contending parties. Indeed, the conflicts in industry are perhaps the most costly to both labor and to the public of any of the various types of group conflict. Thousands of families suffer, homes are disrupted, hatred developed, frequently violence occurs, and even national interest is jeopardized. In such a case you have war within the body politic between conflicting classes of society. Table 3 shows the trend of strikes in the period from 1920 to 1940: [2]

TABLE 3

STRIKES IN THE UNITED STATES, 1920–1940

Year	Strikes	Number of Workers Involved	Man-Days Idle Because of Strikes
1920	3,411	1,463,054	...No data...
1925	1,301	428,416	...No data...
1930	637	182,975	3,316,808
1935	2,014	1,117,213	15,456,337
1940	2,508	576,988	6,700,872

[2] World Almanac (1942), p. 116.

Race Conflicts. Race conflicts in the United States are struggles chiefly between whites and Negroes, whites and Orientals, or Jews and Gentiles. The attacks of the whites on Negroes in the South, sociologically speaking, grow out of the disturbance of the status of the two races consequent upon the Emancipation Proclamation of President Lincoln and the final issue of the War Between the States. So long as the inferior position of the blacks was established by law and common consent, there was no question as to the relationship of the two races. However, upon the political emancipation of the blacks, the question of the relationship between the two races became critical. Habit, custom, and tradition had fixed in the mores of the people of the South the inferior status of the blacks. When they were given political equality after the close of the War Between the States, naturally friction between the two races developed.

From 1882 to 1940 there were 3,404 Negroes lynched in the United States. While the numbers have varied from year to year, rising from 64 in 1882 to 162 in 1892, the trend since 1892 has been steadily downward. In 1940 only four Negroes were lynched. The States that show the largest number of lynchings of Negroes between 1882 and 1940 are: Alabama, 299; Arkansas, 226; Florida, 250; Georgia, 482; Kentucky, 141; Mississippi, 528; Louisiana, 334; South Carolina, 154; Tennessee, 201; and Texas, 345.[3] It is generally supposed that most of the lynchings of Negroes occur because of attacks on white women. A study of the figures, however, shows that 80 per cent of the lynchings of Negroes are for offenses other than rape.[4] State and city interracial committees are being formed for the purpose of adjusting relationships between the whites and the blacks in an equitable manner. Certain Southern States are passing laws giving the Negro victim (or his family) a right to sue the county that allows a lynching, and serious efforts are being made everywhere to adjust these difficult relations.

The root of conflict between the whites and the Orientals on the Pacific Coast is somewhat different. Fundamentally it is economic in its nature, although social considerations enter also. So long as the Chinese and Japanese immigrants were content to take the part of servants in the household there was no trouble. When, however, they began to launch out in the economic field on their own account and with their lower standard of living were able to compete successfully with their white neighbors in industry, agriculture, and business, then it was that trouble

[3] *World Almanac* (1942), p. 583.
[4] *Negro Yearbook* (1921–1922), p. 72.

began. Their family standards, as well as their standards of living, their custom of working on Sundays, their insistence that their children should attend school with white children, and the rising social status that economic success brought in its train, aggravated the situation. The occasional marriage of a white woman to a Japanese or a Chinese, while not of great significance, served to excite the imaginations of the whites with fear of social equality, much as it does when some Negroes, chafing under social restrictions to their own race, insist upon their rights to intermarry with the whites and be accorded equal social privileges.

With the increase of the Jewish population of the United States, especially in our large cities, some resentment of the Jews has appeared. Generally the Jews who cause the difficulties are immigrants accustomed to a lower standard of living in European countries. They colonize in our large cities and enter into competition with the American workers and with American shopkeepers. In addition to this fundamental economic pressure certain customs and traditions mark them off as a people apart. Where, as in America, the Jews are not discriminated against politically, educationally, or economically, many adopt the standards of living of this country, join the labor-unions or organize new ones, accept American standards of business, adopt the customs of their new homeland, and rapidly assimilate with the people of the country.

In Palestine in recent years conflicts between Arabs and Jews were immediately religious, but fundamentally induced by fear on the part of the former that the latter would obtain political and economic ascendancy. In Russia the Jewish problem has been largely solved by the Soviet revolution, inasmuch as many of the leaders of that movement are themselves Jews. From present appearances it seems that the Jewish problem will remain unsettled.

Religious Conflicts. In Asia and Africa, where the Mohammedan culture comes in conflict with the Christian and the Jewish, intense religious hatreds arise and conflicts occur. In India this clash occurs between Hindus and Mohammedans; in Turkey, before the organization of the Turkish Republic, it occurred between Mohammedans and Christians. In a country of religious freedom, that is, where all religions are given equal opportunity and none special privileges, conflict tends to become competition, violence tends to give way to the subtler conflict, and the outcome is the adjustment of all religions to the demands of the people. The more active and flexible religious organizations tend to borrow and adapt to their purposes ideas and practices that have commended themselves. Under such conditions the fierce religious conflicts die out, the tolerant spirit spreads, and those religions which most effectively commend themselves to the beliefs of the people survive while others fade away.

Cultural Conflict. Another type of group conflict is represented by the conflict of different cultures. By the culture of a people we mean all those ways of doing things, points of view, customs, traditions, and habits which make up the warp and woof of everyday life and thinking. For example, consider the difference in culture between the American Indians when the whites came to this country and that of the whites. There was little difference in the agricultural techniques of the colonists and the Indians. But there was a vast difference between the methods of government, religion, personal and group ideals, and traditions. The Indian had no weapons except the bow and arrow and the stone hatchet, or club. The white man brought with him the gun, which had developed out of the discovery of gunpowder. The religion of the Indian was a sort of animism culminating in the concept of the Great Spirit, Manitou. The white man's religion was the result of a long period of development. While the Indian's theology was chiefly a mythology, the white man's religion was shot through with certain dogmas that he held to be of absolute validity. The Indian had no sacred book, the white man had his infallible Bible. A definite set of traditions had attached themselves to his religion, as well as definite practices in the celebration of its rites. The Indian's government was a government based upon blood-relationships, real or assumed. It was in the hands of clan and tribal leaders. The white man's government was based upon written instruments tracing back to the Magna Carta of King John. Its basis was not blood-relationship, but residence within a given geographical area. Moreover, economically, while the Indian practised agriculture, he lived chiefly by hunting. Naturally he could not understand why the white man insisted upon robbing him of his hunting-ground. On the other hand, the white man had passed much beyond the hunting economy; he felt that the Indian used the land wastefully and therefore that he himself had a right to use it more efficiently. This brief outline of some of the different elements of culture of the Indians as compared with those of the white men perhaps gives one a clearer notion of the conflict that inevitably ensued. Subtly working in the white man's mind was the opinion that his culture was superior to that of the Indian, and therefore the latter deserved no consideration at his hands. The Indian, on the other hand, felt as we would feel, should invaders with a different culture settle upon our borders and proceed to divest us of our rights, to crowd us out of our land, and to subject us to their will. This was a conflict of culture.

The unrest in Oriental countries at the present time is largely the result of the conflicts of culture. China and India, with their long history and proud culture, feel that they are superior to the men who bring to them the materialistic culture of the West, with its physical science and its emphasis upon highly organized industry. On the other hand, the white man who has invaded these Eastern countries has a sense of his superiority. In the language of almost every people the name of that people indicates their sense of superiority. No wonder, then, that long-separated cultures which come into contact excite a high degree of emotion on both sides. The natives of India, while they recognize the important contribution made by the British Government, are stirred to their depths by the manifestation of what they believe is a sense of assumed superiority on the part of the whites.

THE GENESIS OF GROUP CONFLICT

Group conflict may sometimes be the result of the personal ambitions of an individual; but usually at the bottom of them lie great currents of human feeling stirred by the consciousness of certain differences and the threatening of interests considered vital.

Economic Disturbance. Frequently class conflict arises out of the introduction of certain economic and industrial changes. Great economic disturbance occurred in the history of England when after the Black Death of 1348, which swept off from a third to a half of the people of England, the old relationships between the lords of the manor and the serfs or vassals were seriously disturbed. The feudal system began to break down, and new methods of agriculture had to be introduced. Because of the demand for woolen goods, sheep-raising became more profitable than ordinary farming, while at the same time it was easier to secure attendants for a flock of sheep than cultivators of the soil. The common lands of whole villages were enclosed to make sheep-runs; large numbers of peasants were reduced to misery; class conflict slumbered until it broke out in movements of one sort or another, often culminating in bloodshed.

Again, the change from domestic to factory industry created a rift in the solidarity of the social population. Large numbers of the hand-weavers were driven to starvation, while factory-owners amassed great fortunes by the exploitation of their workers. Naturally a class psychology arose on the part of the worker as well as on the part of the employer. While the old status of inferior and superior growing out of the feudal relationship, once established, resulted in little or no conflict because the relationships were personal, the new class consciousness generated by the Industrial Revolution, because interests were no longer identical but conflicting, had a very different effect. A similar growth of class consciousness appears whenever there is radical change in economic arrangements. Thus, in the United States the growth of great corporations with absentee ownership and the consequent separation of owner and worker in personal acquaintanceship led to the growth of class consciousness and class conflict. Strikes and lockouts resulted. While a number of experiments in resolving the intensity of the conflict have been tried, such as welfare work for employees, stock ownership by employees, shop committees for the adjustment of grievances, and plans for joint control over conditions of work and rates of pay, the clash of interests between owners and workers has not yet been allayed.

Changes in Culture. A difference in the culture of groups within a given population often results in conflict. When William the Norman conquered England and several thousand of his retainers became the overlords of the country, the elements of a new culture were introduced into that land. A new language became the official language; a somewhat more highly developed religion was introduced by the conquerors; the status of the conquerors was superior and they made their superiority felt by their subordinates. For a generation or two the consciousness of difference between the conquerors and the conquered was very sharp. Frequent clashes occurred. A process of adjustment began, which in the course of centuries was virtually completed, and class consciousness disappeared.

When immigrants from another country arrive in large numbers, differences in culture are soon recognized. Hence, in this country, when large numbers of the Irish arrived in the early part of the nineteenth century, culture differences between them and the people already settled here were recognized on both sides. Again, with the coming of large numbers of Italians with different customs and traditions, a different language, and a different standard of living, the older inhabitants became conscious of the intrusion of an alien culture and dubbed these people "Wops" and "Guineas." While these differences in culture did not always result in conflict, they formed the basis of an attitude of superiority toward the new immigrants. Such attitudes increase the difficulty of what we call "Americanization," that is, the assimilation of these people into our culture. This consciousness of difference in culture accounts for many of the difficulties in forming labor-unions in those industrial groups in which there are large numbers of immigrants of different nationalities. Labor leaders find it very much more difficult to present a united front when cultural differences interfere with understanding and coöperation. Such cultural differences also affect progress in schools, health programs, the development of recreation, housing, and many other social problems.[5]

While many of these conflicts due to differences in culture do not break out into open violence, they are none the less conflicts in the social process. They retard social unification, prevent people of different cultures from looking at things in the same way and uniting for common purposes. They constitute one of our chief social problems.

Religious Innovations. Often religious differences give rise to group conflict more or less sharp. The conflict of different religions is not here referred to, although such conflicts are an inevitable result of the contact of different religions in a common area. However, within a given area changes are constantly taking place in the development of any single religion. This is illustrated by a large number of Mohammedan sects, the different varieties of Buddhism, the orthodox and liberal varieties of Judaism, and of Christianity. Rooted as most of these innovations are in social conditions, and constituting as they do a response on the part of a few leaders to changed conditions in the lives of people, these religious innovations frequently lead to terrific group conflicts within a given organization. Consider, for example, the upheaval, which historically has been called a revolt, brought about by the Lutheran Reformation in Germany and the surrounding countries. All of us are familiar with the terrible results of that upheaval. It disturbed the social solidarity of Europe for centuries and remains even to-day a basis of frequent conflict. The Lutheran Reformation was only one of a series of innovations that have disturbed the peace of the Christian Church from the first centuries of the Christian era up to the present time. Perhaps the latest to develop is that rather fundamental division which has come about in the strife between the Modernists and the Fundamentalists in Protestant Christianity.

Assumption of Group Superiority. The most fundamental cause of class and group conflict is the attitude of superiority on the part of one class, or group, toward another. It may be pride of race, of nationality,

[5] Herman Feldman, *Racial Factors in American Industry* (New York, 1931), Part I.

of culture, of religion, or of political system. It may take any one of a number of forms. As long as it is conceded by all people that there are higher and lower orders of social classes, and the relationships of these classes have become stabilized, there is very little danger of conflict growing out of superiority and inferiority. However, let democracy, or a doctrine of equality, enter into the minds of men as it did in the Western world in the latter part of the eighteenth century, and these stabilized relationships between the higher and lower classes receive a rude shock, class consciousness develops, and class conflict is probable. As indicated above, the conflicts going on in India and China and all the Eastern world at the present time are reactions against this attitude of superiority on the part of the representatives of one kind of culture toward those of another. Moreover, in subtler ways this attitude of superiority appears in any given social group. Consider the gulf fixed between the common people of any State and the educated classes. Too often the educated people, especially those with higher education, feel superior to the common run of mankind. They show this feeling; they look with some degree of contempt on the untutored workingman, or the unlettered legislator. This has its results when university appropriations appear before the legislature for approval. The educated specialists despises the ignorance of most people on matters that are commonplace to him, and he allows this contempt to affect his whole attitude toward the common people. As a compensation these common people repay this contempt with interest and look upon him as a strange kind of human being. While the learned may dub the common people "boobs," they return the compliment by calling him a "high-hat," or a "professor," or a "high-brow."

The same attitude of superiority appears among the rich with regard to the poor. Too often the man who has been successful in accumulating wealth looks down upon those who have not as inferior creatures.

RESULTS OF CLASS AND GROUP CONFLICT

Out of this clash between classes and groups certain important social results appear, some socially good, and some bad.

Good Results. There is no question that certain socially good products have come about as a result of group conflict. The early struggle of tribes and groups of people resulted in the selection of those who were fitted to survive in a given situation. In that early period of group conflict, without question, war favored the survival of the superior. "Superior" in this case meant the class, group, or individual best fitted to survive in a given situation. That advantage was not, of course, unalloyed, and there were evil by-products even in that early day.

Even among modern groups something of the same good social results grow out of conflict. The superiority of a given culture often is demonstrated in violent conflict. To-day, however, conflict is more on the basis of applied science and ideals than on the basis of physical strength or of mental ability. The inevitable result of conflict, no matter how severe it may be, between groups and classes, is either the imposition of certain elements of culture upon the conquered, with perhaps some modification of the culture of the conquerors by infiltration from the lower culture, or a compromise between two rather equally matched groups and the integration of opposing views. As illustration of this point consider what happened in the Norman conquest of England and what happened after the Protestant revolt in Germany. One would suppose that a conquest as thorough and complete as that of the Norman conquest in England would have the result of overwhelming the culture of the Saxons and Danes by that of the Normans. As a matter of fact, however, that did not occur. The basis of Anglo-Saxon law, the language of the country, the religion, and the customs and traditions remained largely those of the conquered people. Certainly they adopted certain elements of culture that the Norman conquerors brought over from France. After two hundred years, however, there had come about an amalgamation of the two cultures into a new culture composed of Anglo-Saxon culture as a base with some modifications introduced by the Normans.

One would think as he reads of the intense conflict between the Catholics and the Protestants following the Reformation that no modification would be possible on either side. One who reads the history after the first burst of hatred had died down, however, learns that such was not the case. The Council of Trent for the Catholic Church introduced certain modifications and took over certain suggested reforms that constituted what has been called the Counter-Reformation. In other words, the Catholic Church attempted to capture some of the "thunder" of the Reformers. Moreover, within two generations after the Reformation had started, the reformed churches took over certain of the Catholic ritual and a large part of the Catholic dogmas and incorporated them into the creeds of Protestant Christendom.

Many other illustrations of this process of compromise and adoption of elements from the opposing culture might be cited.

Evil Results. Certain evil products have appeared as the result of class conflict from the earliest period of history until the present time. One of the most outstanding of these is *the riving of the social solidarity* consequent upon class or group conflict. Open conflict brings to expression all the hidden hatred and suspicion that lie at the base of a conflict. The gulf already opening between classes is made deeper and wider for the time being. Take for example the conflict between the North and the South in the War Between the States. The consciousness of difference that had been growing for nearly a century became sharpened and fixed as a result of that great struggle. The resolution of each side for the time being was stiffened. After nearly eighty years the gulf between the North and the South has been only partially bridged. Misunderstanding between the two sections is still easily excited. It is true, however, that the lapse of time heals old sores. In the end social integration will probably take place.

Another evil result of class conflict is *waste of effort*. Consider the useless words spoken, the fruitless efforts spent, on sectional divisions over public questions in the United States. How much more constructive measures could have been adopted in our political problems in the United States, for example, had the issues not been confused by the memories of the hatred and strife of the War Between the States! How fruitless is much of the strife between Fundamentalists and Modernists over dogmatic problems! How much constructive coöperation has been prevented by the strife between the Catholics and Protestants in this country! These class conflicts have drawn "red herrings" across the path of progress and have diverted the attention of men from problems of greater social importance, which needed settling so badly. How much money has been spent by both labor-unions and employers in maintaining their respective so-called "rights" in the industrial conflict! There is no question that class conflict means enormous waste of effort.

Another immediately evil result of class conflict is *the weakening of the bonds that hold us to some of the old loyalties,* such as the family bonds, church bonds, and patriotism. Perhaps this is not wholly evil. Perhaps this means in the end the creation of a finer loyalty to family, church, and state. Nevertheless, immediately it has decidedly disastrous results upon these social institutions. How frequently religious disputes cut across family lines and dissolve family loyalty! Some of these evil results appear in the divorce statistics in the cases of families established by the marriage of Protestants and Catholics, or of Christians and Jews. Many times these age-old conflicts result in the disruption of a family.

Consider the effect upon religion—Protestant, Catholic, Jewish, Mohammedan, or Hindu—of race antipathy or class conflict. A good example is provided by what happened in the First World War. Consider the predicament in which the Catholic Church was placed, with its adherents ranged on both sides of the great conflict. No less difficult was the dilemma of the Protestant churches, who had adherents on both sides. The church as a whole is in a peculiarly difficult situation in our industrial conflict. Which side shall it take in that strife which has risen over labor questions? Shall it hold with the property-owner, the employer, the capitalist, or shall it take the side of the workman? It requires wise statesmanship to steer the ship of church in the troubled waters of industrial conflict.

The First and Second World Wars alike have shown us the difficulties for thousands of our immigrant citizens and their families in maintaining loyalty to the country of which they are citizens rather than to the country from which they or their parents have come. Our German-American citizens and more recently our Italian-Americans have been in a very difficult situation. They loved both countries, the old and the new. The war period has been a time of severe testing for many of them. In all these ways great class and group conflicts produce results that in their immediate aspects are evil.

FACTORS THAT MITIGATE GROUP CONFLICT

In the previous paragraphs numerous hints necessarily had to be dropped which showed that these group conflicts ultimately are settled. Let us now look at those devices which mitigate the sharpness of the conflict and tend to bring about compromise and adjustment.

In the Economic Field. In the economic field new inventions giving opportunity to rise from one class to another, wide distribution of ownership of property, rapid industrial development providing a chance for energy and genius and for steady employment, lessen class and group conflict. Moreover, provisions for safeguarding the health, old age, or employment of workers, such as health-insurance, old-age and unemployment insurance, or other devices that lessen the hazards to health, age, and employment, tend to ameliorate the conflict between classes. Agencies providing for those who are unfortunate, and devices for settling disputes between industrial groups or between nations cut down the occasions for conflict and mitigate the struggle. Moreover, as we look back over history, we see how many of the great group and class

conflicts could have been avoided had there been an appeal not to prejudice but to scientific investigation and a fair and full presentation of unbiased facts. The probabilities are that the First World War would not
have occurred had there been some impartial investigating body that
could have studied the facts and presented an unbiased report. Many
industrial disputes would not occur were there clear understanding on
the part of both sides of the facts with reference to each side of the conflict. Science applied to all these fields and to many others may yet solve
class conflict.[6]

In the Social Field. Widespread educational opportunity giving the
chance to all who are capable of profiting by it is, in the long run, a mitigating influence on group conflict. That is the justification for the provision of education suited to the needs of the people which has been
made by the United States.

Another mitigating factor in the social field is the shifting of attention to new social values away from emotional prejudices and hatreds.
For example, shifting attention to service to one's country, or to his
city, frequently solves present conflict. As people widen the range of
their interests, taking in philanthropy, art, literature, civic virtue, or
any other great social object, class conflict, resting upon elemental emotions, tends to be dissolved and to disappear.[7]

Widening political opportunity, giving every one a chance to share
in government to the extent of his capacity, tends to lessen the ancient
strife between the privileged and the unprivileged. The coming of a
democracy, while bringing new sources of class division and strife, closes
the gulf between ancient classes. Where, as in England and America, the
humblest citizen, by his gift or the exercise of his talent, may rise to the
highest office, the significance of the ancient political classes has entirely
disappeared.

Moreover, equality before the court and the law, an ancient dream not
yet realized, so far as it is achieved softens the asperity between classes.
Once the peasant had no rights before a court, that his lord was compelled to recognize. In theory each man to-day is equal before the judge.
In actual practice this has not yet been realized. The man with money
or influence sometimes still has the advantage. The setting up of the public defender, *viz.*, a man to defend the poor man against charges brought
against him in the court, is a movement in the direction of equality be-

[6] John A. Fitch, *Causes of Industrial Unrest* (New York, 1924), Part IV.
[7] Herman Feldman, *op. cit.*, Part II.

fore courts of law. Legal-aid societies, which provide good lawyers for the man who is sued for a small sum or to whom is owed a small sum, are moves in the same direction.

Finally, socialized religion, that is, religion suited to the needs of the common man and adapted to the social problems of the day, is another factor ameliorating group and class conflict. Could all religions unite, the conflicts and struggles that have marked the history of dogmatic Christianity would fade away!

If this brief survey of the significance of group and class conflict has any value, it makes clear to us how these conflicts arise, how certain of them are inevitable, and how constantly there are working in human society certain forces and influences that mitigate their severity, lead to compromise, and increase the unity of the various groups. The real problem is how to bring about the union of different cultures and different groups of men devoted to contradictory principles and practices, with the least evil results and with the ultimate combination of all that is socially useful. Cooley has pointed out that these conflicts tend to become less personal by reason of the fact that men's loyalties are organized increasingly across different classes. A man is not only a Republican, for example, but he may be an employer or a laborer; a Presbyterian or a Roman Catholic, an educated or an ignorant man; a lover of art or a lover of fine stock. Group conflict is one of the inevitable results of social evolution. With the development of communication and transportation, men become acquainted with each other, groups learn to appreciate each other's culture, and the fundamental basis of class strife tends to be mitigated.

REFERENCES

"Education for Social Control," *Annals of the American Academy of Political and Social Science* (November, 1935).

COOLEY, Charles H., *The Social Process* (New York, 1918), pp. 241–268.

ELLIOTT, Mabel A., and MERRILL, Francis E., *Social Disorganization* (New York, 1941).

FELDMAN, Herman, *Racial Factors in American Industry* (New York, 1931), Part I.

GABRIEL, Ralph H., *The Course of American Democratic Thought* (New York, 1940).

JOSEPHSON, M., *The Robber Barons* (New York, 1933).

KALLEN, H. M., *The Decline and Rise of the Consumer* (New York, 1936).

"Public Opinion and Labor Unions," *Fortune Magazine* (April, 1938).

Ross, E. A., *Principles of Sociology* (New York, 1938, 4th Edition), Part IV.

WOOFTER, T. J., *Basis of Racial Adjustment* (New York, 1925).

QUESTIONS AND EXERCISES

1. Explain why in the Middle Ages *inferiority* and *superiority* in social status did not create class conflict, while to-day the ostentatious assumption of superiority by any class results in resentment by those who, by inference, are inferior.

2. Bearing in mind that education tends to make a group more articulate, what effect does universal education have upon class conflict? What is the ultimate effect on the standards of the entire group? Give examples.

3. What is the effect on class consciousness if the social structure is such that it provides unqualified opportunity for the individual to pass from laborer to capitalist?

4. List factors (1) increasing and (2) decreasing class consciousness in industrial relations at the present time. What is your appraisal of these factors?

5. What is the basis of the conflict between the two divisions of organized labor: between the American Federation of Labor, on the one side, and the Congress of Industrial Organizations, on the other? Why is the fight between these two divisions of labor so bitter?

6. Explain the following statement: "In general, the growing complexity of interests tends to increase the number of conflicts between groups and to decrease the severity of these conflicts."

7. Name two of the most severe group conflicts that are evident in your community, and show in each case: (*a*) what is the issue of the conflict; (*b*) which groups are the challengers or initiators of the conflicts; (*c*) what are the methods used by each against the other; and (*d*) what is the basis of the claim of each to public approval?

8. Are the issues and goals of group conflict always apparent and clearly defined, or are they often obscured by appeals to patriotism, social justice, honor, and interwoven with prejudices? Give two illustrations.

Chapter 4

THE BASIS OF RACE CONFLICT

GENERALLY problems of race relations have been referred to as "the race problem," and too often the inference has been that the trouble is confined to certain problematic races, while "WE," the white race—or to be more exact, the Nordics—are the ones annoyed and bothered. Looking at the subject thus we have befogged the real issues—and worse, we have vexed and offended "the other fellow" to the point where relations with him have become more problematic instead of improving. There are, to be sure, "race" (*i.e.*, human race) problems—problems of over-population, problems of degeneracy, problems of depletion by military selection—such as are so forcefully presented in Professor Edward M. East's monumental book, *Mankind at the Crossroads*,[1] but such studies are seldom referred to as "the race problem."

There are scores of problems that involve race relations—standard of living, community-building, education, politics, industry, public recreation, travel conveniences, citizenship, business—and to lump all of them together and to speak of them collectively as "the race problem" is merely to create an emotional attitude toward race relations, instead of challenging the use of careful research, thoughtful study, and sound judgment—all of which are essential to progress in human relations in any and every field. So long as questions of race relations rest upon an emotional basis there is no answer to them, other than what has been too generally characteristic—mob violence and war.

THE BASIS OF RACE FRICTION

History is, to a large extent, made up of race conflict, of race conquests and race subjugations; and few chapters of the world's history are more illumined with the fires of race prejudice than are those which recount the making of these United States. What is the explanation?

A race tends to spread and migrate—either drifting or driven in the direction of escape from hunger, adverse climatic conditions, disease, persecution, or servitude, or in pursuit of adventure, fortune, greater freedom for self-expression, political or religious gains. Whenever mi-

[1] 1923.

gration takes place great changes, social, political, and economic, result. Whether voluntary or forced (as was the case of the American Negro), migration invariably gives rise to complicating and difficult problems of human relations.

When members of one race migrate into the midst of another race *recognized* as different in *cultural background* and *physical character-istics* [2] there results a complication of human relations that soon begins to express itself in one way or another. If the number of the migrants is relatively small, they may be accepted with curiosity and more or less indifference; but as their numbers increase, this attitude of indifference gives way to a growing race prejudice; and this race prejudice persists just as long as either the cultural or the physical differences remain recognized by either of the races.[3]

With the increased number of "strange" people struggling for a living, for power, for position, and for prestige, there develops in the native population a feeling that the culture and prestige of its own people— their "position," their "dominance"—is being threatened by the "trespassing" race. *Hence, in all the social institutions and in those aspects of social life where social prestige is expressed and recognized, the "color-line" becomes definitely drawn.* The one race comes to regard the other race as being inferior, or undesirable, and possibly both. The race claiming superiority resents any effort on the part of the other race to assert social equality or to compete with the members of the "dominant" race for social position and prestige. Furthermore, the "dominant" race, while assigning lower social status to the "inferior" race, finds it easy to justify exploitations, and to erect a double standard of justice—one standard for the control of the relations between its own members, and another standard to regulate the relations that its members may have with the "inferior" race.

Whenever the "inferior" race refuses to accept the rating of inferiority, and demands recognition as a social equal, and a right to share the prestige of the "superior" race, then it is that trouble begins. The "superior" race insists that the "inferior" race "must keep its place," and it is seldom satisfied with lawful, orderly measures in enforcing its de-

[2] Jerome Dowd, *The Negro in American Life* (1926), p. 359.
[3] Dowd, *op. cit.*, p. 424, defines culture roughly as follows: "(a) The energy or urge to create, and (b) the expansion of sympathy through the development of common interests, group sentiments, and organization, and the acquisition of habits, technique, patterns, or what the anthropologists call trait-complexes. Primarily, culture is a subjective phenomenon; secondarily, it is objective, and recognizable by tools, machinery, buildings, and all material products and contrivances."

mands on the "inferiors." Such measures are too slow of action, too impersonal, too deliberate, to satisfy the emotions of jealousy, fear, and hatred that boil over when the prestige of the race is at stake. Lynch-law is substituted for orderly justice, and the mob metes out its quick, violent, terrorizing vengeance as a warning to the other members of the "inferior" race, that they must either "keep their place" or perish.[4]

A PRESENT-DAY WORLD PROBLEM

History is full of records of bloody wars and race conflicts that demonstrate the principles that we have just outlined. Wherever a nation is composed of dissimilar races, the embers of race prejudice are easily fanned into fierce flames. This is a fact abundantly attested in the history of almost every people. But no period in history was more vexed with conflict that at bottom is essentially race war, than is the present.

We have already noted how the Jews have been quite generally persecuted. The Jewish culture resists assimilation probably more than does the culture of any other people, and often the Jews are disdainfully inconsiderate of the culture of the other people with whom they are destined to live and trade. This trait caused the ancient Jews no end of trouble during Old Testament times, and the modern "Gentile" seems hardly less resentful. Not many years ago we were shocked repeatedly at the awful persecutions and massacres of the Jews in Russia and Poland. To-day the Jew is confronted with similar hardships at the hands of Nazi Germany. There, as elsewhere, the Jews have been thrifty, aggressive, and aspiring. Their accumulations of wealth gave them a considerable stake in the economic life of the nation, and power to command recognition and position. Then in the minds of the hate-crazed Nazis came the exaggerated picture of Jewish dominance; and Nazi leaders professed foreseeing the honor of the "Fatherland" dragging in the dust. At once race prejudice was whipped up, and terrorizing raids were launched against the Jews and even "anyone with Jewish blood in his veins." Hitler, himself, became the leading rabble-rouser against the Jews.

The Orient has presented an interesting assortment of problems in race relations. In Japan Americans and Europeans dare not assume the air of "Nordic superiority." The Japanese insist on being considered the equals of the best the world over. In Japan the Japanese prestige is dominant and foreigners must respect and obey their customs, laws, and authority. Even in world politics, and especially in the disarmament con-

[4] J. E. Cutler, *Lynch Law* (1905).

ferences, the voice of Japan was heard and respected. Even in Japan's ruthless carnage in China, the United States and European nations long excused one insult after another from the Japanese army and navy.

China traditionally has been a divided nation and one too weak in capital resources to protect her ancient pride and demand recognition as an equal. Hence America, Japan, and European countries, taking advantage of her weak political and economic situation, have imposed upon China their "superiority" complex, and thereby justified economic exploitation of China and her resources. They set up their own government, side by side with the Chinese Government, insisting that the foreigners be subject to their own law and not the law of China. It is easy to see how gross exploitation of every sort would thrive under such circumstances. China's heroic stand against the Japanese invaders will no doubt bring greater unity and prestige to her.

THE PROBLEM OF RACE RELATIONS IN THE UNITED STATES

We have noted that the basis for race friction lies in the recognized differences of cultural background and in physical differences. Are these factors merely artificial and capable of being eliminated, or are they of such a permanent nature that the solution to the problem of race relations involves the hopeless task of altering human nature?

Not a few scientists, chiefly biologists,[5] and a considerable number of American writers take the view that the races are not equally endowed, and that the white man inherits a greater capacity for brain development than does the Negro.[6] If this were true, the problem of race relations in this country would resolve itself into that of devising ways and means for obtaining a change in the Constitution of the United States to permit the establishment of a white man's protectorate over the colored population!

However, most of the anthropologists and students of ethnology are agreed that racial differences cannot be interpreted as implying that some races are superior to others in intellectual capacity, enterprise, morality, and physique. "The answer to such criticism," says Kroeber, "is first of all that racial inferiority and superiority are by no means self-evident truths. Secondly, the belief in race inequalities is founded in emotion and action and then justified by reasoning. That is, the belief is rationalized,

---

[5] See Dowd, *op. cit.*, Ch. 48, for a carefully compiled list of the scientists and writers holding that the differences are biological, hence incapable of being changed, or smoothed out.

[6] W. B. Smith, *The Color Line* (1905); Lothrop Stoddard, *The Rising Tide of Color* (1920).

not primarily inferred by pure reason. It may be true, but it is not proven true." [7] Great efforts have been put forth by anthropologists and ethnologists to find proof that would justify the belief in the superiority of the Caucasian race; but they are frank to admit that they have not as yet come across any real proof.

The acceptance of the belief in the inferiority of the Negro to the white must then be due to other than scientific proof. It is interesting to note that in most fields of thought, *observed similarities* form the basis of our beliefs; but in matters of race relations the exact reverse is true—instead of basing belief on similarities, we have emphasized the social and individual diversities. Perhaps there is no other aspect of the problem of race relations that needs more consideration than that of collecting and presenting accurate information regarding the Negro and his relations to the white race—his economic, his cultural, and his social progress and achievements. In our discussions of race relations we too often leave these matters out of consideration altogether, and emphasize the "criminality of the Negro," the "immorality of the Negro," and the "illiteracy of the Negro." If we were to use the same process of reasoning in forming our estimates of Chicago, St. Louis, Memphis, and other American cities, it would not be difficult to believe that the whole of the human race has fallen into an extremely low state, and that civilization is doomed! But to present the facts in regard to the race relations has not been the popular approach; emotional acceptance of rumor and half-truths crowds back the sober consideration of facts that would further interracial harmony. For example, if the same attention were given to the attacks of white men on colored women that is given to attacks of Negro men on white women, it is indeed doubtful whether much more would be said about the superiority of the whites in regard to morals! The presence of from three to five million mulattoes in the Negro population speaks for itself, and is a clear indication that the problem of race relations is not entirely a one-sided affair.

Then, too, if the problem of race relations rested upon permanent innate antipathies, it would be a universal phenomenon wherever divergent races associated together. But this is not the case. James Bryce, in describing the peoples of South American countries, observes: "Race repugnance is no such constant and permanent factor in human affairs as members of the Teutonic peoples are apt to assume. Instead of being, as we Teutons suppose, the rule in the matter, we are the exception . . . and since the phenomenon is not of the essence of human nature, it may

[7] A. L. Kroeber, *Anthropology* (1923), Ch. IV, p. 59.

not always be as strong among the Teutonic peoples as it is today." [8]
Thus in Brazil, where the Negroes are more numerous than in any other
South American country, there is no color-line—not even against inter-
marriage!

Consequently, if the physical differences form no permanent barrier
to race harmony, if the dogma of superiority and inferiority has no basis
in fact, then we must examine the cultural backgrounds in order to find
the real basis for the problem of race relations in the United States. We
shall presently see that differences in cultural background constitute our
major problem of the "melting-pot" in America. [9] But it is perhaps easier
to fuse the many nationalistic cultures of our foreign-born population
than it is to harmonize the two race cultures that are of our own making
—i.e., the American culture of the whites and the culture of the American Negro. Undoubtedly the difference in these two American-made
cultures constitutes the most persistent and real basis for our problem of
race relations. It is, in short, our home-made cultural difference, more
than difference in the physical make-up of the American and the African,
that creates the problem. This does not imply that the solution to the
problem of race relations is thereby easy. Artificial though they are,
cultural elements, like tempered steel, will resist much wear and ham-
mering, and bend only to fly back again when the pressure is removed.

SLAVE CULTURE

From the time "Angele," the first Negro slave, was landed on the Virginia coast in 1619 to the close of the War Between the States, we, the
people of the United States, were engaged in the development of two
very different types of culture—one for the white man and the other for
the Negro. Slavery existed in the West Indies for more than a century
before it was introduced into the United States, [10] and many of the slaves
came to the United States from the West Indies, though many more were
brought directly from Africa by Dutch, English, French, and Spanish
ships, and later by the colonists themselves. Slavery existed in all the
colonies.

In Boston, New York, and Philadelphia, Negro servants were as common
as in Charleston. Among the aristocratic people of Boston, the slaveholding
families included such names as Hopkins, Williams, Stiles, Edwards, Win-
throp, Mather, and even Faneuil. In New York, the slaveholding families
included the Murrays the Chamberses, the Roosevelts, the Bayards, the

[8] James Bryce, *South America* (1912), p. 480.
[9] Chapter XIX.
[10] Dowd, *op. cit.*, p. 10.

Duanes, the Courtlandts, the Livingstons, the Nichollses, the Jays, and others whose names are still perpetuated in the designation of the streets of that great city. . . .

In all the colonies, special laws, known as Black Codes, were made for the regulation of slave labor, and while these laws differed somewhat, the actual treatment of the slaves was everywhere substantially the same. Generally the slaveholders in all the colonies were the most enterprising class of people, and as a rule treated their slaves humanely; but there were many slaveholders of a low order of intelligence, and of irritable and vicious tempers who treated their slaves with great brutality. In proportion to the Negro population, there were about as many burnings of Negroes, and other barbaric ill-usages of them, in Massachusetts, New York, and New Jersey, as in Virginia, South Carolina, or Georgia.[11]

But the trend of the economic development in the colonies and the climatic conditions finally led to the concentration of the bulk of the slave population in the Southern States. After the major work of clearing the land had been completed, and the population had turned to more intensive agriculture and the development of industries, slavery became unprofitable in the North and only a few of the more well-to-do families could afford to maintain them as servants. Traffic in slaves finally disappeared from the Northern States, and "by the time of the adoption of our Constitution, it had been legally terminated in all the Northern States except Delaware."[12] Thus for almost a century prior to the War Between the States, slavery had been concentrated in the Southern States, where extensive agriculture and single crops were the rule, and where the climate made it less expensive to house and care for the slaves. Because the Negro was unprofitable and required more care in the North, many of the Northern communities prohibited even free Negroes remaining in them, and enforced the rule, "NO NEGRO DARE STAY IN THIS TOWN OVERNIGHT." Had the Negro remained an economic asset to the North, as he did in the South, it is doubtful if Emancipation would have come as early as it did.

Consequently, we must regard the institution of slavery in this country as definitely a responsibility belonging to the North as well as to the South; and the sentiments that later arose against slavery sprang more from the pocket-book than from the heart. Both sections of the country have had a hand in the building up of the two incompatible cultures—the slave culture for the Negro, and the free culture for the whites. Curiously enough, however, the attitude taken by the two sec-

[11] *Ibid.*, pp. 11–12.
[12] *Ibid.*, p. 12.

tions toward the problem of race relations is vastly different: the South, as we shall see, has a dread and fear of the Negro action in mass, though it appreciates and often feels real affection for the individual Negro; the North, on the other hand, concedes equality to the Negro in mass, yet views with suspicion and disdain the individual Negro. These attitudes both arise out of the conflict of the free culture with the slave culture, but their difference comes from the difference of the association that the two sections have had with the Negro population.

Whatever the original culture of the African in his native land may have been, it was very largely supplanted by the culture that developed under slavery.[13] Allowing for the difference in temperament, it is quite possible to find in the slave culture ample explanation for most of the "Negro characteristics" that hamper his progress, and which are often ascribed to his original inferior nature.

A brief examination of the slave culture and the social system that fostered it will help to make more clear the bearing they have on the current problem of race relations. In the first place, we must remember that the Negroes were brought to America and marketed in much the same manner as were domesticated animals; and substantially the same policies governed their treatment as governed that given to live-stock by plantation-owners and live-stock-breeders. Hence the whites came to regard the Negroes in the category of "black beasts," treated them kindly so long as they were obedient, faithful, and productive; using the lash when they were sullen, disobedient, treacherous, or unproductive.

They were given no more share in the white man's culture than was given to the mules and oxen. Because they were ignorant, and had no knowledge of the technique of agriculture, they were worked largely in gangs in the fields, and only the more favored and more apt were trained for servants about the house of the owner. They were not schooled in farm management. They were not even concerned with managing their own households; everything was provided for them; all thinking was done for them. They did what they were told to do—no more—and in the absence of the lash or threats of the lash, there was no hurry about doing that. Like the mule and the ox, they had no cares beyond those of the labor enforced upon them. There was no future, or "rainy day," no social position, no expanding standard of living—nothing of the sort to stimulate the initiative or arouse the ambition to self-development and personal attainment. Generally, therefore, the Negroes on the planta-

[13] See Jerome Dowd, *The Negro Races*, Vol. II, for an interesting description of the original culture of the Negro races.

tions were of a care-free, happy-go-lucky, jovial, playful, childlike nature. Their owners did all the worrying, planning, providing, managing, and directing. Like children who are ever in fear of a flogging, the Negro quickly learned that a lie would sometimes "save his skin," and little wonder that he became quite an adept at "spinning appropriate yarns" —it was nothing more than an indication of his ability to adapt himself to the requirements of survival! [14] Then, too, the Negro is no less endowed with an impelling curiosity than is the white man. It did not take him long to note that his owner was enjoying good things to eat, wearing a watch, drinking mint juleps, and smoking cigars or a pipe. He possessed much the same urge that we may every day notice in normal children—to sample or examine the things that grown-ups seem to enjoy. Consequently the Negro slave found it convenient to develop a habit of "sneaking things" or "toting." This is a cultural trait not at all foreign to the white race, especially when compelled to live under conditions of restraint and oppression. For example, the Armenians have these cultural twists of lying, stealing, and cheating, without any compunction whatever, because for so many generations they have lived in a "buffer state" and under a political régime where such practices seem almost a requisite for survival.

When suddenly the Negro found that he was a free man, he continued to look upon his cultural background in much the same way as the whites looked upon theirs. He was not conscious of the severe handicaps of three centuries of habits formed under slavery. To a large extent he continued to live as he had always lived—any other way was foreign to him. Nor could he be expected to change rapidly. The whites looked upon these cultural twists with much misgiving and even alarm, whereas they had not thought of them as being much out of place in a slave. Many writers, like Dr. W. D. Weatherford, have attempted, in a more or less sympathetic way, to explain that such characteristics belong to the nature of the Negro—an index of his inferiority to the white.[15] But it is hardly necessary to go to Africa to find explanations of, or foundations for, cultural warp and twist. The shiftlessness, lack of foresight, easy-going nature and indifference still characteristic of so many Negroes are traits that could only be expected to develop out of the slave culture we have just described.

[14] Harry Stillwell Edwards, *Eneas Africanus* (Macon, Georgia, 1932). This is a humorous tale based on the faithfulness of a typical "old-time" Negro who displayed a considerable capacity for enlarging on the truth.
[15] W. D. Weatherford, *Present Forces in Negro Progress* (1912).

Another prominent feature of the slave culture is that which relates to the family system and the question of morals. Here also many writers go back to the "primitive nature" of the Negro for explanation. This is hardly necessary, nor is it likely to prove the point. Slavery gave to the Negro a family system altogether different from that of the white owner. As we have just noted, the Negroes were regarded in the same category as live-stock. Pure monogamy, chastity, and a deep sense of family unity were not compatible with slavery, in which Negro women were not only valued as servants and field-hands, but perhaps even more as breeders. Added to this were the living conditions, which became as deeply rooted in slave culture as did any other factor. The little one-room cabin (by no means extinct even to this date) without a glass window, with only an open fireplace for heating and cooking, and with practically no furniture, housed not only single families but often several other adults, male and female. There was not sufficient privacy to permit of the development of any high standard of morality. The fact that the Negro population withstood more than three centuries of this sort of moral stunting, and at the end of it were able to rise, is in itself perhaps the clearest evidence of racial possibilities. It is not to be wondered at that there still exists a considerable amount of moral looseness, juvenile neglect, family desertion, neglect of the aged, and cruelty.[16] Especially have writers generally called attention to the low conception that the Negro has of morals, and some have indicated that this "defect in character" may best be described as "unmorality" rather than immorality.[17] But in view of the degree of social isolation that has characterized the Negro life since the War Between the States, it is to be expected that the old slave culture would hardly yet have given way entirely.

Still another phase of slave culture that must be considered is that related to his intellectual development. Slavery offered practically no chance for the Negro to obtain even the rudiments of an education beyond a training in the art of serving his master, and this art the great majority seem to have learned well and performed with a faithfulness that won for them "a warm spot in the hearts of the true Southerners." But slave education did not extend to those matters which would help to make the Negro an independent thinker, or capable of looking after his own affairs. In a sense he was made to believe, like the Russian

[16] A. B. Hart, *The Southern South* (1912), p. 116.
[17] *The Negro in Chicago*, Report of the Chicago Commission on Race Relations (1922), pp. 438, 447; H. O. Odum, *A Study in Race Traits, Tendencies and Prospects* (1910).

peasant under the Czarist régime, that education was not for him; that
it would make him unhappy, create trouble for him. The majority of the
slaveholders opposed education of the slaves on the ground that it made
them unmanageable and "no account." The great majority of the plantation Negroes knew nothing of farm management, and little about
methods of horticulture. They knew cotton, cane, corn, or yams, but
nothing more. They had not learned how to till the ground effectively
even for these crops. Seldom did they have a garden-spot of their own.
All their needs were looked after by the plantation boss, who told them
each day what to do and how to do what they were told. They had no
money and would not have known what to do with it if they had had
any. Some few knew how to count sufficiently to make change of small
amounts, and perhaps 10 per cent of the Southern Negroes could scrawl
their names. Very few indeed knew what the inside of a school looked
like.

But, cared for as he was, busy as he was, he was happy and loyal.
When we stop to think of what little educational equipment the Negro
had, and how little he knew of the practical arts of living and of shaping
an independent career, we are not astonished at the fact that such a large
majority remained with their old masters even after being emancipated.
One look into the great unknown world of "independence," with all
that it required in the way of responsibility, planning, worry, risk, and
competition, was quite enough to make him feel satisfied, at least for a
time, with an oral contract with his old master, enabling him to live in
much the same fashion as before the Emancipation Proclamation.[18]

We have touched upon merely a few of the major aspects of American slave culture—a culture that, as we have said, grew up alongside the
American free culture, and which became so fixed in the habits of
thought of both blacks and whites that it is as difficult for the Negro to
emancipate himself from it as it is for the whites to forget it. It is the
conflict between these two cultures, both the products of white Americans, North and South, that forms the main basis for the problem of race
relations in the United States.

HOW EMANCIPATION AND THE PERIOD OF RECONSTRUCTION
AFFECTED THE PROBLEM

In 1863 there were 3,960,000 slaves in the Southern States—a population almost equal to the total population of the United States at the time

[18] W. H. Holtzclaw, *The Black Man's Burden* (1915), pp. 16-17.

of the first census. The total value of the slaves was approximately $2,000,000,000, or an average of $500 per slave. The total Negro population in the United States in 1860, including those in the Northern States, was 4,441,830, or 14.1 per cent of the total population of the nation, though 92.2 per cent were concentrated in the Southern States. But even in the South the distribution of the Negro population was not uniform. There were many counties, especially in the highlands, where there were very few, and there was very little shift after emancipation.[19] Consequently, this vast Negro population was concentrated in the rich agricultural belt, known as the "plantation belt," and in many of these counties the Negroes far outnumbered the whites. Thus in Beaufort County, South Carolina, there were ten Negroes for every white person, and in the whole state of South Carolina there were seven Negroes for every five whites. In the Mississippi delta they outnumbered the whites two to one, and for the State as a whole there were three Negroes for every two whites. The population of Louisiana, Alabama, and Georgia was practically half Negro, and many counties were almost wholly black.

Now let us apply the principles of race relations that we outlined at the beginning of this chapter. Here were two races with widely divergent cultures: one a free culture and the other a slave culture, one the culture of the white race and the other the culture of the blacks. So long as blacks remained in slavery there was little race friction. Slavery fixed the status of each race so that there was not even the semblance of competition for prestige, place, or power. The white race, though in many places a minority race, was dominant. Every item of the slave culture unfitted the Negro for self-government, to say nothing of sharing the responsibilities and prestige of the whites. *The whites of the South did not hate the Negro*—on the contrary there was often a profound affection for the "Ol' Uncle Mose" and the colored "Mammy." Nevertheless, the whites regarded the Negroes as vastly inferior beings. The Southern prosperity rested upon black shoulders, and the whites recognized this fact; but at the same time, the whites sincerely believed that the Negroes would starve to death if allowed to manage things for themselves—that they were by nature incapable of self-direction.

Then, suddenly, by the Emancipation Proclamation, this fixed status was swept away, and the Negro was made a free man. Theoretically, at

[19] E. G. Murphy, *The Present South* (1910), pp. 182–201, quoted in A. B. Wolfe, *Readings in Social Problems* (1916), pp. 677 ff.

least, he was on a par with his former owner—he was at liberty, despite his slave culture, to compete for power, place, and prestige with the white man and his free culture.

The whites of the North expected the Negroes at once to rise to the occasion, take the reins of government, and exterminate all white opposition that stood in their way. That is what they (with their background of free culture) would have done, had they been enslaved and oppressed, and they imagined that the Negro felt the same way about the matter. They looked on, but to their utter amazement nothing very dramatic was happening. They could not understand why, unless it was because the Negro was being intimidated and was afraid to act. They did not understand, and many to this day do not understand, why a people will not quickly discard an inferior status and adopt at once a superior one when given the chance. The feelings that the Northern emancipators had for the slave were rooted in a far different cultural background. The Negro might imitate the white man, but he could not feel at home in doing so—not until he had completely freed himself from the habits of thought, the standards of conduct, and the concepts of responsibility and duty that had become "second nature" to him during the two hundred and fifty years of slavery. Consequently, he remained inert and, to a surprising extent, satisfied with the status to which he had become accustomed.

Thus, not fully understanding the true situation, the Northern whites began a campaign designed to establish the Negro in his newly granted rights. It was a campaign hardly less humiliating and terrorizing to the Southern whites than were the campaigns of the Northern armies while the war was at its worst. The armies had shattered the hopes of the Confederacy and had wrecked Southern prosperity and reduced them to wretched poverty, but the Southerners might still cling to their dignity, their pride, and the dominance of the white man's culture. But now, as if to add insult to injury, the Northern whites were intent upon compelling them to recognize the Negro as their social equal and to share power, place, and prestige with their former slaves. To the Southerner this meant the surrender of white culture to the culture of the Negro—that inferior, "beast" culture which we have just briefly described. Thus it was that the problem of race relations began to take on the fierce and horrifying aspects of race conflict, though the major alignment was not as much against the Negroes as it was against the activities and aims of the Northern whites.

The Northern whites launched their ill-advised campaign on two dif-

ferent fronts: (1) through establishing and conducting schools for the
Negro, and (2) through sending political delegates and organizers, now
known as "carpet-baggers," to lead the Negroes into rebellion against
the Southern whites and to establish the Negro in power politically.
While the motives back of the educational drive were no doubt largely
sincere and honest, the motives back of the carpet-baggers are now
candidly admitted by historians to have been corrupt, scheming, and exploiting. Most of the carpet-baggers were personally motivated by desires to share the spoils that might easily be had by "advising" the ignorant Negro office-holder. Incidentally, the Republican party saw in the
movement the possibility of gaining the Negro votes, and thus perpetuating that party in power. Against these movements the Southern whites
threw every power and resource at their command. They would not
have objected so much to the establishment of schools for the Negroes
had not the carpet-baggers extended their interests in them and attempted to force the white and colored children to attend the same
schools. Then, too, many of these schools were used by the carpet-
baggers as propaganda centers, and the Negro was not given the instruction he so much needed. "The teachers and the supervisors of the
schools were largely carpet-baggers. Many of the White people regarded the public schools and also the Freedmen's Bureau schools as only
a disguised scheme of the carpet-baggers to enslave the White people,
and place them under the domination of their former slaves." [20]

Two general types of schools were thus established by the Northern-
ers for the education of the Negro—the public schools, and the schools
conducted with Federal Government aid administered by the Freedmen's Bureau, Washington. The schools conducted by the Freedmen's
Bureau were aided, financially and in providing teachers, by the Northern missionary societies and religious organizations, and these organizations continued many of the schools on their own account after the
Freedmen's Bureau was discontinued at the close of 1869.

It was a pathetic sight to see old gray-haired people crowding into the
schools alongside the children, with the inarticulate feeling that reading and
writing would carry them upward. The Northern missionary societies kept
up these elementary schools, and then began to found schools and colleges
for the training of the most gifted members of the race. Out of their funds,
and with the aid of the Freedmen, they put up school houses, collected
money to establish institutions like Fisk University in Nashville, Leland
and Straight Universities in New Orleans, and Atlanta University. Such
colleges were on the same pattern as colleges for Whites both North and

[20] Jerome Dowd, *The Negro in America* (1926), p. 149.

South, adopting the then almost universal curriculum of Greek, Latin, and mathematics, along with smatterings of other subjects; they included preparatory schools, which, as in some White colleges both North and South, included the larger number of students.[21]

The Freedmen's Bureau, during its five years of existence, established 4,239 schools of varying terms, employed 9,307 teachers of very meager training, and reported a total enrolment of 247,333 pupils. When the Bureau was closed it reported 1,327 Negro teachers employed in these schools.[22] Most of the teachers were at first Northern whites; but gradually the Southern whites took possession of the schools, and at the close of the carpet-bag régime heartily supported the public schools, which made separate provisions for white and colored children.[23] An interesting side-light on the character of these schools is given in the biographical sketch of William Holtzclaw, who, through sheer pluck and great faith, established one of the leading institutions for Negro education in Mississippi, Utica Institute and Training School:

> I distinctly remember that there were no Colored school-teachers at that time (the latter days of the Reconstruction) and, in my locality, there were no Northern White teachers. The few Colored schools that existed at all were taught by Southern white men and women. Before I was old enough to attend school myself, I used to go along now and then with the others, and I remember that one of these Southern White teachers took a great liking to me, and, passing our house one day on his way home, predicted to my mother that I would some day be a lawyer. I did not know what that meant then, but I got the impression that it meant that I was going to be something great, and I never forgot it.
>
> Almost as soon as the Negro pupils got as far as 'baker,' and certainly when they got as far as 'abasement,' in the old blue-backed speller, they were made assistant teachers, and in a short while, relieving the White teachers, they became the only teachers we had. When I was seven years old there was not a White teacher in the community. The Colored teachers were doing pretty good work, but the best of them had advanced only about as far as the fourth grade. There was one thing, however, that they had learned to perfection, and that was to use the rod, and of this kind of education I got my full share every day.[24]

As we have just said, it was not so much the founding of Negro schools that aroused the bitter resentment of the Southern whites; but it was especially the aims and activities of the carpet-baggers. Living, as they were, surrounded by a Negro population that far outnumbered their

---

[21] A. B. Hart, *The Southern South* (1912), pp. 309-310.
[22] Dowd, *op. cit.*, p. 149.
[23] *Ibid.*
[24] William Holtzclaw, *The Black Man's Burden* (1915), p. 14.

own; knowing the intensely emotional character of the Negro; also knowing how ignorant he was of public affairs, and how incapable he was of self-direction—knowing all this, the Southerners could not help regarding the activities of the carpet-baggers with deep concern. They had faith and confidence in the Negro taken individually; but they dreaded what he would do under the spell of mob psychology, and under the leadership of unscrupulous carpet-baggers. It is impossible to describe the horror and fear that possessed the whites at the prospects of black dominance under such leadership. Consequently, the bitterest part of the War Between the States was fought during these terrible first few years of the period of Reconstruction. And this, it must be admitted, the Southern whites won!

The Southerners faced a situation with which reason and orderly justice could not deal, and especially while the South was still occupied by Northern troops. The carpet-baggers, "Negro sympathizers," and aggressive Negroes were rounded up and roughly treated. Every community had its secret vigilance committee; and the hooded "night riders" of the old Ku Klux Klan with flaring torches and brandishing "cat-o'-nine-tails," swooped down nightly, seized those who were suspected of urging "race equality," and "hustled them away."

When the carpet-bag régime had finally been driven from the South, the whites of the South settled down to the sober task of protecting themselves and white dominance from future "invasions," and to the working out of policies and programs of race relations that would insure supremacy of the white free culture. We shall deal with these policies and programs in a later chapter; it is sufficient here to point out that the Southern whites have employed every possible legal and social device to insure white supremacy and avoid social competition with the Negroes.

IS THE CULTURAL DIFFERENCE FADING?

Whatever our feeling may be in regard to the matter, we are forced to the conclusion that the problem of race relations between the American whites and the American Negro springs from the almost complete incompatibility of their cultures. Then, too, the slave culture of the Negro is tagged to him—the color of his skin acts like a sort of black magic that brings up the ghosts of the past. Will he ever be able to shake himself free? Since the signing of the Emancipation Proclamation millions of illiterate foreigners with strange and "questionable" cultures have come to our shores, and in the course of two or three generations most of them have been absorbed into the culture of their adopted country. Perhaps it would be more accurate to say that their culture has blended with that of the communities into which they moved. But slave culture—though an American product—cannot be blended. There is nothing in it that is useful or favorable to progress. *It must be completely uprooted and forgotten.* Its place must be taken by the culture of the whites or something nobler and finer.

What progress has the American Negro made during these sixty years of "freedom" toward throwing off the yoke of his slave culture?

Perhaps the best indexes of the progress of the Negro are to be seen in the transformation of his economic and material conditions and in his achievements in education. In both these fields the American Negro has a record of accomplishments unparalleled by any race. Scarcely eighty years ago he began his climb out of the depths of slavery. He had almost no property to start with, his training was only such as qualified him for work in the fields or for domestic service, and only 10 per cent of his group could be classified as literate. While the Negro population has increased from approximately 4,500,000 in 1865 to 12,865,518 in 1940, an increase of 264 per cent in the seventy-five years, the economic and educational progress has been much more rapid than the rate of population increase.

TABLE 4

ECONOMIC PROGRESS OF THE NEGRO, 1866–1936 *

	1866	1936	Gain in 70 Years
Homes owned, including farms	12,000	750,000	738,000
Farms operated	20,000	880,000	860,000
Business establishments	2,100	70,000	67,900
Banks owned and operated	None	23	23
Bank capitalization	None	$2,000,000	$2,000,000
Bank resources	None	$15,000,000	$15,000,000
Wealth accumulated	$20,000,000	$2,500,000,000	$2,480,000,000

* *Negro Yearbook* (1937–1938), pp. 1, 93.

Educational progress made by the Negro population in the 17 Southern States and the District of Columbia, as shown in Table 5, has the greatest significance. Here is where 80 per cent of Negro school population live; 20 per cent are in the Northern cities where they have the advantages of the most progressive school systems. Furthermore, it is in these Southern States that we find the separate schools for the Negroes,

TABLE 5

EDUCATIONAL PROGRESS OF THE NEGRO IN THE 17 STATES, AND DISTRICT OF COLUMBIA, HAVING SEPARATE SCHOOLS FOR NEGROES, 1866–1936 *

	1866	1936	Gain
Negro population	4,200,000	9,595,417[a]	5,395,417
Percentage literate	10%	90%	74.7%
Children in public school	100,000	2,500,000	2,400,000
Schools in higher training			
High schools	None	800	800
Colleges	15	47[b]	32
Teachers in public elementary and high schools	600	55,000	54,400
Property for higher education	$60,000	$65,000,000	$64,940,000
Annual expenditures for all education	$700,000	$61,700,000	$61,000,000
Funds raised by Negroes	$80,000	$3,500,000	$3,420,000

* Negro Yearbook (1937–1938), pp. 1, 210.
[a] 1930 Census.
[b] In 1936, forty colleges and universities for Negroes were on the approved list of the Southern Association of College and Secondary Schools, seven more having probationary listing.

and in most instances there is a wide disparity between the educational standards of the schools for the two races. Nevertheless, the progress is toward more equal opportunity: in 1915 there were only 91 public high schools for Negroes in these 17 states; in 1930 there were approximately 1,000; and in 1938 this number had increased to almost 2,000. In 1920 only 50 per cent of the Negro children of school age were attending school; in 1938 approximately 85 per cent were in school.

While opportunity in the professions is largely limited to serving people of their own race, the increase in the number of Negroes who have climbed the professional ladders—some of them to positions of fame—is another index to their amazing progress.

TABLE 6

NEGROES IN PROFESSIONS, 1890 AND 1930 *

Profession	1890	1930
Artists, sculptors, and teachers of art	150	430
Dentists	120	1,773
Physicians and surgeons	909	3,805
Trained nurses	None	5,728
Total in all professions	34,184	136,963

* Negro Yearbook (1937–1938), p. 267.

In the Northern States the educational opportunities for the Negro are practically on a par with those of the whites. In the sixteen Southern

States, however, there is still considerable difference both in regard to the length of the school terms and in the per capita expenditures for the children of the two races. In these sixteen Southern States, from 1918 to 1928 the average increase in the school year for white pupils was 16 days, or 11 per cent. During the same period the Negro schools increased 11 days, or 9 per cent. This increase was shown in the schools for white children in all of the sixteen States; but only ten of the sixteen States increased the length of the school term for Negroes—Mississippi, for example, decreased the length of the school year for Negro schools (1927–1928) 28 days. The average length of the school year in the Negro schools of these Southern States was 131 days in 1927–1928.[25] In 1933–1934 the length of the school term was 164 days for the whites and 142 days for the Negroes; South Carolina had the shortest school term for the Negroes of any of the Southern States, and it also had the greatest discrepancy between the terms provided the whites and the colored, giving a term of 171 days to the whites and 117 days to the Negroes.[26]

In all except three of the sixteen former slave States, there is a considerable discrepancy in the per capita expenditure for education of the white and the Negro children, Alabama, for example, spends $37.50 per white child and $7.16 per Negro child; Louisiana spends $40.64 per white child, and $7.84 per Negro child; South Carolina presents the greatest discrepancy, $52.89 per white child, and $5.20 per Negro child. On the other hand, Delaware, Kentucky, and West Virginia spend more on the education of the Negro child than they spend on educating the white child.[27]

But it is not in the schools alone that the Negro is making real progress towards independence. An equally great advancement is seen also in the progress of *agricultural* education among the Negro farm operators. There are 17 Negro land-grant colleges in the Southern States. In 1934 the combined staffs of these schools numbered 754: 476 men and 278 women. Included in this number were 136 agricultural agents and 72 home demonstration agents. The work done by these educators is far-reaching, not only from the standpoint of improving the crop production of the Negro farmer, but also in improving the relations between the races. Added to these is the work of a number of excellent independent Negro schools.[28]

[25] *Statistics of the Negro Race, 1927–1928* (United States Office of Education, Pamphlet No. 14, December, 1930).
[26] *Biennial Survey of Education, 1932–1934*, Ch. II, p. 94.
[27] *Negro Yearbook* (1931–1932), p. 204 (figures for 1930).
[28] *Biennial Survey of Education, 1932–1934*, Ch. IV, p. 437.

Further contributing to this progress is the development of agricultural courses in the public schools, in the Rosenwald schools, and in the independent Negro schools and normal schools. Especially in agriculture, the indications are that the next generation of Negroes will make more progress toward independence and efficient living than has been made since the day of emancipation; they are in a better position to build for themselves, since the old slave culture is rapidly giving way to a new and more *liberating* culture.

The outlook of the Negro in industry, however, is hardly as hopeful as are his prospects in agriculture. Approximately one third of the Negro population now lives in the city, and to a large extent they are employed as day-laborers in industry, though a considerable proportion are employed as domestic servants. Generally speaking, even where there is no discrimination in matters of wages and working conditions, they are assigned to the least paid and least agreeable jobs. But perhaps of even more significance is the fact that they are housed in the poorest quarters, where there is most danger to health and morals. Bad as is the housing of the Negroes on the plantations, it is not nearly as menacing as are the conditions that exist in the typical Negro quarters of our industrial centers.

It is supposed to be the strain and stress of industrial conditions that causes the increase in insanity among Negroes since emancipation. Doubtless, too, social disease and liquor—both curses of which the "old-time Negro" knew nothing—have contributed much to this mental breakdown.[29] A similar effect of urbanization is to be noted in the unfavorable contrast of the infant-morality rates and the general death-rates of the city and rural Negro populations. From 1933 to 1935 the infant-mortality rate in the birth registration area of the United States was 56 per 1,000 births; but for the Negroes the rate was 86.1 per 1,000 births; while the white population lost but 53 per 1,000 births. The infant-mortality rate in the Negro population of cities, for the same year, was 96.3 deaths per 1,000 births, while the rate for the whites was 52.1 per 1,000 births.[30] This, with few exceptions, is the contrast that most industrial centers show with the general population. This same situation is reflected in the general death-rates: The death-rate for the registration area of the United States in 1933, including all classes, was 10.7 per 1,000 of population—11.5 per 1,000 in the cities and 9.9 in the rural popu-

[29] James Bryce, *American Commonwealth* (1916), II, p. 523.
[30] *Infant and Maternal Mortality among Negroes* (Washington, D. C.: Federal Children's Bureau, Bureau Publication No. 243, 1937).

lation. However, the death-rate for the Negro population of the United
States for this same year was 14.1 per 1,000 population—17.2 per 1,000
in the urban centers of 10,000 population and over, and 12.2 per 1,000 in
the rural population. The following table further indicates the comparative conditions of selected urban and rural areas, North and South.

TABLE 7
WHITE AND NEGRO DEATH-RATES IN SELECTED STATES, 1933 *

	Northern States				Southern States		
State	All	White	Negro	State	All	White	Negro
Illinois	10.5	10.3	15.4	Georgia	10.7	9.1	13.7
Urban	10.3	10.	14.4	Urban	15.7	12.4	21.5
Rural	11.	10.7	28.1	Rural	9.2	8.1	11.2
Wisconsin	9.9	9.8	12.7	Mississippi	10.6	8.8	12.4
Urban	9.5	9.5	6.3	Urban	16.5	13.5	21.1
Rural	9.6	9.5	20.7	Rural	9.5	7.6	11.2
Michigan	9.6	9.5	12.5	Tennessee	10.6	9.4	16.
Urban	8.5	8.4	10.8	Urban	14.4	12.1	19.9
Rural	11.3	11.1	29.7	Rural	8.7	8.1	12.3
Indiana	11.5	11.4	15.	Virginia	11.7	10.	16.1
Urban	11.2	11.	14.	Urban	13.7	11.3	19.6
Rural	11.4	11.3	29.3	Rural	10.5	9.1	14.4
New York	11.5	11.3	15.5	South Carolina	11.1	8.9	13.8
Urban	11.	10.8	15.2	Urban	19.2	15.1	25.9
Rural	13.	13.	20.8	Rural	9.5	7.6	11.8
				Louisiana	10.7	8.9	13.8
				Urban	15.9	13.1	22.
				Rural	7.8	6.3	9.9

* *Mortality Statistics, 1933* (Bureau of the Census, 1936), pp. 9–11.

While, as a worker, the Negro is proving satisfactory—in a measure
meeting the needs of expanding industry since the great restriction of
immigration—it is increasingly apparent that the stress and strain of industry and the unfavorable living conditions are serious obstacles to his
real success.[31]

INFLUENCE OF POPULATION SHIFT ON THE PROBLEM OF RACE RELATIONS

The first noticeable drift of Negro population following the War
Between the States was from the rural communities of the South to

[31] L. I. Dublin, "The Health of the Negro," *Annals of the American Academy of
Political and Social Science*, pp. 77 ff. (November, 1928).

the cities of the South. Migrations to the North from 1860 to 1910 amounted to only 3.2 per cent of the Negro population, while in the twenty years 1890 to 1910 the urban population grew from 19.8 per cent of the Negro population to 27.4 per cent. Thus, down to 1910 the problem of race relations was essentially a problem centered in the South. From 1910 to 1920 there was a migration of 3.8 per cent of the Negro population out of the South—in other words, during that decade there was a greater migration than had taken place during the previous fifty years. This decade also showed the greatest shift from the rural to the urban community of the Negro population, a shift that amounted to 6.6 per cent of the total Negro population. In 1920, 14.8 per cent of the total Negro population was located in the North and West, and 34 per cent lived in the cities. (See Table 8.) Since 1920 the movement has been even more pronounced. In 1940 the census reported that 9,904,619

TABLE 8

DISTRIBUTION OF THE NEGRO POPULATION, 1860–1940 *
(Expressed in Per Cents)

Census Year	Negro Population in Southern States	Urban Negro Population	Rural Negro Population
1860	92.2	—	—
1890	90.3	19.8	80.2
1900	89.7	22.7	77.3
1910	89.0	27.4	72.6
1920	85.2	34.0	66.0
1930	78.7	43.7	56.3
1940	76.9	47.9	52.1

* W. S. Rossiter, *Census Monographs* (United States Bureau of the Census, No. IV, 1922), p. 124; 1930 data from *Negroes in the United States, 1920–1932*, p. 3; 1940 data from Bureau of the Census releases.

of the total Negro population of 12,865,518 were still in the South—an increase of 5.5 per cent over the South's Negro population in 1930. The North, however, had 2,790,193 Negroes in 1940—an increase of 16 per cent in the decade.

The shift of Negroes from the rural sections to the urban centers of both the North and the South which began during the First World War has continued to the present time. Negroes in rural non-farm areas increased by 4.8 per cent during the decade from 1930 to 1940, but the Negro farm population declined both in numbers and per cent. Taken as a whole, the rural Negro population declined by 1.3 per cent, with about 90,000 fewer Negroes living in rural areas in 1940 than in 1930, despite the increase of almost a million in the total Negro population. On the other hand, urban Negro population increased by 19.6 per cent, or more than a million in actual numbers. Moreover, the rates of increase of Negro population were highest in the North and West sections of the country, being greatest in the Middle Atlantic (20.5 per cent) and in the Mountain (14.6 per cent) divisions, as compared with the lower rates in the sections most densely populated by Negroes, the South Atlantic (6.5 per cent), the East South Central (4.7 per cent), and the West South Central (4.8 per cent).

A number of explanations have been advanced for this rapid drift to the North and to the cities. Some attribute it to the harsh treatment of the Negroes in the South. Others point out that the First World War uprooted thousands of Negroes and gave them their first real opportunity to get away from the traditional setting. Still others find the chief reason in the recurrent failure of the cotton crops owing to the ravages of the boll-weevil. However, perhaps the most potent factor behind the increasing migration has been the wage offered in the industries of the North, and the activities of Northern corporations in recruiting Negro labor. Some concerns have had employment representatives in the South since before we entered the First World War and their representations to the Negroes have not always been true to fact. Whatever the causes, the fact remains that shift of population has been taking place very rapidly—and it is this speed, perhaps even more than the volume of the shift, that has created the most acute problems of race relations in the Northern industrial centers. Thus, the problem can no longer be regarded as belonging solely to the South; it is now a problem of national scope, and, if anything, more disturbing to the North than to the South, because there have not developed in the North definite policies and programs of race relations to safeguard the interests of either race. The situation, as it now stands, wavers on the unstable basis of crowd emotionalism, and there is a most urgent need for the development of sound and sane policies and programs that will permit the two races to live together without friction.

REFERENCES

Annals of the American Academy of Political and Social Science, "The American Negro" (November, 1928); "The Coming of Industry to the South" (January, 1931).

Biennial Survey of Education in the United States, 1932–1934 (Washington, D. C.: United States Office of Education, 1937), Bulletin, 1935, No. 2.

Dowd, Jerome, *The Negro in American Life* (New York, 1926).

Feldman, Herman, *Racial Factors in American Industry* (New York, 1931), Part I.

Grant, Madison, *Conquest of a Continent* (New York, 1934), Ch. 15.

Negro Yearbook (Tuskegee, Alabama, 1931–1932).

Radin, Paul, *The Racial Myth* (New York, 1934).

Reuter, E. B., *American Race Problem* (New York, 1927).

White, Walter, *Rope and Faggot* (New York, 1929), Chs. 5, 6.

Woofter, T. J., Jr., "The Status of Racial and Ethic Groups," *Recent Social Trends* (New York, 1933), Ch. XI, pp. 553–590.

QUESTIONS AND EXERCISES

1. What *is* the race problem? Is it merely a problem for the Negroes and whites of America to solve?

2. Why is it that the United States has a problem of race relations affecting the Negro, while no such problem is apparent in tropical South America, though the Negroes are as numerous there as they are in the United States?

3. Is there any race prejudice in your community? Explain the reason.

4. Under what conditions does race friction develop? How great a part do the emotions play?

5. What are the chief features of the culture that developed in the Negro population under slavery? Contrast the slave culture with that of the Southern whites.

6. Why were the Negroes so slow to take advantage of their rights after the declaration of emancipation? How far can you change old group customs and habits by act of government?

7. What were the conditions and circumstances that gave rise to the old Ku Klux Klan? Are there any similar conditions and circumstances developing to-day that would cause such an organization to reappear? Why is it that people are not satisfied with orderly measures in dealing with the Negro *en masse?* What do people hope to gain by "taking the law in their own hands" in such matters?

8. The text states that the South fears the Negro *en masse*, but has affection for him individually; whereas the North tends to idealize the Negro's position, while disliking him as an individual. Show how these opposite attitudes have grown out of opposite cultural settings.

9. What evidence is there that the Negro is making progress toward social and economic independence? What sort of educational program is most needed to make progress more rapid and certain? Is it likely that the Negro will be as successful in industry as he has been in agriculture?

10. The 1920–1930 decennial increase of 63 per cent in Negro population in the North dispels any thought that the northward migration was merely a war-time phenomenon. What possible relation do you see between this increase and the drastic restrictions placed on immigration after the First World War? What changes in the attitude of the North

must be brought about as a result of the increase in the Negro population?

11. In what ways can the North and the South be of mutual help in accomplishing the needed adjustments in their respective "Negro problems"?

Chapter 5

POLICIES AND PROGRAMS OF RACE RELATIONS

Now THAT we have noted the nature and importance of the problem of race relations in the United States, we are faced with the equally puzzling question of what to do about it. We have seen how the migration of the Negro to the North and to the industrial centers makes it necessary to consider the problem no longer as an affair of the South, but one that is national in scope and perhaps more menacing to the industrial centers of the North than to the rural communities of the "Black Belt." Consequently, any policy or program aiming to solve the problem of race relations must be viewed from a national point of view.

We should, however, be mindful of the fact that discussion of a national policy or program of race relations is of itself dubious. The mere assertion that such a policy and program is necessary to the promotion of the best interests of both races is at once met with a flood of protest. On the one hand, bitter resentment is quickly voiced by many mulattoes, who for the most part live in the North and who consider themselves superior to the "hat-in-hand obliging niggers" of the South.[1] Their attitude is seconded by a group of political theorists among Northern whites who have never come into close contact with the problem. Both of these groups declare emphatically that any suggestion of a national policy or program of race relations "is incompatible with the ideals of democracy." They insist that such efforts defeat the very ends which they aim to achieve; that unconsciously such policies and programs deepen the "race complex" in the public mind, and invariably lead to a separation of the races, instead of bringing them together. Even the use of the word *Negro* is offensive to many leaders of the black race, as it seems to imply inferiority and something ugly. They deplore the way in which the newspapers always report them as "Negroes," sometimes spelling the word with a small *n!* [2] They would prefer that no mention be made of race, that no attention be focused upon it, and that they be called simply "American," in the same category as the whites. But the mulatto, whose

[1] *The Negro in Chicago* (1922), pp. 518–519; W. H. Thomas, *The American Negro* (1901), p. 292.

[2] *Negro Yearbook* (1931–1932), pp. 16–26.

white blood puts him in a class almost by himself, nevertheless is regarded as belonging to the Negro race. His welfare and progress are
bound up with the welfare and progress of that race. Such objections
must, therefore, be overruled; and attention must be directed to the
difficult task of developing a sane and just policy and program that will
lessen race friction and at the same time protect the best interests of both
races.

Even before the War Between the States certain public men and social
reformers devoted considerable thought and effort to the betterment of
race relations. But the Emancipation Proclamation placed the problem
in the front rank of American issues. Especially since the adoption of the
Thirteenth, Fourteenth, and Fifteenth Amendments to the Federal Constitution there has been no issue that has been more persistently or more
passionately before the American public. There has not been a single
national party convention, nor a single session of Congress, since the
close of the War Between the States that has not debated some phase of
the problem of race relations.

The very nature of most of the proposed policies and programs shows
how deep the problem of race relations has cut into the public mind.
But unlike problems of commerce or industry, there has been very
little *rational* and *scientific* thought applied to it. Race relations seem
so to arouse the emotions as to inhibit rational understanding and just
consideration. This largely explains why it has not been possible to
unite either race behind any one remedy.

POLICIES AND PROGRAMS PROPOSED AND ATTEMPTED

The champions of policies and programs on race relations are divided
into eight different camps: (1) A large group believe that the problem
of race relations can be solved through *political action*—through granting full and unrestricted civil rights to the Negro, equal in every respect
to those granted to and exercised by the whites. (2) A smaller and perhaps a less stable group advocate *race amalgamation*, i.e., they would
wipe out the "color-line" by encouraging intermarriage of the races.
(3) Another group, and one that dates back further than perhaps any
other, sees no hope of the two races' solving the problem on the same
soil. They believe that the Negro should be *returned to Africa*, where
he can set up his own government and social institutions. (4) One group
sees the possibility, and more or less remote probability, of a separate and
independent *"free state"* for the Negroes in the South—setting aside, as

it were, a definite section of the South as exclusively belonging to the Negroes, in much the same manner that the Indian problem was handled. (5) Another group is composed of those who are firmly convinced that the Negro is by nature inferior to the white man, and that the white man is therefore his natural guardian. They would *revise the present constitutional rights*, which, so they say, "were mistakenly and hastily granted the Negro" and establish a sort of caste system guaranteeing white supremacy. (6) A more hopeful group believes that the Negro is here to stay and that the most expedient solution of the problem of race relations is through *race segregation*. (7) Another group, noting the recent trend of migration of the Negro population, believes that this offers the key to solving the problem of race relations; that by *scattering* the 13,000,00c Negroes among the 120,000,000 whites the Negroes would thereby be a negligible element socially and politically and thus not be able to endanger white supremacy anywhere. (8) Finally, there is a growing group in both races who put their trust in *education* and *interracial cooperation*. Content with temporary programs based on expediency, they are aiming to soften race prejudices by equalizing educational opportunity and by developing a social organization that will enable the two races to live and work together in harmony.

In these camps there is by no means unity of opinion. Leaders in each camp are divided between "conservative opportunists" who prefer to move along lines of voluntary action, and the "radicals" who desire to speed up the solution by compulsion.

POLITICAL ACTION AS A SOLUTION

It is an American practice to attempt to solve any and every sort of social problem through political action. As a result, our statute-books are loaded with "dead-letter" laws that are not enforced simply because public opinion does not respect them, nor does it feel responsible for them. We seem to overlook the fact that in a democratic society social reform must have public opinion behind it.

It is little wonder, therefore, that a large proportion of the Negro population as well as a considerable number of whites should pin their faith for a solution to the problems of race relations on this American obsession for *political action*. They are convinced that if the Negro were given full and unrestricted use of the ballot, and allowed his "rightful and proportionate place" in politics and governmental positions, as was intended under the Thirteenth, Fourteenth, and Fifteenth Amendments to the Constitution, then the injustices and vexing discriminations would be corrected.[3] This was the cardinal doctrine of many of the old Abolitionists and was the chief aim of the carpet-bag régime.

But, idealistic and democratic as this proposal may seem, there is not the remotest possibility of its being realized. Public opinion among the whites, North and South, wherever the Negro is at all numerically significant, is stubbornly and unqualifiedly opposed to it. The memory of Reconstruction days and of the fate of the whites in Haiti when the Negroes came to dominate is by no means dead. The whites who sense the temper of most of the Negro press to-day feel quite sure that such a policy would not be to the best interests of either race. The prejudice and hate openly expressed by many Negro editors would scarcely allow the orderly discharge of civic duties if Negroes were allowed the privilege of holding administrative or judicial office. While the Southern whites receive most of the abuse and blame for withholding equal political and civil opportunities from the Negroes, the people of the North are no more ready to grant them these privileges than are the people of the South.

We admit frankly that if political equality had meant the election of Negro mayors, judges, and a majority of Negroes in the city council the Whites would not have tolerated it. We do not believe that the Whites of Chicago would be any different from the Whites of the South in this respect. We have been able to extend the essentials of citizenship to the Negroes freely because the Whites are dominant in numbers. All the essentials are in the possession of the Negro. He is not jim-crowed by law. A line is drawn by usage. The law forbids what is actually done (the separation of the Negroes in cars). It is a futile law because it encounters instinct.[4]

But even though the Negro is allowed to vote in the Northern cities, it seldom gets him the opportunity to hold any public position beyond that of janitor in a public building or a job as an elevator man. As a general rule the Negro vote is shamelessly "managed" to the advantage of white office-seekers, and the Negro politician is generally a mere tool for corrupt politics.[5]

We may then conclude that political action will not solve the problem of race relations. The Negro may be conceded his constitutional rights in communities where his vote is a negligible quantity; but wherever the Negro population is sufficiently strong to endanger in the least white

[3] See *Negro Yearbook* (1931–1932), pp. 27–32 ("Nineteen Years' Civil Rights Struggle").

[4] *The Negro in Chicago* (1922), p. 551.

[5] H. J. Seligman, *The Negro Faces America* (1920), Ch. VI.

dominance, there he will find the door to political action closed to him.[6]

This does not mean that the Negro should take no interest in the civic affairs of his community, State, and nation. He may lack the vote but, if he is intelligently and unselfishly concerned in the promotion of the best interests of his race, his voice is not unheeded. Some time ago the State of Mississippi passed a law providing for county agricultural high schools for whites only. When the law went into effect an intelligent Negro refused to pay his taxes on the ground that this law made no provisions for the needed educational opportunities for his children. The Supreme Court of the State upheld the Negro's objections and declared the law unconstitutional. But many of the thoughtful and enterprising Negroes felt that such a law was needed for the proper training of the children of both races, and began working for a bill that would provide two such schools in each county, one for the whites and one for the Negroes.[7] The petitions that they sent to the legislature were read and discussed with as much consideration as the petitions from the interested whites. The new laws thus made provisions for both races, and now in many counties there are already splendidly equipped schools for both white and colored children.

Booker T. Washington saw the futility of attempting to solve the problem of race relations through political action:

"In my mind there is no doubt but that we made a mistake at the beginning of our freedom of putting the emphasis on the wrong end. Politics and the holding of office were too largely emphasized, almost to the exclusion of every other interest." [8]

AMALGAMATION AS A SOLUTION

Closely allied with those who advocate political action is a group of those who advocate the amalgamation of the two races through intermarriage. The advocates of this policy assume that all races are equal and if given the same environment, the same social and economic opportunity, their attainments would be the same.[9] Some biologists are of the opinion that the result of such a racial mixture would be beneficial.[10] Conservative scientists, while granting that races differ, do not interpret this difference as signifying that one race is superior to another. There

[6] Jerome Dowd, *The Negro in American Life* (1926), Ch. 62.
[7] William Holtzclaw, *The Black Man's Burden* (1915), Ch. XVIII.
[8] Quoted by Dowd, *op. cit.*, p. 508.
[9] Dowd, *op. cit.*, p. 362.
[10] L. C. Dunn, "A Biological View of Race Mixture," *Publications of the American Sociological Society*, XIX: 54.

seems to be no conclusive evidence to prove that the Negro is inferior to the white in native ability. But the assumption that mixed blood is better than pure blood can nowhere be substantiated. The hybrid stock *may* not be inferior to the parent races when given the same opportunities for growth and survival, but it may be taken as a general principle that *too much interbreeding of divergent human races leads to "general and permanent deterioration" of the human stock.*[11] *Random mating* of various breeds of dogs produces the mongrel, and this same general principle is as true for divergent human races as it is for dogs.

Some of the advocates of amalgamation point to the historical incidents where interracial peace was purchased by intermarriage of the leaders of contending races. But such politically arranged marriages, which are frequent even to-day, cannot be regarded as having any serious bearing on the problem. The royal blood of European nations has been carefully mixed; but this has not harmonized the populations of those nations.

Others believe that the trend of history is in the direction of amalgamation of all races; that the improved means of transportation and travel and the growth of commerce will eventually mix all races into one. They point out that the New World is already a mixture of almost all the racial stocks of Europe, and that amalgamation of the whites and the Negroes in the United States has reached the point where between one fifth and one third of the total Negro population are mulattoes.

There is no disputing the fact that there has been a considerable amount of interracial mixture. But this cannot be taken as proof that it is a good thing. The question is not one that can be treated purely as a biological problem. The social consequences are so far-reaching and so disadvantageous as to outweigh any biological benefits if there are any. In the first place, intermarriage seldom takes place except in the lower classes of both races. "From the earliest times marriage of Negroes with White persons in this country was considered highly undesirable, and in the Colonial period such marriages came to be prohibited by law in nearly every Colony." [12] These prohibitions persist with even greater force to-day. The better classes among the whites and the Negroes consider interracial marriages as "disgraceful" and "repugnant." Thus, a white woman who marries a Negro is socially ostracized by the women of both races; and a white man who marries a colored woman is asked to resign from the social clubs of which he is a member, is shunned by

[11] Arthur Dendy, *The Biological Foundations of Society* (1924), pp. 167–169.
[12] Dowd, *op. cit.,* p. 445.

his former associates, and finds no welcome in association with the Negroes. Children born to such marriages—fortunately they are few—share the social ostracism accorded their parents. Under such circumstances, antisocial traits are most likely to develop both in parents and children.

Would the advocates of this solution carry out their doctrine when confronted with the possibility of their own children's marrying into the other race? In any case it is certain that the mere mention of race intermarriage excites violent resentment among the Negroes as well as among the whites, especially among the Southern whites. In spite of its seeming religious foundation, a policy favoring amalgamation would arouse more antagonism and intensify the problem of race relations instead of helping to solve it.

COLONIZATION AS A SOLUTION

Many early leaders of the American democratic movement viewed race diversity as a stumbling-block to the progress of a popular government. They advocated the establishing of a colony on the West Coast of Africa where the American Negroes might be sent and allowed to work out their salvation. Thomas Jefferson, Henry Clay, and Daniel Webster were among those who most ardently supported this program. "In 1777 Thomas Jefferson proposed a colonization scheme to the General Assembly of Virginia, but no action on his proposal was taken. In 1793 he advocated a plan of colonization to be carried on by the several States and by the National government, and he continued to urge this ideal until his death in 1826." [13]

While the prospect for the success of such a plan has never been encouraging, the idea has never been completely abandoned. Numerous organized attempts have been promoted by both Negroes and whites—some of them achieving at least a beginning, but the number of Negroes sent to these colonies was negligible compared to the annual increase in the Negro population.

Lincoln, during the War Between the States, advocated the colonization of the Negroes who came into the custody of the Federal Government. Congress appropriated $600,000 for this purpose, and an unsuccessful attempt was made to establish colonies on the islands off the coast of Haiti.[14]

[13] *Ibid.*, p. 458; James Truslow Adams, *The Epic of America* (New York, 1931), p. 104.
[14] Dowd, *op. cit.*, pp. 460–461.

The ability of the United States to land over two million troops in France during the First World War gave renewed hope to many advocates of this plan. Up to that time it was believed impossible, even over a long period of time, to accomplish the movement of so large a population.

Perhaps the most significant movement for colonization was headed by a Jamaica Negro, Marcus Garvey, promoter and organizer of The Universal Negro Improvement Association and African Community League. He was often referred to as the "Negro Moses." In 1921 this organization fitted out its own ships and sent to Liberia, Africa, a staff of engineers, carpenters, health workers, community-planners, and other specialists to plan and lay out "ideal communities" to which colonists might later be sent.

Perhaps the plan promoted by Marcus Garvey would have aided the problem of race relations by making it possible for the dissatisfied and embittered Negroes of the United States to find a "haven of refuge." If rightly managed it might have proved a real success for those who entered into it.[15] But it is not likely that the plan could have noticeably reduced the Negro population of this country. The assumption that all Negroes are oppressed and unhappy, and thus looking for a "Moses," is of course unfounded. The fact that millions of Negroes, especially in the South, are making rapid economic, educational, and social progress militates against colonization as a practical solution to the problem of race relations.

A "NEGRO RESERVATION" OR "NEGRO FREE STATE" AS A SOLUTION

Some students, especially geographers, regard the establishing of a Negro Reservation or a separate Negro State as both a practical and a feasible solution to the problem of race relations. They point out that the United States found this a practical and satisfactory means of disposing of "the Indian problem." Why not use it to dispose of the even more troublesome Negro problem?

They point out further that the Negroes themselves are showing a mass preference for this plan, in that certain sections of the South are every year becoming more settled by them; that the whites are moving away from these Negro settlements, leaving them to become definitely Negro sections. Some students believe that, if left wholly to the voluntary movement of the Negro population, within another quarter of a

[15] See *Negro Yearbook* (1931–1932), for a brief summary of the exploits of Marcus Garvey.

century certain sections of the South might be wholly taken over by the colored people. If this point were reached, they contend, there would be nothing to prevent the Negroes from managing their own governmental affairs within their sections. This would lead to setting off those sections as separate States. The Negro would then be removed from social competition with the whites, and the problem of race relations would be solved.

There are a number of forces that militate against this happy solution to the problem. While it is true that certain sections of the "Black Belt" are becoming more definitely Negro settlements, it is not due so much to the sectional increase of the Negro population, either by natural increase or by migration, as to the migration of the whites to the urban centers. The land is still, and much will continue to be, in the hands of the whites. Furthermore, the rapid changes in methods of agriculture are substituting machinery for farm labor, thus reducing the economic opportunity of the present Negro population. Thus it is that many Negroes, as well as whites, are leaving agriculture and seeking their economic opportunities in industry and business. This is, no doubt, the major cause for the vast and rapid shifts of the Negro population since the First World War. The tendency, therefore, is more definitely away from, rather than toward the concentration of the Negro population into sections that would make possible a separate State. Finally, the vast tracts of free land that made possible the creation of the Indian Reservations are no longer to be had. But even if lands were available, it would not be possible to force or persuade the entire Negro population to live there without taking away from them the large measure of liberty they now enjoy. No policy or program that must depend upon force for its success can succeed.

THE POSSIBILITY OF A CASTE SYSTEM AS A SOLUTION

There are many honest white people who sincerely believe that the Negro is, by his very nature, inferior to the white man. The white race has always found it hard to divide equally with any other race. Its history seems to indicate that it must either rule or ruin other races. We have come, of late, to refer to this particular characteristic as "Nordic Superiority," which often includes much that is neither Nordic nor superior!

The supporters of this doctrine point out that nowhere are the dark-skinned races making any progress without being under the direction of the whites. Consequently the white race has adopted the convenient philosophy, "The people who can make the best use of a piece of this planet have a right to it." [16] While this point of view makes exploitation easy and has often justified it, it must be admitted that this is not always the case in the relation between the whites and the Negroes in the United States. Generally, the whites, especially in the South, have taken a benevolent attitude toward the Negroes. Senator Bilbo of Mississippi, editor of *The Free Lance*, admittedly belonged to this group, who feel that the white man is superior to the Negro and thereby his guardian. He said:

> We believe that the Negro ought to be treated fairly, but keep his place. . . . So long as the Negro stays in his place and occupies the sphere intended for him through Providence, environment, and capabilities, all will be well. . . . But, in the name of the White man's civilization, and for the sake of our institutions and for the supremacy of our race, when the Negro demands more it will be moving day for him.[17]

The trouble with this policy of race relations is that a caste system can last only so long as educational and economic forces contribute to keep one group dominant over another. But the Negro is rapidly improving his educational status to the point where all the avenues of science and learning are open to him. He is likewise rising in the economic scale to the point where he not only commands considerable wealth, but in proportion as he proves himself useful he is given influence and respect, not only by the members of his own race, but by the whites as well. In the face of this progress, caste is doomed; the Negro may develop his racial possibilities alongside his white neighbor without being either an intruder or an inferior. Under the circumstances, caste would have to depend upon force in order to persist; and since force breeds fraud, the problems of race relations would be even more troublesome than they are now.[18]

SEGREGATION AS A SOLUTION

Segregation has come to be used to designate the policies and programs that are the expressions of the natural disposition of races to live apart from each other and for each to develop its own social life with its own social institutions. The use of the term *segregation* in this connection is unfortunate. It seems to imply too much forced isolation and

[16] Quoted by Dowd, *op. cit.*, p. 495, from Thomas Carlyle's essay, "The Nigger Question."

[17] Quoted from *The Free Lance* by *Information Service* (New York: Federal Council of the Churches of Christ in America, March 15, 1924).

[18] Hornell Hart, *The Science of Social Relations* (1927), Ch. XII and pp. 508–509.

subordination; and thus it arouses a feeling of resentment. *Separation* would have been a happier and a more accurate term, and would have given the radical Negro editors less to complain about.

All over the world there is a tendency for divergent races to want to live to themselves and not blend their living with other races. The League of Nations recognized this principle in attempting to work out a program for promoting world peace.[19] The Negroes and the whites in the United States are not exceptions to this rule. Since Colonial days they have lived apart in spite of their close economic contacts. Both races have a sensitive "consciousness of kind" that impels them toward separation "in all things that are purely social." In the rural South, as we have already noted, the tendency is toward the formation of all-Negro communities; and even where the Negro farms are scattered among those of the whites, each race prefers separate group life. The same is true of the urban communities. Wherever the Negro population becomes sufficiently large to enable them to have their own social institutions, such institutions spring up. Separate churches, pool-halls, restaurants, lodges, and barber-shops often spring up before there has developed a distinctly separate Negro residential district. As a rule, Negroes want separate churches first, and very often they are aided financially by the whites to obtain church property and even to pay the preacher.

While segregation seems to be desired by both Negroes and whites, it is not always obtained in a manner satisfactory to each race. This is especially true in matters of housing and ownership of property, educational facilities, transportation facilities, playgrounds, and recreation places. In the South where the Negro population is densest the policy of separation has become fairly settled and agreed upon by leaders of both races—though in matters of equal educational facilities and equal travel accommodations the Negro has ground for complaint. In the North, however, where the policy of separation has never been understood by the whites and where, until recently, the Negroes were too few to provoke problems of race relations, these questions are giving rise to serious protests, race riots, intimidations, and vexing discriminations.

In almost every Northern city the question of Negro housing and ownership of property has become a serious strain on the harmonious relationship between the races. Here we find Negro segregation a fact. As a rule, they can obtain housing only in the least desirable residential sections, where they gain possession by paying a higher rental than was

[19] Dowd, *op. cit.*

paid by the South Europeans and Russian Jews, who are thus induced to live elsewhere under more favorable conditions. When the Negro with means attempts to secure residence in a better neighborhood among white neighbors he is at once met with opposition—legal and social. Real estate men in many cities have inserted clauses in their land contracts to prevent sale or rental to Negroes. This means of segregating the Negro was challenged in the courts, and carried to the United States Supreme Court. The Supreme Court in a decision rendered May 24, 1926, declared such contracts valid and constitutional. Thus segregation in the Northern industrial cities works a serious hardship on the Negro. Hemmed in, as the "Negro quarter" generally is, and as individuals unable to obtain residence in better neighborhoods, they are compelled to live under conditions that are a menace to their health, morals, and social welfare.[20]

Separate schools for Negroes and Negro teachers to teach them are demanded whenever the Negro population is large enough to make a showing in the community. The demand usually comes from the whites; but the Negroes generally would much prefer this arrangement if they could be sure that their schools would be on a par with the schools for whites. Some of the Northern Negroes, especially mulattoes, have opposed separate schools on the ground that educating the children in the same schools would help the races to understand each other better and thus lessen race prejudice. But the Northern whites are no different from the whites of the South on the question of segregation. The action taken several years ago by eight hundred high school students of the Emerson High School, Gary, Indiana, illustrates this fact. Gary is a city built around the steel industry on the shores of Lake Michigan. It is comparatively new not only in location and structure, but also in regard to its population—the majority of the white children in the high school being native-born of foreign-born parents. When high school opened in September, 1927, there were twenty-four Negro students enrolled. The Negroes were also new to the city. The white students objected to the Negroes entering their classes and demanded that a separate school be provided for them. When the school board rejected their demands, they walked out of their classes and refused to return to school until their demands were granted. This incident reflects the growing race antipathy in many of the Northern cities where the Negro population has increased rapidly owing to recent migrations.

Separate travel accommodations for the Negroes and whites in street-

[20] *The Negro in Chicago* (1922), Ch. V.

cars, busses, and passenger-trains—popularly known as the "Jim Crow" policy—have also met much opposition from many Northern Negroes, and especially Northern mulattoes, and have been criticized by many Northern whites who are not familiar with the "institution." The policy of separate travel accommodations is as rigidly enforced against the whites as it is against the Negroes, and was instituted for the primary purpose of preventing race friction. It was not designed, as some folks think, to embarrass and antagonize the Negro. In the Southern States separation is required by law. In the street-cars and busses, as a general rule, there is no discrimination in regard to the nature of the service— Negroes and whites ride in the same vehicles, separated only by a portable sign that fits on the back of the seats. In passenger-trains, however, the railroads often take advantage of the situation and furnish inferior accommodations for Negroes, and since few Negroes would travel in Pullman cars, they are not allowed Pullman or dining-car accommodations unless especially contracted for by a group. This often works a hardship on the Negro traveler, and especially on the educated and cultivated Negro. However, even in the absence of legal separation there is a general preference for separate travel accommodations. This is well illustrated in Chicago, where a law prohibits transportation companies from applying the "Jim Crow" principles; nevertheless a line is drawn by usage, especially in the cars and trains that pass through Negro settlements.

In the South, where the races understand each other better, there is a clearer understanding as to where the races should separate in playgrounds, parks, recreational centers, and theaters. In the Northern cities, however, the lack of this understanding is the cause of much race friction and serious trouble.[21] At least one of the most serious race riots, in which thirty-eight persons were killed, resulted from inadequate separation of the races on the bathing-beaches and in the recreational parks of Chicago. An imaginary line had been drawn by usage but it was challenged by some of the more "aggressive" Negroes, and it was this challenge which caused the trouble.[22] In general, the Negroes prefer separate amusement and recreational accommodations and have usually organized and provided their own play, where separate public accommodations for them were lacking. Even in athletics they have seldom sought to compete with the whites, especially where their numbers were large enough to permit their keeping to themselves.

[21] Ibid.
[22] Ibid., pp. 596–602.

In the Southern states, where two races are thrown together in great masses, there would be perpetual clashes and outbreaks of violence in schools, churches, hotels and in places of amusement if there were not some local regulation of racial contact. Legalized separation of the races in the South pertains to schools, hotels, restaurants, theaters, street cars and railway cars.[23]

This policy in the South has been in practice almost from the beginning and the races have adjusted themselves to it, and have provided accommodations accordingly. In the North, the policy is gradually finding public approval, but accommodations are in many instances lacking. In many Northern cities it is difficult for Negro travelers to find a place to sleep. The better hotels have "all rooms taken" when the Negro attempts to register for a room; restaurants and dining-halls are "out of food" when he seats himself at a table, or he is handed a menu with prices especially designed to discourage his patronage.

In general, segregation has not only been the means of preventing race friction, but it has also given the Negro his major opportunities to advance. It has saved him from the deadening and dwarfing conditions of a caste system. Many Negro leaders and educators recognize this fact.

This division of the races is an advantage to us as a people, in so far as it permits us to become the teachers of our own people. No better discipline can be given to a people than that which they gain by being their own teachers. They can have no greater opportunity than that of developing within themselves the ideals and the leadership which are to make them not merely in law, but in fact, the masters of their own fortunes.[24]

E. B. Reuter has observed:

. . . To the extent that the races became separated and the Negroes gained in independence and developed a sense of racial pride and self-reliance, there was a place for an educated class within the race; there was a need for teachers and preachers, for physicians and lawyers, for business men and entertainers. . . . With the rise of a middle-class, the race was able to support a professional and leisure class; previously the educated Negro was an idler and a parasite. Isolation of the race forced the Negroes to depend upon their own educated men and so to make a place for such men.

The separation of the races freed the Negro professional and business men from the competition of the better trained and more efficient White men and consequently gave them an opportunity to rise out of all proportion to their native ability and training. The plane of competition became one on which they could hope to succeed. The older—the slave and reconstruction plane of adjustment—was an accommodation on horizontal lines. The White man was at the top, the Black man was at the bottom. It was a caste distinction that prevented the rise of the capable individual out of his group.

[23] Dowd, *op. cit.*
[24] B. T. Washington, *The American Negro of Today*, pp. 67 ff.

In the newer arrangement the opportunity to rise was limited only by ability and the industry of the individual man. There was no superior caste above him.[25]

However, segregation—unless supplemented by an effective means of interracial coöperation—may lead to grave misunderstandings, super-sensitive racial resentments, damning prejudices, and wanton injustices. Herein lies the chief difficulty with segregation as a policy and program of race relations. It cannot be trusted by itself to work as a final solution to the problems of race relations. It must increasingly be supplemented by more efficient and more positive policies and programs of interracial understanding and coöperation.

MIGRATION AS A SOLUTION TO THE PROBLEM OF RACE RELATIONS

Some entertain the hope that migration of the Negroes to the North, East, and West will eventually solve the problem of race relations. They point out that the Negro is getting a better education and is gaining in self-reliance, and is thus less hesitant about leaving the South, where he has been "looked after." They further believe that our restriction of foreign immigration will increase the demand for Negro labor in the industrial centers, and thus lead him to seek the more "advantageous" economic opportunities. It may take some time, but eventually, they think, the Negro will become adjusted to industry and to the urban life of the North.[26] It is thought by some that the Negro will not multiply as fast in the city as in the rural districts, and this will further lessen the number in proportion to the whites. The Negro population thus being scattered, the dominance of the whites will be everywhere assured.

The trouble with this all too hopeful outlook is that it does not take many Negroes to make a crowd, and this is more true in the cities of the North than it is in the South. It will be remembered that the ratio of Negro children to white children in the Emerson High School of Gary was only twenty-four Negroes to eight hundred white—3 per cent—yet there was a problem of race relations. Such a proposal, though used to encourage Negro migration from the South, should not be given serious thought as a solution to the problem of race relations.

EDUCATION AND INTERRACIAL COÖPERATION AS A SOLUTION

There is no panacea for the problem of race relations. A plan that may work well in one community cannot be expected to accomplish

[25] E. B. Reuter, *The Mulatto in the United States* (1918), p. 359.
[26] Alain Locke, "Enter the New Negro," *Survey* (Harlem number, March 1, 1925), pp. 631–634.

like results in all communities. But whatever the plan, its degree of success must depend upon two factors: (1) *The extent to which it has fostered and furthered a program of sound education;* and (2) *the extent to which it has built up and established sound policies and programs of interracial coöperation.*

What should be the central aim of a sound educational program? What sort of education is most needed by the Negro population? Negro leaders themselves are not agreed on this point.[27] But the results already demonstrated leave little room for argument. People who are useful, no matter what happens to be their race or origin, come to be liked and respected. Consequently, the central aim of a sound educational program should be to teach people to be useful.[28] It is this aim which gains for the Negro his greatest freedom and his greatest happiness, and it is this aim which calls forth the hearty support and enthusiastic approval of the whites.

When William Holtzclaw went to Utica, Mississippi, forty years ago, he was met by Colonel Chapman, a white man and successful attorney in that section of the State. The "ol' Colonel," a veteran of the War Between the States, had always lived among Negroes and he knew their needs. "Well," said the Colonel to Holtzclaw, "if you have come here to teach the 'nigger' to be useful, you will find the best White people will be with you; but if you have come to educate him to dress up and quit work, my advice to you would be to pass on." Holtzclaw welcomed this bit of information and advice. He was a graduate of Tuskegee Institute and a close follower of his great teacher, Booker T. Washington. He had in fact come to Utica to prove himself useful and to teach others how to be useful. Utica Normal and Industrial Institute with its 1,600 acres of good land, offering training in twenty different trades as well as academic subjects to hundreds of Negro boys and girls, and conducting demonstrations and institutes among the farmers of the state, stands as a monument to the man who came to educate his fellows to be useful. Perhaps Hampton Institute or Tuskegee would have served better to illustrate the success of this educational aim; but Utica represents the third generation of Negro schools founded on this principle—Hampton and its great founder, Samuel C. Armstrong, handed the torch to Booker T. Washington, who founded Tuskegee, and it was at Tuskegee that Holtzclaw gained the inspiration for his great work. White people the

[27] Dowd, *op. cit.,* Ch. LXV.
[28] Hornell Hart, *The Science of Social Relations* (1927), pp. 521–524.

nation over, North as well as South, have joined hands with the Negroes to build and develop these schools.

The late President Taft, also one-time president of the board of trustees of Hampton Institute, was greatly interested in the advancement of Negro education. "The result has demonstrated," said Taft, speaking of the work of Hampton, "that in the principles that Armstrong taught is to be found the solution to our race problem in this country. Here is to be found the explanation of the marvelous progress which statistics show has been made by the Negro race in the half century of 'up from slavery.' " [29]

While a few of the Negro colleges shun this educational aim as "servile" and "degrading," the vast majority of them—including the State agricultural colleges and normal schools for Negroes—have as their central aim the training of their students to be useful—not only useful in occupation, but useful in the betterment of the civic and social welfare of their communities.

Since these schools are furnishing the teachers for the expanding and improving public schools for the Negroes, and providing the major leadership for the race, it is a hopeful sign that the solution to the problem of race relations—at least from the Negroes' side—is within reach.

But the educational problems of the Negro are not quite the same as those of the whites—and this is another reason for separate schools. As we noted in the previous chapter, the Negro has come "up from slavery," and is still impeded in his progress by the vestiges of the old slave culture—the habits of living, the ideals, the methods and manner of doing things, the stifled initiative, and the happy-go-lucky attitude toward the future. All these he must change if he is to be really useful to-day. He must learn to be self-reliant and plan for the future. He must study improved methods and make himself an efficient producer. He must come to understand the economic system under which he lives, and learn to free himself from the debt-forming habits to which he has become accustomed—he must school himself in thrift. He must strive for farm and home ownership, and free himself from the wasteful and inefficient life of the "cropper tenant," and from the still more wasteful and blighting neighborhood life of the Negro city renter. He must strive for good homes and put much thought and quiet pride into making them beautiful—not gaudy and pretentious, but dignified and artistic. He must talk

[29] Quoted by Dowd, *op. cit.*, from a bulletin published by Hampton Institute.

less of politics, and do more to gain a clearer vision of the community and civic needs of his race.[30]

There is another side to educational aims that relates as much to the whites as it does to the Negroes. The educators of both races have much to accomplish before the schools become *socially efficient*—efficient in giving to young America *the point of view, the knowledge, and the training* that they must have in order to be of highest usefulness in meeting the problems of *human relations*. Our schools—most of them—have become efficient in teaching people to be *readers, listeners, and onlookers;* but there are lacking those essential guiding principles by which this efficiency may improve human relations. It is a sort of *aimless efficiency*, which is as likely to spend itself in a riot as in a love-feast. *Aimless reading* has made a market for tons of "printed trash" that flares from every news-stand and feeds the imagination on the products of sordid minds and morbid discontent. *Aimless listening* has made us easy prey to the rumor-monger, the propagandist, the sensationalist, the mob psychologist. *Aimless onlooking* does not discern the false from the true, the sham from the meritorious, the worthless from the able. Thus it is that we are becoming more and more erratic and more craze-ridden in matters affecting human relations.[31]

Both races need, therefore, to examine carefully their educational aims and the social attitudes that are being formed by them. One-sided presentations of questions affecting human relations; substitution of flimsy opinion for facts; emphasis on difference instead of likeness; tirades on inequalities instead of vivid pictures of opportunities; getting the dollar-sign in front of the service ideal—to the extent that these practices are reflections of our educational methods, to the same extent we may expect our problems of human relations to become more difficult and more menacing.

Segregation—as we have just pointed out—will enable the Negro to adapt his schools and educational aims to fit the peculiar needs of his race, but *it is evident that in matters of education, as well as in other matters of community life and economic advancement, there must be sound policies and programs of interracial relations.* Without whole-hearted coöperation it is hardly possible to correct the harmful tendencies that create race friction, or to strengthen the bonds of relationship by sympathetic understanding. It is only through such coöperation that

[30] Dowd, *op. cit.*, Ch. 71.
[31] *And Who Is My Neighbor? An Outline for the Study of Race Relations in America* (National Conference on Christian Way of Living, 1924).

a healthy public opinion can be created and the press be made to reflect a saner and more just attitude in the treatment of questions relating to race relations and the Negro.[32] Since the Negroes cannot hope to gain anything through political action, there is no method other than coöperation by which their civic and community needs may be fairly met, and a just and equitable distribution of public revenues be made.

Both races benefit from coöperation. "If the Negro can afford to be wronged, the White man cannot afford to wrong him. To the extent that the Negro is 'kept down,' the White man must stay down with him. . . . The 'natural place' for any race is the highest level to which it is capable of climbing." [33]

Interracial coöperation has been slowly developing. But it has been a policy largely left to local communities to apply as they saw fit. Perhaps the first organized effort to promote interracial coöperation was that begun by the Y. M. C. A., through the leadership of Dr. W. D. Weatherford, formerly president of the Y. M. C. A. College at Nashville, Tennessee. This work of the Y. M. C. A. has been directed chiefly toward educating people to an appreciation of the true nature of the problems of race relations.[34] Other groups have made important contributions to promoting a public opinion that would further the movement of coöperation. Some of the most important of these groups are: the Southern Sociological Congress, the University Commission on Race Relations (composed chiefly of Southern universities), the Commission on Interracial Coöperation, the clergy in the various church bodies in the Southern States, the women's organizations, and the semi-official commissions of the various States of the South.

Through these organizations much has been accomplished to stamp out lynching and other lawless activities that were directed chiefly against Negroes. They have vastly improved the treatment of the Negroes before the courts, bettered the conditions of Negroes in jails and penal institutions, improved and enlarged other institutions for Negroes. They have given encouragement to Negro education all along the line —in the public schools, in secondary education, in colleges, and in the home education of adults through public-health nurses, home-demonstration agents, farm-demonstration agents, and traveling libraries.

But perhaps of even greater value in the promotion of a sound policy and program of interracial coöperation is the development of interracial

---

[32] *The Negro in Chicago*, 1922, Ch. IX.
[33] Dowd, *op. cit.*, p. 548.
[34] *Ibid.*, p. 550.

relations committees, particularly under the auspices of the Commission on Interracial Coöperation mentioned above. In the South, where there are now more than eight hundred towns and cities having such organizations, these committees are semi-official bodies composed of an equal number of members from each race, appointed, as a rule, by the mayors. In the North the committees are unofficial, as a rule, and frequently affiliated with the National Urban League. In addition to these permanent bodies, there are in some cities temporary commissions, made up of members of both races. Generally these temporary commissions are appointed for the specific purpose of investigating conditions and making recommendations for the organization and development of a permanent policy and program of interracial coöperation. The Chicago Commission on Race Relations was of this temporary sort and concluded its work with the publication of its report and recommendations—*The Negro in Chicago*.

The program of the National Urban League deals generally with the problems of race adjustment under a new situation and is therefore usually committed to a "social work" program. However, it does attempt to meet the larger problems, such as work on a housing program, newspaper policies, school relationships, industrial relations, recreation and playground policies and provisions, treatment of Negro offenders, and probation.

The interracial coöperation committees, especially in the South, are more committed to the task of racial *readjustment*, for the purpose of promoting harmony of race relations, and for furthering the economic and social welfare of the community as a whole. Perhaps the functions of these committees can be made clearer by taking as an example the program and accomplishments of one such committee that has been in operation for a number of years—the Interracial Relations Committee of Winston-Salem, North Carolina.

Winston-Salem is a city of approximately 50,000 population, of which about 25,000 are Negroes. Knitting-mills are the chief industries, and they have always depended upon Negro labor. The population, both white and Negro, is almost wholly native-born, and the city grew—like most cities of the South—with its typical "Negro quarter" located in the lowlands along the railroads and behind the warehouses. This "Negro quarter" was a dingy, muddy, smoky, unsightly eyesore on the otherwise beautiful and prosperous city. It was here that most of the Negroes lived, except a few of the more educated and prosperous, who formed a suburban district known as Columbia Heights.

Columbia Heights is located on a beautiful hilltop site, where the State normal school for Negroes is located. It is an attractive site for homes, but for years the streets leading to it were unimproved and it was too inaccessible for the mill-hands. Consequently the more thrifty mill workers who wished to improve their living conditions attempted to obtain homes and property in the highlands occupied by the whites.

Attempts had been made to secure legislation compelling the Negroes to remain in the "Negro quarter," where they had always lived; but such attempts did not stand the test of the courts. A serious situation was rapidly developing, which might at any time ripen into a race riot. But Winston-Salem could not afford a race riot, because it could not afford to lose its much-needed Negro labor.

The city, under the leadership of the mayor, began to give the question of race relations serious consideration. They called upon the Negroes to express themselves and they did. The result was the formation of an Interracial Relations Committee to work out a program and a definite policy. The results of this were that the whites agreed to divide the city's public improvements on a "fifty-fifty" basis with the Negroes. The streets of the Negro residential district were improved, and these improvements did not stop at the city limits but extended out through Columbia Heights. Three large school buildings were built for the Negroes. Tracts of land adjacent to the schools were purchased and converted into parks and playgrounds for the Negro children. Street-lighting, sewers, and water-mains were extended to the Negro residential district (notice that the "Negro quarter" gave way to the "Negro residential district").

Rapidly the Negroes began spreading out over Columbia Heights. It was agreed that the whites would not attempt to buy property on that side of the city, and that the Negroes could extend their home building as far out as they desired.

In 1925 a new two-wing municipal hospital was opened—one wing for the service of the whites and one for the Negroes. The city now divides its appropriations equally between the whites and the Negroes. The property holdings of the Negroes have increased in value to the point where there is no longer any question about the "white man paying all the taxes"—the assessed value of the Negro property about equals that of the whites.

Winston-Salem perhaps may be regarded as one of the most successful ventures in interracial coöperation; but it is fairly representative of the movement. It illustrates what can be done to bring about peace and harmony between two divergent races that, by the nature of things, must live in the same community and yet live separated. It illustrates also the possibility of a program of race segregation that is neither humiliating nor debasing. It proves the contention of the great Negro leader, Booker T. Washington, when he said (holding up one hand with outspread fingers): "In all things that are purely social we may be as separate as the fingers, yet as one hand in all things essential to material progress."

REFERENCES

BRYCE, James, *American Commonwealth* (New York, 1916), II, pp. 524–539, Ch. XCV.

CHADBOURN, J. H., *Lynching and the Law* (Chapel Hill, 1934).

FELDMAN, Herman, *Racial Factors in American Industry* (New York, 1931), Part II.

Fundamentals in Negro Education (Washington, D. C.: United States Office of Education, Bulletin, 1935, No. 6).

MATHEWS, Basil, *The Clash of Color* (New York, 1924).

MOTON, R. R., *Finding the Way Out* (New York, 1920).

The Negro in Chicago, Chicago Commission on Race Relations (University of Chicago Press, 1922), pp. 640–652, Introduction, and "Recommendations."

OLDHAM, J. H., *Christianity and the Race Problem* (London, 1925).

Report of the Advisory Committee on Education (Washington, D. C.: United States Government Printing Office, February, 1938).

REUTER, E. B., *American Race Problem* (New York, 1927).

WEATHERFORD, W. D., and JOHNSON, C. S., *Race Relations* (Boston, 1934).

WHITE, Walter, *Rope and Faggot* (New York, 1929).

WOOFTER, Thomas J., *The Basis of Racial Adjustment* (New York, 1925).

——, "The Status of Racial and Ethnic Groups," in *Recent Social Trends* (New York, 1933), Ch. XI, pp. 591–601.

QUESTIONS AND EXERCISES

1. Why is it increasingly necessary that we should adopt a national policy on race relations? Why not continue the time-honored *laissez-faire* policy, and let competition determine the outcome of the race problems?
2. At what stage in the growth of the Negro population should a city begin to develop a definite program and policy of race relations—*i.e.*, Should the city wait until a certain per cent, say 5 per cent of the population, is composed of Negroes? Explain.
3. In communities where there is a considerable colored population, would it be a practical or a desirable policy to insist that both races use the same schools, cars, theaters, and beaches, without being separated? Would such a policy increase or lessen race friction? Explain.
4. What are the advantages and disadvantages of a policy of race sepa-

ration in those fields where the two races are likely to come into conflict?

5. How has the use of the term *segregation* affected the solution of the race
problem? Suppose you were told that you could live only in a *segregated*
section of the city, how would you feel about it? What term is better?

6. What is the rôle of the mulatto in America's race problem? Do you think
the State laws prohibiting the intermarriage of whites and blacks are
weak laws? What would be the effect of the removal of all legal barriers
to the intermarriage of the two races?

7. Make a list of the arguments *for* and *against* political action as a solution
to the problem of race relations, using your own thought on the matter,
as well as the information you have gathered from your general readings
and from public discussions.

8. How may colonization affect the problem of race relations? Can it be
taken as a practical solution of the whole problem? Explain.

9. What effect has migration of the Negroes to the Northern industrial
centers had upon the problem of race relations? Are Northern whites
any more considerate and liberal with the Negro than the whites of the
South? Can we expect migration to distribute the Negro population
eventually so that the major issues of the problem of race relations will
disappear?

10. Outline briefly what you think should be the national policy of race
relations and show how it would work.

11. What difficulties are there in promulgating a national policy in regard
to race relations?

Chapter 6

THE SOCIAL THREAT OF WAR

WHEN THE CURTAIN first rises on the stage of history, men are fighting. The myths and hero tales imbedded in the early literatures of peoples celebrate the heroic deeds of warriors on battlefields. Even back beyond the written literature, since archæologists have dug up the ruins of old cities, explored caves and camping sites, we know from the battle-axes and other implements of warfare, from the cleft skulls, from the weapons buried with the deceased hero, that mankind had learned the art of warfare. There may have been an idyllic period in the history of mankind. So far, however, there is little evidence of it. True, the stone implements found among the remains of paleolithic man do not seem to be as well adapted to warlike purposes as those of neolithic man. Nevertheless we know that, whatever weapons he had, with them he succeeded in slaying animals as large as the elephant, which would seem to indicate that with them he might also slay his fellow-men. Whatever the truth about the antiquity of warfare, for at least fifteen or twenty thousand years man has been engaged in the gentle art of making war upon his fellows.

PEACE AND WAR A PROBLEM IN SOCIALIZATION

With the dispersion of the races and peoples of mankind from the cradle of the human race, wherever that may have been, differentiation between groups set in. With the separation of groups differences of language, customs, traditions, inevitably arose. Within the last two thousand years of history have occurred those differentiations in language and other elements of culture characteristic of the Latin peoples, even in so narrowly confined a region as southwestern Europe. Given the long periods of time since man first appeared in Europe, it is not difficult to understand how enormous changes took place in what may have been an original single culture; these changes would enable us to account for the differences in the cultures of the different groups, which when they later met, would make them alien to one another. The points of concentration of population were determined by economic resources, such as wells in the desert, hunting and fishing grounds, pasture-lands, and fertile valleys. The conquest over nature and greater control over the food supply cut down mortality and stimulated population growth. With the growth of population, inevitably groups came in contact with each other. Peoples with different cultures coming into contact with one another and competing for access to natural resources often came to blows. It must not be concluded, however, that the struggle was solely a struggle for survival, as it is among all other forms of life. The idea that population pressure has been the chief motivating force of intergroup conflict even among primitive peoples has been modified in recent years. The desire for plunder has been a potent factor, since it has afforded a means of getting something for nothing. Similarly, the development of slavery, by which one group can be compelled to do the hard work of another in return for mere subsistence, has put a premium on the capture of members of outside groups or tribes. Both of these motives arouse a sheer lust for power or a desire to dominate for the sake of easier living, quite apart from any acute pressure of population upon the resources available to support it.[1]

Furthermore, we must remember that in the early history of mankind all social relationships were based upon kinship bonds. One who was related by blood either in fact or by fiction was a member of the group, therefore a friend. In the struggle for existence the qualities of courage, resourcefulness, invention, agility, and cunning were developed. Along with these qualities, however, the struggle for existence also produced between members of the group kindliness, sympathy, and mutual helpfulness.[2] But such mutual aid did not extend to those outside the group except under extraordinary circumstances, since broad human sympathy developed very much later than sympathy for kin.

The results of these various conditions were conflicts and wars. Sometimes one group drove out the other, which then moved on to other places. At other times when the strength of the two contending parties was nearly equal, treaties seem to have been made, as well as some kind of a working arrangement for the occupation of the same territory. In the case of both conquest and treaty sometimes assimilation of culture occurred, occasionally amalgamation of the two groups took place by reason of intermarriage, and finally such union of both stock and culture as made these groups one people came about. This we call "socialization." An illustration is provided by the probable history of the

[1] Alvin Johnson, article on "War," in the *Encyclopaedia of the Social Sciences*, XV: 331-334.
[2] P. A. Kropotkin, *Mutual Aid: A Factor in Evolution* (1904).

twelve tribes of Israel. It is quite likely that the people of Israel were the
result of such amalgamation of various groups and the resulting socialization that came about by living together in a common area, sharing the
same culture, and finally developing common institutions and a common political system. That the socialization was not complete is shown
by the fact that in the later history of the people of Israel a political
division took place between the south and north areas of Palestine.[3] The
same process can be traced quite clearly in the history of the people of
the British Isles.

THE BASES OF PRIMITIVE AND MODERN WAR

Despite the enormous contrasts that readily suggest themselves between the tribal, hand-to-hand fighting of primitive times and the mass
assault of whole peoples against one another in present-day war, there
still are certain basic similarities in the background of both types of conflict. Not only are the fundamental urges for power and booty which
were mentioned a moment ago still present, but the underlying problems
of socialization still prevail. The patterns of intergroup competition and
intragroup coöperation are basically the same as they have always been.
Whether the group be large or small, its members become interdependent, one upon another. The individual finds that he has greater security
and can enjoy the use of a greater variety of goods and services if he
shares the work of life with others. As a result of this interdependence
between members of the group, there develop feelings of loyalty to the
group as a whole, a jealousy of its security and continued ability to function. Anything that seems to menace that community of interests from
the outside will at once arouse the antagonism of its members toward
the potential enemy. It is, in effect, a *segmental* socialization. The world
never was—and is not yet—a complete, single unit. There are all sorts
of cleavages, racial, class, religious, occupational, as well as economic
and political, which create opposition among social groups. Each of them
arouses loyalties which are intense enough, in many cases, to create
strong feelings of group difference and conflict, even within a small
community of people. The problem, then, is to harmonize the objectives
and loyalties of the various competing groups so that compromise can
be accomplished on higher planes than those of sheer violence. Yet curiously, the problem becomes more complicated as the conflict grows
sharper and more inclusive, since local or internal differences become
submerged in a common enterprise against any force threatening from

[3] Louis Wallis, *Sociological Study of the Bible* (Chicago, 1912).

the outside; and any partial sympathies that may have extended to other groups or peoples are destroyed. Thus, in war, whether in primitive tribes or between modern nations, internal group solidarity becomes greater, intolerance of the outsider becomes more intense, hope of reasonable settlement of the points of difference diminish. The longer a struggle continues, the more likely it will be to destroy the possibility of peaceful coöperation between the contestants even after the hostilities have ceased.

In modern times, however, we have an increasing emphasis on economic resources as the basis of social life. Similar at its root to the ancient hunger for watering-places, hunting-grounds, pasture-lands, and arable soil, the competition for economic resources at the present time is much more varied in its objects by reason of the fact that we can make use of many resources that once were unusable, so that economic resources supply very many more human wants than they supplied to primitive man. There are scholars who insist that all wars have had their root in economic desires. That, however, is too narrow a view. Cultural wants have increased enormously with civilization; consequently the demand for natural resources that can minister to these wants has greatly expanded in modern times.

With nations taking the place of tribes, political ties and political ambitions have more scope. The emphasis upon group aims and rights is perhaps even more intense than with a primitive tribe. Political doctrines have been developed to justify political aims and purposes. Moreover, the political ideas have taken up and worked into a consistent system cultural and economic desires, binding all these interests together in a doctrine of political sovereignty, and providing for war a justifying ideology that was lacking among primitive people. The economic aims are still there in full force; the cultural aims have not disappeared, but all these are tied up into a consistent system by the political scheme ordered and glorified by political doctrine. This characteristic of modern states has given a new basis for war by shedding on it the glory of a complex of social aims and purposes.

Moreover, through civilization populations have multiplied, means of communication have increased, transportation has been developed, and inventions have given man control over his world such as has never been seen in the history of mankind. All of these things have multiplied conflicts by bringing into closer contact the various nations of mankind. With a distinct national consciousness and national pride, and with increased possibility of contact, conflicts were inevitable.

The *nation* still is our largest effective political agency; and we become sharply aware of its complete influence over most of the other phases of our lives when we travel from one country to another. It determines the laws under which we live and supplies us with our protection both at home and abroad; our movements are freest within the national boundaries; culture elements of language, custom, and historical tradition are largely defined by identity with the nation. Thus, it is to be expected that our loyalties are strongest to the nation to which we owe our allegiance; and *all* of us are compelled to be citizens of *some* nation.

On the other hand, no nation is self-sufficient. It must import many of the things it uses; it must depend on foreign markets to absorb its own surplus products; the giant industries often are fed by foreign materials, and in many cases are owned by business organizations which know no national allegiance. The result is obvious: it is no longer a matter of mere "contact" between national groups. Rather, our economic life has almost completely transcended political boundaries, even while our loyalties still are confined to national groups. Thus, we find ourselves confronted with many problems of a world community, while our largest social unit, the nation, still is only a segment of the whole society. We have, in effect, a network of global relationships beyond the power of even our largest nations to deal with conclusively. The likelihood of friction and conflict therefore reaches enormous proportions.[4]

Making a bad matter worse, also, is the fact that modern inventions have given a new destructiveness to war. Science has made its contribution by providing a knowledge of the processes of nature and applying our knowledge of these things to destruction, so that to-day war is a more serious matter than ever before in the history of the world. This development of science in the interest of warfare has reached a point such that the mind of mankind has been overwhelmed by the social disaster attendant upon war. Unquestionably the most urgent of all our social problems to-day is the problem of maintaining peace, and how to achieve collective security among all the peoples of the world.

THE CHARACTER OF MODERN WAR

The tremendous and catastrophic drama of the Second World War is completely without historic parallel. It therefore is extremely difficult for us, without the benefit of historical perspective, to analyze fully either its nature or its implications. However, it has given us a realiza-

4 Kimball Young, *An Introductory Sociology* (New York, 1937), pp. 85–87.

tion of the meaning of "total war" which even the First World War failed to instill; and we have every reason to believe that the post-war adjustments will be unique and far more difficult than those of any other war. From the character and reality of "total war" as it developed in the Second World War, we may detect some of the more important lines of social disaster which it portends.

1. *Mechanization*. The First World War was only partially a war of machines. There were many refinements of the traditional implements of war; but the instruments still were chiefly *weapons*, whose effectiveness depended very largely and directly upon the use made of them by the individual soldier himself. Consequently, the strategy and tactics of warfare still remained essentially as they had been for centuries. Yet, two new elements made their appearance in that war which were to have a profound effect upon the character of the Second World War: tanks and airplanes. The airplane remained largely a military novelty throughout that war; and while its effectiveness was considerable, very few even among military experts foresaw its importance in the years to follow. The tank was a vital factor in breaking the stalemate of the trench warfare; yet it was a far cry from the relatively crude three- or four-ton affair of that war to the monstrous cannon-mounted seventy-ton tank of the Second World War.

The great strides in airplane, tank, and transport design together conspired to make the Second World War conspicuously a war of movement. The swift hammer blows that felled the north countries and more especially the strong lowland countries to the south—Holland, Belgium, and France—campaigns lasting only a very few weeks, gave force to the concept of *blitzkrieg*, or "lightning war." It was said that in all these campaigns, German combat forces of less than 50,000 men were actively engaged at any one time. But this is hardly a full statement. The fact is that machines were substituted for troops to a very high degree. Airplanes and tanks, especially, are fearfully destructive even though operated by a mere handful of men. But they require servicing, just as any other machinery does; and tremendous ground and technical crews are necessary to supply and repair them under battle conditions. Thus, the British thousand-plane bombings over Germany were said to require the active coöperation of about a half million persons, even though probably not more than five or six thousand aviators actually flew in such raids.

The development of mechanized warfare also depends heavily upon the industrial system, from which it stems. As equipment has grown

larger and more complex, it demands the application of larger amounts
of labor power, and larger and more complex outlays of capital goods.
Thus, the soldier of our Revolutionary army was maintained by the
efforts of one or two civilians, while by the year of 1865, it probably
amounted to three or four; but in the Second World War, it was estimated that it required from fourteen to twenty workers to back each
member of the combat forces. Putting it another way, the cost of each
battle-death has risen from perhaps 75 cents in Caesar's Rome, to $3,000
in Napoleon's time; the cost was about $21,000 in the First World War,
and undoubtedly will exceed $50,000 in the Second World War.[5] This
is understandable when one realizes that the character and mass of military requirements is such that armies no longer can depend much on
forage to keep them going in the field.

2. *Regimentation.* Such an enormous undertaking as modern, mechanized war clearly cannot be organized in a short span of time, nor can it
be done without far-reaching sacrifices by whole populations. Vast as
has been the expansion of productive capacity of the world since the
development of the Industrial Revolution, there simply is not enough
resource for both war and "business as usual." Both the industrial equipment and the natural resources must be marshaled to keep the war machine going; and since the security of the nation is the most basic need
of all, provision for civilian needs necessarily is reduced to the barest
essentials of life.[6] It is clear, too, that such a condition is not peculiar only
to the period of actual combat. In the years just before the Second
World War, the total *annual* world expenditures for war purposes rose
from about $3,800,000,000 in 1932 to about $17,600,000,000 in 1938.
The approximate annual expenditures of the principal nations is detailed
in Table 9. With the advent of actual warfare, the portion of national
income used for war purposes has been estimated to rise as high as 70
per cent.[7]

To achieve such concentration of effort and production, the governments of the various nations assume increasingly broad control over
the lives of their citizens. Each specifies ever more closely the nature of
production, the conditions under which people may buy things for their
own use, digging deeper into the income of the private citizen by levy-
ing new taxes, directing the type of work a person shall do, and the terms

---

[5] J. H. S. Bossard, "War and the Family," *Sociological Review*, p. 339 (June,
1941).

[6] Horst Menderhausen, *The Economics of War* (New York, 1940), pp. 85-95.

[7] Stuart Chase, *The Road We Are Traveling, 1914-1942* (New York, 1942), p. 50.

TABLE 9

NATIONAL DEFENSE EXPENDITURES OF THE WORLD, 1932–1938 *
(In Millions of Dollars)

	1932	1933	1934	1935	1936	1937	1938
World total (60 countries)	3,783	3,962	5,031	8,776	12,976	15,468	17,581
United States	677	540	710	911	964	992	1,065
Britain	426	455	480	595	846	1,263	1,693
France	509	678	582	623	834	909	1,092
Germany	253	299	381	2,600	3,600	4,000	4,400
Italy	270	241	263	778	916	573	526
Russia	282	309	1,000	1,640	4,002	5,026	5,400
Japan a	199	253	271	296	305	1,129	1,755
China	93	108	112	93	95	95	95

* Adapted from *Information Service*, Vol. XVII, No. 33 (October 15, 1938).
a It later became apparent that Japan had been preparing for ten years prior to her surprise attack on Pearl Harbor, hence this report would hardly reveal her true war budget.

upon which he shall perform his duties.[8] Prices are fixed arbitrarily, credits are controlled sharply, and commodities are rationed in various ways—all with a view to reducing civilian consumption, creating large national stock-piles of goods or materials which cannot be produced or imported in time of war, and making the nation strong in military power. If ever war was a spontaneous expression of instinctive antipathies or pugnacity, it cannot be so regarded to-day. War has become a deadly and calculated enterprise of competing nations and touches directly the life of every individual in the world.

3. *Universality*. Enough already has been said to indicate the complete inclusiveness of the demands of the modern war machine. Yet one other aspect of modern warfare was clearly shown in the development of the Second World War. The areas of battle, and the objectives of military attack have been expanded to include whole countries. Even in the First World War, the actual roar and destruction of battle took place in comparatively small areas. Radio still was not available for civilian use; airplanes had a very small range of flight and small bomb capacities. Thus, areas not far removed from battle zones still were fairly safe from attack and destruction. To-day, whole peoples may be subjected to assault of propaganda and misinformation, a psychological "softening up" process which confuses and makes them easy prey to the swift annihilation of *blitzkrieg* tactics. Mass air assaults become so destructive

[8] This process was developed earliest and probably most ruthlessly in Germany. See Henri Ernst, *Hitler Over Europe* (New York, 1934), Ch. V.

that a new word, "Coventrize," springs into the language as a result of the wholesale desolation wrought upon that English city by aerial bombing.

Moreover, if wars are made by nations as a whole, the bitter sting of defeat now is felt by nations as a whole. Where armies formerly foraged on the countryside over which they traveled, to-day the whole national area is seized upon and exploited to the highest possible degree, so great is the need for material and equipment in modern war. Thus, the Second World War witnessed the wholesale plunder of nation after nation: Whole populations were moved away as forced labor to man the factories and fields of the conqueror; capital wealth was removed from shops and office-buildings; reserves of goods and raw materials were confiscated for the use of the invaders; even the commercial stocks of consumer goods were plundered by ingenious systems of monetary subterfuge.

Perhaps the most significant aspect of this new universality of war is the very fact that it *is* universal. No class of people nor geographical area is exempt from paying tribute to the Juggernaut. The profit of war to the "war-monger" fades to a wishful dream as factories collapse and ships go down *the world over*. The very frightfulness and completeness of the ravage of modern war may prove impelling enough to assure a determined effort in the years to come to establish a really effective system of international conciliation and control over world resources. Indeed, such a development *must* come about. The only alternative is anarchy and eventual mass suicide of the human race itself.

THE MENACE OF MODERN WAR

We have just seen that modern war alters greatly the political and economic life of the nations. Increasingly, war casts its shadow even over groups of people who have no part in it and who in some cases have not prepared for it at all. The full effect of war, however, is not to be measured in quantity alone—that is, in its widespread destruction of life and wealth. Nor is it to be measured wholly by the objective changes that war brings about in the patterns of economic and political relationships. War also sets in motion new forces and attitudes that affect the course of human development quite as really as the more obvious changes which we have just been considering. Indeed, their effect may be more crucial than that of the others, since they affect the very fiber of individual human beings.

1. *It impairs the biological quality of the race.* Few would deny that

warfare calls into military service and combat the best manhood that a country can muster. Military, naval, and air service requirements are well known to be high; the selectivity is from the best on down through the less capable, as the war continues. Thus, the sifting process tends to shield the poorer specimens from the caldron of war, while the better stocks are thinned by death and disability.

Apologists for war insist that it is a counterpart of the continual struggle that occurs in nature, and that like the natural struggle it results in the "survival of the fittest." It would appear that war tends to result rather in the survival of the *least* fit, insofar as it takes its heaviest toll among the "fittest" *of both sides*. Nor is the analogy between war and the struggle for survival in nature quite valid. It is true that the species compete with and prey upon one another, and it is also true that the weaker yield to the stronger. But nowhere in nature do we find anything approaching the mass struggle *within a given species* to parallel human warfare. It is questionable, to say the least, whether fitness among humans is rightly measured in terms of adeptness at self-destruction. It has been well remarked that man's worst enemy is—himself.

The unfavorable selectivity of war is not confined to men, but reaches out also to affect women in a similar fashion. The destructiveness of battle in terms of death and disability results in a distinct unbalance of numbers between the sexes. This unbalance, moreover, is heaviest within the age group upon which, normally, rests the major responsibility of propagation of the race. Many of the "fittest" women of child-bearing age must therefore face the alternative of remaining unmarried and childless, or marrying less desirable men than they would otherwise consider. Not only does such a situation have unfavorable biological implications, but also it creates new dangers of unhappiness and maladjustment within the marital relationship. As a result, both the biological heredity and the social training of the oncoming generation are likely to suffer.[9]

While these observations are true among all nations engaging in war, they vary in intensity in specific cases. Every war is different from every other war; and this applies to the biological aspects as well as the military and material phases. Long wars clearly will have a more devastating effect than short ones, and those entailing much hand-to-hand fighting will exact a greater toll than those which are characterized more by strategy and movement. Moreover, the effect may vary between the different nations competing in the same war. Obviously, the relative

[9] J. H. S. Bossard, *loc. cit.*, pp. 342–344.

power and equipage of the competing nations will be reflected in their respective losses; the nation upon whose soil the fighting takes place is likely to pay a higher toll in civilian lives; and offensive war is usually more costly in battle casualties than defensive.

In the Second World War, the people in conquered areas were subjected to wholesale removal from their homelands. Millions of families were broken by internment, forced labor, or extended retention of military prisoners of war, while still other groups (especially Poles and Jews) seemed singled out for virtual extermination. The loss of life in actual combat during the first year of the war was remarkably small; yet as the war continued, it became clear that it was to be a war of men as well as of machines. The total biological cost of the war, including the toll of shock and maiming consequent upon aerial warfare, will not be known for many years to come.

2. *It threatens the cultural heritage of the race.* Modern warfare is so completely devastating and utterly ruthless that it negates virtually all of the standards and ideals by which the human race has struggled to the levels of civilization that we now have at our disposal. The destruction of historical landmarks, churches, libraries, and public buildings, as epitomized by the so-called "Baedeker bombings" in England, necessarily shocks the fundamental sense of continuity and security of the people who experienced such catastrophe. On the other hand, the "scorched earth" policy, by which retreating countrymen destroy anything that might be of possible value to the enemy—factories, warehouses, dams, bridges, crops, and even in some cases the fertility of the soil itself—may well have even more cataclysmic effect upon those who execute such destruction. In such cases they are called upon to put the torch to their own homes and properties. How, under circumstances such as these, can people retain their everyday ideals of industry, thrift, and charity which they have lived by and taught to their children? Indeed, the family itself—the primary object of all social and economic activity—is torn asunder; and principles and aspirations give way to the primitive device of traveling with the pack and exploiting the opportunity of the moment as a sheer matter of survival.

On the positive side, mankind fares no better when confronted with the reality of warfare. We have already spoken earlier in this chapter of the all-inclusive nature of modern war. This regimentation permeates governmental activity both in peace-time preparation for war, and in war; and the process is likely to become increasingly oppressive so long as war remains an active threat. The policy of "guns for butter" which Hitler proclaimed prior to the Second World War, a policy of bending every thought and effort toward preparation for war in time of peace, necessarily must be matched by other nations—however "peace-loving" they may be—if they are to preserve their independence and security.

The cultural sacrifice which such a policy entails is enormous. The individual becomes simply a pawn of the State, with his life's activities prescribed and his training pointed wholly toward making him an efficient agent in the work to which he is assigned. Science is advanced primarily in the lines in which it can be of service to the State, while the subject matter of letters and the arts suffers even greater degradation. Scientific laws cannot be altered; but historical fact, the emotional possibilities of letters and the arts, and the principles of the social sciences can be twisted, falsified, and regimented beyond truthful recognition. Lacking free access to impartial sources and intercourse with the world outside the nation, whole populations thus are indoctrinated with the bigotry of national aggrandizement; and they are easily whipped into misguided and fanatical service to the State and the purposes of its leaders.

Such a setting provides fertile soil for the growth of *militarism*, which is the domination of all other classes in society by the professional war-maker, or the soldier class motivated by the logic of *rule by force*. Unquestioning and unwavering obedience to those in authority is the first law of military efficiency. Undoubtedly, such discipline is necessary so long as a nation must defend itself by force of arms. Nevertheless, the whole-hearted support of large numbers of men in military service results in a tremendous concentration of physical power in the hands of the military hierarchy; and the resources of the nation tend to be channeled more and more to meet the desires of those leaders. The armed forces become the favored class; and the ideals and objectives of the nation as a whole become more and more those insisted upon by the military leaders. The show of force naturally is alarming to neighboring countries, who thus are constrained to follow suit. Tension between nations inevitably increases, and competitive armament takes place; and one of them eventually must spring at the other, to justify the steadily mounting burden of preparedness. Thus militarism, whether it be predatory or not, is a particularly dangerous development in society. At best, it breeds only suspicion, while it drains the best resources of a country. At worst, it provides the means of exploitation by one class of all others, and sets loose progressively more severe destructiveness and carnage.

3. *It increases the friction between the classes.* The integration of the economic life incident to the prosecution of war is not without its beneficial results. One of the few clear-cut gains of war-time industrial activity is the great increase of productive efficiency. The scarcity of labor which arises from the induction of large numbers of workers into the armed forces, and the need for vast amounts of equipment, impel a greater economy in the use of labor power and a greater reliance upon machine power. New technological processes, new materials, and new types of products are developed with intense rapidity under the necessity of war needs. Thus, out of the First World War developed notably the widespread use of assembly-line production, greatly improved engine design, and the phenomenal growth of the airplane and radio industries. Similarly, it became evident even while the Second World War was still in progress that many new plastic materials, new fuels, new synthetic substitutes, and radically new automotive design would be available for civilian consumption following the war.

Such developments unquestionably have a wholesome effect insofar as they tend to break down the lines of class distinction within society. When vast quantities of goods of uniform design are made available at comparatively low cost, then the consumption habits of the classes become more nearly alike. It becomes easier for the shop hand to emulate the office worker and for the stenographer to assume much of the manner and appearance of the society girl. Competition tends, to some extent, to be based more on native abilities and less on superficial distinction and advantage.

Such gains, however, are dearly bought; and one may well question whether the quickening of the rate of social change brought about by war is worth the cost. With greater productivity resulting from mechanization stimulated by war, comes also a reduction in the demand for labor. Yet as the armies are disbanded, the supply of workers is greatly increased. Employment and wages therefore tend to decline sharply soon after the war emergency is past. Depression is the inevitable effect, sooner or later; so that the great mass of people in the end are no better off than before, despite the low cost and wide variety of new goods which are the products of the war-time developments. The employers, on their part, are forced to reduce their overhead; and business organization becomes more centralized—and more powerful. As a result, we have class lines being drawn more and more sharply: the unemployed becoming increasingly resentful of the apparent advantage of the propertied groups, the latter in their turn becoming more fearful of the growing unrest and radical spirit of the underprivileged. Within the industrialized nations in the period between the First and Second World Wars there was a steadily mounting bitterness of class toward class. The rise of the dictatorial States, both communist and fascist, showed clearly the ruthlessness with which either side will attempt to gain superiority over the other.

THE CONTROL OF WAR

The world-wide scope and utter destructiveness of modern war has led in our generation to a steadily mounting conviction that the process of settling disputes by resort to war must be checked. Indeed, it may well be that the victor in the Second World War will so completely dominate the vanquished that war may become impossible. Renewed opposition would require long and intensive coöperation of large numbers of people; and such preparation could be easily detected, and as easily suppressed by a determined hegemony.[10]

1. *Early Attempts to Secure the Peace.* Treaties and compromises have characterized group relationships from a very early period of history. Early civilized societies like the Greek city-states found it important to provide methods for settling their differences and for combination in the face of a common enemy. There resulted the Amphictyonic Council. With the rise of the Roman Republic and the Roman Empire these movements for peace were made unnecessary because of the so-called *pax Romana.* In the Middle Ages, however, again occurred attempts at international arbitration. Frequently also among the feudal overlords disputes were arbitrated by bishops or archbishops, by the Emperor of the Holy Roman Empire, by the King of France, and by the Pope. In fact, the church took the lead in the development of this international arbitration. The incessant warfare of the sixteenth, seventeenth, and eighteenth centuries led to the decline of such efforts. However, in 1729, by the Treaty of Seville, England and Spain established a mixed commission for the settlement of claims growing out of searches and seizures on the high seas. This, however, was not strictly arbitration, since the commission was composed of an equal number of citizens of each country. These early attempts seem to have had very little influence upon modern peace measures.

The Hague Conference. The most important modern development before the First World War was the Hague Conferences. The first one

[10] See Nicholas Doman, "The World We Approach," *Annals of the American Academy of Political and Social Science,* 222: 97-98 (July, 1942).

met at The Hague in 1899 on the motion of Nicholas II of Russia. It
failed to achieve any limitation of armaments, but did result in three
conventions and three declarations, each of which was to be a matter
for separate ratification. The first convention provided for the pacific
settlement of international disputes and instituted a Commission of Inquiry and a Permanent Court of Arbitration accessible at all times to
contracting powers. The second convention was a formulation of the
laws and customs of war on land, with the intent of defining them more
precisely and of laying down certain limits for the purpose of modifying their severity as far as possible. The third convention adapted
to maritime warfare the principles of the Geneva convention of 1864.
The declarations attempted to prohibit the discharge of projectiles and
explosives from balloons and by other similar new methods, to prohibit
the use of projectiles containing asphyxiating or deleterious gases, and
to prohibit the use of bullets which expand or flatten easily in the human
body.

The second Hague Conference convened in 1907 through the initiative of President Theodore Roosevelt, although the honor of summon-
ing it went to the Czar, who called the first conference. Certain improvements of the Permanent Court, which proved to be the most fruitful work of the first conference, were made, the most important of
which was the restriction upon employment of members of the Permanent Court as counsel in cases before it. Some agreement was reached as
to the matter of opening hostilities, the laying of automatic submarine
contact-mines, the status of enemy merchant ships at the commencement
of hostilities, certain restrictions on naval capture, others dealing with
the rights and duties of neutrals in war on land as well as at sea, and the
creation of the International Prize Court. The conference recommended
that a third peace conference be called within a period corresponding
to that which had elapsed since the preceding conference; but that conference was never called by reason of the outbreak of the First World
War.

2. *The World War Interlude*. The most effective effort to preserve
the peace in the period between the First and Second World Wars was
the League of Nations. The League was generally linked with President
Wilson's name, largely because he was its chief proponent; yet the idea
of the League and its characteristics were derived from many sources.
It was to be essentially a voluntary association of free and independent
States, to deal with the important phases of international relationships.
There was to be active coöperation in matters pertaining to their com-

mon welfare, such as in labor policies, "the traffic in women and children, and the traffic in opium and other dangerous drugs," freedom of trade, the control of epidemic disease, the "just treatment of the native inhabitants" of colonies and mandated areas, and "the general supervision of the trade in arms and ammunition with the countries in which control of this traffic is necessary in the common interests." [11] As a further means of maintaining international peace and security, a Permanent Court of International Justice was instituted, which was to arbitrate disputes brought before it by member nations. The League was to function through an Assembly, a Council, and a permanent Secretariat; the Assembly being largely an open forum, the Council dominantly the policy-making body, the Secretariat serving chiefly as a continuously functioning administrative agency. The League was in no sense a governing body, since the member States retained their independent autonomy; and membership was wholly voluntary and could be terminated after due notice had been given. Its decisions required unanimous vote; and any State dissatisfied with the decisions of the League or the Court could renounce the decision by withdrawing from the organization.[12]

Dominant political opinion in America was opposed to the League and the motives behind it. Criticism centered especially on Article 10, which stated:

The Members of the League undertake to respect and preserve as against external aggression the territorial integrity and existing political independence of all Members of the League. In case of any such aggression or in case of any threat or danger of such aggression, the Council shall advise upon the means by which this obligation shall be fulfilled.

Moreover, Article 16 stated, in part, that when such aggressive action had been committed, certain economic sanctions or boycotts should be imposed on the offending State; and further, that "it shall be the duty of the Council in such case to recommend to the several Governments concerning what effective military, naval, or air force the Members of the League shall severally contribute to the armed forces to be used to protect the covenants of the League." The United States people were not pleased with the results of the Versailles Treaty, to which the League became attached and for which it seemed a guarantee. The United States, of course, did not enter the League; and while there were many other reasons for the failure of the League, the aloofness of the United

[11] Article 23 of the Covenant of the League of Nations.
[12] W. R. Sharp and G. Kirk, *Contemporary International Politics* (New York, 1940), Ch. XXII.

States doubtless was an important contributing factor. The League accomplished a great deal in promoting international coöperation; yet as a means of preserving the peace, it never took a militant stand; and by 1939 its power had been quite thoroughly discredited.

Many other proposals were made, and activities were carried on in behalf of peace in this period, but the movement toward war was as inexorable as it was unsuspected by most people. During the first decade following the First World War, many conferences were called to "disarm" by mutual agreement, to scrap obsolete materials and forego new construction; yet they failed, basically, because the nations refused to consider any other basis for such a reduction than the maintenance of "parity" of power. Revelation of the intrigue among the Allied powers regarding the "spoils" to be divided following the war, and the influence of international investment and government finance as a cause of war,[13] led to demands for "neutrality" laws, "conscription of capital," and "nationalization of war industries." How inadequate such measures were in dealing with the basic causes of war, of course, has been borne out by subsequent developments.

Nevertheless, one of the most powerful influences substantiating such a position developed with the exposure, about ten years following the First World War, of the nefarious activities of the "armament ring." To be sure, trading with the enemy was nothing new; but never before had it reached such proportions and apparent brazenness. Thus, for example, it was recorded that:

Germany throughout the War had urgent need of nickel, aluminum, and chemicals like glycerin for explosives. France, because the rich Briey basin and other sources were out of her control, had to scratch hard for iron and steel. Continuously, therefore, what one nation lacked, the armament manufacturers of an enemy nation did their urgent best to provide. Month after month, during the War, German heavy industries exported an average of 150,000 tons of scrap iron, steel, or barbed wire to Switzerland where, having been smelted to a more convenient form, it was then transshipped to France. France, in her turn, shipped chemicals to the Lonza Co. (a Swiss industrial concern, German controlled, but with directors who were French, Italian, and Austrian as well) from which they reached munitions works in Germany. It was all very profitable—and the splendid War went on and on.[14]

Similarly, it was shown that patents and designs pertaining to armament were exchanged by the armorers of the competing nations; that in-

[13] See, for example, Walter Millis, *Road to War* (Boston, 1935).
[14] Copyright, *Time* Inc., 1934 (*Fortune*, March, 1934).

ternational distrust and consequent demand for increased armament were deliberately instigated by manufacturers of arms; that the companies were controlled by large financiers whose holdings transcended national boundaries, and whose profits were derived in the last analysis from the purchases of friend and foe alike.[15]

The result of these revelations was that American public opinion was swung still further toward isolationism. Nevertheless after the first flush of idealism in the First World War and the subsequent disillusionment of the peace settlement, there had been a movement toward practical revision of the terms of the Versailles Treaty. During the decade following that war, there had been many conferences and treaties regarding economic and political readjustments. Faltering efforts had been made to reduce armaments, while the Pact of Paris of 1928 purporting to "outlaw" war by mutual renunciation of it as a national policy seemed a possible basis for bolstering the weaknesses of the League. But the disclosure of the sordid war-time dealings of the arms makers was a severe blow to any inclination of the United States people to continue the search for collective security among the nations. They felt that their efforts had gone for naught, and that they had been cruelly duped in being drawn into world affairs at all. In addition, there already had been rumblings of new wars to come in the Japanese penetration into Manchuria in 1931, while Mussolini had begun to bluster about the Mediterranean Sea being the *mare nostrum* of Italy, and Hitler had openly denounced the Versailles Treaty and shown some promise of making good on his dream of pan-German expansion. The United States

[15] For fuller detail, see H. C. Engelbrecht, and F. C. Hanighen, *Merchants of Death* (New York, 1934); or George Seldes, *Iron, Blood, and Profits* (New York, 1934). How much of this illicit traffic in war supplies survived into the Second World War era cannot, of course, be ascertained. There is considerable evidence to support the belief that the policy of "appeasement" may have been in part, at least, impelled by a concern for the preservation of business interests. For example, the connivance of England in aiding the Spanish insurgents in 1936, and the United States trade with Japan during the first four years of Japanese penetration into China are hard to explain in terms of international justice. It was commonly remarked that some of the British political leaders had large security holdings in German chemical works in 1939, which was offered by some observers as a factor in the prolonged military inactivity through the fall and winter of 1939. There were reports that Dutch-English oil deliveries were continued to Germany in the early months of the war, while Germany and France exchanged iron ore and coke by way of Belgium during the same winter, and mutually avoided damaging attacks on one another's mines and munitions factories within the battle zone. Again, it was reported at that time that Japanese agencies delivered American goods to "Free China" forces over the Burma Road, while high German officials traveled on then-neutral Italian vessels under French passports.

Congress, reflecting public sentiment, began enacting laws that should assure our neutrality in the foreign struggles that seemed ever surer to come. From 1935 even into 1940, our attitude was distinctly one of withdrawal from world affairs, and a determination to keep clear of what was regarded as other people's profit-making wars.

3. *Charting a Peace Settlement.* Whatever may have been the circumstances surrounding the international relations prior to the Second World War, and however one is to interpret the hesitancy in military operations in the months following the fall of Poland in 1939, the character of the war changed rapidly in the spring of 1940. It may well be, as one author suggests, that the fall of France marked a decisive shift in the psychological issues of the war as well as the military. He says:

> Where the war has been the government's war, the cabinet's war, the prime minister's war, or the king's war, the forces of the Axis have been able to do exactly as they liked; but once in any country it has become a people's war, then the Axis Powers have been halted. It was the government's war in the countries that were overthrown. It was the government's war in England until Dunkerque. At Dunkerque it suddenly became the people's war. The Government was out, the people were in—and Hitler was stopped. That is the record of this war all through.[16]

Certain it is that with the complete subjugation of whole countries by the conquering armies, and the wholesale confiscation or destruction of capital wealth as well as of consumption goods, there could hardly be much question that the struggle was to be one for actual survival itself. And as the war continued, the ruthless expropriation of the peoples of the conquered countries, the mass executions and reprisals, and the transplanting of millions of common people from one country to another, showed ever more plainly that the conquerors meant to impose their will completely *and permanently* upon the lives and properties of *all* the vanquished.

Even before the battle-line was completely drawn by the Japanese attack on Pearl Harbor and the resulting declarations of war between the United States and the Axis Powers, President Roosevelt and Prime Minister Churchill made a joint declaration regarding the aims of the anti-Axis Powers. The text of this "Atlantic Charter," signed August 14, 1941, is as follows:

> The President of the United States of America and the Prime Minister, Mr. Churchill, representing His Majesty's Government in the United King-

[16] Frank Kingdon, "Being an American in Wartime," *Annals of the Academy of Political and Social Science*, 222: 1 (July, 1942).

dom, being met together, deem it right to make known certain common principles in the national policies of their respective countries on which they base their hopes for a better future for the world.

FIRST, Their countries seek no aggrandizement, territorial or other;

SECOND, They desire to see no territorial changes that do not accord with the freely expressed wishes of the peoples concerned;

THIRD, They respect the right of all peoples to choose the form of government under which they will live; and they wish to see sovereign rights and self-government restored to those who have been forcibly deprived of them;

FOURTH, They will endeavor, with due respect for their existing obligations, to further the enjoyment by all States, great or small, victor or vanquished, of access, on equal terms, to the trade and to the raw materials of the world which are needed for their economic prosperity;

FIFTH, They desire to bring about the fullest collaboration between all nations in the economic field with the object of securing, for all, improved labor standards, economic adjustment and social security;

SIXTH, After the final destruction of the Nazi tyranny, they hope to see established a peace which will afford to all nations the means of dwelling in safety within their own boundaries, and which will afford assurance that all the men in all the lands may live out their lives in freedom from fear and want;

SEVENTH, Such a peace should enable all men to traverse the high seas and oceans without hindrance;

EIGHTH, They believe that all of the nations of the world, for realistic as well as spiritual reasons, must come to the abandonment of the use of force. Since no future peace can be maintained if land, sea, or air armaments continue to be employed by nations which threaten, or may threaten, aggression outside of their frontiers, they believe, pending the establishment of a wider and permanent system of general security, that the disarmament of such nations is essential. They will likewise aid and encourage all other practicable measures which will lighten for peace-loving peoples the crushing burden of armaments.

This is indeed a remarkably broad and penetrating review of the fundamental tenets of lasting peace; and it is to be hoped that the principles included in it may be given full expression in fact. There are tremendous problems to be met, both in resettlement and in rehabilitation of the victims of the war. New and ancient hatreds need to be allayed. But the greatest task of all doubtless will be the formulation of new patterns of economic, political, and social behavior. Those patterns will not concern only the formal agencies of social organization but the whole fabric of the lives and thinking of individual people. It is a task that staggers the imagination; and the realization that our generation in a very literal sense "has a date with destiny" makes the job no easier. The passion and self-interest that have characterized former peace settlements must be set

aside completely. We must approach the task with calmness, delibera-
tion, earnestness, and a proper sense of humility. Any other course means
disaster both for ourselves and for untold generations to come.

4. *The Basis of a Durable Peace.* The Second World War is unprecedented in its character, in its background, and in the problems it presents
with regard to the peace and the long period of reconstruction which
must follow it. More than with any other war, the peace cannot be made
quickly, both because the problems are so great and because the security
of the world for generations to come may well be at stake. It would be
presumptuous, indeed, for us to say here what should or should not be
done in settlement of that war in the years to come. Nevertheless, our
brief survey of the problem of war seems to suggest that certain factors
will be of considerable importance in the establishment of a durable
peace.

First, it should be evident that some sort of international government
must be established, to control the affairs of all the independent nations
insofar as those activities affect the relations of the nations with each
other. Moreover, this body necessarily must have the power of compulsion to make its decisions binding upon the nations. Whatever the shortcomings of the League of Nations may have been, the Second World
War has made clear that the nations must relinquish their rights to independent action in matters involving the security of one another.

Second, we must not quickly abandon the rigid and effective controls
over price levels, raw materials, and the flow of goods which were built
up during the Second World War. These must be maintained to assist
in the feeding and rehabilitation of the millions of destitute people in the
war-shattered nations. The creation of an international authority may be
necessary to administer the supplies during the long and trying period of
reconstruction. How extensively we shall return to "business as usual"
policies is a matter that only the future can determine.

Third, there must be a realistic approach to the problem of force. We
cannot depend alone upon the good will or the finer impulses of the
people of any nation; nor can any of the "United Nations" retire to a
policy of isolation as was done following the First World War. We
have seen too clearly how disastrous the sudden seizure of power by an
unscrupulous group can be to the rest of the population—both domestic
and international—to permit the possibility of such a *coup* to remain.
Undoubtedly such a program will involve the complete disarmament of
those nations which have shown aggressive designs in the interval between the First and Second World Wars. It likewise will require the

policing and internal administration of those nations by foreign powers for some years to come, to prevent the repetition of secret organization for a new bid for world power.

Force also must be controlled indirectly, in terms of international accounting of industrial production and foreign trade. The years prior to the Second World War showed great changes in the character and amounts of the foreign trade of the various nations—changes which pointed plainly to policies of war preparation; yet no authority existed that was powerful enough to check those activities. *The use of force is both necessary and inevitable in any type of social organization.* But the instruments of force have reached such power and character that their use must be rigidly controlled, as is the use of any other dangerous instrument or agent.[17] *Force must be used judiciously and kept in the custody of responsible authorities;* and this can be assured only by close and implicit coöperation of all the nations of the world.

Fourth, the soundness of the measures thus far proposed can be assured only insofar as democratic principles are extended over *all* the fields of human relationships.[18] The basic inspiration of democracy, of course, is the equality of every individual with every other, an equality of privileges, duties, and voice in the determination of the rules by which the group shall live. It provides for the free and continual adjustments of differences between classes of the gross inequalities that are bound to spring up between classes when one or another of them seizes the reins of control for its own advantage. Whether it be in matters of politics or of economics, of religious or racial differences, the democratic recognition of the underlying equality of the members of the group and the determination to preserve the unity of the larger group by compromise, provide the only certain way to maintain peaceful relations. As soon as these democratic principles are violated and various groups become oppressed, then the relationship is maintained only by exerting force, and, sooner or later, resentment is bound to reach explosive, revolutionary proportions. The process is the same, regardless of whether we are considering local organizations or the world community of nations.

Fifth, we must see to it that we develop competent and responsible leadership to direct the course of affairs in the future. The combination of competence and responsibility is imperative to assure that the con-

[17] Nicholas Doman, "The World We Approach," *Annals of the American Academy of Political and Social Science,* 222: 96 ff. (July, 1942).
[18] See Harold Laski, "Democracy," *Encyclopaedia of the Social Sciences,* V, pp. 76–84.

centration of power that has become characteristic of modern life shall not be perverted to antisocial uses or to the aggrandizement of a particular group or class. The special training of personnel for government service has long been practiced in various countries and has in recent years had some attention in our own country. This is a distinct advance as a means of assuring capable administration. But no economic or political system of life, not even the democratic, is in itself capable of guaranteeing equitable relationships. *It is rather the spirit of the people and of its leaders that give life and character to the social structure.* It occasionally happens, of course, that the spirit of the people and the leadership it has are at loggerheads. Leaders, to put it another way, may gain their position of leadership by deception, or by taking advantage of the confusion or indecision of the people in times of distress. In that event, as we have become so tragically aware, the consequence can be disastrous to both the home people and even the world at large.

The concentration of power in the hands of but few leaders now is an accomplished fact. It no longer can be otherwise, even if we would have it so. It therefore is imperative that those who are entrusted with the direction of that power shall really reflect the will of the people they lead. The best assurance of a wise selection is an alert and well-informed world citizenry, since we may safely assume that the overwhelming majority of people desire not war, but peace. In the light of world history, it is only natural that we should feel no little apprehension as a result of the pyramiding of national and world policy-making into the hands of fewer and fewer leaders. But let us remember that there is no necessary connection between mass, and the individual's, freedom. The citizen of the United States of to-day has lost none of the essential freedom that was enjoyed by his great grandfather in 1789.[19] As a citizen of the world, he will gain still more freedom to the extent that the democratic processes are given more universal application in the free expression of the people's will and choice of their leaders.

REFERENCES

Annals of the American Academy of Political and Social Science, "Public Policy in a World at War" (November, 1941); "Winning Both the War and the Peace" (July, 1942).

BOSSARD, J. H. S., "War and the Family," *American Sociological Review,* pp. 330-344 (June, 1942).

CHASE, Stuart, *The Road We Are Traveling* (New York, 1942).

DOMAN, Nicholas, *The Coming Age of World Control* (New York, 1942).

[19] Doman, *loc. cit.,* p. 101.

Encyclopaedia of the Social Sciences, "Revolution and Counter-revolution,"
    XIII: 367–375; "War," XV: 331–341.
ENGLEBRECHT, H. C., and HANIGHEN, F. C., *Merchants of Death* (New York,
    1934).
HENRI, Ernst, *Hitler Over Europe* (New York, 1934).
MENDERHAUSEN, Horst, *The Economics of War* (New York, 1940).
MILLIS, Walter, *Road to War* (Boston, 1935).
PARMELEE, Maurice, *Bolshevism, Fascism, and the Liberal Democratic State*
    (New York, 1934).
SELDES, George, *Iron, Blood, and Profits* (New York, 1934).
SHARP, W. R., and KIRK, G., *Contemporary International Politics* (New York,
    1940).
STRACHEY, John, *The Coming Struggle for Power* (New York, 1933).
YOUNG, Kimball, *An Introductory Sociology* (New York, 1937), Ch. 4.

QUESTIONS AND EXERCISES

1. What is meant by the statement in the text that peace and war are problems of socialization? Is the mobilization of the national unit toward the war psychology also a problem of socialization? Explain.
2. What would you say to the statement that modern science has made war more likely?
3. How does the business of equipping and supplying modern military and naval units affect the character of war? How does it affect the problems of world peace?
4. What happens to the "four freedoms"—free speech, free press, free religion, free assembly—when a nation prepares for, or engages in war? How is the educational system affected?
5. What are the effects of modern war upon the biological quality of the population?
6. Why could not the Hague Conference and its Permanent Court of Arbitration prevent the First World War?
7. What were the chief objections of the opponents in the United States to the League of Nations Covenant?
8. The opposition of the United States to the League of Nations, *et al.*, has been likened to the similar contest between States' rights and a strong federal union during the Constitutional Assemblies and the subsequent struggle for Constitutional ratification. Do you consider this a valid analogy? Why, or why not?
9. In what sense might the Second World War be referred to as the "People's War"?
10. Why has the maintenance of peace become more imperative than ever before?
11. What appear to be the fundamental requirements for establishing a lasting peace?

Chapter 7

THE NATURE OF THE POPULATION PROBLEM

MAN, one of the most slowly multiplying of all earth's creatures, has, nevertheless, increased with such astounding persistence that he alone has peopled the whole earth. Other forms of life can live only in such areas as naturally provide them with the requisite means of subsistence. They may increase only up to the limit of the naturally available food supply plus certain geographical limits set by range of temperature, humidity, and altitude. Beyond this, a ruthless struggle for existence in competition with their fellows and with representatives of other forms of life for the same food and space kills them off. They have no course other than that of effecting biological variation through evolution: the formation of a new and differing variety capable of existing outside the mother area and under a new set of conditions. But "man is Nature's rebel." He alone has been able to defy her and to fit her for his purposes rather than to change himself to meet her whims. He has learned to consider himself the Lord of Creation because of this superiority and because of the ceaseless multiplication that has placed him in control of the whole earth and of all its forms of life. Even though races are represented by biological differences some of which have demonstrable survival values for certain climatic conditions, such as the pigmentation of the skin in the tropics, any race can adjust itself to life anywhere on the planet. Man can protect himself from the tropic sun or clothe and house himself to withstand the northern cold. If the proper sort of food be lacking, he will import and store it. Against enemies and pests he has provided protection. If a Panama Canal cannot be dug because of the ravages of yellow fever, he conquers the mosquito that bears the germ. Man storms Nature's barriers and presses ever forward.

INCREASE AND THE STRUGGLE FOR EXISTENCE

Natural selection and the struggle for existence make up a far more terrible fact than we of the twentieth century are able to realize. In order that life should survive at all, it was necessary for nature to provide each species with powers of multiplication concomitant with its death-rate. Carr-Saunders presents some interesting data in this field:

The number of eggs found attached to the edible crab in the breeding season varies between half a million and three million. . . . A single pair of flies can produce 20,000 larvae. . . . The least prolific of the British fish is the herring, in which the number of ovarian eggs varied from 21,000 to 47,000 in four specimens examined. . . . If all the progeny of one oyster survived and multiplied, its great-great-grandchildren would number thirty-six with thirty-three noughts after it, and the heap of shells would be eight times the size of the world. . . . Huxley calculated that if all of the descendants of a single green-fly survived and multiplied they would, at the end of the summer, weigh down the population of China.

Not Waste but Insurance. Why is it that nature has made it possible for every species to increase at such a rate "that, if not destroyed, the earth would soon be covered by the progeny of a single pair"? We speak of nature's prodigality and wastefulness. But this is not mere waste, it is insurance. Conditions of life for the lower animals are such that the maturing and survival of the young depend upon a favorable combination of environmental accidents. Given a favorable medium in which to hatch, favorable humidity and temperature, and protection from enemies, the egg may hatch. Once it is hatched, more accidental combinations determine its continued survival, maturation, and further reproduction. Nature can only guarantee continuity through a most prodigious reproductiveness. The higher the form of life and the greater the amount of protection that can be guaranteed by the parents, the lower the birth-rate can safely be, and the lower it actually is. Each species, then, has a birth-rate that, if unhindered, would swamp the earth, but which actually no more than insures the perpetuation of the species without any very marked increase except as the balance in a territory is disturbed. This balance is, however, maintained only by an utterly ruthless natural selection and struggle for existence.

The Persistency of Human Increase. What about the human animal? Few forms of life breed more slowly, and yet none has spread more persistently. In none has the survival-rate been so large. The offspring of a single pair, unhindered, might also cover the face of the earth in a comparatively short time. Granted that there was need of this potential fecundity in the case of our primitive ancestors, is there still need of it in this day of highly assured survival? *The answer is that man's potential fecundity, which once was our survival guarantee, is now the root of a most pressing social problem.* Man has succeeded in domesticating many plants and animals. He feeds them the proper foods and surrounds them with such measures of protection as will guarantee the maximum amount of multiplication and survival. Nature does not produce such crops as are found in our grain-fields. The animal packs of the forest have no such survival-rate as the herds of our barns and pastures. But man is not interested in their survival for further reproduction, but for immediate consumption. Of the wheat grown, but a very small fraction is saved for seed. Of the sheep and cows and swine raised on our farms,

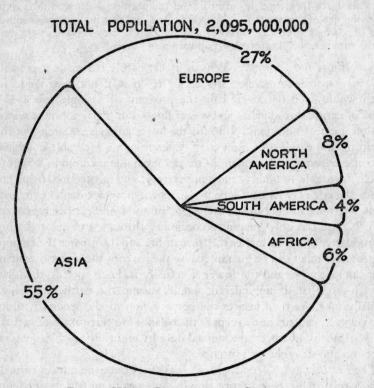

TOTAL POPULATION, 2,095,000,000

FIG. 3.—WORLD POPULATION, BY CONTINENTS
Data adapted from *Foreign Commerce Year Book* (Bureau of Foreign and Domestic Commerce, 1937), pp. 367–368.

the major portion find their way to our stock-yards. Were this not so, but a few generations of domestication would produce a most serious plant and animal overpopulation. Man is in a similar position. He is a *self-domesticated* being. He has arranged for himself far more and much better protection than he has afforded the animals he has domesticated. But to what end? Merely that of survival! *He is an end in and of himself!* He is not weeded out as are food-plants and animals. Every child born is surrounded with every possible life assurance for the sole purpose of being brought to physical maturity and in turn becoming a breeder himself.

A PROBLEM OF SUPPLY AND DEMAND

The population problem is in the main but another aspect of the universal problem of supply and demand. Physical existence of course depends on the supply of standing-room on the earth and on the available supplies of natural resources thereon and therein contained. Naturally a direct relationship exists between the number of people (consumers) and the amount of space and natural resources. While man cannot increase the amount of the material resources of the earth except in the line of directive and selective use and breeding, he can increase their availability. There was just as much iron in the world in the days of Pithecanthropus as there is to-day, but he knew neither how to get it nor how to use it if he had it. For him, since it was not available, it practically did not exist. Till an improved and inexpensive process of extracting aluminium from clay was invented in the laboratory by a student at Oberlin College in Ohio, the supply of aluminium was strictly limited, though it was in existence in unlimited quantities in the earth. Human life, in fact all life, depends upon the supplies of the bases of life. These are: sufficient and suitable standing-room for the operations of life; sufficient and suitable natural resource materials for food, clothing, shelter, and protection; and further resources for the production of the tools whereby these and the refinements of life can be produced.

MAN'S INSATIABLE WANTING CAPACITY

The demand for these possessions of Mother Earth seems to be insatiable. Man's wants are not limited to mere subsistence, as is rather uniformly the case in the plant and the animal world. Man is not satisfied with a full stomach, a comfortable lair, and a mate. There is no limit to the standard of life to which he may aspire. He does not demand the impossible of the scientist in bringing into existence new goods and larger supplies, but he does demand a share of newly created wealth as it becomes available. He may talk of "the simple life" and of "the good old days," but he does not want to live them. He speaks of "oversupply" and of "glutting the market," but there is no supply over and above what he could and would use. It is not that too much has been made available for the use of man, but that too much has been produced to make available for general use by means of our existing system of distribution.

It is doubtful if we could produce more than we could consume. Over a period of time, whenever a larger supply is in sight, either an encouraged birth-rate provides increasing numbers to consume it, or an increased share for each raises the standard of living.

Man wants not only subsistence but also a guarantee of the same for the future. He wants the prestige and power conferred by greater stores, and hence more power and security, than his fellows. As soon as he has subsistence, he wants better subsistence, and with it leisure. It is this "plus" element that distinguishes human from animal life. We can understand this standard-of-living concept better if we think of it first in terms of actual, available size and content of the individual or family share of this world's goods, and second, in terms of the size and content of the share one would like and is willing to fight for. The great product of modern civilization is opportunity; opportunity to observe, learn, enjoy, and do. Here also the demand is always treading on the heels of the supply and the quarrel between classes is not so much for more social opportunity as for a fairer distribution.

Because of man's insatiable wanting and his potential fecundity, both unusual and abnormal, undersupplies of both goods and opportunity are a distinct possibility for the future. Hence, in the study of the problems of human population we are vitally interested in the matters of actual and potential supplies of natural and social resources.

THE SUPPLY OF AND DEMAND FOR HUMAN BEINGS

Man's insatiable demand for consumption goods is further complicated by his potential fecundity and the tendency for populations to increase in number rather than to remain stationary. We thus are compelled to strike a balance between two variables—a changing supply of consumption goods and a usually increasing number of consumers. The former, the increase of goods or the increased availability of goods, is usually accomplished only with difficulty and increased exertion. In the case of the latter, the increase in the number of consumers, no problem at all exists, for at the present time in practically every advanced civilization we face on the one hand the problem of increasing the production of goods and on the other, that of checking the natural increase of human beings.

The movement of the first factor, the supply or availability of consumption goods, is not constant. It depends on the stage of social and technical development at which the group has arrived.

Before the coming of the whites to the North American continent it was already showing signs of population pressure. This was evidenced by the chronic warfare waged between native tribes and by other checks to population increase. We are told that for the Indian's manner of life twenty-five square miles of territory was required to supply the needs of the individual. To-day, in the period of advanced production that has replaced the Indian's hunting-and-finding economy, this same country is capable of supporting not one individual to twenty-five square miles, but more than twenty-five individuals to one square mile. The geographical area is unchanged, but man has progressed; he has learned to make available materials and forces that were denied to the original inhabitants of the area. Furthermore, this much larger population is able to live in far greater security and comfort, and there are evidences that a still larger population can be accommodated. We are justified in concluding that, for any given stage of technique, and within a given geographical area, there is a supply of human beings that will function with the maximum efficiency and to the maximum advantage of all. This is the point of most favorable balance between numbers of people and available supply of consumption goods. The sociologist calls this *the point of optimum numbers*.

The question of the supply of numbers of human beings is not a static problem that can be solved once and for all. It is complicated by the factor of the development of science and man's power of increasing the availability of natural resources. We are fond of the expression that the railroad "opened the West." It is equally correct to say that the railroad made available supplies of natural resources and standing-room which in turn made possible the support of more human beings. Every invention increasing the availability of economic goods makes possible a larger local or world population. It may be, however, that the populations of the areas affected will choose rather to maintain the same numbers at a higher standard of living than to support a larger number at the old standard of living. In India, at least, one of the effects of British occupation has been the introduction of commerce, industry, and more efficient agricultural methods. But the Indians have used the resulting surplus mainly in supporting an increased population, rather than in raising the general standard of living. In Japan the opposite has been the case. It is true that serious population pressure is present, but this is because Japan has used a large part of her increased productivity in raising her standard of living. Other factors have stimulated her rate of population increase; a matter of increased rate of survival rather than of an increased birth-rate. Having accomplished this higher standard of living, having experienced it, she is now striving to maintain it. Were she to drop back to the old standard of living, the present numbers could easily be maintained.

The problem of optimum numbers, then, is the problem of securing and maintaining for any given stage of social advance the best man-land ratio. Either too small or too large a population will produce less per individual, and consequently result in a lower level of subsistence than a population which keeps a proper balance between men and resources.

OPTIMISM AND THE RACE-SUICIDE BUGABOO

In no other field have we been so complacently optimistic. This optimism has usually been connected with periods of normalcy, and has appeared in areas of prosperity such as the United States. But the cataclysmic results of the First World War have again sobered us, and we find the world in a proper frame of mind once more to consider seriously the possible relation between the balance of population and abnormal social conditions. This is one strange characteristic of the human mind. It refuses to be anything but optimistic except in the face of crisis. When the flood comes and towns are swept away, we are moved to mend the dam. We seldom lock the stable till the horse has been stolen. We do not pass immigration laws till our population has been swamped with more outsiders than can be comfortably cared for and the standard of living of the whole be maintained. Then we are apt to go to the other extreme and exclude beyond all reason. It is strange that even so keen a mind as that of Theodore Roosevelt should have been stampeded by the "race-suicide" bugaboo. The facts were at hand. True, the birth-rate is smaller, but the survival-rate is much higher. It does not require higher mathematics to estimate what would happen if we continued to produce families of a dozen and continued, also, to reduce the mortality-rate as we have done through modern medicine, sanitation, and hygiene. It is entirely possible for a group to double itself in size in the course of a single generation. It is theoretically possible, though not probable, to increase its size fourfold. If each couple brought into the world but six children who attained maturity and followed a similar program, then each couple would replace themselves and add two more couples to the total population. Even on the basis of trebling our population each generation, it would require but three centuries for a single pair to become the ancestors of one million souls. Of course this takes into account only normal death from old age and not such "acts of God" as snatch us from this earth before our time.

There is no problem of more vital significance. Unlimited breeding with the certainty of untimely and unnecessary death results in economic, social, and biological waste. Unlimited breeding with normal survival dooms the standard of living. Unlimited breeding from the scrubs in the human stock invites disaster. National prosperity does not depend on mere numbers, else China would be the most prosperous nation on the face of the earth. As it is, she is the poorest. National prosperity depends on the proper balance between men and the available means of subsistence. Furthermore, it depends upon the quality of that man-power. There is a vast difference between a nation of half-starved coolies and a nation of vigorous and intelligent workers.

THE DANGER OF GAMBLING IN FUTURES

We have made great strides in learning how to use and aid nature; in learning how to insure crops and to eliminate waste in the processes of production; in controlling water-supply; in deriving power from new and unexpected sources; in producing synthetically certain materials of which Mother Nature has been somewhat niggardly; and in perfecting processes for the extraction of materials that Mother Nature has compounded with others. At present we are looking for more and more easily accessible stores of nitrogen, and the time may come when we shall easily extract it from the air. The time may come, also, when the problem of power will be as easily solved. We cannot afford, however, to gamble in futures. It will be time enough to meet it when that day comes. Furthermore, not even our wildest conjectures as to what the synthetic chemists can do for us warrant the optimistic belief that we need take no account of the numbers of the social population. After all, the amount of the earth's surface is limited, and likewise standing-room and space for crops, factory buildings, and channels of communication. All we can hope to do is to utilize what is present with increasing economy and intelligence. As invention and discovery make available new and unknown sources of supply, human beings will be here to take advantage of them and, if desirable, to increase up to the new point of diminishing returns and thus establish a new optimum in numbers.

EARLY APPEARANCE OF THE POPULATION PROBLEM

The population specter has been present since the beginning of human society, and with good reason. As a matter of fear of too few for safety or of too many for comfort, it was perhaps more keenly felt, though less clearly recognized, in the beginning than it is to-day. At least our present situation is less precarious than that of primitive man, with his ineffective methods of coping with the forces of nature and the constant danger in which he lived. There was continually with him the desire for the extra fighter and producer and at the same time the fear of the extra mouth to feed. "The view once widely held that the principle of population must inevitably keep the mass of people close to the verge of the bare means of subsistence was no statement of a desirable ideal. It was a nightmare; a nightmare none the less, though it may haunt us yet." The Egyptians felt it necessary to get rid of the first-born of the Hebrews; and the Greek philosophers not only recognized the problem, but expressed themselves freely as to what should be done about it. Attitudes have varied with periods because time's changes have brought with them now the need for encouragement and now the desirability of the discouragement of population increase. Times of plenty and times of scarcity are reflected in the varying attitudes toward the problem. Periods of pessimism and of optimism alternate. The unfortunate thing is that societies forget the experiences of the past and are apt to imagine each time that they have discovered the final truth of the matter.

PRACTICES PRODUCING INCREASE

The practices that have been in vogue for the increase of the social population are too numerous to catalogue. Early groups made a general practice of killing the males captured in war and retaining the females as secondary mates. This increased the potential productivity of the conquering males without a corresponding increase in the number of food-consumers. Premarital intercourse was frequently tolerated in order that females might demonstrate their fertility before being taken as permanent mates. The barren woman was thus excluded from the marriage market and probably soon disappeared from the social horizon. Early marriage defeats its purpose in that with it is apt to come early sterility, but it does have the effect of increasing the number of generations to the century. The Chinese father has one major desire, and that is to see his sons married and fruitful at as early an age as possible and to hold, if Heaven be so kind, his grandchildren in his arms before his death. With regard to his daughters, his main interest is to replace them in the home with daughters-in-law. Persecution of the bachelor and elimination of the barren woman have been found effective in some times and places. The prestige of parenthood and the elevation of motherhood have had their effect. It is interesting to conjecture what were the actual numerical fruits of the famous Roosevelt and Harding letters to the parents of exceptionally large families. There can be no question that social recognition of this sort might be eagerly sought in certain social strata in which it is not highly desirable to encourage the birth-rate. At any rate, these letters did bolster up large-family prestige. Society is remarkably sensitive to family-size traditions, and standards as to what is expected of a couple are fairly effective. These large-family and early-fecundity traditions take the form of social sanctions enforced in the main through public opinion and religion. Nazi Germany has done much to encourage child bearing even to the extent of condoning illegitimacy.

PRACTICES PRODUCING DECREASE

So long as the patriarch holds life-and-death authority over his children and his female possessions, he is at liberty to accept or reject the children with whom his wife or wives present him. The practices of infanticide and abortion are natural concomitants. Prostitution is common where marriage is too long postponed either in deference to public opinion or because of economic necessity. It also follows social degeneration. Both prostitution and late marriage are effective in cutting down the general birth-rate. The encouragement, and sometimes the elevation, of celibacy and virginity have the same effect. They are deleterious in that they more often discourage fecundity among those who should be and are fitted for parenthood than among those who are not. An almost universal practice has been that of the persecution of undesirable groups. Spain rid herself of her Moors, Jews, and heretics, thus eliminating at the same time skilled workmen, traders, and thinkers. Unfortunately, when this method is used, the persecutors are apt to be very poor judges of desirability. It is interesting to note that in old Japan emigration was a capital offense, while the new Japan is committed to a policy of finding an outlet for her surplus population. Finally custom and tradition, in the social approval of small families and the general astonishment expressed over families of "good old size," keep the family down as effectively as under different circumstances they keep it up. Of course, social approval implies some method or means whereby its desire can be accomplished. This may be found in the postponement of marriage or in the various more or less modern contraceptive devices that have for their purpose the control of conception. Fortunately infanticide and abortion are no longer as common as they formerly were. This is due to the fact that they are no longer as necessary. Instead of destroying infants after they are born, it is now customary to prevent their conception. Unfortunately knowledge of this more modern technique is under strict legal ban in most States and is more a possession of the upper than of the lower classes.

We should mention the further fact that the stages of civilization, progress of the arts, and physical environment, while in no wise furnishing programs, affect both the birth-rate and the survival-rate.

BASIS OF PRACTICES AND PROGRAMS

The need of the time is the mother of morals and of socially recognized programs. We rationalize that which is opportune, socially approve it, and accept it into the body of our mores. Society has possessed plenty of population attitudes and agencies, even programs, that were no more nor less than the blind application of pragmatic tests. Indeed, society does not yet possess a national group with a carefully thought out, scientifically derived, and consciously applied population theory, aim, and program. It is possible that the ancient Spartans came closer to having and practicing such a program than any other people has ever done. We may say further that existing populations are in the main the accidents of natural evolution. Of these the most fearsome and grotesquely haphazard has been that of peopling the United States of America with the representatives of every race, nation, civilization, religion, political persuasion, and social and economic stratum in existence.

As has already been intimated, while there were population attitudes and practices among primitive men, there were no population theories in the accepted sense of the term. Blind, groping practices were rationalized and accepted. Children were born and must have died in tremendous numbers. Life was hard and existence precarious. War was the normal state, and famine lurked ever near. Under conditions such as these it is not strange that the normal population need should be for larger numbers. The problem was mainly that of replenishment. It is entirely logical, then, that the only policy of primitive men should be one of encouragement. We do find cases, of course, of favorably located groups in more or less definitely limited areas, e.g., small oceanic islands, where the problem is less a matter of maintaining numbers than of maintaining food supplies. Here practices are resorted to for the purpose of curbing numbers, but such cases seem to be exceptional.

As man progresses, life becomes more secure. Violent and unnecessary death decreases in amount and the older practices become less necessary. It is at this point that the modern population problem begins: the problem of adjusting numbers to the potential food supply. Man has never been able to rid himself entirely, however, from these fears engendered in the childhood of the race. To-day as then, in the popular mind numbers and security seem to go together; there is an eternal fear of group extinction.

We are prone to take the short-time and opportunistic view, forgetting that environmental conditions are in constant flux. We will not remember that the words, "Be fruitful and multiply and replenish the earth," were uttered to a very small boat-load of survivors from a certain well-known marine disaster. We insist on continuing the attempt to replenish already over-replenished areas. A Chinese sage said to a *young* and *growing* people, "Of the three great evils, the greatest is to die without posterity." The same dictum, however, still operates as a sanction in the same country in its *old age* and *exhaustion* from overpopulation.

MALTHUS AND MALTHUSIANISM

Unfortunately the uninformed are in the habit of referring to any attempt to cope with the population problem as "Malthusianism" in much the same manner as they refer to evolution as "Darwinism." Population theories are no more Malthusianism than modern astronomy is astrology, or chemistry, alchemy. These sciences have progressed far beyond the limits of their strange beginnings, and so also have population theories outgrown the limited vision of T. R. Malthus and the closing years of the eighteenth century. It is not that Malthus has been discredited; he has been superseded. We have traveled with, but beyond, him.

Both Darwin and Malthus based their studies on the knowledge of their day, added their bits, enunciated their theories, and rested their cases. No one would have the temerity to suggest, as the use of their names would sometimes indicate, that there the matter stopped, that there is no more to the theory of evolution, for instance, than was set forth by Darwin nearly a century ago.

Since Darwin's day we have discovered additional facts, but the biological organism in the physical evolution of which he was interested has not changed perceptibly. Social evolution, however, proceeds very much more rapidly than physical evolution, and the social life of to-day is very different from that of Malthus's time. The purely biological phenomena underlying his theory remain the same, but the more important conditioning social phenomena do not. Therefore any modern follower of the doctrines of Malthus must reckon with certain social and psychological factors that had not then appeared.

It would seem almost like a waste of time to go into detail over the Malthusian theory of population were it not for the fact that, during the century and a half since the first appearance of that famous document it has gone through such numerous printings and such continual discussion. Almost at once Malthus found himself the center of a heated controversy, which has not yet abated.

What was the astounding statement that could attract so much and such continuous attention? Simply this: *Populations tend to increase faster than material sustenance can be increased and be made available for them.* It was the law of chronic want for, or scarcity of, material goods. It was merely a statement of a fairly regular tendency for populations to outgrow the food supply *unless checked.* This thesis was explained, expanded, and defended, and a wide range of facts was presented for its proof. Into such detail did Malthus go that his second essay has justly earned the title of "the book everybody talks about and no one reads."

His Three Main Propositions. Malthus took his stand on three propositions:

1. Population is necessarily limited by the means of subsistence.

2. Population invariably increases where means of subsistence increase, unless prevented by some very powerful and obvious checks.

3. These checks, and the checks that repress the superior power of population, and keep its effects on a level with the means of subsistence, are all resolvable into moral restraint, vice, and misery.

Malthus recognized that "the first of these propositions scarcely needs illustration"; it is a self-evident fact. Since living implies subsistence, life is limited thereby. With regard to the second, he felt that he had made a very conservative statement by adding the latter portion. He felt that while there might be extreme cases where populations do not keep up to the level of the means of subsistence, they are so unusual as to have no effect on the general application of the law. It is the truth or falsity of this second statement that is the crux of the entire population problem. The third proposition is of negligible importance. We are interested, of course, in the checks to undue population increase, but these checks vary, as we shall see, with times and periods. We might easily accept Malthus's classification of restraints, but we would have to reinterpret them in terms of our own times. We find no difficulty in accepting his three propositions, but we do find some difficulty in accepting all that he said about them.

The Unfortunate Corollary. A corollary to these three propositions lay in the recognition of the tremendous reproductive powers of all forms of life. Plants bear seeds by the dozens, fish lay eggs by the thousands, animals bear their young in litters, and poor indeed would be the form of life that was prepared by nature to no more than double itself in a single generation. And yet Malthus asks us to consider what would happen if only this were to be the accomplishment of the human race. Given subsistence in sufficient amount, any normally healthy group could easily double its numbers with each generation; it could do more. Suppose families of a dozen were the prevailing size and there was no problem of food supply. Making liberal allowance for deaths, a group could quadruple in size in one generation. From this Malthus draws the conclusion that population increase is represented by a geometric ratio —that it tends to increase by doubling. Noticing the difficulty with which the food supply is increased, he deduces the fact that subsistence tends to increase by arithmetic ratio or by mere addition.

Whether or not this corollary is true or contains truth, it is particularly unfortunate that Malthus made the statement, for this is the peg on which most of the opposition to his theory has been hung. It has been comparatively easy to cite cases in which the population has not increased according to a geometrical ratio, and in which the food supply has increased at very much more than an arithmetical ratio. America is the stock example. In spite of our tremendous population growth, the standard of living has certainly increased more rapidly. It has made little difference that Malthus said that, other things being equal, there was a *tendency* in this direction. Here we have a statement, and on this statement he has been universally attacked. It is similar to the use that has been made of the monkey in refuting Darwin.

The Rise of Neo-Malthusianism. It would be impossible to pass Malthus by without mentioning the Neo-Malthusianism that followed. Let it not be thought that this movement, which might quite properly be called the father of modern birth-control, met with his approval. Careful scientist and keen analyst that he was, he was nevertheless a clergyman, and repudiated, in accordance with the clerical opinion of the time, any tampering with the Divine plan once the sacrament of marriage had been effected. Having called the attention of the world to a serious social problem, he stopped short of a practical solution. His "positive checks" are merely a statement of some of the unfortunate things that happen to societies under conditions of population pressure. Societies will never willingly use them. Social programs always exist for the purpose of conquering them. His "preventive checks" are particularly useless in a normally virile society. Continence in marriage and indefinite postponement of marriage with chastity are ideals difficult of attainment in actual practice. His followers, still using his name, sought means of limiting the number of births that were no part of the original Malthusian program.

Since Malthus wrote, three important tendencies have been observed that were not, to an equal extent, operating in his day. They are the phenomenal *decrease in the birth-rate* in most civilized countries, the even more marked *decrease in the death-rate*, and the very rapid *increase in populations* despite the smaller number of children born per parent. The first has given rise to fears of race suicide, fears of national degeneration and much solemn warning. The second we have hailed as an evidence of advancing civilization. The third has stirred pride, spurred patriotism, and conferred a sense of security, but seldom has lulled our fear of the evil results of a decreasing birth-rate. In the popular mind they are apt to be treated as separate facts rather than as an $A - B = C$ proposition. Let us examine these three tendencies, placing special emphasis on the nineteenth century, and see what has been happening.

The Trend of the Birth-Rate. We may well start by asking what a normal birth-rate is, what birth-rates will result in population increase and what ones in population decrease, and how much the increase or decrease will be. Of course this question cannot be answered except in terms of numerous other conditioning factors, which vary with time, place, and stage of culture. First of all it must be answered in terms of the death-rate, for the mere birth-rate is not so important as the rate of survival. Again the problem has been complicated in the United States by immigration, a source of population increase independent of the local fecundity. For instance, France under present conditions is able to maintain a fairly static population with a birth-rate usually fluctuating between 19 and 20. China, on the other hand, with a birth-rate no one knows how high, but certainly close to the maximum, is also just holding her own. Neither population is very much affected by either emigration or immigration. In 1925 France's birth-rate was 19.6, but her death-rate the same year was 18.0, leaving an excess birth-rate of 1.6 or a rate of increase of but .16 per cent for that year. In the same year the United States showed a birth-rate of 21.4 and a death-rate of 11.8 or an excess birth-rate of 9.6, an increase of almost 1 per cent for that year from this source alone; and to this must be added the increase due to immigration. It is clear, then, that we cannot say that a birth-rate of 20 or 30 or 40 is high or low. All depends on the stage of culture, success in saving lives, the volume of either emigration or immigration, and the average duration of life. We may say at least that a population will remain stationary if every individual born at least replaces himself during his lifetime. A thousand individuals must produce a thousand new individuals to take their places. Roughly placing the average duration of life at fifty years (it is actually sixty-three in the United States at the present time), we see that 1,000 replacements distributed over fifty years will necessitate a yearly replacement of 20. This estimate is more suggestive than scientific, but does indicate that a birth-rate of approximately 20, where the average duration of life is fifty years, would be just sufficient to maintain the status quo.

Let us turn now to the history of the birth-rate and see what has been happening. Unfortunately, up to a fairly recent date most countries have not considered the official recording of births of sufficient importance to take the trouble. In some European countries we have fairly accurate parish records. In Sweden we have records going back to 1750. Massachusetts has the longest American record. Even yet the registration of births is a matter that is entirely in the hands of the States.

Such figures as we have for the earlier periods of European and American experience indicate clearly that the trend of birth-rates has been downward. From a rate of 35.1 births in each 1,000 population in 1750, Sweden has reduced her fecundity by almost two-thirds, to 13.76 per thousand in 1935. England, the United States, and Germany alike have more than halved their birth-rates since the Franco-Prussian war, while France herself shows the sharpest decline of all, from 25.5 births per thousand population in 1870 to 14.7 in 1937. Italy has been slowest to reduce her supply of children; and it is interesting to observe the relative effects of the campaigning in Italy and in Germany during the decade of 1930 to stimulate the birth-rates.

That the rates of birth are not universally low is suggested by the data in Table 10 on page 154; yet excepting only British Guiana and Egypt, the tendency is quite generally toward somewhat lower birth-rates even in the countries still showing comparatively high rates.

It is no wonder that the race-suicide alarmists are perturbed. If this general decline continues, it is easy to prognosticate a time in the not far distant future when there will be no children at all. This, however, would be as absurd a conclusion as the forecasts already mentioned of a world population of many billions in the near future on the basis of the probable continuance of the present rate of population increase. *Birth-rates have a tendency to adjust themselves to death-rates and liv-*

TABLE 10

BIRTH-RATES PER 1,000 POPULATION IN NATIONS WHERE ACCURATE RECORDS
ARE KEPT *

(Rates for 1915 and 1935)

Country	1935	1915	Country	1935	1915
United States	16.8	25.1	Hungary	20.8	23.6
Australia	16.6	27.1	Irish Free St.	19.6	22.0
Austria	13.2	18.4	North Ireland	19.2	23.2
British Guiana	34.3	31.3	Italy	23.3	30.5
Chile	34.1	38.6	Japan	30.0	33.1
Denmark	17.7	24.2	Netherlands	20.2	26.3
Egypt	44.1	43.4	New Zealand	16.1	25.3
England & Wales	14.7	21.8	Norway	14.6	23.6
Estonia	15.9	22.6	Scotland	17.8	23.9
Finland	18.5	25.4	Spain	25.7	30.8
France	15.2	11.3	Sweden	13.7	21.6
Germany	18.9	20.4	Union of S. Africa	24.8	29.3
			Uruguay	20.4	28.6

* *Births, Stillbirths, and Infant Mortality Statistics, 1935* (Washington, D. C.: United
States Bureau of Census, 1937), p. 6.

ing conditions. Where life is precarious, high death-rates are offset by
high birth-rates. Where the death-rate is high, the birth-rate is apt to
be high. In newly opened countries or communities enjoying rapid expansion, this need not be the case. We may have the phenomenon of a
high birth-rate and a comparatively low death-rate, but this is due to
possibilities of rapid population expansion. As soon as life becomes standardized, it is impossible to have any very wide discrepancy between the
two. Other things being equal, the lower the stage of civilization and the
degree of the advancement of the arts, the higher the death-rate will
be found to be. Civilization and scientific progress bring with them more
effective insurance against both natural calamities and the ills that flesh
is heir to.

There is at least a tendency, though vague, uncontrolled, and often
misunderstood, for societies to produce no more babies than are needed.
This tendency, however, is mainly in evidence in the more prosperous,
advanced, and dynamic groups and, even there, shows a definite lag
behind the actual birth demands of the moment. The birth of a child
represents a distinct expenditure of both money and vitality. The bearing and rearing of children has its economic and its social costs, and no
national deficit is so great as that caused by over-breeding and a concomitant high infant-mortality rate. It is useless to burden the reader

with endless statistics. Suffice it to say that the birth-rates of 50 and even more that were in evidence a century ago have been cut in half, and that those countries which are enjoying economic prosperity and showing evidences of social progress now have birth-rates below 20. Still their populations continue to increase at a rate that gives some cause for alarm.

The Trend of the Death-Rate. No less astonishing than the movement of the birth-rate has been the history of that of the death-rate. As we have already seen, natural selection among the lower plants and animals requires an enormous mortality. In stationary populations it is naturally as high as the birth-rate. Among primitive peoples struggling for a precarious existence it is appalling. Among peoples like the Chinese, where population pressure has pushed the standard of living down to the mere subsistence level, births and deaths must strike a balance. Many estimates have been made as to the probable magnitude of these two rates in China, but the fact remains that at best they are guesses and no one knows. Certain it is, however, that the birth-rate of this people is very close to the maximum and the mortality-rate is as high. Under conditions of this sort life is cheap. Life is thoughtlessly called into existence and thoughtlessly allowed to pass out of existence. The death of an infant is not an unusual calamity; it is an unusual piece of good fortune if the infant survives.

The figures in Table 11 represent a tremendous saving and prolongation of life during sixty years represented. We must remember, too,

TABLE 11

DEATH-RATES IN SEVEN EUROPEAN COUNTRIES, 1870–1934 *
(Number of Deaths per Thousand of the Population per Year)

Country	1870	1900	1910	1925	1934
United Kingdom	22.4	17.6	14.9	12.2	11.8
Germany	27.2	20.8	17.4	11.9	10.9
France	24.4	20.7	19.1	17.7	15.1
Austria	31.9	24.8	22.2	14.9	12.6
Hungary	35.9	26.9	24.7	17.1	—
Spain	30.9	27.9	23.9	19.4	16.0
Italy	30.2	22.6	21.1	16.6	13.3

* Adapted from table in E. B. Reuter, *Population Problems* (1923), p. 146. The 1934 figures are from *Annals of the American Academy of Political and Social Science* p. 85 (Nov., 1936).

that saving lives is an even more effective method of increasing population than is bringing a larger number of new lives into existence. The decreasing birth-rate experienced during the past century would have astounded Malthus, but it need cause us no worry so long as the death-rate is also decreasing. As Ross so aptly puts it, "The new mortality is more contagious than the new fecundity." In the United States the "good old families" of a dozen or more children no longer abound. A family of sixteen once would have scarcely caused comment. To-day it is worthy of newspaper "story" and causes high executives to write letters of commendation. But populous family lots in graveyards are also a thing of the past. The census gave the 1939 death-rate as 10.6, and even the year of the influenza epidemic boosted it only to 18.0. Unfortunately the United States is particularly lacking in dependable vitality statistics for earlier years. Data for Massachusetts, however, show a remarkable fluctuation of the death-rate from 1850 to 1890, ranging between 17 and 23. In 1892 a new peak was reached (nearly 21), but from that year on, except for minor deviations and the year of the "flu," the drop has been precipitous; in 1939 the death-rate stood at 11.8. For the country at large the drop during twenty-nine years, from 1910 to 1939, was 4.4 points or from 15.0 to 10.6. A study of the Swedish data extending back to 1749 shows a remarkable amount of fluctuation, but a gradual decrease, up to 1880. During the seventy-two-year period 1749 to 1820 inclusive there are no death-rates of less than 20; 83 per cent of the years show rates between 20 and 30, and 17 per cent are over 30, with one extreme case of 52. In the following 100 years, 1820 to 1920, we find sixty-three cases, or 63 per cent of the years, showing death-rates of 13 to 19, and the remaining 27 per cent in the 20's. For the first period (1749 to 1820) 52 is the maximum rate and 21.7 is the minimum. During the second period (1820 to 1920), the maximum rate recorded is 28.9 and the minimum is 13.3. Since 1875 Sweden has not reached the 20 mark in her death-rate record. Thus, the world over, unnecessary death is being conquered and normal death postponed.

Dr. Louis I. Dublin has thrown light on the subject in an address before the American Public Health Association (Minneapolis, 1929). He was reported by the New York *World* as follows:

The expectation of life has increased, but the span of life has remained stationary.

A fundamental distinction must be made between these two. The former, which is the average length of life of people in a stationary population, has shown appreciable gains and will continue to increase as public health improves and more and more diseases are brought under control.

The latter has remained stationary for a long time and it is altogether unlikely that man will be able to do anything to change it.

The span of life seems to be fixed by the nature of man himself. His internal structure wears out after so many years of work and use and he appears unable to master its weakness or give it stamina to last longer.

The breakdown of the human body occurs well on this side of the century mark, except in a few isolated instances. We hear much about the number of centenarians in the United States. There are about 5,000 persons in this country claiming they have reached this age, but the great majority are mistaken as to their age—most of them honestly so.

Practically every investigation of centenarians has disclosed the woeful lack of reliable records of their true ages.

The span of life for the great majority of persons seems to be closer to eighty years than a hundred.

That twenty years have been added to the average length of human life, since public health work began to be actively practiced in the early 80's of the last century, is true.

But this gain can be traced to the reduced mortality of infants and to the cutting down of the unnecessary and preventable deaths of young people from typhoid fever, diphtheria, scarlet fever, smallpox and a host of other diseases which, for the most part, affect persons under 40 years of age.

Improvement, after the age of 40, has been slight, and almost altogether limited to women.

Such campaigns as center around the annual physical examination are very desirable, but their value, so far as they go to extending the life span, is questionable. Their greatest worth is in making old age freer of discomfort.[1]

The Trend of Increase in Population. The third tendency that we must examine is represented by what we may call the "excess" rate. This is merely the difference between the birth-rate and the death-rate. Usually the birth-rate is higher than the death-rate, but in case it is smaller, the excess rate is represented by a minus quantity. Another method used is that of the vital index. This is merely a statement of what percentage all births are of all deaths (births multiplied by 100 divided by deaths). Here a resulting number larger than 100 indicates an increasing population, while a number less than 100 represents a decreasing population.

We have noticed that both the birth-rate and the death-rate have been declining, but what of the distance between them? It is this element in which we are primarily interested, for it indicates what is really happening to the population. In Sweden since 1749 excess rates have ranged all the way from −26.9 to +17.2. To be sure, only five times in the 172 years of the period covered has the balance showed an actual deficit. It would be nearer the truth to say that the excess rate has varied between 0 and 17.2. In the earlier years of the period, the fluctuation of this rate was violent, but after 1870 it remains quite steady, fluctuating between 10 and 13. Before 1870 the excess rate seems to be increasing. After 1870

[1] *World Almanac* (1930).

the movement is very gradually in the other direction.

Fig. 4 visualizes the process in Sweden and illustrates what is happening elsewhere in the world. The first graph on Fig. 4 shows violently fluctuating birth-rates and death-rates and a precarious differential or

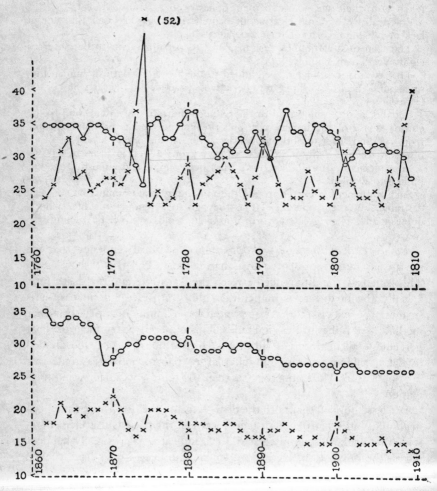

Fig. 4.—A Comparison of the Birth-Rate (o) and Death-Rate (x) Trends in Sweden During Two Periods One Century Apart: 1760–1810 and 1860–1910

excess rate between them. This is typical of the eighteenth and preceding centuries. The second graph on Fig. 4 illustrates the stabilization of these rates that has come with nineteenth-century progress and prosperity.

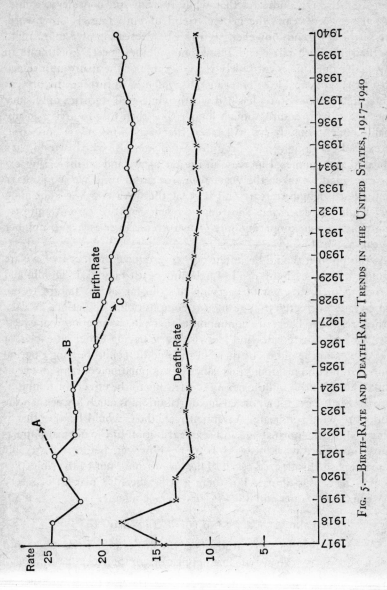

Fig. 5.—Birth-Rate and Death-Rate Trends in the United States, 1917–1940

Fig. 5, page 159, indicates that while there is still considerable fluctuation between years, the general trend of both rates is downward. The birth-rate trend, however, seems to be decreasing at a more rapid rate than the death-rate trend. How soon will they meet? To attempt to answer this question is extremely risky because of the many unforeseen factors that are capable of entering and violently disturbing the present trends. The United States has had worth-while vital statistics only since 1915, and it will require a much longer time than that to arrive at any tenable conclusions. If we had taken the years 1919, 1920, and 1921, for example, we might have prognosticated trend A, which would have indicated a phenomenal increase in the birth-rate and an increasing excess rate. Had we taken the years 1922, 1923, and 1924, we would have been able to demonstrate (trend B) that the birth-rate was remaining level while the death-rate showed a tendency to decrease. Manifestly we are justified in comparing only general trends over as large a number of years as possible.

At this point it would be unfair not to recognize the fact that we are arguing on the basis of crude birth and death-rates. Dr. Dublin has warned us of the danger of carrying this too far and of failure to use refined rates corrected for age and sex composition. Populations do vary in these respects. There are communities that possess an abnormal excess of either males or females and likewise those having either an excess of the young and the old or of those in the middle (child-bearing) period of life. Dr. Dublin maintains that, since our population contains an excess of individuals in this middle period of life, due to the effects of immigration, the birth-rate, for a normal age distribution, is much lower than the crude rate would indicate. A refined rate, then, would be one that is corrected for the normal age and sex distribution of the normal population. Much more work needs to be done, however, before we are able to accomplish this desired result. This is a warning not to overinterpret the present census figures. But there is still a healthy margin of safety between the two rates and it is a far cry to race suicide.

LAND RESOURCES AND POPULATION GROWTH

The new lands that were available at the beginning of the nineteenth century are nearly exhausted. The populations of the world have flooded into the supermarginal areas and only those which are at or near the margin remain. It is easy enough to estimate the area of our own unused Western plains, and the vast interiors of South America, Africa, Australia, and Asia. To be sure, we can find plenty of mere area, but we may be equally sure that if the areas have been left they are no Gardens of Eden. If they had been, they would be populated at the present time. This does not mean that no more unused land remains, but that the land remaining in disuse suffers certain handicaps owing to which it has not yet been brought into use. It is less productive and nearer the margin, and therefore less desirable. It can be made to produce and much of it will be brought into use, but only at greater cost and hence with decreased profits.

Land Situation in the United States. In the United States, with an area of 1,903,000,000 acres, it has been estimated that 879,000,000, 46 per cent, are in farms, but that of this amount only 478,000,000 acres, 54 per cent are improved, that is, in crops, fallow, or used for farmstead or pasture. The remaining 401,000,000 acres are unimproved, probably handicapped land. In other words, but 25 per cent of the land area of the United States is under improved cultivation. Some years ago, two noted leaders of radical movements deplored this condition. Here, they held, we have land in plenty that is denied productivity. Consequently food is scarce, prices are high, poverty is rampant, and we are compelled to deny admittance to the worthy poor of Europe who could so easily be fed. One blamed the capitalistic régime and the other our present system of taxation. Neither seemed remotely interested in any of the scientific data available. They argued from the standpoint of area alone. Estimates by the United States Department of Agriculture, however, are sobering.[2] These figures furnish us with as reliably scientific and non-hysterical data as can be obtained. The conclusion is that to the 478,000,000 acres in improved farms in 1910—the figure rose to about 514,000,000 by 1935—still another 322,000,000 acres could be added, making a total of 800,000,000 acres, or 42 per cent of our total land area. This might be achieved by adding 30,000,000 acres of irrigable desert, 60,000,000 acres of drainable swamp-land, 82,000,000 acres by the development of dry farming, and 150,000,000 acres of reclaimable forest. Of the remaining 58 per cent, or 1,103,000,000 acres, 80,000,000 acres will have to be used for cities; 360,000,000 acres, for forest and woodland; 425,000,000 acres will still continue to be useful only for range and pasture; while 238,000,000 acres are irreclaimable for any purpose and will continue to be so.

Increase in Area and Increase in Population. From the estimates given above it is seen that we cannot even double our present agricultural food-

[2] See O. E. Baker, and H. W. Strong, *Year Book* (Washington, D. C.: United States Department of Agriculture, 1918).

bearing area; we can increase it by but 56 per cent. Increasing it by this amount, however, does not mean that we can look forward to increasing the population by 56 per cent, for the additional land we have brought into use is land that we have brought from below the margin of cultivation at great cost. It is less productive and will support a smaller number of people than the older supermarginal land that was the first to be brought into use. East estimates [3] that, if we roughly consider the new land that is to be brought into use to be only half as good as that which is now under cultivation, "on a productivity basis, just about 35% can be added to our present holdings." In other words, not taking into consideration future improvements in agricultural methods, *on the basis of the present advancement of the art*, we can look forward to the possibility of increasing our population by that amount through the use of new lands alone.

How does this estimate compare with the "classic" that appeared in a New York newspaper in 1921 to the effect that Texas alone, if intensively cultivated, "could feed every person on the planet"? After long residence in China, the writer is inclined to believe that if we adopted China's standard of living, Texas, plus the rest of the United States, could nearly do it, but at what an "animal" level of existence! At what cost to civilization!

This is the situation in the most favorably situated country on the face of the globe. In Europe there is little expansion area available. In Asia more intensive cultivation, if that be possible, and the utilization of her sparsely populated areas will be hardly sufficient to raise the standard of living of her already teeming millions to a humane level. The interior of Australia is largely arid. The major portion of South America is tropical. For Africa we cannot prognosticate the future. It is sufficient to conclude that the world's possible increase of agricultural area is very strictly limited. Supposing that it could even be doubled, and this is a wild conjecture, what does that mean to a world population which is capable of doubling in a single century? The problem is serious.

The Problem of Preserving Soil Fertility. But our population problem does not rest here. The soil itself, once it is brought into use, is not a static possession. Its value changes with use. We mine its fertility as we mine our mineral deposits, but with this difference: the fertility of the soil can be restored, while the riches of our mines, once extracted, cannot be replaced. So long as our country was sparsely populated and there was free land for all for the taking, we thought little of allowing

[3] E. M. East, *Mankind at the Crossroads* (1923), p. 156.

individual families to operate farms of thousands of acres by the most wasteful methods. These farms produced bumper crops, but we have already seen their virgin fertility disappear. It was mined—squandered because a young and optimistic people refused to consider the future. Now, while we can possibly support an additional forty or even fifty million people by bringing into use certain lands that are now neglected, we cannot support more—no, we cannot even maintain those we now have—except by the most strenuous efforts. It is not merely a matter of continuing to use the same old land in the same old way and consequently supporting the same population in the same way. Even to do this we must invent means of maintaining the fertility of the soil, which is extracted by every crop that is grown. Even to maintain the *status quo*, to say nothing of supporting a larger population at a higher standard of living, we must exert ourselves tremendously. The nineteenth century for the Western world was a mad holiday of spending; the twentieth century is already beginning to count up the costs. The virgin fertility of the soils of the Old World long ago disappeared. By the most strenuous efforts and by methods most repulsive to our Western tastes, it has, year by year, been restored. Many of these older countries have for centuries been overpopulated and gaunt from starvation. Unless we succeed in maintaining fertility and continue to accelerate production, we are faced with one or both of two alternatives: a decreased population or a diminished standard of living.

The Prospects of Intensive Cultivation. While we can undoubtedly maintain the fertility of our soil, it is a question how far we can go in increasing the productivity of already fertile land. One may see in New England mile upon mile of tobacco-fields all growing under canopies and truck-gardens of but ten to twenty acres so intensively cultivated and so carefully fertilized that their operators under favorable conditions can make more money than the Western farmer on his 160 acres. It is not difficult to imagine all land as intensively cultivated as this, but not all land is so strategically located with reference to markets. In the province of Chihli in North China the writer found families existing— but merely existing—on the product of a single acre of land. But this too is a process subject to the law of diminishing returns. It cannot be continued endlessly.

At the present time, the product per acre of most of our crops is below that of European countries. In the years 1915–1919 we produced 14.8 bushels of wheat to the acre, and the United Kingdom produced 31.8. We held the record for corn (maize). We produced 92.7 bushels of potatoes per acre and the United Kingdom produced 218.9. As for beans, the ratio stood at 10.1 to 27.8, and again the ratio was in favor of the United Kingdom. During the past century, our own agricultural production, due to improved agricultural methods, has undoubtedly increased. East feels that it may have increased 50 per cent in half a century. There is no reason to fear that we cannot reach the European standard of production. This will require less than a doubling of our present rate. It can undoubtedly be done. But the persistent question is: how long can we keep producing at a substantially increasing ratio? Sooner or later, the point of diminishing returns is bound to be reached; populations cannot go on endlessly expanding at a constant rate for the simple reason that the production of food cannot do so.

The Problem of the Margin of Safety. In conclusion we must face the problem of the margin of safety. Do what man will, Nature does not always coöperate with him in the production of crops. She sometimes withholds the requisite humidity, and again deluges us with it. She sends us biting frosts and scorching winds. We are compelled to fight pests, and sometimes the game is a losing one. It is the experience in a certain section of the country that if a farmer can depend on one bumper crop in four, he can survive. This being the case, we must figure on a margin of safety or surplus to carry us over the lean years. This is the trouble in the Orient to-day. The standard of living is based on the expectation of a normal crop each year. So low is the standard of living that it cannot be reduced without the most serious consequences. We read of their famines, but forget that a famine with them would be merely a crop failure with us. It is not a difference in the character of the phenomenon, but a difference in its social consequences. A famine is merely a crop failure without a sufficient margin of safety.

If we are to maintain a population that is optimum with regard to number and the standard of living, we shall have to consider most carefully the law of diminishing returns as it applies to the human consumers and producers of this world's goods. The basic materials from which these goods are made are strictly limited, even though man's ingenuity is not. Man's fecundity, relatively, is not limited. On the one hand, we must look forward to making the best possible use of the finite world in which we find ourselves. On the other, we must see to it that this world of ours is not swamped with more human swarms than it can well accommodate.

SOCIO-PSYCHOLOGICAL FACTORS IN POPULATION GROWTH

Plant and animal populations, except when domesticated, are affected in their rates of increase entirely by the external factors discussed in the two preceding sections. Human populations alone are affected in addition by another set of factors that are *internal* or spiritual in nature. These are the social and psychological causes which exist because man is man, because he is a thinking being and capable of self-domestication. The lower animals are creatures of their environment and are subject to the laws of rigid and arbitrary natural selection. Their natural environment both makes them and breaks them. Man alone is capable of purposeful progress; of setting his course and mapping out his own destiny. The lower animals are creatures of blind and highly fixed instinct, while man has replaced instinct with social habit.

Only man is able to appreciate an *optimum-numbers* concept. Human societies alone are capable of programs that have for their object the balance of population; of either speeding up reproduction or reducing the excess and weeding out the unfit; of facing the problem of numbers before it has arrived. The pack, in a sort of blind fury, will fall upon and destroy a wounded member. Fowls in the farmyard will fly at and peck at the individual of the flock that behaves queerly. This is, however, but a blind and instinctive reaction. Man has at his disposal much more effective agents.

Social Restraints and Encouragements. Death, disaster, and privation limit numbers. Numbers are also limited by potential human reproductivity. They are increased by peace, plenty, and protection. These are material agents. Restraints and encouragements are also present that are of a non-material nature. They run the whole gamut from the most incidental social approvals and disapprovals embedded in custom and tradition to the strictest sanctions that may be found in law and religion.

We have, for instance, very definite styles in the size of families. These styles change; they vary with time and place even within the same nation. Furthermore, different styles exist within the different social and economic strata of the same general population. In New York City what would be considered as normal on Park Avenue or Riverside Drive would be thought a very poor showing by the denizens of the Lower East Side. At the present time a couple producing four children are thought to have fully met their social obligation, while no surprise is expressed if there be but two. "Four children! What a nice family!" or "Six children! You certainly have a job on your hands!" are the commonly heard reactions that indicate to us what society expects. Our colonial ancestors would have remarked, "What? only ten! My mother had sixteen."

Styles in the size of families have long been on the side of decrease in practically all of the more civilized nations of the world. There was a time when the terms *spinster* and *old maid* carried more of a stigma than they do at the present time. Our modern women have demanded the same right to "single blessedness" that men have had, the home is no longer their only possible career, and one does not speak of herself as a "bachelor girl" with any sense of apology.

Public opinion goes much farther than merely setting styles in the size of families. It determines all those factors which have to do with securing a mate and establishing a family. It limits the relations between the sexes before marriage, the degree of freedom that each shall enjoy, the range of choice in finding mates, woman's sphere, the age at which and the conditions under which marriage may be contracted, the standard of life that must be maintained, the respective duties of husband and wife, and the social values and ideals connected in general with the home and family life. All of these affect the span of the generation, the marriage-rate, and the rate of genetic increase. We are scarcely conscious of these regulators. They seem to us to be merely reflections of things as they are. But we obey them. Public opinion is usually remarkably sensitive to changes in the material conditions on which it is based. Population pressure, a disappearing frontier, a threatened standard of living, easily may encourage stricter marriage taboos, while increasing prosperity and economic security may work in the opposite direction. Custom may, however, be so deeply embedded and firmly intrenched as to defy change and time. This seems to have been the case in China for a thousand years. Family styles have remained unchanged in the face of every catastrophe that overpopulation has wrought.

Legal and Religious Sanctions. Sometimes society has not been satisfied with control through slow-moving, easy-going public opinion, and the laws of God and man have been called upon to furnish the penalties and rewards necessary to accomplish the task. Accordingly we have sanctions now enjoining and now severely penalizing prolicide. The Spartans used it to insure a vigorous citizenry. The Chinese have used it in the main in the case of female infants as an economic measure, while with us in America it is a major crime. Bachelors have in various ways been penalized, reproduction has been rewarded, and parenthood has been subsidized. In some countries birth-control clinics are operated, or at least tolerated by the State. In America it is against the law in most States for a physician to give counsel on the subject. We even question the right of the physician to allow the hopelessly defective infant to die. It has been in the past, but fortunately is not at present, a fine ethical question in the case of childbirth when both mother and child could not be saved, as to whether the physician's main duty was to the mother or to the child. Should the mother be sacrificed that the child might live, or was the mother's life the main consideration? Prostitution is usually deplored. Illegitimacy is frowned upon, and the unmarried mother is made to feel the burden of her sin. In some few States there are sterilization laws for cases of certain types of insanity and of feeble-mindedness, but with the exception of California they are fairly inoperative. In some States medical examination is required in order to secure a marriage license. In general, however, society either remains quiescent or frowns upon any and all attempts to control by law the reproduction of even the unfit.

The hand of religion is seen in all matters affecting morals, but more especially in those having to do with sex. Here its pronouncements are made in no uncertain voice, and woe betide the trespasser! In general, however, its sanctions have to do with the protection of the marriage vow and the family tie. It encourages marriage, and, where it speaks at all on the subject, seeks to insure and increase reproduction.

Effect of Social Conditions on the Birth-Rate. Not only by custom and tradition, by law and order, is the birth-rate regulated, but also by the individual's reaction to his manner of life. A low standard of living, poverty, and economic hopelessness unfortunately do not discourage fecundity. Where these conditions obtain, whether it be in a nation or in a social stratum, we are apt also to have a high birth-rate. Perhaps we should call it thoughtless marriage and hapless reproduction. Fortunately (or unfortunately) a high death-rate is apt to obtain in the same areas. Where a fairly high standard of living is endangered by marriage, we find marriage postponed and economy practiced in the bringing of children into the world. This seems to be the first economy adopted where the standard of living is high enough to be worth fighting for.

Democracy, social opportunity, education, and the advantages that go with them discourage unrestricted multiplication. This is not because selfishness and love of ease are thereby bred, but because these conditions breed foresight and caution. They result in the heedful replenishment of the population rather than in heedless reproduction and consequent overpopulation.

REFERENCES

Annals of the American Academy of Political and Social Science, "The American People" (November, 1936).

CHASE, Stuart, *Rich Land Poor Land* (New York, 1936).

DELL, B. N., and LUTHERINGEX, G. F., *Population, Resources, and Trade* (Boston, 1938).

DUBLIN, L. I., *Population Problems* (New York, 1926).

EAST, Edward M., *Mankind at the Crossroads* (New York, 1936).

FURNAS, C. C., *The Next Hundred Years* (New York, 1936).

KRANHOLD, Herman, *The International Distribution of Raw Materials* (New York).

Ross, E. A., *Standing Room Only?* (New York, 1927).

———, *Principles of Sociology* (New York, 1938, 4th Edition), Ch. II.

Technological Trends and National Policy, Report of National Resources Committee (Washington, D. C.: June, 1937), Part I.

The Balance of Births and Deaths in Western and Northern Europe (Washington, D.C.: Brookings Institution, 1930).

THOMPSON, W. S., *Danger Spots in World Population* (New York, 1929).

QUESTIONS AND EXERCISES

1. Why is the population problem one of the most important problems with which society is faced to-day? Is it more of a problem to-day than formerly? Why are we awakening to its importance?

2. What are the adverse conditions in the world population situation that make it a social problem?

3. What are the specific adverse conditions in the population situation in the United States that give rise to our population problem?

4. What is meant by an *optimum* supply of human beings? How can an optimum population be maintained?

5. What are the various current attitudes in regard to population problems? What expressions of these attitudes have you noted in the press recently?

6. What was the Malthusian position? Was it tenable? Do you think it has deserved all of the attention that has been given to it? Restate Malthus's three points in terms that you think would be acceptable to-day.

7. How does progress in science and technology affect the problem of population pressure? Has the phenomenal progress in technology in the United States insured the country against population pressure? Illustrate your answer.

8. Why has nature provided for such a tremendous rate of increase in the plant and animal worlds? Has this not resulted in a needless volume of destruction of life?

9. What are the advantages and disadvantages among human beings of a potential rate of increase far in excess of that which can survive?

10. What are the trends in the birth-rates and death-rates of the world?

11. What factors have contributed to the rapid decline in the American birth-rate?
12. What is the official attitude of your church toward birth-control?
13. In your particular group, when and under what conditions may young people marry, and what is considered the normal family?
14. What is the agricultural situation in the United States, and what are the prospects for future increase in the supply of farm produce?
15. Why worry over the agricultural situation so long as we are rich in manufactures and are prosperous commercially?
16. Compare tariff barriers with strict immigration laws as a means of protecting the American standard of living. What are the effects of each upon international relations?

Chapter 8

POPULATION SHIFT AND COMPOSITION

WE HAVE at our disposal but one means of increasing the total human population of our world. This is by *genetic increase* or surplus of births over deaths. This type of increase is affected by a host of factors that make it slow in some areas and rapid in others. It also varies according to stage of culture and civilization. These matters were discussed in the preceding chapter. We now turn our attention to local increases and decreases in population that are due entirely to small- and large-scale shifting and to resulting problems of composition and distribution.

Writers on the subject are in the habit of using the convenient term *movement* of population in two senses. The first is *numerical* and refers to movement in terms of increase or decrease as such. The second is *spatial* and refers to shift, or the movement of people or populations from one locality to another. In this chapter we shall be speaking in the main of spatial movement, and treating the numerical movement as a by-product.

I. MAJOR OR INTERNATIONAL POPULATION MOVEMENT

History records innumerable cases of population movement from one geographical area to another. The Bible furnishes some of the earliest of such examples in the wanderings and varied fortunes of the Children of Israel. Population pressure, in the form of famine, forced them to find refuge in Egypt, where they were welcomed much as America welcomed the first influx of immigrants from Europe. While there they increased in numbers to such an extent that they became a menace to the established economic order and the Egyptians were compelled to take strong measures against their further increase. This brought about their final emigration from that country and the problem of finding a new area in which to settle. In the valleys of the Tigris and Euphrates rivers populations were seething caldrons of humanity competing with each other for the land that was the chief means of subsistence. The conquest of one group by another sometimes meant the very nearly complete extermination of the conquered and the repeopling of the area by the conquerors. Even before the time of Christ the Chinese people found it necessary to build a tremendous wall, extending for thousands of miles across valleys and plains and following the ridges of mountain chains, for the purpose of protecting themselves against foreign invasion from the north.

Similarly we find the descendants of the mythical Jimmu Tenno, the Japanese, exhibiting remarkable variations in physical type, from the hairy Ainu of the north to the sleek and diminutive inhabitants of the islands to the south. Siberia, Korea, various Chinese latitudes, and the South Sea Islands have made their contributions and have left their imprint. Because of the smallness of the Island Empire her culture, except for that of the backward Ainus, is one; but even so it is not indigenous to the soil.

We are more familiar with the major movements that determined the present distribution of European population and which resulted in the repeopling of the Americas. These include the advance of Roman arms, depredations from the north, retaliations from the south, and the various invasions by North African and Asiatic hordes. They also include all more modern attempts at colonization in Asia, Africa, and the Americas. They reach their climax in the most tremendous movement recorded by history, that of the steady migration to the North American continent of the representatives of every race and nation on the face of the globe.

Looking at the races and nations of the world in this light, it is difficult to convince ourselves that it is possible that there exists to-day a single pure (original) race. We are a mixture of racial stocks; and modern means of communication are accelerating the process of cross-breeding among these stocks. In America "our Niggers are already half 'yaller,' " and wherever East meets West we have our Eurasian communities. Following the First World War it was even necessary in some cases to hold plebiscites to discover predominant national predilections.

TYPES OF POPULATION MOVEMENT

Ever since there have been populations, there have been population movements. About the prehistoric movements we of course know nothing except that they inevitably took place. We are able to recognize the periods of the Piltdown man, Neanderthal man, and Cro-Magnon man. Each in turn disappeared and was replaced. These early movements, when man was peopling the earth, cannot be designated as conscious and purposive migrations. They were wanderings, mainly, in as yet unoccupied territories, in quest of better food supplies and in response to changing climatic conditions. They were slow movements, which we might designate as peaceful penetration. They preceded the dawn of history and scattered man to all quarters of the globe.

Instinctive wandering has brought about its own cessation. As soon as any area has become completely populated, its people are under the necessity of either competing with each other for the possession of the soil or turning pioneer and discovering new fields for their surplus numbers. People have another alternative: they may become inventors and discoverers and thus find new and improved methods and resources for supporting their increased population within the same territory. Thus does instinctive wandering change into conscious movement.

When the Children of Israel came to Egypt they brought their depleted possessions with them. When they departed they left *en masse*, taking their greatly increased movable possessions and forced donations from the Egyptians. They wandered, an entire migrating population, for more than a generation seeking a permanent location. When the Mongolian hordes invaded Europe in response to the pressure behind them, it was no mere advance of a conquering army. It was a mass movement of an entire people with all their goods and chattels. Nor were these expeditions accomplished in a few years, for whole lives were lived on the move. Wives, children, slaves, goods, tools, and even flocks and herds were taken along, which of course made rapid advance impossible. It was not a matter of transplanting individuals and families, but entire populations. The earlier movements were of this sort. They were population movements in the literal sense of the term. Another typical movement of this sort was that of the Goths. They spent two hundred years en route to Rome. Young men and women started that famous journey whose descendants of several generations later finally arrived. Mr. Wells, in his *Outline of History*, presents a map of Europe and West Asia in which he shows the "tracks of the various migrating and raiding peoples between 1 A.D. and 700 A.D." Its lines or "tracks" form a veritable network and indicate the widespread character of the movement. Invasions of this sort are not necessarily for conquest, though fighting is usually present. In the main they represent the advance of a swelling tide of humanity that cannot be stemmed.

Movement for the purpose of conquest is apt to be of quite a different sort, and is best illustrated by the growth and spread of the Roman Empire. Here the way is prepared by armies and fleets, and the result may be merely the subjugation of populations for purposes of trade and tribute, or the establishment of colonies as well.

Colonization is another type of population movement, one that is more familiar to our generation. In this case, an entire population does not pull up stakes and move, but a new group is selected out of the old and, as a new population, is transplanted to a new environment. Thus it was that the *Mayflower* came to our shores.

Contrasted with these types of population movement, all of which are still more or less in operation in different parts of the world, we have a much more modern form that has been made possible through progress in means of travel and transportation, and which constitutes one of the main problems of modern civilization. It is that which we designate as emigration and immigration. Americans are apt to see but one aspect of the problem, that of immigration; but we must not forget that behind every immigrant coming to our shores, and thus creating a problem, is the problem of emigration in the country from which he comes. The two are complementary problems and, perplexed as Americans are over what to do with the surplus numbers arriving, more perplexing still are the problems of emigrant countries to know what to do with the surplus numbers they are producing. In this more modern form of population shift we have not a mass movement of greater or smaller magnitude, but an individual or family migration to a new home. It would seem as though this would, of necessity, be a slow process; but the nineteenth century migration from all parts of the world to the North American continent presents a phenomenon in comparison with which the hordes that overran Europe sink into insignificance. It is with this type of movement that we are mainly concerned here.

It must not be understood that these various types of movement are distinct and mutually exclusive. A mere *wandering* may grow into a mass movement. Conquest may be present, colonization may result, and individual immigration may follow it up. In the peopling of the American continent we start with colonization. The movement to the West represents wandering, conquest, and colonization. Since 1820 our numbers have been extensively augmented by individual and family immigration.

PROBLEMS OF EMIGRATION

The problems of emigration precede the problems of immigration, since here we must consider the reasons why men leave old environments and seek new homes. We must start by recognizing the strong pull of home ties—the fact that men do not easily uproot themselves and start life anew amid unfamiliar scenes. Familiar paths are pleasant paths. "Be it ever so humble, there's no place like home," so long as it provides reasonable security and means of subsistence. Social habit and personal loyalties retard immigration. The urge must be a strong one that will cause a man to decide to transplant himself and his family to a new environment, there to make over his life, fearfully adopting the new, regretfully discarding the old, adjusting himself to new articles of consumption, new activities, new methods of production, a new tempo of life, different means of recreation, new ideas, and a new way of living, thinking, and reacting.

No mass movement occurs so long as conditions at home are favorable. We do not know why the Goths started on their invasion of South Europe, but it is a reasonable surmise that they were either forced out by population pressure and insecurity at home or lured by the prosperity that lay before them. The Mongolian invasions of Europe occurred at a time when the Chinese were strong enough not only to keep the Mongolians out of China but also to encroach on the territories that the Mongolians already held. Usually we find both pressure from behind and lure ahead stimulating these great movements. Colonies are not made up from the successful and the satisfied of the mother-population. Dissatisfaction may arise because of political, religious, economic, or social conditions in the homeland. Often it is a combination of the four. Europe was often guilty of recruiting her colonists from among her paupers and law-breakers. It was a good way to get rid of them. For the emigrant it represented an opportunity for a new start in life, a new prospect that could not be worse than the old. Even when colonies are well established, as in the case of English colonies in India, it is not easy to go. It is the lure of luxury, higher remuneration, and a higher social position that causes men to make the break with home ties. Consider the strength of the urge that was necessary to persuade thousands of families, bound for America, to embark in frail sailing-vessels on a perilous voyage across an uncharted ocean to the stern and rock-bound coast of a little-known continent peopled with savages. Consider the urge that would be necessary to persuade us to pull up stakes and move to another country, renouncing old loyalties and espousing alien dress, customs, manner of life, language, and even ideas. People may do this in order to escape death or imprisonment or in response to a consuming religious impulse, but whatever the stimulus, it must be strong. Emigrants do not represent a cross-section of the populations from which they depart. They are not the successful and secure of their respective communities. Neither do they represent the lowest types, the ones who have not sufficient initiative and strength of purpose to be willing to pay the price for the new start in life. They are those who feel that they have much to gain by making the move, that the price they are paying in breaking home ties will be compensated by the advantages they will gain in the new environment. Invading hordes did represent a cross-section of the home population, but modern emigration does not.

The causes that produce migration, whether group or individual, exist both within and outside the individual; but in either case they are more or less closely connected with population pressure upon the means of subsistence. The climate and soil may prove such as to make the struggle for existence unduly hard. Climatic changes and the failure of natural resources may endanger continued existence. Populations may increase to the point where survival itself is endangered—where the share that goes to each individual is so small as to render life precarious.

Those who are not under the compulsion of adjustment to external natural forces are the victims of clash with the dominant social organization. This may be economic, political, religious, or social; it is usually a combination of all. Men feel that they are being unduly exploited, resent the indignities heaped upon them, chafe under the restrictions they must bear, and dream dreams of a new life in the country to which they expect to migrate. They are "underdogs"; and as such they will get out. Even these social maladjustments may frequently be traced to the conditions of overpopulation that breed them.

So long, then, as a condition of *optimum numbers* obtains within any population, there will be little thought of or need for emigration. But when the point of diminishing returns has been reached and the pressure of numbers is felt, we may expect both the people and their rulers to cast about for means of reducing the surplus numbers. Thus, emigration from Europe has been in waves, sometimes inundations and sometimes but a normal flow. It is interesting to note that the volume of emigration from Europe or from any given country has been closely correlated with conditions of economic prosperity and business depression on both sides of the Atlantic. Prosperity in America has acted as a lodestone, and depression at home has been an expulsive force. Similarly, it is undoubtedly a fact that if our Western States had been as open to Asiatic immigration as the Atlantic Coast was to Europeans from 1850 to 1900, we would now have a preponderantly yellow population in that section of our country.

As water seeks its level, so population pressure seeks uniformity. The flow is from areas of high population pressure to areas of low pressure. It breaks through natural barriers and beats upon the dikes erected to hold it back. Our immigration laws are such a dike. They are a protection to us only so long as we are in a position to enforce them.

EMIGRATION A FALSE HOPE

Emigration is no solution of the problem of population pressure, even in countries which have reached the point where such pressure is acute. At best it is but a temporary relief—an opiate. It is like dipping water out of a tank that is filling too rapidly rather than reducing the inflow by turning off the spigot. We have already seen the amazing rapidity with which the populations increase; their ability to populate their own territories without outside aid. We also recognize their inherent right to do so. We look upon the outsider as an invited guest and reserve the right to withhold invitations. Unless we break down all barriers and allow free movement of all populations to all parts of the world, thus equalizing the pressure in all parts and reducing the population problem to one single world problem, we can only solve the problems of pressure by attacking them in the respective countries in which they arise. If European or Asiatic populations are reproducing with too great rapidity, their only salvation lies in the direction of cutting down on home production rather than finding foreign outlets, for such foreign outlets will in time also be glutted. This is, for example, the fallacy of Hitler's demand for *Lebensraum* for the expanding population of Germany.

Emigration, then, represents the attempt to find temporary relief from excess numbers. It is indicative of underlying problems of economic and social maladjustment, however, which are not solved by emigration. Fortunately for the country from which the migrants depart, nature takes its course, and those countries usually are not compelled to face the problem of selecting those who go. The best risks stay, and those who have not met with success leave. Even in case of religious and political persecution it is the dissenters—the socially disapproved—who emigrate. This last class of *emigrés* may and often does represent a really superior element in the social population, but such elements do not leave unless driven out.

PROBLEMS OF IMMIGRATION

The problems of immigration are complementary to the problems of emigration. Both movements take place in all countries, but either one or the other predominates; only one of the movements constitutes a problem in any one country. In the main the older and more densely populated countries are the emigrant nations, while the newer, more prosperous, and less densely populated ones face the problems of immigration. As such, countries to which immigration takes place are relatively young, vigorous, progressive, and prosperous. The standard of living is comparatively high, and greater equality of social and economic opportunity exists. They are magnets attracting the underprivileged of the world. We must not forget that they are also apt to be countries of rapid natural increase, since conditions are favorable to early marriage and large families. They are not apt to be countries, except in their beginnings, that require the aid of immigration to populate them.

Three problems are faced by countries receiving immigrants in large numbers. They have to do with *numbers* or too rapid increase, *quality* or the type of immigrant coming, and *culture* or the type of social life produced by a mixture of widely divergent cultural elements.

So long as no barriers exist, population exchange between countries will continue as fast as transportation facilities permit and until equalization of pressure has been attained. This includes the equalization of the standard of living and of economic opportunity, but the equalization is apt to be a one-sided affair. The emigrant country, already reproducing with too great rapidity, is merely protected against the danger of lowering her standard, while the immigrant country will receive surplus numbers till her standard of living and opportunity has been reduced to such a point that she is no longer a force of attraction. Any population desiring to maintain a high standard of living or to insure a rising standard must consider the problem of the balance between probable numbers and potential food supply. It must safeguard itself against too rapid genetic increase, but even more against an inundation of immigrants who are usually adults at the reproductive age and of large family stocks.

Unrestricted and undirected immigration is automatically selective. Neither the best nor the worst physical and mental types are attracted; nor does the immigrant represent the average. He is apt to be drawn from the lower middle classes and as such is not representative of the stock from which he comes. This is not the case if the motive force impelling him is political or religious persecution at home and promised toleration abroad. Such a situation has often resulted in the expulsion of the finer elements of a population. This, however, is the exception rather than the rule. To-day especially, immigrants are in search of better economic opportunity, and as economic opportunity in emigrant nations improves, progressively lower cultural and economic types are emigrating.

"Melting-pots" not only produce new and complex physical types, but new and perplexing cultures as well. Americanization programs are but a last resort and a faint hope for the preservation of our civilization, if we may be so bold as to assert that we still have one. It is idle to hope that the immigrant casting his lot with us will ever discard the loyalties and social values of his youth. We may go far in changing his children, but so long as he has them out of school hours, the traditions of the fatherland will continue to germinate. So long as communities are predominantly German, Italian, or Jewish, they will retain the complexion of the cultures from which they sprang and persist as focal areas for their spread. This is no idle fear. We have German, Scandinavian, French, and other communities in America that have retained their distinctive characteristics since long before the War Between the States. They have retained their native languages, customs, and traditions. They even operate their own schools, and both teach and worship in a foreign tongue. If our desire is to produce a cosmopolitan culture, free and unrestricted immigration is the surest road. If we feel justifiable pride in the culture we have and wish to preserve it, immigration must be carefully controlled and the newcomer must be guided into becoming a *naturalized* member of American life.

Immigrant countries are faced with the problem of what the immigrant will do to them as much as with that of what they will do with him. It is a serious problem which cannot be set aside with a mere emotional reaction and idealistic sentiment. It is a practical problem of telic progress, the type of civilization in which we will to live.

THE AMERICAN IMMIGRATION PROBLEM

The American immigration problem is not the problem of what might have been, but the problem of the situation that we face as the result of more than a century of practically unrestricted influx of alien elements. Realizing, with the close of the First World War, that a new high tide of inflow was imminent, we set up new and drastic restrictions. The "gentlemen's agreement" with Japan was scrapped, and immigration of Chinese and Japanese was limited to one hundred persons annually from each of those countries. European nations were put on a quota determined on the basis of the number of their nationals already in this country. The desire was not to discourage immigration from North Europe, which was already represented by large numbers here and hence was allowed large quotas, but to discourage immigration from the South and East European peoples. The actual administration of the law has been defective in many respects. It has been fumbling and inconsistent. American-born women, wives of foreigners, have suddenly found themselves and their children debarred. Families have been broken. British subjects whose children happen to have been born in Abyssinia have found that their children must come in under the Abyssinian quota and that if this quota was closed and the British quota was open, the parents were welcome, but the children were not. Furthermore the law has had the effect of encouraging the smuggling of immigrants across our long borders, and once they gain access to our country there is little hope of discovering them. Be this as it may, a law as drastic as this requires time for adjustment, and it has had the effect of greatly reducing the numbers of immigrants entering. At Ellis Island some time ago, an official apologized for having so little to show: "There were only sixty to-day and most of them are already cleared. It is not much like the old times when we handled as many as five thousand in a single day."

It is incorrect to say that America has been peopled by immigrants. The original settlers were colonists; it was not till the year 1820 that immigration reached sufficient proportions to be recognized as an important factor in the peopling of the continent. Strictly speaking, the colonial period ends with the recognition of the new republic by England in 1782. Between that time and 1820, when the first immigration records were systematically collected, it has been estimated that approximately 250,000 immigrants came in. These were mostly from the United Kingdom and from North Europe. The colonists were from the same stocks. This resulted, long before 1820, in the firm establishment of English standards, customs, and traditions, to which the few immigrants from other countries were led to conform. Their assimilation was quick and fairly complete, and presented no problem. Plenty of land and a constant demand for labor made them desirable. They had not come in numbers large enough to create a social problem. The economic problem of immigrant competition with the native born had not yet arisen, and only from the standpoint of religion or politics might immigrants be considered undesirable. Some restriction of the entrance of paupers and criminals was aimed at, but it was not till the turn of the century that Europe realized what great possibilities lay in this direction and began the systematic dumping of her human refuse on our shores.

After 1820 three general periods may be recognized: the old immigration, which lasted till approximately 1880; the new immigration, which lasted till the First World War; and the period of restriction, which we entered at the close of that war.

The first period was one of unparalleled activity in opening up, settling, and exploiting the resources of the new continent. Immigrants
were welcome because they were helpers in this vast project. They came
from both the East and the West. In 1848 there were some fifty Chinese
on the Pacific Coast, but with the discovery of gold in California their
number increased to 25,000 in that State alone by the year 1851. In the
year 1820, 8,000 immigrants entered our gates. In 1830 the number increased nearly threefold. In 1840 it was 84,000, and in another ten years
we find 370,000 entering in a single year. During the unsettled days preceding and following the War Between the States the numbers went
down, but only once were they under the 100,000 mark. In the year
1870, 387,000 entered, and in 1880 immigration was within less than
50,000 of the half-million mark. Or, looking at the matter in terms of
decades, we find that during the first decade of this period (1820–1830)
less than 150,000 entrants came, while during the last decade of the
period (1870–1880), the number had risen to nearly 3,000,000.

Most of the more than 10,000,000 immigrants who came to America
between 1820 and 1880 were from North and West Europe. They were
people of similar customs and traditions and created no insurmountable
problem due to different cultural backgrounds. The majority of them
were either farmers or craftsmen of one sort or another. Comparatively
few of them were wholly unskilled laborers. They fitted into our national life, most of them taking up their work where they had left off
in the old country. Germans showed a tendency to migrate to Wisconsin; Scandinavians, to Minnesota and the Dakotas; while the Irish remained in the East.

The period was not without its problems, however. Transportation
facilities were a scandal. The new-comers were exploited both on leaving and on arriving. They huddled in slums. There was little effort directed at selection, and hence there were included an undue number of
paupers and criminals. Many were diseased and entirely ignorant, and
there was no adequate means for their reception. It was a period of chaos
with control, for the most part, in the hands of the individual States.

The period had its ups and downs. Three peak loads are to be noted.
The first, in the 50's, coincided with the famine in Ireland and war in
Europe. It was followed by the panic of 1857 and the Civil War, only
to build up twice more to the panics of 1873 and 1882. Periods of increase were periods of harmony and prosperity, but periods of business
depression and immigration decrease were marked by waves of antagonism and hatred directed against the "foreigner." It is interesting to

note that the famous Know-nothing movement, which was aimed chiefly against the Irish in the East, was employed by the Irish in the West against the Chinese. It was an "America for Americans" movement and as such was directed against the latest comer, whoever he might be.

During this first period the million-mark was attained only in a decade of time; but during the period that followed, it was six times accomplished in a single year. Up to 1900 it fluctuated around a half-million; but from then till the First World War it soared. The character of immigration also changed. No longer were the immigrants coming from North and West Europe, but from South and East Europe. Unskilled

TABLE 12

THE SHIFT IN THE SOURCES OF IMMIGRATION, 1860-1910 *

Country of Origin	Immigrant Arrivals in Each Decade					
	1861–1870		1881–1890		1901–1910	
	Number	Per Cent	Number	Per Cent	Number	Per Cent
All countries	2,314,824	100	5,245,613	100	8,795,386	100
United Kingdom	1,042,674	45	1,462,839	28	865,015	10
Germany	787,468	34	1,452,970	28	341,498	4
Italy	11,725	0.5	307,309	6	2,045,877	23
Austria-Hungary	7,800	0.3	353,719	7	2,145,266	24
Russia	2,512	0.1	213,282	4	1,597,306	18
All others	462,645	20	1,456,494	27	1,800,424	21

* Norman M. Kastler, *Modern Human Relations* (Boston, 1940), p. 326.

laborers predominated. They came from vastly different cultural strains, and with far greater difficulty adapted themselves to the new environment. They filled the slums, congested the cities, did underpaid manual labor, filled almshouses and prisons, created a serious strain on charity organizations, and made more difficult the maintenance of order. America finally began to realize the seriousness of her immigration problem. In 1923 President Coolidge wrote:

American institutions rest solely on good citizenship. They were created by people who had a background of self-government. New arrivals should be limited to our capacity to absorb them into the ranks of good citizenship. America must be kept American. For this purpose it is necessary to continue a policy of restricted immigration. It would be well to make such immigration of a selective nature with some inspection at the source, and based either on a prior census or upon the record of naturalization. Either method would insure the admission of those with the largest capacity and best intention of becoming citizens. I am convinced that our present economic and social conditions warrant the limitation of those to be admitted. We should find additional safety in a law requiring the immediate registration of aliens. Those who do not want to be partakers of the American spirit ought not to settle in America.

Thus it required a full century for America to realize the seriousness of its immigration problem and to take definite steps toward its abatement.

During the past one and a quarter centuries, more than 30,000,000 immigrants, or the equivalent of almost a fifth of our present population, have entered our country. Allow 1,200 of these individuals to the mile and we have a procession circling the globe. During the year 1910 they entered this country at the rate of nearly five per minute. Every one of these new-comers needs to be fed, clothed, and housed. *If they are allowed to enter, they should be guaranteed equal treatment in industry and the opportunity of becoming respectable, self-supporting members of society. It is as much to the advantage of the United States as it is to their advantage to do so.* They are different from ourselves in many respects, but no matter how different, if we admit them, both we and they must look forward to the time when they will be citizens and able to stand in equality and with the right to vote beside the purest colonial blood of the country. We have all too recently discovered that this we have not been doing. We have welcomed them as cheap labor, but deplored their outlandish ways, low standards of living, and teeming undernourished families. We have not realized that they were becoming an integral part of our national life, that they set the standards for large sections of the country, that they often were *used* for the control of elections, and that they accomplished a virtual transplantation of foreign cultures into our midst. Now we should have no quarrel with such transplantations provided we can assimilate them and select those elements which fit our purposes. We can undoubtedly learn from many nations. What we should avoid is the possibility of our being swamped.

The distribution of the foreign born has been poor. They have tended either to congest our cities or to congregate in colonies. Their assimilation has not been accomplished. According to the census of 1930, while 89.7 per cent of our population was white and 72.3 per cent was native white, *only 52.3 per cent was native white of parents born in this country.* Unfortunately we have no statistics showing the percentage of those whose grandparents were born in this country, but it would undoubtedly be small.

II. The Passing of the Frontier

The peopling of America through an extraordinarily high genetic increase and the most tremendous influx of foreign elements that any people ever experienced has resulted in vast and rapid social and economic changes on this continent. Our own grandfathers were the pioneers who braved the wilderness, fighting their way step by step across mountain, plain, and desert to the "promised lands" beyond. Older men and women now still living can remember the days of the covered wagon, before the palatial, air-conditioned Pullman which now transports us farther between sunrise and sunset than they could travel in a month. What but a few decades ago was unbroken wilderness, with grazing buffalo and wandering tribes of savages, now teems with cities, factories, and prosperous farms. A very network of steel and cement ties together East and West, North and South, carrying the never-ending procession of freight and express trains, pleasure cars and trucks, which make this country one. The postal and telegraph services extend to the most out-of-the-way places. The farmer enjoys as regular a delivery of mail at his door as does the city-dweller. The radio not only entertains him with everything from grand opera to jazz, but also provides him with weather reports and market tips. The grandparents of many of us moved from New England to the Middle West, their sons moved on to the Dakotas, while still others found opportunity in the Southwest. Horace Greeley's advice, "Go West, young man! Go West!" was heeded by millions. They went West. They grew up with the country. They took advantage of the exceptional opportunities offered them. Free land was to be had for the taking. Rich natural resources were there for the exploiting. The only capital needed was youthful vigor, a clear head, a sound body, and a willingness to work. The world was theirs. All over this country are scattered great fortunes that had their foundation in an unparalleled early opportunity. The result was a tremendous impetus to the growth of population.

But that day has passed. Opportunity is no longer to be had for the asking; it must be made. The frontier has disappeared, and with it free land and unlimited natural resources. The coast has been reached, and already the tide has turned back in the opposite direction. Lands and resources that were neglected or scorned in the first successive waves of advance have been requisitioned by the backwash. The extensive exploitation of the pioneer has been replaced by intensive cultivation and development by his grandchildren and the continuing ripples of migrants from the East. They are in a keener competition for the good things of life, and the result has been a decline in the rate of population increase. Families are smaller, and now we have taken steps to cut down immigration.

The problem of the past was that of conquering the frontier. The problem of to-day is how to get along without it. As late as 1850 the States east of the Mississippi held 91.4 per cent of the total population. By 1930 the population had moved westward to such an extent that more than 30 per cent lived in the Western States. But the abruptness with which the center of population checked its westward march is an index of the fact that the frontier has been reached and exhausted. Until 1890 the center of population had moved westward at a rate of from fifty to sixty miles per decade. During the last fifty years it has moved in all only ninety-eight miles, or an average of but twenty miles per decade.

PROBLEMS CONNECTED WITH THE DISAPPEARANCE OF THE FRONTIER

The first problem is that of the tragic exploitation of what should have been the heritage of many future generations. The advance wave of tremendous progress resembled nothing so much as the invasion of a looting horde. It swept across the country, robbing both forest and soil of their richest resources, taking no thought of the future, leaving depletion behind it. Our present problem is one of conservation and of intensive, rather than extensive, development—*we must use efficiently what remains.*

Both immigration and westward migration were accomplished only through a process of human selection, both physical and spiritual, which has left its mark within the country and on the country as a whole. Up to 1880 the *immigrating* type, and till well into the 60's the *migrating* type, were of pioneer caliber. This means that they were vigorous both mentally and physically; they were the bolder and more adventurous spirits, the potential leaders. Ross says: "In the rougher parts of New England to-day one finds old towns that touched their zenith eighty [now more than a hundred] years ago. The elite of the young people have regularly migrated, formerly to the West, of late to the rising cities of their own region. Aside from the aliens that here and there have seeped in, the inhabitants are of the blood of those *who always stayed behind.*" He paints a vivid picture of the listlessness of the children and youth of these "fished-out" communities, the shiftlessness of farms and farmers, of villages and villagers, the rarity of intellectual craving in the very place where it once abounded, the disappearance of vigorous community spirit, the languishing of morals, and the deadness to higher things.

The comment of the State Superintendent of Public Instruction upon the classical academies which once flourished in these towns is pertinent. "Out of these academies went a steady stream of sons and daughters who were, other things being equal, always the strongest of the generation, for otherwise they would not have gained this education. They became lawyers, or physicians, or clergymen, or schoolmasters, or business men in the cities, and the girls went with them prevailingly to be their wives. The unambitious, the dull, the unfortunate boys and girls of the old country-side, who could not get to the academy, as a class remained behind and became the dominant stock. And the old academy, having sorted out and sent away the ambitious stock, is now dormant." [1]

Since these words were written, nearly thirty years ago, other changes have taken place in New England. Aliens in droves have flocked in and taken up the worn-out and deserted farms, intensive market gardening has grown apace, and the net result seems to be a measure of new prosperity and the infusion of new South European elements into the population. Still the bright and ambitious of the native-born are selected out, this time by the lure of the city. Ross continues:

If the moral sag is deepest in certain New England spots, it is only because nowhere else in the North has a rural population been so skimmed and reskimmed. But the thing has a wider range than people suspect. The disfranchisement of seventeen hundred citizens of Adams County, Ohio, for selling their votes lets in a pitiless ray on the dry rot of the lifeless communities that have missed the electrifying touch of railroad or city. The knots of gaping, tobacco-chewing loafers that haunt the railway-station in some parts of Indiana suggest that the natural pace-makers of the neighborhood have moved on to create prosperity elsewhere. In southern Michigan, in Illinois, and even on into Missouri, are communities which remind one of fished-out ponds populated chiefly by bullheads and suckers. [2]

Thirty years later Professor Ross's observation is still pertinent. In spite of the coming of the automobile, the radio, and the cinema and the building of cement highways, the process goes on apace. The sorriest sight the Middle West has to offer is that of the hamlets and villages which have lost their reason for existence. One such might be cited here. It was started in the early days by a group of highly cultured New Englanders on the shores of the lovely Lake St. Croix. It was a prosperous port of

[1] E. A. Ross, *Changing America* (1914), pp. 151 ff.
[2] *Ibid.*, pp. 156–157.

call for the river steamers plying between St. Paul on the Mississippi and the upper reaches of the St. Croix. The railroad came in, and it looked for a time as though the little village so strategically located was bound to have a future. Then came the decline of the lumber industry, the disappearance of steam-craft from the river, and the growth of other centers. The railroad, up to a few years ago, continued to operate a train a day, not because there was any profit in it, but because the railroad's charter required it. The academy on the hill now houses a sorry grade school. The social life of the town is gone. A few representatives of the old families remain, but for the most part they have intermarried with new-comers, and their places have been taken by a group who have brought with them a strange tongue and vastly different social values. The little old church is falling into decay, while above it on the hill is a more prosperous one where worship is conducted in another language. The pool-hall, the dance-hall, and the taverns are the main centers of social activity. There are prosperous farms about, but no longer is it a trading center, since the automobile makes it so easy to go to the more pretentious town to the north. And who lives there, and why? Only those who have been caught in the eddy and have not sufficient energy to swim out. Summer folk come from the cities and rusticate for a brief space on The Point across the bay, but they are "dudes" and make little impression on the stagnation of the no longer "quaint" New England village. The Middle West possesses many such towns, with struggling churches and starving small colleges, mute reminders of a day when the populace was predominantly one of leaders.

We must not conclude, however, that the fishing-out or skimming process was due solely to the westward movement of the population. A companion to that process was the movement toward the cities. Growing industrial cities have been a lodestone that has continued the work. The problem of the present is to revitalize rural life, to make it a life worth living. Perhaps the time may come when it will be the shiftless who will be forced out of the rural districts and the operation of the process of selection will be reversed.

Migration is not an evenly progressing onward rush. It is a succession of waves, and with each wave a reselection of types takes place. For this reason we notice a marked change in energy and attitude as we move from East to West. The sleepy conservatism and fearfulness of taking a definite step, so characteristic of the rural East, give place to the fervent Rotarianism of "God's Country" and of the "Native Sons of the Golden West."

Thus has the disappearance of the frontier accomplished not only the exploitation of our *natural* resources but the exploitation and redistribution of our *human* resources as well.

THE SLACKENING OF EXPANSION

"The public thinks that a great social change can hinge only on some great event: a battle, treaty, law or party struggle. The sociologist, however, knows that among the greatest happenings are the things which do not occur at any particular time or place." The disappearance of the frontier was such a catastrophic change. Its disappearance was such a gradual affair that it was not appreciated till it was all over and readjustment to a new situation was already under way. The American people, who had developed in the presence of unlimited resources and who had developed modes of activity and types of mental attitude in accordance therewith, gradually came to the realization of the fact that the old order had changed and that a new type of struggle for existence faced them. The frontier that had molded them was gone, and a new set of factors was in operation. Freedom to move on was a thing of the past, and with it the attitudes which it bred. We see the slackening of expansion in the reduced rate of population increase, the decreasing number of acres per individual, the slowing advance of population and of agricultural production centers, the decreasing expansion of the food-bearing areas, and the increase of land values and of food prices.

That America is awake to her problem is evidenced by the vigor of the conservation movement in all quarters. The churches, the universities, business organizations, scientific societies, and the States vie with each other in their study of our new problems: how redeem the country, how make the city a more effective servant of society, how make production the most economical and the most effective, how secure the proper distribution of social opportunity so that no section will suffer? These are the problems which are being attacked. We hear much these days about the "back to the land movement," the Resettlement Administration, the Subsistence farm movement, the A. A. A., the decentralization of industry, the Coöperative movement—all representing efforts directed at finding a way to do without the frontier. What we need is not more farms and farmers, but better ones. A most effective Department of Agriculture at Washington, similar bodies in every State capital, and numerous agricultural colleges are making farming a business and a profession. Rural communities and villages are being surveyed and studied to such an extent that they are beginning to regain their confidence in themselves. The sociologist is developing both rural and urban sociology. We are combining as never before to make good the loss of the frontier.

Problems of population shift, whether from one country to another or within a given country, give rise to a host of problems having to do with the *composition* and *distribution* of the people. Let us now turn to this problem in the United States.

III. THE COMPOSITION AND DISTRIBUTION OF THE SOCIAL POPULATION

The composition and distribution of the social population is not a simple problem; it is infinitely complex. Viewed from a distance, populations present a remarkable dead level of similarity. They are human beings, male and female, old and young, pigmented and unpigmented. They are like a regiment on parade. As viewed from the reviewing stand, the regiment looks like a throng of duplicates. Functioning as a group they are of interest, but one has the feeling that they would be monotonous as individuals. Each soldier is similarly uniformed and equipped, he carries himself rigidly erect, keeps step, and acts in unison with all the others. We know, however, that in spite of careful selection and training, each soldier is an individual. Taken in their own setting and in clothes of their own choice, these individuals have vast differences in temperament, ideals, habits, and mental and physical characteristics. They come from widely varying environments; they possess different aptitudes, likes, and dislikes; and they represent unlike problems to their officers. Notice again a group of students in a class. They have been selected out of the population at large because of their similarity in respect to educability. They come very largely from the same social class in society. They hope to qualify for professional work of some sort. They are in the same age group and are living much the same daily round of life. Here we should have almost the maximum of similarity, but still great differences exist. Each has a dominant interest, a type of mind, a degree of physical energy, an amount of mental ability, and certain social values.

When populations are subjected to closer scrutiny, we find that their differences extend far beyond the more obvious age, sex, and color variations; that they are varicolored mosaics forming a large variety of patterns. *On the composition of the social population depend, to a remarkable extent, the social characteristics of the group.*

Distribution is the companion problem of composition. Not only do we find marked variations, but we find types of variation predominating in given communities. Similarly, while we speak of our population of more than 132,000,000 and of our continental land area of more than 3,000,000 square miles, we are faced with the fact that this population is very unequally scattered. In 1920 our population density was 35.5 to a square mile. To-day it is over 44, but this means little when we consider that densities in the various States, as reported in the 1930 census, varied from .8 in Nevada to 644.3 in Rhode Island. In the Mountain States (Montana, Idaho, Wyoming, Colorado, New Mexico, Arizona, Utah, and Nevada) there was but one individual to each 164.8 acres, or 4.3 persons per square mile of land, while in the Middle Atlantic States (New York, New Jersey, and Pennsylvania) there was an individual for every 2.9 acres, or 262.6 persons per square mile. Thus the distribution of individuals stood in a ratio of better than 50 to 1 in the two areas. Excluding the Middle Atlantic area with its Greater New York congestion, we find that the New England States could show but 5.4 acres per individual, which represents a 30 to 1 comparison with the Mountain States.[3] *Not only the distribution of types but also the physical proximity in which people live is a determiner of group attitudes and activities.*

SEX COMPOSITION AND DISTRIBUTION

Nature has so arranged matters for us that in general from 104 to 106 males are produced to each 100 females. This ratio is called the masculinity rate. Males are produced slightly in excess of females, perhaps to even matters up by the time reproductive maturity has been reached. From both the biological and the sociological standpoints it is desirable to have an equal distribution of the sexes at maturity. The best interests of society demand it. Yet the world over we find the widest variations actually existing. In China female infants are not wanted. When and where infanticide is practiced it is on the girl babies and not the boys. In the United States in 1920 there were six States that showed, as the effect of distribution and not of excess of births, more females than males in the total population. At the same time there were four States in which the males were at least 20 per cent in excess of the females. In the case of Nevada, the excess was 48.4 per cent. For the country as a whole there were 104 males to each 100 females in 1920. In New England there were only 98.5 males to each 100 females; but as one moved west the ratio increased till it reached its maximum (115.7) in the Mountain States. In the Pacific States it was 113.9. (See Fig. 6.)

By 1940 the situation had changed considerably. Nevada was the only State in which the preponderance of men recalled the traditional mascu-

[3] *Statistical Abstract of the United States, 1937,* pp. 2-3.

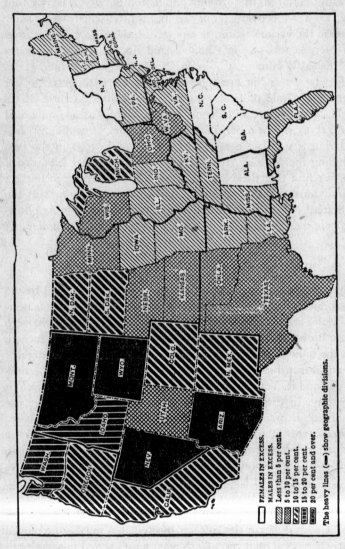

FIG. 6.—RATIO OF MALES TO FEMALES IN TOTAL POPULATION, BY STATES: 1920

Fourteenth Census of the United States (United States Bureau of the Census, 1920). District of Columbia females in excess not shown separately on the map.

FEMALES IN EXCESS.
MALES IN EXCESS.
Less than 5 per cent.
5 to 10 per cent.
10 to 15 per cent.
15 to 20 per cent.
20 per cent and over.

The heavy lines (——) show geographic divisions.

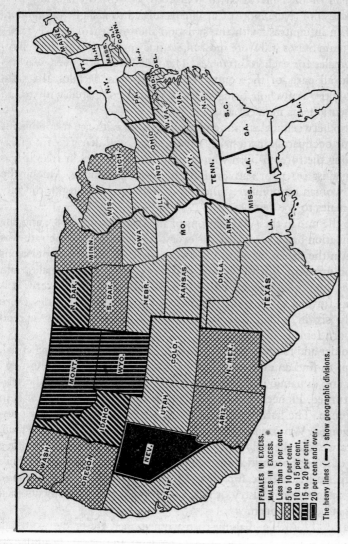

FIG. 7.—RATIO OF MALES TO FEMALES IN TOTAL POPULATION, BY STATES: 1940

Statistical Abstract of the United States, 1941, p. 14. District of Columbia females in excess not shown separately on the map.

FEMALES IN EXCESS.
MALES IN EXCESS.
Less than 5 per cent.
5 to 10 per cent.
10 to 15 per cent.
15 to 20 per cent.
20 per cent and over.

The heavy lines (——) show geographic divisions.

linity of the West, the ratio being 123 males to 100 females. At the other extreme, the number of States in which there were a higher number of women than of men increased to fourteeen, two of them being west of the Mississippi river. North Carolina returned to a slight preponderance of men in contrast with the situation there in 1920. (See Fig. 7.) The Mountain States still were most masculine among the divisions, having 108.2 males for each 100 females. The unbalance, however, was less extreme in all parts of the country than in former decades, the ratio for the country as a whole being 101.1 in 1940 as compared with 104 in 1920 as mentioned a moment ago.

The ratio between males and females also varies with the predominant industry or occupation, nationality composition, and density of population. Among the foreign-born whites in the United States in 1940 it was 111.1 as against 101.2 for native whites of native parentage. Among the Negroes, women outnumbered men by a considerable margin, the rate being 95 males to 100 females.

In 1930 the rate in the rural sections of the country was 108.3 and the farm population had 111.0 males for every 100 females, but the rate was only 98.1 in the urban sections. Of seventy-five cities with populations of 100,000 or more, but thirty-one had more males than females, and these cities are predominantly either heavily industrial or Western. It is interesting further to note that in these same seventy-five cities there were only six in which foreign-born males did not greatly exceed foreign-born females in number.

In the older and longer-established countries, other things being equal, we are apt to find an even distribution of the sexes; while among new, growing, and dynamic populations the balance is more likely to be seriously disturbed. Pioneers need their women folk, but they need also an excess of men. The hard work of the lumber camp precludes the presence of women. Women are less necessary on farms nowadays than men, and hence we find them flocking to the cities to take advantage in office and shop of the opportunities there to be had. In Troy, New York, where collars are made, the rate for men is but 84.7, while in Akron, Ohio, famed for its rubber industry, it is 138.9. In migratory movements men predominate over women.

Ross says: "Less hedged about than women, men are readier to break home ties and try their fortune in a strange land. In our earlier immigration males were to females as three is to two; but in the new immigration, coming for high wages rather than for land, they are three to one. Districts which have lost by emigration have more women than men." This is true of the countries that have furnished us with our millions of immigrants. It is true of the "fished-out" areas that furnished the material for the peopling of our West. And what are the effects of this disturbance of the balance between the sexes? Either male or female traits will

TABLE 13

SEX RATIO AND PER CENT MARRIED FOR VARIOUS POPULATION GROUPS 15 YEARS AND OVER, UNITED STATES, 1930 *

Population Group	Sex Ratio, 1930	Males, Per Cent Married	Females, Per Cent Married
United States total	102.5	60.0	61.1
Rural-Farm	111.0	57.9	66.0
Urban	98.1	60.5	58.5
Negro	97.0	59.8	58.5
New England States	97.2	58.7	55.8
East North Central	104.1	60.8	62.9
South Atlantic	99.6	60.6	60.0
West South Central	103.3	61.9	64.0
Pacific	108.7	57.2	62.3
Massachusetts	95.1	58.0	53.7
Montana	120.0	52.6	65.4
Boston	96.4	52.1	48.9
Charleston, S. C.	83.8	60.9	50.3
Cleveland	103.0	59.0	60.4

* R. E. Chaddock, "Age and Sex in Population Analysis," *Annals of the American Academy of Political and Social Science*, November, 1936, p. 191.

predominate. In either case—a superabundance of bachelors or a superabundance of maiden ladies—normal social organization is impossible. We have no striking examples of predominantly female communities, but the Western frontier has shown us what to expect when men are not bound by home ties. Such populations are in a constant state of flux. They are restless and unsettled, they are prone to quick and ruthless exploitation in order to "get back home" to "God's country." Law and social restraints are weak and morals are low, though vices are apt to be the open and aboveboard vices of strong men rather than the petty ones of weaklings. But "women make homes and the home favors stability and the sense of responsibility."

AGE COMPOSITION AND DISTRIBUTION

Civilizations, nations, and communities vary in age and are affected thereby much as individuals are. Young communities are apt to be active, dynamic, and pushing, while older ones move more slowly and are more conservative and "settled down." Communities also vary as to the predominant age of the individuals composing them. Just as communities may be predominantly male or female, so they may be made up of an undue proportion of the old or the young or the middle-aged. Older communities having little contact with the outside world are apt to possess a normal distribution of the various age groups, but young, dynamic, and active communities frequently give evidence of a more or less serious disturbance of the balance.

Age distribution is affected from within by all the factors that affect the marriage-rate, age at marriage, the birth-rate, and the various mortality-rates. Numerous births and early and numerous deaths will result in the flattening out of the population pyramid, while smaller families and longer lives will make it steep.

The decline in the size of the American family, together with the increasing success in saving and prolonging life, is changing the age composition of the population. This is clearly indicated in Table 14. It is

TABLE 14

A CENTURY OF POPULATION TRENDS IN THE UNITED STATES, BY AGE GROUPS *
(Expressed in Per Cents)

Age	1880	1940	1960	1980
Under 5 years	13.8	8.0	6.7	6.1
5 to 19 years	34.3	26.5	22.2	19.6
20 to 44 years	35.9	39.0	37.6	33.9
45 to 64 years	12.6	19.7	23.3	26.0
65 and over	3.4	6.8	10.2	14.4
Total	100.0	100.0	100.0	100.0

* Adapted from U. S. Bureau of the Census release (1941).

estimated that the persons over 65 years of age will, by 1980, constitute over 14 per cent of the total population.

The factors that bring about migration from one area to another result in making the pyramid irregular and unbalanced. Just as cities attract more women than men, so they attract people in early maturity. "Fished-out" communities lose not only their men, but also those in the flush of life.

Ross remarks, "age composition may reflect itself very clearly in the collective spirit. The community with a large proportion in the early productive years, e.g., young and rapidly growing settlements and towns, display unusual fluidity, energy, initiative and adaptability. On the other hand, an excess of young children and of the elderly lessens venturesomeness and makes for pessimism, timidity, and the want of prompt decision."

RACE AND NATIONALITY COMPOSITION AND DISTRIBUTION

In considering race and nationality compositions, the fact must be recognized that primarily these rest on different foundations. Race is a *biological* fact. We most commonly distinguish between races by color, which is their most evident distinguishing feature, but more scientifically by a large group of physiological variations, such as color, cephalic index, cross-section of the hair, and facial angle. Nationality is a *social* fact. A given nationality may belong to one racial group or another, but it is distinguished as such by its social inheritance in language, religion, government, and other social institutions in general. It would be difficult to determine how many nationalities there are on the face of the earth, since political affiliations are continually changing.

The history of the world has been one of racial and national contacts and combinations but, with a few exceptions, most nations to-day represent one predominant racial and national strain. The United States is the most outstanding exception to the rule. It presents one of the most complex large-scale ventures in combination that the world has yet seen. Racially the United States is about 10 per cent colored. At least one-tenth of its population belongs to races of such marked difference that full coöperation is impossible. (See Table 15, page 196.) Moreover, our colored elements are not equally distributed. The yellow races are more or less concentrated on the Pacific Coast and the blacks in the South. In the "Black Belt" we find the percentage of Negroes in the total population varying from more than 50 in Mississippi and South Carolina to 15.9 in Texas. In eight of our States the population is 30 per cent or more black. The Negroes and Mongolians to a considerable degree represent elements injected into the body politic that, while *in* it, are not *of* it.

The United States Bureau of the Census has made the practice of dividing our population into native white of native parentage, native white of mixed parentage, native white of foreign parentage, foreign-born white, and colored.

There are not many nations that would find it worth-while to enumerate their populations under these divisions. The mass of their populations would fall under the first head and "native white (black, or yellow) of native parentage" would imply a long succession of generations of such parentage. In America it is a distinction to be able to trace one's ancestors back to the American Revolution or to the landing of the *Mayflower*. In

TABLE 15

POPULATION OF THE UNITED STATES, BY RACE AND COLOR, 1940 *

Race	Population	Decennial Increase, 1930–1940	Males Per 100 Females
All classes	131,669,275	7.2	100.7
White	118,214,870	7.2	101.2
Native-born	106,795,732	10.9	100.1
Foreign-born	11,419,138	18.3	111.1
Negro	12,865,518	8.2	95.0
Other races	588,887	−1.4	140.5
Indian	333,969	.5	—
Chinese	77,504	3.4	—
Japanese	126,947	−8.6	—
Filipino	45,563	.8	—
All others	4,904	−16.7	—
Region			
North	76,120,109	4.2	100.4
South	41,665,901	10.1	99.6
West	13,883,265	16.7	105.7

* Sixteenth Census release (U. S. Bureau of the Census, 1941).

England the Norman Conquest takes the place of these events. In China one may trace his ancestry back to the time of Christ or before. In comparing our country with other countries it is startling to learn that 65.3 per cent of our entire population is native and of native parentage, but it is even more astonishing to learn that but 55.3 per cent is native white of native parentage. *But what does native white of native parentage mean?* Not a native ancestry for five hundred years, or even a hundred years, but for one generation, or about twenty-five years. A person's grandparents may have been born in Germany, later settling in Milwaukee where their children were born and brought up amid German customs and traditions. He (the grandson) may attend a German Lutheran church and speak German familiarly with his friends and English but brokenly, but for the purposes of the United States census he is a native white of native parentage.

Fig. 8 gives us some idea of the way the United States compounded the nationalities of the world into her population. With immigration practically closed, there has been but very little change in the relative composition since 1920. But statistics do not give us all the information we need to get a full picture—the Jews, for example, are distributed in the nationality data of Fig. 8, and it is difficult to find out just what

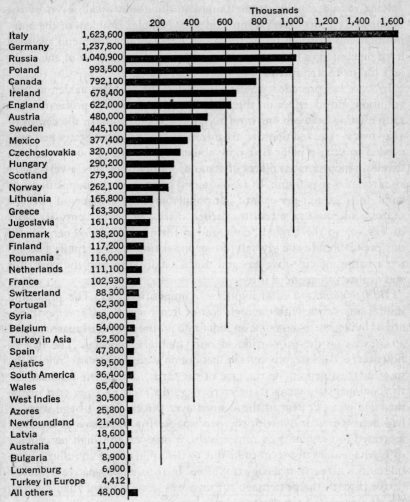

		Thousands
Italy	1,623,600	
Germany	1,237,800	
Russia	1,040,900	
Poland	993,500	
Canada	792,100	
Ireland	678,400	
England	622,000	
Austria	480,000	
Sweden	445,100	
Mexico	377,400	
Czechoslovakia	320,000	
Hungary	290,200	
Scotland	279,300	
Norway	262,100	
Lithuania	165,800	
Greece	163,300	
Jugoslavia	161,100	
Denmark	138,200	
Finland	117,200	
Roumania	116,000	
Netherlands	111,100	
France	102,930	
Switzerland	88,300	
Portugal	62,300	
Syria	58,000	
Belgium	54,000	
Turkey in Asia	52,500	
Spain	47,800	
Asiatics	39,500	
South America	36,400	
Wales	35,400	
West Indies	30,500	
Azores	25,800	
Newfoundland	21,400	
Latvia	18,600	
Australia	11,000	
Bulgaria	8,900	
Luxemburg	6,900	
Turkey in Europe	4,412	
All others	48,000	

FIG. 8.—FOREIGN-BORN POPULATION OF THE UNITED STATES, BY COUNTRY OF BIRTH: 1940

Sixteenth Census Release (Washington, D. C., United States Bureau of the Census, 1942).

the Jewish population is, although their number was estimated as having been about 4,770,000 in the United States in 1937.

OTHER FACTORS

Lack of space prevents the complete discussion of all, even of the important, factors entering into this very complex problem of the composition and distribution of the social population. In the end we shall have succeeded in little more than indicating the character of the problem and its special intensity in the United States.

In what has preceded we have suggested the problem of density distribution and its effect on the social life. A part of this problem is the ratio existing between our *rural and urban* populations. In the census of 1940 it was revealed that the urbanization of the United States had proceeded to such a point that now about 56 per cent of our population dwells in incorporated places of 2,500 or more inhabitants, a very slight rise from the 1930 figure. In 1880 some 70 per cent of the population was rural. In 1930, 49.1 per cent of our population lived in places of 8,000 or more; while in 1830, a century earlier, there were but twenty-six cities of that size in the United States, and in them lived but 6.6 per cent of our population. In the growth of our population we are rapidly becoming a nation of city-dwellers and this is vitally affecting the character and quality of our social life.

Marital condition is an important composition fact. The prevailing impression is that, with the high cost of living and the advancing standard of living, there has come an indefinite postponement of marriage and an increase in the proportion of our voluntary celibates. The fact is, however, as Ross so aptly puts it, that not only are Americans "one of the most married peoples on the face of the earth," but "their fondness for the conjugal state seems to be increasing." In 1890, 58.3 per cent of the men and 68.2 per cent of the women over fifteen years of age were or had been married. By 1930 the percentages for these two groups had increased to 65.9 and 73.6 respectively. Moreover, this high percentage of marriage does not seem to be due to the influence of an influx of immigrants with early-marriage traditions. In 1930, among native whites of native parents, the percentage for men was just 0.4 lower than the 65.9 for all classes; and for women it was but .8 less.

It is also interesting to note that rural communities are more married than urban communities, that the South is more married than the North, and that the East is more married than the West. It is highly favorable to find such a high percentage of marriage in general, but that 70.7 per cent of all males twenty to twenty-five years of age are still single and 46.5 per cent of the females of this age group indicates a trend toward later marriages. We have advanced the age of marriage, but in time we *do* get married.

Our *illegitimacy* rate is much lower than that of Europe, and may reflect our proneness to marry or our resort to contraceptives. It is higher in the South than in the North, and in the East than in the West. Among the Negroes it is far in excess of that among the whites.

With regard to *illiteracy*, the showing of the United States is excellent in comparison with some countries and a national disgrace when compared with others. Naturally the influx of tremendous numbers of foreigners and the possession of a vast mass of underprivileged Negroes affects the rate adversely. Nevertheless, since they are here, their degree of illiteracy affects that of the whole body. While the amount varies widely with geographical location, nativity, color, occupation, and class, 3.7 per cent illiteracy was reported in 1940 among those twenty-five years of age and over. For native whites it was only 1.3 per cent, but for the foreign-born it was 12.2 per cent, and for Negroes, 10 per cent. It was higher also among rural than among urban populations. "But," comments E. A. Ross, "these figures, originating with the heads of families interested in not confessing the truth, are no good. They are further invalidated by the revelations of the training camps. In 1917, 24 per cent of the men 21 to 31 years of age could not write a letter home." Very well, so much the worse! In 1930 more than one voter in twenty was unable to read and write.[4] Since 1930 a number of the "works projects" have attempted to reduce the illiteracy, and reports of the work would indicate that much has been accomplished.

TABLE 16

EDUCATIONAL ATTAINMENTS OF WHITE MALES SELECTED FOR MILITARY SERVICE *

Level of Education	Per Cent of Selectees	
	World War II	World War I
All	100	100
College	11	5
High school graduate	30	4
High school non-graduate	28	12
Grades, and no schooling	31	79

* Bureau of the Census Release, 1942.

Finally, what about the composition of the population with regard to its *quality*? No problem could be more difficult to handle, because we

[4] *Statistical Abstract of the United States, 1937,* p. 43.

have as yet no adequate measures of quality and the census helps us very little. On the one hand we are a nation that is going to school as never before, but on the other, an alarming proportion of our youth is dropping out as soon as (and often sooner than) the law allows. We do not know how many of these are forced out by economic necessity and how many are the unfits for whom an education is an impossibility. Certain it is that the number of our low-grade and defective mentalities is alarmingly high. This subject will be treated more at length in another chapter.

WHAT IT MEANS TO BE AN AMERICAN

From the biological standpoint it means little to be an American. We are already a composite—a heterogeneous mass of crossed and recrossed strains. Socially it means a great deal. Our nation was started with certain very definite ideals in mind. We have not realized all of them, but they still exist as a part of the unfinished business before us. Americans are Americans because of a complicated set of attitudes toward life. These attitudes and social values have been highly responsible for attracting immigrants to our shores. For the most part they represent, in the case of the later accretions, but vague and little-understood longings and aspirations. Our problem is to carry forward the work started by the founders of our republic—to complete the experiment. The ingestion of great masses of foreigners without thought of digestion has hampered the process. Our first problem is that of calling a halt, either temporary or permanent. This we have done. The second will be that of taking stock of what we are, what the past century of immigration has made us, and, progressing on that basis, of moving forward toward our national aims.

REFERENCES

Annals of the American Academy of Political and Social Science, "Economics of World Peace," pp. 7–12 (July, 1930); "The American People" (November, 1936).

CARR-SAUNDERS, A. M., *The Population Problem* (Oxford, 1922).

CREAMER, Daniel B., *Is Industry Decentralizing?* (Philadelphia, 1935).

DUBLIN, L. I., *Population Problems* (New York, 1926).

GOODRICH, Carter, and others, *Migration and Economic Opportunity,* Report of the Study of Population Redistribution (Philadelphia, 1936).

HANSEN, Marcus L., *The Immigrant in American History* (Cambridge, 1940).

Our Cities, Their Role in the National Economy (Washington, D. C.: National Resources Committee, Research Monograph, 1937), pp. 7–29.

Recent Social Trends, Report of the Hoover Committee for the Study of Social Trends (New York, 1933), Ch. I.

Ross, E. A., *Principles of Sociology* (New York, 1938, 4th Edition), Ch. I.

Thornthwaite, C. Warren, *Internal Migration in the United States* (Philadelphia, 1934).

Wells, H. G., *Outlines of Man's Work and Wealth* (New York, 1936), Ch. 13.

QUESTIONS AND EXERCISES

1. List the earlier types of population movements preceding our modern migrations, and the primary motives of each, so far as we have been able to interpret them.

2. What distinguishes our modern emigration and immigration from those earlier movements?

3. List (1) *favorable* and (2) *unfavorable* influences of past immigration on American life.

4. What groups or organizations in America favor immigration? What groups oppose it?

5. Briefly trace the development of our immigration policy. Why has the trend been toward increasing restriction?

6. What are the reasons for the absolute exclusion of the yellow races from the United States? Is it because of the difference in color?

7. Why are the nationals of northern and western Europe given such liberal quotas in our immigration law?

8. The motives instigating the settlement of the Western frontier were essentially the same as those prompting foreign emigration to the United States. Explain the pioneer's and immigrant's motives in terms of population pressure.

9. What would happen under a condition of unrestricted immigration? What would happen if we restricted all immigration but eliminated all tariff barriers to international trade? Under which arrangement would there be the greater security?

10. Why do we apparently have relatively few conspicuously "self-made" men among the present younger generation?

11. In your estimation, does continued immigration constitute a menace to the best interests of American development? Briefly explain.

12. Where might one find predominantly male communities? What problems are created when a proper balance between the sexes is not maintained? Where is the shift most pronounced to-day?

13. What is the racial composition of the United States?

14. Is your community made up predominantly of home-owners or of renters? How does this affect the nature of community life?

15. What changes are taking place in the composition of the population of your state? Are these changes reflected in your immediate community? What are the causes of these changes, and how do the changes affect the nature of the social life?

16. Compare the present social attitudes of the East with those of the West; the South; the Middle West. How do you explain the difference?

Chapter 9

THE QUALITY OF THE POPULATION

1. OUR HERITAGE

NATIONAL WELFARE, as we have already seen, does not relate to the mere numbers of the social population but to the *quality of the individuals composing it*, as well. The quality of these individuals depends in part on their training and partly on the social and physical environment within which they develop. It depends in part also on their heredity; on the inborn traits and characteristics that predetermine how much or how little training an environment can profitably give them. These two determiners, environment and heredity, make the individual what he is. The study of the first set of factors is called *euthenics*, and the study of the second, *eugenics*. Children are born into the world who are normal or defective, healthy or ailing; some are abounding in vitality and very active, while others are weaklings. Just as we find them born to be tall or short, rosy or swarthy, so we find a group of mental differences. Some are always dull no matter what advantages surround them, and others are quick-witted and keen even if unschooled. We may notice also a great number of special aptitudes for some particular type of work or mental activity, but it is difficult to assign these definitely to heredity, in spite of the fact that it may be impossible to discover any factor in the environment that might have produced those abilities.

Children are not merely born into the world in general, but each into a particular environment. The content of each child's mind, his training for life, his habits and attitudes, and even his physical health and vigor are either determined or limited by the environment. Seeds sown in stony and in fertile soil develop differently. So it is with children. Type environments, such as city and village, town and open country, villa and hovel, tenement district and restricted residential suburb, leave their imprint on the unfolding human being.

HEREDITY OR ENVIRONMENT, WHICH?

There can be no question that heredity and environment working together make the individual what he is. But which is the predominant force? Which plays the more important rôle? This question has been argued interminably but to no avail. Naturally the biologist sees the importance of heredity, while the professional social worker, who is mainly interested in improving environments, answers the question in the light of the fruits of his work. The sociologist doubts that the question can as yet be answered. He carefully avoids a bias in either direction. The two forces work together inextricably. Each is necessary to the other; each is incomplete without the other. He refuses to waste his time defending either against the other. He demands, however, that each be fully recognized. The old illustration of the potter and the clay serves us well here. It requires good clay and a good potter to make the finest porcelains. Clays are of various grades. Some are good only for the most clumsy jars, while others are suitable for the finest vases. Potters have varying degrees of skill. If a skilled potter is given poor clay to work with, we may expect only as good a product as can be made with that material. If the best clay is placed in the hands of a clumsy potter, we shall likewise merely get the best job that he can do. Heredity is the clay. It is the basic material with which the potter (environment) has to work. Good heredity and good environment make the best combination, but either is handicapped by a deficiency in the other, and neither can completely triumph over the other. We can say only that the basis of individuality is in the inherent quality of the individual and that this is played upon by stimuli supplied by the environment, the finished product being thus produced. To produce a fine vessel we must start with good material, but it must be worked upon by a skilled potter as well. And which of the two is really responsible for the excellence of the finished product? To answer is to argue in a circle.

Any one who will consider for a moment the careers and development of individuals he has personally known will find it difficult to explain what has actually happened in terms of heredity and environment. The accounts that follow are of actual cases which illustrate the point. The first example is that of three boys from the three "first" families of the small community. There was nothing to indicate anything but the best heredity. The fathers were successful business and professional men. They were leaders in the community and one had been the governor of his State. The mothers were women of intelligence and culture, also leaders in church and social life. Their homes were affluent. They all went to college. And how did they turn out? They sowed all of the "wild oats" possible at the time and place. They were all sent home from the Eastern colleges they attended. Each went into his father's business, married, reared a family, and made a place for himself in the community. Twenty-five years later one is a suicide, one a bankrupt, and one is awaiting trial. Another is the case of a little girl with an insatiable desire to draw pictures. Her heredity was good but not exceptional. Neither of her parents was artistically inclined and there was little enough in the small-village environment either to call forth or develop the trait. Still, she was made of the clay of which artists are made, her parents were sympathetic, and the village encouraged her. She was sent to one of the best art schools and to-day is on the road to fame as an artist. In still another instance, the son of an eminent father and of a mother of exceptional talent has played the violin since he was large enough to hold the instrument. To-day he is one of the well-known artists in his field. His heredity is of the best and the environment in which he was reared furnished every stimulus toward the development of his talent. Which did it? Heredity or environment? The answer is, undoubtedly both. We may hear of exceptional talent coming from the slums and exceptional failures coming from seemingly the best of environments. We see the best heredity producing scrubs and wonders done despite what looks like the worst heredity. We cannot afford to be dogmatic as yet. We are made by our heredity plus our environment, and it behooves us, if we are interested in the quality of the human race, to study the means for the improvement of both.

THE THREEFOLD NATURE OF THE PROBLEM

The quality of any given population, whether it be a race, a nation, or a section, depends on these two determiners, as well as one additional factor. First, *what sort of people are we breeding?* What is the general heredity of the stock from which they spring? Are we breeding in the main from the scrubs in the stock or are the superior elements contributing their full share? Second, *what type of environment are we furnishing them for their further development and unfolding?* Is it such as to develop each individual to the fullest extent of his latent powers? Does each individual receive as much education and training as he can profitably use? Is he brought up in a socially and physically healthy atmosphere? In a word, are we using the best possible "potters" for the working up of the "clay" at our disposal? Third, *what is the quality of the individuals we are accepting from the outside?* This is the problem of the quality of the immigrant accretions, and is no less important than the problem of the types we are producing at home. Do they represent a fair sample of the quality of the groups from which they come? Are they predominantly from the superior or the inferior strains?

The heredity of the American people is based on an original ancestry composed of a highly selected group of early colonists who were in the main of superior stock. They were the dauntless souls who were driven from their homelands by political and religious persecution. We must not, of course, forget that there were those who were adventurers only, without the ideals that motivated most of the New England colonists, nor that America was early used as a dumping-ground for paupers and a haven of refuge for criminals. These, however, were typical neither of the blood nor of the spirit of the original ancestry. All in all, they were a vigorous group of risk-takers; alert and capable, willing to brave the dangers of the deep and to take their chances in a new and undeveloped country. To this original ancestry have been added in a century and a quarter some thirty million later accretions. They have come from every part of the world, but represent Europe in the main. Their blood has been mingled with that of the native American strains, and the germ-plasm of the nation now represents a mixture of widely diversified stocks.

THE ECONOMY OF QUALITY

The problem of quality is also a problem of economics. Farmers do not find it economical to breed from the scrubs in the herd. They often pay huge prices for fine breeding animals in order to insure the quality of the herd. They also take heed of the environment of their animals that they may develop to the best advantage: to the maximum of their latent powers. Feeding, pasturage, and housing are given careful attention for the simple reason that they pay dividends. Similarly there is no economy in breeding anything but the best human beings, and it represents a serious short-sightedness to allow them to develop to anything but their fullest powers. Yet we tolerate the multiplication of the manifestly unfit, and allow great sections of our population to develop in environments which are so bad that they cannot possibly produce individuals who are normally socialized or adequately trained for an efficient and productive life.

It is strange that society should have continued for so long a time to refuse to consider the population problem from anything but the emotional angle. To have a spouse and beget a family is a God-given right, we say. But is it a God-given right to pass on serious hereditary defects to countless succeeding generations? Perhaps from the standpoint of the individual it is; but society as a whole must be considered as well. So far as society has had any program in the past, it has been in the main a program for the purpose of encouraging unlimited numbers. We have already seen that such a policy defeats its own purpose. There has been practically no attention paid to the improvement of heredity, and only sporadic attempts have been made at the improvement of the environment. To be sure we have wonderful school systems, very effective sanitation and hygiene, and building codes and regulations, but we still allow people to live in slums and to procreate freely in poverty. We allow large numbers of our social population to be overprivileged, and still greater numbers to be underprivileged. Social opportunity is a sort of nourishment. It is shortsighted to economize on physical nourishment for the growing child. But in society we do economize on social nourishment and feel that we have accomplished a great saving when we have done so. A mayor or an administration often points with pride to budgetary frugalities, the real fruits of which may be borne by a handicapped coming generation. *The greatest possible economy lies in the direction of encouraging the best heredity and developing each individual to the maximum of his powers.*

THE ADVANTAGE OF GOOD HEREDITY

The advantage of good heredity is the advantage of a good initial start in life. As yet the hereditary factor is not so well understood as that of environment, and in democratic America we are apt to hold it a bit under suspicion. Here men have risen from the ranks to positions of power and honor. We hail the self-made man. We hold that the boy "who has the stuff in him" can and will make his mark. In one sense this is a recognition of the fact that America furnishes an environment which makes such achievements possible. In another sense, it admits that he must be made of "good clay" to begin with. Heredity is *original* capacity. It can be either limited or developed by environment *but it cannot be changed*. It is not democratic. Good heredity is more like an aristocracy. Favorable environment may be the result of chance, but good heredity is a favorable bond of connection between the generations. Heredity cannot be improved by training or environment, since we transmit acquired characteristics to future generations to but a very small extent if at all. *Heredity can be improved only by selection.* Animal-breeders know that no amount of scientific feeding will make a scrub produce anything but scrubs. They know that a superior herd must be bred from a "blooded" ancestry. Luther Burbank, the plant-wizard, did not produce his marvels by the cultivation of his plants, but by planting acres of specimens and searching for the hereditary variations that most nearly represented the type he was trying to evolve. From these he continued the process, selecting and reselecting, till at last the new variety had appeared and its heredity was proved pure. For seed purposes farmers select only perfect ears of corn and use only the perfect kernels from the main body of the ear. Seed houses supply pedigreed seeds, and some of the most valuable services of our agricultural colleges have been in the direction of improving plant and animal breeds through selection. In other forms of life we know the value of good heredity, but in human life, since we are human beings, we have been loath to apply the same findings to ourselves.

Hereditary differences between individuals and between strains are great. Shakespeare said that "some are born great, some achieve greatness, and some have greatness thrust upon 'em." Here we see a recognition of the importance of heredity, training, and environment. No man is the product of one, but rather of the combination of the three. One cannot but be impressed, as he looks back and recalls what has become of his childhood playmates. There was a democratic equality then, but what has happened since? Some of them entered the ranks of unskilled labor. Many dropped out of school because they were incapable of continuing; the competition was too much for them. Others went on for the simple reason that they were capable of doing so; because they "had it in them." We remark that a boy is "a chip off the old block," that "blood will tell," and many other similar bits of folk wisdom.

There are hereditary strains in any village in our country that are marked by generation after generation of superiority, mediocrity, or inferiority. Any community, large or small, if carefully studied will show definite strains of defective inherited traits. A few years ago a county in northern Wisconsin was studied, and all its problem families were traced back to three original family stocks. In a later and more careful study, these three were found to spring from one. Any case worker in any charitable organization in the country knows that he is dealing with family strains rather than with individuals. He knows that many of the strains are inherently inferior and that in working with them he seldom effects a complete rehabilitation. The best he can do is to improve the environment, keep such individuals under continual supervision, and make them as efficient members of society as their inherent inferiority will permit. Undoubtedly the greatest disillusionment of the young social worker comes when he discovers that among the great majority of his clients, in normal times, improvement is limited by capacity; and that the lives of the unfit represent a permanent problem so long as the breed continues.

The advantage of good heredity is the advantage of a normal or superior physical and nervous organization. It lies in the absence of an original handicap. It is the advantage of being so constituted that good environment will be able to produce good fruits. Heredity sets the limits for possible future development, while environment offers the opportunities for such development.

We cannot go into the problem of the mechanism of heredity. For our purposes we will have to accept it as a fact. A person's heredity represents a linkage of cells, a linkage of the past with the present. It is a continuous thing. Every time a child is born, certain characteristics of his ancestors reappear in his body. Many additional characteristics lie dormant in his germ-plasm but may reappear in the bodies (somato-plasms) of his children. The individual's chief importance, genetically, is as the agent of a line of physical heredity, a combination of traits that will be passed on by him to future generations. He is the custodian of hereditary quality. The only way to get rid of poor quality is to prevent its reappearance. The best way to insure high quality is to encourage its continuity.

THE ADVANTAGE OF GOOD ENVIRONMENT

Some plants represent dwarf varieties. It makes little difference how carefully we train them or what supports we give them on which to grow. They are dwarfs and will remain so. The support may hold them a bit straighter and give them more room to spread, but at best they are dwarfs that have been given a good chance. Other plants are climbers and will climb if given the opportunity. If we fail to provide the trellis they will twist about on the ground in an effort to perform their normal function, but they will never grow as large and as luxuriantly as they would have done if the support had been provided. The dwarf was a dwarf to begin with and the other a climber. The support merely represents an opportunity. It is environment. The *advantage of good environment is the advantage of a favorable opportunity to develop, but no amount of opportunity will make a climber out of a dwarf.*

There is a limit to the amount of water that a sponge can absorb. There is a similar limit to the amount of opportunity by which an individual can profit. It is wasteful to give a dwarf vine a ten-foot trellis.

Similarly it is wasteful to force a boy through a college training that he is incapable of absorbing. In the case of the human being the waste is more serious, since we force him into a sphere where he will never fit and prevent him from taking the place in society where he really belongs. Overprivileging is thus as serious a mistake as underprivileging and has produced for us a vast army of "white-collar" misfits.

The effects of environment are much more evident than the effects of good heredity. From birth till death, environment is at work influencing physical, mental, and social development. At birth and before, the physical health of the infant depends in large measure on the health and care of the mother. During infancy the physical development of the child is determined by its feeding and care. Many individuals are physically handicapped for life because of the ignorance or neglect of their parents. The fond mother who puts "just a wee drop of coffee" in her infant's milk is showing a bit of misplaced love, and little wisdom. The child brought up in a home of poverty where proper nourishment and clothing are impossible does not get a fair start in life. So on through life the habits of the individual, the conditions of sanitation under which he lives, his diet, clothing, and housing, the amount of exposure and strain that he endures, the hygiene that he practices, the climate that he lives in, and his opportunities for healthful living in general determine his physical development. Some are born physical weaklings, and some are born robust. Good environment cannot make a healthy man, but it can make him as healthy as his original endowment allows.

Men are born with various grades of native ability, but their mental patterns come from their social environment. Their degree of socialization depends on the habits and attitudes of mind that society implants. "It is a great advantage to a child to be born into a family where the mother tongue is spoken correctly, where good habits are maintained, where manners are gentle and where conversation is ennobling. . . . And so with training. Regular attendance at school, frequent travel and visits to art museums confer an inestimable benefit upon the child." Both the slum and the residential section, the street and the playground, the railroad tracks and the park, the back alley and the summer camp, the alley gang and the boys' club, are making our future citizens. Every child approaches adult life indelibly stamped with the environment that has furnished him with his personal habits and his social ideals.

What is the object of our school systems, churches, libraries, social centers, parks, galleries, museums, playgrounds, summer camps, and other allied institutions and programs? It is to aid in the physical, mental, and social development of individuals. It is an attempt to make the environment fit for humanity. Still we doom millions to lives in environments that can only stunt growth and development. We continue to build our best schools where they are the least needed, to beautify streets in prosperous sections, and to establish parks where the poor cannot get to them. Slums are in part the product of the people who live in them, but even more are the people the product of the slum. Their streets are dirty because careless people live in them, but also because municipalities pay more attention to cleaning their boulevards. The public takes care of its show places but allows charity, through social-settlement programs, to assume the responsibility of furnishing opportunity for the poor. The writer once lived in a settlement-house in a vicious section of New York. The room he chose for his own opened on an air-shaft, as did those of the tenements fifteen feet across the shaft. No light ever entered the room, and floor and furniture were perpetually covered with a film of oily dust. Through the windows came not only the odors from innumerable wash-tubs and frying-pans, but indescribable sights and sounds as well. There were tired, irritable, and slovenly mothers alternately bending over wash-tub and kitchen stove. They were existing in an environment and under conditions that could never be made to produce a home. In the very nature of things they were not and could not be fit companions for their husbands and children. Tired, sweaty, begrimed husbands came home to such conditions as these; and who could blame them for stopping at the "poor man's club" on the way? Half-wild children in from the streets, surly sons from work, gaudily dressed and painted daughters, home for what? To eat and later to sleep, escaping between times to the social life of the gang, the pool-hall, the tavern, the "movie," and the dance-hall. Blocks and miles of this with Fifth Avenue but a few steps away, and the only attempts at counteracting the situation being made by the social settlements and similar charitable agencies.[1] And what did the environment produce? Exactly what one might expect: stunted lives, crime, vice, low ideals, social inefficiency, misfits. No business man would tolerate antiquated, inefficient methods of business and production. We have learned our lesson in that field, but in the production of our crop of citizens we are unbelievably lax.

---

[1] The "slum clearance," "low-cost housing," "subsistence farming," and "resettlement" programs carried out as a part of the heroic effort to provide socially useful employment for the unemployed, have brought considerable change in the situation. But there remains much yet to do.

Environment determines opportunity. The social ideal of democracy is that of an equal chance for all. But an equal chance has been cleverly defined as an equal opportunity for every man to prove his inequality. In other words, it is the chance for every man to develop as far as he is able to go. It involves not wasting opportunity on those who are incapable of profiting by it.

THE PHYSICAL AND THE SOCIAL ENVIRONMENT

Fairchild says:

Man does not have to sigh for new worlds to conquer. He is already faced with a new challenge—the challenge of the human environment. The happiness of mankind is in the last analysis the happiness of the individual, and the well-being of the modern individual is at least as dependent upon human environment as upon the physical. The human environment is vastly more complex and baffling than the physical. This is due largely to the fact that it is a dynamic factor rather than a static. . . . The world has always been essentially the same at every stage of man's development. . . . All he needs to do is to learn about the world, and the knowledge holds good. But the human environment has been built up from nothing to its present proportions during the space of man's own existence. Every change in the physiological features of the human being, every additional convolution in his gray matter, every invention and discovery, every new institution, every advance in the mastery of nature itself has had its repercussion on the human environment. As fast as adaptations were made new adaptations were required. As a consequence, man's adaptation to his human environment has never been very accurate, and at the present time the maladjustments are glaring. We know a good bit more about the organization of industry than we do about the organization of society. We know a good deal better how to produce wealth than we do about how to distribute and use it. We understand much better how to control the forces of nature than the forces of the human heart.[2]

INDEXES OF POPULATION QUALITY

The Distribution of Wealth. The amount of wealth an individual possesses is not necessarily an index either to his social worth or to his inherent ability. In a country, however, where there are comparatively few inherited large fortunes and where the *self-made man* is still the rule, the acquisition of wealth may easily mean some sort of superiority. But however the wealth is acquired, whether by accident or by ability, it does represent social opportunity for those possessing it. This wealth may be wisely or foolishly used; it may not bring the social opportunity it inherently represents; but certain it is that *insufficient wealth*, no

[2] H. P. Fairchild, *Foundations of Social Life* (1927), p. 151.

matter how economically it is used, does represent a serious social handicap. Poverty involves a low standard of living, insufficient nourishment and clothing, improper housing conditions, and an inadequate surplus for insurance and incidentals. It makes the normally efficient life impossible, and the handicap is seen in the impairment of physical health, mental vigor, and social outlook. *The distribution of wealth is an inadequate index to inherent ability, but is a most potent determiner of social environment and of acquired ability.*

In a study of income, some years ago, the Brookings Institution found that the common explanation of economic depression as being caused by "overproduction" is largely untrue. The faulty distribution of national income is the more logical explanation. The vast proportion of the population lacks the purchasing-power to get what it wants and needs. Of the 25,205,000 families in the United States, over 6 million, or 21.5 per cent, received less than $1,000 in 1929, the last of the boom years; 12 million had income of less than $1,500; over 16 million had less than $2,000; and more than 19 million, 71 per cent of the total, had incomes of less than $2,500. Only about one family in twelve received as much as $5,000 annual income. On the other end of the scale we find that 220,000 families, approximately eight-tenths of 1 per cent, get over 20 per cent of the national income. The 36,000 families at the extreme apex of the population pyramid receive in the aggregate an amount equal to that obtained by the 12 million families with incomes of less than $1,500, or over 300 times as much per family.[3]

It is perfectly evident that $1,000 per year is an utterly inadequate amount on which to maintain a family of five and produce socially, mentally, and physically efficient citizens. It is equally evident that other families or groups of families, fortunately few in number, possess annual incomes of such huge proportions that by no stretch of the imagination can they profitably and efficiently consume their incomes. The remainder may be squandered, hoarded, or reinvested and made to multiply; or it may be doled out to a grateful public in the form of libraries, foundations, and endowments. In any case, little enough of this surplus gets back to, or alleviates the condition of, the handicapped masses.

The Health and Physical Fitness of the Nation. The span of life is, as we have seen, increasing. The mortality-rate shows an encouraging trend, and the morbidity-rate for most diseases likewise is declining. We are saving more of our infants, getting them through the perilous first

[3] *Income and Economic Progress* (New York: Public Affairs Pamphlet, No. 1, 1936).

year of life. There are fewer industrial accidents and occupational diseases. We are discovering germs and conquering plagues. Our land

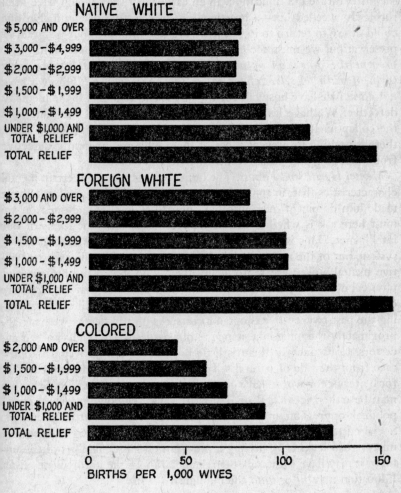

FIG. 9—BIRTH-RATES IN THE UNITED STATES, BY INCOME GROUPS: 1930

From Clyde V. Kiser, "Birth Rates and Socio-Economic Attributes in 1935," *Milbank Memorial Fund Quarterly*, April, 1939, p. 146.

s dotted with hospitals and sanitariums. Boards of health and sanitary commissions are on the job everywhere. We are safeguarding our ailing as never before. This is as it should be, but there are certain by-products of sanitation and hygiene that are worth noticing. We are not only saving life but also insuring the lives of the unfit. We are preserving them for future multiplication. In an earlier day they would have been ruthlessly weeded out—a heartless but an effective program. No one could desire to return to it, but if we are to continue in our program of preservation, we must accompany it by a program of selection. *If we prevent the operation of natural selection, we must substitute some form of artificial selection or suffer the consequences.* This we have not done. We have hospitals for the insane and schools for the mentally defective. We have institutions for the deaf and dumb, the blind, and the epileptic. If we salvage them or fit them for life in society again, there is nothing to prevent those of them who are inherently defective from marrying and passing on their hereditary defects.

Mental Health and Fitness. The human being possesses certain mental characteristics that, in spite of his comparative physical weakness, have made him dominant over all other animal beings. But the question we must here ask is whether or not we are maintaining the levels of our intelligence. This is not a question of the effectiveness of our school system, but of the rate at which different grades of intelligence and native mental ability are reproducing their kind. Since the processes of physical evolution are so slow, there is little evidence that the structure of either the body or the brain has undergone appreciable change during the past twenty-five thousand years. As human beings we have approximately the same inheritance as our earliest historically known ancestors. Consequently there is little hope for the improvement of the race from the side of natural selection. What changes there are, either for better or for worse, have come through selective breeding. Selection may be either accidental or designed. War, religious intolerance, and political oppression may strip populations of their fittest members. Social customs may work in either direction. Charity may create more misery than it relieves, placing a premium on larger families of the unfit, or it may have for its aim the rehabilitation of the unfortunate misfit. Education may *fit* or *unfit* the individual for life.

Mental tests and their widespread application in schools and to draftees for the First World War have given us the first scientific grounds for the mental classification of our population. It must be admitted that these tests are still in the experimental stage and that the tests made in the army camps were made under far from uniform conditions. Still the results are, to say the least, astounding, and we are faced with the fact that we have a far larger percentage of low-grade mentality than we had dreamed. It is difficult to estimate the amount of genius and of mental inferiority in our population. A mere enumeration of the numbers in hospitals and other institutions for the mentally handicapped gives us little or no idea of the problem, since the vast majority of our defectives are not in such institutions. Their defect is of such a nature that they are able to marry, maintain families, and engage in unskilled labor, and are allowed to vote and function as normal citizens. The ratio of actual certified insanity cared for in institutions in 1936 was 276 per 100,000 of the population, but many were privately cared for. Moreover, this does not take into account the volume of feeble-mindedness to which we pay little attention and for which we have few institutions.[4] The ratio of feeble-mindedness is variously estimated at from 2 to 5 per 1,000 of the population; but when we consider the findings of the draft examinations and the experience of schools with mental tests, we suspect that they far understate the truth.

In order better to understand the problem, let us briefly define and explain the terms we are using. In a class by itself is *insanity*, which is a legal term to define a person whose brain is diseased. Insanity may be hereditary or acquired and may be either curable or incurable. A *feeble-minded* person, on the other hand, is one who possesses a functionally dwarfed brain, one that is incompletely developed. It has been normal up to a certain stage, where further development has been arrested. Feeble-mindedness is largely an innate or hereditary quality. Some determiner of mental capacity is absent from the germ-plasm in such cases. Degrees of feeble-mindedness are measured in terms of mental age. Mental and physical age are not necessarily the same, for an individual of forty-five may have attained a mental growth of but ten. "The degree of intelligence which marks the line between the feeble-minded and the normal person has been defined as that degree below which the possessor cannot manage himself and his affairs with ordinary prudence." In terms of the mental age, this point is placed at from twelve to fourteen years. Below this point, a person is feeble-minded, and above it he is normal. The feeble-minded class is further divided into three groups. The *idiot* does not surpass the intelligence of a two-year-old child, is helpless, and needs constant physical care. The *imbecile* may attain the intelligence of a seven-year-old, and can perform simple routine tasks, but only under direction. He also needs physical care. The *moron*, the real social problem, may attain a maximum mental age of from twelve

---

[4] *Statistical Abstract of the United States, 1937*, p. 70.

to fourteen years, can take care of himself physically, and can perform so many functions that it is difficult for the average person to recognize him.

The insane person, the idiot, and the imbecile are easily recognized. Their defects are sufficiently serious to induce us to provide institutions for their care, and they are seldom a menace to heredity, since they are usually incapable of marriage and procreation.

The moron, however, can pass as normal among laymen. Like the twelve year old child, he can understand instructions and perform fairly intricate tasks. He can read and write, feed and clothe himself, can take interest and discuss the events that transpire about him, but no matter what his physical age and size, he is always a child in his power of discrimination, of self control, of planning, and of initiative. To leave him on his own resources out in the community, forced to compete with his normal fellows in industry, to live up to the standards of morals evolved from the complexities of modern civilization, when he has not the inherent qualities necessary to enable him to do so, results in the ne'er-do-well, the unemployable, the vicious, the immoral and the criminal. To study the available statistics on the subject is to realize the vital necessity of a more general recognition of the moron as a part of the feeble-minded group if the progress of civilization is to continue. *A large portion of the defective delinquents are morons.*

Let us now turn to the findings of the First World War draft, remembering that they cannot be accepted at face value, but that if we qualify them by 50 per cent, they are still astounding. The draft represented a perfectly fair cross-section of the young manhood of our nation. It included more than 1 per cent of the entire population. It drew men from every geographical section and from each social and economic stratum. It was what the statistician would call a *fair sample.* Goddard, in his *Human Efficiency and Levels of Intelligence,* has made one of the best studies of quality from the results of these tests. The following is adapted from his findings:

Three general levels of intelligence may be recognized: superior, average, and inferior. Those of superior intelligence (Grades A and B) are endowed with marked intellectuality. They have qualities of leadership and represent the *successful* college-student type. From this group came the major portion of the officers. Average intelligence (Grades C+, C, and C—) present a wide range of ability. In terms of mental age it extends from 11.5 to 16.5 years. This carries it from slightly below the border-line up to a fair degree of ability. Those of high average intelligence (C+) are capable of finishing high school, with all that that indicates with regard to their general ability. Those of low average intelligence (C—) are probably incapable of getting into high school at all and are capable only of routine work. When we realize that this general "average" group represents the mass of our population or of any population, and when we realize that it is the group which "just gets by," which is distinguished neither by marked failure nor by marked success, it somewhat dampens our hope for the great middle class. Those of inferior intelligence (Grades D and D—) were exactly what the word implies. Their mental age ranged from 11.5 years to 10 or below. This means that they were morons, were apt to be illiterate, were incapable of finishing the grades in schools, and were capable only of manual routine work. These are not the "scrubs" in the herd; they are below even that.

With this in mind, the results of the army tests may be visualized as shown in Table 17.

TABLE 17

INTELLIGENCE OF DRAFTED MEN IN THE FIRST WORLD WAR

		Percentage
A	—ssssssss	4.5
B	—sssssssssssssssss	9.0
C+	—AAAAAAAAAAAAAAAAAAAAAAAAAAAAAAA	16.5
C	—AAAAAAAAAAAAAAAAAAAAAAAAAAAAAAAAAAAAAAAAAAAAAA	25.0
C—	—AAAAAAAAAAAAAAAAAAAAAAAAAAAAAAAAAAAAAAA	20.0
D	—IIIIIIIIIIIIIIIIIIIIIIIIIIIIIIIIIIIII	15.0
D—	—IIIIIIIIIIIIIIIIIIIIIIIII	10.0

s = Superior.
A = Average.
I = Inferior.

From this we may gather that 13.5 per cent were of superior intelligence; 61.5 per cent, average; and 25 per cent, inferior. This is a serious showing, but the results have not received wide credence for the simple reason that they have been considered too astounding to be true. Be that as it may, they are a testimony to the fact that our social population is cumbered with a vast load of low-grade intelligence. This condition is complicated by the fact that the lower the grade of intelligence, the weaker the inhibitions, the earlier the age at marriage, and the larger the number of children born. A class of this sort is a special danger because there is always a tendency for them to outbreed the average and superior elements.

The criticism has often been made, and with justice, that our present mental tests do not actually isolate and measure innate ability: that they are vitiated by a certain amount of environmental influence which cannot as yet be excluded. Whether or not this is true, they do measure ability (either inherent or acquired) and as such and for our purposes are a valuable index of quality.

A further index to ability or quality is found in the occupations in which the males of our population are engaged. Obviously not all unskilled workmen are such because of intellectual inferiority. They may find themselves in that position because of adverse social conditions and inadequate social opportunity to develop. Likewise, not all professional men and successes in trade and industry are such because of exceptional ability. Accidents of environment may have made them what they are. Nevertheless, in a country of such general equality of opportunity as the United States, we may expect the type of work a man does to represent somewhat his ability. With this in mind, compare the numbers of our unskilled laborers who are working by the day at routine manual tasks with the numbers of our professional men engaging in professions that require a high degree of training, skill, initiative, self-direction, and individual responsibility.

Compare also the size of incomes, which, while an imperfect indication, is suggestive; and consider the populations of our slums and tenements. The numbers of our population who are inadequately nourished, clothed, housed, and paid may be an inadequate index to inherent quality, but it is a good index to acquired or developed status.

Social Health and Fitness. How shall we measure our social health or the degree to which our citizens have been adequately prepared for citizenship—the degree to which they are socialized and are efficiently functioning parts of the social whole? Or, conversely, how many of them are parasites, refusing to coöperate, to earn an honest living, to abide by the social standards of the group and, in a word, to play the game according to its rules? For an answer visit our courts, prisons, reformatories, and workhouses. Go to our probation officers and to our hospitals filled with drug-addicts and the venereally diseased. We shall be tempted to conclude that large numbers of our population are making a *land of liberty* a *land of license*. It is generally agreed that "the United States is the most criminal country in the world." The city of Chicago alone has to its discredit each year more murders than the British Isles together. It has been recently estimated that the cost of crime in the United States runs to the amazing figure of $15,000,000,000 annually. This amounts to nearly $115 per capita. "At all times about 200,000 persons in the United States are under lock and key. But these 200,000 represent less than one-fifth of the active criminal population—

men, women and children who are definitely anti-social and certain to be charges of the state for some part of their lives." [5]

The problem of the quality of the social population is, of course,, much wider than can be indicated here. The evidences or indexes are much more numerous, but this will be sufficient to call attention to the important fact that the quality of the individuals we are producing, either by physical heredity or by social environment, is of even greater importance than their numbers.

II. The Problem of Insuring Quality

We have noticed the various programs for the insuring of an abounding quantity of population. Usually they have to do merely with mores and with the social frame of mind. Seldom, however, have definite programs been successful. The Roman Catholic Church stands opposed to any voluntary curtailment of the birth-rate; yet it is not evident that the fecundity of Catholics of the same economic class shows a markedly different trend from that of Protestants. The Italian dictator, Mussolini, threatened the alternative of larger families or certain penalties. It has not appeared that the penalties, as such, were effective. Populations are, on the other hand, remarkably sensitive, and react subconsciously, to social and economic situations. The age at marriage, the volume of marriage, and the average number of children per family reflect the social and economic outlook and the standard of living toward which the group is striving. If the sanctions of the Catholic Church were effective, then we might expect it to be made up of consistently large families, but such does not seem to be generally the case. In the matter of reproduction people will not obey orders, but they do respond with alacrity to indirect social stimuli. Fecundity is controlled not so much through reason and legislation as through the emotions. There are few examples of definite programs directed toward limitation of the size of the population. The Spartans exposed defective children, but not to limit the size of the population; certain Oriental nations practice infanticide, but not as a social policy; abortion and contraception are fairly common the world over; and Americans have cut down on accretions through immigration. But, with the exception of our strin-

[5] The United States Bureau of Census report, *Prisoners in State and Federal Prisons and Reformatories, 1935,* indicates that on January 1, 1935, there were 138,316 prisoners in the State and federal prisons. Over 30,000 more were in juvenile correctional institutions. Certainly, these figures do not represent more than one fourth the number now under lock and key in our county jails and city lock-ups. Therefore, 600,000 would come closer to the number locked out of society.

gent immigration laws, which do not have to do with reproduction, these practices are, at the present at least, purely individual affairs and unconnected with any general program or practice.

It seems evident, then, that human reproductivity defies *definite* social control. We are dealing with one of the most complex of emotional reactions, both on the part of the individual and on the part of society. A multitude of factors are in force that may operate either to increase or to decrease the rates of birth. All the statesman can do is to keep his finger on the social pulse, *keep society informed as to its condition*, and let nature take its course. He can modify conditions here and there, but he cannot produce direct and sweeping changes. He can tax bachelors or he can spread propaganda of imminent economic prosperity—and the latter course will be far more effective than the former. *The size of the population is the direct result of the reaction of people to their social and economic environment. It is affected by the level and the trend of the standard of living. It is influenced by social opportunity, intelligence, and the breadth of the social horizon.* The best we can do, in attaining the desired optimum numbers, is to keep the people intelligently informed, and to take such intermediate steps as will indirectly produce the desired results.

THE INSURANCE OF QUALITY

The problem of insuring the quality of the social population is one that allows more direct treatment. We cannot control the reproduction trends of a people, but we can direct their choice of mates and prevent breeding from obviously defective stocks. Thus far we have made many and varied attempts to control quantity and have done little about the control of quality.

Who Are the Inferior? Before we can tackle the problem of improving the breed we must know who are the inferior. This is no task for the tyro. It must not be left to the reformer or to the statesman. It is a question for the biologist and the psychologist to answer; and when they feel reasonably sure that they know, the sociologist can begin to build a program. We know that there is a vast amount of inferiority, but we do not know how much of it is due to environment and how much to heredity. Hence, we do not know whether to tackle it from the standpoint of euthenics or of eugenics. We visit our slums and stagnant villages and wonder why these people are there. Have they been produced by their environment or have they themselves produced it?

We note all too frequently a certain type of laborer at work. He, like the horse, has his physical strength to market. We talk with him and note the dullness of his face, his lack of any specific training, and the emptiness of his mind. And why? Is he inherently inferior, or has he suffered from the effects of an underprivileged environment? We visit our schools and note that the children have been sorted out according to their mental ability and assigned to special classes. One class is for the slow ones, and special teachers are provided who excel in their ability to deal with them. Another class is for the exceptionally bright students, who have been thus placed by themselves in order that they may advance as rapidly as their superior ability permits. But why the difference? Why has one group a higher intelligence quotient (I. Q.) than the other? Is it innate, or is it merely because the inferior students came from inferior environments? We may go to our prisons, workhouses, reformatories, hospitals, asylums, schools for the feeble-minded, and other institutions for the socially or physically defective; here we certainly can find a congestion of the inferior. If we go to the judge, to the juvenile court, to the charity organization society and the social worker, we shall find among their charges many of low intelligence who, nevertheless, are still a part of the body politic.

The unfit, then, are those people who have been so handicapped by either heredity or environment that they are not normally efficient members of society. They are the ones who are unable to stand the strain of normal competition, social and economic, with their fellows. They are our failures even though not all of them are in prisons, hospitals, asylums, poorhouses, or other public and charitable institutions. The vast majority of them are society's marginal hangers-on. We tolerate them, allow them to do our dirty work, scorn them, pity them sometimes, but in the main take them for granted and allow them to go their way, marry, and perpetuate their kind.

There are two possible root causes of their inferiority, heredity and environment, and two possible points of approach to the solution of the problem, eugenics and euthenics. The sociologist is not concerned with *determining* which it is; that is a problem of another science. He merely wants to know which in order that he may direct the attack.

The Euthenic Program. The euthenic program has for its object *the provision of such an environment that each individual will have the opportunity of developing up to the limit of his latent powers.* To do anything else is social waste and economic folly. Therefore, even though we are not making the best of the heredity that we have, what can we do to improve the environment and at least bring every individual and class up to the limit of his or its potential ability?

In the first place, we may take for granted that in a country as resourceful as our own, and one in which great fortunes are so numerous, *there is no possible reason why any normally efficient man should earn less than a normal subsistence wage.* If his work is worth anything at all to society, it is worth enough to make it possible for him to maintain himself and his family at the minimum standard of efficiency and decency at least. We know what kinds of food, and how much, he and his family should have, what housing conditions, what clothing, and what insurance and incidentals. It is easy to estimate the minimum for social and physical efficiency. When so many are maintaining standards far in excess of this level, even to the point where their consumption habits are detrimental to their physical and social health, why should there be any excuse for poverty except among the physically unfit? This, of course, is primarily a problem of the distribution of social wealth, but it results in the serious handicapping of many otherwise normally endowed families and individuals.[6]

Second, *those who are so handicapped or inefficient that their labor is not worth a day's full pay certainly should be the wards of the State.* At present we provide "homes," asylums, hospitals, and poorhouses for the hopelessly defective and dependent. This is as it should be. Society should not tolerate idleness or too low pay for the normally efficient, and it should assume the burden of responsibility for the demonstrably unfit, whom it has either allowed to be born such or has produced in the unfavorable environments that it maintains. We have too large a volume of unskilled labor that is unskilled simply because of the lack of training. We have many others who can do unskilled manual labor but can never be normally efficient workers because of some inherent deficiency. These prey upon society, keep our slums going, and furnish an undue proportion of the next generation. It would be cheaper in the long run for society to assume the burden of responsibility for these. Society should not, of course, keep them in idleness, but should assure them a decent minimum standard of living in return for whatever work they are able to do. It will be possible for society to limit the reproduction of the classes thus segregated.

Third, *continue the present program of improving the social environment.* Slums pay dividends only to the owners of tenements and cost

[6] *Your Income and Mine* (New York: Public Affairs Pamphlet, No. 20, 1938).

society huge sums. Playgrounds, recreation centers, and directors cost money, but they cost far less than alley gangs and their products. Clean streets, sanitary precautions, breathing-spaces, fresh air, and sunlight are more necessary for the poor, who have not the means to live in restricted areas, than for the rich. Education should be for life and should be adapted to the needs of the individual and his probable future. Latin grammar is fine for the boy who has prospects of entering Harvard, but of little use to the boy who can look forward only to learning a trade and becoming an efficient, skilled workman. We should not tolerate a condition that allows any normal boy to leave our school system till he is definitely fitted to earning a living. Girls may be prepared to earn their living too, but it is even more important that they be taught to be home-makers. If the native ability of an individual is so low that he cannot profit by such an educational opportunity, he should undoubtedly become a ward of the State.

It may be objected that it is useless to provide conveniences and comforts for many of the poor, since they do not want them and do not know how to use them. They clutter up the fire-escapes of their tenements in spite of the fact that their own safety demands access to them. We are told of cases where porcelain bathtubs have been used for the storage of fuel. The conclusion is that it is useless to try to improve their condition, that we might as well leave them as they are in their dark, crowded, and unsanitary quarters. We can answer that so long as we do leave them there they will never learn the better way. People who have spent the major portion of a lifetime in such quarters and under such conditions have become inured to the handicaps of their environment and will not easily change. But their children need not continue the life. They can be reached and changed. Through the children the lives of the parents can also be modified. We shall never attain the goal in either city or country by adopting the *laissez-faire* policy.

The Eugenic Problem. The logic of the euthenic program is self-evident. That of the eugenic program is still under fire. While the majority of our biologists are convinced of the existence of hereditary inequalities and of the hereditary character of many types of inferiority, there are those who refuse to recognize anything but the environmental factor in the production of differences between individuals. The latest theory from Europe is that latent genius is present in every man, and that it merely remains for society to discover and develop the latent power. Certain it is that much potential genius is allowed not only to lie fallow and undeveloped, but to be smothered out as well. If this be true, well and good. Our duty is to press the euthenic program to its logical conclusion. But whether it be true or not, the purpose of the euthenic program is to make the best of the material in hand. If it be false, then we may use the eugenic program for the purpose of improving the material itself. The sociologist is inclined to the belief that the biologist knows what he is talking about and is disposed to canvass the field and see what can be done about the improvement of the human breed. But, we are reminded, human beings cannot be bred like cattle. We are human beings, God's handiwork, the climax of creation. You cannot breed human beings for intelligence and physical superiority as you can breed Jersey cows for milk or Leghorn hens for eggs. This is true. The home cannot be supervised as the barnyard is. Further, society does not want the standardization for which the plant-breeders and animal-breeders strive. It might be possible to breed human beings for specific physical and mental qualities, but a standardized race would hold out a most uninteresting prospect.

In the eugenic program we are interested for the present only in the process of breeding out the unfit—of getting rid of the scrubs in the human stock. If we can do this in the course of a century, we shall have done well. This one problem is sufficient to command all of our attention and ingenuity. We do not know definitely as yet who the inherently unfit are, but as they are designated to us by the expert, there are certain things that can be done.

THE DEVELOPMENT OF INTELLIGENCE AND SOCIAL CONSCIENCE

The first step in the development of intelligence and social conscience has nothing to do with sanction and legal enactment; it is what Ross so aptly calls "falling in love intelligently." Romantic love is thought of as the flower of our civilization. We stand aghast at the very idea that Oriental parents choose mates for their sons and daughters, but we could do very well in the Occident with a larger measure of more mature parental control in this all-important matter. Of course this implies that the parents will also be intelligently motivated and make their choice on the basis of physical, mental, and social quality rather than on that of social prestige and money. So long as we bless marriages and approve unions on the ground that two immature persons of opposite sex are in a condition of emotional instability and are *madly in love* (with each other or *with love*), marriage will continue to be a gamble. At present the purpose of marriage seems to be the honeymoon. Young people are left to discover later that it implies a home, a family, and a lifetime of fairly unromantic living together. It is a sharing of sorrows as well as of joys; of responsibilities as well as of privileges. Its real importance lies not so much in the comfort and happiness of the contracting parties as in their success in rearing and training the children of the next generation—those who are to take their places, pass on their heredity, perpetuate their cultural heritage, and bring into the world the following generation. In many groups to-day it is still considered scarcely decent for young people to recognize frankly the fact that parenthood is in store for them. It is a dead secret, and even their parents must broach the subject to them only indirectly and under a veil.

Of course it will be impossible ever to rationalize marriage completely. "Marriage must be mainly a matter of the emotions; but it is important that the emotions be exerted in the right direction. The eugenist seeks to remove the obstacles that are now driving the emotions in wrong channels. If the emotions can only be headed in the right direction, then the more emotions the better, for they are the source of energy which is responsible for almost everything that is done in the world." It is not necessary to allow the emotions to run wild even in the matter of mating and marriage. There is no reason why the choice of a husband or a wife should not lend itself to as careful and intelligent consideration as the selection of a profession.

Thus our first problem is that of intelligently motivating marriage and mating. This must be accomplished in the main through popular education, though we may turn to legislation for the prevention of certain unquestionably undesirable types of union. There are many agencies that can be used for the purpose of creating popular sentiment on the subject: preaching, teaching, writing, lecturing; drama, art, literature. One difficulty has been that so few of our writers, teachers, and preachers were themselves sufficiently well informed on the subject. The process is slow, but public sentiment is already changing.

Ross sums up the fruits of the application of this social intelligence on the part of the individual and the family somewhat as follows: There will be greater attention to family history and the better keeping of family records when the contracting parties, represented by contracting families, realize that it is a new line of heredity which is being sanctioned rather than a mere honeymoon. There will be, and should be, a tendency to coöperate with the Eugenics Record Office in its effort to lay the foundations for a sound knowledge of American heredity. There will be more inquiry by parents into the state of health and family history of wooers and less concern over financial prospects. The

romantic ideal of marriage will be modified by bringing into consideration by both parties the question of the heredity of their prospective
children. A new social conscience will be developed with regard to the
knowledge of the possession of probable heredity defects. The conscious possessor of such defective germ-plasm will be as severely cen-
sured by public opinion as the transmitter of a vile disease who nevertheless marries and subjects his innocent mate to contamination. Normal
people possessing such defects will refrain from marriage; or, frankly
facing the issue, the contracting parties will agree to refrain from having children. Near kin, knowing the situation, will feel under the obligation of giving evidence.

It is most important to note that *obvious* defects present in the so-
matoplasm will take care of themselves. A person whose handicap lies
on the surface and exposed to view has less chance of winning a mate
than has a person of normal structure. The hereditary defect, however,
is often masked. A seemingly normal person may be the carrier of defects that will crop up only in a future generation. For this reason it is
imperative that the new social conscience be encouraged and developed.

But, it may be asked, will not this attempt to rationalize marriage
strike the death-blow to our cherished institution, the home? Is not the
home, as at present based on romantic love, the outstanding feature of
Western civilization? The answer is that the foundations of the home
seem to be less secure in Western than in Eastern civilization at the
present moment. Our divorce record in America, where individual
choice is allowed the greatest scope and where romantic love has the
greatest freedom, beats the world. Our home has become a filling-station
and a parking-place. It no longer plays the rôle it once did or that it
plays at present in the Eastern world. Furthermore, from personal observation and intimate knowledge, the writer does not find the freedom
of individual choice and unlimited romantic love result in happier families in the West than a very different system does in the East. In one
case, one falls in love *before* marriage, and in the other case, *after* marriage—and the latter system actually works! It is likely that we have
gone to an extreme from which there must be a retreat. Undoubtedly
the Orient, representing the opposite extreme, will also have to modify
its course. There can be as little advantage in too little premarital acquaintance and familiarity as in too much; in having all the "say" as in
having no "say" at all. A Chinese told the writer one day that he was
about to be married. He was forty years old and this was to be his
fourth wife. The writer treated the matter lightly, asking him where

he had met her, if she was young and handsome, and the like. Though he was the writer's servant, the Chinese drew himself up in all his Oriental dignity and asserted that he was "not that sort of a man," that he had "never seen her." Still, they are very happy together and as much in love as any Occidental might wish or expect a man and his fourth wife to be. Every culture group defends its own institutions and fails to see how any other *modus operandi* can work. The family is an old institution and has been variously controlled and operated. There is no reason why our own method of mating should not undergo modification in favor of a bit less fervent emotional heat and a bit more cool-headed sanity.

THE DEVELOPMENT OF A PROGRAM BY THE STATE

The trouble we now face is that the program outlined above is ineffective in cases of antisocial individuals and individuals who are so defective as to be incapable of appreciating their social responsibility in this delicate matter. Morons are not sensitive to social sanctions and are inherently lacking in the possession of normal inhibitions. Their sex urge is feebly controlled. Society will have to be safeguarded against individuals such as these, and normal individuals deserve such assistance as the State can give.

1. Let the State study the quality of its members with as much care as it does that of horses on farms, and devote as much attention to this study as to the study of commerce and industry. The census operations of the Government bid fair to increase in the future rather than to decrease. This is a matter in which the State should be vitally interested. At present it records births and deaths, enumerates and classifies the population, notes occupation and physical condition, but stops short of those analyses and that information which are of vital importance to any eugenic, or even euthenic, program. At present we have a privately endowed Eugenics Record Office and laboratory at Cold Spring Harbor on Long Island. It is attempting as best it can and quite without official backing to collect family histories and other eugenic records.[7] This should, and in time will, be a function of the State, one of its most important functions. Perhaps then we shall know as much about our human stocks and their pedigrees and transmissible traits as we now do about our cattle and sheep.

[7] The Human Betterment Foundation, Pasadena, California, is also making an important contribution with its educational program, promoting a better understanding of the nature and significance of sterilization of the unfit. California had sterilized 15,220 insane and feebleminded wards of the State up to the end of 1941.

2. Let us have a thorough and efficient physical and mental examination of every child. This can best be done in connection with the school, through which every child is expected to pass. Through such inspection, remediable deficiencies can be discovered and dealt with. Through it inherent deficiencies will be spotted. Such inspection should be official in nature and applicable to all, irrespective of social position or rank, and careful records should be kept.

3. All persons of definite hereditary taint, whether it be feeblemindedness, epilepsy, or physical deformity, should be registered. License to wed may quite properly be withheld from certain classes of inherent defectives such, for instance, as morons.

4. Let us have adequate provision for the care and supervision of the defective. This would include special classes for defectives within the school system so that they can develop to their greatest efficiency. It would involve the custodial care of many more than are now the wards of the State, together with the building and manning of many additional institutions for their care, and, where necessary, their segregation. It might well include the establishment of industrial or agricultural colonies where many of the less seriously handicapped could live a life as close as possible to the normal and partially support themselves.

5. Let us have sterilization in exceptional and undisputed cases for the present, and let it be more widely practiced when we know more about heredity. At present twenty-nine States have sterilization laws aimed at the insane and the feeble-minded. In the past these laws have not only been remarkably inoperative, but have been also aimed in the main at insanity, which is of minor importance in comparison with the feeble-mindedness that has been allowed to breed on unheeded. A beginning has been made, however, and California stands at the head of the list with a record by 1941 of more than fifteen thousand sterilizations of feeble-minded individuals.

It should be added that modern scientific sterilization requires but a very minor operation in the case of the male. For the female it is more difficult, but not serious. It does not incapacitate for either physical or mental efficiency. Marriage and the normal marriage relation are possible; but such unions are sterile. In many cases it would be cruel and inhuman to doom adults, sexually mature but mentally twelve years old, to sex segregation in institutions or on farms where they would spend the reproductive years of their lives in isolation from the opposite sex. Provided they are sterilized, society can allow them to mate and live as family pairs without danger of their perpetuating their defect.

But such a program would cost money! Yes, it might easily cost a billion, but what of the saving? Society spends that much and more every year in charity for its ineffectives; in operating the courts, the major portion of the work of which is caused by them; and in the losses to society through their economic inefficiency. We would not tolerate an out-of-date machine in a factory if its upkeep cost more than its product was worth. That sort of waste we can understand. The perpetuation and even encouragement of inefficient human machines is a very similar matter, but more difficult to grasp.

It will be noticed that this program makes no attempt to breed for a specific type; it does not invade the sanctity of the home, nor does it attempt to dictate the selection of mates. It merely attempts the isolation of the inherently unfit. It is a process of breeding the unfit *out* of society rather than one of selecting certain desirable traits and breeding only from them. If we do this in the next century, we shall have accomplished more than is at present in sight. The problem of *breeding out* is ours; that of *breeding up* may well be left to another generation.

REFERENCES

Annals of the American Academy of Political and Social Science, "Postwar Progress in Child Welfare" (September, 1930).

DAVIES, S. P., *Social Control of the Mentally Deficient* (New York, 1930).

ELLIS, Havelock, *A Study of British Genius* (London, 1927).

ELLIOTT, M. A., and MERRILL, F. E., *Social Disorganization* (New York, 1941), Chs. XIX, XX.

FURNAS, C. C., *The Next Hundred Years* (New York, 1936).

GILLIN, J. L., *Poverty and Dependency* (New York, 1937, 3rd Edition), Chs. XIX, XX, XXI.

GUYER, M. F., *Being Well-Born* (New York, 1927).

MENDERHAUSEN, Horst, *The Economics of War* (New York, 1940), Ch. 12.

MILLSPAUGH, A. C., *Public Welfare Organization* (Washington, D. C.: Brookings Institution, 1935), pp. 252–276.

NORTH, C. C., *Social Differentiation* (Chapel Hill, 1926).

POPENOE, P. B., and JOHNSON, R. H., *Applied Eugenics* (New York, 1926).

"Urban Housing Conditions in the United States," *Labor Information Bulletin* (Washington, D. C.: United States Department of Labor, June, 1938).

WIGGAM, Albert E., *The Fruit of the Family Tree* (Indianapolis, 1924).

QUESTIONS AND EXERCISES

1. What is the relation of heredity, environment, and personal choice in the making of social adjustments by the individual? In this day of complex living and of increasing demands for dexterity rather than physical

strength, would you say that the environmental factors are making larger or smaller demands upon eugenic selection? Explain your answer.

2. Is the self-made man necessarily superior? Why, or why not?

3. How would you detect what have been called the "over-privileged, white-collar misfits"? What policy would you pursue relative to their training and propagation?

4. "It is well known that only a small part of the feeble-minded in the United States are in institutions established for their care." Explain the significance of this statement, both in terms of population quality and of *optimum numbers*.

5. Which is the better method of dealing with serious hereditary defects, *segregation* or *sterilization*? Why?

6. Outline the major points of a program for the creating in youth of a sense of the social significance of marriage. Is marriage and parenthood an "inherent and inalienable" right of the individual, regardless of physical and mental fitness?

7. How do you account for the widespread opposition to birth control?

8. Is a more liberal attitude regarding birth control socially desirable? If so, how should the dissemination of information as to technique be controlled and administered? If you believe it socially undesirable, give your reasons for objection.

9. Former President Hoover is quoted as saying, "If we could have one generation of properly born, educated, and healthy children, a thousand other problems of government would vanish—." Evaluate this statement.

10. What facts are needed if we are to be sure that slum clearance and programs for improved housing for the working population will not result in merely transferring the slums from one place to another? Is there such a thing as a "slum stock"?

11. List the objectives of a sound euthenic program.

12. List the objectives of a sound eugenic program.

13. Discuss the relative feasibility of eugenic and euthenic programs in the light of current social thought.

Chapter 10

PRIMARY SOCIAL PROBLEMS OF INDUSTRY

In an earlier chapter we called attention to the vast social changes that are rapidly taking place in our industrial society.[1] We noted how the Industrial Revolution—still going on with increasing momentum—has made *capital* the dominant factor in our economic relations and has widened the gap between the employer and the employee. We noted how the close personal relations that once existed between manufacturer and worker have given way to the *impersonal*—placing the laborer in much the same category as the machine, a commodity to be bought and sold in the market at a price determined by the economic law of supply and demand. We noted how the old concepts of "equal opportunity" and "freedom of contract" are being revised in terms of *group action* and *public regulation*, which are becoming more and more prevalent. With these facts in mind, we may now turn our attention to some of the major social hazards that grow out of this revolutionized industrial life.

CONFLICT BETWEEN CAPITAL AND LABOR

The most alarming and perhaps the most evident social hazard of modern industrial life is to be seen in the bitter and wasteful conflict being waged between capital and labor. On the one hand, we see many employers—the owners of industries, mines, railways, and business enterprises—combining into associations, mergers, and holding-companies to effect a greater efficiency of management, to control prices, and to facilitate their struggle to keep the upper hand on the labor market. On the other hand, we see organized labor growing in strength; extending its fields to include every type of worker; becoming more and more class-conscious; getting better educated, better disciplined, better equipped financially, better able to bargain with the employers—in recent years even under the protective arm of the Federal Government.

We cannot here consider in detail the tactics used by the opposing sides in the struggle over the *right to organize* and the question of *recogni-*

[1] Chapter 2.

tion of the union. It must be admitted, however, that these two issues form the pivotal centers of present-day industrial conflict. These are the issues upon which the success or failure of the other issues largely depends, since the individual worker is no match for the corporation-employer in bargaining about terms of employment. It is a mistake, moreover, to think that the struggle has been terminated by the activities of the Government in recent years with reference to labor organization. It is true that since 1933 Congress has passed a number of far-reaching laws, which we shall discuss presently, that greatly facilitated the organization of unions. But the assistance was *only* facilitation: basically, it simply reduced some of the traditional legal barriers to unionism and provided the machinery for establishing recognition of a union as the bargaining agent for the employees of a given plant. There was nothing in the law that made labor organization, or its recognition, mandatory; and in 1942 at least two-thirds of the wage-earners still were unorganized.

TABLE 18

NATIONAL UNION MEMBERSHIP, 1940, BY UNION TYPES *

Type of Union	Total	A. F. of L.	C. I. O.	Independent
Total	8,641,800	4,374,700	3,624,000	643,100
Craft	718,300	467,200	—	251,100
Amalgamated craft	3,918,400	3,110,400	436,000	372,000
Industrial	3,545,100	547,100	2,978,000	20,000
Locals directly affiliated with national	460,000	250,000	210,000	—

* Computed from Table 29, pp. 351–357, of C. R. Daugherty's *Labor Problems in American Industry* (Houghton Mifflin Company, 1941, 5th Edition).

Behind the growth of industrial conflict lie the uncertainties and discontent that grow out of the great industrial changes: the increasing trend toward the introduction of elaborate automatic machines, which displace every year tens of thousands of laborers; the increasing value of this capital, which every year commands a larger voice in the shaping of industrial policies; the centralization of opportunity for employment and livelihood into the hands of fewer and fewer men who control the large corporation wealth; the disappearance in fact, if not in theory, of the guaranteed rights of "equality of opportunity" and "freedom of contract." The struggle, therefore, at bottom, is a struggle to gain control over industry—a struggle for a job, for *property rights* on the job, for security of the job (comparable to the security of investments), for a larger share in the wealth produced by the job.[2]

The individual worker—union and non-union alike—seeks (1) to secure a wage that will provide for himself and his family "a decent standard of living"—a standard that is by no means stationary, but ever advancing and expanding; (2) to secure improved working conditions that will give him protection against uncertainties of employment; (3) to secure a shorter working day to enable him to enjoy a larger measure of the fruits of his labor and to liberate him from the mechanical drive and speed increasingly set by machine industry; (4) to secure protection from the health hazards; and (5) to provide for old age.

The position of the *public* in regard to these issues in labor disputes is a shifting one. The traditional attitude was one of hands-off and of leaving such matters to "private initiative" and "rugged individualism." But a decade of severe economic distress prior to the Second World War forced the American public to do some rethinking. As we become better acquainted with the actualities of the interdependence of all the various groups in our economic life, we see that these aims of the worker are not only reasonable but more and more necessary to the economic stability and general prosperity of the entire population. Wholly aside from the humanitarian considerations and social justice, and looking at the wage-earners merely as consumers of the products of our farms and factories, we are forced to the conclusion that low wages, long hours, irregularity and uncertainty of employment, hazardous working conditions, and inadequate provisions for retirement not only destroy the workers' prospects for a decent standard of living, but jeopardize the economic security of the whole nation. Not long ago the success of a business or industry was measured almost solely by the *profits* it paid to the investor. To-day the measure of success is rapidly shifting from profits to *wages and working conditions*. Profits are not as effective as wages in distributing purchasing power. The raising of the American standard of living depends more upon wages and working conditions than upon the payment of big profits. As a pioneer nation, our problem was one of *production*; as a matured nation, our problem now is one of *distribution*. It is safe to conclude, therefore, that the public is to-day more interested in the basic aims of the labor movement than it has been at any time during the more than fifty years of modern unionism.

[2] William H. Kiekhofer, *Economic Principles, Problems, and Policies* (New York, 1941), p. 14 ff.

Labor relations to-day are vastly different from what they were in the last quarter of the nineteenth century, when modern unions were getting a foot-hold in American industries. Indeed, the relative position of the opposing sides to-day is quite unlike what it was in the 1920's. Prior to the passing of the National Industrial Recovery Act in 1933, labor unions were in a relatively weak position. Three major conditions combined to put them at a disadvantage: (1) organized employers were in a stronger position legally and had used various devices such as company unions, blacklists, labor spies, subtle anti-union propaganda, and even physical violence against union organizers, to keep the control of the labor market in their own hands; (2) union leadership was weak and in many instances corrupt and racketeering (still an ever-present danger); it was often content to raise wages at the expense of unorganized workers and consumers; it was dominated by craft unions, though technical change had rendered craft unionism obsolete in many major fields; (3) the depression further weakened the unions when unemployment made it impossible to keep up the payment of membership dues or to keep up morale. By 1933, union membership had dropped to almost the 1914 level, i.e., about three million members.

Many important changes occurred in United States labor relations, beginning in 1933. Most significant, undoubtedly, was the shift in the attitude taken by the government agencies, resulting from the change in administration and the introduction of the "New Deal" program. This was an especially significant situation, since prior to that time the Government had entered into the field of labor relations only piecemeal and exercised its authority spasmodically. Moreover, the legal tradition was largely opposed to any sort of labor organization, even though it long had been plain that unionism was necessary to any sort of equality in bargaining power between employers and workers. For at least a century the common law had been invoked to stifle organization of workers on the ground of "conspiracy"; and it had been given added force by the application of the Sherman Act of 1890 to proscribe unions on the basis of their being "in restraint of trade." Even the Clayton Act of 1914 had proved of little value in liberating labor from that restriction. By 1933, then, the time was ripe for a revision of our policies in regard to industrial conflict. Unemployment was widespread; the unions were obviously fighting a losing battle; employers themselves—both individually and as a group—were quite incapable of dealing effectively with the steadily mounting spiral of depression; and the public grew ever more fearful of the consequences of continued economic hardship and insecurity. So it was that despite the conservative tradition of governmental policy with regard to industrial relations, an almost completely new approach was undertaken by the administration which was swept into office with an impressive mandate by the voters to take positive action.

The first important innovation in the development of the new governmental policies came with the National Industrial Recovery Act of June, 1933. This Act aimed at improving standards of competition and other business relations by formulating codes of fair business practices to which business and industry were expected to conform. It also included the highly significant and well-known "7A clause," pertaining specifically to labor and providing, substantially, that:

(1) . . . employees shall have the right to organize and bargain collectively through representatives of their own choosing, and shall be free from the interference, restraint, or coercion of employers of labor, or their agents, in the designation of such representatives or in self organization or in other concerted activities for the purpose of collective bargaining or other mutual aid or protection;

(2) . . . no employee and no one seeking employment shall be required as a condition of employment to join any company union or to refrain from joining, organizing, or assisting a labor organization of his own choosing.

These provisions were opposed bitterly by many employers, with a result that strikes became rampant as workers attempted to force the code authorities to live up to the spirit of the clause rather than merely to the letter. The President then appointed the National Labor Board, which was to deal independently with that portion of the Act. The company unions, which in many cases were established by the employers just prior to the National Industrial Recovery Act, were tacitly approved in some instances, and the matter was one of a number of points of friction that grew up between the Code Authorities and the Board. The Board, on its part, took a liberal view in interpreting the Act; and, so far as it had the power to do so, the Board insisted on free elections among the workers, absence of counter-measures against union members or union organizations, and complete acknowledgment of the authority of the union as the bargaining agent of the workers. The Board, however, had no clearly defined legal status or authority, so that the Code Authorities and recalcitrant employers alike disregarded its findings and "orders." Although the Board later was reorganized in an attempt to remedy these shortcomings, the labor sections of the National Industrial Recovery Act still remained chaotic in their status when the whole Act was declared unconstitutional by the United States Supreme Court in May, 1935. Nevertheless, the problems encountered and the policies adopted in this period were of inestimable service in the formulation of the provisions of the National Labor Relations Act of 1935.

The *National Labor Relations Act* (often called the "Wagner Act") provides that the employees of an establishment may select, by means of a majority vote in a "fair election," the group to represent their interests in bargaining with the employer. The National Labor Relations Board, created by the Act, has the power to set up the machinery for the enforcement of the Act in all industries and businesses affected by interstate commerce—except the railways, which are served by an agency of their own, the National Mediation Board. The National Labor Relations Board has the power to hold elections of employees or to determine in some other satisfactory manner whether any labor organization has a majority. It also has the power to determine the appropriate bargaining unit—whether it should be the whole plant, the company, a craft, or a subdivision. In addition, the Board rules upon complaints of "unfair labor practices" which the law specifically forbids. Among these provisions are the following: (1) employers shall not refuse to bargain collectively with the authorized representatives of their employees; (2) employers are forbidden "to interfere with, restrain, or coerce employees" in the application of their right to bargain collectively; (3) employers may not encourage or discourage membership in any organization by "discrimination in regard to hire or tenure of employment or any term or condition of employment"; (4) employers are not "to dominate or interfere with the formation of any labor organization or to contribute financial or other support to it"; and (5) employers are not allowed "to discharge or otherwise discriminate against an employee because he has filed charges or given testimony under the Act."

The agents of the Board act in the capacity of both prosecutor and judge and may appoint the necessary legal assistance to take and present the evidence against employers. The Board selects trial examiners to hear the evidence and charges presented by both sides, and *full consideration must be given to the evidence and complaints presented by both sides*. This *complete* hearing is then reviewed by the Board before it issues its decision. The Board may dismiss a case or issue an order to the offending employer or union requiring compliance with the Act. When the Board finds that the employer's actions have caused losses to the worker, it may require him to make good those losses. Thus it may require the reinstatement of discharged employees, either with or without pay for the lost time.

When an employer refuses to comply with its orders, the Board may appeal to the United States circuit court for an enforcing order. Similarly, the employer has a right to appeal to the appropriate federal court for an injunction against the Board's order, if he feels that the Board has not been fair. The court reviews the Board's findings, and if they are supported by the evidence, it issues a court order demanding compliance with the order of the Board. Violation of the court's orders are punishable under contempt-of-court proceedings.

Although the National Labor Relations Act specifically states that nothing in it shall be construed as limiting in any way the right of workers to strike, it was believed that the law paved the way for an *orderly* approach to the settlement of such disputes as might arise between employers and workers, and that enforcement of the law would make strikes unnecessary. Unfortunately, this expectation has not been realized; and there are many persons who feel that the application of the Act has been greatly impaired by the hundreds of strikes that have occurred since its inception. Nevertheless, although the situation was made much more difficult by internal schism within the ranks of organized labor (the struggle between the American Federation of Labor and the Congress of Industrial Organizations), a period of adjustment was inevitable; and the later reports of the Board show an encouraging trend in its ability to deal effectively with industrial conflict.

The National Labor Relations Act, and more especially the Board, have been assailed bitterly by both wings of organized labor, by employers' associations, by various associations of lawyers, and by much of the press. It is to be expected that any effective agency attempting to settle labor disputes would be subjected to plenty of abuse. The very fact that the Board has been attacked from all sides suggests that its decisions might well be striking a fair average of justice. During its first five years of existence, the Board handled 2,888 strike cases and settled 2,161 of them. In addition, 869 threatened strikes were averted by its action. It must be admitted that there are serious weaknesses in the Act; but doubtless they will be remedied as time goes on. There is no longer any question but that some such agency acting in the interest of the public must be clothed with the authority to adjudicate industrial disputes and promote orderly peace between capital and labor. Under our form of government, such a national agency will require the coöperation of similar State bodies. A number of States have created such State Labor Boards or Commissions; and their experience has been significant in contributing toward the discovery of a sound and democratic path to industrial peace.[3]

THE PROBLEM OF WAGES AND HOURS

1. *The Problem of Wages.* There are at least two income hazards that are ever-present causes for anxiety in the average wage-earner's family: (1) *adequacy of the income* for meeting the needs of a growing family and for giving them the necessities and comforts regarded as essential for "the American standard of living"; and (2) *regularity of income* to enable the family to get along without alternating periods of deprivation and plenty.

When we speak of *adequacy of income* it is not the *money wage* that we have in mind, but it is what the money wage will buy. It is the *real* wage—the *purchasing power* of the wage—that we are thinking about. When we compare the higher wage of to-day with the wage paid before the First World War, we notice that there has not been much actual increase in prosperity: taxes have risen, the cost of living has advanced, and the 1942 dollar purchased about the same amount of groceries that sixty to eighty cents would purchase in 1914. Almost always wages lag behind price advances. Indeed, it is this lag of wages which gives rise to a large part of the industrial unrest and labor disputes. Wages usually fall as prices come down—and fall faster and farther. By the time retail prices have reached the lowest point, the income of the worker has either stopped because of loss of employment or has been seriously reduced by outright reduction or acceptance of part-time employment.

Adequacy of income, in the last analysis, means little in most cases unless the income is received with a fair degree of *regularity*. It might almost be said that regularity is an important determining factor in the adequacy of income. It is plain that income can be much more judiciously used if it is certain to be available from week to week and month to month. The individual then is able to budget his expenditures, to plan his occasional purchases with relation to the resources he has, and to anticipate such items as taxes, insurance premiums, or installment payments by setting aside for these obligations comparatively small portions of the income as it is received. On the other hand, if the income is

[3] For a fuller account of the National Labor Relations Act, see C. R. Daugherty, *Labor Problems in American Industry* (Boston, 1941), pp. 940–958.

irregular, then the budget becomes of little value. The individual, in effect, is reduced to a condition comparable to that of the primitive tribesman who faced feast or famine, depending on the luck of the tribe in the hunt. Irregularity of income leads to borrowing and impairment of credit, to impulsive and wasteful purchasing, to unstable living, and to improvidence with regard to future needs. As a result, even though the total income might be sufficient for a fair standard of living under normal circumstances, it might well be inadequate under the abnormal conditions incident to irregularity of work and life which uncertainty of income entails. In other words, a smaller total income, if assured as to its regularity, generally is more satisfactory in promoting the welfare of the worker and his family than one that is considerably higher but of uncertain duration.

The matter of regularity of income also is significant in the struggle between employer and worker, which we have just discussed. The dispute over wage rates is understandable enough. It is directly to the interest of employers to keep wage rates low and for the workers to secure as high rates as possible. But, owing to seasonal employment, poor management, or high turn-over of labor, high wage rates do not necessarily result in large earnings over a period of time. And the confusion of wage rates and earnings often arouses much public impatience with the demands of workers. This is especially true in the case of the building trades, transportation, and mining, which affect the public more or less directly. Daily wage scales for workers in these occupations are comparatively high; but the work is so seasonal that the workers are idle for as much as a third or a half of their time. The result, obviously, is that the annual earnings as a rule are not conspicuously large. Moreover, as we saw a moment ago, wage rates, and even average annual earnings, mean little if the income itself is received irregularly. Thus, we are confronted with the problem of irregularity of employment; and this problem is itself so important that we shall consider it separately in the following section.

In any consideration of the adequacy of wages, moreover, it is well to keep in mind that *the struggle in America is not a struggle for existence; it is a struggle for standards.* The wage-earner not only wants to live in better houses than the workers lived in a generation ago; the public and the law also *require* it and largely *arrange* it. Health regulations, fire protection, and civic pride have forced better housing in most cities. Most wage-earners of the cities now are provided with city water, sewage-disposal, garbage-collection, sanitary conveniences, and paved streets. The worker not only *wants* to give his children a better education than he received; the law *requires* it and makes it difficult for the child to secure any employment that would be of much assistance to the family income. Lack of shoes or clothing—in many cities lack of food—is no longer adequate excuse for a child's remaining out of school. If the parents cannot provide these necessities, the school or some one else will. In almost every phase of family life the American standard of living demands more than was demanded a generation ago.

The wage-earner who is the head of a family, and must maintain that family on the "decent" standard of living, faces a difficult task in that the wage he receives is not altogether a *family* wage. Society, in its other phases, has recognized the family as the fundamental unit; but industry and business enterprise generally have developed wage systems based upon the bargaining power of the individual, not upon the needs of the family. The non-family men and women and children have been—and still are—competitors in the labor market with the man who is the head of a family. The tendency of this competition is to pull the wage scale downward toward the point where it is sufficient to meet the needs of the non-family worker but not sufficient for maintaining the family man on the same plane as his fellow-workers who "enjoy single blessedness." When the wage is decreased, the retrenchments made by the *non-family man* may be an inconvenience; but the retrenchments that must be made by the *family man* amount to this inconvenience multiplied by the number in the family—which often means want, suffering, working mothers, undernourishment, exposures, sickness, and lapse of insurance. This fact, however, has not seemed to block marriage seriously. It is either taken for granted that the sacrifice is "a part of the game," or blind faith is placed in the false assumption that "two can live as cheaply as one." Undoubtedly, however, the failure of the wage to maintain for the married man the standard of the non-family worker is a cause for *some* of the increase of divorce and family desertion.

Many employers oppose recognizing these "sentimental factors, which are foreign to sound economics," in setting wage rates; they insist that competition in the labor market is the only sound basis for an economic wage. Nevertheless there seems to be a growing sentiment that recognizes family hazards under such a competitive wage and considers these hazards as a part of the costs of production: if not chargeable to industry, they are charges to society at large. The income tax has recognized the family as a unit, and to some extent the problem of financing the family, by allowing exemptions for the dependent members of the household. Most of the social-insurance plans—especially the Federal Compensation Act and most of the compensation provisions of the various States, which provide for employee compensation in case of accidents—recognize the family as a unit and adjust payments on the basis of the number in the family who are dependent upon the wage of the injured employee. Many of the labor-unions maintain mutual insurance funds for strike benefits, unemployment, and sickness and provide for payments in accordance with the family needs. In practically all discussions and controversies over what constitutes "a fair wage" this problem of financing a wage-earner's family occupies the center of interest. There seems to be a definite trend toward lifting the "fair wage" from a scale set entirely by the non-family worker to a scale dictated to a larger extent by the family needs.

2. *The Problem of Hours.* An adequate wage implies "a fair wage for a fair day's work." It is based upon the assumption that any kind of job that is worth hiring some one to do, day in and day out, is worth at least a living wage for the worker and his dependents. Living wages are not easily determined in every case, of course; but it is clear that the wage paid must be high enough to persuade the worker to keep on the job; and from the social point of view it should be high enough to assure that the worker and his dependents will be normal, reasonably healthy and happy members of the community.

But what is a fair day's work? Before the Industrial Revolution, it was generally considered to be from dawn till dark; and when industrial production began, the traditional fourteen- or even sixteen-hour day was carried over into factory and mine. The results were disastrous. It is one thing to work long hours at farming or shipping or fishing, where operations are simple even though physically wearisome, and where there are intervals when relaxation is possible. It is quite another matter to work at noisy machines in rooms that often are poorly ventilated and badly lighted, and where the rhythm of untiring machines permits no relief from the need for alertness and agility. It has been said that it took England at least two generations to recover from the toll of accidents and poor health that resulted from the unrestricted expansion of industry at the turn of the nineteenth century.

It is obvious, then, that hours of labor must be set with due consideration for the nature of the work and the welfare of the worker. When it became apparent that long hours entailed serious losses of life, limb, and health, there began a steady pressure by various groups toward

reducing hours to more satisfactory levels. The Federal Government as
early as 1840 set the length of the work day at ten hours for government
work, although a twelve- or fourteen-hour day still was general at that
time. Shortly after the War Between the States, there was a concerted
move toward the eight-hour day among union workers, who in varying degrees have retained that gain through the years, while the general average settled between nine and ten hours. Many studies in years
past have suggested that the shorter day actually resulted in more production, up to a point, as well as reducing costs by curtailing accidents
and health hazards. So in recent years the question has been raised as to
whether further shortening of the work day might be even better; and
before the Second World War, there was considerable pressure to set
six hours a day and five days a week as the standard work period. Widespread unemployment, moreover, gave force to the proposal in that the
shorter work period would tend to "stagger" the work and create jobs
for more workers.

How far we can rightly go in curtailing hours of labor, however,
presents a real problem in both economic and social policy. Insofar as
a shorter day increases production or reduces the *costs* of production,
there can be no question of its desirability. Yet the question is not altogether an economic one. The desire of workers to cut down the number of hours of work is based upon the perfectly natural inclination,
which all of us share, to exert themselves as little as necessary to get the
things they want. And the point of view is not without some degree
of social justification. If the machine is to replace the need for labor
power, it would seem that labor itself also should share its benefit in
terms of reduction of effort. But still more evidently, an individual with
some time and energy remaining after the work day or work week is
over, is likely to be a better citizen than if he were completely exhausted. He will be in better health and spirits, and his attitude will be
reflected in more wholesome family relations and in more bonds of
common interest and experience between parents and children. Moreover, such a worker is in a much better position to enter into the social
life of the community and to participate actively as a member of its
organized activities of various sorts. To be sure, added leisure also gives
more time for the individual to get into trouble, which may well suggest that more active guidance will be needed for the agencies meeting
leisure time needs of the community. Nevertheless, the worker with
both leisure and energy remaining after his work is done is likely to be

a better informed citizen than he otherwise would be, capable of voicing intelligent opinions and casting a really considered ballot.

Nevertheless, how far we are justified in reducing hours beyond the point where such reductions are economically gainful, is a question which necessarily raises strong differences of opinion. When production actually begins to diminish, then the reduction of hours begins to place a burden somewhere. The employer must be willing to accept less income from his investment and his managerial efforts, the worker must take a reduction in his cash wage, or the two somehow must share the costs. A rise in prices basically is futile as a general policy, since it reduces purchasing power of wages by encouraging high prices all down the line; and we already have seen that workers as a rule receive an income that is hardly adequate to what we have come to consider a fair standard of living. Employers can be expected to protest that the added burden of reduced hours is unbearable; and to some extent, they are quite justified in their position. In the first place, we cannot expect to share what does not exist. Thus, if we arbitrarily increase employment by cutting hours, production is not increased; and the total product then must be shared by a larger number of people. Furthermore, even though no increase of employment is anticipated, continued shortening of hours necessarily results eventually in a smaller production— which means smaller income and less money available to pay out in wages. To this extent, labor perhaps must regard the reduction of hours itself as an item in a higher scale of living, for which it may be compelled to make some financial concession. And, finally, such a situation puts the employer at a distinct disadvantage in competition with other producers. The company that operates with minimum labor costs can easily outbid the one that has high costs, because it can offer the goods at lower prices and has greater resources to use on promotional schemes to extend its markets.

The question of wages and hours, then, becomes basically a question of distribution of income. This is a matter which concerns no isolated group of workers or their employers alone, nor can it be adjusted by direct bargaining between the two groups. It concerns all of us, together. The relations between industries and territorial sections of the country are so closely enmeshed that no particular segment of them can work out their own salvation alone. It thus becomes a matter of public concern; and broad policies must be devised to strike a fair balance among the interests of capital, labor, and public welfare.

3. *Legislative Action*. Recognition of the importance of the problem of wages and hours to the public welfare is reflected by the persistent effort to secure legislative protection for the workers in these matters, despite the many obstacles and complicating factors attendant upon such action. The right of governmental agencies to regulate the working conditions of their own employees never has been questioned; and both federal and State bodies have limited the work day generally to eight hours. Similarly, the right of governmental units to specify the work conditions on work done by contractors in governmental service also was early established and has been exercised quite extensively. The control over private enterprise has been much more difficult to accomplish, although the States have been experimenting with laws regarding hours and wages for at least fifty years. Early laws attempting to shield the health and safety of workers by reducing hours of labor usually were nullified by Constitutional guarantees of "freedom of contract"; yet they were more successful in occupations such as transportation where public safety was shown to be involved. Laws regarding wages were even less successful than were those applying to hours, since they were still more clearly a challenge to the right of free contract.

Nevertheless, under the pressure of unemployment and the severe unbalance of both income distribution and bargaining power that became apparent during the depression years following 1929, the demand for government action in the field of protective labor legislation grew apace. The result was that under the plea of public necessity and emergency, fairly comprehensive public policies developed during the New Deal period. The National Industrial Recovery Act marked the initial entry of the Federal Government into the field of direct regulation of wages and hours in private industry. Under the Act, the various Code Authorities (trade or industrial associations) fixed wage and hour scales for their respective industries. The general point of departure was a forty-cent minimum hourly wage rate and a forty-hour week; but adjustments were made to compensate for prevailing geographic variations in labor conditions. Women, apprentices, and handicapped workers were completely exempt from the operation of the Code regulations.

The operation of the federal power over wages and hours faltered for a time with the rejection of the National Industrial Recovery Act by the Supreme Court in 1935. But just as it had paved the way for the passage of the National Labor Relations Act to cope with the problems of industrial conflict, so also did the National Industrial Recovery Act lay the groundwork for the subsequent and more comprehensive, more satisfactory system of control which was to be expressed in the Fair Labor Standards Act. This Act, often called the "Wage and Hour law," was passed in 1938 and was designed, as President Roosevelt expressed it, "to put a floor under wages and a ceiling over hours." It provided a minimum hourly wage of 25 cents for the first year, 30 cents till 1945, and 40 cents thereafter, while hours were to be scaled down by 1940 to a standard basic work week of 40 hours.

There were many exceptions and qualifying features in the Act which sharply limited its effectiveness. Wage scales were to be adjusted to local conditions, taking into account price levels, prevailing wages, and union-management wage scales, while the forty-hour week placed no limit on hours actually to be worked but was to be the point at which wages were to be increased to time-and-a-half overtime levels.

Nevertheless, the arrangements written into the Fair Labor Standards Act probably are as satisfactory as any that could be devised, taking into account the immense diversity in wage and hour schedules from one section of the country to another. Such problems as the lower wages of women and of part-time or handicapped workers, and the low wages and long hours so prevalent in the South, together with the seasonal fluctuations in various industries and the fundamental differences in living standards and variations in skill of labor from one geographic section and class of workers to another, makes the administration of such a law a colossal undertaking. However, one of the fortunate features of the law is that it provides for continually functioning commissions that will help to make the transitional adjustments much easier than would be the case if the schedules were fixed once and for all for immediate application throughout the country. The most serious shortcoming of the law undoubtedly is that it excludes large classes of the working population of the country. Executives, salesmen, professional persons, and transportation workers are excluded; but these in general have fairly satisfactory conditions of employment. On the other hand, agricultural workers, sales clerks, and domestic servants also are excluded, and these groups obviously include many workers who are in need of such protection. These exclusions undoubtedly were based on both economic and political considerations, since extensive changes in these fields necessarily would result in widespread economic readjustments that could not be accomplished without drastic effects upon the price structure at the present time. Altogether, it is estimated that probably 14,000,000 workers—about a third of the total number in the country—are covered by some phase of the Act.[4]

The Second World War created many dislocations in the adminis tration of the Act, because of the urgency of need for production and the scarcity of labor. Nevertheless, the existence of the Act is itself recognition of the importance of the problem of wages and hours in American economic life; and it provides a framework for a consistent socialized approach to the adjustment of that problem.

THE PROBLEM OF UNEMPLOYMENT

Unemployment is a condition in which a person, able and willing to work and normally dependent upon his earnings to provide the necessities of life for himself and family, is unable to obtain gainful employment. There is probably no fear that hangs more heavily over the head of the average worker than the fear of losing his job. There are, to be sure, a considerable number who are chronically unemployed the men who "won't work," hobos, tramps, and "psychopathic person alities." While many of these may have started their shiftless habits through failure to find proper vocational placement, the major propor tion of them are victims of other social or personal ills than those con nected with our changing industrial life. Our discussion of the hazards of unemployment, therefore, is not so much concerned with these in dustrial derelicts. Our chief task is to see the hazards that confront the great body of workers who are capable of and desire steady employ ment.

The reorganization of industry and the introduction of labor-saving machinery are important causes of much unemployment—either for a short period during the reorganization or installation of the machines or for a long period owing to complete displacement of labor by the machines. But just how many workers are every year forced out of work through this cause, we cannot say. However, we do know that since the First World War—on farms and in mines and factories—labor saving machinery has displaced more workers than during any equal period since the beginning of the Industrial Revolution. Undoubtedly this was a major factor causing widespread unemployment following 1929. In this displacement the traditionally skilled workers have gen erally suffered more than have the unskilled; though the unskilled are generally the first to be "laid off." The new automatic machine requires

[4] For a fuller account of the Fair Labor Standards Act, see C. R. Daugherty, *op. cit.*, pp. 837–852.

but little skill or training to be "fed," and the unskilled workers, even women and children, can easily become machine-tenders.

Some employment is casual, offering steady work perhaps for a few hours or for a few days and then offering nothing for a while. The work

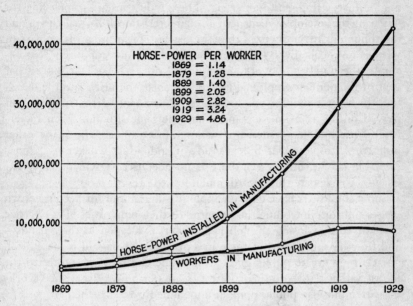

FIG. 10.—GROWTH OF HORSEPOWER AND WORKERS IN MANUFACTURING, 1869–1929

Norman M. Kastler, *Modern Human Relations* (Boston, 1940), p. 104. Data from Harry Jerome, *Mechanization in Industry* (National Bureau of Economic Research, 1934), p. 217.

of the longshoremen and dock-hands in the shipping industry is of this sort. The men work hard while there are ships to load or unload; but ships are not always in the harbor, and the amount of work depends upon the number and size of the incoming and outgoing cargoes. Likewise, many small industries provide a fringe of this haphazard type of employment. Most of these workers could doubtless find more steady employment, but there seems to be a fascination about this type of work which holds them, and they seem to live in constant expectation that "next week will be a busy week." The casual nature of the work makes it difficult to dovetail these occupations with other employments that would provide work during the time now wasted. Casual employment not only makes the income uncertain and inadequate for the families depending upon it, but it also has a demoralizing effect upon the worker himself.[5]

Other industries are seasonal in nature and can furnish employment for only a certain part of the year: like the clothing industry, coal-mining, harvesting, and lumbering. These industries are responsible for much of the unemployment that is characteristic of normal times, and the thousands of workers in these industries constitute a major part of what is now called the *labor reserve*. In the canning industry, for example, the number of workers employed during March is but 18 per cent of the number employed in September; in the brick and tile industry, the winter months employ but 61.4 per cent of the number employed during the summer; and much the same situation is characteristic of the building trades, the manufacturing of ice, and many other industries. Employment bureaus aid the individual workers to a considerable extent, but as yet there is no adequate system of labor exchanges to alleviate this hazard, much less to prevent it.

Some employers have used unemployment as a tool for keeping down wages and for controlling the activities of their employees. They realize that the fear of losing the job is a powerful weapon in their hands—and they have used it. But these practices cannot be said to be ethical, nor do they create public good-will. In the end they are costly to the industry that resorts to them. They create not only a dissatisfied working force but also public opinion unqualifiedly resents them.[6]

Thus we see that even under comparatively normal conditions, unemployment is a distinct social hazard. But the most serious aspects of the unemployment problem are not those of normal times but the longer and more trying periods of *industrial depression*. Industrial depressions are rather regularly recurring periods—following periods of unusual prosperity—when industries close down, prices tumble, and credit is difficult to obtain. Many theories have been offered in the past to explain the occurrence of business cycles. These economic and social dislocations have been attributed to such causes as overproduction, underconsumption, overexpansion of credit, cycles of optimism and depression of the public mind, dislocation of business enterprise due to war, the tariff, or to technological changes in industry. Some have even suggested that these cycles are due to natural cycles of change in the weather, variations in sun spots, or caprices of the planets.

Whatever the cause may be, it is true that throughout American eco-

[5] Lascelles and Bullock, *Dock Labor and Decasualization* (1924), Chs. V, X.
[6] D. L. Hoopingarner, *Labor Relations in Industry* (1925), pp. 281–282.

nomic history there have been alternating periods of prosperity and trying years of depression, unemployment, and slow recovery. Indeed, we have had more years of depression and hard times than we have had of prosperity.[7] Moreover, our periods of business and industrial depression appear to be increasing in severity and duration, if not in frequency. As a result, the business cycle idea itself is being questioned; and it has been argued that these fluctuations are in response to long-time influences which transcend even the business cycle. If this be true, we are confronted with a challenge to some of our most fundamental tenets of social equity and economic distribution. That such may be the case is suggested in the fact that "lack of sound social and economic planning" has in recent years been regarded by many as a significant cause of unemployment. Acceptance of this point of view reduces the business cycle idea to being hardly more than a poor excuse for public negligence, a sort of rationalization for traditional *laissez-faire* concepts that leave such matters as employment and trade to personal liberty and private initiative. At any rate, the experience of recent years, and especially of the decade prior to the Second World War, has taught us that unemployment *is a public problem*. It cannot be left to private business to find a solution. Furthermore, we have learned that it is not a problem belonging wholly to the local community, or even to the several States individually; it is *a national* problem. Therefore the Federal Government must take a leading rôle in the shaping of the program and providing the machinery for dealing with the major aspects of the unemployment problem. This is, indeed, almost a complete reversal of the traditional American policy in regard to such matters.

As late as 1932 we in the United States still were trying to handle the problem of unemployment essentially on an emergency and local basis. It is true that specially organized committees and boards were handling the situation with considerable adroitness, and the relief of the unemployed and their dependents was, generally speaking, both adequate and well distributed. Yet "relief" naturally was not forthcoming till the unemployed individual had quite exhausted his resources; and all efforts to stimulate reëmployment were largely futile. Standards of living were reduced, insurance policies were dropped, families "doubled up" to conserve heat and rent, bank accounts dwindled, if indeed they were not lost completely through the widespread failure of banks in that period, and debts mounted to the limits of creditors' willingness or ability to advance loans. And along with such retrenchment went the

[7] H. U. Faulkner, *American Economic History* (New York, 1938), p. 753.

psychological hardships that attend unemployment: worry, reduction of skill, impairment of health, loss of self-respect, a withdrawal from ordinary social contacts with friends and neighbors.

Nevertheless, we had made considerable progress beyond the techniques which had been used during depression periods prior to the First World War. The old indiscriminate soup kitchens and bread lines were largely gone. Employment facilities, though still far from being efficient, at least were fairly well coördinated; and employers were coöperating with them so far as circumstances would permit. Demoralization of the unemployed probably was as little as ever could be expected under such restricted policies pertaining to remedial effort. But unemployment and its attendant distress grew steadily worse, and President Hoover insisted throughout his administration that the intervention of governmental agencies, and particularly those of the Federal Government, should be kept at a minimum. Consistent adherence to such a policy had one benefit, at least: it proved quite conclusively that more aggressive action was imperative. The public was quite ready to accept the new approach under "New Deal" guidance in 1933.

The Federal Government made a distinctly new approach both to the relief of the distressed, and to the matter of stimulating reëmployment. The Federal Emergency Relief Administration was set up at once to attack both of these problems together. Private agencies were not driven out, but neither were they helped, in most cases, as they previously had been to some extent. Instead, a vast program of federal public relief assistance was inaugurated, operating through State and local *public* agencies, and simultaneously extensive work programs were projected, notably the Civil Works Administration, the Public Works Administration, and later the Work Projects Administration, the National Youth Administration, and the Civilian Conservation Corps. Of most lasting character and worth, however, undoubtedly has been the development of the United States Employment Service and of the unemployment compensation provisions of the Social Security Act, administered by the Social Security Board of the Federal Security Agency. The two agencies have worked in close coöperation, and together they constitute the most comprehensive approach yet made by the Federal Government to the problem of unemployment.

Under the Wagner-Peyser Act of 1933, the United States Employment Service was greatly expanded, both in the scope of its services and in the number of its offices. These offices are set up in State or municipal areas. Financing is on a matching basis, contingent upon agreement of the States or municipalities to maintain certain minimum standards of equipment, personnel, and policy prescribed by the federal agency. All of the States have taken advantage of this opportunity; and the effectiveness of the work of these offices is enhanced by the fact that the unemployment compensation payments are cleared through this agency. Close touch thus is maintained with the unemployed worker, and it is possible to put him in touch with employment opportunities as they develop, as well as to reduce greatly the likelihood of payment of such benefits after the worker secures new employment.

The framework for the provision of unemployment benefits set up in the Social Security Act is comparatively simple, chiefly because the bulk of the details and administration of unemployment compensation is left to the several States. The Federal Government levies a pay-roll tax of 3 per cent on employers of eight or more workers who are employed for a period of not less than twenty weeks in any year, the amount of the tax having been stepped up from 1 per cent at the time the Act went into effect in 1936. The coverage thus excludes the seasonal workers to a large extent, as well as those in small enterprises. In addition, certain other large segments of labor are excluded, among them being farm labor, domestic or home employees, some classes of transportation, government workers, and most forms of quasi-public service such as charity, scientific, or educational organizations. These exceptions approximate the exemptions made in the Fair Labor Standards Act pertaining to wage and hour practices, and, as in that case, the limitation doubtless was inspired by both political and economic considerations.

The administration of the Act is driven into the jurisdiction of the several States largely by the expedient of tax remission. In States having suitable systems of unemployment compensation, the employer paying the federal tax may deduct up to 90 per cent from that tax to pay his State tax for the same purpose. The portion paid to that State in turn is remitted to the United States Treasury, and the sum is earmarked for that State as a reserve or fund from which the benefits that may become payable in that State are paid. The remaining 10 per cent is paid to the Federal Government directly by the employer and goes into the general funds to offset the federal costs of administration of the Act. Obviously, it is to the interest of each State to enact such laws, in order to recapture for its own use the bulk of the payments by the employers within the State. The resort to such seemingly roundabout procedures was taken to assure the constitutionality of the Act; and of course the national scope was sought to remove the competitive disadvantage which such payments would create, were the more progressive States to impose purely State systems upon employers within their borders engaging in interstate trade.

All the States have enacted acceptable laws and are now providing unemployment compensation protection for large portions of their workers. There are wide variations in the exact provisions among the States, both as to coverage and as to benefits.[8] Some of the States, for example, include workers in businesses employing less than eight workers, and include some of the occupations excluded by the federal minimum basis. Benefits vary as to amount, length of payment, and length of the waiting period that must elapse before the worker is eligible for benefit payments. Another important point of difference is whether each employer should maintain separate reserves, or whether the funds should be pooled for the whole State. There are advantages either way. But in both cases there undoubtedly will remain necessary provisions for reducing payments by employers who stabilize their working staff and so reduce the uncertainty of employment. This is one of what may be regarded as the two primary objectives of the Social Security Act, the reduction of unemployment by supplying an incentive to employers to regularize their employment—the other being, of course, the direct benefit of the compensation payments to the unemployed worker himself.

The Social Security Act obviously cannot eliminate unemployment. No one agency can do that. And as it stands, the Act still leaves much to be desired, both in coverage of employed workers and in the amounts payable. Furthermore, the Federal Government assumes no responsibility for the care or placement of the definitely unemployable classes such as the aged, disabled, deficients, or transients, who were thrown back to the care of local and State groups in 1935. It is still too early to judge fully of the effect of the Federal Government's direct entry into the field of employment problems; but we have every reason to be confident that at least it will afford a means of sharing the burden of unemployment among the whole population, as it should be borne, and of mitigating the acute distress that traditionally has befallen the unemployed worker and his family.

[8] For a fuller account of the provisions of the Social Security Act as they relate to unemployment, the State variations, and fiscal and administrative problems, see Ewan Clague, "Unemployment Compensation," *Social Work Year Book, 1941,* R. H. Kurtz, ed., p. 567.

THE PROBLEM OF OLD AGE

Not least among the social hazards of modern industrial life is old age. In the early days, before machinery came into use, the worker with his own tools set his own pace of work. Whether one man could do more or less than another did not materially interfere with his having a part in producing things. The older man found his pace of work and did what he could. He had the satisfaction of feeling that he was at least useful and could be independent and largely self-supporting.

With the development of modern industrialism all this has changed. Industry to-day calls for the maximum efficiency of the laborer. This is essentially a demand for the laborer who is still in his youth or in the prime of life. Since he "must have experience," he is not wanted much before he is 25 years of age. He then has about 25 years of fairly certain economic opportunity in normal times. But even before he has reached 50 years of age he is facing increasing difficulty in holding his own in the labor market. The pace set by the machine is a pace that only the strong can endure; and even they do not endure for long periods of time.

In 1932 a study was made of the employment policies of selected manufacturing establishments representing the major branches of American industry. This study revealed 31.7 per cent of the establishments as having a maximum age limit beyond which no employees are hired. These establishments represent 28 per cent of the total number employed in all industry. Some industries have a maximum age limit as low as 40 years. In many others, notably the steel industry, the maximum age for hiring new workers is between 40 and 46. In the other industries covered by the study there is no definite maximum hiring age, but in practically all these plants employment managers stated that requirements of the job determine the age policy, and in most cases they admit that not many men over 50 would be employed, except in cases requiring especially skilled employees where it would be impossible to secure young men.[9] Furthermore, the opportunities for gainful employment for the older worker grow leaner each year. The 1890 census showed 73.8 per cent of the men who were 65 years of age or over were gainfully employed; the 1910 census showed 63.8 per cent still drawing pay; the 1930 census revealed 54.7 per cent employed, and estimates for 1938 ranged from 15 to 31 per cent of these older workers as still clinging to their jobs. Nor is it merely the policy of employers that is more and more discouraging to the older worker. Both organized labor and the

[9] *Handbook of Labor Statistics, 1936*, p. 456.

public generally also seem to be more concerned about getting the older worker out of the labor market than they are in finding creative employment for him. To an increasing degree, therefore, the industrial worker has a narrowing span of years in which he may find opportunity to use his earning capacity to the fullest extent.

The plight of the older worker in modern industry is strangely out of line with the trends in the social population. We noted, in our study of the composition of the population, that the proportion of the older age groups is increasing.[10] Whereas, in 1860, only 2.7 per cent of the population of the United States were 65 years of age or over, the 1930 census found 5.4 per cent, or about one person in nineteen, in that bracket; and it is estimated that fifty years hence, one person in twelve will be in this group. The growing proportion of "ripe old age" is, of course, due in large part to the shrinking of the birth-date, the reduction of infant mortality, and improvement in health services. Thus, for example, from 1911 to 1935 the expectation of life *at birth* among the industrial policy holders of the Metropolitan Life Insurance Company increased from 46.6 years to 60.2 years—a gain of 13.6 years in less than a single generation! [11] Nevertheless, it likewise is true that medicine and surgery have cut down the toll of disease, increased bodily vigor, and added more years to the average adult life as well. In either case, the fact remains that as time goes on we shall have larger proportions of people living to years extending well beyond those usually occupied with gainful employment.

The industrial worker thus faces a strange and disconcerting paradox. He is cheered by the prospect of many more years of health and vigor than were accorded any previous generation of workers. On the other hand, he is pushed off the pay-roll long before he has reached a reasonable retirement age. Such a situation at once raises a serious question: Is the industrial worker—especially the great body of unskilled and semi-skilled workers—able to earn and save enough money during this narrowing span of years to maintain the coveted American standard of living through the years of uncertainty that stretch on beyond the maximum employment age?

Despite the unfavorable conditions which we discussed earlier in this chapter relative to wage levels, there nevertheless are some who have insisted that there is no reason why the working-man should not be able

[10] Chapter 8.
[11] L. I. Dublin and A. J. Lotka, *Twenty-Five Years of Health Progress* (New York: Metropolitan Life Insurance Company, 1937), pp. 33–42.

to save enough to take care of himself in old age. They do not see why society or the State should be concerned about old-age pensions or plans for the care and treatment of the aged. "My contention is," writes one employer, "that it is possible for the great mass of our people, out of current earnings, to amass $5,000 by the time they reach the age of pensions, if they will conscientiously try to do so. . . . The fear of old-age dependence is a wholesome fear. It is one of our most precious assets. If we allow it to be taken away, by the assurance that in old age the State will step in and assume responsibility, we shall be giving up a good thing for the sake of a much less valuable thing." [12] But even in the presumably prosperous pre-depression year of 1928 when there were more than 53 million persons with savings accounts, the average account amounted to only $534, which was about $223 less than the average account in 1913. The great majority of the accounts were much smaller, since two-thirds of the savings of the American people are made by the 2 per cent of the population with incomes of more than $10,000 a year.[13] More than a third of the non-farm families have been unable to save anything at all; and during the depression years following 1929, there were many industrial communities where as many as a quarter of the families were destitute or on relief. Growing old under such circumstances is, to say the least, not encouraging.

Being unable to gain the feel of social security through savings, the industrial worker has turned increasingly to various types of life insurance. From 1911 to 1935, the number of weekly premium-paying industrial policyholders increased from 8,000,000 to 17,000,000. As a rule, however, such insurance pays little more than the burial expenses of the insured, or at best provides the beneficiary of the wage-earner with but a few hundred dollars. The weekly premium itself is a commentary on the meager resources of the average worker and affords the least protection per dollar expended because collection costs and cancellations are high. "Building an estate through life insurance" has the same limitations as the savings account: the family man with an income of less than $1,500 a year simply cannot afford it. Moreover, the small life insurance policy offers little as a potential source of security for the assured or for his beneficiary. It can hardly serve them both.

The plight of the discarded industrial worker, then, is pressing a

[12] G. E. MacIlwain, "In Behalf of the Poorhouse," *Open Shop Review*, p. 251 (July, 1927).

[13] *Income and Economic Progress* (New York: Public Affairs Pamphlet No. 1, 1936), p. 15.

greater responsibility upon our public and private agencies for working out a satisfactory and adequate program for social security. It is plain that the individual worker generally is unable to save enough during his working years to provide for his old age. And for various reasons, he cannot look to his children for much help, as was often the case in former years. Our population is increasingly urban, and there is little room for aged parents in the modern home. Living costs and standards have risen to such an extent that these extra persons in the household create a strain on the family purse that few younger families can sustain. Even in rural areas the growth of tenancy and of mechanized farming makes the old folks, especially old men, less serviceable and more difficult to accommodate than was the case a generation or two ago.

Traditionally, almost the only alternative which old people had, if care could not be given them by relatives, has been the poorhouse (now euphemistically called the county infirmary or county home). Its limitations are obvious, being reflected in the opprobrium with which such institutions and their inmates alike still are commonly regarded. Their utility always has been kept at a minimum, both in the types of service they have rendered and in the numbers they have served. It is significant, too, that male inmates have outnumbered female inmates quite consistently by approximately two to one. It appears that older women are more useful and acceptable to the modern family life than are older men. At the same time, since men usually are regarded as the breadwinners, such an unbalance of men in the county homes gives added emphasis to the contention that the aged wage-earner presents an especially troublesome facet in the general problem of the care of the aged.

Public outdoor relief, or assistance to the needy living in their own homes, also has been niggardly and grudging, even for the aged. To this general situation, however, there is one important exception. The United States has always been the most generous nation in the world in its beneficence for the veterans of military service. Thus, during the fiscal year 1939–1940 alone, about $127,500,000 was paid to nearly 160,000 veterans and 58,000 veterans' survivors of the Spanish-American War, and nearly $28,000,000 to some 2,381 veterans of the War Between the States and 50,141 dependents of deceased veterans.[14] While ostensibly the pensions have been regarded as a form of deferred payment for services

[14] Irene Grant, "Veterans," *Social Work Year Book, 1941,* R. H. Kurtz, ed., p. 578.

previously rendered, it nevertheless is true that such bounteousness has had an important part in mitigating the destitution of the aged.

As the needs of the aged dependent grew more urgent, however, they commanded attention among the more sensitive individuals and groups in society as a whole; and private agencies have tackled the problem with rising vigor, especially since the turn of the twentieth century. Many private homes for the aged have been set up by religious, fraternal, charitable, and labor organizations; and various systems of financial benefits have been devised to supplement the work of such homes, especially by the fraternal organizations. Indeed, the growth of more adequate and humane public systems of pensions and institutions may be ascribed in large part to the pioneering work done by these private groups. Cities began to pension their superannuated policemen and fire fighters, and teachers were provided with retirement funds by many cities and States, some on the basis of length of service, most of them on a contributory basis. The Federal Government in 1920 created a system of old age retirement for its employees. And finally the movement for a universal system of old age retirement benefits took shape in the various States following the First World War. Alaska was the first to put such a plan into operation in 1927, with six States following its lead the next year. At the close of 1934, the year before the enactment of the Federal Social Security Act, twenty-eight States, four territories, and the District of Columbia had passed legislation for old age pensions. Most of these State laws followed the same general pattern. All were *enabling* acts, none being State-wide or mandatory with the counties. Some permitted the counties, cities, and other local units of government to provide such a pension fund without aid from the State, while most of the States assisted the local governmental units setting up pension systems by assuming from a third to a half of the annual cost. Most of the laws based the pension award on proof of need, and set the age of eligibility at 70. In most instances, $30 per month was the maximum allowance, and a limit was set upon the amount of property which a pensioner might own.

The very similarity of most of the old-age pension plans enacted by the States during the early years of the New Deal foreshadowed the coming of the federal act covering these phases of the problem of social security. Indeed, by the time that President Roosevelt appointed the Committee on Economic Security in 1934, it was almost a foregone conclusion that the Federal Government would take some action in the matter. The later State acts were fashioned with a view to the probable requirements of such an act; and when in fact the Social Security Act was passed by Congress in the following year, the adaption to the federal system was hardly more than a formality for many of these States.

The section of the Social Security Act pertaining to the provision for the aged included two types of benefit payments: pensions to the aged dependent, and contributory old-age annuities for superannuated wage-earners. The two types will both be necessary permanently; but it is expected that the scope of pension requirements will stabilize at much lower levels as the annuity benefits develop to the full limits of their potential effectiveness. The first type of assistance substantially is a matching plan, by which the Federal Government undertakes to assist the States by transferring from federal funds sums equal to the sums granted by the several States to their aged poor. In addition, the Federal Government grants 5 per cent of its assistance for administrative purposes, making a total grant of $52\frac{1}{2}$ per cent of the amounts expended by the States. In return, the Federal Government makes various requirements as to standards of assistance and administration, including provision for appeal and fair hearings for those denied assistance by the State boards. The State must grant such assistance to needy persons at not less than 65 years of age, at which age the federal grants become effective, while the matching provisions obtain up to a maximum of $40 total monthly benefits in each individual case.

Of much greater interest and importance for the aged wage-earner from a long term point of view, is the system of old age annuities set up in the Social Security Act. The Act is not universal in scope, however, the excluded occupational groups being substantially the same as (but not identical with) those in the case of the unemployment section discussed earlier in this chapter. But all other employers *and workers alike* now pay a 3 per cent tax on their pay-roll or earnings, respectively, up to $3,000 annual earnings per employee. These payments are credited to the account of each worker, the sums being invested by the Secretary of the United States Treasury at 3 per cent. Subsequently (since 1940), at 65 years of age the worker who retires from active employment is to be eligible to receive a monthly payment or annuity. The amount of the payment is computed on the basis of his earnings; but by the terms of the Act, the monthly benefit may not be less than $10, nor more than $85. Death benefits depend upon the individual circumstances. If the worker involved dies before he reaches the age of 65, his estate is paid a sum equal to $3\frac{1}{2}$ per cent of his earnings since

January 1, 1937, the date that the Act became effective. If he dies after 65 years of age, then his estate is paid 3½ per cent of his earnings subsequent to January 1, 1937, less the amount he has received in monthly benefits. Clearly, if the worker lives long enough, he actually will receive more than his normal share, since the benefits are paid as long as the assured lives.

These are the major aspects of what is perhaps the boldest attempt, from point of sheer mass, ever made to achieve collective security by any nation. There are many minor provisions for applying the Act to specific instances and groups, and of course there are many serious problems, shortcomings, and criticisms of the Act which cannot be considered here.[15] Enough has been said, however, to suggest that the traditional public policy in the United States in regard to the aged has been modified greatly. It is to be hoped that the problem of security for the aged can be reduced further, as time goes on, by refinements in the application of the principles of the Act.

REFERENCES

Annals of the American Academy of Political and Social Science, "Appraising the Social Security Program" (March, 1939).

BROOKS, Robert, *When Labor Organizes* (New Haven, 1937).

CATLIN, W. B., *The Labor Problem* (New York, 1934), Chs. 4 and 5.

CHASE, Stuart, *A New Deal* (New York, 1932).

DAUGHERTY, C. R., *Labor Problems in American Industry* (Boston, 1941).

DOUGLAS, P. H., HITCHCOCK, C. N., and ATKINS, W. E., *The Worker in Modern Economic Society* (Chicago, 1925), Ch. 17.

ELLIOTT, Mabel A., and MERRILL, Francis E., *Social Disorganization* (New York, 1941), Chs. XIV, XVI, XVII.

EPSTEIN, Abraham, *Insecurity, a Challenge to America* (New York, 1936).

FAULKNER, H. U., *American Economic History* (New York, 1938), Ch. 22.

Handbook of Labor Statistics (Washington, D. C.: 1936 Edition). United States Department of Labor, Bureau of Labor Statistics.

REYNOLDS, L. G., and others, *Labor and National Defense* (New York: Twentieth Century Fund, 1941).

RUBINOW, I. M., *The Quest for Security* (New York, 1934), Book VII.

Social Security Yearbook, 1939 (Washington, D. C.: Federal Security Agency, Social Security Board, 1940).

[15] For a fuller study of these provisions of the Social Security Act, see articles on "Old Age Assistance" and "Old Age and Survivors' Insurance" in *Social Work Year Book, 1941,* R. H. Kurtz, ed.; C. R. Daugherty, *Labor Problems in American Industry* (Boston, 1941), pp. 805–822; *Social Security in America* (Washington, D. C.: Social Security Board, Publication 20, 1937), which contains also the text of the Act; or the *Social Security Year Book, 1939* (Washington, D. C.: Social Security Board, 1940).

Social Work Year Book, 1941, R. H. Kurtz, ed. (New York, 1941).

YODER, Dale, *Labor Economics and Labor Problems* (New York, 1933), Ch. 5.

QUESTIONS AND EXERCISES

1. What changes in industry have given rise to the modern industrial conflicts? What social hazards result from these conflicts? Have any social benefits been gained from these conflicts? Discuss.

2. What are the arguments for and against outlawing strikes?

3. What is group bargaining? What are the advantages and disadvantages of group bargaining? Is it likely that labor would obtain the same advantages by bargaining as individuals? Explain.

4. What are the main provisions of the National Labor Relations Act? How has the operation of this law affected the problem of industrial relations? What are the major criticisms of the law, as reflected in the first few years of its operation?

5. Why is the discussion of wage levels so often confusing or misleading?

6. What is meant by the terms "living wage," and "decent standard of living"? Can American economic resources support a high standard of living for the working population?

7. Is it true that shorter work-days must result in lower wages to the individual worker? Defend your point of view.

8. What are the difficulties facing the attempt to control wage and hour problems by legislative action?

9. Describe the chief provisions of the Fair Labor Standards Act. What appear to be its principal shortcomings?

10. What are the causes of unemployment? What causes are due chiefly to the individual worker? What causes grow out of faulty industrial organization?

11. List what you regard as the major social hazards resulting from unemployment.

12. Is governmental action regarding the problem of unemployment really necessary, or are workers and employers shifting their own responsibilities to someone else's shoulders?

13. What three approaches to the problem of unemployment were taken by the government under the "New Deal"? Briefly describe and evaluate each.

14. How does the progress of modern industrialism affect the social security of the older worker? What is the trend of industrial policies in regard to the maximum age at which new workers are hired? What is the public's attitude in this matter?

15. From your own observation in your community, make a list of the occupations and gainful employments followed by the men and women whom you regard as belonging in the old-age group. Do these occupations provide an income equivalent to the standard wage of the community?

16. About what proportion of the people you know in this age group are

self-supporting entirely? What proportion are partially self-supporting? What proportion are totally dependent?

17. What public measures have been taken to assist the aged?

18. Describe the provisions of the Social Security Act that pertain to the aged.

Chapter 11

SECONDARY SOCIAL PROBLEMS OF INDUSTRY

In the previous chapter, we discussed social problems of modern industrial life as they affect practically all of us directly, in one way or another. Questions of industrial conflict, unemployment, wages and hours, and old age touch each one of us whether as workers, employers, or consumers. But there are other problems, less direct and less inclusive, which nevertheless are serious and merit our consideration. Chief among these, perhaps, are matters of industrial accidents and sickness, vocational adjustment, the place of women in our industrial framework, and the problems attendant upon the employment of other marginal groups of workers such as children, Negroes, and convicts. Such are the problems to be dealt with in the present chapter.

INDUSTRIAL ACCIDENTS AND SICKNESS

1. *Extent.* One of the oldest, most persistent, and in many ways most troublesome of the social problems raised by modern industrialism is that of accidents which hurt, cripple, or even kill the worker on the job. Yet the average individual who has no direct contact with work conditions in factory, office, mine, or commerce seldom is aware of the tremendous human costs of the high standard of living he enjoys as a result of our industrial development. To be sure, he reads of the spectacular mine disasters, train wrecks, factory explosions, fires, or the like that take a heavy toll of life in no time at all. On fairly rare occasions, such calamity descends upon his own community, so that he has first-hand—and memorable—experience of what they entail in human misery and property loss. But the total costs, the day-in-and-day-out toll exacted as a price for the vast increase in economic production during the past century and a half far exceeds the average individual's comprehension.

For that matter, *no one* knows exactly what the frequency or cost of industrial accidents may be, because it is impossible to derive accurate and inclusive definitions. When, for example, is a worker to be accounted as injured? Everyone agrees, probably, that a worker who is incapacitated for a week or more can be considered as injured. But what if he is able to return to work in a day or two? Or if he suffers only a badly cut finger but is able to resume work as soon as the wound is dressed? And suppose a worker suffers a brain concussion, as sometimes happens, as a result of a blow on the head, and resumes work within the hour—but later suffers complications that result in a long illness or even death? It must be clear, then, that estimates of the extent and costs of industrial accidents are very largely *guesses*, based on what one chooses to include in his reckoning.

Nevertheless, the record of accidents as reported by careful and reasonable students of the matter, is startling enough. It is true that accidents necessarily vary considerably from year to year, depending upon the extent of employment and the *speed* of industrial operations. There also are long-term trends which, generally, show a slow decline (considering the larger number of workers and resulting increase of *exposure* to accidents), which is due to the improvements in preventive measures. Yet in continental United States in recent years the estimates run between 15,000 and 20,000 fatal accidents per year in industry, and from one to two million non-fatal accidents serious enough to result in loss of time and to afford basis for claims for compensation. Many interesting comparisons and correlations have been made in an attempt to dramatize the human costs of production, to give us an idea of what they mean in terms of common experience. For example, a million tons of coal is said to cost the lives of about four miners; and industrial fatalities have exceeded battle deaths even in time of war. However that may be, it is sobering enough to realize that *two lives are sacrificed every hour, night and day*, to keep us supplied with the things we want, while the interval between non-fatal, but more or less serious, reported accidents is a matter of but a few seconds.

Industrial sickness and occupational disease are even less tangible and less appreciated than are industrial accidents. Estimates are hard to make, since obviously there is no satisfactory general test for the degree of a worker's efficiency or for the extent to which his inefficiency is a result of impaired physical condition. It is significant that no exhaustive studies or estimates have been made, comparable to those in the field of accidents. Moreover, the legislative measures pertaining to health hazards have lagged far behind those relating to accidents, both as to coverage and as to extensiveness. All of the States but Mississippi had made at least some provision for the protection of workers against industrial accidents by 1940, while only half of them had taken cognizance of health hazards. It is true that the average citizen is "health conscious" to a degree not at all reflected by the complete absence of industrial health provisions in the Social Security Act. But the fact remains that so far as tangible measurement of the incidence of health casualties in our industries is concerned, we are only on the fringe of an appreciation of its magnitude. Nevertheless, it is probably safe to say that all things considered, the economic loss from industrial health hazards probably is as great as—if it does not exceed—the burden of industrial accidents. Daugherty places the man-days of labor lost to American industry at about 250,000,000 annually, with cash losses to employers and workers together in the neighborhood of $5,000,000,000.[1]

2. *Causes*. The causes of industrial accidents and sickness are many and varied. They are necessarily woven one with another in actual life circumstances, so that in any given accident or illness one is likely to find a host of contributory factors which provide the setting for, or lead up to, the disaster. For example, a worker may lose a finger at a lathe, apparently due to his own carelessness. But other factors are likely to be found present upon closer study: the shop may be working long hours, or overtime; the lighting may be poor, or the man's vision may prove to be defective. It may even be that the worker is untrained or temperamentally unsuited to the job—that he took the lathe work as a make-shift because his regular trade afforded no opportunity for employment at the time. It is easy to see, then, that we often cannot place the blame for an accident at just one point. Nevertheless, it is well for us to review the various causes and call to mind some of the principal factors that go to make the problems of industrial safety and health so hard to grapple with in actual practice.

Among the direct, contributing causes of industrial illness, one of the most important is that of *dust* and *fumes*, either of which may be an irritant or a poison to the lungs, membranes of the nose, or even the skin. In most cases, their effect is not immediately apparent; and this constitutes one of the chief difficulties in combating their menace. Akin to these, but generally less disastrous, are the industrial processes that involve *extremes of temperature*, of *humidity* or *aridity*, or even of *air pressure*. In the case of air pressure, of course, disaster will overtake the diver or the tunnel worker who rises or descends too quickly between his work and the normal atmosphere. Then there is the *danger of infection*, either through open wounds, or from lesions directly caused by such substances as *acids*, *oils*, or *dyes*. In some occupations, such as those involving meat-cutting, or the handling of chemically active substances like *phosphorus* or *radium*, the danger can be serious enough to menace

[1] *Labor Problems in American Industry* (1941), p. 114.

life itself. And finally, there are those hazards which are common to both the health and safety of the worker: such matters as *poor lighting, poor ventilation, poor adjustment* of machines or benches to the stature of the worker's body, *monotonous* motion, or *cramped* positions.

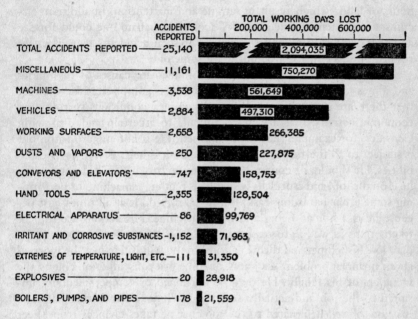

	ACCIDENTS REPORTED	TOTAL WORKING DAYS LOST
TOTAL ACCIDENTS REPORTED	25,140	2,094,035
MISCELLANEOUS	11,161	750,270
MACHINES	3,538	561,649
VEHICLES	2,884	497,310
WORKING SURFACES	2,658	266,385
DUSTS AND VAPORS	250	227,875
CONVEYORS AND ELEVATORS	747	158,753
HAND TOOLS	2,355	128,504
ELECTRICAL APPARATUS	86	99,769
IRRITANT AND CORROSIVE SUBSTANCES	1,152	71,963
EXTREMES OF TEMPERATURE, LIGHT, ETC.	111	31,350
EXPLOSIVES	20	28,918
BOILERS, PUMPS, AND PIPES	178	21,559

FIG. 11.—INDUSTRIAL ACCIDENTS AND WORKING DAYS LOST IN WISCONSIN, 1937

Norman M. Kastler, *Modern Human Relations* (Boston, 1940), p. 114.

Accidents which menace the safety of the worker obviously are more sudden than are the disasters which directly threaten the health of the worker. It must be borne in mind, of course, that the very existence of health hazards is an important cause of accidents; and accidents, in turn, may result in permanent ill health. Thus, the worker weakened by long and repeated exposure to dust, fumes, or poisons, sooner or later must be caught up by his own diminishing efficiency; and if resulting accidents are not fatal, they very often maim or create permanent invalidism. Aside from the condition of the worker himself, however, there is an infinite number of causes of industrial accidents. Among the commonest of such causes are the poor lighting, ventilation, and monotonous and fatiguing bodily movement which were mentioned with reference to health hazards; breakage of tools, machines, or the materials upon which they are being used; falling objects and insecure footing; exposure of gears, pulleys, levers, conveyor or power belts and chains or other moving parts of tools and machines; noise, speed, rhythm, and long hours of labor which result in fatigue and inattention. In addition, circumstances often produce "freak" accidents that no one could foresee and that are very unlikely to recur. Yet such accidents may as easily result in losses that must be borne by some one.

So much for the more obvious and immediate causes of disabilities and illness in employment. But our problem is complicated by the fact that there are many more subtle and complex conditions surrounding economic activity that are more difficult to ascertain and deal with. Consider, for example, the worker himself. He is not an automaton but is subject to all the failings to which the flesh is heir, as well as its capabilities. He should, of course, "pay attention to what he is doing" when he is on the job, and especially when he is tending a machine or performing some other hazardous task. But he *doesn't* do it at all times, just because he is a human being and not a machine. His actions are subject to emotions as well as to reason and habit. If things do not go right, he may lose his temper and throw caution to the winds. He may be worried about financial problems, sickness, or some grievous affliction among the members of his family. He may be untrained or temperamentally unsuited to the job and actually fear the machine; on the other hand, he may be so *well* habituated to the job that he takes chances from sheer overconfidence. Again, he may be the victim of poor living conditions, his health impaired not by the requirements of the job but by the fact of poor diet, poor housing, improper habits of life.

When we enter upon the matter of living conditions among workers as a potential determinant of industrial safety and health, we are in a category where individual and social responsibility are joined. The individual worker has very definite obligations to society to use his income wisely, to live temperately so as to be capable of performing his day's work with reasonable efficiency, to shoulder his fair share of the problems of the community in which he lives. But in many cases, too much is expected for too little. Long hours of labor, meager wages, and inadequate training put the worker at a tremendous handicap even though he be determined to live according to the rules. As we saw in the previous chapter, these adverse conditions confront the average worker more often than not; and to that extent, society itself is at fault to a greater degree than is commonly recognized for the frequency and severity of industrial accidents and sickness.

"Society," of course, is a broad term, and includes workers as well as employers, public officials, and consumers. Each of the four must assume its share of the responsibility as a class. As we have seen, workers have an obligation to keep themselves as fit for their jobs as possible. Employers must bear the lion's share of responsibility for the *immediate* causes of accidents and sickness among their workers, inasmuch as they control almost entirely the physical equipment their workers use and to a somewhat smaller degree the terms and rules under which they work. Public officials have the responsibility to enforce legal regulations and standards. Consumers are responsible to the extent that by their patronage they voice their desires as to the objectives of production, indirectly giving tacit assent to the policies of the companies whose goods they buy.

It must be remembered, however, that we cannot retain such sharp distinctions between workers, employers, and consumers in actual practice. Any single individual at one time or another plays all three rôles. Most of us have to work for our living, and more often than not we work as employees. Yet we all occasionally hire some one to work for us, to repair our houses or automobiles, perhaps, or to give us some other special service which for one reason or another we cannot perform for ourselves. Obviously all of us are consumers of one another's products. So in the last analysis all of us together, in our dealings with one another, are directly instrumental in shaping the terms of our economic life and formulating the collective attitudes toward the group problems that arise from those relationships.

It is argued that employers, being bent on maximum profit, necessarily will try to buy cheap and sell dear—the purchase of labor being no exception. The critics thus point out that proper safeguards for workers are expensive and so tend to reduce profits, and that employers will not take these precautions unless driven to do so by organized pressure of labor-unions or by governmental authority.

There is some truth in this position. The old *laissez-faire* philosophy which reduced legislative restrictions to a minimum and unloosed the force of unlimited competition compelled people to fend for themselves as a matter of economic survival. As a result, the employer who attempted to protect his workers actually was at a competitive disadvantage, since he was assuming costs which other producers were throwing on the workers themselves; and so he could not sell as cheaply as could his competitors.

However, the argument that capitalism alone is to blame for the vexing problem of industrial accidents is not sound. The assertion that competition was ruthless is true enough; yet the unbalance of bargaining power between individuals had not become acute until perhaps the period following the War Between the States. The legal disabilities that came to be so onerous for the workers as accidents became more numerous and severe were not strictly a "capitalistic" device but had roots in the common law extending far back into the Middle Ages. Moreover, it was no mere coincidence that comprehensive provisions for injured or diseased workers came slowly. Medical and surgical assistance for the afflicted was not impressive till the last quarter of the past century, when anaesthetics and antiseptics were discovered and began to come into general use. And finally, it must be admitted that "accidents will happen," regardless of the ideology under which economic activity takes place. It is as illogical to blame capitalism for *all* industrial accidents as it is to blame that system for accidents which result from errors in judgment or lack of caution on the highways or in the home itself. Consequently, regardless of the economic system under which a society may function, there inevitably will be problems of devising means for assuring health and safety to its members and care to the victims of disease and accident.

3. *Remedies.* The most natural thing to do when one is confronted with any kind of danger is to try and remove the source of the danger; and this was substantially the policy that was pursued in regard to the menace to health and safety developed in modern industry. Of course, knowledge was quite incomplete in regard to the extent or character of those dangers; yet certain among them seemed to stand out. Thus, the early legislation regarding hours of labor, which we noticed in the previous chapter, was in part an effort to reduce accidents. The menace of open gears and the old-time shaft and belt power transmission was soon apparent; and the earliest legislation called for suitable guards to shield them. Later, as the matter of safety was studied more carefully, further refinements were added, such as those regarding lighting, ventilation, guard rails, and sanitary facilities.

Accidents and disease, however, continued almost unabated; and it became clear that other measures were necessary, both to assure the enforcement of the safety laws, and to provide some sort of assistance for the incapacitated worker. While the laws provided penalties for non-conformity, nevertheless they had to be enforced to be effective; and adequate enforcement without large numbers of inspectors was impractical. So while the laws still are a very important phase of the campaign to reduce the hazards of accidents and sickness, they had to be linked with incentives more powerful than mere punitive fines to make them effective; and as casualties among workers mounted, the problem of their care became more insistent. The two problems were linked together into a very ingenious system of "workmen's compensation" laws which we shall presently consider.

Prior to the development of the compensation laws about the only practical way the worker had for securing relief from the distress arising from industrial injuries was by suing his employer in the courts. Such a procedure, however, was not at all effective in most cases. The body of common law that had developed pertaining to this remedy through the centuries provided that the employer should have "reasonably" safe equipment and personnel in his shop. The worker was expected to be aware of the risks he was assuming when he agreed to work for the employer and to shoulder the responsibility for negligence on the part of himself or his fellow workers insofar as their activities affected him. Obviously the chances for collecting damages under such conditions grew more remote as industry became more complex. "Reasonableness" can become a very vague concept when applied to industrial practices and conditions that have become less uniform; and workers themselves knew less and less about the details of the risks they assumed and were compelled by necessity to accept work conditions and fellow workmen as they found them. Moreover, the condition was not altogether satisfactory even to the employer. Even though he *usually* went scot-free under these laws, his civil liability nevertheless was unlimited; and the *occasional* success of the worker in securing a judgment created a constant and sometimes disastrous threat to the financial solvency of the employer. The workmen's compensation laws, although they were at first regarded with considerable suspicion by both workers and employers, have proved to be of distinct advantage to both by reducing these hazards. The worker is assured of some protection, while the employer's liability is placed within fixed limits; and in most cases both of them are spared the losses and uncertainties of long and expensive court proceedings.

The first compensation laws were enacted in Germany in 1884, followed by those of Great Britain of 1897. They were introduced into some of the States in America early in the present century; but it was not until 1911 that New York and Wisconsin passed the first laws to stand the test of constitutionality in the courts. By 1941 all the States except Mississippi had some sort of compensation provisions for their workers, although the inclusiveness and effectiveness of many of the States' provisions left much to be desired.[2] As might be expected, the laws have found their fullest development, with but few exceptions, in the industrial States of our North and East.

In general, the objectives of these laws are to provide compensation for injured workers according to fixed schedules of benefits and injuries to be covered. Usually there is a waiting period before benefits begin, in the case of non-fatal injuries, the period varying from one day to as much as two weeks. Benefits also vary, but in general they include medical care, compensation for wage loss, and frequently assistance in rehabilitation if the worker is rendered incapable of his regular job but is able to do something else. In the case of fatal accidents, the benefits are paid to the victim's survivors or to his estate, sometimes in a lump sum, sometimes over a period of years. In any case, the benefits thus paid are limited in duration and amount.

Settlements sometimes are made by the employer or his agent (usually a casualty insurance company), or they may be fixed by a State board or commission (or, in a few States, by the court); but the private settlement also is subject to approval by the State agency. Benefit payments are financed entirely by employers; and these funds are raised in various ways, but always in accordance with insurance principles. Employers may insure directly with approved insurance companies or pay their premiums to a State fund. Larger employers sometimes are permitted to segregate some of their own resources for this purpose. Another point of variation pertains to whether the premiums are kept separate for each employer or are pooled for all the employers together. In either case, however, the payments of individual employers are assessed on the basis of their accident records.

The compensation laws appear to be economically sound from every point of view. They release the worker from the major portion of the financial burden of accidents, yet the benefits are small enough that malingering is reduced to a minimum. They provide sufficient incentive for the worker and employer alike to avoid accidents, for the former to

[2] For a short comparative discussion of the variations in the State workmen's compensation laws, see Marshall Dawson, "Workmen's Compensation," *Social Work Year Book, 1941*, R. H. Kurtz, ed., pp. 609–613.

assure his wages, for the latter to reduce the payments he must make to maintain his reserves. In the long run, moreover, when all competing employers approach the practical minimums of accident experience, then the price of their commodity tends to rise to offset their costs. This, too, is defensible, since the consumer should expect to bear the full cost of the goods he buys.

There are many shortcomings of the laws, as is so generally true of the various types of social legislation. One of the most serious, undoubtedly, is that there are no federal standards of coverage or benefits, since the laws still are enacted and administered entirely by the States. As a result, the usual problems of interstate trade arise, the employers in the more progressive States being put at a competitive disadvantage. Benefits are generally very low and of short duration, and the waiting periods are too long in most cases. Coverage is much too narrow, since whole categories like agriculture and home employment are exempt, and the laws apply only to employers of many or at least several persons. Moreover, the problems of industrial *diseases* have hardly been touched. Only about half of the States make any provision at all for this type of disability, and even among them the list of compensative sicknesses is distinctly limited. Nevertheless, with all their shortcomings, the workmen's compensation laws have greatly mitigated the hazards and suffering arising from industrial accidents.

THE PROBLEM OF VOCATIONAL ADJUSTMENT

Still another perplexing aspect of modern industrialism is the ever-growing problem of vocational adjustment: the problem of finding the right sort of job and of adjusting the worker to it. This problem has become more and more apparent with each advance of machine industry and with the continued increase of specialization in industry and business.

In this, as in the other problems of modern industrialism, American public opinion has been slow to abandon the traditional doctrines of rugged individualism. The pioneer regarded each individual as "the architect of his own fate," and it was felt that any young man with ambition and the will to work could achieve success in "this land of opportunity." There still are many influential people who believe that opportunity for success is as great to-day as it was in the day when farms and forests could be had for a few cents an acre. Opportunity, they say, is even greater to-day than at any time in the past, and there is an abundance of "room at the top" in every business and profession.

The exponents of this all too hopeful doctrine overlook the fact that the "top" is every year getting narrower; that business and industry are rapidly integrating, and every year sees the business and industrial establishments growing larger in size but fewer in number. Even the field for independent executives is getting narrower, and to an increasing extent the men who a generation ago would have risen to be "captains of industry" must now be content to become the efficient, specialized hired experts of corporations. But, after all, the vast majority of the working population could not expect to become executives, or even hired managers—and it is with this rank and file of the vast working population that we are here chiefly concerned. It is with the rank and file of American workers that the hazards of vocational adjustment have a real meaning and are an ever-present threat.

We might group these hazards of vocational adjustment into two general classes: (1) the hazards of finding the specialized occupation suited to the individual boy or girl, and of getting the proper education and training required for success in it; (2) the hazards that grow out of the improvement of processes and methods of industry and the invention of labor-saving machinery—processes and machines that displace human skill and do the work of thousands of hands. The first group of hazards involves the problem of vocational guidance and training; the second group involves the even more difficult problem of beginning anew, perhaps late in life—after having learned one trade—and developing skill in and becoming adjusted to another occupation.

Vocational Adjustment of Youth. In former days there was not much question about what the young man or young woman would do for a livelihood. It was generally taken for granted that the boy would follow in the footsteps of his father, and the girl would get married and become a home-maker. If the father was a craftsman, the boy was expected to become an apprentice, then a journeyman, and finally a skilled artisan himself. The son of a professional man or merchant generally entered the office or business of his father, and it was expected that eventually the young man would carry on the enterprise when the older man retired. When our country was still predominantly agricultural, the farmer's boy—when he was ready to "make his own way"—either purchased a part of the old homestead from his father or moved on to the West and homesteaded for himself, in either case effectively settling the question of choosing a vocation.

For the great majority of young men and women, the problem of finding an occupation no longer is simple. Only a very small percentage

—even of the farmer's children—follow the parental example. In the rapidly changing industrial life of to-day such a plan would not be possible for the majority, even if it were desirable. Not less than one out of every two of our boys and girls drop out of school before completing high school, because their parents are too poor to keep them in school, or because they cannot make a success at the college-tuned curriculum of the modern high school, or because they are overanxious to earn their own money. Consequently, most of our boys and girls look out upon the confusing and changing multitude of narrow, specialized occupational niches of modern industry and business, and, through an awkward trial-and-error process, seek the jobs that seem to pay best. They are not willing to accept reduced pay with an opportunity to learn a trade or to become skilled in a specialized occupation that offers some future advantages. The twenty-five to fifty cents per hour paid for unskilled, common machine hands looks large to them. The employer may need skilled workers and may offer attractive apprenticeship opportunities, but the average boy or girl looks at the present rather than the future. What skill they happen to acquire—if they are fortunate enough to acquire any—they get in the course of wandering from one job to another. In this process many become "floaters," workers on the job to-day and gone to-morrow. Many become dissatisfied with their lot, feel embittered against the "capitalistic system" which they think keeps them down, and develop a sort of religious zeal in a "war on capitalism." Thus we see that the "blind-alley" jobs of unskilled labor— jobs which the average boy or girl can do as ably as men and women— stand in the way of the vocational guidance and training which would cut down the hazards of occupational adjustment.

By the opening of the present century the seriousness of the problems growing out of the failure of thousands of new workers to find satisfactory vocational adjustment began to be recognized. Forward-looking educators and employers began to discuss the prospects of developing vocational guidance as a new profession. "By vocational guidance is meant the provision of expert advice as to what vocations offer most promise of successful permanent employment based upon a careful examination of each candidate and a knowledge of available opportunity." [3] The first vocational guidance bureau was opened in Boston in 1908 by Dr. Frank Parsons, and on the basis of accomplishments of this first bureau the National Vocational Guidance Association was organized.

[3] Dale Yoder, *Labor Economics and Labor Problems* (New York, 1933), p. 149.

Vocational guidance has developed into vocational *counseling* and *coördinating*. Instead of prescribing specific vocations, the individual is given an understanding of as large a range of vocations as possible. During the past few years there has been increased recognition of the value of this service. Vocational schools have led other educational institutions in giving specialized attention to this problem, though universities, high schools, and many grade schools have been attempting to meet the situation by assigning members of the teaching staff to this task in addition to their regular teaching duties. It must be admitted, however, that as yet no really sound and effective plan has been developed; much of the advice and counseling amounts to little more than guesswork. Much research has yet to be done before a sound system of vocational counseling can be developed.[4]

The slowness with which sound vocational counseling has developed and the growing intensity of the need for such a service have provided almost unlimited opportunity for the quack and the cheat. Thousands of job-seekers, including many who are apparently intelligent and well educated, are the victims of such organized frauds. It is amazing and pathetic to see them awaiting their turn to have their careers revealed to them by an "expert" who "reads" their palms or "deciphers" their handwriting, or who employs some other pseudo-scientific device of "psychoanalysis" that may create a more professional impression but in fact has no more validity than crystal-gazing, astrology, phrenology, numerology, or any other clairvoyant trick. Not far behind this group of quacks and cheats are the hundreds of so-called "schools" which promise to prepare the desperate job-seeker for profitable employment in a skilled occupation "in a few short lessons, on an easy payment plan." Many States have attempted to control or prohibit such exploitation by licensing private counselors and requiring correspondence-study schools to meet the standards prescribed by the State department of public instruction. But even in the face of these legal safeguards, millions of dollars are annually filched from gullible job-seekers.[5]

Vocational Adjustment of Adults. The reorganization of industry and the introduction of labor-saving machinery every year throw thousands of workers into the unhappy quandary of rebuilding their occupational footing and of starting anew to work up to a satisfactory wage income.

[4] See *List of References on Vocational Guidance* (Washington, D. C.: Office of Education, United States Department of Interior).

[5] Ella Woodyard, *Culture at a Price* (New York: American Association for Adult Education, 1940), recounts first-hand experiences with correspondence schools of various types.

Must the worker, then, go to school perennially in order to be prepared to make the shift from one trade or occupation to another? If so, there is need in most States for some far-reaching changes in the educational machinery: changes that would provide a program of *adult* education suited to the needs of the working population, one recognizing the problems of vocational change.

TABLE 19

NUMBER OF EMPLOYEES PER MILLION OF POPULATION FOR SELECTED OCCUPATIONS, 1850 AND 1930 *

Occupation	1850	1930
Agriculture	103,568	85,294
Boiler makers	68	407
Boot and shoe workers	5,644	2,482
Clerical occupations	4,369	49,805
Coopers	1,884	92
Electricians	†	2,283
Harness and saddle workers	982	62
Iron and steel workers	528	6,731
Millers and millworkers	1,199	316
Paper and pulp mill workers	128	1,094
Rubber factory operatives	7	896
Sailors and deck hands	3,044	527
Wagon and coach makers	673	34
Wheelwrights	1,323	†

* *Monthly Labor Review,* pp. 1017–1018 (November, 1933).
† None listed.

Historically, the first great adjustments of artisans to the march of machinery came in the textile industries. Thousands of weavers found their trade taken from them by the introduction of machines, and most of them had to turn to other occupations for earning a living. A few years ago printing was dependent upon the type-setters, but the invention of the linotype machine shattered this aspect of the printers' trade. Glass-blowers until a few years ago produced most of our glassware; but now the Owens Bottle Machine does the work of thousands of glass-workers. Machinists have seen the same sweeping changes come into the rapidly growing machine industry, and many had to be content with becoming tenders of huge automatic machines, or becoming repair-men in garages—only the better educated could step up into the professional class of machine-designers and mechanical engineers. Telegraph operators have been displaced by the installation of automatic machines that transmit messages from one typewriter to another. The adding-machines, billing-machines, tabulating and recording machines have lessened the need for thousands of bookkeepers, clerks, and office help. Almost every aspect of business and industry furnishes us equally striking examples of labor displacement.

It is interesting to note that business and industrial periodicals, which a few years ago devoted a great deal of attention to labor management, industrial welfare, and employee education, are now stressing the *use of improved labor-saving machines as means of cutting down costs and increasing output.*

Trade-unions were at first opposed to the introduction of labor-saving machines; but soon they realized that such opposition was futile and not in harmony with progress. Most of the trade-unions to-day offer no open resistance to these changes, but attempt to regulate them in such a way as will insure the job for the union worker and keep the wage from falling. Unions have done—and are still doing—a great deal to bring about occupational adjustments for their members. But generally the methods used by trade-unions have not been favorable to the full use of machines—they have been more of the nature of restriction of output.

Doubtless the building of vocational schools, the development of scientific vocational guidance, and the organization of a scientific system of employment bureaus will not only aid the new worker entering industry, but will eventually become the route by which the displaced worker can find satisfactory readjustments. There must be a closer relationship between the school, the employment bureau, and industry in order that industrial changes be better understood and the worker properly prepared for readjustment. The employer must give more consideration to the laborer's problem, and not proceed as though the readjustment of the worker is no concern of his. Many employers are doing more than their just share in aiding these changes—and are finding that it pays in the long run. But many more employers are either indifferent to or opposed to policies aiding readjustment which, they say, are "dictated by the exponents of organized labor." In fact, many industries have found the introduction of labor-saving machinery "a means of emancipating themselves from the grip of organized labor," and for this reason refuse to consider a program of readjusting their employees. Doubtless a sound public policy is needed before full coöperation of all employers of labor can be had.

Some cognizance has been taken of this problem by both the State and federal governments, in their vocational rehabilitation services. The

Federal Vocational Rehabilitation Act of 1920 provided federal funds for the use of the States in expanding their vocational educational programs, the allotments being made on a matching basis. The scope of federal assistance was further extended under the Social Security Act. These allotments, however, have been directed chiefly at rehabilitation of *incapacitated* workers, and mainly among those who, it is felt, can be restored to normal earning capacity. At best, only a fraction of workers eligible for such assistance have taken advantage of it, largely because the maintenance of the workers and their families during the period of retraining remains their own responsibility in most cases. The problem of the *displaced* worker has hardly been touched at all by these measures.

THE EMPLOYMENT OF WOMEN

1. *Extent.* Probably no other phase of labor problems has had more attention in public discussion than the entry of women into gainful employment. The trend was sensed and regarded with some curiosity before the First World War; but the presence of large numbers of women in "war industries," coupled with the rapid demobilization of the troops following that war, brought the matter more sharply to the attention of men, who have continued to regard themselves ever since as being confronted with a new source of competition for their jobs. The employment of women is not a new phenomenon, however. As far back as 1880, one person in seven gainfully employed was a woman. The proportion had risen to about one in five by 1910, which was substantially the situation ten years later, after the First World War. In 1940, the figure stood at just under one in four, and later was increased considerably by the demands of war industry. Moreover, the proportion of employment among women has been approximately the same as the proportion of women among the total number of employed persons.

Nevertheless, the *number* of women employed has increased greatly since 1880. The comparatively small rise in the proportion is more startling when we take into account the fact that the population also has been growing. Moreover, men always have been employed to a much higher degree than women, the figure having hovered around 80 per cent during that period; yet among men, the proportion actually is falling slightly, owing to the growing industrial and public assistance policies of retiring industrial workers at earlier ages. Thus the contrast becomes more impressive, considered numerically. The number of women employed increased from about 2,650,000 in 1880 to nearly 12,850,000 in 1940, a gain of almost 400 per cent; while among men, the numbers increased only about 170 per cent during the same period, or from approximately 14,750,000 to about 40,000,000.

Women are to be found in almost all the occupations to-day, being excluded from a few such as mining, steel manufacture, or construction work chiefly because such work is physically incompatible with the welfare of women. Domestic and personal service engaged about three employed women in ten, while clerical jobs of one sort or another occupied about two more. Manufacturing took a somewhat smaller proportion, but more than agriculture, trade, and the teaching profession, each of which occupied about one in ten. Most women gainfully employed are young, about 60 per cent of them in 1940 being under 35 years of age. More than 85 per cent of the employed women in 1940 were white, while about 15 per cent were Negro.

2. *Development.* Women have always had an important part in the productive work of the world; but from primitive times down to the beginning of the Industrial Revolution their work was largely of a *domestic* nature: it was performed in or about the home. They performed much of the agricultural labor, as, indeed, they still do in areas where agriculture itself has not yet become mechanized. They prepared and stored most of the food supply and did the spinning and weaving. They not only bore the children but gave them much more of their early education than they now do. The average home required but little from the outside, either in things consumed or in equipment used. The husband and wife, together with the grown children, actually produced most of their own living. The chief industries outside the home were fishing (in coastal areas), agriculture, and commerce; and these activities were engaged in dominantly by men, as they still are, since they required strength and stamina beyond the average capacity of women.

The coming of the factory system and the growth of modern business enterprise have removed from the home the major part of its productive work, placed that work in an altogether different setting, and created a new set of social relationships. Women were deprived of their economic value in fulfilling their traditional rôle of keeping the home together as a "going concern." Moreover, since more of the things the family needed were bought, there developed a greater need for cash expenditures.

It was only natural, in the light of the new conditions created by the

Industrial Revolution, that women should follow their age-old occupations out of the home into the factory. This was especially noticeable, for example, in the case of textiles, which was one of the first great "large-scale" industries to develop. The work was comparatively easy, although tedious and to some extent hazardous. Nevertheless, even in the early development of industry, there was a direct clash of interest between men and women. The technical developments began to make their impact felt in many of the crafts and industries which formerly had been carried on by men. Displacement of labor in such fields began to appear very early in the history of the Industrial Revolution; and the combination of lack of labor organization and the tremendous drive for increased production to meet the demands of foreign markets put the workers at a disadvantage. Unorganized workers could do little to forestall the pressure for long hours of work and low wages; so the mite which the employed women added to the family coffers of individual workers was both necessary and welcome, even while the competition which the employment of women afforded was a contributing factor to the desperate problems confronting the workers. It was, indeed, a "vicious circle."

It has already been suggested that women have always been more or less of a "drug on the market" of labor supply. While they have always done useful work, the fact is that until the domestic activities gave way to such a large extent to the expansion of factory production, a *price* had not generally been put on their work; and they never were considered an appreciable supply of employable labor. Consequently the system of economic production for exchange had grown up with the labor supply limited mostly to men. And when large numbers of women began to enter the labor market, the inevitable result was that conditions of labor grew steadily worse. This process still is going on to a considerable extent, although there are mitigating factors, such as an expanding labor market and the restriction of labor supply by means of legislative action and the growth of unionism among the workers themselves.[6]

3. *Present Conditions of Work.* As might be expected on the basis of the background of the employment of women in industry, the conditions under which women have worked have never been favorable. The abundant supply of potential women workers has been a powerful factor in keeping their wages low, and the terms of work, such as hours

[6] See Mary van Kleeck, "Women in Industry," *Encyclopaedia of the Social Sciences*, XV: 451-456.

and shop conditions, have been largely what employers saw fit to provide. While hours of labor are being increasingly restricted by legislation in regard to products made for interstate and local consumption
alike, the laws are far from uniform, and many are of very limited
scope. Despite legislative protection, wages still are extremely low for
women generally. Various studies indicate that women's pay lags behind men's by as much as one-third or even one-half, even for services
that are more or less comparable; and women's wages vary widely between geographic sections and between races, as do men's.[7]

There are other vital factors, however, that still operate against
women workers, even though the conditions of women in industry
have improved greatly since, let us say, the period before the First
World War. It still remains true, even in the face of legislative protection, that it costs more to employ women and that women themselves
are *able* to work for less than are men. Regarding the costs of hiring
women, it is well known that absenteeism, or days absent from the job,
is higher among women. This is due partly to their biological make-up,
partly to their tendency to tire more easily, and partly to the fact that
many women have other duties at home, whether they have homes of
their own or whether they live with their parents. These factors suggest
further items of higher costs in employing women: more rest periods,
more rest rooms and sanitary facilities, and better conditions of ventilation and lighting are needed to keep fatigue and disability at a minimum
among women than among men. It is also well known that the majority
of women stop work at, or soon after, marriage; hence the costs of
labor turn-over are higher. The very fact of legislative restrictions on
the hours of labor for women also increases the unit cost of machinery
and plant upkeep, since they are idle for a greater share of the time.
Granting these points, however, it is doubtful whether the lower wages
that prevail among women are wholly justifiable. It would seem that in
most jobs employers would prefer hiring men if the costs to him were
equal; men are steadier, require less consideration, have long-time interest in their jobs.

The unfavorable position of women workers is further intensified by
the conditions surrounding women as a group. We have already noticed
that women enter employment much less permanently than do men.
Most young women expect to marry; and this, coupled with the fact
that so many machine and light assembly jobs require a minimum of

---

[7] See C. R. Daugherty, *Labor Problems in American Industry* (Boston, 1941),
pp. 217–218.

training, makes for much competition among women for the comparatively unskilled jobs. Many women are only partially self-supporting, inasmuch as they may draw on other members of their families for assistance. Furthermore, even those that are wholly self-supporting often can get along on a smaller cash income than men, due to their common ability to cook and sew for themselves; although it is likely that a goodly portion of those who do such "light house-keeping" in addition to a day's work "on the job" are driven to it by the very fact that their wages are small. And lastly, women undoubtedly are generally more conservative than men, being less inclined to band together to improve their own conditions.

4. *The Problem of "Equal Pay."* Our discussion of the reasons for women's wages being substantially lower than men's even for comparable work may help to throw some light upon the problems involved if we are to try to provide "equal pay for equal work." This slogan long has been an expression of the opinion of many, that women should not be penalized with lower wages for reasons of sex alone. It also is offered as a "solution" for the problem of competition of women with men in the labor market, it being argued that if we raise women's wages to a parity with men's, then large numbers of women will be forced out of employment due to employers' general preference for men if other conditions are equal.

It must be remembered that women *do* constitute a substantial *labor reserve*, which is tapped only under special conditions. As was stated earlier, our labor economy was built on the premise that men constitute the bulk of the paid labor supply. If, then, we raise women's wages "equal" to men's, the result must be that more women will be attracted to enter the active labor market. That is to say, the supply of labor will increase relative to the demand for its services, and the scale of wages for *all* workers will decline. The only way it can be avoided is by legislative and union restrictions on the supply of labor; the alternative is "equally" *low* wages for all workers, men and women alike.

It is not at all certain that women have displaced men in industrial employment. It is true that in some lines of work such a development seems to be taking place. But much of that displacement can be as reasonably laid to the introduction of machinery itself. Many displaced workers are absorbed by new industries, of course; but the gradual and steady rise of unemployment through the years has been too consistent and unrelated to the fluctuations in the employment of women to warrant general claims that the employment of women has driven men out of work. The problem of unemployment, at which the "equal pay" proposal is leveled, is too much a product of our general economic dislocation to be explained categorically by the employment of women in industry.

5. *Improving the Conditions of Work.* Efforts to improve the conditions of employment of women have taken a somewhat different route from those designed to improve the working conditions of men. Men have used their unions and group bargaining in matters relating to wages, hours, and days off. Women do not seem to be so successful in developing strong labor organizations. Hence they have not been able to wield organized force to protect their best interests or to obtain industrial advantages. The National Women's Trade Union League has been an active force in building up unions wherever possible and in promoting the legislation that would strengthen the position of women in industry. But the membership of women in these labor-unions is small compared with the total number employed. Even with the ever-ready assistance from the men's organizations, it is hardly possible for the organized women workers to affect materially the working conditions of women in industry.

Consequently, the most effective efforts for improving the industrial outlook of women workers have been directed at obtaining *legislation* and *public action.* This means, of course, that the legal provisions regulating and safeguarding the employment of women will vary widely from State to State, and the effectiveness of such measures depends to a large extent upon the degree of education and the strength of public opinion relative to working conditions for women in the various States.

In general these public measures fall into three principal classes: (1) measures directed toward establishing a minimum that would not be oppressive, by limiting hours of work or establishing minimum wage-rates; (2) measures directed toward improving working conditions and obtaining the facilities and adjustments for meeting needs of women workers—rest-room facilities, seats, and safety equipment; (3) restrictive measures directed toward excluding women from those occupations which are most detrimental to their health and well-being.

Sixteen States by 1941 limited the work day for women to eight hours, sixteen others had a nine-hour day, while only four had failed to make at least some provision in this matter. Seventeen States regulated home employment. Twenty States prohibited or restricted night work for women, while twenty-nine had minimum wage laws for women. Forty-five States had mothers' aid laws, although their inclusiveness varied widely, and only forty-two had plans which had been approved by the Social Security Board for federal participation.

6. *Gainful Employment and the Status of Women.* One of the most interesting by-products of the employment of women in industry, from the social point of view, is the impact of such employment upon the status of women in present-day society. It is a matter which must be approached with some caution, however, since we are apt to generalize too freely and credit the economic opportunity of women with more benefit than is its due. Stern has well pointed out that "throughout history class lines have cut across sex lines with the result that women of the ruling classes have enjoyed privileges denied to the men as well as the women of the submerged classes; within each class, however, women have been at a disadvantage as compared with the men." [8]

Of all the classes of women, the women of the middle class undoubtedly have benefited the most from the Industrial Revolution. It was they who formerly were burdened with the bulk of comparatively easy, yet essentially monotonous, household tasks of cooking, canning, weaving, and sewing which were taken from the home and placed largely in the factory. Lower-class women, relieved of the domestic tasks at home, nevertheless had to follow them into the factory because their husbands —farmers and artisans, largely—were being harassed by other phases of the Industrial Revolution, and the need for additional cash outlay to supply their daily needs increased. To the extent that they contributed to the family's maintenance financially, the women of the lower classes began to command more respect than formerly from their husbands, since their assistance was more visibly indispensable—and measurable. The middle-class women, however, found their husbands capable of "supporting" them, since their share of the benefits from the technological advance was larger. So for the first time in history, there arose a large "leisure class": a considerable segment of women largely released from toil and given a world of opportunity for self-expression. Whether that opportunity has been well used cannot be stated in final terms. There has been a good deal of lost motion and time-squandering in what has been termed competitive consumption—"keeping up with the Joneses"—a good deal of frustration in trying to keep busy about something that at least seemed worth-while. On the other hand, the great leaders among nineteenth century women who advocated legal, political, and social liberties for their sex as a whole, were dominantly women

---

[8] Bernard J. Stern, "Woman, Position in Society," in *Encyclopaedia of the Social Sciences*, XV: 442, New York, 1937.

of the middle class. It was they, too, who for the most part led the many groups seeking social reform during the same period: they looked toward better care for children, toward temperance, toward better hospital care and improved treatment for dependent and deficient classes generally. Many have sought "careers" and contributed much to the arts and professions and sciences, as well as to the more practical world of commerce and politics.

Women as a whole also have found in the effects of the Industrial Revolution an economic equivalent and alternative to marriage, which gives them much greater independence in their dealings with men in general and potential husbands in particular. As a result, more of the "bonds of matrimony" have come to be the silken cords of inclination rather than the iron chains of necessity! [9]

THE COMPETITION OF SUBSTANDARD WORKERS

Unfortunately, women are not the only group of workers that is able to compete with men who, by tradition, as husbands and fathers, have been the "bread-winners" for their families. The average wage-earner is expected to maintain our "American standard of living"; but there are various other types of workers who, like women, are able to compete for his job on less than even terms. The presence of such groups in the labor market increases the supply of labor available to industry, and so threatens both the wage rates and work conditions in the whole field. Thus they are called *substandard* workers, since they work under conditions and for wages below the levels generally considered necessary to maintain "average" or normal living conditions for themselves and their families. Among these we already have considered the direct competition of Negroes, for example, who by reason of their traditional status and lack of organization, have been able to enter industry and secure jobs in preference to the white workers.[10] Still other groups of this nature which create distinct social problems are children, home workers, prisoners, and "casual" labor—and in the latter group we may classify the so-called "poor whites." Only the first three will be discussed here, however, since for the most part the casual worker is an agricultural rather than an industrial wage earner.

1. *The Employment of Children.* To some extent the employment of children in industry followed the same patterns of development as did the employment of women, which we have just discussed. When we

[9] See Chapter 12 below.
[10] Chapter 4.

remember that the universal education we attempt to provide for our children here in the United States has not always been universal, we realize that child labor is hardly a problem of modern origin. When hand labor was prevalent, every pair of hands was at a premium; and children were not exempt. Indeed, they learned most of their practical knowledge by actually doing things and by imitating their parents at work. So when the Industrial Revolution developed, it seemed to some but a reasonable step to put the children to work, earning while they were learning. Furthermore, it had been felt for long that "the Devil finds work for idle fingers"—especially, it seemed, among children. We still find in some sections of our country a considerable abhorrence of leisure time and recreational activities.

In 1910, the census reported nearly two million employed children between the ages of ten and fifteen years, or about 18 per cent of all the children in that age group. By 1920, the number had been almost halved, being a little over a million, while the percentage had dropped to 8.5. In 1930 there were some 667,000 child workers, who constituted about 4.7 per cent of the total number of children. In 1910 at least one worker in twenty was a child not more than fifteen years of age; by 1930 there were on an average hardly three such children among two hundred workers.[11]

Boy workers quite consistently have outnumbered girl workers through the years by at least two to one, a situation explained by the fact that child labor has been and still remains largely a rural phenomenon. It is true that most of the girls are employed in agriculture, too; but farming traditionally is a man's job, and it is felt by many that farming is best learned "by experience." Thus among all children gainfully employed in 1930, three-fifths of the girls and three-fourths of the boys were working on farms; yet of the total of about 470,000 rural workers, about 343,000 were boys and only about 126,000 were girls. Numerically, the boys and girls engaged in manufacturing were about equal, both being approximately 35,000. On the other hand, boys greatly outnumbered girls (about 57,000 as against 7,000) in trade and messenger service, while the girls exceeded the boys in domestic and personal service, at nearly 36,000 to 10,000. Only 3.3 per cent of the white children were employed, while a little more than 16 per cent of the Negro children were at work.[12]

[11] *Census of Occupations, Abstract Summary* (U. S. Bureau of the Census, 1932), pp. 3–5.
[12] *Ibid.*, tables 22 and 45, also p. 86.

The cold figures of child employment do not give a very adequate picture of the evils of child labor. Everyone will agree that children need the discipline of work and responsibility as a part of their training for adult life later on; but the work and responsibility they are expected to shoulder should be *commensurate with their years.* Thus the moral hazards for boys in street and messenger service are high, as are those for girls in domestic and restaurant service. In both cases the children are placed in adult situations requiring maturity and judgment which obviously children cannot be expected to have. Then there are the physical costs of child labor. Industry and agriculture are probably the chief offenders here, since they require long periods of repetitive application to the job, often under conditions of abnormal posture, whether it be cramping or stretching to use oversize equipment. None can gauge the loss entailed by the limitation of education resulting from child employment, nor the ill effect upon the progeny of the child worker who reaches adulthood in poor health and in ignorance. Economically it seems an ironic commentary that there should be any child labor at all at times when millions of adults go unemployed; and it is questionable whether even the employer of child labor gains much in the long run. If one were to count the losses from high labor turn-over, excessive accidents and sickness, and spoilage of materials, together with the damage to consumer good will, it is unlikely that the child worker is an asset to his employer.

Despite the evident costliness of child labor from virtually every point of view, the struggle to remove or even to control it has been a long and difficult procedure. Moreover, contrary to common belief, the matter has not even yet been fully adjusted. There are various considerations and groups which still oppose such regulation as might be really effective; and even the developments during the first two terms of Franklin D. Roosevelt left many loopholes for lax administration of such legislative provisions as were made for federal control over the matter. Employers commonly are opposed to federal acts; farmers as a rule have been dead set against any restriction of the labor of children in agriculture; many political leaders are jealous of the apparent encroachment of the Federal Government upon the domain of States' rights; and even religious bodies have expressed fear lest government reach too far into the sphere of family relationships.

The control over child labor still remains largely in the hands of the individual States, and, as one might well expect, the legislative provisions pertaining to child labor have varied widely regarding hours of labor, age of children protected, industries covered, educational minimum requirements, health 'standards, and work conditions. It long has been clear that child labor legislation to be effective must be of a federal nature, to meet the problems presented by interstate competition; but the development of federal control has been very slow. There has been the active opposition to such control which we mentioned a moment ago; and the opponents have had in the past an effective weapon in the question of the constitutionality of such acts. The Congress attempted such measures first in 1916, as an act to regulate interstate commerce, and again in 1919 by imposing a prohibitive tax; but both acts were declared unconstitutional. A constitutional amendment, putting regulation of child labor in the hands of the Federal Government was passed by Congress in 1924 but still remains unratified by the necessary number of States. The National Recovery Administration codes (which defined fair business practices) generally ruled out child labor in industry but left the problem untouched in agriculture; and the whole National Industrial Recovery Act was invalidated by the Supreme Court in 1935. The Fair Labor Standards Act has gone farthest among the federal acts regulating child labor, providing that no child under sixteen years old may be employed on articles of interstate commerce; and it quite generally excludes children from fourteen to sixteen years of age in mining and manufacturing industries. However, the effectiveness of the Act will become apparent only as policies become established through the years. There are broad exceptions regarding employment of children by their parents; and in other cases, considerable authority rests with the federal Children's Bureau to determine the limits within which child labor shall be deemed socially acceptable and at what point such employment becomes detrimental. Under such conditions it is clear that policies still are likely to be fixed on the basis of personal bias of administrators or the pressure exerted by partisan groups.

2. *The Home Industries.* We used to hear a great deal about the "sweat-shops" and of the exploitation of women and children by the "sweated" industries. For some reason not so much is said any more about those old survivals of domestic industry. But because the furor has subsided does not mean that industrial work has disappeared from the homes and tenements. Attempts at licensing and inspection have improved some of the worst aspects of it, but the "sweating trades" are still with us. In spite of efforts to improve them, they are still a menace to and a blight upon the health and welfare of thousands of women and child workers.

In general, there are two types of "sweating." (1) The small shop, set up in a tenement or dwelling-house, where the subcontractor crowds in the necessary machines and employs the women of the neighborhood to come in and do the work under his direct "supervision." The typical sweat-shop of this sort is small, poorly lighted and ventilated, usually insanitary and with no adequate sanitary equipment. (2) The other, and now more prevalent type of "sweating," is the subletting of the work to be done in the homes of the workers. In this way the worker is assisted by all the available members of the family who happen to be at home nights. The homes are often small, overcrowded, neglected, and poorly lighted. Sickness in the family is generally more of a reason for taking in work than for withholding it—the consuming public does not know the difference between a garment made in a sick-room (with the aid of the diseased) and a garment made under "strictly sanitary" conditions!

The first type of sweat-shop is gradually disappearing, owing to enforced legislation regarding standards of places of employment, and owing also to the demands made by the organized clothing workers. But the work done in the homes, where no inspector has an opportunity to set standards of cleanliness, lighting, and hours of work, is where the problem offers resistance to solution. Under such conditions the worker legally is an independent contractor rather than an employee; and on this basis he is not protected by factory and other labor laws. Thus in large cities and their immigrant sections it is easy to obtain the labor of women and children on contracts for "home work," especially in the neighborhood of factories and businesses which are irregular or seasonal in their employment, and where the efforts of almost every member of the family are needed to supplement the small income of the father.

The manufacturing of artificial flowers, finishing of gloves, millinery work, making garters, picking the meat out of nuts, making men's neckties, stringing beads, hemstitching, finishing children's clothes, hemming aprons, sewing and working buttonholes on men's suits—these are a few of the things that are furnishing "opportunity to work in the home."

The National Consumers' League, the National Federation of Women's Clubs, the State and national health agencies, and numerous other groups have helped to educate the public to demand the abolition of the "sweated" industries. The National Consumers' League has furnished its label to mark goods that are made under approved conditions, so that the consumer might be guided in his choices. But the consuming public seldom looks for more than the price tag. Hence the chief means of controlling this type of work is through legislation, employing the police power of the State to the ends of protecting the public health and welfare. In some States the minimum-wage law has been employed to take away the abuse of low wages in these home industries. But such industries continue—and continue largely as parasites, exploiting the labor of women and children. It is in the inaccessible home that working conditions are perhaps more unfavorable to the workers and more costly to the public health and welfare.

3. *The Use of Prison Labor*. The employment of prison inmates at productive labor has been a source of bitter controversy ever since it first began to take shape about a century ago. Prior to that time, prisoners usually had been forced to do hard but not very profitable work, such as crushing rock, splitting wood, or picking oakum. Indeed, even these tasks were a marked improvement over the early non-productive effort required for purely disciplinary purposes, such as the crank or the tread-wheel. As the machine gained perfection, it appeared quite logical to move machines into prisons and set up shops for the prisoners to work at more productive jobs. There was a good deal to recommend the practice, since it helped to remove the tedium of prison life and made prison discipline easier because men could feel some pride in such work; it gave prisoners some training or experience that would be useful to them after they were released; and by selling the product of such labor it was possible to reduce the cost of prison maintenance for the taxpayer. Moreover, when small wages were paid, the prisoners were able to contribute at least something to the support of their dependents or to build a reserve to help reëstablish the convict himself when he was released.[13]

Various systems were worked out by which prisoners could be worked profitably, and many of them still are used. Under the *contract* system, for example, contractors supply materials and machines, while the State provides buildings, power, light, and guards and receives from the contractor a stipulated fee for the labor of the convict. A variation of this arrangement is the *lease* system, wherein the contractor takes complete custody of the prisoner in return for a fee to the State. The *State use* system provides for production *and use* of the prison-made goods by the State itself, while the *public account* system provides for production *and sale* of the prison-made goods by the State.

Some of these arrangements have appeared to be more satisfactory

---

[13] J. L. Gillin, *Criminology and Penology* (New York, 1937), Ch. XXI.

than others; but regardless of their relative acceptability, there has been persistent opposition to any sort of prison labor at all. Extremists still challenge the idea on the ground that convicts should go to prison for punishment and not to make a living. They argue that prison life should be made as severe as possible; and they are quite right in their belief that enforced idleness is one of the cruelest forms of punishment. The unsoundness of such a policy, however, is shown by the fact that brutality breeds only resentment; and the discharged prisoner reëntering society with a "chip on his shoulder" is not likely to make a satisfactory social adjustment.

There are sounder objections to prison labor, however, even apart from the ill effect upon prisoners of some of the more unsatisfactory systems such as the contract or lease systems. The most valid contention, no doubt, is that prison labor competes with free labor. If the goods are sold on the open market, they can undersell goods made by free labor, since the production costs are so much lower. Even when the goods are not sold, the prisoner still competes with the free laborer, since his products otherwise would have to be bought by the State in the open markets. It is true that the total amount of prison labor is very small, compared to the number of free workers. In 1932 there were only about 82,000 employed convicts in federal and State institutions, while there probably were more than 49,000,000 free workers.[14] The difficulty is that the products of this prison labor tends to segregate in *certain types of industry.* Thus in 1923 more than one-eighth of all the jute bagging was made in prisons, a fifth of the twine and rope, nearly a third of the linen.[15]

The problem of prison labor is far from settled. It is quite generally agreed that some sort of productive work among prisoners is desirable. The payment of wages also is receiving increasing support. It generally is felt that the States should use the products in their own institutions so far as possible and that when prison-made goods are offered for sale, they should be offered only at current market prices. Laws also have been passed requiring labeling of prison-made goods. To some extent, the growth of prison schools has provided a valuable *alternative* to economic production and has been a factor in the steady decline of the percentage of prisoners engaged in economic production. Nevertheless, there still has remained the general problem of the competition of

[14] *Prison Labor in the United States: 1932* (Washington, D. C.: Bulletin 595, U. S. Bureau of Labor Statistics, 1933), p. 6.

[15] L. N. Robinson, *Should Prisoners Work?* (Philadelphia, 1931), pp. 55-57.

prison-made goods with the free; and that competition has been felt in interstate trade especially by those industries in which prison labor has been centered. The Congress of the United States therefore passed two acts, the Hawes-Cooper Act of 1929 and the Ashurst-Sumner Act of 1930, under which the respective States are permitted to establish their own policies regarding the prison-made goods of other States, and federal authority is extended to forbid the shipment of prison-made goods into States that choose to forbid their sale within their borders. Not all the States have elected to exercise this privilege, however; so a federal law was passed in 1940 that forbids the shipment of prison-made goods among the States.[16]

REFERENCES

Annals of the American Academy of Political and Social Science, "Women in the Modern World," Part III (May, 1929).

CATLIN, W. B., *The Labor Problem* (New York, 1934), Chs. 6, 7.

DAUGHERTY, C. R., *Labor Problems in American Industry* (Boston, 1941).

DOUGLAS, P. H., HITCHCOCK, C. N., and ATKINS, W. E., *The Worker in Modern Economic Society* (Chicago, 1925), Chs. 14, 15, 16.

DUBLIN, L. I. and LOTKA, A. J., *Twenty-Five Years of Health Progress* (New York, 1937).

ELLIOTT, Mabel A., and MERRILL, Francis E., *Social Disorganization* (New York, 1941), Ch. XV.

EPSTEIN, Abraham, *Insecurity, a Challenge to America* (New York, 1936).

GILLIN, J. L., *Poverty and Dependency* (New York, 1937), Ch. XVI.

HEINRICH, H. W., *Industrial Accident Prevention* (New York, 1931).

MANGOLD, G. B., *Social Pathology* (New York, 1932), Ch. 9.

ROBINSON, L. N., *Should Prisoners Work?* (Philadelphia, 1931).

Social Work Year Book, 1941, R. H. Kurtz, ed. (New York, 1941).

United States Department of Labor (Children's Bureau), "The Illegally Employed Minor and the Workmen's Compensation Law" (Bulletin 214, 1932); reprint from *Monthly Labor Review,* "Trend of Child Labor, 1927 to 1936" (December, 1937).

United States Department of Labor, "Occupational Progress of Women, 1910 to 1930" (Women's Bureau, Bulletin 104).

VAN KLEEK, M., "Women in Industry," *Encyclopaedia of the Social Sciences,* XV: 451-456.

YODER, Dale, *Labor Economics and Labor Problems* (New York, 1933), Ch. 12.

[16] C. R. Daugherty, *Labor Problems in American Industry* (Boston, 1941), pp. 827-828.

QUESTIONS AND EXERCISES

1. Are industrial accidents increasing or decreasing? Why? Do you think it would be possible to prevent all accidents in industry? Why, or why not?

2. How have the compensation laws given impetus to the apparent increase in industrial accidents?

3. What are the health hazards of modern industry? Why is it more difficult to obtain compensation for a case of occupational disease than it is to do so for an accident that causes a similar loss of wage?

4. To what extent are employers responsible for the industrial hazards to the safety and health of the worker? To the worker himself? To society as a whole?

5. What has been done in the past to reduce the hazards of accident and ill-health in industry?

6. Describe (a) the theoretical bases for the compensation laws; (b) the manner of operation of the laws. What criticisms have been made of them?

7. It is commonly observed that industry to-day favors the younger man. Why is this true? Does it mean that, as the late Judge Gary said, "Young men and women have never before had such fine opportunities for success"?

8. Why is the problem of selecting and finding an occupation so hazardous to-day? What relation has this problem to industrial unrest and "radical movements"?

9. Why is it that the average boy and girl are not willing to accept lower pay at the start even if by so doing they are given an opportunity to enter a skilled occupation or gain promotion? What program would you suggest to guard the new worker against "blind-alley" jobs?

10. Why is it that so many workers are compelled to change their occupations in middle life? What hazards confront the worker in making these changes? How can he be aided best in making such occupational readjustments?

11. What is a substandard worker? Give examples.

12. What is the extent of the employment of women in gainful occupations? Is the trend in the direction of increase or decrease of gainful employment of women?

13. What occupations are women entering in the greatest numbers? What relation does their gainful employment bear to the work that women have traditionally had to do?

14. Compare the ages of women and men who are gainfully employed. How do you account for the difference?

15. Enumerate the chief hazards that grow out of married women's seeking employment outside the home.

16. "The wage paid for a given grade of labor should depend entirely on the *value of the service rendered*, and should be paid alike to all performing that service, irrespective of age, sex, or marital condition of the worker." Discuss.

17. What has been the effect of gainful employment of women upon the status of women in society?
18. What is the extent of child labor in the United States to-day? How would you explain the fact that boy workers outnumber girl workers about two to one?
19. From the social point of view, are the deleterious effects of "boy labor" any more or any less important than those of "girl labor"? Give reasons for your answer.
20. What legal safeguards does your State provide for the protection of children in gainful occupations?
21. What issues are involved in the protest of free labor against convict labor? What justification is there for prison labor? How would you resolve these conflicting interests?

Chapter 12

•THE FAMILY IN TRANSITION

THE ORGANIZATION and control of the sex life of individuals is probably one of the oldest and most primary problems society has faced. For sex represents a perpetual urge that not only *must be* but *is* gratified. It is a primary biological function, in and of itself demanding outlet and expression. It is preserved in all its intensity by natural selection in that the most highly sexed are apt to pass on this character to the largest number of offspring, whereas those deficient in this respect permit their deficiency to die with them. The fact that sex life, in, of, and for itself, as a companionship and "play function," is the primary motive might as well be faced and accepted. Offspring or the perpetuation of the group is distinctly a by-product. Seldom indeed are unions formed, either temporary or permanent, that have for their avowed and honest purpose procreation alone. The scramble for mates and sex prerogatives is and always has been potent with disharmony, jealousy, hate, intrigue, exploitation, and brute force. Wars between nations have been fought over the respective rights of contending monarchs to an individual desirable female. Fights, often to the finish, between males all too often result from the same cause. Nor can we say that the possibility of conflict from this cause is limited wholly to males; females have been known to indulge in fierce hair-pulling frenzies to gain sole rights to some male. If mere procreation were the motivating factor one female would do nearly as well as another; but where sex partnership is concerned, marked differences are recognized.

Thus to the individual the outstanding fact is sex and the happiness and satisfaction and sense of "completion" resulting from normal sex life. To society, however, the individual's happiness and sense of "completion" in this respect is no more important than in any other department of his life. Society is interested only in keeping him sufficiently satisfied to be amenable to social control, and if more attention is paid by society to this function than to others it is because it has greater socially disruptive possibilities. To society the by-product, children, is the main concern. Society is interested in perpetuating itself and is profoundly interested in the preparation of its members for future citizenship and carrying on. Of course, individuals *do* desire children. They plan for them before they are born and devote their lives to them when they have come into being. Mother-love and father-love are very real human attributes, perhaps the finest and highest sentiments the human being is capable of. Still, they are the products of the mating instinct rather than its producer. The basic fact is that "male and female made He them"; and the higher the animal in the scale of creation the more definite the differentiation between them, and the more definitely sex life and procreation, though interdependent, become separate facts. While societies and individuals desire children, in the modern world they seldom desire them in unlimited numbers. They always do desire, however, the best conditions of life and surroundings for the number that they consider adequate.

Thus is society squarely faced with a complicated problem that is always the same, though time and place through social change may alter its aspect. The first phase of the problem is that of regulating and guaranteeing the sex life of individuals. The only way of avoiding the disorder that results from the fight for females is to lay down certain rules for the members of the group which will guarantee a fair and equal chance for each Jack to have a Jill. The powerful may be able to indulge in polygyny, while the poor and the downtrodden must console themselves with polyandry; but still strict regulation is there, and absolute promiscuity is not evident even in the most savage tribes. The march of civilization has always been in the direction of monogamy or the equal apportioning of mates, since under normal conditions their numbers, at maturity, tend to be equal.

The second phase of the problem is concerned with the by-product, or children. Society is interested in insuring itself or guaranteeing its perpetuity. Children, therefore, must be born in adequate numbers. But this is not enough. Society must guarantee that these children will reach maturity properly nurtured and prepared for the duties of adulthood. Thus the problem boils down to one of satisfying individual desire and social demand. The solution of the problem has been found in the institutions of marriage and the family. Throughout all ages these twin institutions are found. Their organization and technique may and do vary widely between times and civilizations; but the fundamental purpose and the problem to be solved are always the same.

THE PROBLEM OF MARRIAGE

Marriage is the institution that regulates and legalizes the acquisition of a mate (or mates or a share in a mate, as in the case of polygyny and polyandry) to have and to hold in undisputed possession within the limitations imposed by the social order. The rules of the game may vary all the way from capture and purchase to the most approved forms of romantic wooing. The necessary formalities prior to the legal recognition and social sanction of the union may vary all the way from gifts to the bride's parents and a community powwow to a medical examination, a marriage license, and the taking of vows. But whatever the rules and forms may be, they are usually enforced with the greatest rigidity, having behind them the sanctions of public opinion, law, and religion. Non-conformers are liable to the severest social ostracism, the condemnation of religion, and legal censure. Few other contracts open to the individual are hedged about with such a variety of safeguards so jealously maintained.

Society further regulates the sex side of life by a host of social, legal, and religious taboos on all varieties of sex expression except those legalized in marriage. Many of them are considered dishonorable, some are seriously illegal, and most of them are branded as wicked. The aim of society seems to be not only to guarantee, safeguard, and regulate the securing of a mate but also to reduce to the minimum all other sexual experience.

Ideally every individual has an inherent right to normal sex life on the attainment of biological maturity. Both physical and spiritual health and welfare demand the normal exercise of this function. Practically, however, society has an equal right to control, postpone, or even deny this function in the interest of health and heredity and social welfare. Where venereal disease is involved the right of the individual concerned is overbalanced by his danger to others. Where bad heredity is manifestly present society has the right to refuse a handicapped by-product —defective children. Society has also the undoubted right to regulate the age of marriage, that is, of biological maturity, in order, in the main, to prevent child marriages and the exploitation of immature females. Society has also forbidden marriage within certain degrees of kinship.

Our American ideal is that a young man shall not marry till he has proved his economic independence and is able, unaided, to undertake the support of a wife and potential family. This is a fine democratic ideal firmly grounded in our individualistic philosophy. The family thus assumes no responsibility for the sex life of the budding adult except on the side of repression. It is a case of "watchful waiting" on the part of parents, during which time anything can and many things usually do happen to the repressed and inhibited individuals watched. With the advance of Western civilization, rise in the standard of living, increase in the cost of living, heightened intensity in competition for opportunities to earn a living, and lengthening periods of preparation for the professions, it is not strange that young men find it increasingly difficult to marry at a relatively early age. The higher a young man's aim in life (provided he is not subsidized by wealthy parents), the more difficult it is for him to marry in the twenties. The intervening years spell cruel inhibition for the vast majority, sublimation with sorry mental twists for some, and ruinous substitutes for altogether too many. These substitutes, while they may in and of themselves degenerate and be degenerate, are ruinous in the main because of the social attitude toward them and the frame of mind in which they must be indulged. Love can be a fine and ennobling thing only so long as society allows one to think of it in those terms. When both parties face the assurance of ostracism and censure if discovered, a fine thing is turned into one that is sordid and the mental state resulting is of greater danger than the physical indulgence.

The postponement of marriage till the late twenties or even into the thirties for many of our young men and women, especially those preparing for the higher walks of life, has a serious side that our very prudery makes it difficult for us to study. For those fearful of race suicide it is of the greatest importance from the standpoint of the bearing of children. The causes of this situation are not simple. They are founded in our mores, which change but slowly, always lagging behind the demand and never giving in till forced to do so. They are determined by all the complexities of modern economic organization, which takes no thought of paying a beginning wage sufficient for the needs of two. If our mores change slowly we may expect changes in the very bases of remuneration to change even more slowly. The situation that we face cannot be legislated out of existence, nor can business and industry be changed to meet its demands. We can evolve out of it through the education of public opinion, but that is a slow process at best. In the meantime there is a tendency for the double standard of morality to give way to a single standard which is less than that formerly demanded of women. One hears more and more of temporary monogamous matings of convenience in our cities. These may and often do bear all the earmarks of true love and fidelity; but in the long run, such are our mores, it is the woman who still pays the price.

The problem of marriage, then, is the problem of making it possible for sound individuals to marry at the normal time. Where this opportunity is not present substitutes must be and are found. Sex is a fact and its complete sublimation is more a surface appearance than a reality. Where normal sex life, defined by society as marriage, is either delayed or denied a host of socially disapproved substitutes appear. The outstanding substitute is prostitution, which has been called "the oldest profession in the world." This profession is not always clandestine. Some societies have organized and even operated it in the interest of the chastity of the rest of its females and in response to male demand. Where it is socially disapproved and outlawed the clandestine professional makes her appearance and plies her trade. The volume of illegitimacy bears testimony to only a small part of non-professional illicit intercourse between the unmarried. Other substitutes reach through the whole field of so-called "unnatural" practices or "perversions" and on into the field of pornographia and other substitutes. So delicate is the sex balance of life, so far is its reach beyond the mere physical act into the very nerve-fiber and spiritual life of man, that most substitutes are probably undesirable if not actually dangerous.

THE SOCIAL FUNCTION OF THE FAMILY

The family is probably the oldest social institution known to man. It is the mother of most other social institutions. It has played the leading rôle in the civilization and socialization of man; and there is little evidence that its day is past and that the time has come to relegate it to the museum of anthropological curiosities. The family, however, has existed in many and various forms, each representing an attempted adaptation to the needs of the time and the place. It has undergone many changes; man in his history has tried every possible experiment with it. It is well not to lose sight of this fact in the present deluge of seemingly new proposals. It is well to remember also that a marriage or a family institution within a given culture does not represent merely restrictive taboo but also the organized sex morality of the group.

The ideal of the family in Western society is that it is a monogamous and permanent partnership, sexually exclusive "to have and to hold, for better or for worse, till death do us part." When marriage is contracted and a family thus inaugurated it is not considered either by the contractng parties or by society as a mere trial or experiment, with possible dissolution in the offing. All parties concerned take it for granted that love so true and deep can result only in a true and permanent union. Fidelity, loyalty, and coöperation are taken for granted. A home is established and within it two living as one will bear and rear children, nourishing them and training them for the duties of citizenship and of the family life that will in time be theirs. No ideal could be higher. Woman is no longer a chattel. She is a voting partner. Man is no longer allowed to be a tyrant. The rights of both women and children are protected by law. The sanctity of the home is protected by law. Infidelity is severely punished both by law and by public opinion.

With regard to the family in its most primitive forms, Miss Goodsell wisely concludes,

We must admit that primitive society has rendered very real service to civilization. It has regulated the relations of the sexes in such wise as to avoid promiscuity, which would have retarded, if not prevented, the development of a body of customary sex morals and the organization of stable family life. The primitive family itself, however unsettled by frequent divorce and divided by polygamy, yet afforded a more or less permanent refuge for men and women from the disordered conditions of life and a nursery for the helpless young who might otherwise have perished. Then, too, the family preserved and passed on to the rising generation those technical skills by means of which primitive man was fed, clothed and housed. Thus a store of knowledge indispensable to life was conserved and very slowly increased. Finally, in so far as the primitive family upheld and inculcated the moral traditions and customs of the group, it rendered valuable service in helping to lay the foundation stones of a more idealistic conception of human relations than primitive man had even dimly perceived.[1]

And the job is not finished. The family is still, in spite of its inadequacies and apparent failures, the foundation-stone on which civilization still builds.

Gillin well sums up the social function of the family. He says:

It is evident . . . that the family represents the unit of social order. Within it people are trained for the larger social life. Not only are they schooled in the art of producing wealth and trained in the rights of property, but also in the duties and privileges of individuals in association. Here they receive the elements of religious training, for it is in the home that the beginnings of all forms of culture appear. Politically the family and the state are entirely separated so far as civil rights and duties are concerned, yet the home gives instruction in political life. It is here that questions of public policy are discussed and members of the family receive their early training in political

[1] Willystine Goodsell, *Problems of the Family* (1928), pp. 22–23.

opinion. It is in the family that the first ethical ideals are imparted, and socialization is begun. Modern child psychology is re-emphasizing and explaining in scientific terms the wisdom in the old adages. "Train up a child in the way he should go, and when he is old he will not depart from it," and "Give me a child until he is seven years old and you can have him all the rest of his life." From the very first moment of his existence the child is conditioned by his experiences. In the home the child receives his first conditioning. His responses made there are likely to become fixed as habit patterns which determine his conduct through life. In spite of many influences which have lessened its influence upon the child, it (the family) still stands as the primary social group in the process of creating a social being.[2]

WHAT IS WRONG WITH THE FAMILY?

The institution of the family, with the finest ideals in the world behind it, is in operation and is working, fortunately, with marked success in at least the majority of cases. Still we hear the rumblings and creakings of the machinery, note with alarm the high percentage of disaster, and wonder if the whole thing is about to crash. The trouble with marriage and the family to-day is not new or different. A necessary institution keyed and adjusted to the tempo and conditions of a past generation finds itself in the whirlpool of rapid modern change. There is nothing new about this and perhaps nothing particularly serious. We take such maladjustments for granted in education, government, and economics. But when it comes to marriage, the family, morals, and sex we like to think of them as inherently right, settled once for all, and incapable of maladjustment. We prefer to think that something is wrong with us rather than with these ancient institutions.

The social trend of the modern family may here be briefly summarized.

1. We note evidences of *decreased parental authority and family loyalty*. In this age the old yoke of authority by parents is no longer tolerated by the younger generation. Influence undoubtedly is exercised by parents over children, but it is a much sugar-coated and becloaked affair in comparison with that of a century ago. Perhaps this is well. It may be due partially to the fact that to-day so many of our elders are parents of children much better educated than *they* are. The children in our modern schools are frequently in possession of more adequate elements of information along certain lines than their parents are. And long before maturity they are well aware of the fact. It has been cleverly remarked that the modern family has become a democracy wherein

[2] Gillin and Blackmar, *Outlines of Sociology* (1930), pp. 187–188.

each member has his vote and there are never any majorities. At any rate one feels in many homes that it is the parents who are "to be seen and not heard" rather than the children. It would be hard to find the old family loyalties that were the rule but a few generations ago. They do not exist because the family seems to have ceased to exist as a unit. We may note an increased independence of the individuals composing the family. Opportunities for employment make it possible for even adolescent sons and daughters to have independent incomes of their own. It is possible for sixteen-year-old daughters to serve notice on their parents that if the latter do not like their friends and actions they will rent a room and pay board elsewhere. No longer do we find the common family purse. Where children do not contribute to their own support they are very apt to be the recipients of independent allowances, which they spend as they please.

2. *Loosened Family Ties.* The family seems to have lost much of its former unity, its central position in the life of the individual, the economic and social interdependence of its members; many of its loyalties, common interests, common amusements, and traditions. The expression "It's just like one big family" has lost much of its former significance. We no longer have "big families," and in the small ones each member is an individual with his own interests, activities, circle of friends, and frequently his own allowance or income. The home has with some justification been likened to a filling-station with parking-space attached. It has been called the place where one goes when he has no other engagements. Of course this is a bit far-fetched, but it is a long cry to-day from the old family unit and unity. Membership therein means a vastly different thing on the surface. It is a question, however, how vitally important these modifications are. If we can demonstrate that a smaller unity has been exchanged for a larger and that new loyalties have taken the place of the old, we are merely discovering that the social order does change. As yet, we are sure only that we are in a period of change that is as yet maladjustment. If these family ties loosen we must find substitutes for them. These substitutes have not as yet adequately demonstrated themselves.

3. *Reduction of the Family Function.* The cry here is that the family has lost its job. Formerly it was pretty much of an independent and self-sustaining social and economic unit. It produced its own amusement, social life, cultural stimulus. These were simple but eminently healthy. They were a coöperative product. It was an economic producer as well. Every member of the family was a producer. The family produced

goods that the family consumed. In this modern day of large-scale factory production of everything from amusement thrills to canned corn, one or more members of the family produce salaries and with these goods are purchased that were formerly produced at home. Good or bad, this condition will not be changed so long as modern commercialism can supply the demand better than the home can.

The father, as producer of wages or salary, is becoming increasingly an absent partner in the home. His duties and his interest lie outside. They are no longer the intimate and personal affair of every member of the family.

The mother has experienced the main loss. She is no longer allowed to produce goods as she once did. Her children have been taken out of her hands during much of the day. No wonder she is turning to trade, industry, and the professions in increasing numbers. It is not strange that, having been deprived of her family she is entering the large field of social welfare in women's clubs, societies, and politics. It is natural that, where unfitted for these activities, her new freedom should be frittered away in fruitless but time-consuming activities.

4. *Training for life and citizenship seems increasingly to be taken care of outside the home.* The new school, the socialized church, and a thousand State and private programs are either entering the home or working with the child outside the home. The idea is to standardize the influences that form the character of the child and to distribute them more equitably rather than to leave them to the haphazard influence of a multitude of individual homes and pairs of parents. One would not think of disbanding the Boy Scouts, disrupting the social work of settlements, schools, and churches, or dismissing family case workers, probation officers, visiting teachers, and visiting nurses. Activities of this sort have come into being because there was a demand for them. Still they definitely encroach on the former functions of the home.

5. It is complained that *the family has ceased to function as a producer of children.* So strenuous are the demands of modern life, so costly, that the support of a real, old-style family has become an economic impossibility for the majority. Certain it is that the birth-rate has declined and that our successful classes are scarcely replacing themselves.

6. *Sanctity.* It is not so long ago that the marriage contract was a purely religious affair. Only the clergy could solemnize it, and their discretion was the only check. Now the church wedding has become an affair of fashion and the part played by the clergy a necessary bit of

local color. It is still more respectable to be married in church, but in no way necessary; the contract is eminently a civil one. Good or bad? Well, marriage licenses and further social control of the license to wed are here to stay. Sanctity or no, we really do not trust the unsupervised discretion of the church.

7. *The home no longer holds the center of the stage.* It cannot compete with commercialized amusement for the attention of the child, or even of the parents. The movies and the dance-hall, the baseball park and the beach, are much more thrilling and spectacular. Why read stories and play games at home when a million-dollar spectacle is to be seen for half a dollar? The females of the home are no longer the producers of economic goods that they once were. Labor-saving devices and apartment-house life have largely done away with the chores and home tasks that once made for family coöperation. Indeed, with the multiplication of outside demands on the interest and attention of the members of the family, the home seems to be becoming more and more of a show place, a place to eat fairly regularly, a place to sleep, and a place to go between outside appointments.

8. *Stability.* Instability is the final indictment. We still take it for granted that marriages will last forever, but an alarming proportion of them survive for less than five years.

The home itself, in the old sense, is disappearing. Domiciles of a highly temporary nature are rapidly taking the place of former family seats of generations standing. We are rapidly becoming a nation of renters. In the more congested areas, our large cities, the home has become a cubicle in a vast pile of brick and stone; a single cell in a honeycomb. There is undoubtedly much virtue in the ownership of a domicile and the sense of stability and belonging resulting therefrom, but modern economic organization of life makes that impossible for the many.

FACTORS RESPONSIBLE FOR THIS SITUATION

What are the changes in the social environment that have produced such marked changes in the family? The number is legion, and they include all those which have gone into the making of the new economic, political, and social life of our time. Most of these have already been discussed in our chapter on social change. Consider the new communication that has given us a wider range of association; the new industry that, among other things, has taken production from the home; the new education that assumes a much wider responsibility for the child; socialized religion, which saves lives for the here as well as for the hereafter; and the revolutionary emancipation of women. Each of these changes stands in first magnitude in and of itself. Each thrusts up social problems of the first order. Each affects every other social institution, and together they, in their own change, affect the family, compelling it to readjust itself to the new conditions. It is not conceivable that the family or any other institution could continue to function without change in the face of such marked change in all departments of life surrounding it.

We must conclude that the present disorganization of the family, which we are prone to define in terms of the family of the past, is the normal result of the tempo of the time. We must recognize also that the changes indicated above are fundamentally desirable and good. Who would return to the simpler and more restricted life if he could? Who would limit the work of either the church or the school? Who would consider the disfranchisement of women? Who would reinstate the old family, even if it did seem to possess greater stability? The social problems of the family and of other social institutions are not problems of innate goodness or badness. They are merely problems of the adjustment of fundamentally sound institutions to the needs and conditions of the time. The family, in some form, is here to stay. Communal breeding and rearing of children is an idle dream. Marriage is a necessary form of the social control of mating and can be made to work. Our problem is not one of destroying outworn institutions but of reconditioning very valuable machinery.

Our outstanding problem is that of increasing the stability of the family insofar as this is desirable. This stability can be increased, in the main, by the measures already discussed that safeguard marriage and entrance into the family life. So long as marriage is a haphazard affair we are justified in looking for haphazard results. So long as we allow misfits to wed we have no reason to expect that wedded life can make them any less unsuited to one another. So long as we have no uniform divorce program, forbidding it absolutely in some areas and allowing it for the most trivial of causes in others, we know exactly what to expect —and our expectation is being realized.

For the rest the social health of family life depends on social education—of the individual and of the public; of the child in school and of the adult. As often as not social problems are basically social ignorance. The time has come in this most important institution and department of life to know the facts, to face them fearlessly and shamelessly, and to plan for the future.

THE BROKEN HOME

In view of these tremendous strains upon the family ties, it is not surprising that a certain number of marriages should result in failure. But since the home is probably our most fundamental social institution, any condition that endangers its effective functioning raises a serious social problem. Moreover, both the number and proportion of broken homes have been rising steadily in recent decades, so we must turn our attention to the conditions and consequences of the breakdown of family life.

The home may be *broken* by the death or incapacitation of either the breadwinner or the home manager. It may also be broken by desertion or divorce. Among these causes those pertaining to divorce and separation [3] probably are the most baffling from the social point of view. The problems of death and sickness, after all, are a concern chiefly of medical science; and we already have seen that marked headway has been made in saving life and ensuring health. Desertion, sometimes called the "poor man's divorce," frequently is resorted to because legal divorce is too expensive. It is a curious fact, however, that a large proportion of desertion is only temporary and may be even recurrent, with the recalcitrant spouse returning to his family after a more or less extended period of "French leave." Sometimes, of course, desertion occurs only technically, since it actually represents an agreement between the parties involved. In any case, the deserter of the family, whether it be the husband or the wife, is one who is not playing the game; and desertion generally is branded with all of the stigma that the word implies. Divorce, however, presents problems that are not so clearly defined; and we shall need to study the various aspects of the matter more fully if we are to gain a better understanding of them.

THE PROBLEM OF DIVORCE

Divorce is a method society has set up whereby the mismated may find legally recognized release. If we grant that divorce is ever and under any circumstances justifiable, then we must defend formal legal procedure for the purpose of bringing it about.

Is it a moral issue? What, then, is the problem of divorce? On what

---

[3] Separation is really a partial divorce, which gives legal recognition to the fact of "separation from bed and board." The principals remain legally married, however, and do not have the legal status of separate persons, as do those who are awarded absolute decrees of divorcement. Some States require a year of legal separation as a requisite to granting a divorce decree.

grounds do we here consider it and why is it receiving such wide attention? For answer let us turn to the church, the keeper of morals and the defender of social values. Among the Hebrews, as we have seen from the Old Testament, divorce was not only recognized but the only grounds necessary seemed to be the husband's dissatisfaction with his wife. Even so, it was not as easy as biblical citations might seem to indicate. In China about the same amount of freedom exists in theory. In fact, however, the husband thus giving his wife a bill of divorce knows that he has her family to deal with and his village knows that it will have to answer to her village. If the wife's family is socially or politically more powerful than that of the husband there is little likelihood that he will send her away, for if he does he will have to reckon with the consequences of an enraged family and the possibility of starting a village feud. It is entirely possible, in that land of eternal compromise, that the elders of his village will persuade him out of the course if they fear that they cannot see the affair safely through. The New Testament also recognizes divorce but greatly restricts it. Woman's position is safeguarded, and divorce can be had but "for the one cause" —that of unfaithfulness in the marriage relation. The teachings of Jesus himself on this point are perfectly clear.

And the Pharisees came to him, and asked him, Is it lawful for a man to put away his wife? trying him. And he answered and said unto them, What did Moses command you? And they said, Moses suffered to write a bill of divorcement, and to put her away. But Jesus said unto them, For the hardness of your heart he wrote you this commandment. But from the beginning of creation, male and female made he them. For this cause shall a man leave his father and mother, and shall cleave to his wife; and the two shall become one flesh. What, therefore, God hath joined together, let no man put asunder. And in the house the disciples asked him again of the matter. And he said unto them, Whosoever shall put away his wife, and marry another, committeth adultery against her: and if she herself shall put away her husband and marry another, she committeth adultery.[4]

The "one cause" is elsewhere mentioned in the later Scriptures but some students of the Bible are of the opinion that it represents an interpolation and not the original thought of Jesus. There is no question that Jesus considered divorce immoral and forbade it except for the one possible cause of unfaithfulness.

How have the modern churches interpreted the teachings of Jesus? What is their attitude toward divorce? The answer is that you can find anything you please from a strictness almost transcending that of the

[4] Mark X: 2–12.

New Testament to those churches which will solemnize any marriage and ask no questions not required by the law. We have on the one hand marriages that require papal authority for their annulment and on the other hand "marrying parsons" who specialize in *re-unions*. One of the Ten Commandments enjoins us not to commit adultery. Sociology would recognize in this a fundamental and necessary law of social control. But does the person who remarries commit adultery? The theologians answer both yes and no. Indeed the Pope does not issue a divorce at all; he merely announces that the marriage never existed, while the more liberal churches are only interested in whether or not a license to rewed has been legally issued.

Since the church has been unable to decide the matter, we are scarcely justified in considering divorce as a moral issue. The Catholic Church stands opposed, but the great bulk of the Protestant Church is for recognition of a legal procedure. We can all agree that divorce may be *immorally used* by individuals who find in it a means for legalized promiscuity. This, however, is an expensive process and not a course open to the man of even average means. A comparatively small portion of the volume of modern divorce is of the front-page-scandal type. Society should welcome any aid from religion in increasing the sanctity of marriage but should deplore the inflexible attitude that makes adjustment impossible even where eminently desirable.

Is, then, divorce merely a matter of social expediency? For the sociologist it is this. He is interested in the economical and efficient functioning of social institutions. He is interested in the success of the family. Hence he is interested in divorce, which may be either a safeguard in exceptional cases against rank injustice, or an opportunity for lax sex relations. He does not question that legalized divorce has proved itself a desirable safety-valve. He may and does question the various legal technicalities surrounding it—making it in some commonwealths a "nickel-in-the-slot" affair, and an impossibility in others. He is more interested in the volume and conditions of divorce than in the fact of divorce. Accordingly we shall discuss divorce from the standpoint of its effect on society and lay aside its moral and religious aspects.

Is divorce evil, or is it caused by evils? When we say that we shall discuss divorce from the standpoint of its effect upon society we must hasten to admit that we are not yet sure whether divorce is a cause or an effect—whether the legal recognition of divorce and the character of the divorce laws tends to accelerate the divorce-rate or whether there are other social conditions in operation that weaken the home ties and result in increased recourse to the divorce courts. If the former, then divorce is, in and of itself, an evil; but if it is the latter, divorce is but a symptom of underlying social maladjustments that call for remedy. It may be that society will discover that truth lies in both directions, that the ease with which divorce can be secured affects its frequency, as do also the unfortunate conditions that reduce the stability of the home.

WHO ARE DIVORCED AND WHY

The popular impression, gained largely from the newspapers, is that the large volume of divorce is of the Hollywood, Reno, and Paris sort. This is far from the truth, for the mass of divorce in this country takes place in the great middle class of society and is accorded but scant publicity by the press. It is this divorce which has increased in volume at such a rate as to cause consternation. This being the case, it is important that we should know the conditions surrounding this middle-class volume of divorce. Who are these people? Where do they come from? What is their religion, occupation, and social condition? If we can answer even a part of these questions we shall understand better the problem of divorce.

1. To begin with, *it is in young and dynamic countries that divorce is on the increase, and in older countries where social reorganization is taking place*. The United States, Switzerland, and Japan are at present heading the list. Again, increased resort to divorce seems to follow the geographical direction of progress—from East to West. This is true not only for the world but within the expanse of the United States as well. Divorce seems, then, to be in some way connected with the social expansion and cultural development of peoples.

2. *Divorce seems to follow the emancipation of women and the extension of educational opportunity*. Here again it appears to accompany progress. No one would be willing to argue that since the according of equality to women has been accompanied by divorce, they should therefore be relegated to their former status. It may be that the emancipation and education of women has made them less quiescent under male dominance, less willing to suffer the petty tyrannies of the past. If this be the case, then the increase in divorce is but a by-product in the new adjustment between the two sexes.

3. *Divorce seems to follow economic prosperity and a rising standard of living*. This too is difficult to understand unless we concede that economic prosperity gives rise to many new and additional interests out

de the home. The father is more and more completely absorbed in the
emands of his business and finds release on the golf-course rather than
n the more simple pleasures of the home. The wife is released from
many former household duties and enters an outside sphere of activity
ompletely foreign to that of her husband. The children have their
chool and the many organized activities that occupy their time and at-
ention outside the home and are little connected with the interests of
heir parents or with each other. Shall we call this the loosening of home
ies, or shall we merely remark that this too is but a stage in the adapta-
ion of home life to new social and economic conditions? If the latter,
hen divorce is here also but a symptom and a by-product.

4. *There is more divorce in the city than in the country.* On the
asis of what has been said this is understandable, for the country is more
onservative than the city and city life moves at a much more rapid
ace. In the city there are more outside distractions to draw the various
members of the family apart and to lessen the importance of the home
o each.

5. *Divorce is more common among Protestants than among Catholics.*
This, of course, is due primarily to the fact that the two communions
xert different social pressure in this matter. It is doubtful if one could
rove that Catholic unions are happier in general than Protestant unions
nd hence result in less divorce. Divorce is simply less available to the
ne than to the other.

6. *Another and a seemingly damning fact is that more divorces are
ranted to women than to men.* This was not formerly the case, for the
ery sufficient reason that divorce was a male prerogative. However,
oes the present situation indicate that, given a new freedom, the women
re proving a less stable element in society, or that more husbands fail to
nake good? Probably neither. There is enough of the old chivalry re-
naining for most men to allow their wives to initiate the action, what-
ver the causes that bring it about.

7. *Divorce varies with occupation.* There are occupations that exert
nore strain on the family life than is the case with others. Certain occu-
ations presuppose more temperament than others and attract the more
igh-strung and emotional types. Other occupations take the husband
way from the home for longer or shorter periods and thus break into
s even tenor. Divorce is low for farmers, but it is high for actors, show-
nen, commercial travelers, musicians, and physicians. This situation
oes not reflect on the character of actors and physicians. It merely re-

flects the effect of occupation on home life, with a resulting degree o
instability.

8. *Divorce seems to reach its maximum about the fifth year of mar
ried life.* If a couple can weather the storms of the first five years, th
chances for the continued success of their venture are greatly increased
This is due to the fact that the family life requires an immense amoun
of readjustment. Each party to the contract must learn to get used to th
matrimonial harness. In an economic system within which it is difficul
for a young man to undertake the responsibility of a wife and famil
before he is twenty-five years of age, habits become settled and readjust
ment to the new relation is made with increasing difficulty.

9. *Finally, divorce is twice as frequent in homes where there are n
children.* Perhaps this is fortunate, since we are mainly concerned ove
divorce as a home-breaker and in its effect upon the children. If ther
are no children to be thus handicapped, society can better afford t
allow the contracting parties to make a new start. The child is th
stabilizer of the home—the central interest that binds parents together
It is the child who gives the home its real purpose. It is around the chil
that the divorce problem centers.

TABLE 20

MARITAL CONDITION OF THE POPULATION, FIFTEEN YEARS OLD AND OVER, BY SE
AND GEOGRAPHIC DIVISIONS: 1930 *

(Expressed in Per Cents)

Geographical Division	Marital Condition and Sex							
	Single		Married		Widowed		Divorce	
	Male	Fe-male	Male	Fe-male	Male	Fe-male	Male	Fe-mal
United States	34.1	26.4	60.0	61.1	4.6	11.1	1.1	1.
New England	35.3	31.9	58.7	55.8	5.0	11.2	0.8	1.
Middle Atlantic	35.6	29.4	59.2	58.9	4.4	10.9	0.5	0.
East North Central	33.1	25.1	60.8	62.9	4.6	10.4	1.3	1.
West North Central	34.5	26.5	59.4	61.9	4.7	10.3	1.2	1.
South Atlantic	34.0	27.0	60.6	60.0	4.5	11.9	0.7	1.
East South Central	31.3	24.2	62.7	62.1	4.9	12.1	1.0	1.
West South Central	32.0	22.9	61.9	64.0	4.7	11.2	1.3	1.
Mountain	36.1	23.4	57.3	64.9	4.6	9.9	1.8	1.
Pacific	35.3	22.3	57.2	62.3	4.5	12.2	2.6	3.

* Fifteenth Census, *Population* (U. S. Bureau of the Census), Vol. II, pp. 853–854.

TABLE 21

MARITAL CONDITION OF THE POPULATION, FIFTEEN YEARS OLD AND OVER, BY SEX,
COLOR, AND NATIVITY, AND PLACE OF RESIDENCE: 1930 *

(Expressed in Per Cents)

Sex and Marital Condition	Color and Nativity			Place of Residence	
	Native White	Foreign-born White	Negro	Urban	Rural Farm
Males	100.0	100.0	100.0	100.0	100.0
Single	36.8	21.5	32.2	33.7	36.5
Married	57.9	70.8	59.8	60.5	57.9
Widowed	4.0	6.6	6.3	4.3	4.8
Divorced	1.1	0.9	1.4	1.3	0.7
Unknown	0.2	0.2	0.3	0.2	0.1
Females	100.0	100.0	100.0	100.0	100.0
Single	29.4	12.7	23.3	27.8	25.2
Married	59.7	70.0	58.5	58.5	66.0
Widowed	9.4	16.4	15.9	11.8	8.1
Divorced	1.3	0.9	2.2	1.6	0.6
Unknown	0.1	0.1	0.1	0.1	0.1

* Fifteenth Census, *Population* (U. S. Bureau of the Census), Vol. 2.

What can we conclude from this brief résumé? We have seen that divorce has been a concomitant to social progress and economic prosperity and that it varies with the varying stability of the home. Shall we therefore defend divorce and conclude that it is necessary to continued social well-being? Or shall we conclude that it is an unfortunate by-product in a period of rapid social change and frenzied readjustment? We certainly shall not attack divorce on moral and theological grounds, but we must view with apprehension the vast numbers of broken homes, the children left without normal home environments, and the general indication of a weakening hold of the home and family life on the individual.

CAUSES OF DIVORCE AND GROUNDS FOR DIVORCE

There is a vast amount of difference between the *causes of*, and the *grounds for*, divorce. By *causes* we mean the real, underlying reasons. It is for these that the sociologist is seeking. It is only by discovering them that the problem can be solved. By *grounds* is meant the legally recognized technical bases demanded by the courts. In the State of New York there is but one legally recognized ground. It is adultery. Therefore candidates for divorce must either admit or pretend this cause if they wish separation under the jurisdiction of that State. In another State no divorce is granted for any cause whatsoever, and accordingly those desiring divorce must become residents of another and more liberal community. The other extreme lies in the granting of divorce for such a trivial cause as "incompatibility of temper." In all there are at least thirty-six different grounds for divorce recognized by the various States of the Union, but no one State recognizes all of them.

The study of court records gives little light on the real causes of divorce. While collusion between the parties concerned is illegal, it is undoubtedly true that very few divorces are granted where either the husband and wife or their legal representatives do not agree on the grounds that will secure results with the least publicity and pain to all concerned. It is interesting to note that adultery as a ground has been steadily decreasing for nearly a century, while cruelty and neglect to provide have been on the increase. This is probably due to the fact that the latter grounds (or excuses) carry with them less social stigma and not that spouses are becoming more faithful on the one hand, or husbands more cruel and less provident on the other.

While we believe that the welfare of society demands that divorce be legally possible, we deplore the two extremes represented by the divorce laws and practices of certain of our States. In some it is either an impossibility or a near-impossibility, and in others so easy as to permit separation on slight provocation. Where divorce is too difficult or expensive to obtain we pay the price in desertion and philandering. Thus, if divorce is impossible and home conditions are intolerable, then another way around the difficulty will be found. On the other hand, if divorce is easy it stands as an ever-ready solution to any petty squabble. It has been the experience of most domestic relations courts that comparatively few divorces are really justified. They all have small beginnings, which grow and become magnified. If the parties concerned can be brought to unburden themselves completely to a sympathetic third party, reconciliation can often be effected. Unfortunately there exists a class of shyster lawyers who batten on marital incompatibilities and make the most of them. It would seem to be true that too easy divorce breeds divorce, and that too difficult divorce defeats its own ends. The divorce laws of the United States are a hopeless tangle. It is even possible for a man to be legally divorced from his wife in one State, and at the same time to be legally wedded to her in another. He may find himself in the uncomfortable position of being the lawful husband of one wife in one State, and a bigamist in the next.

THE FRUITS OF DIVORCE

The primary and immediate result of divorce is the broken home, and most of the fruits are the result of this unfortunate break. The child who is brought up with but one parent is handicapped, for he needs the influences of both father and mother. He is brought up with the consciousness that all is not well, that one parent has been wronged by the other, or both *have not played the game*, that he is differently situated than other children are. The lessons of love and sympathy between parents are absent from his life. Often each parent appeals to his sympathy as against the other. If the child be motherless because of divorce, he loses the softening influences of that companionship during the major portion of the day. If he be fatherless, he misses that part of his training. Such a child is fortunate indeed if he does not grow up with a complex of one sort or another due to the unnatural or incomplete environment in which he is reared. On the other hand, it must be admitted that it might be better for some children to have but one parent, rather than to live in the discord caused by the continued union of the two that he has.

There seems to be a startling correlation between broken homes and juvenile delinquency. It is easier for a child from such a home to go astray. This may be due to the fact that he has insufficient supervision or it may be due to the fact that his delinquency is a defense reaction to the unnatural situation. Ellwood found in 1909 that of some 7,500 children in State reform schools, nearly 30 per cent came from families in which there had been divorce or desertion, and only a few came from normal homes. This effect upon the child, whether it result in delinquency or not, is the chief fruit of the broken home that troubles us.

No less serious, but unfortunately not so commonly recognized, are the consequences of divorce to the divorced persons themselves. The tug and strain between parents of children has already been suggested. But even when there are no children, the price of marital freedom for those who seek divorce is high. Obviously when a home is broken by divorce, the whole chain of habits and social relationships is broken for both of the divorced people. The sexual readjustments incumbent upon both the man and the woman are obvious. Similarly all the rest of the intimate details of daily living must be reorganized, with each of the

divorced persons being forced to "live alone and like it." Such a necessity is, in effect, a serious crisis in the life of the individual; and a profound sense of loneliness is likely to result. Inevitably, too, there is a
lingering sense of failure which is not easy to throw off. In addition,
there are the hard problems of finance—whether alimony is to be paid,
how much, and for how long. The payment of alimony is a burden upon
the husband, who is then forced to maintain two establishments. The
wife often is confronted with earning her own living comparatively late
in life, and not infrequently for the first time. Friends of the couple
most often "take sides" in favor of one or the other of the principals,
with a result that many confused situations are bound to occur in planning social functions. Society still ostracizes the divorced person to
some extent; and frequently the divorced man or woman is forced to
extremes of conduct, and acceptance of associates of questionable character in the struggle to restore a sense of his or her own importance.

THE STABILIZATION OF THE FAMILY

How shall family stability be increased and unnecessary divorce be
checked? To begin with, the solution of none of our social problems is
simple. It is difficult, as we have already seen, ever to place the finger on
an even approximate single cause. Most problems have a wide range of
interrelationship and cause and hence call for a wide range of readjustment in order to effect cure. Boiled down, the cures for most of our
social problems are remarkably similar. In treating an institutional disease the prescription usually advises society to clear up a host of very
obvious difficulties. Every step in the direction of general social efficiency and harmony will react on every individual institution, promoting harmony and efficiency therein. The cure of general social ills of
maladjustment lies in the direction of correcting individual maladjustments wherever we find them, of a general attack all along the line.

To be more specific, we offer the following suggestions in regard to
the stabilization of the family:

1. *Education for Marriage and Family Life.* We start with education
because we consider it the true starting-point. What we shall have to
say about it is but part and parcel of the larger program of education
for social life in general. Its effect would be felt not in the family alone
but would carry over to every other department of life as well.

Is it not strange that the social sciences still play so slight a part, generally, in our educational system? A study of the curricula of American
schools from grade schools to colleges reveals the fact that the study

of social life plays an exceedingly minor rôle. Language, literature, history, and the exact sciences form the bulk of the educational offerings. No respectable school is without its definite requirements for graduation in each of these fields, whereas courses in the social sciences are more apt to be in the "elective" group. The great majority of our institutions of higher learning have done very well in meeting the new demand, but in the lower schools this vast field of training has begun to come into its own in very recent years. If the youth of our nation is to be ready for the duties of citizenship and of family life it will be necessary to begin to acquaint them with the requirements of social life at an early age.

Regarding the twin institutions of marriage and the family, could anything be more important than information in this field? What does the average youngster know of the deep social significance and importance of either? His attitude is apt to be either one of sloppy sentimentality or one of licentious eroticism. Beyond this, marriage and the family are just taken for granted as things that are and always have been. We plunge our youth into marriage without warning, without preparation, inadequately informed, to sink or swim, and to make port as best they can. No wonder many of them fail to reach the harbor. Still the conspiracy of silence continues. The subject is either too sacred or too "indelicate," as you will, to present to the adolescent mind. The educational program is and always will be the first step in the solution of any social problem. "Forewarned is forearmed" is as true to-day as it ever was. Solutions may come from other sources, but to put them into effect requires an intelligent public opinion.

2. *Raising the marriage and family ideals* is a direct by-product of the educational program. Romantic love is a pleasant diversion but a poor foundation for permanent wedded happiness. No problem is more complex than that of the adjustment of two lives to the strain of living together day by day as one person. Marriage is more than a sex exploit, and the family is more than a necessary evil. Let the veil be lifted, and more healthy ideals will obtain; a life partnership will then appear as an even more desirable consummation but also as a contract not to be entered upon too lightly.

The only popular ideals of marriage we at present have are those of love (a condition of emotional instability between two individuals of opposite sex); chastity, which is not overly stressed; and economic competence and independence, which may or may not be present. The popular ideals in the case of the family are higher. They include love (of the enduring sort), fidelity, honor, confidence, and absolute and unending coöperation. In our schools we provide domestic science for our girls in order to make them better housekeepers and manual training for our boys in order to prepare them for possibly earning a living, but we have scarcely begun to prepare them for the life that starts with the most solemn covenant to "love and honor, to cherish in joy and sorrow, in health and sickness, in prosperity and adversity, to be faithful and never to forsake" one another. Yes, the ideals of marriage, on the emotional side, are high enough. On the practical side they must be expanded. Still their realization depends primarily on the ideals surrounding marriage, and yet those ideals too often take no thought whatever of what is to follow through the years.

3. *Uniform marriage laws* might be made to prevent many unfortunate unions. We definitely need, as has been pointed out earlier in this chapter, not only stricter scrutiny of applicants for marriage licenses and regulation of the license to wed, but even more we need greater uniformity among the various States. These would include, as already indicated elsewhere, permission, legal or parental or both, physical and mental examination of both applicants, and due notice or legal banns. The purpose of uniform marriage laws is not negative, that of preventing marriage, *but rather to aid marriage and to insure the proper marriage to each other of those properly mated.*

4. *We would most seriously suggest a right-about-face on the part of* a large section of the Christian Church. In theory the church sanctifies marriage. The taking of marriage vows is eminently a religious ceremony. If the church really takes the vows it administers seriously, it will not administer them indiscriminately to all who apply on presentation of due license to wed. One church marries only its own members and these must be communicants in good standing. It is thereby condemned and accused of narrowness and intolerance. It is a fact, however, that it thereby strengthens the power of the vows thus taken and does not cheapen itself. What greater travesty than that of the solemn dignity and beauty of the church wedding of two individuals to whom the office is but dignity and beauty, a bit of lovely pageantry symbolizing their joy; who do not and cannot join in the religious spirit of the moment? The churches might well reserve their sanctification for those who definitely accept it as such. For the remainder the purely civil marriage is logical. Civil marriage need not be unlovely. It can be decked with all the trappings desired. Let the ceremony stand, however, for what it honestly is.

5. We come last to *uniform divorce laws and a socialized divorce court*. We believe that this is placing the emphasis where it belongs. The most important step is preparing individuals for married life. The second is that of getting the right people wedded. The third is that of correcting the mistakes that still may have been made. This is the work of the divorce laws and courts. With regard to law chaos exists. There is no uniformity. The widest possible gulf separates the legal standard of South Carolina and Nevada in regard to divorce. Uniformity is both logical and possible and neither extreme is desirable. Divorce should be available but only after the most serious consideration. Just as we have juvenile courts for the consideration of that highly specialized problem, so we should have courts of domestic relations prepared to consider these even more complicated problems of the family. The ordinary divorce trial with its attendant publicity and duplicity is eminently bad for public morals and a danger to the institution of marriage and the family.

We need a more careful study of justifiable grounds for divorce. The matter of separation should receive as careful attention as the matter of marriage. Society has decided that marriage should not be entered into lightly. It is even more necessary that it should not be terminated lightly. It has been said that "marriage is a gamble," that it is a "lottery." This need be the case only when it is entered upon unthinkingly, and when either or both parties to the contract are unwilling to play the game honestly, to give as well as to take, and to make a real effort toward its success. Divorce should be legally possible, but not so temptingly easy as to constitute an invitation.

6. In conclusion, we need, in order to control divorce, a more effective control of marriage. We do not need stricter divorce laws so much as we need stricter and more uniform marriage laws. In order to stabilize the family we must stabilize the individuals setting up families. Until society, the State, and the church look marriage and the family frankly in the face, recognizing the fact that they represent the union of human individuals rather than of either devils or angels, and prepare these entirely human individuals for both the duties and delights awaiting them, the "gamble" will continue.

REFERENCES

Annals of the American Academy of Political and Social Science, "The Modern American Family" (March, 1932).

BABER, R. E., *Marriage and the Family* (New York, 1939).

ELLIOTT, Mabel A., and MERRILL, Francis E., *Social Disorganization* (New York, 1934), Part III.

ELY, Mary L., and CHAPPELL, Eve, *Women in Two Worlds* (American Association for Adult Education, 1938).

GROVES, E. R., and OGBURN, W. F., *American Marriage and Family Relationships* (New York, 1928).

KRUTCH, J. W., *The Modern Temper* (New York, 1929), Ch. IV.

PRUETTE, Lorine, *Woman and Leisure* (New York, 1924).

REUTER, E. B., and RUNNER, J. R., *The Family* (New York, 1931).

Social Work Year Book, 1941, R. H. Kurtz, editor (New York, 1941).

WESTERMARCK, E., *The History of Human Marriage* (London, 1921, 5th Edition).

White House Conference on Children in a Democracy, 1940 (Washington, D. C.: Department of Labor, Children's Bureau, 1940).

WOOLF, Virginia, *A Room of One's Own* (New York, 1929).

QUESTIONS AND EXERCISES

1. What is the social purpose of the family? Of marriage?
2. What forms of marriage and the family have preceded that now practiced in our country? (See Gillin and Blackmar, *Outlines of Sociology*, Ch. X.)
3. Is polygamy in and of itself immoral and wicked? If so, why? If not, do you still deplore the practice, and why?
4. Consider the case of your own home. Where do you live, and why? What common interests do the members of your family share? In what common occupations do they engage? What are the individual interests and occupations not thus shared? Can you justify the continued existence of your home? What necessary and legitimate functions does it perform?
5. Do you plan to marry, have a family, and establish a home? Of course you do; but, frankly, why?
6. Would you, if a man, be willing to have your wife economically independent of you, with a professional career of her own, and from her own income hire cook, nurse, and maid to care for your home?
7. What would you, if a woman, think of the idea of swapping places with your husband, leaving him home to care for the house and children and yourself earning their support? Would you trust him with your children?
8. Why is it that we consider divorce a social problem? What is the problem? Is it that divorce is immoral or that it is anti-social?
9. State the attitude toward divorce (*a*) of the early Christian Church; (*b*) of the Roman Catholic Church; (*c*) of the Protestant Churches; (*d*) of the State; (*e*) of public opinion.
10. Are the legal grounds for divorce an accurate index to the actual causes of divorce?
11. Why are the great majority of divorces granted to women?
12. What are the real social causes of divorce?

13. Are modern education, and all other agencies that make for increased individualism, also increasing divorce?
14. Has woman's winning of a place for herself in the world—economic independence, intellectual equality, equal opportunity, and suffrage—resulted in happier or unhappier homes? More or fewer divorces?
15. We have suggested education as a factor in solving the problem of divorce and the unstable family. What should the young man and the young woman be taught? Work out a program.

Chapter 13

SOCIAL PROBLEMS OF EDUCATION

THE ADJUSTMENT of children to society has always been one of the major problems claiming the attention of social groups. The social pattern is not inherited; and the growing child must not only be trained regarding the modes of conduct approved by the group, but he must also be fitted so far as external influences can aid to take an active and useful part as an individual in the society of which he is a member. Education may therefore be defined as the process whereby the young individual is adapted to the group pattern of conduct and whereby his natural powers are developed in ways that will enable him to take an active part in group life.

EDUCATION IN PRIMITIVE SOCIETIES

Primitive peoples devised various methods for the accomplishment of these purposes, among them being (a) family guidance; (b) storytelling; (c) taboos; (d) pressure on community opinion by the elders; and (e) ceremonialism.

Just as the family is the ultimate social unit, so must it be regarded as the first educational influence that is exerted upon the child. The injunctions of parents, to say nothing of more strenuous forms of *family guidance*, seem to have had their effect among all peoples.

In the *folklore* of primitive peoples commonly are found explanations of the physical universe, hero tales of great leaders, personal experiences, and glimpses into the mysterious world of the spirits, all charged with an emotionalism and set forth with a dramatic eloquence calculated to impress and to inspire the young listener. In this manner not only are the ideals of the group passed on and rekindled, but modes of action successful in the struggle for existence and for social prestige are commended from the personal experiences of the raconteur. The subject-matter of folklore is of two types, mythical and objectively true, but the social effects are in every case the same—to instruct the listener in ideals and modes of conduct. The tales of the heroes to be found in Homer's Iliad and Odyssey reveal the ideals and patterns of action held by the Greeks of that day, and abound in stories that were used for the inculcation of such ideals and actions in Greek youth. The stories found in the early books of the Old Testament are largely hero tales of the early Hebrews. How the blood of Hebrew youths must have leapt at the story of Samson in his lone-handed fight with the Philistines! How they must have chuckled, as about the fireside or on great occasions in the life of the group, the story of Jacob with his dependence upon God, his sly cheating of Esau out of his birthright, and his clever manipulation of affairs to overreach his father-in-law Laban, were told with all the art of the story-teller! The folklore of our American Indians provides many stories of similar import.

Among primitive peoples, *taboos* constitute one of the most effective means of impressing upon the younger generation the rules of social conduct. Many of these survive in our superstitions of the present day. The taboo widespread among primitive peoples against eating the sacred animal is an illustration. The taboo against women approaching the men's house, against revealing the secrets of the men's society to the women, forbidding the man to see the face of his mother-in-law, the ban upon doing things in any other way than that which had come down by tradition from the past, are all illustrations of educational measures of enormous effect upon the conduct of youth.

The pressure of *public opinion* is a mighty influence on the conduct of all people, and in primitive groups this is usually exercised by the elders. The young and the inexperienced always stand in awe of the dogmatism of age, and when this dogmatism is backed by tradition as it is in many primitive groups, all other opinion tends to defer to it. Slogans and proverbs are familiar and subtle tools of age in molding the conduct of the young.[1]

The reiteration of group ideals and beliefs is accomplished for all sections of the population and among practically all groups by some sort of *ceremonialism*. In primitive societies the rites of initiation for boys and girls at adolescence have been perhaps the strongest ceremonial influence in the education of the young. The consuming desire of children is to become men and women. The rites are surrounded with an atmosphere of secrecy and solemnity that gives them great power. Among the Australian aborigines the ceremonies consist of very elaborate preparations, instructions by selected guardians who accompany the boys, an impressive series of dramas during the initiation exercises, and the

---

[1] F. E. Lumley, *Means of Social Control* (1925); E. A. Ross, *Social Control* (1901); W. I. Thomas, ed., *Sourcebook for Social Origins* (1909), pp. 258–264; W. G. Sumner, *Folkways* (1907), p. 629.

undergoing of severe physical pain for the purpose of testing the self-control of the lad. Concerning these ceremonies, Howitt says:

The intention of the ceremonies is evidently to make the youths of the tribe worthy members of the community, according to their lights. Certain principles are impressed upon them for their guidance through life—for instance to listen to and obey the old men; to generously share the fruits of the chase with others, especially their kindred; not to interfere with the women of the tribe, particularly those who are related to them; not to injure their kindred, in its widest sense, by means of evil magic. Before the novice is permitted to take his place in the community, marry, and join in its councils, he must possess those qualifications which will enable him to act for the common welfare. . . .

In the ceremonies mentioned, with few exceptions, there is a similar mode of assembling the meeting for initiation, the making of a circular earthen mound, the removal of the boys from their mothers' control, the knocking out of the tooth, the investment in some tribes of the novice with a man's attire, the formation of a new camp by the women, and the showing of the boy to his mother, with the severance of her control over him by a formal act, and finally the period of probation under severe conditions. I have elsewhere referred to the belief inculcated as to the existence of a great supernatural anthropomorphic Being, by whom the ceremonies were first instituted, and who still communicates with mankind through the medicine-men, his servants.[2]

The efficacy of these various methods of primitive societies in the education of children and youth is attested by all travelers who have observed them. The pressure of the established patterns of conduct and belief is so great that it is only the exceptional child or youth who does not habituate himself to these group ideals and patterns. He who refuses to conform is selected for death and thus disappears as a disturbing influence.

EDUCATION IN A COMPLEX SOCIETY

1. *Why Primitive Methods Are No Longer Effective.* In civilized societies conditions are so much more complex that the old means of social control tend to fall short of their purpose. They are inadequate for our modern conditions. Although still used, their effectiveness is much less than in a simpler society. The home still serves as an educational institution but with lessening influence; group traditions survive; impressions are made on sundry ceremonial occasions even now, but everywhere the close adherence to group patterns is breaking down and variant forms of conduct are appearing. Family ties are loosened, chil-

[2] Howitt in *Sourcebook for Social Origins*, W. I. Thomas, ed. (1909), pp. 231-232.

dren are less restrained, regard for the aged is less than in a primitive society.

The individual, in short, is rapidly tending to become anonymous; and one of the principal reasons for this is the *increasing size of the group*. Practically all modern civilizations, and particularly that of the United States, comprise large populations spread over a wide area, a state of affairs that was never present among primitive men. Modern means of communication and transportation, as has been pointed out in an earlier chapter, have enabled a nation of one hundred and thirty-two million people to become a society as truly as the primitive tribal group of a few hundred, with the important difference, however, that the face-to-face relationship which enabled all members of the tribe or village to know one another personally is no longer present in the larger society. As a result, the rigid uniformities of conduct made possible by education in a limited group through personal contact are no longer possible.

Moreover, the possible relations of life, economic, political, social, are much more numerous. There is in modern society a *greater variety of interests* for the individual than was possible in more primitive groups. Division of labor has reached an unprecedented development. Functional classes have arisen that were rare under primitive conditions. Interests are organized in more definite groups over a much wider territory.

The *rapidity of change* which is a characteristic of modern social life is a further reason why the old methods of education no longer suffice. Society is no longer static. It is necessary that new possible reactions be evaluated at once. These new evaluations cannot often be the result of long-continued testing and inculcation. Because of the size of territory and the rapidity of change, it is impossible for the group to standardize the reactions and to maintain control of them, approving some and effectually disapproving others. Educational means have had to be devised to make the individual adaptable to these changes.

Coincident with these changes in modern social life has come the *enlargement of the social horizon*. While the inherent urges of children are the same as those in the primitive child and youth, the surroundings are different. In primitive societies these urges and impulses were constantly under an effective control. About the child and youth constantly were kindred persons who were closely observant of his conduct and ready to bring effective pressure against any variation. The patterns of conduct presented to him were those upon which there was agreement by the whole group. To-day the youth who leaves his home, whether for business or for education or for pleasure, meets with a varied assortment of patterns. Thousands of alternatives surround him from which he may—in fact, *must*—choose. Hence the inhibitions that guarded primitive childhood and youth are largely loosened; and incorrigibility, disorderly conduct, truancy, and delinquency, to say nothing of breach of propriety, have become frequent among the children and youth of our present day.

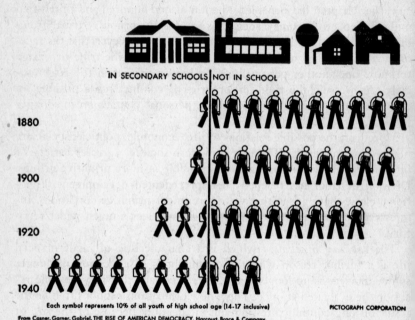

IN SECONDARY SCHOOLS | NOT IN SCHOOL

1880

1900

1920

1940

Each symbol represents 10% of all youth of high school age (14-17 inclusive)

PICTOGRAPH CORPORATION

From Casner, Garner, Gabriel, THE RISE OF AMERICAN DEMOCRACY, Harcourt, Brace & Company.

FIG. 12.—GROWTH IN SECONDARY SCHOOL ENROLLMENT

2. *The Purposes of Modern Education.* From the social point of view, the purposes of modern education are much the same as those of education among primitive societies. In either case, there is the attempt to condition the individual to the requirements of the group in which he lives and to train him, as well as might be, to shoulder his share of the work and responsibilities inherent to group life. The education of young men and women in democratic societies, however, probably is unique in the attention it gives to the welfare of the individual—not simply as a group member, but for himself alone. This has been made possible by

the greater economic security of modern living and the transfer of much tedious and dangerous effort from the human being to the machine. Thus we may say that the basic purposes of modern education are to help the young to adapt themselves to the circumstances of life in such a way as will enable them to bring the world of things and of men to their service, and to enable them to contribute better adjustments in social relationships. Such purposes will require that we undertake various types of instruction, among which the following are fundamental:

a. *Understanding the Universe.* It is possible for the child to-day to know more about the nature of the universe than the wisest man of a thousand years ago. Indeed, within the last hundred years there has been greater extension of knowledge concerning the world in which we live than there was in all the previous experience of the human race. All of our applied science, our machinery, our control over nature, is based upon such knowledge. Moreover, the happiness of the individual himself, his freedom from fear, his ability to control the forces of nature, his sense of order, depend in large part upon his being furnished with the knowledge that modern science has brought regarding the natural world in which we live. Only by understanding this universe of physical things and natural forces can he find the answers to the deep questions that arise to plague him, and only by such understanding can he make use of them most efficiently for his own and for his fellow's needs. The record of all these achievements modern education attempts to hand over to the child and the youth.

b. *Understanding Society.* Modern education likewise endeavors to give to the child and youth our recent gains of knowledge concerning the world of men and their institutions. The history of the past, and our knowledge of prehistory, give us a picture of how man has dealt with his situation in the world during the last thirty millennia. Never before has he needed so much to know the history of man's institutions, of his ideals, and the fundamental principles upon which social welfare is based: the ways in which groups act and react toward one another. Social relationships are so complex to-day that unless the youth understands something of their nature and the conditions on which society depends, he cannot be a really intelligent citizen. The possibilities of friction are so much multiplied, and the men and the groups with which he must deal are so much more numerous than ever before, that such knowledge as we possess of the social relationships which exist in the world must be a part of his equipment. How shall he judge of the value of the family to-day unless he knows something of its past? How shall he judge of our business relationships unless he understands how they operate and how they have come to be what they are? How shall he help prevent the international frictions and disagreements that lead to war unless he understands how they develop and the processes by which misunderstandings can be obviated? Hence education tries to hand on as much of our social knowledge as possible so that the youth may know how to adjust himself to the world of society with the least possible friction and with the greatest efficiency.

c. *Formation of Social Values*. Modern education further attempts to present to the developing mind of the child and the youth certain social values. It is evident at once that we are here face to face with the problem of determining the very objectives of society itself. Society at various times and places has placed above all else the need for a high regard for the wisdom and judgment of the elders and for a strict conformity to the traditions and customs handed down from the past. It has, on occasion, demanded complete subservience to the will of the leaders of the group, whether military, religious, economic, or political. In our own society, of course, we try to free the young from the fears and superstitions that have enslaved men through the ages and to inculcate such ideals as honor, honesty, loyalty, and concern for the general welfare. We are trying, though often not too consciously or successfully, to fulfil those purposes of education which unite freedom for self-development with a corresponding service to the group in return. Whatever the goal that is to be sought, however, education has as one of its functions to impart to the young an understanding of what society expects of them and what they may expect of society.

d. *Development of Social Usefulness*. Since the family has been superseded as the institution to train people to make a living, and since the shop has given way to the factory, it seems to be incumbent upon the school to prepare its students to be economically useful. This purpose, however, has not been everywhere recognized, and is realized only in part even now. The movement for vocational schools and vocational guidance is a recognition of this purpose in modern education. Our colleges and universities similarly are adapting their curricula to meet the needs of the wide variety of technical and professional groups so essential to modern life.

It must be borne in mind constantly, however, that specialization can become something of a menace to both the individual and society itself. One cannot attain maximum usefulness, in most instances, unless he be fully aware of the dignity and the function of his occupation *within the social pattern as a whole.* He may find employment difficult to obtain if his specialization is so great as to restrict his adaptability; and without proper perspective, he may fall easy prey to manipulation by misguided or unprincipled leadership.

e. *Preparation for Living.* And finally, the young must be given some training in the matter of "getting the most out of life." This does not necessarily mean, of course, that education should present patterns for "the good life," as ideals that the young should strive for in later years. Such matters, after all, are so much influenced by individual temperament, by regional and class—and even religious—environment that generalizations would be futile. Nevertheless, there are many practical problems of every-day living in which the individual needs a store of accurate information. Thus, for example, it is as much to the individual's interest as to society's that he should have a knowledge of the functioning of his body, methods of preserving health, and the adjustments necessary to promote physical efficiency. There are also many practical problems of family and marital adjustments which our schools have begun partially to recognize by instituting courses of study in both colleges and high schools on marriage and family problems. A further need that still remains largely unrecognized pertains to budgeting and purchasing and other problems of private finances of the individual. We have too long stressed the need for making a living and left the individual consumer to the wiles of merchandizers and creditmen, apparently assuming that once having earned his living, he "naturally" will know how to spend it to his best advantage.

SOME PROBLEMS OF MODERN EDUCATION

Obviously the modern school system does not function perfectly. It is as new as our modern industrial civilization. It is not surprising if, emerging little more than a hundred years ago, it has not been perfectly adapted to our rapidly changing situation. What is said about its problems is in no sense a criticism of the army of devoted men and women who are administering it and are no less concerned with its problems than the sociologist. All of us have a stake in it, since it is such an important social institution, and every one of us should thoughtfully consider these problems in the hope that together we may more perfectly adjust it to the needs of our children and youth.

1. *School Mortality. a. Extent.* The United States undoubtedly is the best-educated nation in the world. Our schools are more numerous, better equipped, and better attended than those of any other country. In

1936, with a total population of about 128,000,000, we had at least 32,000,000 individuals going to a school of one sort or another—not less than a quarter of our entire population. Illiteracy, too, had been reduced to about 4.3 per cent for the nation as a whole by 1930; and while the rates for immigrants and Negroes were considerably higher

TABLE 22

School Enrollments in the United States, 1936 *
(Figures Are in Round Numbers)

Type of School	Enrollments
All schools	32,658,000
Kindergarten and primary grades	23,000,000
High school	6,000,000
Vocational schools	1,250,000
College and professions	1,000,000
Correspondence schools	850,000
Normal schools, teacher colleges	150,000
Schools for mental deficients	120,000
Commercial schools	100,000
Nurse-training schools	80,000
Vocational rehabilitation (disabled)	40,000
Training schools for delinquents	30,000
Schools for the deaf	25,000
Schools for the blind	13,000

* Adapted from *Statistical Abstract of the United States, 1938.*

(9.9 and 16.3 per cent respectively), the proportion of illiterates from 10 to 20 years of age had been reduced by 1930 to a fraction of 1 per cent for most classes, with rural Negroes remaining conspicuously high at 10.3 per cent.[3]

More than 4 out of every 5 of our children 17 years of age and under are in school; but it is well known that large numbers of them drop out of school at an early age. For example, let us trace the group that started to school in 1925. There were 4,048,598 of them in the first grades of the public schools that year. By the time they were in the eighth grade, their numbers had been reduced to 1,681,520; and only 1,064,467 reached the last year of high school. Graphically, their history is recorded in Table 23. It will be noticed that the number actually increased between the eighth grade and the first year of high school, a phenomenon characteristic of the depression years from 1930 onwards, when many older children were returning to the schools for lack of em-

[3] *Statistical Abstract of the United States,* 1938, p. 531.

TABLE 23

PROGRESS OF THE PUPILS ENROLLED IN THE FIRST GRADE OF THE PUBLIC SCHOOLS IN
THE UNITED STATES IN 1925 *

Year	Grade	Number of Pupils
1925	1	4,048,598
1926	2	2,819,896
1927	3	2,695,615
1928	4	2,632,474
1929	5	2,408,979
1930	6	2,256,249
1931	7	2,041,280
1932	8	1,681,520
1933	9	1,816,317
1934	10	1,540,254
1935	11	1,229,295
1936	12	1,064,469

* *Biennial Survey of Education, 1934–1936* (U. S. Office of Education, Department of the Interior, 1937), Part II, No. 2, p. 8.

ployment opportunity, or for other reasons.[4] Even so, only about 806,000 of the 4,000,000 children who started out together in 1925 actually graduated from the high school in 1936.[5] The total enrollment in our schools of higher learning in 1936 included about 1,200,000 persons,[6] while less than 100,000 were granted degrees.[7]

b. Why Children Quit School. There are many reasons which explain the child's failure to stay in school. Some of them may be directly traced to the fault of the teachers or to the school administration. Too often efforts of the school are thwarted by ignorant, indifferent, or even greedy parents—parents who view the child's present earning power with more concern than they do his future success in meeting the problems of living. Often, too, parents and teachers fail to understand the child and make bad matters worse by scolding, shaming, and ridiculing him. In other cases ill health, defective vision, bad teeth, and many other noticed or unnoticed physical defects prevent the child from putting his best efforts and spirit into his school work. He gets discouraged and falls behind, finally quitting school at his first opportunity. We have already noted that the home no longer affords employment for the members of the family, and there are many attractive opportunities for earning spending money, many outside attractions to

[4] *Biennial Survey of Education, 1934–1936*, Part II, No. 2, p. 8.
[5] *Statistical Abstract of the United States, 1938*, p. 107.
[6] *Ibid.*
[7] *Biennial Survey of Education, 1934–1936*, Part II, No. 2, p. 3.

pull and tug at the child's interests. Getting in the habit of thinking and following these outside interests absorbs his time and attention from his school work, and he gets out of step with his class, becomes dissatisfied, and marks time until he can quit school. Adolescence itself brings impulses and ideals that often result in loss of interest in school. Almost every child who drops out of school offers a unique combination of reasons, and most of these reasons can be removed if properly studied and thoughtfully considered.

Environmental factors also play their part in reducing the child's interest in school. Every study of problem children in school shows clearly that the *homes* from which the children come often poorly prepare them to receive full benefit from the school. Many parents do not coöperate with the school; they do not understand the home surroundings necessary to make the child's educational process a success. *Industry and business* go their way without considering what are the effects, direct and indirect, of their methods upon the development of childhood and youth. Few business men and industrial leaders have asked themselves how much they are responsible for the failure of the schools. If, however, the wages paid do not provide for a decent home, is not part of the failure in the production of citizenship due to business? Moreover, the *neighborhood* conditions often draw the growing boy and girl into the coils of degeneracy and destroy the effects of the educational process. We have not yet fully accepted the fact that one of the responsibilities of a city is to provide for proper use of the leisure time of boys and girls. *Conservatism* is also partly responsible for the failure of childhood and youth. The older people often fail to remember the feelings of childhood and youth; they become harsh, repressive, unsympathetic with the youth and his house of dreams. Finally, *the school itself* must shoulder part of the responsibility for its failure. The very fact that it is a system, more or less inelastic, attempting to train great masses of young people, and including among its teaching body many who are ill-prepared to deal competently with the problems of childhood and youth, shows that it cannot shift its responsibility entirely to family, neighborhood, and business.

2. *The Education of Special Classes.* In the beginning our educational system proceeded on the theory that all children should be given the same education. Longer experience, however, has shown us that education should be adapted, so far as possible, to the particular situation of each child. For example, there is the crippled child, the mentally

deficient child, and the superior child; and there is the whole class of adults whose education has not been adequate.

a. The Physically Handicapped Child. The education of the physically handicapped child presents many difficulties. The number of cripples, fortunately, is small. Yet that very smallness of numbers presents pedagogical problems, since the handicaps of each pupil are likely to be somewhat different from those of every other. Providing adequate instructional and medical care necessarily is costly; and the parents, most often, are not in a position to contribute much to offset those special costs. Fortunately, all of our States are now making provisions whereby these children can have the best medical and surgical care that modern science affords. However, their school life is bound to be interrupted unless care is taken. After even the best has been done that science knows, perhaps some physical disability will still remain. The child's impaired condition may have set him back so far that he has become discouraged, or his disability may have made him conspicuous and the object of rough jokes or of too much pity by other children. This is especially true, probably, in the case of children suffering from poor sight or hearing, since they *appear* to be like other children. Their condition is not easily discovered; and in many cases the children themselves are unaware of their handicap, because they assume that *everyone* has similar trouble. Consequently the child falls behind and may be considered a dullard, even though in reality he may be exerting extraordinary effort and ingenuity to get on as well as he does, with what he has to work with. Modern educators, however, have not forgotten the disabled child, and many of our city school systems have made special provision for them. Special busses may gather them up and take them to and from the school-room; equipment suited to their impaired condition is often provided; special teachers are employed in some places to give attention to these pupils so that they can "catch up." If means are provided whereby the child can compensate for the disabilities that he suffers, often his social development will go on quite as steadily and as hopefully as that of the normal child.

b. The Mentally Handicapped Child. It is important that special attention be given to mentally slow or emotionally unstable children in the schools. Special classes or special rooms where the work is adapted to their deficiencies have been established as experiments in the attempt to keep them in school as long as they can profit from it and to relieve them from the results of competition with brighter children. The "op-

portunity room" (as these experimental rooms are called) is proving to
be the salvation of many of these children who in former days became
thoroughly discouraged and dropped out or who became delinquent.
With them the training must be as individualized as possible, to make
use of whatever abilities they may have for the practical purposes of
life, and for the enrichment of their own personality. Jessie Taft describes the problem of the dull-normal child in these words:

He is not allowed by law to leave the public school when it gets beyond
him, yet to face failure, ridicule, reprimands, day after day, is something
that human nature cannot do without efforts to escape from so unbearable
a situation. The child will either run away in body or in spirit. He is bound
to gain a sense of importance somehow—if not by good conduct, by bad.
He will take refuge in sullenness, indifference, or in more active, aggressive
attempts to counteract the boredom and inferiority of his position. If he
cannot shine in school, he can perhaps become the terror of the neighborhood. There is only one possible treatment for this type of child, and that
is to offer him legitimate avenues of successful expression. If school or work
offers him a chance to act successfully, he will seek social approval, just as
he apparently sought social disapproval before. All you need to do to prove
this statement is to put such a child into a school that gives him work in
which he can succeed. He becomes the simplest of case problems. His energy
goes over into useful activity and drains off from the unsocial channels.[8]

c. *The Superior Child*. The superior pupil often presents grave difficulty in the school if there is a rigid system of promotion, or if he is
held back by the poorer pupils in the class. Experiments are being tried
nowadays to require more of these superior students and to advance
them more rapidly. Says Wile concerning the superior child:

The superior child is a potential asset to the community. Is it not, then,
to the community's best interest to develop him to the point of fullest self-
expression and greatest service? While no prediction can be made as to the
part an individual superior child may play in the guidance of his generation,
it is undoubtedly true that these children, as a group, will provide nearly all
of the leaders in art and science, in the professions, and those who, by creating new ideas and ideals, must contribute to the progress of civilization. Such
children are too few for the school system to neglect them. The time-mark-
ing system for these bright, capable, natural students is mentally harmful
and, viewed socially, is responsible for a far greater loss to the community than can ever be atoned for by attempts to raise the mental achievements of children of inherently inferior mental powers. School progress is
checked and mental growth retarded, with disastrous results to themselves
and to the community when these vigorous minds are permitted to remain
idle or to work at half speed. Most careful thought should be spent upon

[8] Jessie Taft, *The Problem Child in School* (1925), pp. 69-70.

the needs of the superior child, for by modification and adjustment of the curriculum it is possible to weave an educational program more in harmony with his mental pattern.[9]

d. The Adult. Finally, there is the problem of the education of adults who as children have been denied the opportunities of the school system. How frequently it happens that because of economic needs or because of dissatisfaction with the schools, the boy or girl leaves as soon as possible and takes a job. After the stress and strain of adolescence have passed, they sometimes awaken to the need of further education. They realize all they have missed, and with proper encouragement they are ready to make sacrifices in order that this lack of education may be made up. The exploitation of this consciousness of need has made rich the numerous correspondence schools in the United States, and accounts for the great success of the university extension divisions in this country. For the most part, these courses are of practical or vocational value. Life's experiences have made the student keenly appreciative of the necessity for such courses. However ill-taught and poorly organized, doubtless they have provided in a way an answer to the deep need felt by many of these people to whom the school system has not adequately given preparation for life. The vocational school movement in some of our States and the promotion of industrial education by our Federal Board of Vocational Education are doing much to meet the need for education with these adults. A comparable service is being performed among the farmers of the nation by the United States Department of Agriculture through its Agricultural Extension Service and the Home Demonstration agents. Colleges and universities increasingly are serving special occupational groups through summer institutes or short courses designed to give these people new insight into their work or to acquaint them with current developments in their respective fields. Town Hall Associates, the American Association for Adult Education, the Office of Education, and others are sponsoring forum and discussion groups for consideration of the broad social, economic, and political problems of society as a whole.[10]

3. *Higher Education.* The colleges are widely accused of turning out young people equipped for nothing in particular and apparently lacking the training or inclination to analyze situations and to adapt themselves successfully to life. The development of intelligent leadership, which is conceived as the aim of a liberal college education, as dis-

[9] I. S. Wile, *The Challenge of Childhood* (New York, 1926), pp. 141–142.
[10] Mary L. Ely, *Why Forums?* (New York, 1937).

tinguished from the more specialized training of the professional or technical school, seems to have suffered under the present system.

Whereas college education used to be the privilege of a small class having a similar cultural background and to a large extent similar ambitions, the present situation finds the higher institutions crowded with students of all classes, with varying economic and social antecedents, and with widely divergent ideas, often quite vague, as to what they wish to do with their newly acquired learning. The magnitude of this problem becomes apparent when we discover that the enrollment in such institutions has increased more than fivefold since the turn of the century, there being 1,350,905 students in 1938 as compared to 237,-592 in 1900.[11] The heterogeneity of the new student population, especially at the great universities, has found the institutions unable to create the social and psychological solidarity that was formerly the heritage of college men.

The greatest problem facing the modern college is to stimulate intellectual curiosity and the development of mental initiative on the part of the average student. Experiments are now in progress in various parts of the country in regard to methods of instruction; touching the alteration of the curriculum; orientation courses; psychological and social distance tests; vocational guidance and closer faculty advice. It is apparent that the problem must be seriously considered both within the colleges and without, if the possibility of a very grave waste of time and money on the part of an important part of the population at a critical time of life is to be avoided.

4. *Academic Freedom.* Education is not the panacea for all the ills of society that many people seem to believe it to be. Educators especially are prone to overestimate the power at their command, contending that primarily through the medium of education we can develop the kind of society we think is right. It must be conceded that the educator has a tremendous opportunity—and responsibility—to mold the thought of the rising generation. But there are subtle and powerful influences upon the educational system itself, determining what sort of precepts shall be presented and how the ideas that are learned will be expressed in terms of social values and conduct. The fortunes of education and educators in continental Europe during the Second World War brought home to us with awful force the realization that education is not a major power in its own right. It is rather a *tool*, which is used by society or some special group within it to project the objectives such groups

[11] *Statistical Abstract of the United States, 1941,* p. 122.

may seek. It has been made clear anew that it is imperative to preserve the right of free inquiry and expression if the influence of the educational process is to be exerted for the cultural enrichment of the human race.

The dangers to academic freedom are not always malicious or the result of selfish interest on the part of those who would have a hand in determining what shall be taught or who shall teach it. Sometimes the materials involved are controversial in nature; sometimes the "facts" of the study involved are open to variable interpretation; sometimes there is a sincere belief that certain types of knowledge, even if sound, would be disastrous in their social effects if generally known or utilized. Thus the question of censorship appears in determining educational policy. Shall we, for example, prohibit the study of the Bible, or of communism, atheism, or evolution in our schools? There are many who honestly believe that these "subjects" should be barred from our curricula. Yet can we arrive at a complete understanding of history, philosophy, or biology if we omit them? And where is the balance between social expediency, real or supposed, and the fundamental necessity for unrestricted inquiry and research?

On the other hand, there are problems in regard to how many and what sort of required subjects we must find a place for in our curricula and what sort of qualifications we shall demand of our teachers. From the traditional "three R's" we have come to be required by law to teach such things as agriculture, health, citizenship, and "coöperation." To be sure, such requirements are defensible to the extent that students—especially at the secondary and primary levels—are not competent to make their own choice of studies. An increase of required courses probably is inevitable as a result of the growing complexity of the world with which the young must be made familiar. But when such requirements, as sometimes happens, result from pressure politics or special interest groups of one sort or another, then clearly we are on the road to perverted use of the educational process. And since education, after all, is what we make it, society as a whole must keep a vigilant watch over the system and those who would use it to their own selfish purposes.

REFERENCES

Bourne, Randolph, *Education and Living* (Boston, 1916), Chs. I, III, IV, V.
Bushee, F. A., *Social Organization* (New York, 1930), Chs. X, XI.

Democracy's Challenge to Education, Beulah Amidon, ed. (New York, 1940).

DEWEY, John, *Democracy and Education* (New York, 1916), Chs. II, VII.

ENGELHARDT, N. L., and ENGELHARDT, N. L., Jr., *Planning the Community School* (New York, 1940).

GROVES, E. R., *Social Problems and Education* (New York, 1925).

MARTIN, Everett Dean, *The Meaning of a Liberal Education* (New York, 1926).

National Resources Committee, "Social Development and Education," *Problems of a Changing Population* (Washington, 1938).

OVERSTREET, H. A., *We Move in New Directions* (New York, 1933), Ch. 7.

PERRY, C. A., and WILLIAMS, M. P., *New York School Centers and Their Community Policy* (New York, 1931).

PITTENGER, B. F., *Indoctrination for American Democracy* (New York, 1941)

Ross, E. A., *Social Control* (New York, 1926), Ch. XIV.

RUSSELL, Bertrand, *Education and the Modern World* (New York, 1932).

TUTTLE, H. S., *A Social Basis of Education* (New York, 1934).

QUESTIONS AND EXERCISES

1. Can you trace to stories told or read to you, or read by you, in childhood and youth any of your social ideals and social attitudes?
2. Can you cite from your own experience any teachers and any subjects in school that were injurious to your social development? Any that affected your social conduct favorably?
3. What conditions of modern life have arisen that have impelled the formal organization of the educational processes?
4. Outline and discuss briefly the purposes of modern education, adding to those purposes listed in the text any others you may believe important.
5. What are the major reasons for children's quitting school?
6. What educational problems are presented by the handicapped child? Why is it also true that the *superior* child may require special handling?
7. What do you understand "socialized" education to be?
8. Could socialized education serve as an aid in adjusting the problems of the family? If so, in what ways?
9. Outline a program for the promotion of adult education that you think your community needs. What agencies would you interest in carrying forward this program?
10. What trends or tendencies in our present economic and social life make it increasingly imperative that we should give more thought in our educational preparation to the intelligent use of leisure time?
11. What is "academic freedom"? Why is it so important that such freedom be preserved? To what extent, if any, should teachers be restrained in the exercise of this privilege?

Chapter 14

RELIGION AND SOCIAL PROBLEMS

WHY IS RELIGION A SOCIAL MATTER?

RELIGION in its simplest and most scientifically acceptable definition is *a belief in the supernatural* in relation to man. A church is the institutionalized form of a system of beliefs pertaining to the supernatural, and a system of devices by which its members hope to utilize the power of the supernatural. Investigators have found no stable society, present or past, without religion. In some form or other it is the cultural property of all social groups. And, whatever their supernatural ingredients,

TABLE 24

DISTRIBUTION OF WORLD POPULATION, BY RELIGIOUS FAITH *
(Estimates Based on Most Recent Information from Various Sources)

Faith	Membership
Total	1,849,000,000
Christians	682,000,000
Confucians and Taoists	351,000,000
Hindus	230,000,000
Mohammedans	209,000,000
Buddhists	150,000,000
Animists	136,000,000
Shintoists	25,000,000
Jews	15,000,000
Miscellaneous	51,000,000

* Adapted from *The World Almanac* (1937), p. 431.

the forms of religious beliefs and the rituals of religious observances are in large measure the product of the group and are passed down the generations as part of the social heritage. When men worship together or hold beliefs in common with other members of a group, not only the individual but also the group is conceived of as standing in a special relation to the supernatural. Therefore the matter of religious belief, and especially the manner in which it is translated into action affecting society, are social affairs. Indeed, religious cults now and again become attached to socially unacceptable standards of behavior, and the State

feels it must intervene. Occasionally, too, religion has been linked with
the State itself, a combination that may easily lead to oppression and
exploitation. Apart from its dynamic possibilities for good, then, religion itself may create problems of social policy. Sociologically, we are
vitally interested in the effect of religion on the individual's social conduct and welfare.

There is no reason to believe that the power of religion is of negligible importance in our modern American society. Institutionalized religion as represented by the church is far from insignificant either materially or spiritually. The total number of church members in the
United States according to the Bureau of the Census tabulation for 1936
was 55,807,366, divided among 256 denominations. If the number of
persons who have been baptized, all nominal adherents, and all those
who in the supreme test of life or death turn to a particular communion

TABLE 25

CHURCH MEMBERSHIP IN THE UNITED STATES, 1935 *
(Principal Denominations)

Denomination	Approximate Membership
Total	57,800,000
Roman Catholic	20,600,000
Baptist	10,200,000
Methodist	9,100,000
Lutheran	4,600,000
Jewish	4,100,000
Presbyterian	2,700,000
Episcopalian	1,900,000
Disciples of Christ	1,600,000
Congregational and Christian	1,000,000
Eastern Orthodox	1,000,000
Evangelical and Reformed	1,000,000

* Adapted from *The World Almanac* (1937), p. 432.

were included in the count, undoubtedly the total would rise to at
least 75,000,000. One must not forget, however, that many of these are
only nominal adherents. The total expenditures for the year 1936 were
$518,953,517 and in the same year the value of church edifices stood
at $3,411,875,467.[1]

At first glance it may appear odd that religion should deserve a place
in a consideration of social problems at all. Yet there is not an organized

[1] *Census of Religious Bodies: 1936.* (Washington, 1940).

religion in the world that takes no cognizance of social life, or which contains no trace of social idealism. From a primitive tribe like the Manus of New Guinea to the semicivilized ancient Semites, and the modern nations under Hinduism, Buddhism, Mohammedanism, Confucianism, or Christianity, there is not one the religion of which does not bear upon social relationships.[2] Organized religion has always concerned itself also with the affairs of men living together. The explanations of this phenomenon are various.

Self-Preservation. Religion as part of the social heritage cannot be self-perpetuating unless it rests on the basis of a healthy social group. One of the primary reasons for the interest of religion in social affairs, therefore, is *self-preservation.* To primitive man, regard for the supernatural is closely linked with group welfare. On the observance of this taboo or of that ceremony depends not only the health and prosperity of himself and his family, but also the preservation of his whole society from epidemic pestilences, from the failure of rain necessary for the pasturage of his flocks, and from the hostility of enemies—or at least the victory over enemies in a conflict. Religion played a direct part in man's economic and social welfare for a very long time. It was considered vital to his existence. His individual welfare depended on the welfare of his group. The welfare of his group depended on the help of what he considered superhuman beings. Hence the vital import of religion in his scheme of things. Religion was necessary to the preservation of himself, his family, and his group. Any interest or activity of the individual, therefore, that tended to crowd out consideration of the larger group, since it meant hazard not only to himself but to the group, was to be controlled by religion in the interest of all. How unfortunate for both religion and for society that the larger aspects of that close connection between religion and social welfare are not recognized as of great importance in modern life! Sex morality, for instance, has always been a matter of intense concern on the part of the Christian Church. The same amount of attention has not been given to the other bodily functions as to those connected with sex. It seems reasonable to suppose, however, that, consciously or not, religious leaders have realized that absorption in the affairs of sex is the one activity which may claim the whole of the individual to the total exclusion of social purposes. Hence the insistence upon chastity and continence. Obviously control of such

---

[2] See Margaret Mead, *Growing Up in New Guinea;* Robertson Smith, *The Religion of the Semites;* Hastings, *Encyclopædia of Religion and Ethics,* articles "Confucianism," "Hinduism," "Buddhism."

affairs cannot safely be left to the individual conscience or will power. In the long run, group pressure to enforce a moral standard is worth any amount of individual exhortation. So the church has supported, built up, and strengthened the group attitudes on sexual morals at all points, thereby acquiring an automatic lever to turn the individual soul toward the supernatural.

The other social policies of the Christian Church can be explained on the same basis. A stable family, which has always been one of the primary concerns of the church, is necessary to the future of religion because it is through the family that the individual receives his first contact with religion. The home circle is the unit of community religious feeling. Unless the fires of belief are kept brightly burning on the domestic hearth, the strong white flame of religious passion that reaches to heaven will become a smoldering smoke-pall to be eventually dissipated.

The church has frowned upon antisocial conduct—of which stealing and lying in one or another of their forms are the most prominent examples—because its prevalence means acute social maladjustment. In the scramble for material things spirituality is lost. Hence the Christian Church's early hostile attitude toward wealth, the taking of interest, etc. The same is true of the church's attitude toward war—favorable when war seems to be the means of spreading religion, as in the medieval Crusades or in the contemporary stand against Hitlerism, opposed when war promises to disrupt spirituality, as in the Truce of God.

Religion Is Socially Generated. Aside from its interest in social life from the point of view of self-preservation, religion takes an active part in the affairs of men because it is in considerable measure the product of men. Although we may believe that religion is divine in its origins, the religious forms and beliefs as they appear objectively are *socially generated and conditioned*. Religion embodies the ideals and hopes of its believers, who are unfortunately obliged to live in a world that is not perfect. And the reason that their world is not perfect is that they have been unable completely to adjust themselves (1) to nature and (2) to their fellow-men. If happiness is the life goal of all men and adjustment is only another word for happiness, we must bear in mind that for the normal individual these two aspects of complete adjustment, social and material, are interdependent. Adjustment to the material environment without adjustment to the social environment, even when it is possible, is only half-happiness; and half-happiness is unhappiness. Religion is a means to surmount the maladjustments of this life. Reality is always beset with difficulties, but religion also attempts to transcend reality, and to solace the soul fatigued by the troubles of reality. If, therefore, religion is to be of any help or comfort to the individual in his quest for happiness, it cannot ignore the social environment, adjustment to which is essential for the individual's happiness.

The Christian Church also has an obligation to face the social problems of the day because many of these modern social problems the church has created by setting up standards of social conduct at variance with the selfish and egoistic motives of men. Therefore it has a responsibility for their solution that it cannot escape. Was it not Jesus Himself who set up the ideal of the Kingdom of God in which men should live as brothers? Was it not St. Paul who said that "in Jesus Christ there is neither male nor female, bond or free, but all are one"? It was another of His followers who said: "If a man love not his brother whom he hath seen, how can he love God whom he hath not seen?" The church has set up ideals of social conduct and standards of social relationship, and by that very fact has created some of these problems. Were it not for the religion of brotherhood, would it be so clear that the enslavement of one man by another is unjust, or that the economic exploitation of one man by another is unrighteous? Economic change may destroy slavery on the ground of unprofitableness, but not on the ground of social injustice.

Religion a Means of Social Control. The Christian Church has often found itself entangled in the affairs of a society because it has been used by those in power as an *instrument for regulating action.* Thus at times when the church sanctioned the belief that political power was foreordained and sent by heaven, kings and nobles could, while posing as God's lieutenants on earth, command their inferiors to do what best suited their ends. Religion has sanctioned wars such as the Crusades, persecutions such as the Huguenot massacres, torture such as the Inquisition. It has also given its sanction to political ideals, as in the American colonies; to the alleviation of poverty in its encouragement of charity; to art, as in the cathedrals of Europe; to education, as in the medieval monasteries. Whenever people have been led to believe that religion was favoring a certain social movement, it has been easier to enlist their coöperation. These efforts have been both worthy and unworthy from the social point of view, but whenever the church was the tool of those working for the social good or for self-interest, it has of necessity found itself in the midst of social life.

In short, religion has also been *historically interested in social affairs.* The Christian Church and prophetic Judaism, out of which the church sprang, concerned themselves with social problems. Social justice slavery, infanticide, exploitation of labor, an honest day's work, the subjection of women, sexual vice, marriage and the family, have all occupied the attention of both the Jewish and the Christian churches No one who studies the writings of the great Hebrew prophets can overlook their interest in social problems. One cannot read the Gospel or the Epistles of Paul and of other New Testament writers without seeing that, in spite of the fact that they expected the return of Jesus in a short time, they did nevertheless concern themselves with the applica tion of the Gospel to social relationships.[3]

Religion as a Means of Emotional Release. It would be easy to show that the emotional satisfaction possible through religious exaltation has both good and evil social results. Religion has had and should have a connection with the problems of social adjustment. Even for the solu tion of such problems, the emotional aspect of religion is not without its value. Because it serves to resolve the emotional strain of doubt and indecision for the individual in a crisis—such as mortal combat with a wild animal or a human enemy, or such as occurs when a new set of cir cumstances not familiar to the individual by experience arises and result in uncertainty as to the proper course—it serves also the group in time of fateful decisions, of great peril to the group, of uncertainty and doub as to what course to pursue before great perplexities. Appealing to superhuman beings for help, or going through certain magical ceremo nies, relieves the strain of suspense, provides through action a channel for the release of the pent-up emotions of the members of the society.

Consider, for instance, the ceremonies engaged in by members of our various American Indian tribes before going on a buffalo hunt, or enter ing on the war-path against an enemy. Or watch the solemn activities of the tribe in a time of drought as it makes supplication to the superhuman beings for the much-needed rain. Or again, think of the historic in stances of appeal to the gods for help in times when great epidemics of disease were threatening the people, or when an enemy was hammer ing at the gates of the beleaguered city. In every case religion served to provide outlet for a highly charged emotional state in the group.

RELIGION AS A POWER IN SOCIETY

Whatever power religion may exert in society, either for good or for evil, is due to the emotional and intellectual appeal that it makes to the individuals coming under its influence. Only in rare instances has re-

[3] Louis Wallis, *Sociological Study of the Bible* (1912).

ligion been able or willing to exert any actual direct physical power. As between intellectual and emotional power religion has most frequently resorted to the emotional, not only because its appeal and its influence are wider, but also because in the last analysis emotion is at the root of religion. They believe in God, if they really do, because they have *felt* His presence and His existence; they want to believe in Him and feel that they cannot do otherwise, all intellectual evidence to the contrary notwithstanding. Once having felt the emotional power of religion they may enlarge upon or rationalize their experience with their intellect, but its essence is emotional. Such is the power of religion on the individual. Thus, in explaining the survival of religion, it has been observed:

As a scientific explanation of the universe religion has lost its old dominion. As a philosophy giving meaning to the universe and to the social relations it has only begun to come into its own. Its chief function has ever been, not explanation, but action. It has been a faith primarily, having only enough mythology attached to give an excuse to the rational faculty for action. Therefore, it has survived, because it has provided man with a working hypothesis on which to adjust himself to the universe and the world of Nature to him. It is the expression of man's faith that there is a way whereby he can bring under his control and for his purposes the forces about him. That faith has released for experiment the energies paralyzed by fear and doubt. Oftentimes the means used were not adapted to his purposes, but the drive of religious faith was still there to find another and better way.[4]

The influence that religion may wield in society is dependent upon the ability of a particular religion to stir the emotions of a number of individuals in a group and to focus them upon some social objective. Organized religion, manifested in the churches of the various faiths and sects, is best able to do this because of its facilities—buildings, machinery of ceremony, and organized memberships schooled in the specific things that they are to believe. Thus organized religion has control over certain social sanctions without which the solution of our social problems will be much delayed, if not indefinitely postponed. Through its pulpit it has a platform of public instruction and discussion the like of which does not exist in any other organization.

Considering only Western civilization and more particularly the American branch of it, a difference is to be noted between the present position of the Christian Church and that which it has occupied in the rather recent past. The paradox of the present situation in regard to religion is, as Lippmann puts it,[5] that we have ceased to believe without

4 Gillin and Blackmar, *Outlines of Sociology* (1930), p. 326.
5 Walter Lippmann, *A Preface to Morals* (1929).

ceasing to be credulous. The point is that a large number of the so-called
enlightened members of the population no longer believe all the doctrines of the Christian Church, but they have not given them up. The
diffusion of scientific knowledge has made it difficult, for the time being at least, for many persons to believe in the supernatural at all, or at
least in the same manner as their forefathers.

Granted that the church is one of our most important influencers of
public opinion because of its contact with large groups of people, the
question arises as to how it is to hold and influence these groups now
that its followers no longer feel it is the direct intermediary between
them and God. Reference to the Bible, for instance, is becoming less
effective as a coercive to action for a growing number of people. The
traditional emotionalism of many of the churches frequently does not
appeal to the average educated man who has become interested in
science, in reality one of the most coldly intellectual, non-emotional
entities in the world. The uneducated and those who do not do their
own thinking are apt to follow the lead of the "enlightened," or to fall
into indifference because they find no appeal in the old religious attitudes.

It is obvious, then, that the church has a hard row to hoe if it is to
keep its members; and without its following, the church is of little importance from the social point of view. The present wisdom for the
church would seem to be to arrest the interest of the people by maintaining close contact with the developments of modern life, at the
same time emphasizing social idealism. Happiness still consists in the adjustment of the individual to his material environment and to his fellows.
While science may help to solve the former, there is a place for the enlightened idealism of religion in the solution of the latter problem that
no individual questing for happiness can afford to overlook.

The spoken prophetic word has not lost its power. It can still, to
paraphrase St. Luke, cast down the mighty from their seats and exalt
the humble. The churches in their doctrines of sin and repentance have
an instrument unequaled in power by which to enforce social behavior.
In their journals and other printed materials, the churches have an educational force that cannot be excelled for sanctioning "right" social arrangements. The fear of hell and the hope of heaven do not move as
many people as they once did; nevertheless, the church still has power
to stir the social emotions of man. Its appeals for sympathy, justice,
brotherhood, righteousness, truth, fairness—all these carry emotional

content long established. In a word, the social idealism of the Christian Church is a power beyond computation.

Limitations to be Recognized by the Church. It is not contended that the church has all the knowledge necessary for solving each social problem. It must take notice of the facts and principles revealed by each of the social sciences. We can go further and say that the church, in its attempt to solve the problems of society, must take into account all knowledge that every science may contribute. It must heed the economist, the sociologist, the psychologist, the biologist, the political scientist, and the educator. Its contribution must be social ideals, motives, and sanctions. To it is committed the responsibility of developing in the individual a social attitude and of seeking in every way to realize in social relationships the ideals of brotherhood, of kindness, of justice, and equality of opportunity. The scientist contributes his knowledge of the way in which things operate. The church contributes its ideals of a righteous society and supplies the motives for the realization of these ideals.

Furthermore, the church must recognize that its method is educational. It will secure social changes in the direction of the realization of its ideals by slowly and patiently teaching those ideals and endeavoring to find ways by which they may be realized in accordance with the findings of science. It will not be satisfied until these ideals are incarnated in the customs, folkways, laws, administrative agencies, and public opinion of the community, so that they may be made really effective.

The rapidly changing conditions of urban life in the United States create problems for every church. The great commercial and industrial communities—with their geographic areas serving different purposes and giving us even a physical stratification of the population with little association between those living in each; separating the people into functional groups having clashing interests; growing and changing so rapidly that even one generation sees the old residential areas decay into rooming-house districts with their transient population, with commercial houses, manufactures, and transportation facilities swamping one after another of the former residence sections—put problems of adjustment before the churches. Downtown churches see their congregations crowded out. New economic and social conditions present problems that the old message of the pulpit no longer fits. No longer is it true, as it was once, in these city churches that "the rich and the poor meet together." The old methods no longer command the allegiance of the people. Many a city pastor and board have wondered what is the matter.

No less striking has been the perplexity of the rural church. The improved roads, the motor-car, and the radio have played havoc with the rural churches as a factor in country life. Their young people drift away. Their members young and old no longer find in the church their social center. The activities at the church interest fewer and fewer of the people of the community.

The results of these changes in American life have seriously impaired the social usefulness of the church. Must it not adjust its message and adapt its functions to these changes? Can it find a way to meet a need in the life of the people, as once was the case?

PROBLEMS FOR THE CHURCH

Christianity, through its history of almost two thousand years, has frequently been obliged to make readjustments in order to adapt itself more closely to the needs of the people at various periods of history. There have been times of general change in thought and belief, of which the present period is a good example. During such times there has apparently been a decay of religion. The church had become adapted to the patterns of thought and of social relationship of a bygone period. These patterns have changed. The church changes more slowly, and so maladjustment results. For example, during the Middle Ages the adjustment between society and the Roman Catholic church came to a climax at the time of Aquinas. Then feudalism gave way to a social order based on commerce. Newtonian science undermined the accepted notions concerning the nature of the universe. Conceptions of social relationships underwent a change. The church had to readjust her whole framework. For a time chaos reigned. But eventually the church, as always, managed to fill a needful place in society.

Without taking the time to recount the history of Christianity we may call to mind a church made up of outcasts in the first few centuries, a church offering the one example of stability and permanency in the dissolute days following the decline of Rome, a church as the sole source of education, charity, and art in the Middle Ages, a church as the center of community and social life in pioneer America.

The church at the present time is undecided as to what place it shall occupy in society; and one of the reasons for this is that it has become unfamiliar with the problems of modern social life. The time has come when it must address itself more directly to social conditions as they exist. The modern man lives in the present. Spiritual leadership is as necessary for this life as it is for the world to come.

It is impossible to name all the problems for which the church has a responsibility. In fact, it is impossible to think of one social problem to which the gospel preached by the church should not apply. If religion is concerned with life, then its application is as wide as life itself. Let us consider three of these problems as typical and perhaps the most pressing at the present time.

Health and Disease. Professor Patten of the University of Pennsylvania once asked the members of a seminar to write on pieces of paper what they thought was the one chief criterion by which to judge the efficiency and liveliness of a church. The different members handed in different replies. Some said that the criterion was the amount of money invested in the church building; others, the number of people attending the services; still others, the number received into the church; and others again, the kind of preaching that was to be heard from the pulpit. Professor Patten, after reading each of these replies and asking why the writer had chosen that particular one, said that he did not agree with any of them. In his judgment, he said that the chief criterion was the death-rate and the morbidity-rate of the community. Naturally, the members of the seminar were very much perturbed by this reply, and wanted to know his reasons. In answer he said that the chief concern of everyone was to live and to live well. He argued that if you had the death-rate and the morbidity-rate you had the basis for judging what was the attitude of the employers toward the employees, the standard of living of the community, regard for childhood and womanhood, the attitude of the community toward vice and crime, the attention paid to sanitation—and the attitude of the church toward these problems, because, said he, the church in any community can modify any of these things as it wishes, if it will. The astonishment of the members of this seminar shows how little we have connected some of the most vital affairs of life with religion.

Says Wilbur, formerly Secretary of the Interior:

Our information at the present time, due to the studies of research workers all over the world, is such that we can say that if any well-situated community of fifty thousand people would adopt and put into practical every-day use all that we now know of medicine and science, and all that we have been actually using in the control of many soldiers in war, there would be such an increase in human happiness and effectiveness, and such a decrease in sadness and inefficiency, that in ten years it would make that city the wonder of the world.[6]

Some day it will be considered as sinful to sell dirty milk as to commit adultery; to work people in places that induce tuberculosis and typhoid as to forge a check, or to steal a neighbor's wash; to exploit one's employees as to hold slaves; to break quarantine as to break into a house; to live in a city with a high death-rate as to live in Sodom and Gomorrah. Why is it not so now? Because we have not connected the church with this vital matter of life and death. From the purely religious viewpoint alone there is morality in good health and the social practices necessary to promote it. By pointing this out and by lending its facilities for reaching and influencing large numbers of people the church can become a vital part of this important social movement and make religion a living force in community life.

The Relations of Capital and Labor. Another problem with which the church is face to face is the relations of labor and capital, or the employer and the employed. The problem is not new but is more pressing just now than ever before. It is at least as old as the New Testament. The problem finds its prototype in the relations between master and slaves in the Roman Empire. The early Christian Church had to face that problem. The Christian solution is indicated by St. Paul as follows:

. . . not in the way of eye service, as men-pleasers; but as servants of Christ, doing the will of God from the heart; with good will doing service, as unto the Lord, and not unto men; knowing that whatsoever good thing each one doeth, the same shall he receive again from the Lord, whether he be bond or free. And, ye, masters, do the same things unto them, and forbear threatening; knowing that he who is both their Master and yours is in heaven, and there is no respect of persons with him.[7]

Moreover, the early Christian Church faced frankly the relations between the hired laborer and his employer:

Behold, the hire of the laborers who mowed your fields, which is of you kept back by fraud, crieth out: The cries of them that reap have entered into the ears of the Lord of Sabaoth.[8]

In spite of dismal departures on the part of the church and its leaders from these high principles through the ages of Christian history, there is no question that religion has now and again, both by word and by action, championed the cause of the oppressed against the oppressor; has

[6] Wilbur, "Health: A Business Asset," *Survey*, p. 679 (March 15, 1926).
[7] Ephesians VI: 6-9.
[8] James V: 4.

urged the dignity of labor upon the worker, and the imperative necessity of treating the poor with justice and kindness. In spite of the increasing secularization of the church after the time of Constantine, again and again the spirit of Christianity burst out against the exploitation of the poor and in favor of the oppressed classes. Many of the early church Fathers saw the danger in monopoly and private property. In the Middle Ages the church forbade interest-taking; it condemned monopoly profit, and taught the doctrine of a fair price and a just reward to the laborer. Many of the monasteries emphasized the sacredness of labor, and all of them provided refuge from the inequalities and iniquities of secular society; and all distinctions of rank were obliterated in the common term "brother." The Protestant sects of Reformation and post-Reformation times also emphasized the protest against the exploitation of the poor by the rich, and preached a kind of fraternity of rich and poor in the church.[9]

Nevertheless, it must be admitted that during the breakdown of the medieval domestic economy and the rise of the modern factory system, religion underwent severe trials. The theological controversies of the post-Reformation period absorbed the energies of the church to such an extent that the church failed to give consideration to the pressing social problems of the day. When almost two centuries later the Industrial Revolution burst upon western Europe, the Christian Church was still so intent upon its factional fights that it could not tackle the problems of the day. Yet here and there arose noble Christian souls who played their part in the protest against the evils of the new industrialism. The Earl of Shaftesbury found the expression of his own religious life in attacks upon child labor and the exploitation of women and children in the mines and factories of Great Britain, and did a great deal to start the movement for the regulation of hours and conditions of labor in that country. On the whole, however, it must be admitted that from the time of the Industrial Revolution until recently, the church has expressed very little interest in the strained relations between employers and employees. Supported largely by the employers, the leaders of the church have too often been blind to the sufferings of the poor, with the result that the working-classes in industrial centers have largely been alienated from the church. Too often the church has counseled patience to the workman, has promised reward in another world for the miseries of this, without attempting to face the conditions that produce the misery and take a stand against unjust conditions in our social and economic life.

9 Walter Rauschenbusch, *Christianizing the Social Order* (1921), pp. 378-382.

The consequence of this attitude of the church has been that false standards of sin have been established. Some day it will be considered as sinful to exploit workers as to swear, as sinful to do poor work as to get drunk. Perhaps some time we shall all go to confession because we have bought a garment that has been made under unfair conditions. It was cheap because it was made by exploited labor in a sweat-shop. In the fight between labor and capital in the industrial conflict of the present day, too frequently the churches have felt that the strikers were dangerous people without taking the pains to try to understand why people would throw up their jobs for a principle, or why good, earnest men, members of the churches, looked upon these strikers as vicious and pestiferous persons who must be shown their places. Too often the churches have followed a policy of "Hands off" in any such struggle. As the self-confessed repository of the Gospel of Jesus the Christian Church has plenty of warrant in His words to bring to bear upon these vexed relationships between men a gospel of brotherhood, kindliness, and justice that would go far to settle the struggle between capital and labor. Perhaps she would be rent in twain in the effort, but that would not be the first time she has become divided. Often splits have occurred over much less important matters. Said the late Bishop Turner, of Buffalo:

The mission of the Church is to foster social justice. She has the power . . . to call a truce in the war between classes of society, to still the angry passions from which the conflict of class interests arises. Hers are not the remedies of the economist, but remedies that go deeper to the root of the evil. In every industrial injustice there is a moral factor, a moral element, and in dealing with this moral element she is at home and no one can deny her competence. The economic cure-all of to-day may be the discarded economic heresy of to-morrow, but hers are the principles of moral justice which never change. It is her prerogative to upbraid the oppressor of the poor, to take her stand as Ambrose did when he compelled the Emperor-murderer to do penance for his sins. It is equally her prerogative to restrain the lawlessness of the oppressed when a lawless course is taken. It is her mission to teach the right use of riches, to inculcate moderation and every kind of sobriety, to rebuke the sins of capital and labor alike and to hold up to all men the divine principles of justice and charity and fair dealing between man and man. It was said recently that our civilization is an economic civilization, that it is founded on material principles and knows only material standards of value. Alas, in common acceptance this is too true. But it is the mission of the Church to make our civilization once more a moral and spiritual civilization, to restore the higher values that one time prevailed and bring justice and charity to reign once more among men.[10]

[10] "The Mission of the Church," *Columbia*, p. 13 (September, 1924).

War. In the early days of Christianity the attitude of Christians was hostile to military service. For a long time no one could be a member in good standing of the Christian Church and be a soldier. With the change in the attitude of the Roman State to the church under Constantine, and later with the dominance of the church over the nascent nations of Europe, a great change came about in the attitude of Christians toward war. After the union of church and State the latter became the secular arm whereby the decrees of the church were carried out, especially with reference to heretics. The result was that the church became an apologist for the warrior, and the warlike State. With the growth of nationalism national churches were recognized. The result was that the position of the church in its early days became compromised, and war became looked upon as a laudable activity, especially if it was in accordance with the aims of the church. The only exceptions were such Protestant sects as the Quakers, Mennonites, and Dunkers.

During the First World War, while a number of the leaders of the Christian churches had begun to look upon war as a great evil, as a whole the churches, both Jewish and Christian, actively upheld the aims of their respective nations. They were used as foci of propaganda for the aims and purposes of each nation. The Germans, led by propaganda to believe that their cause was just, felt that God was on their side; the Allies, believing that Germany had broken faith with little Belgium and was carrying on a war of aggression, felt that a just God could not feel otherwise about it than they themselves. Both prayed to the same God for victory. One cannot but wonder what an All-wise God thought about the situation. Practically the only religious body that came out of the war with its standards untarnished was the Quakers. Often misunderstood, nevertheless they persevered in bringing to the suffering non-combatants on both sides of the conflict their ministrations of help. They consistently refused to fight but earnestly proposed to help those who were in need.[11]

In the Second World War, the position of the churches was quite different from what it had been in the earlier conflict. They were able to profit to some extent by their mistakes of the former period. Even more important, however, the churches had been subjected for several years prior to the conflict to an increasing hostility by the Axis powers; and the outbreak of the war itself found the churches in those countries exposed to active suppression by the military and political authorities. Thus there was a greater bond of unity between the churches of the

[11] L. M. Jones, *The Quakers in Action* (1929).

United Nations and the remnants of those in the Axis nations. The English and American churches alike took a realistic view of the conflict for the most part, acknowledging the need to support the war effort as a matter literally of self-defense, as demonstrated by the bitter experience of the Axis nations' churches, yet insisting that their people look to the causes for which they fought and to the terms of the peace which was to follow. They spoke less of national peril and more of the direct threat to the survival of Christianity itself. The character of the struggle reduced greatly the feasibility of efforts to ameliorate the sufferings of the belligerents, although again some relief was made available to refugees and prisoners of war by the Quakers, the Y.M.C.A., and the Red Cross.

THE CHURCHES DRAW THEIR LINES

The churches cannot influence the decisions that are made in dealing with the problems of society unless they state definitely what opinions are in accord with Christian principles. Some one obviously must interpret and apply the precepts of Christianity to specific social problems. The task is no less difficult for laymen, lacking full knowledge of Christian dogma, than it is for church leaders who are to some extent laymen in the field of social science. The attempt to be definite is surrounded with dangers of partisan bias, incomplete understanding of practical problems involved, and consequent error. Nevertheless, it is an essential part of making Christianity an active force in the relations of human beings with one another; and the various church groups rightly have declared their position from time to time. Interesting comparisons suggest themselves in a study of the following pronouncements by representative churches in the United States.

The Roman Catholic Church. The members of the Administrative Board of the National Catholic Welfare Conference, deputed in the 1941 annual meeting of the Bishops of the United States, prepared a statement which said in part:

Observing the fiftieth anniversary of the Magna Charta of labor, the *Rerum Novarum* of Leo XIII, His Holiness Pope Pius XII, on June 1, 1941, spoke of "three fundamental values" which must be kept in mind for the reconstruction of the world after the present devastating war.

The first of these values has to do with the use of material goods. His Holiness quotes from the letter which he addressed to the American Hierarchy, *Sertum Laetitiae*, on November 1, 1939, in which he stated "that the goods which were created by God for all men should flow equitably to all, according to the principles of justice and charity."

The second fundamental value considered by His Holiness is human labor. He says: "The duty and the corresponding right to work are imposed on, and conceded to, the individual in the first instance by nature and not by society. . . . The duty and the right to organize the labor of the people belong above all to . . . the employers and the workers. It devolves upon the State to intervene in the field of labor and in the division and distribution of work according to the form and measure that the common good, properly understood, demands. Every legitimate and beneficial interference of the State in the field of labor should be such as to safeguard and respect its personal character."

The third "value" emphasizes the importance of the possession of private property by the family. His Holiness insists that, of all goods which can be held as private property, "none is more conformable to nature than the land." The Holy Father lays stress on the social significance of widespread ownership of land in the form of the family homestead. To him, the function of the family as the root of a nation's greatness and power is bound up with family ownership of "the holding on which it lives, and from which it draws all or part of its subsistence." Without that "stability which is rooted in its own holding," the family cannot be the "cell of society" which nature destined it to be.

Domestic progress and peace depend on securing vital space for the rural family, as world progress and peace depend on securing living space for all the nations of the world. Accordingly, an adequate solution of the problems of emigration is of major importance in bringing tranquillity to a confused world.[12]

Elaborating the position relative to industrial relations, the same statement said, in part:

We express again our sympathy for labor and we appreciate the difficulties of maintaining family life with the mounting cost of living. In union with the Holy See, we have, on many occasions, condemned the evils of unrestrained capitalism. At the same time, in union with the Holy See, we hold that "our first and most fundamental principle, when we undertake to alleviate the condition of the masses, must be the inviolability of private property."

Pope Leo XIII declared: "Religion teaches the laboring man and the workman to carry out honestly and well all equitable agreements freely made; never to injure capital nor to outrage the person of an employer; never to employ violence in representing his own cause, nor to engage in riot and disorder; and to have nothing to do with men of evil principles, who work upon the people with artful promises, and raise foolish hopes which usually end in disaster and repentance, when too late. Religion teaches the rich man and the employer that their work-people are not their slaves; that they must respect in every man his dignity as a man and as a Christian."

Popes Leo XIII and Pius XI expressed their approval of unions for the workers. As we think of the present difficulties in labor and trade unionism,

[12] *Crisis of Christianity* (National Catholic Welfare Conference), pp. 9, 10.

we express the hope that the leaders will be well advised for the welfare
of the workers of the nation; that they will keep before them the common
good of the country; that they will refrain from doing anything that is
harmful to the general welfare, and that they will come forth from the
emergency of national defense united in closer coöperation with all right-
minded employers and deserving the commendation of the general public.[13]

The Protestant Churches. It was mentioned earlier in this chapter that
there are upwards of 250 religious groups in the United States. The
great majority of these denominational churches and sects are Protestant
Christian organizations, with membership lists ranging from several
hundred up to several millions. Most of them hold national or regional
conferences at more or less regular intervals; and more often than not,
these occasions are taken to formulate and publicize statements of their
positions in regard to the social problems of the day. In most cases, however, such gestures are largely ineffective, since the groups are small
and the opinions expressed usually represent the sentiments of the delegates present rather than that of the membership of the church as a
whole. Moreover, the individual church organizations do not have the
resources to make a thorough study of the social problems they are
considering or to undertake any program of action to make their con-
victions felt in every-day life.

A number of the larger denominations, becoming aware of their
sectarian limitations in applying their ideals to specific social problems,
united in 1908 to form the Federal Council of the Churches of Christ
in America. Representative of the Council's social objectives at that
time is its statement regarding industrial relations:

We deem it the duty of all Christian people to concern themselves directly
with certain practical industrial problems. To us it seems that the churches
must stand—
For equal rights and complete justice for all men in all stations of life.
For the right of all men to the opportunity for self-maintenance, a right
ever to be wisely and strongly safeguarded against encroachments of every
kind. For the right of workers to some protection against the hardships often
resulting from the swift crises of industrial change.
For the principle of conciliation and arbitration in industrial dissensions.
For the protection of the worker from dangerous machinery, occupational
disease, injuries and mortality.
For the abolition of child labor.
For such regulation of the conditions of toil for women as shall safeguard the physical and moral health of the community.
For the suppression of the "sweating system."

[13] *Ibid.,* pp. 15–17.

For the gradual and reasonable reduction of the hours of labor to the lowest practicable point, and for that degree of leisure for all, which is a condition of the highest human life.

For a release from employment one day in seven.

For a living wage as a minimum in every industry, and for the highest wage that each industry can afford.

For the most equitable division of the products of industry that can ultimately be devised.

For suitable provision for the old age of the workers and for those incapacitated by injury.

For the abatement of poverty.

To the toilers of America and to those who by organized effort are seeking to lift the crushing burdens of the poor, and to reduce the hardships and uphold the dignity of labor, this Council sends the greeting of human brotherhood and the pledge of sympathy and of help in a cause which belongs to all who follow Christ.[14]

The Federal Council of the Churches of Christ in America now is supported by some twenty-two denominations and continues to perform commendable functions in the field of social service. It is essentially a fact-finding and coördinating agency, serving to guide the efforts of the member denominations notably in the fields of race, industrial, and international relations and in the techniques of social work administration.

The Interchurch World Movement, which ceased to function in 1920 and which has been pointed out as a dismal failure in the attempt to apply Christianity to a great industry, nevertheless through its report on the steel strike, in 1919, brought to a focus public attention on that strike, its causes and results, which doubtless had much to do with the later development of better conditions in the steel industry. A new attempt at world organization of church groups, the World Council of Churches, was initiated in 1942, headed by the Archbishop of Canterbury.

The response of the church to the cataclysm of the Second World War is indicated by the resolutions adopted by nearly 400 delegates attending a "National Study Conference on the Bases for a Just and Durable Peace" at Delaware, Ohio, early in 1942. While this conference did not represent any official action by the churches, it was significant in that it was attended by individuals prominent in the activities of such widely diversified churches as the Unitarian, Lutheran, Christian Scientist, Congregational, Methodist, Presbyterian, and Episcopalian; and its

[14] *The Church and Modern Industry* (The Federal Council of the Churches of Christ in America), pp. 17, 18.

resolutions suggest a possible trend in the development of the position of the churches. Among the significant points agreed upon were the following:

We declare as the major premise that the Church is a spiritual entity, one and indivisible, which as such is not and cannot be broken by human conflicts. Therefore the Church is in a unique position to heal the wounds of war and bind the world together in a just and durable peace. We recognize the particular rights and responsibilities of the State in connection with the secular order. But we reaffirm the Christian truth that the Church in its essential nature is an ecumenical, supranational body, separate from and independent of all States, including our own national State. The responsibilities of the Church and the service which it may render the State derive not from the claims which the State may make but from the freedom and autonomy of the Church itself under the Lord Jesus Christ who is its living head. . . .

We are deeply disturbed by the economic distress of millions of our fellow men and by economic conditions that threaten the extension of the Kingdom of God on earth.

We view the economic tensions and distresses of our day as symptoms of a general world disorder. In our era production has been carried on primarily with a view to monetary gain. Profit has been the principal incentive relied upon to turn the wheels of industry and to bring forth the fruits of the soil.

This system has in recent years developed grave defects. There have occurred mass unemployment, widespread dispossession from homes and farms, destitution, lack of opportunity for youth and of security for old age. These calamities, which have often been accentuated by short-range, self-seeking trade policies of various nations, have made for war. . . .

In this chaotic situation there has arisen in certain countries an alternative way of production which is based on complete management and control of all economic life by government. With this has come a system of compulsion which deprives the individual of freedoms, economic, intellectual and spiritual, necessary to human dignity.

We do not believe that we are limited to a choice between these two alternatives. If this seems the only choice, it is largely because the Churches have failed generally to inculcate Christian motivation. . . .

As Christians we must be vitally concerned for the preservation of human values in any and every system. . . .

Any economic program which allows the quest for private gain to disregard human welfare, which regiments human beings and denies them freedom of collective bargaining, thus reducing labor to a mere commodity; any program which results in mass unemployment or dire poverty in mine or factory or farm; any program which fails to conserve natural resources . . . is manifestly wrong. . . .

We are convinced that industrial democracy is fundamental to successful political democracy. We therefore recommend that labor be given an increasing responsibility for and participation in industrial management. The principle of democracy in economic relations should be accorded wider expression by the development of stronger *voluntary* producers associations, farm organizations, labor organizations, professional groups, and consumers organizations, and their integration into some form of national economic council, for planning in coöperation with the government for maximum production and consumption and the abolition of unemployment. . . .[15]

The Malvern Conference, a gathering of English church people in 1941 in the very midst of the Second World War, was extraordinary in the lengths to which it went in appraising the fundamental tenets of our traditional economic and political life. And while again it did not claim to formulate the official position of the English Church, nevertheless the fact that it was attended by many of the most notable leaders within that church (including the Primate of England, then Archbishop of York) suggests a likely trend in the development of that church's position. Regarding social problems, one of its basic points of agreement was the following:

There is no structural organization of society which can bring about the coming of the Kingdom of God on earth, since all systems can be perverted by the selfishness of man. Therefore, the Church as such can never commit itself to any proposed change in the structure of society as being a self-sufficient means of salvation.

But the Church can point to those features of our existing society which, while they can never prevent individual men and women from becoming Christian, are contrary to divine justice, and act as stumbling-blocks, making it harder for men to live Christian lives. . . .

In our present situation we believe that the maintenance of that part of the structure of our society by which the ultimate ownership of the principal industrial resources of the community can be vested in the hands of private owners, may be such a stumbling-block. On the one hand it may deprive the poorest members of the community of the essentials of life. On the other, while these resources can be so owned, men will strive for their ownership for themselves. As a consequence, a way of life founded on the supremacy of the economic motive will remain, which is contrary to God's plan for mankind.

For one or both of these reasons, the time has come for Christians to proclaim the need for striving toward a form of society in which, while the essential value of the individual human personality is preserved, the continuance of these abuses will be no longer possible.[16]

A committee of economists, industrialists, and representatives of labor was organized by the Archbishop of York on the recommendation of

[15] *The Living Church*, pp. 6-9 (March 18, 1942).
[16] "Malvern and After," *Living Church*, p. 12 (March 4, 1942).

the Malvern Conference itself and was able to agree on a report which included these statements:

> Every citizen should have assured liberty in the forms of freedom of worship, of speech, of assembly, and of association for special purposes not contrary to human well-being. . . . Every citizen, every people, and every government should regard the resources of the earth as God's gifts to the whole human race, to be used and conserved with due consideration for the needs of all mankind in its present and its future generations. . . . With these primary needs we associate as necessary to social justice and public welfare the conservation and stabilization of the family, the provision for all of such education as will develop the gifts of each to the full in a living fellowship and with growing realization of personal responsibility, the ending of unemployment in the sense of enforced idleness, and a fairer distribution of the results of industry. . . .
>
> During the 19th century the main concern of the industrial and commercial world was to increase production. This was done partly by allowing great freedom to initiative and enterprise, with the accompanying risks. Today, the most widespread demand is for greater security of different kinds —e.g., against war, against invasion, against want, and against unemployment. Freedom from want and freedom from war are the two most urgent preliminaries to full personal development. But freedom from want and freedom from unemployment are not identical, nor in practice always found together, yet freedom in both these forms is requisite.
>
> It is not always recognized that this can only be obtained by the loss of some measure of freedom—for security can only be reached by "planning" (and, even so, of course, will never be absolute), and "planning" involves control by some central authority, international, national, or regional. We have to choose how much of freedom should be surrendered as the price of a specified increase of security. And in all inquiries vigilance must be exercised lest in the search for security of tenure and fairer distribution of the products, production itself should fail to be maintained up to the necessary standard.[17]
>
> We now come to ways and means, and five fundamental issues call for separate comment:
>
> (a) The pressure of competition in forms which lead to intolerable conditions of labor and life. . . . In this whole field it is vitally important to remember the basic principle that the aim of economic activity is to promote human welfare as a whole, and that the right course may be one which does not produce the maximum of economic wealth. . . .
>
> (b) The misdirection and abuse of the profit motive. . . . It must be admitted that the desire to improve one's position in life is not in itself necessarily harmful, nor can we either expect or wish that men should ever cease to aim at benefiting themselves and those closest to them. But we must try to prevent the misdirection of this desire in ways that influence production to the injury of the State or its citizens. . . .

[17] Living Church, p. 14 (March 4, 1942).

(c) *Non-participation by labor in control of production.* The lack of any participation by labor in the control of production is a manifest sign of the broken fellowship of our economic life. . . .

(d) *Far-reaching changes in the present system of land ownership are required.* . . . Serviceable ownership must be both subject to discipline if it fails in its stewardship, and also admissible to remedial assistance if unforeseen or natural causes hinder fruitful stewardship. . . .

(e) *The Monetary System.* . . . The essential purpose must be to secure that money becomes a genuine register of economic fact, and, so far as it is also a force affecting that fact, is directed by consideration for the public welfare alone. . . . It is therefore urged that the State should control the issue and cancellation of money or credit utilized as money. . . .

A change is taking place in our social life, so great as to deserve the name of a revolution. It is of supreme importance that it should be a Christian revolution. The principles set forth above are offered as a guide and call to Christian revolution.

Such a revolution would not be violent; it would be inspired by a new energy of good-will and be supported by members of all social "classes." But that revolution of good-will is bound to be frustrated, and ill-will with or without revolution must prevail, unless Christians under the impulse of their faith accept the full burden of their social responsibility.[18]

The potential implications of such a development can hardly be overestimated. Its immediate influence on American religious thought, for example, may be surmised by the similarities apparent between the Malvern and the later Delaware declarations cited above.

The Jews and Social Problems. In June, 1941, the Central Conference of American Rabbis published what they called a "Program of World Reconstruction." Its text, substantially, is as follows:

Basic to any civilization is the belief in the religious principle of man as a child of God. Therefore, man's personality is sacred, his soul immortal. Thus, every man has inalienable rights which come from God and which all other men must recognize. In this divine fellowship, men of all races, of all creeds are included, for in God's sight, all men are equal. . . .

Men will never accept slavery, and freedom is the heart of human dignity. The totalitarian state cannot be tolerated. Tyranny of every form must be destroyed. Any state which denies to human beings the right to self-government, which exalts the state above the individual and man above God, cannot endure.

The development of facilities for transportation and communication, especially of the airplane and the radio, have shrunk the world and have brought peoples more closely together. In such a world greater international coöperation has become imperative. Such coöperation could best be effected through some international organization. . . .

The Prophet Micah recognized that swords can only be beaten into plough-

[18] *Living Church,* pp. 19-21 (March 18, 1942).

shares "when every man shall sit under his vine and fig tree and none shall make them afraid." Our age too must recognize this. The widespread unemployment of men able and willing to work, the unnecessarily low standards of living, the specter of economic insecurity, the fear of impoverished old age, the inability to secure available medical treatment, the blight of child labor, and other similar social evils, create hostilities and hatreds which mar human life and jeopardize the peace of all men. Social justice for every individual must be the cornerstone on which the structure of world peace is erected.

International coöperation must not be merely political. It must also be economic. The raw materials of the world must be available to all the children of men who need them. Nations must cease to regard each other as hostile competitors. The economy of the world must be recognized on the basis of friendly coöperation between all nations and races and the recognition of the sacred rights and privileges of every individual.

Upon all men we urge the recognition that all wealth is of God and that individuals or nations which possess it are merely its stewards. Verily, "The earth is the Lord's and the fullness thereof." All that man possesses is but a temporary trust. Ownership carries with it moral and social obligations. Those who fail to recognize these social implications menace the well-being of society and delay the dawn of the Kingdom of God.

This moral law applies to all ownership, whether of power or of might, of authority or rulership, or of the ownership of land, machines or money. There must be no denomination of any class in society over any other on the basis of these possessions. All elements of humanity must support this ethical truth, this basic teaching of prophetic religion, this important commandment of God. . . .[19]

The Social Work of the Churches. It should not be inferred from this presentation of church thought relative to social problems that the various church bodies are engaged primarily in telling other people how to run their own business. To the contrary, with religious beliefs and discussion has been combined generally a very practical motive of brotherhood and service. Indeed, many of the fields and methods of social service work have been pioneered by the religious groups. The origins of our hospitals, our care of the insane, our provision for the aged poor, the destitute, the widowed, and the dependent child can be traced to movements of considerable antiquity within religious organizations. That they have become more completely *public* services in recent years has come about largely by the fact that church groups had awakened the conscience of people to their responsibilities toward the unfortunate to such an extent that the burden of administration became too large for the churches to carry on alone. Nevertheless Catholics, Protes-

[19] "Program of World Reconstruction," a statement adopted by the Central Conference of American Rabbis at its annual conference in 1941.

tants, and Jews alike still carry on quite sizable undertakings in the field of practical social service.

The welfare work of the Roman Catholic Church in the United States is administered chiefly through the diocesan "Catholic Charities" organizations, there being 75 such agencies located chiefly in the more thickly populated areas, and the work is adapted to the needs of each diocese. The extent of direct relief work is indicated by the fact that 46 of the dioceses reported $640,000 expended in the first nine months of 1939 for this purpose. Child welfare activities occupy a major place in the work of the Catholic Charities. In 1938, 72 agencies placed about 15,000 children in foster homes, and nearly 40,000 other children were cared for in 326 institutions. There also are about 95 Catholic day nurseries operating at the present time. The Society of St. Vincent de Paul, an organization of Roman Catholic laymen, sponsors extensive activities in the field of family problems, having reached more than 100,-000 families comprising about 500,000 individuals in a variety of services in the fiscal year 1938–1939, at a cost of more than $3,000,000. There are about 140 institutions caring for at least 16,000 aged dependents, while nearly 1,000 hospitals and medical centers with staffs totaling more than 125,000 ministered to more than 2,000,000 persons in 1939.[20]

Quite similar to the Roman Catholics in their long tradition and closely knit church organization, the Jewish charities are highly organized; yet they are distinctive among all the religious groups in the lengths to which they go in caring for their own church members who are in need. Thus, although the total Jewish population in the United States is only about 5,000,000, 70 per cent of whom live in the 11 largest cities of the country, there are Jewish charity councils in at least 50 of our cities. Direct family welfare work was carried on in nearly 55,-000 cases in 1939, with relief expenditures of about $1,900,000. In addition, refugee services involved about 6,000 cases cared for monthly in 1939, at a total cost for the year of $1,300,000. There are 46 Jewish Children's Homes, while about 12,000 children received foster-care in 1939. Jewish inmates in public homes for the aged are notably few, since Jewish social service is so comprehensive. There are upwards of 60 private Jewish Homes for the Aged, sheltering about 6,000 aged persons. There are 38 general hospitals which gave more than 2,700,000 days' care to patients in 1939, in addition to 20 other hospitals offering more specialized services.[21]

[20] *Social Work Year Book, 1941*, pp. 92–96.
[21] *Ibid.*, pp. 277–280.

The Protestant church group is distinctive in that it does not have the institutional framework of either the Catholic or the Jewish churches, and its numbers are divided by denominational lines. Its approach is more evangelical and probably more adaptable and exploratory. It has not wholly neglected the field of social service, as is shown by the fact that there were in 1938 at least 353 Protestant hospitals with a bed capacity of nearly 40,000, while there were in 1940 probably not less that 212 Protestant Homes for the Aged and 400 children's institutions. It is likely that as a rule Protestant social welfare activity has been expressed more fully in the support of secular agencies. Nevertheless, Protestantism shares with other churches, and perhaps expresses more militantly than the others, the recognition of the pastoral opportunity of social service work—holding that the equilibrium and stability of the individual served is the ultimate function of all the welfare activities of the church.[22]

THE NECESSITY OF THINKING

It must be recognized that such utterances and activities do not represent the united sentiment of all leaders within the churches. Some are hesitant or doubtful. We may assume, however, that they do represent the opinion of those who feel that the churches should take an active part in the solution of social problems. They are the individuals who are making an honest attempt to answer a question that cannot longer be evaded: What, if any, is to be the place of religion in the social order of the future?

That the organized form of religion, the church, will be called upon to make radical changes is being prophesied by many reasonable thinkers. Whatever changes may take place, it is safe to say that religion will not disappear, nor will the organization of religion fade from our culture. Judging from the experience of the past, it is man's nature to be religious, although perhaps not always in the sense in which professional churchmen define the word; and it has always been the characteristic of the followers of religions, when living in society, to organize.

Assuming, therefore, that religion seems destined to have a place in the social order of the future, whatever it may be, three possibilities stand out: (1) no change will be made; (2) the present Christian Church will adapt itself to the changes in social life; (3) an entirely new form of religion, presumably better adapted to the needs of society, will evolve. We may dismiss the first possibility as containing the seeds of its own

22 *Ibid.*, pp. 403–410.

downfall; it will dream itself into extinction or be driven to some social backwater by the rising tide of change. Between the last two choices, it would seem, in view of the fact that it is already a firmly imbedded part of our culture pattern, that the present religion through adaptation holds the greatest possibilities. It will be considerably quicker and more effective socially to remake the old religion, difficult as such a program may seem, than to undergo the spiritual upheaval of making ourselves a new form of belief. If a new religion grows up in our midst, it may in time prove itself fitter than the old forms. But for the time being, the present organization seems capable of infinite possibilities for the social good. The ideals of our own religious tradition, shorn of their dogmatic trappings, are at least the equals of any others. The efforts of the church to adapt itself to the social needs merit the serious attention of all champions of the social good.

The burning words of Amos, Hosea, and Micah, of Isaiah and Jeremiah, the penetrating utterances of Jesus in the Sermon on the Mount, cannot be stifled. However men may seek to keep apart their business, their politics, and their religion, it cannot be done. Life is an all-embracing entity and includes all the various phases of man's thought and activity. Slowly but surely as we try every other remedy and see it fail, and as we perceive the depth and meaning of religion for daily life, an increasing number of men are becoming convinced that the age-old struggle of human kind with the circumstances of life cannot be solved except by the application of the principles of the great leaders and prophets of mankind to the problems that arise. War will not be prevented by a balance of power alone. The economic struggle will not be settled by a stalemate of force. Inevitably, we shall fail to solve these problems unless we come to look upon each other as brothers whose struggles and whose difficulties are common and whom we are willing to meet on common ground in a spirit of fraternity, fellowship, and helpfulness. The Sermon on the Mount has not lost its power. St. Paul's pregnant utterance that "God has made of one blood all men for to dwell on all the face of the earth" has a significance for our social relations. The Golden Rule of Jesus has a meaning for both employers and employees that needs only to be applied in order to settle difficulties. Paul's statement that our bodies are the temples of the Holy Spirit cuts deep into our disregard of health measures. Jesus' saying, "They that take the sword shall perish by the sword," cannot be ignored in the presence of international misunderstanding. The Apostle's question, "He who loveth not his neighbor whom he hath seen, how can he love

God whom he hath not seen?" goes to the root of human selfishness and
has a relevancy to the problems of social and economic relations of man.

REFERENCES

ABRAHMS, Ray H., *Preachers Present Arms* (New York, 1933).
BRADEN, C. S., *Modern Tendencies in World Religions* (New York. 1935).
BREASTED, James H., *The Dawn of Conscience* (New York, 1934).
ELLWOOD, C. A., *The Reconstruction of Religion* (New York, 1922).
LIPPMAN, Walter, *A Preface to Morals* (New York, 1929).
Malvern, 1941: The Life of the Church and the Order of Society (New York,
    1941), Sections B, C (The Proceedings of the Archbishop of York's
    Conference).
MECKLIN, J. M., *The Story of American Dissent* (New York, 1934).
MELAND, Bernard E., *The Church and Adult Education* (American Associ-
    ation for Adult Education, 1939).
PATTEN, Simon N., *The Social Basis of Religion* (New York, 1911).
STRACHEY, John, *The Coming Struggle for Power* (New York, 1933), Part III.
WALLIS, Louis, *Sociological Study of the Bible* (Chicago, 1912), Parts IV, V.

QUESTIONS AND EXERCISES

1. Why are we interested in religion as a social problem?
2. Why is mankind universally religious in the broad sense of the term?
3. What is your opinion of the statement that "religion is an opiate to put
   to sleep the social aspirations of the downtrodden"?
4. What is the difference between religion and the church?
5. In your opinion, may an individual who is not connected with a church
   have a socialized "personal religion"? If so, how? If not, why not?
6. Explain the basis for the church's interest in social problems.
7. To what extent have the churches entered upon the practical application
   of religion to the problems of public welfare?
8. Explain the modern opinion that the church should stay out of politics. How do you reconcile this with our contention that the church
   should face social problems?
9. What are some of the difficulties of establishing a unified church sentiment in regard to social problems?
10. How did the position of the churches with respect to their attitude
    toward war differ in the Second World War from what it had been
    in the First World War?
11. Defend, or attack, any one of the statements of the various church groups
    regarding their approach to social problems as quoted in the text.
12. Secure from the pastor of a church of your own denomination a copy
    of its most recent statement similar to those referred to in the previous
    question, and analyze it.
13. Make a list of five suggestions that you would offer for making the
    church more helpful socially.

Chapter 15

PROBLEMS OF DISEASE AND PUBLIC HEALTH

IMPORTANCE OF HEALTH FOR EFFICIENCY AND HAPPINESS

IMAGINE a gigantic weighing-scales constructed on the principle of a druggist's balance. Into the pan of one side pile enough dollars to represent the value of all our material assets in this country—mines, railroads, farms, live stock, timber, manufactured goods of all kinds, houses and their furnishings, factories, and all other items of our wealth. Into the other pan pour enough dollars to represent the value of our 132,000,000 inhabitants considered only as economic producers. At first thought many of us would expect the material wealth of the country to outweigh by far the economic value of the people. But according to conservative estimates, the pile of dollars representing the value of the people would be five times as great as that representing all the material assets of the country combined. Our national wealth in material goods in 1929 was reckoned as being nearly 400 billions of dollars; the total vital assets were estimated as more than $1,500,000,000,000.[1] So from the strictly economic viewpoint national health is of the greatest importance.

Moreover, a human being is also one of the most expensive things we produce. Consider first only the time it takes to grow a man or a woman in comparison with any of our domestic animals. Swine attain maturity in seven or eight months from birth; cattle and horses in two or three years. It takes fourteen or fifteen years for a child to come to puberty and a fifth of a century to come to full physical development. In most countries the young are not considered to be mature enough to vote before they are from eighteen to twenty-three years old. Next, consider the cost of rearing a child. Dublin has estimated that in a family with an annual income of $2,500 a year, the cost of rearing a child to the age of self-support, including food, shelter, clothing, education, etc., is $7,238. If one includes interest on capital and makes allowance for the cost of those who do not survive the age of eighteen, the amount rises to somewhat more than $10,000.[2]

---

[1] L. I. Dublin, *Health and Wealth* (1928), p. 6; Evans Clark, *Internal Debts of the United States* (New York, 1933), p. 9.

[2] Dublin, *op. cit.*, p. 3.

On the other hand a mature man considered as a wage-earner is the most valuable animal we raise. Basing the calculation again on a group of families each with an income of $2,500, Dublin calculated that at age eighteen the present net worth of a man's future earnings, *i.e.*, his gross earnings less his minimum personal expenditures, is about $29,000. At age twenty-five his net worth is more than $32,000. Human beings have a dollar-and-cents value. Health means wealth.

However important good health is economically, that is not the whole story. "Life is more than meat and the body than raiment." Life is not to be measured in dollars and cents, but in happiness, which is the excess of the satisfactions and joys of existence above its dissatisfactions. The importance of the organic basis for existence has been aptly pointed out in the remark that whether or not life is worth living "depends upon the liver." Aside from occasional exceptions, health is the foundation of human happiness. And a sound mind in a sound body has been the ideal of seekers after efficiency since the time of the Greeks. There is good evidence that health is a major basis of human progress and that lack of it is one of the predisposing causes to national decay.[3]

Other things being equal, good health makes for physical efficiency, bodily comfort, a sense of well-being, and develops energy, alertness, and keenness. The relation of good health to social welfare is well summarized in these words:

There should be a keen sense of enjoyment of all life's activities. As William James once said, simply to live, breathe and move should be a delight. The thoroughly healthy person is full of optimism; "he rejoiceth like a strong man to run a race." We seldom see such overflowing vitality except among children. When middle life is reached, or before, our vital surplus has usually been squandered. Yet it is in this vital surplus that the secret of personal magnetism lies. Vital surplus should not only be safeguarded, but accumulated. It is the balance in the savings bank of life. Our health ideals must not stop at the avoidance of invalidism, but should aim at exuberant and exultant health. They should savor not of valetudinarianism, but of athletic development. Our aim should be not to see how much strain our strength can stand, but how great we can make that strength. With such an aim we shall, incidentally and naturally, find ourselves accomplishing more work than if we aimed directly at the work itself. Moreover, when such ideals are attained, work instead of turning into drudgery tends to turn into play, and the hue of life seems to turn from dull gray to the bright tints of well-remembered childhood. In short, our health ideals should

[3] Irving Fisher, "National Vitality, Its Wastes and Conservation," *Report of the National Conservation Commission* (Senate Document No. 676, Sixtieth Congress, second session, 1909), III: 739–741.

rise from the mere wish to keep out of a sick bed to an eagerness to become a well-spring of energy. Only then can we realize the intrinsic wholesomeness and beauty of human life.[4]

EXTENT OF THE PROBLEM OF PHYSICAL INEFFICIENCY

1. *Death—Mortality-Rates.* Deaths caused by pathological conditions of the organism—in other words, deaths not due to old age—are regarded by the medical profession as largely avoidable. Since at present by far the largest percentage of all deaths are due to abnormal causes, the mortality-rates of a country show the degree to which disease control has progressed. Death-rates are expressed in terms of the number of deaths per 1,000 of the population. In the registration area of the United States for 1939 the death-rate was 10.6, while by that year the average expectancy of life was 60.6 years for males and 64.6 years for females.[5] Mortality varies in the different countries of the world. The lowest rate for the period 1931 to 1935 inclusive was 8.2 in New Zealand, while the highest rates reported for the same period were Chile and Ceylon, 24.7. The following table shows death-rates for the different parts of the world for the two periods, illustrating the decline in mortality that has taken place in practically all countries during the first part of the present century.[6] Furthermore, the death-rate ranges higher in the city than in the country; the death-rate of the colored people

TABLE 26

DEATH-RATES IN TWENTY COUNTRIES: 1901–1905 AND 1931–1935 *

Country	1901–1905	1931–1935	Country	1901–1905	1931–1935
Australia	11.8	9.0	Netherlands	16.1	8.9
Austria	24.3	13.5	New Zealand	9.9	8.2
Ceylon	26.7	24.7	Norway	14.6	10.4
Chile	30.8	24.7	Ontario	13.0	10.2
Denmark	14.8	10.9	Scotland	17.1	13.2
England	16.1	12.0	Spain	25.9	16.4
France	19.6	15.8	Sweden	15.5	11.6
Germany	19.9	11.2	Switzerland	17.5	11.8
Italy	22.0	14.1	United States	16.2	10.9
Japan	20.5	17.0	Uruguay	12.9	10.4

* *Mortality Statistics: 1936* (United States Bureau of the Census, 1938), p. 4.

[4] Irving Fisher and E. L. Fisk, *How to Live* (1916), pp. 5–6.
[5] *Abridged Life Tables, 1930–1939* (Preliminary); (United States Bureau of the Census), p. 14.
[6] *Mortality Statistics: 1936* (Washington, D. C.: United States Bureau of the Census, 1938), p. 4.

greatly exceeds that of the whites; that of the poor surpasses that of the rich.

Death-rates have been decreasing during the last few centuries. In London during the seventeenth and eighteenth centuries it was between 40 and 50, while between 1680 and 1720, a period of epidemics, it rose as high as 80. In Havana, Cuba, following the American occupation, the death-rate fell from over 50 to about 20.

The *infant death-rate* has fallen much more than the adult, the number of infants who died in the first year of life having declined in the United States from 100 per 1,000 live births in 1915 to 46 in 1940.[7]

With the exception of the Japanese, the various *colored races* in the United States have a substantially higher death-rate than the white population. While the white death-rate in 1930 stood at 10.4, the rate among the Negroes was 15.3; it was 16 among the Indians, and was highest, 17.7, among the Chinese. The Japanese death-rate was lower than that of the whites, the figure being 8 per 1,000. The situation undoubtedly reflects the tremendous influx of Japanese women during the preceding twenty years; their number increasing from about 9,000 in 1910 to 57,000 in 1930, while Japanese men increased less than 20,000: from 63,000 in 1910 to about 81,000 in 1930.[8] As a result, the Japanese population in the United States was unusually young, and death-rates correspondingly were lower than for a more balanced distribution of age groups. Tuberculosis seems to be the principal cause of the comparatively high death-rate of the colored races, but it is accompanied by other diseases, such as cancer and diseases of the circulatory system.

Decrease in mortality-rates varies with different diseases. The death-rate from tuberculosis in England is only one-third of what it was seventy years ago. The death-rate from typhoid fever has been decreasing very rapidly in recent years. Another disease that has shown a remarkable decrease in death-rates is smallpox. Between 1846 and 1870 in Prussia the death-rate per 100,000 from smallpox was 24. In 1874 vaccination was made compulsory, and as a consequence, the rate fell during 1875 and 1876 to 1.5. In 1793 during the epidemic of yellow fever in Philadelphia one-tenth of the city's population died within six and one-half weeks. Since the discovery that this disease is transmitted only through the mosquito, it has practically disappeared in America.[9]

[7] *Statistical Abstract of the United States, 1941*, p. 96.
[8] Figures derived from *Mortality Statistics: 1930* (United States Bureau of the Census, 1932), p. 9, and *Population*, Fourteenth Census, Vol. II, p. 42. See also *Statistical Abstract of the United States* (1941), p. 11.
[9] Irving Fisher, "National Vitality," *loc. cit.*, pp. 624, 625.

Every decrease in the death-rate means lengthening of life, the prevention of needless expense, greater economic usefulness and the increase of human happiness. Health has been called "a purchasable article" *i.e.*, by wisely spending money we can cut down the incidence of disease.

2. *Ill Health*. On the basis of a number of investigations it has been found that there is a fairly definite percentage of the population, ranging between 2 and 3 per cent, that is at all times incapacitated on account of sickness. An additional 2 to 4 per cent feel the effects of illness but continue to work. On this basis, it is fair to say that at least 6,000,000 people at any given time are more or less ill. Each day at least a million and a quarter of our 54,000,000 gainfully employed persons are not able to report for work owing to sickness. An equal number of less seriously ill are, but should not be, at work.

According to Farr, the English statistician, for every death there is annual average sickness of two years. To put it another way, for each death per year there are two persons sick throughout the year. This would mean that there are 3,000,000 persons on the sick list all the time, or an average of about thirteen days of sickness per capita.[10]

In 1908 *tuberculosis* in all forms caused the greatest number of deaths of any disease. In 1939 *diseases of the heart* stood first, the tuberculosis rate having fallen and the rate from diseases of the heart having steadily risen. Other diseases that have increased are cerebral hemorrhage, and cancer and other malignant tumors. Influenza and pneumonia following it have a very irregular graph. Deaths from these diseases fluctuate more than those from any other.

3. *Accident-rates*. In 1939 the number of deaths due to *accidental or undefined external causes* was 92,782, or about 70 per 100,000 of estimated population. Of these 31,947, or a rate of about 24.5, the result of automobile accidents, constituted the largest group.[11]

4. *Economic Loss Due to Sickness*. Louis I. Dublin, statistician of the Metropolitan Life Insurance Company, has estimated that the total annual cost of sickness in low wages, reduced production, and medical expenses amounts to $2,250,000,000. He also estimated that the total capital value of preventable deaths, based on a capitalization of the average expectancy of earnings for the deceased, is something more than $6,000,000,000 each year.[12]

[10] *Ibid.*, p. 625.
[11] *Statistical Abstract of the United States, 1941*, p. 94.
[12] L. I. Dublin, *op. cit.*, pp. 7–10.

TABLE 27

Total Expenditures for Medical Care *

(All Figures in Thousands of Dollars)

Service	Total	Sources of Funds			
		Patients	Govern-ments	Philan-thropy	Indus-try
Physicians in private practice	1,090,000	1,040,000	—	—	50,000
Dentists in private practice	445,000	445,000	—	—	—
Secondary and sectarian practitioners	193,000	193,000	—	—	—
Graduate nurses, private duty	142,000	142,000	—	—	—
Practical nurses, private duty	60,000	60,000	—	—	—
Hospitals: operating expenses	656,000	278,000	300,000	54,000	24,000
Hospitals: new construction	200,000	—	100,000	100,000	—
Public health	121,000	—	93,500	27,500	—
Private laboratories	3,000	3,000	—	—	—
Orthopedic and other supplies	2,000	2,000	—	—	—
Glasses	50,000	50,000	—	—	—
Drugs	656,000	656,000	—	—	—
Organized medical services	29,000	7,790	16,000	210	5,000
Totals	3,656,000	2,885,790	509,500	181,710	79,000

* Final Report of the Committee on the Costs of Medical Care, *Medical Care for the American People* (University of Chicago Press, 1932), p. 14. With a few minor exceptions, the data apply to the year 1929. They are probably representative of any normal year of recent times.

5. *How Much Is Preventable?* It is now known that we can prevent about 45 per cent of the deaths and save that proportion of the waste which sickness and early death involve. Doubtless the better sanitation of our cities, the hygienic control of our water and food supplies, have had much to do with the lowering of death-rates from certain gastric diseases and from certain other diseases that are water-borne or food-borne. Much yet remains to be done, however, to make available for the preservation of human life the knowledge we have. Our statistics have not yet enabled us to discover how much of the sickness and ill health and death is due to overfatigue in work. That much of it is so produced, however, is indicated by the fact that in England under sickness insurance much greater regularity in attendance upon industry has come

about since the worker has had access to the physician without paying a fee. That economic conditions are closely related to infant sickness and death is indicated by the studies of the federal Children's Bureau in a number of our American cities. These studies show that as the wage of the father increases, the infant mortality steadily decreases.

While we have not by a long way yet approached the conquest of the diseases we now know how to prevent, we are making progress. We have lengthened the average duration of life from 40 years in 1880 to 55 or 56 years in our cities. For the registration area of the United States the life-expectancy of a baby born in 1901 was 49 years; now it is more than 63 years. We cut the infant-mortality rate by one-half in the twenty years between 1920 and 1940. We have almost wiped out typhoid fever in the cities of the North. Since 1900 the death-rate from tuberculosis has been cut by almost three-fourths. The death-rate from diphtheria dropped from 43.3 per 100,000 in 1900 to 3.3 in 1934.[13]

SOCIAL RELATIONS OF HEALTH AND DISEASE

Health is the great desideratum; upon it depend the achievement and the happiness of men. The energy for creative enterprises depends upon it; the joy of existence is rooted in it; the inventiveness that perfects our civilization is closely related to it; the hope and ambition that drive us to service for our families and our communities have some vital relation to it. On the other hand, sickness and death bring many evil results. Poverty follows in their wake; crime breeds where sickness and death-rates are high; hopelessness and despair, laziness, and broken homes follow in the train of sickness and death. Consider the following picture painted by a social worker of the advantages of health on the one hand and the consequences of sickness and death on the other:

We have been so greatly concerned in the past because the poor have not been able to enjoy the full fruits of what they create that we have not appreciated the perdition caused by the inability to experience the joy that comes from achievement. If it is poverty to lack some considerable part of the economic goods and services necessary for decent and wholesome life, it is also poverty to be prevented from producing to full capacity one's share of the spiritual and economic goods and services which are the hope of the world.

Into this Hell, sickness is continually driving humanity. It does so by robbing man of his most valuable asset, by depriving him of his vitality.

"What is a man without energy?" writes Mark Twain in one of his let-

[13] Ibid., pp. 11, 12; Statistical Abstract of the United States, 1941, p. 96; National Resources Committee, op. cit., pp. 171, 184.

ters. "Nothing—nothing at all. What is the grandest thing in Paradise Lost—the Archfiend's terrible energy! What is the greatest feature in Napoleon's character? His unconquerable energy. And today, if I were a heathen, I would rear a statue to energy and fall down and worship it!"

Vitality, indeed, is the power that has made possible the great achievements of history. The great writers, the great artists, the great statesmen, the great business men have abounded in it. It is the men who have had vitality over and above that which they needed for the routine of life, who have outstripped their fellows in enriching the world.

This physical essence of man is the object of sickness' every attack. Acute and chronic illness of the kind discussed thus far in this paper feed upon it. Of that we need no proof. More insidious, more subtle and more difficult to ascertain is the effect upon vitality of what, to borrow from the biologist, we might call *recessive* sickness, the sickness which only the diagnostician can recognize, which the patient himself overlooks, and which, if included in health surveys would bring the percentage of sickness in the general population far above the proportion of three in one hundred.

This is the sickness that people do not consider important enough to justify consultation with a physician, the sickness that expresses itself in a fleeting pain, in an occasional ache, and which preying on vitality, results in an inability to think and act at the top of one's powers. This kind of illness is an almost universal experience; yet by reason of its very nature it is difficult to discover or to subject to statistical analysis. Social agencies learn about it usually only when the disease has reached the advanced stage in which definite and easily recognizable symptoms develop.

An illustration of this is to be found in the experience of Antonio Cardeleo, who for years had been an unsatisfactory sort of person. He was lackadaisical and without energy, a "no account" fellow who seldom had employment and who frequently deserted his family. The cause of his depleted vitality and consequent unproductiveness was not discovered until he returned home from one of his periodic absences, suffering from a hemorrhage. A diagnosis of tuberculosis in an incipent stage was made. Three months elapsed before the sanatorium could admit him. During this time he was under the instruction of a dispensary, and when his turn to go away arrived he had made such progress in learning how to regulate his life and diet that it was possible for him to return to work. A job as a railroad switchman was secured for him. This position he has held ever since. He is buying his own home and has continued to live with his family. Obviously many things entered into making this man into a productive citizen, but among them, certainly, the restoration of his vitality played an important part.

Even more elusive was the cause of Joseph Brown's inefficiency. He was described by one visitor as looking like a Greek God, having the sort of physique which made people instinctively say of him—there's a man for the army. Nevertheless he was ineffective. The neighbors said he was lazy and so indeed he appeared to be. It was only when his condition became so serious that his power to grip things with his hands failed that tuberculosis of the spine was discovered. The disease has since been arrested sufficiently to enable him to work regularly.

Again, the cause of the inertia of another man was not ascertained until one morning he went to bed because the noise which his children made irritated him. A neurologist found that the trouble was locomotor ataxia. The disease was discovered early enough to enable this person for a time at least to become partially self-supporting.

A few weeks ago there died in a tuberculosis hospital a patient who for nearly three years by sheer power of will had forced his body to do work for which it had not the energy. Could any torture be greater than the growing sense of impotence and ineffectiveness which this man felt and struggled against during the months when for the sake of supporting his family he cast aside his hope of recovery?

Here, indeed, is where the destruction of the poor is their poverty. The pressure upon them is to work to the last minute, to ignore disease in its incipient stages, and to neglect those slight chronic digestive troubles and minor defects in the circulatory system that feed upon the energy which men and women need to function adequately as human beings.

Perhaps the first to recognize the dangers of *recessive* sickness has been the successful business man. Against the poverty that comes from a loss of vitality the capable executive guards himself vigilantly. He is careful about what he eats. He is particular about relaxation and recreation. He focusses every effort toward keeping himself at the peak of his energy during the hours when he must make decisions. Any casual disorder is a red signal that meets with instant attention.

But the big business man or the successful professional man is the exception. The rule is the poor man who must often perforce neglect the aches and the pains which accompany his loss in vitality. Without the means or the courage to learn why, he finds himself less and less able to do his best. Even worse, he may never have known what it is to be at one's best. Sickness like another Dracula has preyed upon his life blood from earliest childhood until he becomes what social case workers find so many families to be —spiritless, hopeless, ineffective, without the confidence that comes with physical well being and lacking the impulse toward accomplishment that springs from accomplishment. Thus he is steadily drawn deeper and deeper down into the perdition of unproductiveness.

Through him this social Tophet threatens to engulf us all. The families under the care of charity organization societies are but symptomatic of a misery that is far more widespread than their limited numbers. For each family that, lacking resources in money, in personnel, and in friends, applies to a social agency there are hundreds that manage to struggle on without taking this last resort. All their lives they have not enough to eat or to wear. All their lives they pass in the Hell of economic insufficiency. But if those who suffer thus are many how much greater are the multitudes of those who experience the torture of unproductiveness, the perdition of incomplete achievement? Into this Hell, one cannot tell when, any of us may sink. Verily the burden of sickness is thrusting us lower than the grave and we shall fall into Tophet.[14]

[14] Karl de Schweinitz, "Sickness as a Factor in Poverty," *Proceedings of the National Conference of Social Work* (1919), pp. 160–162.

PRESENT METHODS OF DEALING WITH DISEASE

So long as he did not know the nature of disease and so long as magical notions constituted his only science, man could not hope to overcome the ills of life. If he was of a philosophic mind, he explained them as the inevitable fate of life; if he was religiously minded, he accepted them as inscrutable acts of Providence, somehow intended by God for his own betterment. Well it was for him if he obtained a philosophy of life that, so long as he could not remedy these ills, gave him the will to meet them with high courage. For how long man wrestled with these problems without hope of overcoming them is indicated by the fact that only two centuries ago did medicine become in any way scientific. Modern medicine, with its hope of finally triumphing over man's ancient enemies, disease and ill health, had very little promise of success until the triumph of the germ theory of Pasteur. Consider the methods that we have to-day to assist mankind in its struggle with disease! Perhaps the following will suggest an adequate picture of the present situation:

1. *Physicians, Dentists, and Nurses.* In 1940 there were 132 physicians per 100,000 population in the United States, a decrease from 173 in 1900. In addition there were about 50 dentists per 100,000 population in the same year.

Both medical doctors and dentists are quite irregularly distributed, being concentrated chiefly in the larger cities; and some parts of the country have very much larger numbers in proportion to population than others. While there is a doctor for every 930 persons in the United States, the ratio varies sharply from one State to another, the figure ranging from about 1 for 500 in New York State, to 1 for about 1,400 in Alabama. The distribution also varies greatly between city and country: urban centers have a doctor for each 525 persons, whereas towns of less than 5,000 have but one for every 1,350. Open country areas are still less well served, there being instances of whole counties being without a physician. Dentists gravitate toward towns and cities even more than do the medical doctors; yet their service to the rural areas appears to be more adequate than is that of the physicians.[15] Since the medical profession has become more highly specialized, it has also become somewhat commercialized. However, their uneven distribution and the fact

---

[15] *Social Work Year Book, 1941,* pp. 326–327; *see also* J. H. Kolb, *A Study of Rural Society* (Boston, 1940), p. 603.

that some people prefer certain doctors to others, probably means that some are starving while others are rushed to death.

The *nurse* is as necessary to-day as the physician. In 1940 there were probably about 300,000 graduate nurses in the United States. Graduate nurses have increased since 1900 more rapidly than either physicians or population. There is much evidence to indicate that the supply of nurses, were they properly distributed, is adequate for ordinary peace-time requirements at the present time. However, the distribution of nurses is as uneven as the distribution of doctors and hospitals. The nurses are concentrated in large cities, leaving the rural sections rather poorly supplied. A recent study showed that in ten representative States the cities of 500,000 and over had 43 per cent of all the nurses in those States, while cities of that size contained only 32 per cent of the total population of these ten States. On the other hand, places under 10,000 had only 14 per cent of the nurses and 42 per cent of the population.[16] The number of nurses' training schools has been growing very rapidly, having increased from 11 in 1879 to more than 1,900 in 1930.

Once the nurse was only a private-duty nurse or a hospital nurse. To-day various other kinds of nursing have developed, such as the visiting-nurse, the school nurse, the dispensary nurse, the tuberculosis nurse, nurses employed in stores and factories, and the public health nurse. Air-line hostesses also are nurses.

Unfortunately, most of these nurses are still concentrated in the cities. With the growth of the movement for the county nurse, an increasing number have been made available to country people.

2. *Hospitals and Clinics.* The modern practice of medicine makes a hospital almost necessary. Hospitals in recent years have grown both in numbers and in number of beds provided. In 1920 there were approximately 4,000 hospitals for community use, but by 1940 the number had increased to at least 6,200. The bed capacity had increased from 311,000 to more than 1,000,000 during the same period. To put the matter on the basis of population, in 1920 there was one bed for every 340 persons, while in 1940 there was one for every 130 persons.

The distribution of hospitals is quite uneven. Facilities are not provided in proportion to the amount of illness. However, from 1920 to 1940 the percentage of counties in the United States having hospitals for general community use increased from 44 to 58. Distribution with

[16] Peebles, *A Survey of Statistical Data on Medical Facilities in the United States* (Committee on the Cost of Medical Care, Publication No. 3), pp. 30-32.

respect to population is very uneven. For example, while in the North Atlantic States in 1928 there was one bed for community use for every 198 people, in the South Central States there was only one bed for 508 people. Wisconsin had the most adequate provision, with one bed for 154 persons, while South Carolina had the worst, with one bed for each 749 persons.[17] Ten years later, it was reported that an eighth of our people lived in areas where hospital bed capacity was as low as 1.5 per 1,000 population; most of them, moreover, lived 50 miles or more from any considerable hospital center.[18]

Almost three-fourths of our hospitals are owned by independent associations, churches, individuals, and partnerships, while 26 per cent are owned by governmental units. However, governmental agencies provide 64 per cent of the bed capacity and render 70 per cent of the duties of hospital service.[19]

Scattered throughout the country, especially in the larger cities, sometimes connected with hospitals, sometimes separate, are a number of *dispensaries and clinics* to which people can come for advice and treatment. These people do not need a bed and are what are called "ambulatory cases."

There has been a very great increase in clinics and health centers since 1910. At that date there were about 600, including out-patient departments, while by 1937 there were more than 6,000. It is estimated that at least 50,000,000 visits are made annually to these institutions. They are maintained by hospitals, private health and governmental organizations, commercial and industrial establishments, schools, colleges, trade-unions, courts, prisons, and charitable agencies. Out of 2,500 of these studied in 1923, 42 per cent were conducted by governmental agencies.

These clinics are of many varieties. It is estimated that there are about 700 tuberculosis clinics in this country. In 1940 there were about 3,000 clinics for venereal disease. In the same year there were about 400 mental clinics. Because of the recognition of the importance of heart-disease, cardiac clinics have grown up. In 1928 there were 187 of these.

Owing to the discussion of the cost of medical care, group clinics under private medicine have developed, especially in the Middle West. There is no accurate estimate of their number, although one authority estimated there were 220 such clinics in 1926, mostly in the Middle West.

[17] *Ibid.*, pp. 36–48.
[18] *Social Work Year Book, 1941*, p. 328.
[19] Peebles, *op. cit.*

In certain of the large cities pay clinics have risen, which charge approximately the cost of the services rendered. The movement seems to have begun in Massachusetts.[20]

TABLE 28

MEDICAL SERVICES NEEDED AND RECEIVED *

Units of Medical Service Received per 1,000 Individuals in Families with Specified Incomes Compared with Services Needed to Meet Standards of Good Medical Care. Data on Services Received, Based on 38,668 White Persons in 8,639 Families Surveyed for Twelve Consecutive Months, 1928–1931.

Unit of Service	Services in Families with Specified Incomes (Number per 1,000 Individuals)						Services Needed to Supply Good Medical Care
	Under $1,200	$1,200–$2,000	$2,000–$3,000	$3,000–$5,000	$5,000–$10,000	$10,000 and Over	
Home, office and clinic calls (physicians)	1,931.9	2,045.9	2,296.7	2,741.4	3,621.4	4,734.4	5,649.5
Hospitalized cases	59.4	52.4	59.4	63.1	79.3	98.0	107.0
Days of hospital care	927.9	666.7	757.4	604.2	840.3	1,200.8	1,384.7
Dental care (persons over 3 years of age)	117.9	184.6	247.5	309.4	446.0	622.0	1,000.0
Health examinations	83.2	68.0	69.1	82.2	121.7	234.0	941.9
Immunizations	68.5	49.2	50.9	59.6	84.3	120.2	185.3
Refractions or glasses	24.5	24.6	39.6	53.8	89.6	159.7	175.0
Home and office calls (secondary) practitioners and cultists	154.6	139.1	230.4	231.1	459.0	569.2	——

* Final Report of the Committee on the Costs of Medical Care, *Medical Care for the American People* (University of Chicago Press, 1932), p. 8.

3. *Medical Social Service.* What is known as medical social service arose partly out of the abuse of hospitals and dispensaries by people who could afford to pay, but who were claiming that they were unable to do so, and partly out of the realization that disease is often the product of the conditions under which people live and work, and that cure depends upon the change in the family and in working conditions which

[20] *Ibid.*, pp. 43–45.

have brought on the illness. The present movement goes back to the establishment of such service in the Massachusetts General Hospital in 1905. By 1935 nearly 600 hospitals had started social work in connection with their patients.[21] Medical social service represents one more extension of human effort to control the conditions that produce ill health and to bring about cure by adjusting social conditions to that end. It is the application of social case work to the healing of disease. It is a recognition that ill health is the product not only of germs, but also of the physiological disfunction which comes about by subjection of the human organism to bad social conditions in the widest sense.

4. *Health Centers.* By the health center we mean any room or building in which health information is given with the purpose of teaching people how to keep well. Frequently clinical examination occurs there, but this is chiefly for the purpose of interesting those who come in the matter of health and providing a means whereby health education can be disseminated. No treatment is given in the health center; and if the need of treatment is discovered, the person is referred to his family physician, or to a hospital or dispensary. Frequently the health center is the starting-point from which the public health nurse gets her clues as to what people she should follow up and give further information. The health center is only one more method devised to teach people the value of health and hygiene.

Social settlements and some welfare associations have seen the importance of public-health instruction. The Red Cross, after the First World War, took up health centers as one of its main activities; boards of health in a number of our States have developed them; and a number of private organizations, such as anti-tuberculosis associations, frequently have organized them and stimulated interest in public health in this way. Often they go under other names, such as child health clinics, or child welfare clinics. Several hundreds of these have been established, some of them giving extensive medical and educational service and others giving only general health information.

5. *Public Health Departments.* In this brief survey of the agencies already at work for the conservation of the health of the people, the public health departments, local, State, and national, should not be neglected. Each of our States and dependencies has a board of health. The income of all these State and Territorial departments in 1938 amounted to more than $40,000,000.[22] In 1939, about 40 per cent of the counties had full-

[21] *Social Work Year Book, 1941,* p. 340.
[22] *Statistical Abstract of the United States, 1941,* p. 239.

time health officers,[23] while urban centers are increasingly turning to full-time health officers to assume the administrative responsibilities of their health boards, and providing these officers with up-to-date laboratories and equipment for inspection.

The duties of the local public health officers vary widely in the different States. The chief duties of the local officers are the enforcement of the quarantine regulations, sanitary laws, and other regulations affecting public health. However, in the larger cities, the health department frequently has a wide program for the promotion of health as well as the enforcement of laws and regulations. Often they hold clinics of various sorts for the discovery of disease. In some of the cities a large force of nurses works under the Department of Health. Often the city Department of Health has laboratories for the purpose of testing water, food, and milk, and for the microscopic examination of specimens sent in by physicians.

The State health department serves chiefly to coördinate the health activities of the localities within the borders of the State, holding the local boards to certain minimum standards of service, and supplementing financial and technical limitations of communities as necessary. It promotes public appreciation of the problems of health by preparing and distributing pamphlets, organizing clinical demonstrations, and recording statistical information regarding the health of the State. It specifies the minimum requirements for milk and water supplies, performs many laboratory and inspection services for both localities and individuals, checks on local sewage disposal systems, and in some instances takes a hand in setting the minimum standards of training and proficiency to be required of local health officials. The State Boards, moreover, are to a considerable extent the agencies through which the federal Health Service makes its findings and suggestions effective.

As the spearhead of the public health service in our country stands the United States Public Health Service. It originated from the marine hospital service that was established by an act of Congress approved July 16, 1798. The original purpose of this service was to furnish care for sick and disabled seamen in hospitals, either those maintained by the United States or civilian institutions with which contracts might be negotiated. To-day, its activities include the following services:

1. Furnishing medical service to American seamen and other beneficiaries.
2. Protection of the United States from the introduction of diseases from without.

[23] *Social Work Year Book, 1941,* p. 427.

3. Prevention of the interstate spread of disease and the suppression of epidemics.

4. Coöperation with State and local boards of health as well as with federal agencies in health matters.

5. Investigation of diseases of man.

6. Supervision and control of biological products.

7. Public health education and dissemination of health information.[24]

In any consideration of public health service it should be noticed, however, that many such services are rendered by agencies not under the jurisdiction of health departments. This is true of both the State and federal governments. The administration of workman's compensation laws, for example, has a profound influence on the health of the individual; and many of the functions ordinarily performed by the State Department of Public Welfare and of the Industrial Commission have important health implications. In the national government, we need point only to such agencies as the Children's Bureau and Women's Bureau of the Department of Labor, the Division of Vital Statistics of the Bureau of the Census, or to the many and diversified services of the Department of Agriculture or of the Federal Security Agency, to realize that concern for the public health permeates the whole structure of government.

6. *Private Health Agencies.* In addition to public agencies supported out of public funds, there are many private agencies promoting health in one way or another, such, for example, as the anti-tuberculosis associations in various States, the National Anti-Tuberculosis Association, the associations against cancer, the heart associations, the Child Welfare League of America, child health associations, and many others too numerous to mention. Most of these actively carry on propaganda in the interest of public health. Then there are the factories and large stores in cities, great industrial plants, and other business concerns that have found it to their financial interest to provide hospitals, nurses, and out-patient clinics for their employees. In addition to these some of the insurance companies, like the Metropolitan Life Insurance Company, send out people to give addresses and publish many bulletins in the interest of public health. In fact, so far has the health propaganda gone that the manufacturers of various products have capitalized the health slogan in their advertising. For example, we hear of "health bran," "health bread," "health underwear," "health toothbrushes," and "health soap."

[24] *Public Health Reports*, Vol. 41, No. 50, p. 2827 (Dec. 10, 1926).

OTHER MEASURES NECESSARY IN THE INTEREST OF HEALTH

Perhaps no other interest of the people of the United States except money-making, education, and religion commands more attention at the present time than health. The present propaganda in the interest of health is certainly greater in volume and better prepared than that in the interest of religion or of education. It is surpassed only by business advertising. In spite, however, of its apparent widespread acceptance. and in spite of the well-organized agencies public and private for its spread, health education has only commenced its great tasks.

While the modern health movement and modern medicine have delivered many from age-long fear, still countless millions live in the shadow of death, as a brief study of our mortality and morbidity statistics shows. Needless death still sweeps off millions. While death ought to occur at the end of a long and useful life, a welcome end to the outworn machine, to-day most of us die untimely deaths. Infants, youths, and men and women in the flush of maturity still perish with life unfulfilled. Moreover, in spite of all the health propaganda, millions spend their lives in sickness and consequent inefficiency. How shall the knowledge now available to the scientists be made the common property of all? How shall the people be provided with the facilities they need in time of sickness? What can be done about the majority of deaths and sicknesses that we do not yet know how to prevent? These are some of the unanswered questions regarding health which challenge this generation.

1. *Scientific Eugenics.* The science of eugenics has two aspects: (1) negative eugenics, which means the elimination through the lack of breeding of the dysgenic stock, and (2) positive eugenics, which means the cultivation of sentiments and ideals that will lead the thoroughbreds to mate only with thoroughbreds and rear adequate families. Eugenicists have suggested that it is possible for society consciously to develop ideals in individuals which will make them shrink from a marriage that promotes degeneracy. Education along the line of positive eugenics, it is believed, will lead to discrimination in the matter of marriage much more generally than is practiced to-day. Young people contemplating marriage should very seriously consider the hereditary background of their prospective mates. If there is a history of insanity, epilepsy, or feeble-mindedness in the ancestors, he who takes the risk is shouldering a great responsibility to the race. This may seem shocking to young, romantic love. Proverbially, love is blind; and this may indeed be the

reason why so many young people fail to take into consideration the heredity of their prospective mates. Modern education has the responsibility of opening their eyes to these important considerations.

On the side of negative eugenics much more strenuous steps must be taken to control the propagation of the incapable than are now to be found in any country. In none of our States have we made provisions for the segregation of the feeble-minded to the extent of as much as one-tenth of the number supposed to be present in the population. Furthermore, consider the responsibility of those who by reason of inherited weakness bring into the world children who all their lives suffer from weakness and disease. Some day perhaps even the foundation of good health will be considered a eugenic matter. Education on the importance of the hereditary basis of good health ought not to be impossible, because many of these people who produce weakling children have minds capable of understanding the importance of this subject. When there is patent weakness in the ancestry, should they take the risk of bringing into the world those who all their life long will suffer from the defective constitutions handed on to them by their parents?

2. *Public Hygiene Measures.* The eugenic measures are for the benefit of posterity. There are other measures, however, that affect the present generation. Hygienic measures based upon our present knowledge as to the prevention and cure of sickness may be realized either through public hygiene, quasi-public hygiene, or personal hygiene. In recent years great advances have been made in all these matters. Streets are cleaned much more effectively than ever before. Sanitary water supplies have been provided in wide areas. City health departments are watching food supplies, regulating quarantine, attending to garbage-disposal and sewage as never before. Nevertheless, much remains yet to be done. There are still cities whose supply of drinking water comes from contaminated rivers and lakes. Because of the agitation of ignorant people, quarantine regulations are not as strictly enforced in some places as they should be. While some cities are providing vaccines of various kinds for the prevention of such diseases as smallpox, typhoid fever, and diphtheria, in some places there is still a determined fight against the use of these preventives. City health departments and State departments of health have still enormous reaches of territory that must be covered more effectively than they are to-day. State health departments have a serious problem in the struggle to prevent people from contracting diseases while on their summer vacations. Many of the resorts ignore the

simplest elements of sanitation. Many a man comes back from his vacation with the germs of typhoid lurking in his system from the water that he drank. The sanitation of the villages and the open country is still in its infancy.

To various State departments also belong the problems connected with the sanitation of factories and other places in which people work. Upon these conditions depends the health of innumerable persons. While many of the States have been working on this problem in various parts of the country, a large number of our States still make very little provision for the protection of the health of the worker in industry. The whole problem of industrial hygiene is just in its infancy. What shall we say of the labor of women just before and soon after childbirth? Studies have shown that the numbers of still-births and of deaths of infants soon after birth were very greatly increased by improper guarding of the mother in factories at that period.

Only a few of our States have provided an adequate compensation law for industrial accidents. The figures often cited indicate that an enormous amount of disability arises from such accidents. Furthermore, traffic conditions on our roads and streets must be more carefully regulated and our people taught the importance of safe driving, else the number of accidents from the automobile is bound to mount.

Again, the lack of proper housing laws and tenement-house regulations in many of our cities is a distinct menace to health. Cities and States must more carefully regulate the building and repair of houses before the death and sickness rates incident to unhygienic housing conditions decrease very materially. The houses of an astonishing number of our American cities still contain dark rooms, in which breed all kinds of disease germs.

While the standards of the medical profession have been rising rapidly in the last few years, there is much yet to be done. There are still to be found medical schools turning out practitioners inadequately trained and some of them of such low character that it is impossible to expect them to bring honor to the profession. Too often the members of the medical profession are so engrossed in the practice of medicine as a business, instead of as a profession, that, instead of seconding with all their power the work of the State and city departments of health, the work of private associations for health education, the multiplication of nurses and other agencies for disseminating health instruction, they are found in the opposition. Perhaps the time will come when more of them than now will find their chief aim to be that of putting themselves out of business by assisting in the program of health education and prevention.

The extensive use of patent medicines, the presence everywhere of quacks of every sort, and the rapid growth of various methods of nonmedical healing are symptomatic of the great work that still needs to be done in the education of the public on public health matters. How little the man on the street knows about the nature of disease and the methods of preventing it! How little impression modern science has made upon him is shown by the fact that thousands of charlatans and quacks live upon the people who prefer them to our regular physicians. Truly, the doctor has his job of public health education cut out for him in the face of the dense ignorance that exists and the belief in these occult practices. If they but had eyes to see it, the doctors have before them in these things a challenge to their best efforts to promote health education. As a whole they are a self-sacrificing and charitable group of men. Very few of them turn away the person who cannot pay; yet too many of them do not realize that public health education, instead of ruining their practice from the commercial point of view, would send thousands to them who now buy patent medicines or go to the quacks.

Much as needs to be done in the line of physical health, how much greater is the need with regard to mental health! Physical hygiene has a start; mental hygiene is in its infancy. But a little while ago insanity was looked upon as a doom, not a disease. Fortunately, that attitude has changed among those who are familiar with the nature of the various forms of insanity.

How far our mental hygiene is behind physical hygiene is shown by the fact that very few people consult doctors for their mental difficulties as compared to those who consult physicians for their physical troubles. Among the populace generally insanity is still looked upon as something dreadful and inexplicable. Enough is known, however, at the present time to enable us to prevent part of the terrible inroads upon the mental health of the people that the various forms of insanity are now making. In some States we have mental hygiene associations, the purpose of which is to instruct people as to the nature of their mental maladies; but how few they are, and how few are the people whom they reach! Insanity is looked upon as a disgrace that must be hidden. Only a few of our States have provided mental clinics to which people can come for consultation, and yet the number of insane people increases steadily. The number will continue to grow until we learn how to teach people the elements of mental hygiene, the signs of mental disturbance, and the fundamental nature of the disease.

3. *Personal Hygiene.* Important as are these various measures of community hygiene, they are insignificant in comparison with personal hygiene. You talk in vain to a man who has no ideals of personal hygiene, when you try to educate him to community hygiene, because your effort has no soil of experience in which to root itself. The difficulties of the public health educator, whether he be doctor, nurse, public health department head, or representative of a private health agency, are primarily due to the fact that the individuals to whom he appeals do not have ideals of personal hygiene. Of what value is it to have pure drinking water supplied to the city if the consumer drinks it out of a glass used by a typhoid patient? What signifies it that inspection of the milk supply be ever so good if the mother feeds it to her baby from an unclean bottle? Of what value are quarantine regulations against children's diseases if the mother whose child is quarantined believes that every child ought to have these diseases when he is young? And how surely are the results of hygienic laboratories negatived by the personal habits of vicious, gluttonous, and bibulous persons?

Our habits of eating from childhood to old age are of the very greatest importance in the preservation of good health. The death-rate of babies has been cut since we have learned better ways of infant feeding. For adults it is an old saying that "we dig our graves with our teeth." One of the lessons that every man and woman has to learn as he grows older is the importance of controlling his appetite for food. Moreover, some individuals can digest certain kinds of food that others cannot. Consequently, one of the great movements of the present day for the preservation of health is careful attention to the hygiene of nutrition. Moreover, sound bodily health depends upon the *proper elimination of the wastes of the body*. Improper elimination of waste means the poisoning of the whole system. Many of us who are sick have poisoned ourselves as a result of our failure to recognize the importance of this matter.

It must be confessed, however, that part of our poisoning of ourselves is directly from without rather than indirectly from within. Numerous poisons have become habits. Perhaps the greatest of these is *alcohol*. Could we do away with the abuse of alcoholic liquors the probabilities are that we should very greatly decrease the amount of sickness and ill health, both physical and mental. Taken in any considerable quantities alcohol seriously interferes with various physiological functions; it is probably a contributing factor in the production of some forms of insanity, as well as several other important diseases. It is a well-known fact that our larger insurance companies inquire particularly about the drinking habits of the applicants for its policies.

Other narcotic drugs, such as morphine, heroin, veronal, and cocaine, since they are habit-forming drugs and lead to the demand for ever-larger doses, are inimical to good health. Often the habit of taking these drugs grows out of the abuse of drugs by the physician for the alleviation of pain rather than attacking directly the causes of the disease; sometimes it is started by patent medicines. These drugs therefore are rather carefully regulated by both the United States Government and the various health departments. However, the real solution of the drug habit is in a growing appreciation by each individual of the importance of remaining free from the clutches of such a habit. Beware of the headache tablet and the patent medicine that has any of these habit-forming drugs in its composition.

A poison of less importance, which nevertheless may be injurious to health if taken into the system in too large quantities, is tobacco. Closely related to tobacco are certain other stimulants widely used, among them coffee, tea, and cocoa. Again, unless used to excess, they are probably not particularly injurious for the normally healthy person.

Another measure of personal hygiene is *proper exercise.* Man in his development has been an active creature. To-day large sections of our population are sedentary. The motor-car has done more than anything else to bring about physical inactivity. We drive to our offices and then have to play golf in order to secure exercise. The recreation movement of the present time is a vital necessity to good health. Sports should be encouraged as a public health measure. The activity connected with outdoor sports stimulates circulation of the blood and activity of the organs that eliminate waste from the system, and tends to promote good health. While we laugh at the golf enthusiast and the old men who join walking clubs, we have to admit that every device that gets men away from their chairs and into active games promotes sound health and lengthens life.

4. *Social Hygiene.* In every life there are two primary urges—the urge for food and the urge for a mate. Both may be abused and such abuse destroys good health. While the abuse of food and sex have many other social ramifications, our concern here is the relationship of sex to health. Men and women are naturally so constituted that the normal exercise of the sex function is as compatible with good health as is the

normal use of food. While it is contended by some that many physical and mental ills are the result of the denial of the normal exercise of the sex function, most medical authorities believe that such denial is not of serious consequence if the individual can find equivalent expression of his love-life in challenging social projects. How often have we seen those who have not married find satisfactory expressions of their love-life in devotion to children, in the care of those who are helpless, and in active concern for the disadvantaged! People differ in self-control as in other matters, but social policy cannot be based upon the ability of the weak. It must be built upon a policy that will have regard for the health of the people. Whatever debates there may be with regard to sexual conduct from other points of view, there is no question that from the standpoint of health irregular sexual relations are of the very greatest menace. Upon such practices depends the spread of *venereal disease*, which causes tremendous losses every year. No method has been devised by which it can be insured that sexual relations outside of matrimony will not result in disease.

So serious is *syphilis* that many life-insurance companies will not issue a policy to a man until four or five years after he has been pronounced cured. This disease often leads to insanity, paralysis, apoplexy, softening of the brain, and locomotor ataxia. Moreover, it is serious in its effects upon unborn children. The terrible ravages of syphilis are beyond computation. Blindness of the new-born is a disease caused by *gonorrhea*. It has been estimated that 25 per cent of all the cases of blindness in the United States have been caused to innocent children by this disease. Also it accounts, we are told, for a large proportion of the major operations upon women. Ill health, especially in the female, is a consequence. How much misery it has caused in human history and how much it is causing at this present moment, no one can compute.

It is impossible to say how widespread such diseases are, because many cases are dormant at any given time, and because the treatment for both syphilis and gonorrhea is increasingly successful. The reporting of such diseases is required of physicians in every State in the union; but many physicians have been quite lax in this regard. Unfortunately, too, many victims of the disease have resorted to the use of nostrums and "self-cures" rather than seeking counsel of competent medical persons. It has been estimated, however, that probably 1 person in 10 is, or has been, a victim of venereal disease, while perhaps 3,500,000 are afflicted actively at any one time.

In recent years, considerable progress has been made in diagnosing and treating venereal disease. The Venereal Disease Control Act of 1938 provided for a Division of Venereal Disease within the United States Public Health Service. Congress provided some $15,000,000 for the first three years' activity of the Division, and the State and local agencies matched the federal appropriations approximately 2 to 1. The federal agency is supplying fresh drugs to physicians in at least 43 of the States.[25] More than 11,000,000 tests were made in 1940, and nearly 7,000,000 treatments were provided in about 3,000 clinics and dispensaries throughout the country. Nevertheless, while science is making great gains in the cure of venereal disease, the treatments (especially for syphilis) are protracted; and prevention still remains the best policy. However we view the matter, there is no question that sex hygiene is one of the most important aspects of personal hygiene.

Education in social hygiene has also grown greatly since the First World War. Forty per cent of the high schools of the country have instituted some instruction to the pupils in sex hygiene. Whereas before 1918 only two States required notification of venereal diseases, now every State and the District of Columbia have this requirement. This again shows that public attention has been focussed on the problem. In spite of these signs of increased interest, however, there are serious problems still to be faced. People easily get tired of hearing about any one subject and lose interest unless continued attention is given to enlisting interest in new ways. Nevertheless, the importance of this phase of personal hygiene is well expressed in the following words:

If the relative importance of the several phases of modern public health is analyzed, it will be apparent to any impartial observer that social hygiene should take first place. It involves not only the prevention of that group of diseases transmitted by sexual contact, in which is syphilis, the greatest killing and disabling disease, and gonorrhea, probably the most prevalent of the serious diseases which afflict the race, but it is related directly to many other phases of life. Social hygiene is concerned with character formation; it influences mental health to a profound degree; it is a most significant factor in marital happiness; in short, social hygiene influences more directly our whole social system and guides more intimately the whole trend of our civilization than any other phase of public health.[26]

5. *Health Insurance.* An adequate program of health protection, both financial and medical, for the individual has developed very slowly in the United States. Every important country in the world, except China,

[25] *Social Work Year Book, 1941,* p. 427.
[26] "Social Hygiene and Public Health," *Journal of Social Hygiene,* January, 1927, p. 19.

India, and our own, has some sort of program of health insurance under governmental auspices. Pioneered by Germany in 1883, the governmental administration of health insurance spread over all Europe, with the exception of Spain and Italy, by 1933; and by 1941 there were 26 governmental systems of compulsory health insurance throughout the world. Russia had gone farthest in this regard, being the only country in which such protection was *universal*.[27] We in the United States have persistently refused to take any concerted action in the matter, despite the undisputed need for it revealed by the findings in the five-year survey made by the Committee on the Costs of Medical Care.[28] The fact that we are the only advanced country in the world without such a system undoubtedly is due to our individualistic tradition. The medical profession regards the movement as an infringement on its professional status, while insurance companies fear the loss of business, and many employers regard it as being a burden too costly for them to assume and still maintain a favorable competitive position.

The essential features of compulsory health insurance plans are much like other phases of the social security program, which we have examined more fully in earlier chapters.[29] Moreover, the objectives of health insurance are quite like those of the other types of protection, being designed to help those who are least able to help themselves, to distribute the burden of misfortune more equitably, and to increase the security of the individual and thus stabilize society as a whole.

In general, the health insurance programs provide for cash benefits, usually a percentage of the worker's wage, and for varying amounts of medical service, including professional, hospital services, drugs, and medical supplies which may be either unlimited or to the extent of stipulated values. The benefits normally extend for a maximum period of about six months in any one year, with longer or chronic cases being taken care of under other arrangements. In the case of women, maternity benefits usually are provided, with the same privileges being extended to wives of insured workers. Death benefits, to offset costs of last illnesses and funeral expenses, also are included, as a rule to a value of about six weeks' wages. In almost all systems, contributions are required from workers, employers, and the State in varying proportions, since it is felt that all three have an interest in maintaining good health

[27] C. R. Daugherty, *Labor Problems in American Industry* (Boston, 1941), p. 798; J. L. Gillin, *Poverty and Dependency* (New York, 1937), pp. 553, 561.
[28] See *Medical Care for the American People*, The Final Report of the Committee on the Costs of Medical Care (Chicago, 1932).
[29] See especially Chapters 10 and 11.

and that all three have it in their power to assist directly in bringing about more healthful conditions of life. Workers' contributions, however, are kept at a minimum, on the ground that their earnings already are extremely limited as a general rule. All the systems, save that of Russia, are limited in that they apply only to low-paid, employed persons and their families and exclude one or more classes even of those workers. The agricultural laborer is most commonly excluded from these systems.

The United States, as has already been said, has been reluctant to institute such programs for its people. Instead, we have relied chiefly upon the governmental agencies to provide the minimum essentials of preventive and remedial medicine and upon private organizations to supplement that work by special research and health services. Nevertheless, there have been certain significant developments in the field of health insurance. Larger companies are commonly providing blanket protection for their employees and their families through group insurance policies. Many of them also have medical staffs and equipment within their organizations, which usually are available also to the immediate families of the employees. Physicians and hospitals also are frequently organizing clinical and hospital care on a group insurance basis within local communities. A number of insurance companies, too, are experimenting with health and accident policies offering various degrees of protection, and sold to individuals on the same basis as other types of insurance. The Social Security Act, while it did not include any direct provision for social insurance as such, made possible a considerable expansion of health service at all levels of government organization. A later bill, introduced by Senator Wagner in 1939, would have enlarged the provisions of the Social Security Act still further, even including a section that would have encouraged (but not required) the States to inaugurate limited health insurance plans or to foster the development of voluntary group health insurance organizations. Stiff opposition and a growing preoccupation with the problems of the Second World War, however, prevented the bill from becoming law. Nevertheless, there is a persistent public demand for some sort of Federal Government action regarding the problems of health security. It may very well be that as the benefits of the other phases of the social security program become more clearly demonstrated and established, the United States will take its place with other leading nations and adopt an integrated system of health protection, service, and insurance.

REFERENCES

Committee on the Costs of Medical Care, *Medical Care for the American People* (Chicago, 1933).

Davis, M. M., *Paying Your Sickness Bills* (Chicago, 1931), Chs. II, III, VI.

———, *Public Medical Services* (Chicago, 1937).

Dublin, L. I., and Lotka, A. J., *Length of Life* (New York, 1936).

Haggard, H. W., *Devils, Drugs, and Doctors* (New York, 1932).

Heiser, Victor, *An American Doctor's Odyssey* (New York, 1936).

Hertzler, A. E., *The Horse and Buggy Doctor* (New York, 1938), Chs. 10, 12.

Hill, F. E., *Educating for Health* (American Association for Adult Education, 1939).

Sand, René, *Health and Human Progress* (New York, 1936).

Social Security Yearbook, 1939 (Washington, D. C.: Federal Security Agency, Social Security Board, 1940).

Social Work Year Book, 1941, R. H. Kurtz, ed. (New York, 1941)

Stern, Bernard J., *Society and Medical Progress* (Princeton, 1941).

Winslow, C.-E. A., "Public Health," *Encyclopaedia of the Social Sciences*, XII: 646–657.

QUESTIONS AND EXERCISES

1. Indicate the economic and social losses entailed by poor health.
2. Name five social problems that are affected by sickness and death.
3. What changes have taken place in the present century in the relative importance of the various diseases that cause death?
4. What is the relation between reduced infant mortality and declining birth-rates? And the status of women?
5. What bearing does the lower infant mortality have upon population quality? Upon living standards? Discuss.
6. How has the disappearance of the old-time country doctor affected the problem of health service in the rural community?
7. How has the development of the telephone, automobile, and good roads affected the health service among rural people?
8. Set down in your own way the different methods now used of (*a*) treating the sick; (*b*) preventing disease.
9. Are these measures adequate to the solution of the problem of disease and untimely death? Why, or why not?
10. Would you favor a system of State medical service, coupled with compulsory health insurance? Give reasons for your position.
11. If medical care were readily available to all, would many people be likely to "enjoy poor health" in the sense that malingering would increase?
12. Outline the chief elements in a program to solve the problem of disease and premature death.
13. What social problems would you expect to solve, partially at least, by such a program?

Chapter 16

PROBLEMS OF POVERTY AND DEPENDENCY

ALL SOCIAL PROBLEMS grow out of maladjustments. The rich and the poor have been with us ever since one man was able to control more desirable objects than another. They did not present serious social problems, however, until methods of trading developed to such a point that a market was established for the exchange of commodities and a scale of values was established in the minds of men. To-day, with business organized on a world basis, with the development of what is practically a world market, and with certain standards of living established in the customs and traditions of men, poverty has become a stark and naked reality in contrast with riches, and dependency stands out in contrast with independence. Differences in the amount of goods possessed by different people may be of great significance even for those above the poverty line. For those below that line such differences may be tragic.

The poverty line is determined by the customs and modes of living of each society. Poverty may be defined, therefore, as *that condition of living in which a person, because of either inadequate income or unwise expenditure, does not maintain a standard of living high enough to provide for the physical and mental efficiency of himself and to enable him and his natural dependents to function usefully according to the standards of the society of which he is a member.* Any one living in that condition is below the poverty line of his particular group. It should be observed, however, that what one person regards as poverty might be thought to be quite a satisfactory plane of living by another. A given individual may be considered well-to-do by his associates, while people in the class next above him regard him as a "climber" and treat him with indifference. An office worker may be quite successful among people of his own class; but if he tries to fraternize with the executives of the company, he is more than likely to find the pace much too swift for him. On the other hand, if the executives were to maintain standards of living similar to those of the office workers, they would be regarded as peculiar by the other people of their own position; they would not be maintaining the standards of the society of which they are members. So we cannot refer to any hard-and-fast poverty line above or below which all of us must fall. There are as many lines of poverty as there are classes within the society one refers to. And what we have said about the tragedy of falling below the poverty line applies with force to any individual hovering about that line, whatever class he may be in.

Dependency in a broad, general sense may or may not be related to poverty or pauperism. The young child is dependent upon its parents, although they may be rich. On the other hand, the child in an orphanage or placed out in a strange family is dependent and may be a pauper. *The only dependency that creates a social problem is the dependency connected with support by some one other than one's natural or legal supporter.* The wife dependent upon her husband for support is a dependent, but constitutes no social problem. However, the wife left without means of support by her husband who deserts, becomes incapacitated, or dies, creates a problem for society. Dependency in the narrow sense of the term, therefore, is synonymous with pauperism.

Thus pauperism may be defined as *that condition of life in which one depends upon some one other than his natural or legal supporter for his sustenance, either in whole or in part.* The child dependent upon its parents *is not* a pauper, while the child dependent upon an orphanage or a child-placing organization *is* a pauper. While her husband is still living and supporting her, the wife is dependent upon him but is not a pauper. If, however, she receives a "mother's pension," she is a pauper and is therefore a social problem. The word "pauper" should carry with it, however, no connotation of social opprobrium. It simply refers, as our definition states, to those dependent upon some one other than their natural or legal supporter. Within the ranks of paupers, however, there are both willing and unwilling recipients of such help. Unfortunately, the willing paupers have come to be identified with the word so completely that we now speak of people being "pauperized" who have become willing paupers; and the concept works both hardship and injustice upon the vast majority of self-respecting, unwilling paupers who are, nevertheless, still paupers and as such create serious problems of social policy.

AMOUNT OF POVERTY

Shortly before the First World War, King estimated that the poorest two-thirds of the people of the United States owned at that time but a petty 5 or 6 per cent of the nation's wealth, and the poorest four-fifths of the population owned scarcely 10 per cent of the total wealth of the land, while the richest 2 per cent of the population possessed almost three-fifths of the wealth. In other words, each of the men in the richest four-hundredth part of the population possessed one hundred times the wealth of the average citizen.[1] Looking at the same problem, Royal Meeker, then United States Commissioner of Labor, in 1919 estimated that American families on the average were not fully nourished until their yearly income reached $1,800, a figure still conservative for a family of four. He pointed out, however, that the average income of the gainfully employed in this country fell well below $1,600; as a matter of fact, it was about $1,350.[2] Nearly a decade later, according to a study by the National Industrial Conference Board, in 1928, for the United States the average income per capita was $650 and per each person gainfully employed only $1,749.[3]

Total and average income, however, mean little unless we also know something of how the income actually is distributed. Even at best, the National Bureau of Economic Research has estimated that if an equal distribution of income could be effected without serious impairment of the machinery of production on which all incomes depend, there would be only a small margin for the normal family above the amount needed to maintain a decent standard of living. One of our most explicit indexes as to the actual distribution of income is the report of the income tax returns, released annually by the Treasury Department. In 1938 these returns showed that nearly two-fifths (39.4 per cent) of those reporting had incomes between $1,000 and $2,000 and received only 18.3 per cent of the national income. Nearly 6 per cent reported incomes of less than $1,000 and accounted for but 1.4 per cent of the total incomes; while on the other hand less than 3 per cent reported incomes upward of $10,000, but more than a fifth (20.72 per cent) of the reported income fell to those having such incomes.[4] However, there is little doubt that such figures fall far short of showing the true conditions regarding the distribution of income. No one is likely to overstate his income to the tax-gatherer intentionally, while millions of workers earned so little that their incomes fell below the minimum exemptions, and they did not file at all. Thus, the National Resources Planning Board estimates that about

---

[1] W. I. King, *Wealth and Income of the People of the United States* (1915), pp. 80–82.

[2] Meeker, "What is the American Standard of Living?" *Monthly Labor Review,* p. 5 (July, 1919).

[3] *World Almanac* (1931), p. 484.

[4] *Statistics of Income for 1938* (U. S. Treasury Department, Bureau of Internal Revenue, 1941), Part I, p. 19.

5 per cent of the nation's 29,000,000 families have annual incomes of less han $1,500.[5]

These are but indications of the actual situation. No one can say exactly what proportion of our people are living on or near the poverty ine. From the standpoint, however, of our definition of poverty, certainly we shall be conservative if we say *a third of our people do not have he necessaries of life to enable them to maintain their physical and mental efficiency and to conform to the standards of decency set by the members of their group.* If we think of the standard as one that implies aking advantage of life's opportunities for the children, doubtless the proportion of those in poverty would be greater. Lack of recreation, a poverty-stricken social life that gives no outlook beyond the bare necessities, absence of opportunities for those social contacts which ennoble personality—that create an aspiration for better things, and inspire a sentiment of patriotic devotion to the country—these dwarfing conditions prevail in all too large a proportion of our population. From he standpoint of social development and good citizenship these disadvantaged people are in poverty.

SOCIAL AND ECONOMIC COST OF POVERTY AND DEPENDENCY

Statistics of the extent and costs of pauperism in the United States have been far more complete since 1933 than they were prior to that ime. It is likely, moreover, that public assistance since then has been more adequate to the need than it was at any previous time, even apart from the enormous expansion of the need for such assistance due to the unprecedented and widespread depression of the 1930's. Rubinow has estimated on the basis of rather careful statistics that in 1928 our country was spending through the public relief agencies from $100,000,000 to $200,000,000 a year. In addition, through private agencies we were spending from $60,000,000 to $100,000,000 on outdoor relief, or a total of perhaps $200,000,000 for social work in general. He estimated that this amount was perhaps only one-fifth of 1 per cent of our national income.[6] For the winter of 1932–1933, he estimated that relief mounted to about $1,000,000,000 a year, with only about 10 per cent of this amount being supplied by private agencies.[7]

---

[5] *Consumers Incomes in the United States, 1935–1936,* pp. 18, 96.

[6] I. M. Rubinow, "Can Private Philanthropy Do It?" *Social Service Review* (September, 1929).

[7] I. M. Rubinow, *The Quest for Security* (New York, 1934), p. 350.

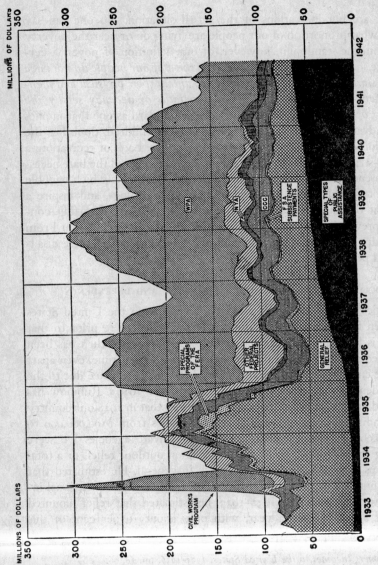

FIG. 13.—PUBLIC ASSISTANCE AND FEDERAL WORK PROGRAMS IN THE UNITED STATES, JANUARY, 1933–APRIL, 1942

Social Security Bulletin (Social Security Board), Vol. 5, No. 6 (June, 1942).

In 1934, the first full year of "New Deal" policies, not less than a quarter of our population was assisted to some extent, either by direct relief benefits, or by work programs, at a total cost of about two and a third billion dollars. The cost of public assistance reached its peak in 1938, with $3,236,600,000 being expended, although the number of persons assisted dropped to a monthly average of approximately 20 millions. More than half of this huge amount was expended in Works Progress Administration projects, while the Old Age Assistance program accounted for more than a tenth, or $392,384,000, of it, a sum more than ten times what it was in 1934; but the number of aged people so helped rose from 123,000 in January, 1934, to 1,776,000 by December, 1938.[8]

What does it mean—no matter whether the cause is the individual's own incapacity or lack of frugality, or social circumstances and economic conditions—that an army of people every year have to depend upon some one other than themselves or their relatives for help? Consider what it means in terms of childhood deprived of opportunities, of sickness that has brought many of these people to need, of the destruction of ambition, of the loss of hope, of despair, of vice, of the sense of futility, and of the lack of self-esteem—of the lack of all that is essential to good citizenship. Consider the slums, rural and urban, where these people live and the bad housing in which they abide, the lack of sanitation, the dirt, the squalor, and all that attends such conditions. Picture to yourself also the economic inefficiency that lies back of this dependency. Think of the changing jobs that have marked the history of these dependent families. Consider the hopelessness with which they looked forward to old age, the destruction of aspiration on the part of their children for something better than their parents had, and the denial of opportunity. Think of the misery and despair of which these things are but indications. Then, above this mass of dependents behold the army of the poverty-stricken, who are not so degraded in spirit, have not lost ambition, have fallen just below the poverty line, and who are struggling against adverse circumstances to attain something of their dreams of prosperity.

Moreover, consider the light that this mass of poverty and dependency throws upon our social stupidity. If we were really a far-sighted people, should we not begin to appreciate that the prevention of poverty and dependency is one of the first steps to economic independence and prosperity? Are not the sums we pay for the care of the pauper a meas-

[8] See "Public Assistance," reprinted from *Social Security Bulletin* (Washington, D. C.: Social Security Board), Vol. 5, No. 2 (February, 1942).

ure of the price of our neglect, and do they not constitute an indictment of our vision? How little insight into causes of social conditions have we when we allow such things to happen without more regard for the consequences! How little social statesmanship we have shown is indicated by these impressive figures. We go on allowing people to drift down from self-support and independence to poverty and dependency year after year and do so little to prevent it. If we looked at the matter simply from the standpoint of good business, would we not make an effort to check this enormous drain upon the resources of the financially able? The average business man is not concerned about it; he cries out against high taxes and forgets that at least 10 to 12 cents of every dollar of taxes is paid for the support of those who have been brought to their present state by reason of his neglect. We have great regard for the engineer in building bridges, constructing roads, and making machines; we do not seem to realize that there is such a thing as *social engineering*. The application of science to the prevention of human misery, the destruction of homes, and the impairment of human efficiency has only just begun to be appreciated by even intelligent people and has not yet been thought of by most of our population.

CLASSES OF THE POVERTY-STRICKEN AND THE DEPENDENT

The poverty-stricken and the dependent fall into many classes. Only a few of these can be mentioned here. Perhaps the outstanding classes are: (1) the dependent children, normal and illegitimate; (2) the mentally defective and diseased; (3) the aged. Let us look at each of these classes briefly in order that we many visualize more concretely the conditions under which these people become poverty-stricken or dependent.

1. *Dependent Children*. All children by the very nature of their age are dependent upon some one. When their parents or other natural supporters are able to care for them, however, the financial aspect of dependency is not important. The only problem then is as to the quality of upbringing that the family is suited to give them. There are problems in such families, of course, but not problems of dependency.

Dependent children fall into several classes. Though a dependent child may have been born in wedlock, his parents may no longer be able to care for him unassisted; or he may have been born out of wedlock and be dependent. With our present social views as to the status of the illegitimate, the latter case is much more difficult to handle. Again, the child may be classed as a dependent child, even though he is living with one or both of his parents, or he may be an orphan dependent child.

In spite of these distinctions, however, the problems connected with dependent children are two: (1) the problem of financial support to enable the child to have the opportunities necessary for his proper development, and (2) social surroundings that will provide for the proper mental, moral, and social development of the child so that he may become a useful citizen.

The problem of the financial support of the dependent child is not a negligible item. As we noted earlier, it costs more to bring the progeny of human beings from birth to adulthood than it does for that of any other animal. A pig becomes a hog in about three months; a colt matures into a horse in about two years; it takes twenty-odd years to rear a baby to adulthood. The significance of this prolongation of infancy for the mental and moral development of human beings can hardly be over-emphasized. A human being is so much the product of his social environment that it requires a great many years to fix in him the habits and ideas necessary if he is to function properly in human society. At the basis of that, however, is the fact that biologically he matures very much more slowly. These two things go hand in hand. In the study made by the Metropolitan Life Insurance Company as to how much it costs to rear a child from infancy to eighteen years of age the conclusion was based upon a study of families with an average income of $2,500. It was found that the cost of rearing a child to that age was $7,250. This figure does not include the cost to the community in the shape of education and other public services, but the cost to the family alone. It is apparent at once that families with small incomes are much more likely to produce dependent children for the community to take care of than are large-income families. While the lack of money is not the only factor that produces child dependency, yet it is apparent that without a proper family income it is impossible to give the children proper attention, provide education, give them a share in the elements of culture, and generate that self-respect and self-confidence which every child ought to have.

Much more difficult than the financial problem in the case of dependent children is the matter of providing them with social surroundings that will conduce to their proper development. Even in the best of circumstances, parents themselves often do not know how to handle their children, with a result that children seemingly with every advantage are poorly adjusted to society and its ideals and standards. Personality of both parents and children is a very important factor in determining the social adjustment of the young, as is shown by the many fine characters that have emerged from childhood environments that appeared to be anything but promising. When the child is taken, for whatever reason, from the surroundings into which he was born, still other problems arise. In the original family relationships to which he has partially adjusted himself, he has built up certain habits, emotional tone, and mental characteristics, all of which are strained when he is compelled to make adjustments in a new home outside his own family. Again, the foster-parents must be of sympathetic temperament and judgment if the strain of reorganization is to be kept at a minimum for the child. This is especially true in dealing with the child burdened with physical defect or mental abnormality. In such cases, there is need for a proper balance between compassion for the handicapped child and firmness in training him to a maximum degree of self-reliance and healthy social attitudes. Unfortunately, few parents or foster-parents, regardless of their station in life, are capable of providing such care; and as a result, a considerable portion of adult poverty and dependency stems from personality warped in childhood.

The Illegitimate Child. It is estimated that 35,000 white children and 40,000 Negro children in this country are born of unmarried mothers every year, which means that about one birth in twenty-five in the United States is illegitimate. Not all illegitimate children are dependent children, of course; but the likelihood of dependency is much greater in such cases; and an increasing number of States are making specific statutory provisions for the care of such children. In 1938–1939, the Social Security Board reported about 8,000 unmarried mothers receiving public assistance for the care of nearly 13,000 children, about one in twenty of all children receiving aid given under the Social Security Act.[9]

Public sentiment condemns most of these innocent children to a position of disgrace, even though the States now are more liberal in the matter of birth registry. Such liberality, however, necessarily releases the father from his just responsibility in many cases, since obviously it is the paternity that remains uncertain. And while, as we have seen, there is greater liberality in public assistance, it still is true that the mother usually is burdened with the support of the child. Even where paternity is established and the father is charged by the court with contributing to the child's support, statistics indicate that collections are discouragingly low.[10]

---

[9] Agnes K. Hanna, "Changing Care of Children Born Out of Wedlock," *Annals of the American Academy of Political and Social Science*, 212: p. 159 (November, 1940).

[10] *Ibid.*, p. 164.

It is significant, too, that some cities have shown that from 40 to 45 per cent of unmarried mothers are also, without question, of such low-grade mentality that it is too much to hope that they can provide their babies with the proper social environment. With low-grade inheritance so common among them, with prenatal and postnatal conditions of care so generally unfavorable, and with economic and social opportunities so limited, it is clear that illegitimate children, as a class, still are destined to a life of hardship, even though important steps have been taken to improve their lot.

Methods of Caring for Dependent Children. Various methods for the care of dependent children have been developed. *The orphanage* is probably the oldest. Such institutions were to be found in the Roman Empire and in early Christianity. The church in the Middle Ages increased the number, and it continues as one of the favorite church charities down to the present time. While it may still have a place for certain types of problem children, opinion is now veering away from it. A second method of caring for dependent children is *the almshouse*. While at one time, even in America, large numbers of children were cared for in the almshouse, in 1923 only 1.1 per cent of the inmates of the almshouses of the United States were children. A third method is by means of *State schools or homes* for dependent children. In 1938, about one-sixth of the 140,352 institutionalized children in the United States were in such schools. Experience has shown, however, that such institutions tend to become filled up with children who are non-placeable. A fourth method of caring for dependent children is *county and city children's homes*. Such homes are apt to be too small and poorly administered for a sustained program of rehabilitation. From the standpoint of pauper child care, they are failures, except insofar as they serve as temporary shelters for delinquent or abandoned children in the larger urban areas. A fifth method is *placing or boarding children out.* This method has been in use for a long time; but because of the lack of supervision, the lack of investigation of the homes into which these children were placed, and the lack of close supervision afterwards, until recently it has not generally been a success. To-day this placing-out of children is looked upon as the most important method of caring for mentally normal dependent children and is now used among about 40 per cent of the dependent children not cared for in their own homes. A sixth method has come into vogue in the present century, namely, the granting of *mother's pensions* to the person having charge of the child. If the home in which the child is found and the mother or other person in charge is a fit person to have charge of the child, and if the administration is carefully guarded, this is a very hopeful method of taking care of dependent children. Such aid is now extended to parents of almost a million children, exceeding by a considerable margin the total number of children under foster-care.

Principles of Child Care. In caring for dependent children, whether born in wedlock or illegitimate, the following principles have been sifted from years of experience:

a. By reason of the fraility of infants it is important that they be kept with their mothers and breast-fed, if possible, until they are at least six months old. At the present time, after all of the work of the past few years in infant welfare, about 1 in every 20 children born dies before the end of the first year of life. The primary principle, therefore, is to take such measures as will insure the survival of the child.

b. Dependent children should have financial support and adequate care, whether placed in free homes, boarded out, or supported by mothers' pensions. That fundamental principle must be kept in mind. Unless support is adequate to provide for food, clothing, shelter, educational opportunities, some degree of culture, kindness, sympathy, and education, the social purpose of child care will not be served.

c. Unless the child is mentally defective or disabled in some way and therefore constitutes a problem child in a special sense, he should be found a normal family home. Normal children cannot be reared successfully *en masse* in an institution. Individual attention and care in the home atmosphere is essential. Moreover, this home must have the elements for successful development of the character if it is to succeed in producing a useful citizen. The careful investigation that is now made by child-placing agencies and the equally careful follow-up supervision are intended to make sure that these fundamentals of care and treatment are secured. These principles apply to the illegitimate child as well as to the child born in wedlock.

2. *The Mentally Defective and the Mentally Diseased.* The mentally defective are likely to become dependent because they do not have the mentality to compete with their normal fellows in the struggle for existence. They find their way into almshouses, or are cared for by public outdoor relief or charitable relief, or by private agencies, or are sent to state institutions where they have to be cared for by the public. The insane and epileptic likewise in many cases are incapable of caring for themselves.

In 1929 it was estimated that 8 per 1,000 of the whole population of England and Wales were mentally defective, a figure which probably reflects the situation in our own country as well. In addition to these patently feeble-minded it has been estimated that at least 10 per cent of the population of our country are so deficient in intelligence that in the complex conditions of city life to-day they find difficulty in supporting themselves and conducting their lives in accordance with our social standards. In Great Britain in 1933 *the insane* numbered 3.7 per 1,000 of the population. In that same year 8 per cent of the total pauperism in the United Kingdom was caused by the dependency of the insane and idiot poor. On January 1, 1940, in the institutions for the insane of the United States were 472,385 persons, or 3.6 per 1,000 of the population. In the United States *epilepsy* is to be found in at least 3 per 1,000 of the general population.

These mentally defective and mentally diseased persons in our population constitute a serious problem that as yet has not been adequately dealt with. Furthermore, in view of the fact that a great many of these people are such by reason of heredity, we have a eugenic problem in connection with them that is of the greatest importance. They reproduce without prudence, and in spite of an enormous infant death-rate, they bring to maturity more children per family than do other people. They cast upon society an increasing burden for their care. The feeble-minded and the epileptic are more likely to become parents of illegitimate children, are vicious in other ways more commonly than normal people, and must be cared for in some way or else they will perish.

At the present time not more than 1 out of 10 of the feeble-minded is segregated, and probably not more than that proportion of the epileptics. In some of our States we are taking proper care of the insane, except that often they are discharged and are allowed to reproduce children even though they have a history of hereditary insanity. They constitute a great class of economic incapables and socially create problems that are very difficult to handle.

The feeble-minded can be handled from the eugenic point of view only by some method that will prevent their reproduction. They can be segregated into *institutions and colonies*, where the higher grades can make a living, and some of them can be trained for certain vocations in which they can make their way on parole. Greater numbers could be let out into society after being properly trained if they were sterilized. A great deal of prejudice, however, exists against *sterilization*, and it is not making the headway it warrants. However, the Supreme Court of the United States has decided that sterilization laws relating to the feeble-minded are constitutional.

In the United States we have attempted to take care of the insane in hospitals, for those who may be curable, and asylums for the chronic cases. No widespread effort has been made to sterilize the insane who have a history of hereditary insanity. This should be done or they should be kept in an institution where they cannot reproduce. Progress has been made in an understanding of insanity in recent years, and we now know that much of it can be prevented. For many years we have given a great deal of attention to *physical* hygiene; we now know enough to proceed to a program of *mental* hygiene, which, if it is carried out in wide areas and under proper auspices, will forestall the necessity of sending many people to institutions for the insane.

The epileptics are particularly to be pitied. Many of them, except for a short time after seizure, are quite capable of work and apparently are normal persons. Yet these people find it difficult to hold a job. They suffer loss of self-respect and usually steadily deteriorate in mind. Only a small proportion of them are curable, but they can be made happy and useful. They can best be cared for in colonies in which they can work and in which they can be properly treated for their disease. However, as late as 1935 only ten States had provided special care for the epileptics in colonies, although several other States cared for them separately in institutions for the feeble-minded or the insane. Colony care has also been provided in some States for the insane and the feeble-minded. These colonies of people working out in the open have proved to be very practicable agencies for handling these defective and diseased people, who constitute a problem that challenges our very best thought.

3. *The Aged*. Less pitiable only than the dependent child is the old person who is nearing the end of his years and has no provision for his care. He may have been, it is true, a worthless member of society; but more often he will be found to have been a useful citizen who was unable to save for old age, who has been deprived of his friends and relatives, or who in his later years has lost his savings, through misfortune of one sort or another. The problem of old-age dependency has been made increasingly more difficult and extensive in recent years both by the growth in the number of aged people in our population and by the development of new conditions in our society that make it harder for people to provide adequately for their old age. We still are inclined to believe that the individual should plan for his own future; yet the ex-

igencies of the years since 1929 have made us recognize that the problems of old age, as we have them to-day, are to a large extent a product of our modern life itself.

It has been remarked frequently that our population is growing older. This does not mean that the period of old age is being extended to more advanced years. It means, rather, that more people are living out a larger portion of the traditionally allotted three score years and ten. In addition we are experiencing a steady decline in the birth-rates, so that the numbers of young people constitute a smaller portion of the whole population than formerly. Thus the balance between youth and age is steadily shifting. Persons over 65 years of age made up only 2.6 per cent of the population in 1850; to-day they approach 6 per cent of the total. On the other hand, the portion of the population that is under 20 years of age has declined in the same period from a little more than a half to about three-eighths at the present time.[11] From this situation, it is clear that an increasingly smaller proportion of younger people is confronted with the task of caring for an increasingly larger proportion of their elders. Furthermore, the years of regular employment are shrinking. Industrial requirements to-day are such that at an earlier age than formerly a man is considered too old to work; while, on the other hand, more of the younger years are spent in preparation for work. In addition, the fact that our population is increasingly urban complicates the problem of old-age dependency. Urban people at any age are much less independent than are rural dwellers. They depend upon one another more directly for the things they need; and there is less opportunity for the aged either to make themselves useful, or even to keep themselves occupied. They find themselves cast aside long before their physical or mental powers have deteriorated beyond the desire for useful activity; and the resulting mental frustrations create a situation hard for both the old people themselves and those with whom they must live.

How Are Old People Cared for in the United States? a. Savings. Why should not everyone save for old age? This has been looked upon as the land of opportunity where everyone who wishes can get a job, where good wages are the rule, and where everybody prospers who is not worthless. That is the popular notion. Doubtless some have no savings because they have not saved when they could. Every study, however, that has been made of the aged has shown large numbers who have been unable to save because of small earnings, irregular employ-

[11] See Louis Dublin, "Longevity in Retrospect and in Prospect," *Problems of Aging*, E. V. Cowdry, ed. (1939).

ment, misfortune, or because of the necessities of caring for other relatives during their best earning days.[12] Thus, savings accounts in 1930
averaged only about $500 despite the threefold rise in the number of ac-
counts from 16 to 53 millions in the fifteen years prior to that time.[13]

b. *The Almshouse*. The almshouse or poorhouse is the last resort of
the dependent in the United States. At the present time more than one
half of the poorhouse inmates in this country are homeless and helpless
old folks. Many—if not most—of them, of course, are not of high social
standing. The stigma these give the poorhouse renders it in many places
abhorrent to respectable old people. However, in some of our States the
movement has developed to make them boarding-homes for old folks
who are infirm and without relatives or friends, and to improve the
physical equipment and the character of the service rendered by the
poorhouse.

c. *Homes for the Aged*. Church organizations, lodges, private phi-
lanthropies, and private individuals have established something more than
1,200 homes for the aged, capable of caring for about 100,000 old people.[14] Many of these homes are of a very fine character. The chief difficulty, however, is that often they have an entrance fee which many
people cannot pay, and furthermore they are quite inadequate in number and therefore touch only a fringe of the problem of the aged poor.

d. *Outdoor Relief*. Many old people are provided for by outdoor
relief (assistance given them in their own homes), by private organizations or by public officials. If this is carefully administered and adequate,
it provides for a class of old people who may have a little home but have
not enough income to care for themselves, and it enables them to continue to live together until the infirmities of old age demand the care
of other people.

e. *Care by Relatives*. Care by relatives is the oldest method and by
far the best, when it is possible, for the care of the aged dependents.
Perhaps a quarter or third of them are cared for in this way, living with
their sons, daughters, or other relatives.[15] Sometimes they are able to pay
their way, but more often they are serious financial burdens. This situation has been modified considerably by the the old-age benefit features
of the Social Security Act; yet the problem will continue to some ex-

[12] Report of the Pennsylvania Commission on Old Age Pensions (1919), p. 11.
[13] Charles Denby, Jr., "Do We Need State Old Age Pensions? Yes," *Annals
of the American Academy of Political and Social Science*, 170: 97 (November,
1933).
[14] *Social Work Year Book, 1941*, R. H. Kurtz, ed. (New York), p. 239.
[15] I. M. Rubinow, *The Quest for Security* (New York, 1934), p. 243.

tent so long as there are aged individuals not eligible for such benefits. At the same time, it must not be overlooked that there are many cases where support by relatives is impossible. The children may have married and have a family that they consider their first responsibility, or the relations between the old people and the children are not agreeable. Living quarters in urban areas are apt to be small and cramped by the presence of the old parent or other relative; and in most cases, there is little that the older persons, especially the old men, can do to be helpful in the urban home, so that the aged person becomes *psychologically* hard to live with.

f. Insurance. Insurance against the exigencies of old age through endowment and annuity policies is an excellent plan. The method, however, is open to the same limitations as is the program of saving for old age, since it is basically the same approach. Every study of the matter has shown large numbers of people are unable to buy insurance without depriving themselves and their families of the necessities of life. Moreover, three-quarters of the policies are of the industrial type, with a face value averaging only a little over $200; and more than nine-tenths of them lapse or are surrendered before maturity.[16]

g. Industrial Pensions. In 1925, 245 firms in the United States had established industrial pensions or service pensions. Twenty-nine of these concerns employed over 25,000 persons each, and together they accounted for nearly three-fourths of the total number of employees covered. In December, 1924, the total number of pensioners of all these firms was only 35,953.[17] Rubinow in 1934 estimated that not more than 100,000 aged persons of a total of some 6,500,000 were provided for in this way.[18] Since workers often change firms, this plan does not meet the exigencies of the situation with respect to industrial workers.

h. Public Service Pensions. The best-known form of public service pension is the soldiers' and sailors' pensions in the United States. In 1941, more than 850,000 such pensioners were drawing over $433,000,000,[19] while Rubinow in 1934 estimated that only 300,000 persons at sixty-five years of age, or more, were receiving federal service pensions of any sort.[20] Doubtless these military pensions have kept many old people out of the poorhouse; but these payments as administered have been a very

---

[16] Charles Denby, Jr., *loc. cit.*, p. 97.
[17] *Industrial Pensions in the United States* (National Industrial Conference Board, 1925), p. 508.
[18] *Op. cit.*, p. 243.
[19] *World Almanac* (1942), p. 107.
[20] *Op. cit.*, p. 243.

costly and often wasteful expenditure of public funds. Since 1920, the civil service employees in the United States Government service have had a contributory retirement system which in 1934 was paying about $43,500,000 to some 44,000 annuitants.[21]

In many States and cities firemen, policemen, and teachers are given old-age pensions after reaching a certain age. In 1930, at least half of the States had pension systems of State-wide scope, and others had pension systems applying to the teachers in only part of the cities. A few of the States also have civil service pensions for other public employees. The number of the aged covered by these pension systems is, however, rather limited, even in the States where they are in effect.

i. Old-Age Pensions. With the number of the needy aged increasing and with the example of old-age pensions in some of the foreign countries, a movement for the enactment of old-age pension laws in the United States resulted in the creation of the Social Security Board by Act of Congress in 1935. A considerable portion of its duties pertains to old-age assistance and annuities, and all of the States are operating under this system. Unquestionably it has helped to reduce the bitter experience of want among the aged, and it will do so increasingly as time goes on. As now set up and administered, however, the Act still does not apply to large portions of our needy aged, since eligibility for assistance is at comparatively high levels, and large classes of the population are excluded from participating in the annuity system. It is unfortunate that these limitations tend to exclude the very classes that need security and assistance the most. It must be remembered, of course, that a system of such proportions involves many problems, and considerable experience is necessary before it can be perfected. It is reasonable to suppose that, as time goes on, the service of the pension and annuity systems in meeting the problem of the aged dependents will increase in efficiency.[22]

CHIEF FACTORS IN POVERTY AND DEPENDENCY

No one case can show all the factors in poverty and dependency, yet a case reveals the concrete realities of the situation better than statistics. Consider the various factors in the following case history:

The John Thomas family. John Thomas had come to an eastern city of the United States from Wales when he was a lad of eighteen. He had been

[21] *Care of Aged Persons in the United States* (Bureau of Labor Statistics, Bulletin No. 489), p. 221.

[22] For a detailed discussion of these various plans for taking care of the aged, see J. L. Gillin, *Poverty and Dependency* (1937, 3rd Edition), Ch. 18.

brought up in a mining community in Wales, and mining was the only occupation he knew. After landing he went to a mining community in Pennsylvania where he got work in a coal mine. He was sturdy, industrious, and
a likeable chap, although he was not especially ambitious and had not many
of the social graces. He had had only a common school education but was
fairly bright and quick to learn.

At the age of 21 he married a girl of 18, whose family lived in this
mining community. Her parents were a rather roving, somewhat ne'er-do-
well family. The father was a hard drinker and a common laborer, frequently
in debt, sometimes in trouble, and consequently the family lived on the verge
of poverty all the time. Her mother was a slovenly woman with a large
family. She was not very bright. The home was located in a rather poor
part of the community and was poorly kept. A younger sister of Thomas'
wife was so mentally defective that she had been sent to one of the state
institutions for the feebleminded. Another was an epileptic in the state
institution for that class of defectives. A brother who could not get on
well in school had become a hard drinker, was sexually loose and became a
vagrant. Another brother became a common laborer and lived a hand-to-
mouth existence. One sister, who was bright, became a school teacher; and
in time she was the chief support of her parents. Two sisters and three
brothers had died before attaining maturity—one in convulsions, the others
from scarlet fever and diphtheria. One sister who was rather slow-witted
at an early age had become the mother of an illegitimate child.

John's family from all that could be learned of his history from his wife,
had been a respectable miner's family in Wales. However, in the family
there had appeared a history of three persons disposed to tuberculosis. Two
sisters and a brother had died of that disease before John came to the United
States. His parents also had died shortly before he left for this country, his
father having been killed in a mine accident and his mother dying of an
attack of pneumonia. John was well but not robust.

When this family came to the attention of a social agency in a mid-western
city, there were five children. The oldest was a girl of eighteen, the mother
of an illegitimate child. The next, a boy of sixteen, not very strong and of
low-grade intellect, had never been able to get beyond the fourth grade
in school. The next was a girl of fifteen who was up to grade in school
but not very well and with a tendency to resist parental control. The two
younger children were two boys of ten and seven respectively who were
weakly, and the older one was behind grade in school.

In 1903 a strike occurred in the mines where John was working, and
he was out of work for a considerable time. For some time he had been
somewhat discouraged with mining, his health was not of the best, and he
desired to get into some occupation in the sunlight. Therefore he moved
his family to a farm some distance away which he rented on shares. With
what little money he had been able to save he purchased the necessary animals and implements to enable him to run the place. During the five years
on this farm he did quite well and had saved in the vicinity of $2,000.
He decided to go west and try farming in a better country. Accordingly he
and his family moved to South Dakota, rented a farm for a few years, pros-

pered, and finally bought a quarter section of land, paid down $2,500 and promised to pay the balance, $1,000 per year, plus interest and taxes. He was doing fairly well when in the first year the hog cholera swept off most of his fine herd and left him behind in his payments. The next year proved to be equally as disastrous by reason of a severe drought which left him nothing for his work.

The next year there was a scourge of army-worms which destroyed part of his wheat; and the Hessian fly and the rust hurt badly what was left, so that he had but a small fraction of a crop, and that was of poor quality. That fall when his corn was in blossom a severe hailstorm battered it into the ground, and, since he had no insurance, left him so far in arrears that the skin-flint creditor foreclosed on the farm. Discouraged, he sold his stock and farm implements, and after he had paid his debts he had $400 left. With this sum he decided to go to a large city of the Middle West and get employment in a factory. The war was at its height, and at once he got a job at fair wages although he had never worked at anything but mining and farming. This work was common labor in the factory but paid a fair remuneration. The family had moved into a rather poor house in a crowded section of the city so that John could be near his work. Here again ill luck was his lot. One day his shirt sleeve caught in an unguarded machine, and his arm was so badly injured that he was idle for about five months. His compensation cared for the family during this time, and he returned to his old position without serious disability. In the factory, however, his health began to fail. He contracted a cold which left him with a severe cough which racked him night and day. Moreover, about this time his wife's health became poor and the doctor finally advised an operation. This required much expense, and the household ran down. While the wife had never been an excellent housekeeper, knowing little of how to save or how to prepare food tastefully and economically, they had been able to get along because until the disaster came on the farm John had earned fair wages. Mr. Thomas kept to his occupation until the slump in industry occurred in 1920. Then he was let out with thousands of others. Weak and discouraged he sought work without success.

While the mother was in the hospital the oldest girl, in charge of the household, began to go out with an attractive but wild boy of the neighborhood. Her father warned her of this boy without other effect than to irritate her. The household was neglected, the younger children left without guidance and control except when the father was home. The fifteen-year-old girl did her best to keep the household going, but was not strong, was busy in school most of the time, and could not manage to meet all of the requirements of the task. The oldest girl was sullen and irritated at the other children. She helped little and was gone most of the time from the household on one excuse or another. For a short time she obtained a job in a ten cent store but was out late at night and would tell her father and the children nothing of her whereabouts. After the mother returned home this daughter was found to be pregnant and some months later gave birth to an illegitimate child. When her condition was discovered, the father had gone to the boy with whom she had kept company and tried to persuade him to marry her. Under duress he promised but at once left for parts unknown. The mother was so ill after she returned that she was unable to look after the home. The younger girl, under the strain of the burden that she had been trying to carry, became ill and ultimately had to be sent to a sanitarium for the tubercular. The eldest boy became unmanageable, was taken into juvenile court, and placed on probation. The ten-year-old boy was getting into mischief in the neighborhood; the younger child was so woefully neglected as to attract the attention of the neighbors. Finally, unable to find work in the community, and discouraged by the difficulties which he faced, and sick, John Thomas set out one afternoon to go to another town in which he thought he might be able to find work. He never came back, and all efforts to find him proved unavailing. A social agency through the neighbors became interested in the youngest child, and another agency made arrangements for the tubercular girl to go to the sanitarium. Finally, in the dire circumstance consequent upon the desertion of John Thomas, the Family Welfare Society took hold of the family in the endeavor to work out a solution. With that solution we are not here concerned.[23]

Let us analyze this case and see the factors that brought this family to need.

1. *Hereditary Factors.* Observe that in the family of John Thomas there is a history of tuberculosis. While one cannot say definitely that the predisposition to tuberculosis was hereditary in this family, it is well known that some people resist tuberculosis and others are predisposed to it. The difference seems to be due in part, at least, to inherited characteristics. Even clearer is the inheritance of mental defect on the wife's side. This seems to be hereditary because it appears in the children of the John Thomas family as well as in the family of Mrs. Thomas. From various studies that have been made, especially of dependents, it appears that 25 per cent of the paupers in almshouses, 10 per cent of the public outdoor paupers, and perhaps 5 per cent of the paupers relieved by private organizations are mentally defective. Of all the feeble-minded, it has been estimated that from one-half to two-thirds are such by reason of heredity. In the remainder the condition is due to accidents at birth, prenatal conditions, and the results following sickness or accidents in childhood. The hereditary factors in poverty and dependency can only be attacked successfully by preventing reproduction. For deficients already born, efforts should be made to adjust the environment to them so that they can make the most of their poor abilities and contribute to their own support as much as possible.

2. *Industrial Conditions.* It will be remembered that a strike in the

[23] Gillin, *op. cit.,* pp. 117-119.

coal mines was the first step in the demoralization of the John Thomas family. From 1901 to 1905, the period in which this strike occurred, there were 2,900 strikes in the United States. These strikes involved some 585,000 workers and continued on the average for about 32 days. In the "New Deal" years prior to the beginning of the Second World War, the number and size of strikes increased sharply, there being nearly 2,300 strikes involving some 582,000 workers as late as 1940; but the *duration* of the strikes, in most cases, has tended to be much shorter than formerly.[24] While it is estimated that the average annual losses from this cause are probably only a twentieth of the total losses from unemployment and industrial accidents and disease combined, it remains true nevertheless that the striker loses the daily wage which he would otherwise have. The resulting curtailment of family income and the irregularity of habit which arise while strikes are in progress, naturally tend to disrupt the life of the family and to upset the well-being of each of its individual members.

3. *Adverse Climatic Conditions and Pests.* Had it not been for the adverse physical conditions experienced by John Thomas in his farming operations, the whole history of the family might have been quite different. The children reared in the country might have turned out otherwise than they did as a result of their return to the city. He seemed to be doing well when the hog cholera swept off most of his herd and the severe drought left him nothing for his work. Then the scourge of army-worms, the Hessian fly, and the rust destroyed most of his crops. Finally a hail-storm destroyed his corn and left him badly in debt. No one knows the extent of damage caused by climate and natural disasters and the pests that afflict the farmer, but there is no question that it is very large.

4. *Sickness.* In this case also we see the physical factor of sickness. Possibly if Mrs. Thomas had remained well and John himself had continued to be healthy, disaster would not have come to the family in the city.

Three-fourths of the cases which come to the charity organization societies come by reason of sickness. When we further consider that in the United States the average member of the population loses thirteen days a year from sickness and that the cost of preventable sickness and death amounts to billions of dollars a year, one can easily see the influence of sickness in producing poverty and dependency.

24 C. R. Daugherty, *Labor Problems in American Industry* (Boston, 1941), pp. 287–289.

5. *Unemployment.* In the Thomas case, as in so many other cases, unemployment was the final demoralizing step in the family situation. Discouraged by all the sad circumstances that had preceded, and unable to get a job, John Thomas left his family, ostensibly to seek work, and never returned. There are many cases, however, where the man does not desert, but is unable to make a living because he cannot find employment. Next to sickness probably unemployment is the most fertile cause of dependency. Careful studies have shown that unemployment ranges from 2 per cent in the most prosperous times among the skilled workers to as high as 25 per cent in times of industrial depression and among the unskilled laborers. Until society finds some way by which it can eliminate unemployment, poverty and dependency are inevitable for large numbers of people, especially those least fitted for the intensive struggle for existence. The unemployment benefit provisions of the Social Security Act are helping to *minimize* unemployment by creating incentives for employers to reduce their labor turnover, similar to the incentives provided in the workman's compensation laws to reduce industrial disabilities. Yet the operation of the Act has resulted chiefly in *regularizing* employment, and to increase to some extent unemployment among the marginal workers—those formerly hired part-time or intermittently —who are the very group upon whom the burden of unemployment rests most heavily.

6. *The Employment of Mothers and Children.* The Thomas case provides illustrative material for the effect of the labor of children outside the home. The oldest girl began to work under the pressure of family need. However, freedom from home restraint and subjection to influence outside the home conduced to the loosening of family control and finally led to demoralization.

Every study made anywhere in this country has shown that the employment of mothers and children outside the home demoralizes the family. The children's physical, mental, and moral welfare is neglected when the mother works outside; often the mothers impair their health, and child labor is usually a sign of inadequate income in the family.

7. *Inadequate Education.* This case shows also the unhappy results that come from inadequate education. Thomas had no broad foundation educationally and was not trained for any particular skilled trade. He illustrates the abbreviated educational life of American children, especially those of the lower economic classes, the lack of a vocational aim in much of our elementary education, and the consequent blind-alley jobs for himself and his children.

8. *Industrial Accidents.* Getting his sleeve caught in an unguarded machine in the factory in which he worked was one more circumstance that diminished the income and discouraged the worker. It is estimated that there are about 15,000 deaths from industrial accidents in the United States every year. A million and a quarter more workers are annually incapacitated, about 100,000 of them permanently, with a financial loss to the nation from such accidents of probably close to $500,000,000 a year.[25] A case study a few years ago in Boston showed that 13 per cent of the intake of the family social agencies of that city was made of families where industrial accidents or industrial disease was a factor.[26]

There are various other causes of poverty and dependency, but these are sufficient to give an insight into the tangled complex of conditions that brings about demoralization of individuals and families in their struggle to make a living. Often these conditions are as inevitable as fate; but sometimes they are the result of the individual's lack of forethought and prudence.

THE SOCIAL APPROACH TO THE PROBLEM OF POVERTY

In the complex conditions of modern society, especially in our cities, it requires careful consideration and adjustment for the individual to find his way from early manhood or womanhood to successful independence. Unless one comes into the world equipped with intelligence and with certain characteristics that produce sound judgment, and unless he is trained to know the complex conditions of the world in which he makes his struggle for life, he is bound to fail. Natural ability must be trained. Out of experience must come lessons for the future. The experience of older and wiser men and women should be heeded by the youth as he starts out on his career.

Our traditional American policy has been to let each man struggle for himself, on the theory that thus the most capable would achieve their ends and the less capable would fail. However, it has been discovered that in this struggle for existence, unmodified by mutual aid and sympathetic help, many who have fine abilities also fall by the wayside. Success or failure in life depends upon the combination of two sets of factors: the natural abilities that have been handed down to us by our parents, and the way in which these abilities are developed by our education, family experience, and life contacts with others. Our philosophy of

[25] *Social Work Year Book, 1941,* R. H. Kurtz, ed. (New York), p. 610.
[26] Pear, "How Boston Meets and Supports its Family Service Program," *Proceedings of the National Conference of Social Work* (1925), p. 489.

"every fellow for himself and the Devil take the hindmost" is not suited to the complex conditions of modern life. Man ought to be able to select better than blind nature. Every effort ought to be made by society to give ability a chance. This does not mean, of course, that we should allow the congenitally defective and incapable to propagate and thus continue their stock. That is quite another matter from giving the capable every chance to make the most of their ability for the welfare of society. Many of our present arrangements, however, do not accomplish that purpose. We allow the degenerates and defectives to multiply with little let or hindrance; we still permit the naturally capable boy or girl too often to struggle without aid, to go into "blind-alley" jobs without advice, to live and work under conditions that invite disease and untimely death. In short, we still quite commonly permit people to be overwhelmed by natural disasters and economic circumstances who, if they were given a chance, might well develop and achieve.

A policy of social engineering is necessary to discover and discriminate between the capable and the incapable, to provide for the incapable protection and direction of their poor capacities (but not permitting them to reproduce), and to give the capable a decent chance to achieve what is in them. While we are attempting it rather blunderingly, we nevertheless are endeavoring to do some of these things through preventive medicine, the care of the sick, mental hygiene, old-age pensions, free public education, various plans to prevent and alleviate unemployment, and taxation systems devised to lay the heaviest burdens of taxation upon those most capable of paying. Much, however, yet remains to be done in the adjustment of *social* to *individual* circumstance in order to enable each person to make the most of his capacities.

REFERENCES

ABBOTT, Edith, *Some American Pioneers in Social Welfare* (Chicago, 1937).

BROWN, Josephine C., *Public Relief 1929–1939* (New York, 1940).

DOUGLAS, Paul H., *Social Security in the United States* (New York, 1939).

DUBLIN, L. I., *Health and Wealth* (New York, 1928).

EPSTEIN, Abraham, *Insecurity, a Challenge to America* (New York, 1938).

GILLIN, J. L., *Poverty and Dependency* (New York, 1937).

QUEEN, Stuart A., *Social Work in the Light of History* (Philadelphia, 1922).

Social Security Act, (Washington, D. C.: U. S. Government Printing Office, Publication No. 271, Seventy-fourth Congress).

Social Work Year Book, R. H. Kurtz, ed. (New York, 1941).

WARNER, QUEEN, and HARPER, *American Charities and Social Work* (New York, 1930).

White House Conference on Children in a Democracy, 1940 (Washington, 1940).

QUESTIONS AND EXERCISES

1. Define *poverty* and explain the significant words and phrases in your definition. Do the same for *pauperism*.
2. What proportion of the people in the United States at the present time are in poverty? What proportion are in pauperism?
3. How do you account for the toleration of such widespread poverty and pauperism in the United States, which has the greatest per capita wealth of any country in the history of the world?
4. Why is it important that children be protected from subjection to stark poverty? How do you account for the fact that some children who grow up in poverty sometimes make very good citizens?
5. What sort of dependent children should be kept in institutions rather than placed in a good family? Why?
6. How could society prevent the tragedy of want and suffering that results from old age?
7. What factors in producing poverty and dependency seem to you the most important?
8. What is the relation between poverty and dependency, and the success of a program of socialized education?

Chapter 17

PROBLEMS OF CRIME AND PENOLOGY

IN PRINCIPLE, the distinction between what we now call the *criminal* and the *delinquent* is as old as the common law, the difference being determined on the basis of the age of the offender. Under English common law, a child below the age of seven was not considered capable of committing a crime. Later the age limit of the juvenile was raised to twelve, then to sixteen, and now it is generally set at eighteen years. The reason for this was that it was believed that the knowledge of the difference between right and wrong was necessary to commit a crime, and a juvenile was not considered as having reached the age of discretion. Upon this distinction between right and wrong rested the theory of responsibility. Hence, in legal parlance, the *criminal* is, in most of our States, an adult offender above the age of eighteen, while the young offender below that age is a *delinquent*. A criminal, according to our legal notions, may be punished; a delinquent is taken into custody by the court for protection.

History shows that often the child actually was treated as an adult criminal, despite the provisions of the common law which limited the responsibility of children in the matter of age. In England, down to a very recent date, children were confined in prison with adults; and occasionally in some parts of our country children are still found in the county jails. However, a little over a century ago some people in the United States began to make the distinction between the criminal and the delinquent. In 1815 in New York City Thomas Eddy, a New York Quaker, and some of his friends began to discuss the importance of erecting a juvenile reformatory so that the children could be taken out of the common prisons.[1] Only recently, after more than a century, could it be recorded that *all* the States now provide juvenile reformatories for their delinquents.

Nevertheless, the criterion of age is not wholly valid as the mark of

---

[1] Bernard Flexner, and Reuben Oppenheimer, *The Legal Aspect of the Juvenile Court* (Federal Children's Bureau Publication No. 99, 1922), pp. 7, 8; George Ives, *A History of Penal Methods* (1914), pp. 126, 130, 179, 180, 234; J. L. Gillin, *Criminology and Penology* (1935), pp. 418, 563.

distinction between the criminal and the delinquent. What about the feeble-minded person forty years old but with the intelligence of a seven-year-old child? Is he a criminal or a delinquent? What shall we say about the adult insane person guilty of a serious offense? The legal distinction between the criminal and the delinquent is sociologically unsound. From the sociologist's point of view, *either a criminal or a juvenile delinquent is one who is guilty of acts believed, by a group that has the power to enforce its belief, to be injurious to society and therefore prohibited.* The only sound sociological grounds for society's taking from the individual his liberty and subjecting him to a course of treatment are: (1) the *protection of society;* and (2) *reformation*, or training the individual so that he may be a useful member of society rather than a menace. As a by-product of the measures necessary to secure these two purposes such treatment of the delinquent and the criminal may result in *deterring* others from the same or similar socially proscribed acts.

From the standpoint of the social purposes of punishment it makes no difference whether these acts are committed by a juvenile or by an adult. It is fortunate, however, in view of the traditional attitude regarding the punishment of criminals, that the distinction between the criminal and the delinquent has been made. Such distinction has made possible under our ancient theory the introduction of sociological methods of treating the delinquent that suggest changes in the treatment of the adult criminal. Here, again, *a little child has led us.* Perhaps some day observation of the results of the treatment of juveniles will lead us to adopt sensible treatment of adults.

EXTENT OF THE PROBLEM

How criminal are we? How can we find out? What does it cost to take care of our criminals and delinquents? Unfortunately, we cannot answer with exactitude any of these questions. In the United States we have official figures regarding commitments to institutions for criminals and delinquents in a given census year, and the *Uniform Crime Reports* record the crime reported to the Federal Bureau of Investigation by the police in our larger cities, which include about half our population. These figures, of course, do not tell us the extent of crime. Many suspects who are charged with crimes are not convicted. Still others are charged with crimes and convicted, but are put on probation or have their sentence suspended. In addition, many who commit acts contrary to law are dismissed because of insufficient evidence or for other legal reasons.

Large numbers of perpetrators of criminal acts, of course, are not even apprehended. Consequently the figures do not give us an adequate measure of the number of criminal acts committed in any year, or of the number of individuals involved.

It is a startling fact that not less than 1 in every 300 of the total population is committed every year to some correctional or penal institution. In 1939, over 66,000 prisoners were received from the courts by State and federal prisons and adult reformatories, which had a total inmate population on January 1, 1939, of over 160,000. It has been estimated that in our 3,700 local and county jails, upwards of 600,000 persons are confined under sentence each year.[2] Among the latter, of course, are a high percentage of minor offenders; yet the number of serious offenses committed in 1940 was estimated by the Federal Bureau of Investigation at 1,517,026.[3] Sellin, in 1933, estimated minor offenses, exclusive of liquor and motor vehicle violations, were in excess of 15,000,000.[4] (This was when the whole country was at the bottom of a severe economic depression.)

As an example of the contrast between our country and Great Britain, Chicago in 1916 had thirty-six times as many murders per 100,000 of population as London; Cleveland, Ohio, thirty times as many as London, while Cleveland had more robberies and assaults to rob than England, Scotland, and Wales put together. Our neighbor Canada had in 1921 no more prisoners than the Joliet State penitentiary of Illinois.

The Cost of Crime in the United States. Various estimates have been made of the cost of crime in the United States. None of these pretends to any great degree of accuracy. The Wickersham Commission in 1931 estimated the annual direct costs of dealing with crime at above $1,119,-000,000,[5] while total costs were estimated in 1937 by J. Edgar Hoover, of the Federal Bureau of Investigation, at between $13,000,000,000 and $16,000,000,000 annually. This latter staggering figure can be easily justified if we take into account such items as the wages of watchmen, the costs of locks and other protective equipment, the losses through fraud, property damage or theft, and the impaired earning capacity of the criminal and sometimes of his victim as well. Whatever be the cost of our struggle with crime, there is no question that it is a heavy burden

[2] *Social Work Year Book, 1941,* pp. 37-44; *Statistical Abstract of the United States, 1941,* p. 85.
[3] *Uniform Crime Reports,* Vol. XI, No. 4, 1940, pp. 202-203.
[4] *Social Work Year Book, 1937,* p. 108.
[5] *National Commission on Law Observance and Enforcement* (Washington, D. C.: Report 12, 1931).

upon the taxpayer and thus diverts money from other uses, such as health
and education.

The Proportion of Each Class of Crime. Among the 1,500,000 serious
crimes estimated by the Federal Bureau of Investigation to have been
committed in the United States in 1940, murder and manslaughter ac-

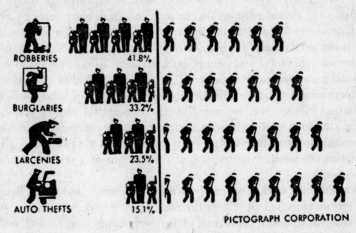

ROBBERIES   41.8%

BURGLARIES   33.2%

LARCENIES   23.5%

AUTO THEFTS   15.1%

PICTOGRAPH CORPORATION

FIG. 14.—HOW MANY ARRESTS FOR EVERY HUNDRED REPORTED
OFFENSES? (UNITED STATES, 1940)

counted for about 12,000; rape, 9,000; robbery, 53,500; assault, 46,500;
burglary, 316,000; larceny, 902,000; and auto theft, 177,500.[6] Other
crimes that came to their attention through their fingerprint service to
the police departments, included about 19,000 cases of fraud and embezzlement, and nearly 29,000 cases involving drunken driving.[7] In England, about the year 1920, 8 per cent of the offenses were against the person, 18.5 per cent against property, and 73.5 per cent other offenses.

Is Crime Increasing or Decreasing? Following the First World War,
a great furore was raised concerning the increase of crime. This was
chiefly "newspaper talk"; the truth being that there are but few statistics
that throw light upon the matter. The Federal Bureau of Investigation
in 1940, basing its estimate on police reports from areas including slightly
more than half of our population, stated that in the previous five-year
period there appeared to be increase in rape, felonious assault, and
larceny, while criminal homicide, robbery, burglary, and auto thefts

[6] *Uniform Crime Reports*, Vol. XI, No. 4, pp. 202–203.
[7] *Ibid.*, p. 203.

showed decline.[8] It is certain that we get used to crimes with which we are familiar; their commission does not impress our imagination. On the other hand, new crimes impress us to such an extent that we feel there is surely an increase in crime. Furthermore, the newspapers, in seeking for the new and the sensational, convey to the reader the impression that there actually is such an increase. However, if one looks back over newspaper discussion and comment in other periods, he will find that every so often there has been a "crime wave." So far as one can tell from the figures, it has been largely psychological. It is also commonly believed that a crime wave follows every war. That may be true. The consensus is that there are slight increases in crime rates following periods of war, and that there is a slowly rising amount of criminality, probably due to the fact of our growing urban settlement, with its greater density of population and extent of personal contact.[9]

Repeaters in Crime. One of the purposes of criminal justice and of the punishment of the criminal is to prevent a man who has once been convicted of crime from repeating his act. We call our institutions "correctional" institutions. How well do they "correct"? Let us see.

In Massachusetts in 1921, of all prisoners sent to the various institutions, 51.3 per cent, and in 1922, 55.1 per cent, were repeaters. In Wisconsin in 1920, of the inmates of the State prison 45 per cent, of the Milwaukee House of Correction 53.5 per cent, had been convicted of crime before. About the same time in the West Virginia State prison 51 per cent, and in the Georgia State prison 42 per cent, were "repeating the course." In Detroit about the year 1920, of 1,800 misdemeanants, 55.4 per cent had had previous contact with the police or the courts. The Federal Bureau of Investigation in 1940 reported that of about 609,000 persons whose fingerprints were sent to the Bureau by police officials of the country, 50 per cent had been previously arrested, while 33.9 had been previously convicted.[10] Among the inmates of prisons and reformatories in 1935, 46.3 per cent were first offenders, and 53.7 were *recidivists*.[11] These figures represent an enormous failure. Practically half of these men have been in difficulty before. What a comment upon our methods of treating the criminal! When our universities send home every year from 2 to 8 per cent of the students enrolled because they have "flunked out," sometimes a great cry is raised against the failure of

[8] *Ibid.*, p. 170.
[9] E. H. Sutherland, *Principles of Criminology* (1939), pp. 31-32.
[10] *Op. cit.*, pp. 213, 214.
[11] *Prisoners in State and Federal Prisons and Reformatories, 1935*, Washington, D. C.: Bureau of Census, (1937), p. 30.

our school system. What if the high schools and the universities flunked half of their students? And yet that is what these figures of recidivism really mean. Half of the criminals in our correctional institutions have "flunked the course" once or more.

It should be remembered, however, that we send to our correctional institutions the failures of our schools and of our communities and then expect those institutions to do what the schools and the playgrounds, the homes, and the probation officials have failed to do. Naturally into our prisons will be sent those who have failed to respond to every other influence to make them good citizens. No more serious criticism should therefore lie against the authorities in correctional institutions for the failure of these cases than is made against the community for the failure to keep them from going wrong. Furthermore, these institutions should not be required to release their inmates when it is known that such individuals are likely to repeat their antisocial behavior. Yet in most of our States the criminal law provides for the ultimate termination of the sentence, in most cases at a very definite period, whether the man has reformed or not. This is a great mistake and accounts for a large part of the recidivists among the inmates of our institutions. These are custodial cases who ought to be kept indefinitely within an institution.

FACTORS IN THE MAKING OF THE CRIMINAL AND THE DELINQUENT

The conduct of every person, including the criminal, is the result, in general terms, of two sets of factors: (1) The native characteristics of the individual handed down in him by heredity from his ancestors, and (2) the various external influences that play upon him as he matures. In order to make more precise the analysis of the factors producing the criminal, we may further divide these two general classes of influence into the following sections: (1) physical environment; (2) physical and mental characteristics of the individual; (3) hereditary characteristics— thus giving special emphasis to the physical and mental characteristics that are inherited, in contrast with those which are developed through the influence of the environment; (4) economic factors; (5) social factors.

The Physical Factors, the Physical Environment. Early in the scientific study of crime and the criminal it was noticed that *crimes vary with geography, the climate, the seasons, and the weather.* Lombroso believed that he had discovered that the minimum number of crimes against the person occurred in level country, a slightly greater portion in areas that were hilly, and the maximum number in the mountainous districts.

On the other hand, his statistics indicated that rape was more common in the level country than in the mountains and hills. Furthermore, he found that the districts of Italy most subject to malaria showed the maximum number of crimes against property. In contrast, those parts of France and Italy where goiter (which may result in cretinism) prevailed had less than the average number of homicides, thefts, and sexual offenses.

It has been observed by certain students that countries with a warm *climate* have a higher rate of criminality against the person, while those in cool climates have a comparatively high rate of crimes against property. Again crimes vary with the *seasons*. In winter crimes against property become more frequent, while in summer the peak is reached in the crimes against the person. This variation of different kinds of crime according to the seasons led to Lacassagne's so-called "criminal calendar." According to this calendar infanticide holds first place in the months of January, February, March, and April; homicide and assaults in July; parricides in January and October; rapes upon children in May, July, and August, with the minimum in December; rapes on adults reached their maximum in June and the minimum in November; while crimes against property seemed to reach the maximum in December and January.

As the result of the discussions which have grown out of these statistical findings it is now generally agreed that *the effects of these physical factors are indirect rather than direct.* That is to say, it is not that cold induces sluggishness, which lessens crime against the person, but that the crimes against the person in cold regions and in the cold season are fewer because human contacts are less numerous during those periods and in those countries. Furthermore, crime against property increases in the cold climates and in the cold seasons because of the greater distress.

More recently some attention has been given to the relationship of *the changes in the weather* to criminality. Dexter's studies indicated that the number of arrests varied quite regularly with the temperature in any given place. He found that as the barometer fell the number of arrests rose, and suggested that this air pressure may affect the nervous condition of people. He found that assaults vary inversely with the degree of humidity and explained this on the basis of the depressing effect of a high degree of moisture in the atmosphere. Similarly, he discovered that on the days when the winds are mild, there is a high pugnacity-rate, while during the days of calm and days of high winds, the number of arrests were less. He found that cloudy days showed the fewest number of personal encounters such as attract the attention of police. Much more extensive investigations will have to be made, however, before these conclusions can be accepted at their face value. Here, too, it is probable that the weather affects conduct, on the whole, indirectly rather than directly. We may hold, tentatively, that in general the physical environment affects man's conduct largely through its influence on his ways of getting a living, its influences on his recreation, the form of occupation that the climate makes possible, the unemployment and therefore the pressure of need due to seasonal occupations, and through the ease or difficulty with which a living is obtained, due to the richness or poverty of the natural resources and the ease with which the resources can be exploited.[12]

The Physical and Mental Characteristics of the Individual. Man in his physical and mental make-up is very much more complicated than any other animal. He has a depth and a breadth of emotional expression impossible to the lower animals. His intellect enables him to discriminate, weigh, and decide a course of conduct in a very much more complex environment than that of the lower animals. His conduct, therefore, more largely than in the case of animals, is the result of his physical, emotional, and intellectual nature. His conduct is not so instinctively determined; his emotions are subject to control by his intellect and consequently find expression in much more devious and complicated ways.

What are the chief physical and mental factors that enter into the production of delinquents?

Consider first the *physical characteristics of the individual.* Society has set up certain standards in its requirements of a human being which can be met only by a fairly well-developed physique. His physical organism must function in certain specific ways in order to meet these requirements. For example, he must have fairly good health; he must be physically well formed and capable of certain economic activities, and his physical appearance must make a reasonably pleasant impression upon those by whom he is surrounded in order for him to get along well economically and personally. If he is not strong enough to work at an occupation that will yield him a livelihood, he is handicapped on the economic side. If he has suffered disablement, either by disease or by accident, it may be impossible for him to hold a job, or he may hold one that pays only a very small wage. Economic pressure may become too great, and he may, by reason of this fact, develop into a thief. Goring's

[12] For a more thorough discussion of the factors of the physical environment see J. L. Gillin, *Criminology and Penology* (1935), Ch. 5.

study of the criminals in Parkhurst Prison, England, showed that the inmates were as a whole physically inferior to the general population of the same age. Similar studies in the United States have shown the same situation. Sleyster, studying the convicts in the State prison of Wisconsin, found that they averaged 1.4 inches shorter than the stature of the average freshman at the University of Wisconsin and 2 inches shorter than the average Harvard student. The Wisconsin convict lacked 1.3 inches of the height of the men and boys who enlisted in the War Between the States, and was 3 inches shorter than the Fellows of the Royal Society of England and English professional men.[13] Moreover, numerous studies of convicts have shown an unusual number of physical defects and diseases.

On the other hand, studies by Healy among juvenile delinquents in Chicago showed that 13 per cent had some abnormality of development as a probable cause of delinquency. From 50 to 64 per cent of the 2,000 juvenile recidivists in Chicago and from 72 to 73 per cent of the females among them were overdeveloped physically.[14] Juvenile physical overdevelopment seems to result in sexual maturity before judgment and self-control have developed equally, often leading to sex delinquency.

Recent studies on the endocrine glands, or the glands of internal secretion, suggest a possible relationship between the functioning of these glands and crime. Research has not gone far enough yet, however, to make certain that the lack of proper functioning of these glands leads to criminality.

The chief mental defects and characteristics that seem to have a bearing upon the making of the criminal are epilepsy, the insanities, and certain emotional disturbances which seem the result partly of inherent tendencies and partly of the individual's reaction to his life's experiences.

Mental defect, or feeble-mindedness, as a characteristic of delinquents and criminals has received marked attention in recent years. The figures differ with the examiner and with different parts of the country as well as with the type of crime. Goring in his study of 948 convicts found that the largest percentage of mental defects appeared among those guilty of setting fire to stacks (52.9 per cent). Then the percentages decrease sharply for arson (16.7 per cent), rape on the child (15.8 per cent), robbery and violence (15.6 per cent), unnatural sexual offenses (14.3 per

---

[13] Sleyster, "The Physical Bases of Crime as Observed by a Prison Physician," *Physical Bases of Crime, A Symposium* (1914), pp. 115, 116.
[14] William Healy, *The Individual Delinquent* (1915), pp. 135, 136 and Book II, Ch. 4.

cent), and blackmail (14.3 per cent), with burglary noticeably less at
10 per cent. Among those guilty of counterfeiting it was practically negligible (3.3 per cent). In the United States figures vary from prison to
prison and from examiner to examiner. There are those who believe that
prisoners are not more often mentally defective than those in the general
population of the same age and sex; others who believe that prisoners are
superior mentally to the free population; and still others who, while ad-
mitting that prisoners show a greater proportion with a low I. Q. than
non-prisoners, nevertheless believe that mental defect, although important in individual cases, in the aggregate is of less importance in criminality than all social conditions. Certainly recent studies have made it clear
that the mental defective is not, because of his defect, predisposed to
antisocial behavior. Rather, his defectiveness operates indirectly. He is
less apt to foresee the consequences of his acts. He is often shunned and
made fun of by others. He is more likely to feel rejected and frustrated
and therefore emotionally disturbed. To compensate, he is more likely
to seek to obtain approval and social status by responding to suggestion
and serving as a stooge for more capable, but more cautious and more
vicious, individuals in a group. In any case, he appears among the inmates
of prisons and reformatories in much greater proportions than among
the free population.[15]

Epilepsy, probably because of our neglect of epileptics, seems to furnish a disproportionate number of criminals and delinquents. Healy, in
Chicago, in a study of 1,000 young repeaters, found 7 per cent that were
known to be definitely epileptic, while in the general population, probably less than half of 1 per cent are thus afflicted.

The *insanities*, thirty-odd varieties of which have now been recognized, have some importance in the production of criminals and delinquents. The number of insane persons incarcerated is considerably
smaller than that of deficients. Nevertheless, extreme mental disorders
sometimes lead to quarrelsomeness and the starting of lawsuits. The person concerned feels that he is unjustly treated, has delusions of persecution, and easily becomes a fraudulent person or even a criminal of violence.

Perhaps even more important are the *emotional disturbances* that result from unhappy life experiences in the young. We have no definite

---

[15] For a more detailed discussion, see Gillin, *op. cit.*, pp. 81–87. In a recent study
of 1,118 inmates of the Wisconsin State Prison and of 629 inmates of the Wisconsin
State Reformatory, 1⅔ times as many prisoners per 1,000 had a mental age of less
than 11 years as the men in the Wisconsin draft for the First World War.

statistics on the number of cases in a given criminal population who have been started on their career of delinquency by reason of these emotional disturbances. Recent studies, however, have shown that a great many young delinquents are suffering from mental conflicts and emotional frustrations which have resulted from unpleasant experiences in their lives. These emotional upsets may result from severe repression at home, lack of appreciation by schoolmates, shock from premature sexual experiences, or from the conflict that may arise between natural curiosity and the moral standards of society. Studies in both the juvenile courts and the schools have shown that many "problem" children are suffering from such emotional disturbances.[16]

Heredity and Crime. The student will sometimes meet the expression "hereditary crime." Naturally the question arises, can crime be inherited? To speak of crime as "hereditary crime" is a loose usage of terms. Crime is a social manifestation in conduct, while heredity is a biological matter. Crime cannot be inherited in any scientific sense of the term. What is meant by those who discuss heredity in connection with criminality is that certain inheritable physical and mental characteristics may result in crime if the environmental conditions suggest or encourage such conduct. Among such traits are the inheritance of early sexual maturity with a lag in mental and emotional maturity, nervous instability, and mental defect. It should be remembered, however, that crime and criminality are social concepts, not in any sense biological or inheritable traits.

Economic Factors. Many writers have called attention to the fact that most of the delinquents belong to the poorer classes, that crimes increase with economic depression and unemployment, and that crimes against property increase in a capitalistic organization of society. There can be no question as to these facts. The question relates rather to the correct interpretation of the facts. Do men steal because they are hungry? Do girls enter a life of prostitution because of need? It is true that some men steal because they are hungry or because their families are in need; and some girls enter a life of prostitution, or that course of conduct which may lead to prostitution, by reason of the pressure of necessity. Unemployment and distress doubtless put upon some individuals a strain

[16] For a detailed discussion of these points see William Healy, *The Individual Delinquent* (1915), Book II, Ch. 10; M. B. Sayles and H. W. Nudd, *The Problem Child in School* (1925) and *Three Problem Children* (1924); S. S. Glueck, *Mental Disorder and the Criminal Law* (1925), pp. 287, 315, 317–318; Miriam Van Waters, *Youth in Conflict* (1925); E. B. Hoag and E. H. Williams, *Crime, Abnormal Minds and the Law* (1923), Ch. 13; *Judge Baker Case Studies*, Ser. I.

that it is impossible for them to bear. On the other hand, some people in the very deepest distress do not commit crime, and some girls in the direst need do not stray from the path of virtue. It is clear, therefore, that in most cases economic factors act indirectly rather than directly. Need becomes a circumstance to which a certain type of individual responds by antisocial conduct. Whether, therefore, the economic factors be direct or indirect in their operations, they provide the stimuli under which certain natures give way and break over the "normal" standards set by society. Statistics on juvenile delinquency and child labor show that there is a very close correlation between them. Moreover, certain trades appear to be especially dangerous morally. Street trades especially are menacing to children. Night work in factories provides circumstances that peril the morals of young women. Working boys have a delinquent-rate from two to ten times higher than that of those who are in school. Boys employed in messenger service seem to be especially liable to delinquency. Compelled to enter all kinds of resorts at all hours of the day and night, they become habituated to scenes of vice and lawlessness that challenge moral standards; and this often results in disaster. Waitresses in hotels and restaurants, commonly living on the smallest of wages and denied the ordinary recreational diversions, are apt to be easy prey to the solicitations of conscienceless men.

Social Factors. The social circumstances of life affect one's conduct. Like the economic conditions, they are a factor in the total environment in which personality develops. If the social circumstances are of such a nature as to bring out the individual's inherent qualities that are adapted to social life and to inhibit those characteristics which lead to antisocial conduct, experience leads us to believe that the individual will develop conduct in accordance with the standards of society. It should be remembered that conduct is the outcome of a double set of conditions, *viz.*, the inherent characteristics of the individual himself, stimulated to expression or repression by the circumstances in which he lives.

The social factors surrounding the individual in our society may be classified broadly as follows: (1) the home; (2) the playground; (3) the school; (4) the community; (5) customs and beliefs; (6) companions; (7) class; (8) religion; (9) the courts and prisons. Frequently social conditions within these areas of social life are inimical to the development of socially desirable personality and conduct. Consider in this connection our discussion of attitudes, group patterns of conduct, and the way in which the conduct patterns of different groups come into conflict in the experience of many persons. In the study of the problem child and

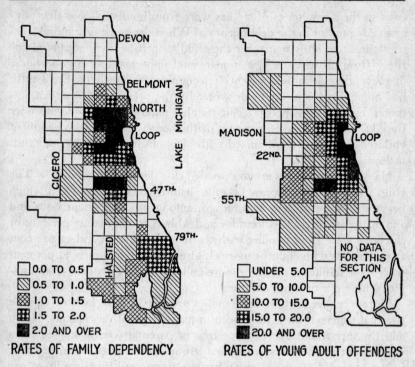

RATES OF FAMILY DEPENDENCY

0.0 TO 0.5
0.5 TO 1.0
1.0 TO 1.5
1.5 TO 2.0
2.0 AND OVER

RATES OF YOUNG ADULT OFFENDERS

UNDER 5.0
5.0 TO 10.0
10.0 TO 15.0
15.0 TO 20.0
20.0 AND OVER

FIG. 15.—DISTRIBUTION OF DEPENDENCY AND CRIME IN CHICAGO

C. R. Shaw and H. D. McKay, *Social Factors in Juvenile Delinquency* (National Commission on Law Observance and Enforcement, 1931), pp. 75, 106.

the delinquent child, and of the criminal man and woman, the results of these clashing standards upon the allegiance of the individual come clearly to view.

The *home* as the fundamental social institution has an enormous influence upon the development of the personality of the children. In the case of the immigrant family, it frequently occurs that the children become Americanized more rapidly than their parents; and thus a great chasm opens between the social habits and traditions of the children and those of their parents. Often, too, the immigrant home is poverty-stricken; and this condition has a decided effect upon the delinquency of the children even from the homes of the native-born parents.[17] A study by Healy and Bronner in Chicago showed that one-fourth of the

[17] Gillin, *op. cit.*, pp. 145-146; Taft, "Nationality and Crime," *American Sociological Review*, pp. 725, 726 (October, 1936).

cases in their new series of studies were from homes so poor that poverty was a factor in the delinquency.[18] When the home is immoral, perhaps the situation is worse for the child than if he were separated entirely from his parents. The fundamental importance of a good home in preventing delinquency is well recognized everywhere. Frequently bad home conditions are made worse by the presence of drunken, immoral, epileptic, insane or feeble-minded parents. Healy and Bronner found that from 20 to 28 per cent of the homes from which delinquent children had come were cursed with alcoholism, immorality, or criminalism.

Many of these homes are so crowded that decency is impossible. The child from his earliest years becomes habituated to scenes from which he should be protected. In Chicago, among 584 delinquent boys and 157 delinquent girls, Breckinridge and Abbott found that 47 per cent of the boys were from families with six or more children and 21 per cent from families with eight or more children. Among the girls 34 per cent were from families with six or more children and 13 per cent from families with eight or more children.

Moreover, even where the families are not broken, lack of capable parental management is to be seen in many cases of delinquents. Healy and Bronner found that extreme lack of parental control ranged from 23 per cent of the cases in the first group they studied to 46 per cent in the second. Extreme parental neglect was found by them in 16 per cent of the second group of 1,000, in which only 5 per cent of the homes were very good.

The lack of *wholesome recreation* in a great city is one of the most potent causes of juvenile delinquency. Undirected use of leisure time is a peril to a child. Thurston found in his study of delinquents in Cleveland that over 50 per cent of his cases spent their leisure time in desultory unguided pursuits.[19] In parallel study of 160 wholesome citizens in the same city, it was found that less than 1 per cent spent their leisure time in such pursuits.[20] No community can afford to neglect playground facilities, with proper supervision of their use, for its children.

The relationship of *education* to crime has often been studied. Very few college graduates are found in our prisons and reformatories. This may mean either that education results in a course of conduct which

---

[18] William Healy, and Bronner, *American Journal of Sociology*, 22: 50, 51 (July, 1916).

[19] H. W. Thurston, *Delinquency and Spare Time* (Cleveland, 1918), Chs. IV, VII.

[20] J. L. Gillin, *Wholesome Citizens and Spare Time* (Cleveland, 1918).

does not end in a prison, or it may mean only that those who graduate from educational institutions do not get caught. There are, however, a number of reasons why the ignorant have a higher crime-rate, other things being equal. The uneducated man usually has greater difficulty in making a living. He has to take a lower wage for his employment; usually he does not have as wide a range of employment open to him; he is less likely to have a varied use of his leisure time and therefore may easily drift into bad companionship.

However, it must be admitted that education in the simple elementary subjects has only an indirect bearing upon the prevention of criminality. It has been found that the type of crime varies with the degree of education. Crimes of violence are more frequently committed by the uneducated, while crimes of skill and cunning, such as embezzlement and forgery, are the crimes of the educated.

Children who do not get along well in school are likely to become truant and to wind up in the juvenile court. Evidently our schools are not yet perfectly adjusted to maintaining the interest of all the children who come to them. Too frequently the children drop out of school from lack of interest and go to work at the first opportunity; and, as we have seen, working children are under special hazard. Too often the schools are built to fit the average student, and too little attention is given to the variant child. The teacher alone, loaded with forty pupils, some of whom present special problems, cannot be charged justly with this result. Consequently the *school system* itself must shoulder the responsibility for making some delinquents in that teachers are commonly too few in number and too often incompetent. Nevertheless, more and more attention is being given to suiting the school system and the curriculum to the needs of the individual child. Some schools are introducing rooms for special classes of students, guidance clinics, and visiting teachers whose business it is to follow up the child who is not doing well in school or who presents special problems, to see that adjustments are made in that child's life and that the school adapts itself to his individual capacities and peculiarities in order to produce a wholesome personality. Too often the teachers are interested only in earning their salaries; but there are some glorious exceptions who follow children into their homes and into their community life in order to help adjust the child to the circumstances of school and community. It is being recognized that the chief business of the school is to form social personality. Mere formal education will not always accomplish that purpose.

The influences in *the community* have a great deal to do with the development of conduct. Young children and adolescents alike are highly susceptible to the attitudes and opinions of the community, more especially of their immediate associates. How often when a delinquent is brought to court the story is told of how he had a good family, and yet had gone astray because of the untoward influences in the community in the midst of which he lives! Sometimes the influences of the community are positively demoralizing. Consider the difficulty that well-intentioned parents have in stemming the effect upon their children of evil influences in the congested district of a great city. The influence of the home is neutralized by the tide of immorality that flows out of taverns, dance-halls, night clubs, and the uncontrolled life of the gang in the alleys, back yards, railroad tracks, or docks of the city. Even when the home is of the best, it has great difficulty in fighting against such influences. This is especially true among the families of the foreign born, whose ideals and traditions seem intolerable to the children who have more rapidly become in a way Americanized in the new environment in which they live.

Moreover, consider the influence of *customs and conduct patterns* that are at variance with the traditions, standards, and ideals of the society in the midst of which a new group of citizens may live. Contemplate the foreign-born family, coming with a set of social standards and traditions from another country, yet subject to the standards and traditions that have grown up upon American soil. Their culture is different in many respects from that which they find in this country; their ideals and customs are apt to be quite different. Consider, for example, the contrast between the sex morals of an immigrant from an eastern or southeastern European country and those which are required in an American community. Struggling with poverty in a great American city, the foreign family sees no reason why it should not take in numerous boarders. Consequently, every available space is occupied, and boarders may even sleep with some of the children. As a result, what we call immoral relations are often established, and the culprits are haled into court. The group mores that held matters in hand in the homeland have weakened and the families have not yet adopted the standards of their adopted country. The drinking habits of many people are a fertile source of delinquency and crime. Numerous studies indicate that of the serious crimes of violence from one-third to two-thirds are due to drunkenness.

Moreover, many beliefs that are at variance with the established standard of conduct become current among certain classes and groups of society. Confirmed criminals are usually cynical and bitter. They see no reason why they should be punished for acts that are similar to other acts which are within the law. According to their standard, open assault on a rich man seems less ignoble than the cautious combinations of fraud sometimes practiced by respectable citizens. The criminal is subject to the public opinion of his own class rather than to that of the general society of which he is a member. Similarly, consider the results of the practice of taking apples from a tree in the country, when such a practice is carried out in the city by taking fruit from a fruit-vendor's stand.

With the social and economic development of a population, classes inevitably arise, both social and economic, and *class hatreds* are likely to develop unless the relations between these classes are very carefully controlled. In every period of social and industrial unrest, of political or economic oppression, class hatreds are bound to arise. Out of these hatreds develop beliefs and standards of action that frequently lead to violation of law. There occurs to one's mind such examples as the violence that often breaks out in industrial strife, the so-called "race conflicts" between the Negroes and whites in some of our great cities and between Orientals and the whites on the Pacific Coast, the religio-racial anti-semitic pogroms in certain European countries, and the friction in America between radical and conservative economic and political groups.

Religion is another social factor that has been considered in connection with crime. One would suppose that a religion which has for its basis the love of one's fellow-men would prevent clashes, would produce tolerance, and would make for peace and good conduct. Curiously enough, however, even Christianity has not always been characterized by such standards. Wars have been fought over religious questions; and study of prison statistics indicates that religion does not always have the effect of curbing the antisocial propensities of men. A study made by Aschaffenburg in Germany has shown that in certain countries of Europe Catholics have a higher criminal rate than Protestants, both of them a higher one than Jews, and all three rate higher than those professing no religion whatsoever. Aschaffenburg suggests, however, that the economic conditions of the people rather than their religion probably accounts for this curious situation. So it must be confessed that religion does not always curb the evil propensities of men. If religion is chiefly of a ceremonial nature it cannot be expected to have much influence upon conduct. The only religion that seems to have a positive contribution to the problem of crime control is a socialized religion, *viz.*, a religion devoted to social ends and purposes.

The courts are the instruments set up by the State to protect the citizens and to bring offenders to justice. On the whole they serve that purpose well. However, it must be admitted that certain practices of the court make criminals instead of curing them. Consider the effect upon the man charged with an offense and brought before a court, who cannot afford to hire a lawyer but has had to take whatever lawyer the court saw fit to appoint to defend him. Whether he is correct in his conclusion or not, he is likely to believe, when he sees rich men defended by very capable lawyers and himself defended by a novice, that justice is not even-handed. The delay in bringing to trial the accused, who perhaps cannot get bail and must lie in jail in contact with hardened criminals, frequently corrupts the young offender. Furthermore, consider the numerous technicalities on which skillful lawyers may cheat justice in the case of influential criminals, in contrast with the speedy hearing and the swift punishment meted out to the poor or uninfluential man. Again, what must be the effect of our theory that no matter what the difference in the persons of different criminals, the same crime merits the same punishment? While the jury is permitted to consider extenuating circumstances, and the judge may in the imposition of sentence consider such circumstances, nevertheless a study of the sentences imposed for crimes shows that even-handed justice is quite impossible under our system. The effect upon the minds of men who feel that they have been discriminated against may be easily imagined. Put yourself in the place of the man who has received a ten-year sentence for a certain crime, when he knows that another man just as guilty of the same crime has drawn a five-year sentence. Those who thus come to feel that they have been unjustly treated may readily develop a grudge against society and turn to crime by way of settling their grudge.

In many of our States our *prisons* are conceived to be institutions for the reformation of the criminal; in others, the theory is that the prison is solely for the purpose of punishing the criminal and then turning him out into society again. If the theory followed by the prison officials is that of punishment alone, then the purpose is to make prison life as disagreeable as possible so as to make certain that the prisoner suffers as much as he made others or society suffer. After that kind of treatment, however, he is likely to go out feeling that he has been mistreated and that he has a right to exact vengeance of a society which has taught him the doctrine of vengeance. Similarly, even under the theory that the prison is for the reformation of its inmates, what must be the effect upon the prisoner's mind when he is treated so that he feels that society, instead of trying to reform him, is brutally punishing him? Moreover, when first offenders are thrown into contact with hardened criminals, the prison becomes a school of crime. Innumerable cases might be cited showing such results from a prison experience.[21]

Civilization itself may be said to account for some criminality. Our social relationships are growing ever more complex. They are most complex in our great cities. Such a civilization requires nice adjustment on the part of the individual. It is easy to imagine the special difficulties that must be felt by the defective or unbalanced individual in his adaptation to the changing requirements of modern urban life. Unless civilization shields and guides him in circumstances in which he cannot fend for himself, civilization itself may be fairly charged with accountability for his delinquency. Again, consider the man reared in the simple relationships of the country who in later life migrates to the city. Often he finds the readjustment quite difficult. If in addition to that he is by nature limited in capacity, his difficulty is doubly great. Or again, contemplate the immigrant habituated to norms of conduct in another country, with different standards from ours, who comes to this country in middle life and attempts to adjust himself to the complex conditions of one of our great cities. Here, again, if civilization does not give him help and guidance, the very complexity of the life in the midst of which he lives will be too much for him. Or, again, consider the immigrant who in his native country has never had a chance to vote—a simple peasant man who worked hard and had to be content to have some one else govern him. He comes to this country and after a few years the ballot is put into his hands. Too often instead of the conscientious citizens of the country teaching him the spirit of our institutions and preparing him for good citizenship, some political boss helps him get his naturalization papers and then through money or influence controls his vote. Such a man is not a criminal in any true sense of the word: he is simply an uninstructed citizen, much less culpable than the man who buys his vote.

When we consider all these conditions surrounding every individual from childhood to old age, realizing that there are great gulfs between the opportunities of different groups and that a considerable number of

---

[21] If the student is interested in reading examples of such cases, let him consult Donald Lowrie, *My Life in Prison* (1912), or Victor Nelson, *Prison Days and Nights* (1932).

our population is somewhat defective mentally, while others lack in education, even though good training to meet these complex conditions is essential to good citizenship, we decide that it is remarkable that no more become criminal. The marvel is that so few fall by the wayside, considering the few and bungling arrangements made by society to help the individual in that great adventure of adjustment to the requirements of social life.

METHODS OF DEALING WITH THE DELINQUENT AND THE CRIMINAL

The Police. The police and other law enforcement officers are the first persons who deal with the criminal. Their chief functions are to preserve order and to arrest and bring to trial those who disturb the peace. Until recent years we have had very few police schools in the United States, and consequently most of the men are untrained except for the practical experience they get on the job. In recent years, however, the Federal Bureau of Investigation has embarked on a program of training groups of selected men sent to their school by coöperating local departments. These men generally are relaying the benefit of their training to their fellow-officers in their own communities, often by more or less formally organized classes. This is an encouraging start, but we still are far from giving our police any special training for their job comparable to that which we give our professional groups or even our skilled tradesmen. But the police of our cities are in most instances much better equipped for their work than are the sheriff and his deputies, or the town constable. Few college men, indeed, look forward to a career in the police. The policeman is often appointed because of his friendship with some politician, or if a sheriff, he is elected by popular vote. If a town constable, he may be appointed by the mayor or elected by the city council or the town board. So long as our civilization was a rural or semi-rural one, almost any man could be a good peace officer. With the growth of our large cities, however, the responsibilities of the policeman have very greatly multiplied. If he is to fulfil his responsibilities, he must be a very much higher type of man; he must be trained for very difficult duties and should be selected with the greatest care. The office of policeman is not looked upon with great favor because of the kind of men who have been appointed to it in the past. The policeman is the butt of all the jokesters and is a favorite theme for the cartoonist. He is usually pictured as quite stupid, large of person, and fat of head. Yet in this man's hand lies the protection of the person and property of the people of our cities. He must know the law and the court decisions as to what a policeman

may do and what he may not do. He may be the bogeyman with which
to scare children, or he may be a constructive force among the childhood and youth of his beat. He may be the one to turn the erring feet
of youth into the paths of good conduct, or through his bungling and
lack of understanding of human nature he may be the means whereby a
reckless youth is turned to destruction. He must not only arrest offenders, but he must also discover evidence on which a trial can be based. He
must understand criminals and their ways, but he must also understand
the psychology of the non-criminal population. A good law enforcement officer can do much to prevent crime.

A new day is dawning for the policeman. We have just begun to appreciate the great opportunities and responsibilities he has. Some day he
will be selected and trained with much greater care; perhaps then we
shall look upon him with as much regard as we give the school-teacher
or the banker. It has been charged that at the present time the police
make as many criminals as they catch. Most of them do not know how
to handle juveniles, and it often appears that they do not understand
how to get along with adults. If ever the policeman measures up to the
opportunities that are his, he will be one of society's finest agents for the
prevention of crime, as well as for its detection and punishment.

The Courts. After a man is arrested, he may be placed in jail to await
trial or let out on bond. In due time he comes before the court for his
trial. He may plead either guilty or not guilty; if the latter, he stands
trial for the charge against him. As our courts are organized at the present time in this country, the trial is a legal battle between the prosecutor
and the defender. The judge is pretty much an umpire in a game. He
conducts the game according to rules of procedure that in many instances
seem quite outworn and technical. The statute covering the offense tells
the judge within what limits he may sentence the man if he is found
guilty. The jury hears the evidence, and in some States the jury decides
what law should be used, as well as what evidence shall be admitted. It
decides whether the man is guilty or not guilty and in some States decides the punishment. In other States the judge pronounces the sentence
and metes out the punishment. In case the man is acquitted, the whole
matter is ended, except for his attorney's fees. If he is convicted, the law
provides for appeals on the part of his attorney to the higher court, on
the theory that every chance should be given to the man to prove himself innocent. However, in the course of time so many technicalities in
regard to court procedure have been developed that it is very difficult
to convict a man who is able to hire good lawyers to defend him. Thus,

for example, a study in St. Louis County, Missouri, showed that of 443 suspects for whom warrants were issued, 137 pleaded guilty, while only 26 were found guilty by the court.[22]

Could we study the number of appeals and the disposition of the cases on appeal, and could we look into the minds of those who escaped punishment and those who were punished, we should have a more adequate picture of the failure of the courts in the administration of criminal justice. Then we should be prepared to appreciate the truth, even to-day, of President Taft's statement that the administration of criminal justice in the United States is a disgrace.

Here and there, however, States are making improvements in the courts which give promise of making them more adequate to their social purposes. Increasingly the courts are making use of clinics in order to study the individual who is on trial. Laboratories to determine how to classify the convicts, and how to fit the treatment more perfectly to the needs of each individual are being introduced in both courts and correctional institutions. Similarly, the juvenile courts more and more have the services of expert psychologists and psychiatrists to aid them in determining what to do with the juveniles who come before these courts. Thus, step by step, science is being introduced into the determination of the nature of the offender in order that the institutions provided by society for his treatment may better perform their duty.

Probation is another device to mitigate the maladjustment of criminal justice to the needs of the individual. We still retain the old theory that the lawmaker should say just what treatment should be handed out to each individual who contravenes a certain law. However, that has worked so unjustly that we have developed a procedure known as *probation* by which the judge is empowered in certain cases to use his discretion as to whether he will send a convicted man to an institution, or whether, in view of all his characteristics and the circumstances surrounding his offense, he might not better suspend sentence and put the man in charge of some one who will give him careful supervision. If probation is carefully used and applied only to those who give promise of doing well at liberty under supervision, and if the probation officers take an active, sympathetic, and wise interest in the person committed to their charge, probation is a most beneficial expedient. The man is saved the stigma of a prison sentence, is put to work, and his earnings are devoted to his family or saved for himself; and, most important, he himself may be redeemed.

[22] *The Missouri Crime Survey* (1926), pp. 154, 155.

Juvenile reformatories were devised to remove from prison juvenile offenders. They are now usually called "training schools." The history of these institutions has not been reassuring. Too often those in charge of them have been men and women without special qualifications for their difficult tasks. As a consequence, they have been largely juvenile prisons. In a study made by Dr. Miriam Van Waters a number of years ago of some twenty-eight girls' industrial schools in the United States, only six were found that were doing constructive work. In all these six cases the schools were manned by people who understood children and youth. Under such circumstances they are valuable institutions, because there are children who will fail on probation and who need an institution in which they may be trained and their habits may be rebuilt for good citizenship. On the basis of experience we may say that a State must place in charge of these institutions trained men and women who understand young people and who know how to arrange matters in the institution so as to bring a new viewpoint on life into the minds of the youngsters. They must be able to awaken idealism and to get the juveniles to form habits of conduct in accordance with the standards of society. Without capable supervision such as this, juvenile reformatories are worthless and may even be schools for crime.

Adult reformatories were started in this country with the establishment of the Elmira Reformatory for Men in New York State in 1876. This was an experiment in applying reformatory methods to young men. It was limited in its original intention to first offenders who had committed certain offenses. Schools were established to provide elementary education and certain trades. In addition, the attempt was made through military drill and physical exercise, medical service, religious services, and certain classes in citizenship and ethics, to bring before the young men new ideals, to establish new habits, and to prepare them to live as useful citizens after their release. Elmira was copied in a large number of States, in most places with somewhat indifferent success. With a few rather notable exceptions these institutions have turned out to be merely young men's prisons. Here, as in the case of the training schools, the difficulty was that those in charge of them were persons not fitted by native endowment or by training to handle these difficult problem cases.

Another method that has been devised to adjust treatment to the individual offender is *the indeterminate sentence*. Unfortunately, the term is a misnomer. It is not absolutely indeterminate but is limited by statute within maximum and minimum lengths of time, the former being reckoned as what the prisoner would have been given in a determinate sentence. The indeterminate sentence, moreover, is invoked only for younger first offenders and for certain types of crime. It must be admitted, however, that it has made the retention of men in prison variable, some being retained longer, others for less time than they would have been under definite sentences. Therefore even the limited indeterminate sentence means some social advance. The sentence, however, should be absolutely indeterminate. That is, termination of confinement should depend upon the judgment of those who know the man best and are best qualified to determine when he is fit to go back into society.

Closely connected with the indeterminate sentence is *parole*, another method of individualizing the treatment of offenders. While probation means supervising the man *before* he is sent to an institution, parole means that *after* a man has spent time within an institution and has shown by good conduct the possibility of his doing well on the outside, he is released under supervision of parole officers. Here again, inefficient officers have been the rule. Without special training for their tasks, frequently they have not understood how to handle the parolees, and they have been too few in number to have adequate contact with their charges. Often men have been paroled who should never have been admitted to parole outside the institution, and as a consequence this method has not had the hoped-for success. The legal limitations on parole, such as that a man may not be paroled until he shall have served half of a definite sentence or the minimum of an indefinite, have hampered its usefulness. In spite of all these drawbacks, however, parole as a method of individualizing treatment has great possibilities under an adequate number of well-trained officers. No one knows how large a percentage of those paroled have done well. Originally the estimates were as high as 85 per cent. The tendency in recent years has been to scale down the estimates, as a result of more careful follow-up and study of these men. But if 50 per cent, or even a third, of the men do well on parole, it probably has justified itself. With carefully selected men for parole, with capable and sufficient officers, parole would be one of our most promising devices for the redemption of offenders.

Our most stringent penal institution is the *prison*. To this institution are committed those convicted of the more serious crimes and those above a certain age who cannot be committed to the reformatory. Its history has been a sad one. Usually the prison is run under the strictest discipline, the rule of silence between the men is common, and frequently the institution is officered by men who have no special qualifications for the task, either by nature or by training. From the standpoint of reforming men and restoring them to society as good citizens, it has been a colossal failure. Even the highest officer in a prison, the warden, usually has had no special educational background for his work. The lesser officials are still less adequately prepared. Hired for a wage that will not attract many capable men, the guards for the most part are uninspiring, repressive automatons. We shall not have different prisons until we pay as high salaries to a warden as we pay to a university president, and select him as carefully. Perhaps we should not expect that the same standards would be applied to guards and to college professors. Nevertheless, it is probable that until we pick these lesser prison officials with at least as great care as we select high-school teachers, we shall not get far in making our prisons really reformatory institutions.

Our prisons go on year after year failing to reform half, or even more, of the men in them. Too often a prisoner's history is that he comes first into the juvenile court, where he is put on probation. Failing on probation, he is sent to the training school for boys. After release there he finds his way to the reformatory for men, and finally he winds up in the prison. After a certain number of years he can go out into society again (in some of our States, at least, even if he has been sentenced for life), provided he has a history of good behavior in the institution. We should recognize that in the prison we have two general classes of inmates: (1) those who ought to be subject to custodial care as long as they live and ought never to be permitted outside, and (2) those who have seen the error of their ways and have decided to reform. The latter should be let out into society as soon as they are fit to return. Every effort within the institution should be bent to prepare them for social life. Cutting across both of these classes are those offenders who are such by reason of their native incapacity or by warps in their nature. These we should treat as such, using our best efforts to retrain them for normal life on the outside. Those who cannot thus be retrained should be kept as custodial cases during their lives.

As we look back carefully over the history of the treatment of the criminal, we see that here society has made one of its most dismal failures. It fails in its detention of the offender before his trial; it fails in its court procedures in trying him. Again it fails when he is sent to an institution that is not properly equipped or manned to exert society's pressure to change his way of life. It often fails by putting the wrong person on probation or by releasing the wrong person on parole and by giving improper supervision in either case. It fails also in its retaining the definite sentence for a great many offenders under the law and releasing them whether they are fit to go back into society or not. And it fails in not applying good educational measures and principles to the treatment of the offender whom it is trying to reform.

We are only just beginning to utilize science in the treatment of the criminal. After all, the place to begin on this problem of crime is at the beginning. Here, again, the old saying is true that an ounce of prevention is worth a pound of cure. If our researches show that the lack of playgrounds makes for criminality, that slums produce offenders against society, that the school is failing to set the feet of young people upon the right path, that even the church may be failing in the great task of directing young people into the paths of social righteousness, that our economic system frequently drives men into crime, or that certain aspects of our political system promote criminality, then we have the keys to an effective program of attack on the problem of crime. Steadily year by year, as our capacities to do so increase, we must apply the fuller and more accurate knowledge which we develop in psychology, in sociology, in education, in religion, in politics, in economics, to adjusting the conditions of life to each person so as to enable him to function so far as possible to the best of his innate ability.

From our research in heredity we learn that certain people born into the world are unable to function under the present organization of our social life. Eugenics suggests that certain of these people should be selected for non-propagation. If we applied as much good sense and science to the production of our human population as we do to our animals we should solve this aspect of the problem in a very short time. The feeble-minded, certain classes of the insane, epileptics, the mentally abnormal, and other defectives challenge us to give our attention to this problem of the racial stock. Some people are less capable of adapting themselves to the social requirements of life than others. Either we must eliminate those incapable of making adjustments, or we should throw about them the protecting arm of society, that is, adjust society's requirements to them rather than make demands upon them that they are incapable of meeting.

REFERENCES

Aschaffenburg, Gustav, *Crime and Its Repression* (Boston, 1913).
Barnes, H. E., *The Story of Punishment* (Boston, 1930).
Gillin, J. L., *Criminology and Penology* (New York, 1935).
———, *Taming the Criminal* (New York, 1931).
Glueck, Sheldon, and Glueck, Eleanor, *Preventing Crime* (New York, 1936).

McKelvey, Blake, *American Prisons* (Chicago, 1936).
Overstreet, H. A., *We Move in New Directions* (New York, 1933).
Parsons, P. A., *Crime and the Criminal* (New York, 1926).
Sutherland, E. H., *Principles of Criminology* (Philadelphia, 1939).
Taft, Donald R., *Criminology* (New York, 1942).
Tulchin, S., *Intelligence and Crime* (Chicago, 1939).
Wilson, Margaret, *The Crime of Punishment* (London, 1931).
Wood, A. E., and Waite, J. B., *Crime and Its Treatment* (New York, 1941).

QUESTIONS AND EXERCISES

1. What is the sociological definition of a criminal? Explain the implications of significant words and phrases in your definition. What interests has society in dealing with the criminal?
2. What is the legal distinction between a criminal and a delinquent? Of what value is this distinction in handling the juvenile offender? Might the same principle be extended to certain classes of adult "first offenders"?
3. How extensive is the problem of crime? Is its seriousness to be measured only in quantitative terms? What other losses might well be considered?
4. List and briefly characterize the factors contributing to crime.
5. Would you agree that "we are all potential criminals"? Or is the criminal inherently "unbalanced"? Explain your position.
6. How may a visiting school-teacher aid in the development of personal attitudes that will prevent delinquency? A child guidance clinic? The church? The Boy Scouts? A playground?
7. Suggest important changes that could well be made in our institutional treatment of the delinquent and the criminal, giving reasons for the suggestions you make.
8. Show the importance of "follow-up" work in reforming the released criminal and delinquent.

Chapter 18

SOCIAL ATTITUDES AND SOCIAL PROBLEMS

THESE VARIOUS SOCIAL PROBLEMS we have been discussing are the results of imperfect socialization, meaning by the term *such adaptation of the individual to the requirements of the group in which he lives as makes his conduct conform to the purposes and ideals of that group; and such adjustment of the machinery of the group, including its ideals, its mores, and its behavior patterns, to the capacities of the individuals in the group as to provide the individual with a degree of expression of his basic wishes adequate to enable him to function happily and usefully in his social relationships.* In other words, the *individual* unable to adapt himself to the requirements that the group has laid down for its members creates problems for that group. These problems may be problems of poverty, of crime, of immorality, of family disorganization, of ill health, and of the breakdown of group solidarity. On the other hand, if *society* has not adjusted its behavior patterns to the capacities of its individuals and has failed to provide in its social institutions and the organization of its life for the less capable members of its group, or if it has failed to provide for the superior members of its group the opportunity to express their fundamental social urges in socially constructive ways, we have lack of socialization.

From the standpoint of social psychology, this adjustment between the individual and his group and between groups within a society depends upon the creation of certain uniformities of patterns of action, of feeling, and of relationship. We might say these social uniformities constitute the framework of our organized society. They define the limits of tolerance beyond which the individual or minority dare not go if they expect to avoid trouble. Obviously society would quickly disintegrate unless its members respect these social standards and coöperate in their enforcement. As indicated in Fig. 16, there is a negative limit to our tolerance, a limit characterized by such ideas as "doing too little," "being too careless," or "failing to provide." There is also the positive limit to our tolerance, suggested by such popular expressions as "going too far," "taking the law into one's own hands," or "disregard of the public welfare." Society has created the *formal* agencies of government to safeguard these limits; and the individual who violates them flagrantly is taken out of society and put where he has time to mend his ways. But perhaps even more significant than the stern clutches of the law which guard society's limits of tolerance, is the power and force of society's *informal* controls. Long before the formal limits of tolerance are reached,

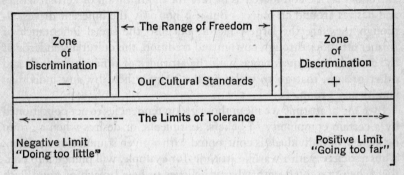

FIG. 16.—HOW WE SET AND ENFORCE STANDARDS OF CONDUCT

the erring one finds public disapproval, criticism, and disdain, which make his way lonesome and uncomfortable. He is still in society, but he is in a zone of adverse discrimination. Society grants full freedom only to those of its members who respect the cultural standards; and it saves its praise and rewards for those who contribute to the strengthening and defense of its common interests and aims.

Fundamentally, the uniformities of culture patterns rest upon the creation of certain attitudes of individuals and of groups toward each other and toward life experiences. Hence the importance of diverse attitudes on the part of individuals and of groups in bringing about those maladjustments which create social problems, and of uniform attitudes as the fundamental condition of their solution. Thus, diverse attitudes by individuals toward the obligations of marriage and the duties of the different members of the family give us our divorce problem, our problem children, and our homes broken by desertion. The different attitude of the trade-unionist from that of the employer gives us our labor problems. In this way also we may account for the international friction lying back of international conflicts, of "race" and culture conflicts. Had the criminal and the judge the same attitude toward conduct, we should have no crime problem. So with the other problems.

An *attitude* is a tendency to act in a certain way. Many things go into the making of an attitude, but in general all attitudes rest ultimately on original human nature modified by custom, tradition, and social contacts. The inherent drives of the individual, such as hunger, sex, and self-preservation, are at the basis of the individual's attitudes. The wishes, desires, and appetites are the strongest factors in their formation. In fact, attitudes may be considered as merely the mobilization of certain wishes and desires around an object.[1] But it is not only the inherent drives, although they are the largest factor, but also the social inheritance of former attitudes through custom and tradition, the cultural standards of the group, and acquaintance with the attitudes of other individuals and other groups, that go to make up the attitude held by any individual and by any group.

By a *social* attitude we mean those group tendencies to act conditioned by a certain community of beliefs, sentiments, or desires when a group or society of individuals is confronted with a given stimulus or situation. Thus a society with a warlike attitude, for example, will plunge into conflict when presented with what it believes to be a breach of good faith on the part of the potential enemy. Obviously, social attitudes are based to a certain extent upon the behavior patterns common to the individuals making up the society. A social attitude is usually more than the mere sum of individual attitudes concerned, but it is impossible to have a group attitude without having at least the majority of individuals composing a society sharing common beliefs, sentiments, folk-ways and mores.

FACTORS CONDITIONING ATTITUDES

An attitude, we have seen, is in its simplest sense merely a tendency to act. The interesting question in this regard is: Why do we find ourselves with tendencies to act in certain ways and not in other ways? In other words, why do we behave as we do? In answering this, we shall have gone a long way toward explaining many of the problems that confront society, for in so far as we can control certain antisocial tendencies to action, we can eliminate some maladjustments resulting therefrom. The factors conditioning our attitudes must be classed under the two familiar but all-inclusive heads of (1) *heredity* and (2) *environment*.

In the first place, every individual comes into the world with a certain *heredity*. We behave as human beings because we are human and are descended from a long line of ancestors who were human. Obviously our human heritage determines attitudes both by *limiting* certain actions

[1] R. E. Park and E. W. Burgess, *Introduction to the Science of Society*, p. 435.

and by *prompting* certain others. Thus, no normal man has a tendency to swing about the trees by his tail for the very sufficient reason that he has not inherited a tail. On the other hand, all animate beings require oxygen; but human heredity prescribes that this be obtained only from the air, which necessitates the act of breathing through the lungs.

In a deeper sense, however, biology has revealed to us enough concerning inborn tendencies to show us that each individual's social behavior depends somewhat upon the characteristics that have been transmitted to him by his parents through the germ-plasm. Not only are such things as the color of our eyes, skin, and hair or the structure of our teeth determined by heredity, but also the basic nervous organization of each individual depends upon his inheritance. How much these inborn characteristics or tendencies determine our responses to given situations we do not yet know. We are quite certain, however, that they determine our bents and trends in a fundamental way.

We also behave as we do on account of our reactions to the experiences of life—in other words, because of the effect that *environment* has upon our inborn equipment. By environment is meant every element surrounding us in life. Obviously the history of an individual's life is largely the account of how his hereditary equipment adapts itself to the stimuli of the environment. Neither the inborn equipment nor the external stimuli can be considered alone in studying the history of any organism. For our purpose, however, it will suffice to consider the environmental factors under the two headings, *physical* and *social*.

Physical environment is obviously the basic form of external influence. There is a school of anthropogeographers who maintain that the institutions of mankind and the reactions of individuals are, directly or indirectly, the results of natural surroundings. To what extent this is true we are yet unable to say. Nevertheless, there seem to be substantial grounds for belief that our physical surroundings have something to do with the way in which we behave. A large number of theorists have attempted to show the importance of the physical environment upon human social behavior.[2] The modern student of social problems, while realizing the importance of physical environment, must avoid giving it too much emphasis.

Even more important than the surroundings of physical nature is the human or *social environment*. Individual personalities are the primary factors in our social environments. From our earliest days as infants we

[2] See Pitirim Sorokin, *Contemporary Sociological Theories* (1928), Chs. II, III, for a critical review of these theories.

are subject to almost unceasing stimulations and checks from other human beings. Our mothers, our nurses, our playmates, our neighbors, our school friends, our college friends, and the personalities who influence us through their books, their pictures, or their music, all stimulate us to respond in one fashion or another. All unconsciously our characters are formed by the way in which we respond to these circumstances of life.

Pressing upon us like an atmosphere of which we are mostly unconscious, and to which we respond by acquiescence or revolt, are the *patterns of behavior* that have been set up as approved by the members of our group. In the family into which we were born certain types of behavior are tolerated and others are tabooed. Adjustment to these patterns of behavior is enforced in different ways by parents. Every group into which we enter thereafter, like the neighborhood play group, the church, the school, the gang that meets on the corner, the little group accidentally meeting at the crossroads store, has patterns of behavior to which we must respond in one way or another. The most common mode of response is acquiescence. These groups have appropriate means by which to bring the recalcitrant individual into line.

It is apparent that at times these various groups present us diverse and even contradictory patterns. When we become conscious of this difference in attitudes, a conflict arises within us. These conflicts provide the problems of maladjustment for the individual. Out of such conflicts within the personality grow those emotional upsets which explain certain types of delinquency elucidated by Healy.[3] They set the stage for the psychoses so often popularly called "insanity." Problem children often are such by reason of emotional tensions due to unsolved conflicts of choice between varying social attitudes. To which pattern the individual will conform is a problem that he must settle for himself. Problems of adjustment also arise for the individual when group attitudes surrounding him change, as often occurs when a person moves from one culture to a new one, when a family changes residence from one neighborhood to another, or when a child develops into adolescence.[4]

In somewhat the same manner as the individual's attitudes are affected by heredity and environment, so also are the group attitudes. A community's attitude toward social affairs may thus be analyzed as the result of the type of stock that makes up its population, the character of the climate and of the physical surroundings, and the contact with and

[3] *Mental Conflicts and Misconduct* (1919).
[4] Thomas has worked out the consequences for the migrant in his (and Znaniecki's) *The Polish Peasant*, and for the adolescent girl in *The Unadjusted Girl*.

effect of the attitudes of other communities upon it. The backwardness of certain small New England communities has been attributed to the fact that the inhabitants who were most vigorous both mentally and physically have gone away. An important factor in the backwardness of Kentucky mountain communities, to cite a familiar example, is their geographical isolation and the poverty of natural resources. The enthusiasm aroused in a "better cities" contest, of which there have been recent examples in several States, illustrates the stimulation of community attitudes by the attitudes of adjoining groups.

LEADERS AS AGENTS IN THE FORMATION OF SOCIAL ATTITUDES

Masses of people seem to have an ineradicable need to bow down not only to great ideals but also to individuals who in their eyes represent such ideals.[5] Personification is an essential element in the formation of social attitudes.

Newton, for example, made the world a rational place in which to live. If the universe is but a machine all that is needed to understand it is a clear, logical, deductive reason. It was to this point of view that Newton turned the thinking men of the world. The Newtonian world of orderly and harmonious law worked itself out in religion, in the new social sciences, in government, and in morality.[6]

Napoleon, to take an example of a leader of action, though a small man and a foreigner, was able to inspire his French soldiers to the greatest military exploits in history up to his time. It is said that Napoleon never argued, but simply ordered. His indomitable self-confidence is recognized as one of the causes of his success.

Whether a man is a leader of thought or of action, there are two essentials in his character: (1) a significant individuality and (2) a broad sympathy. The first is necessary in order that people may feel that he has something to give them which they do not have. The second is essential if the leader is to influence large numbers of people; if he is to make himself intelligible to potential followers of limited and diverse understandings.

Leadership is both a cause and an effect, but it can hardly be considered apart from its social background. In one sense, the leader merely focusses the social attitudes of his time in some definite direction or about some definite object, as President Wilson did when he led the United States into war in 1917. A leader is a cause when he creates new attitudes

---

[5] R. Michels, *Political Parties* (1915), pp. 64–68.
[6] J. H. Randall, *The Making of the Modern Mind* (1926), Chs. XII–XV.

on the part of the group or effects a transference of objects. A political speaker "changing the mind of his audience," an artist patiently building a new style, a prison warden gaining the confidence of his men, are examples of leadership in its causal aspects.

Leadership has an aspect of sympathy and conformity, as well as one of individuality and self will, so that every leader must be a follower, in the sense that he shares the general current of life. He leads by appealing to our own tendency, not by imposing something external upon us. Great men are therefore symbols or expressions, in a sense, of the conditions under which they work.[7]

There are several means that are used by all leaders in altering, creating, and controlling social attitudes:

1. The leader inspires his followers by his own *example.* By demonstration he gives them the confidence to imitate him and at the same time furnishes objective evidence of his authority. Bryan's abstinence from alcohol was doubtless a factor in his temperance leadership; McFadden's luxuriant head of hair enables him to prescribe certain physical-culture treatments for the scalp; Dr. Meanwell's string of basket-ball championships at Wisconsin has won many converts to the "Meanwell System" of play.

2. The leader has an apparently unending supply of fresh *ideas.* He thus seems to have a solution for the problems of his followers. Where lesser men are "stumped" the leader has "something up his sleeve." A good football coach has always a new combination of plays and an unending flow of advice for his men. A successful politician is at no loss for an issue; he is constantly offering new solutions for the troubles of the country.

3. It is furthermore the characteristic of leaders to be filled with a boundless *self-confidence.* In this way they create an illusion of success before it has actually been achieved. The captain of an ocean liner very seldom shows signs of perplexity or agitation even in the most desperate situations. A leader must never admit, once he has taken his stand, that there is any other possible.

Except as a person trusts and cherishes his own special tendency, different from that of other people and usually opposed by them at its inception, he can never develop anything of peculiar value. He has to free himself from the domination of purposes already defined and urged upon him by others and bring up something fresh out of the vague underworld of subconsciousness and this means an intense self, a militant, gloating "I." [8]

[7] C. H. Cooley, *Human Nature and the Social Order* (1902), p. 321.
[8] Cooley, *op. cit.,* pp. 293–296.

4. Another corollary of leadership is *prestige*. "Prestige is the mainspring of all authority. Neither gods, kings, nor women have ever ruled without it." [9] Prestige is a rating of superiority and is usually greater or less than a person's actual ability and worth, its inaccuracy being due to ignorance on the part of one person of another's ability, or to unscientific methods of making the evaluation.[10] "The fame and power of man often transcend the man himself. . . . Thus we may say of all famous and admired characters that, as personal ideas, they partake of the nature of gods, in that the thought entertained of them is a constructive effort of the idealizing imagination seeking to create a personal symbol of its own tendency." [11] It is largely on account of prestige that leaders are considered to be carriers of authority. They are credited with special ability in choosing the real thinkers and experts.[12] Henry Ford is interviewed on international affairs; Gene Tunney is asked to give his views on Shakespeare; and one has but to look at the advertising pages of the magazines to realize the authority that the endorsements of a diversity of leaders seems to carry respecting merits of all manner of products, from cigarettes to motor-cars, frequently almost completely disassociated from the individual's main field of achievement. Their *saying* an idea is true *makes* it so in the minds of many people.

5. In addition to these requisites it is essential that a leader have *good physical equipment*, especially if his leadership is of the type that brings him in personal contact with his followers. As a compensation for his short stature Napoleon is said to have taken pains always to appear before his soldiers on a horse. In a study of executives, it was found that practically all business leaders, college presidents, and foremen were taller and of greater weight than the men under them.[13] Not only is an impressive appearance necessary, but also a great deal of energy both mental and physical is the common attribute of leaders. "Fierceness and tenacity of purpose go far in getting opinions accepted by others, partly because of the natural dislike of most men for controversy, and partly owing to the presumption that an opinion sincerely and strongly held is more apt to be true." [14]

In its last analysis leadership is merely a form of suggestion. Through his personality, originality, example, self-confidence, prestige, vitality,

[9] Gustave Le Bon, *The Crowd* (14th impression, 1922), pp. 147 ff.
[10] E. S. Bogardus, *Fundamentals of Social Psychology* (1924).
[11] Cooley, *op. cit.*, p. 569.
[12] A. Lipsky, *Man the Puppet* (1925), p. 48.
[13] E. B. Gowin, *The Executive and his Control of Men* (1915).
[14] Lipsky, *op. cit.*, p. 49.

and physical attributes the leader touches the emotions of men, inducing his followers to accept his attitudes and follow the behavior that he suggests. "Men in a crowd lose all force of will and turn instinctively to the person who possesses the quality they lack," [15] and this is only a little less true of men in more remote associations with one another.

Leadership is therefore a very important factor in the formation of social attitudes. While a leader must appeal to fundamental human attitudes and values, much depends upon where he places the emphasis. Most men are capable of surprising extremes of thought or action once they are properly aroused. Indeed, all of us even have latent attitudes that need only to be called into activity to produce forms of unsocial behavior. Thus a labor leader is frequently in a position to encourage or avert industrial conflict, depending upon whether he suggests violence or arbitration as the best means of realizing the demands of the workers, which in either case will be the same. The president of a college class is often able to inculcate a spirit of constructive interest in campus affairs within the student body or, on the other hand, to turn the tide of favor to aimless social functions, depending upon the attitude that he chooses to foster. A preacher can often head either a congregation of public-spirited citizens or one of uncoöperative denominationalists, depending upon whether he emphasizes a socialized or an intolerant religion.

In the interest of averting and solving social problems, it is essential that society (1) afford ample opportunity for the discovery and development of leaders, and (2) furnish adequate training for their responsibilities. Leadership is a scarce commodity and it should not be allowed to go to waste. Schools and industries should provide chances for the young individual to show his aptitudes. And once discovered, leadership should be equipped with social ideals so that it may exert its influence for the social good.

AGENCIES IN THE FORMATION OF ATTITUDES

The Rôle of Public Opinion. When we speak of agencies in the formation of social attitudes we must recognize that attitudes thus formed are the result of the creation of public opinions, which are the oral aspect of social attitudes. Public opinion is just the opinions of individuals plus their differences. "There is no public opinion where there is no substantial agreement. But there is no public opinion where there is no disagreement." [16] Opinions often rest on a basis of habit rather than on

[15] Le Bon, *op. cit.*, p. 137.
[16] Park and Burgess, *op. cit.*, p. 832.

one of rationality. "The pitfall of the established concept is that it ignores nice distinctions that are oftentimes the very substance of issues." [17] Just as there are many opinions, so there are many publics within a society.

A public is organized on the basis of a universe of discourse, and, within the limits of this discourse, language, statement of fact, news will have, for all practical purposes, the same meanings. . . . The public has not only a circumference, but it has a center. . . . The focus of attention : . . is constantly shifting. The shifts of attention constitute what is meant by the changes in public opinion. When these changes take a definite direction and have or seem to have a definite goal we call the phenomenon a social movement. . . . When the focus of public attention ceases to move and shift, when it is fixed, the circle which defines the limits of the public is narrowed. As the circle narrows, opinion itself becomes more intense and concentrated. This is the phenomenon of crisis. It is at this point that the herd stampedes. . , . The sentiments and tendencies which we call public opinion are never unqualified expressions of emotion. . . . The public is never ecstatic. It is always more or less rational. . . . Public opinion fluctuates. . . . Social customs, the mores, change slowly . . . but they change in one direction and they change steadily. . . . Changes in the mores are only slightly under our control. They are not the result of agitation; rather they are responsible for agitation. . . . The mores represent the attitudes in which we agree. Opinion represents these attitudes in so far as we do not agree.[18]

Agencies in Forming and Directing Social Attitudes. A number of agencies are active in forming and directing our social attitudes. Not only do they serve as channels for the distribution of attitudes among the population, but they are also molds, that is, attitudes and suggestions passing through them tend to be modified. The agencies that we shall consider here are personal intercourse, the press, advertising, propaganda, the radio, the theater, the platform, and art.

1. *Personal Intercourse.* Attitudes are formed and passed along in the personal relationships between individuals. *Gesture and facial expression* are among the most elementary means of the expression of attitudes. A smile, a frown, a lifted eyebrow, the wave of a hand—any of these may serve to indicate the individual's attitude. Shaking hands is merely a conventionalized gesture to indicate friendliness. In the use of words, *gossip* plays an important part in the formation of attitudes. It has very little mixture of fact; rumor and imagination are its chief ingredients and personality its chief concern. *Conversation,* when it can be distinguished from gossip, is on a somewhat higher plane, embodying more content of

[17] A. D. Weeks, *Control of the Social Mind* (1923), p. 43.
[18] Park and Burgess, *op. cit.,* pp. 791–833.

fact and reason. The conditions that favor conversation are (*a*) increase of leisure, (*b*) unification of language, (*c*) diffusion of common knowledge, and (*d*) equalization of rank. *Correspondence*, which is merely conversation carried on at a distance, depends upon the above conditions together with (*e*) travel and (*f*) cheap and adequate postal service.[19]

Discussion is a more specialized form of exchange of attitudes. In its organized form it becomes a means of group thinking and problem-solving. The thought process as described by John Dewey goes through the following stages: a problem is raised by disturbing facts; an idea is suggested as the key to it; the development of that idea's leadings follows. "In the first stage, where concentration is a requisite, 'solo' thinking has the advantage. But at the second and third stages the special requisite is that a variety of promising ideas shall come to mind. Here . . . group thinking has the advantage of a greatly extended range of mental associations. . . . Not majority win or compromise, but consensus (of opinion) is the Ideal Aim" of intelligent organized discussion.[20] The *platform*, by which we mean all forms of public speaking, although not as influential as formerly, is still a very important factor in the formation of attitudes, through the spread of information and the creation of new values.

2. *The Press.* The influence in the formation of attitudes of the printed word is enormous. News is the raw material from which opinion is made, and the editorials and special articles that fill our publications are compilations or evaluations of facts written with the purpose of assisting or coercing the reader into forming certain opinions. In a democratic country it is essential that all members of the population be as well informed as possible concerning public affairs if they are to be in fact as well as in theory the real rulers of the country. What is needed, therefore, is *facts*—the account of events and conditions as near to objective truth as possible. Distortion of or tampering with the news in the interest of advertisers or other groups perverts public opinion.

In 1939 the 2,040 daily newspapers in the United States alone put an average of nearly 43,000,000 copies (17,150,000 morning and 25,800,000 evening) into circulation every day, or one paper for approximately every three persons in the country. In addition to the dailies, there were in 1939 more than 1,000 weeklies, 2,300 monthlies, and nearly 700 quarterlies, which together with other periodicals made a total of more

---

[19] W. J. Shepard, "Public Opinion," *American Journal of Sociology*, XV: 44–59 (1909–1910).

[20] A. D. Sheffield, *Joining in Public Discussion* (1922), pp. viii–xiii.

than 14,000 publications issued regularly in the United States. In 1939 approximately 135,000,000 copies of monthly publications were circulated each month, and 56,000,000 copies of weeklies each week. Outside the periodical field, new publications in 1939 comprised 9,015 new books, and 1,625 new editions of old books.[21]

The most significant modern trend in the periodical field, especially in the newspaper, is the increased amount of advertising and the influence that the commercial motive has upon news and editorial policies. In 1940, there were more than 1,000,000,000 agate lines of advertising in our newspapers, while in the single month of September of that year, there were more than 7,500 pages of advertising in the pages of our magazines.[22] Moreover, the proportion of space allotted to advertising and news stories has been steadily shifting during the past forty years toward a preponderance for advertising, so that well over half the space in the newspaper is devoted to advertising matter. It is also well known, of course, that advertising constitutes by far the greater proportion of the periodicals' incomes, the actual proportion being more than two to one. Since the periodical press is a large commercial enterprise, entailing heavy expenditures for plant and equipment, it is not remarkable that its public functions as disseminator of news and comment should be influenced to some extent by commercial considerations. It must be remembered, however, that such considerations will be a far greater factor in local affairs than in those of larger State and national matters. More than 75 per cent of the advertising in 1940 was devoted to retail and department store advertising, the rest being scattered between automotive, financial, classified, and general advertising.[23] On the larger issues, the policies of newspapers are more likely still to reflect the political position of the editors and owners.

It has been suggested, to avoid the influence of the advertising interests, from whom the largest part of the newspapers' incomes is derived, that the press be endowed by the Government in the same manner as the schools or the postal service have been. There is reason to believe, however, that this plan would only remove the press from the influence of business men to put it under the influence of bureaucrats and politicians. At least, it seems that the press would thus become an organ for the policies of the Government and would lose its freedom of criticism, which is essential in democratic countries. Under this plan the press

---

[21] World Almanac (1942), p. 528.
[22] R. M. Dobie in Editor and Publisher, p. 24 (November 15, 1941).
[23] Ibid.

would serve as the organ of the majority—of those in power—but the minorities would be denied a voice. We have only to recall the complete domination and exploitation of the newspaper by the totalitarian powers in recent years to appreciate the dangers inherent in such a plan.

It would seem, therefore, that we must allow the press to continue as a private enterprise, recognizing that advertising is and probably will continue to be its life-blood. This being the case, there appear to be two lines along which protection of the public against garbling and distortion of the news may·proceed: (1) development of ethical standards in the journalistic profession and (2) the development of an intelligently critical attitude on the part of the readers.

It has been only within the present century that journalism has aspired to be a profession. A larger number of schools of journalism in the universities are now offering full courses for future writers and editors, and a dozen periodicals are devoted to the interests of the profession. Several hundred teachers of journalism in the colleges and universities are devoting their time and energy to the problems of the press.[24] Whether with the rise of these new arrangements, with the growth of better education, and with the attraction of a higher type of individual, journalism will assume its social responsibilities in the future remains to be seen.

A healthy skepticism on the part of the reader is necessary. The slang phrase, "You can't believe all you see in the papers," is an indication of a step in the right direction, but the reader must also be able to decide what he can believe. The following practices are helpful in this regard. (a) Visit your newspaper plant, see how the paper is made. When you realize the shortness of time in which the reporter must gather the news, the speed with which it must be transmitted to the office, edited, put into type, proof-read, and printed, you will understand that absolute infallibility, even with the efficiency of modern newspaper methods, is often impossible. It is the responsibility of the reader to add that pinch of salt to the news which, through sheer lack of time, the daily journalists are unable to add. (b) Analyze the sources of the news. If the mayor gives an opinion concerning the State university, ask yourself just how much his opinion is worth and in what ways he is qualified to speak on the subject. If there is a strike, ask yourself if the employer who gives a statement concerning the good conditions of the workers is really giving you the entire truth. (c) Make allowances for biases and distortions on

[24] R. R. Barlow, *Directory of Teachers of Journalism in the United States and Canada* (Department of Journalism, University of Minnesota, 1923).

the part of the paper. These are frequently unconscious as well as conscious. It will not take you long to discover that the *Christian Science Monitor* is a poor medium for medical news, that the *Chicago Tribune* will give you only a small amount of raw material for building an attitude in favor of "New Deal" policies, that the *Washington Star* invariably supports the Republican party. (*d*) Read periodicals expressing opposite points of view. You should see both the Republican and the Democratic papers of your city; read the *American Magazine* and the *American Mercury;* read the *Saturday Evening Post* if you want to, but also one of the critical weeklies like the *Nation*, the *New Republic*, and the *United States News*. In this way you will be able to balance opinion against opinion and be able to arrive at something more nearly approximating the truth than if you allow the organs of only one point of view to form your attitudes for you.

All of this is to assist you in avoiding stereotyping and lumping. All of us have our stereotypes.[25] We tend to think of all villains as sleek individuals with black mustaches; all successful bankers are large gentlemen with top-hats; during the First World War all Germans were bullet-headed individuals with an irrepressible habit of killing little children; because a few Jews have hooked noses and disagreeable manners certain people tend to lump all members of that group in a similar category. Stereotyping and lumping are forms of generalization from the particular, an unreflective setting up of specific instances in our experience as the prototypes for all succeeding instances of a similar nature. It is much easier to pigeonhole each succeeding villain or German or Jew, as the case may be, who comes into our sphere according to the stereotyped picture that we carry in our heads, but it is also much less satisfactory from the point of view of social adjustment.

3. *Advertising*. Advertising is the effort to create a favorable attitude toward a purchasable commodity so that you will buy it. Advertising relies upon suggestion, and its most usual method is to make a prospective buyer feel a strong desire for the advertised commodity. We are told that our brains will be jarred to the point of nervous breakdown unless we wear rubber heels, that death in an accident is almost sure to result unless we use fog lights, that our competitors will outdistance us unless we employ the telegraph, the long-distance telephone, the adding-machine, the dictation-recorder, and other machinery. Vanity is called upon to create a desire for many articles, including clothes, houses, and automobiles of the more luxurious types. We desire such nonessential

[25] Walter Lippmann, *Public Opinion* (1922).

things as cigarettes because of their fragrance, household appliances because of their convenience, trips to foreign countries because of the
supposed social distinction that they confer, after having these points
brought to our attention by the advertisers. Advertising is usually
bought and paid for and can be readily distinguished as such. The principal forms are periodical, outdoor (billboard), street car or city bus,
mail, radio, and novelty advertising. This method of creating social attitudes is obviously under the control of private interests. Its undesirable
effects have to do with the stimulation of unnecessary purchasing. The
whole purpose of it is to establish certain attitudes favorable to the
purchase of advertised articles. It does so by appealing to motives growing out of already established attitudes and values.

4. *Propaganda.* Propaganda is the art of making up the other man's
mind for him, and in our usage to-day the word implies doing so without revealing your method or your intentions.[26] Unlike advertising,
which is usually a frank attempt to induce you to buy a represented
commodity, propaganda disguises its objects and applies itself to many
fields other than the commercial. Its most famous historical use has been
in connection with the spread of religious dogmas, and it reached a
peak of development, in both quantity and technique, during the Second
World War.

As distinguished from simple education, propaganda places its emphasis upon the feelings and emotions. An analysis of the propaganda of
both sides during the First World War has shown the following to be
the principal aims of war propaganda: (1) Hatred must be mobilized
against the enemy by representing him as a menacing, murderous ag-
gressor, an obstacle to the realization of the cherished ideals and aims
of the nation. These representations of the enemy must be supplemented
by assurances of ultimate victory. (2) The friendship of allies must be
preserved by stressing our strenuous exertion and our hearty consent to
the war aims of the ally. (3) The friendship of neutrals must be preserved and, if possible, their coöperation procured by leading them to
identify their interests with the defeat of the enemy. (4) The enemy
must be demoralized by leading him to substitute new hates for old,
mainly by spreading discouragement and an attitude of defeatism,
whereby a receptive mood is formed for violent campaigns against allies,
the governing class, national minorities, and the unity of the State.[27]

[26] K. Young, *Social Psychology* (New York, 1935), Ch. 27.
[27] Harold W. Lasswell, *Propaganda Technique in the World War* (1927),
pp. 185 ff.

Within a given country there are three tactical principles observed by the propagandist: (1) Suggestions are circulated that promise to arouse the interest of specific groups, such as the educated, the non-educated, farmers, business men, Protestants, Catholics, etc. (2) Suggestions are chosen to nullify inconvenient ideas that cannot be suppressed. (3) Untruth, which is likely to be contradicted before the achievement of the strategic purpose, is avoided.[28] "The forms of suggestion are few and elemental but the possible occasions and carriers are infinite."

The following account of the activities of the propaganda organization of our own country during the First World War gives an idea of the variety of instruments that were used in influencing public opinion.

Thirty-odd booklets were printed in several languages. Seventy-five million copies were circulated in America, and many million copies were circulated abroad. Tours were arranged for the Blue Devils (French Soldiers), Pershing's Veterans, and the Belgians, and mass meetings were arranged in many communities. Forty-five war conferences were held. The Four Minute Men commanded the volunteer services of 75,000 speakers, operating in 5,200 communities, who made a total of 755,190 speeches.

With the aid of a volunteer staff of several hundred translators, the Committee supplied the foreign language press of America with selected articles. It planned war exhibits for the state fairs of the United States, a series of inter-Allied war expositions, and secured millions of dollars worth of free advertising space in the press, periodical, car and outdoor advertising forces of the country.

It used 1,483 drawings prepared by volunteers for the production of posters, window cards and similar material. It used a daily newspaper with a 100,000 circulation for official use. It ran an information service and syndicated feature articles for the press. Plate matter for the country press, and specialized material for the labour, religious, and women's press was supplied. Moving pictures were commercially successful in America and effective abroad, such as "Pershing's Crusaders," "America's Answer," and "Under Four Flags."

Over two hundred thousand stereopticon slides were distributed. Still photographs were prepared, and a stream of 700 pictures per day of military activities were censored. Cable, telegraph and wireless were employed by an official news service. A special mail and photograph service was also built up for the foreign press. Reading-rooms were opened abroad, schools and libraries were fitted out, photographs were displayed prominently.

Missions were sent to the important districts of the world to look after American propaganda on the spot.[29]

[28] *Ibid.*, pp. 200–209.
[29] *Ibid.*, pp. 211–212, adapted from George Creel, *How We Advertised America* (1920).

We devote this much space to wartime propaganda because it is the best example of organized publicity that history has to offer us. Activities of the same sort, only on a lesser scale, are going on about us all the time in an effort to "make up our minds" for us. Many of these campaigns, such as those in favor of hygiene and good health, physical culture, education, and travel, are beneficial and to be encouraged, but the powerful tool of propaganda is also used by selfish interests in an effort to induce favorable attitudes to causes that from the social point of view are less commendable. For this reason, every citizen should train himself to identify and evaluate propaganda.

5. *Radio.* The radio has become an important factor in the formation of attitudes. At the end of 1941 there was an estimated total of 56,000,000 receiving sets in operation in the United States. During 1941 alone 13,000,000 new sets were sold, and the total value of radio sales during that year amounted to $610,000,000. There were 765 broadcasting stations in the United States in 1940, 457 of them network and 308 non-network and these stations together employed about 22,000 persons full-time with a weekly pay-roll of more than $1,000,000.[30]

Unlike any other major country in the world, we in the United States have not undertaken to establish a rigid public control over the program of our radio stations. In other countries, the radio has been very closely regulated, both as to materials to be broadcast, and as to the privilege of having receiving sets. The latter are taxed to support the programs; and commercial broadcasting as we know it in America does not exist elsewhere. Moreover, in the United States, within certain broad limits of propriety and expediency, any person can buy broadcasting time in behalf of any organization or idea which he may wish to advance. Thus radio has not been fully exploited as a means of shaping unanimous public opinion. Nevertheless, individual broadcasters are known to build up tremendous followings among listeners; and the influence of the radio as an agency in forming social attitudes must not be underestimated.

6. *Motion Pictures.* Thousands of persons who seldom read books or attend lectures, go frequently to the "movies." It is estimated that 80,000,000 admissions are paid every week in the 17,500 theaters operating in the United States. About 700 short films and 530 features were released in 1940. The film industry represents an investment in the United States of more than $2,000,000,000 with 282,000 persons continually employed and some 276 different industries and crafts involved.[31]

30 *World Almanac* (1942), pp. 859–860.
31 *Ibid.*, p. 864.

The motion picture, like the radio, has been used chiefly as an agency for entertainment. As a vehicle of planned educational activities, it has been developed to a much smaller extent than has the radio, due to the obvious limitations imposed by greater complexities of production and the larger expenditures involved.[32] However, the unique appeal of color, motion, and sound inherent in the modern motion picture makes possible a wide scope of dramatic and emotional appeal with reference to the locality or period depicted by the individual production. And like the radio artist, the motion-picture actor or actress builds up large followings and influences the daily thought and action of his or her public to a very impressive extent.

7. *Art.* Art in each of its forms and various stages of excellency or degeneracy finds a clientèle for whom it symbolizes the social values and for whom it synthesizes the factors that create new attitudes. It is especially effective in its graphic forms, including the wide use of photographs, comic strips, and editorial cartoons in newspapers and magazines. Art is the organization of emotional values and of social attitudes. For this reason its healthy development is important for the well-being of any society.

THE RÔLE OF ATTITUDES IN SOCIALIZATION AND SOCIAL DISORGANIZATION

The attitude of the individual, whether determined by his inherent nature or by his experiences of the past, often creates problems for society to solve. Only as society, through its various institutions and organizations, permits the individual to realize his fundamental wishes in ways consistent with the patterns of the group, is conflict prevented. Certain wishes and values the individual possesses. If they are consistent with the aims and customs of the society to which he belongs, then the problem for society is to discover methods by which he may adopt those patterns without denying his fundamental wishes.

The conflict of new behavior patterns with established attitudes and mores of the people creates many social problems. This fact is illustrated from many fields of social life. Let us take the attempt in Wisconsin to regulate public dance halls as an example. Says a report:

In estimating the effectiveness of this system of county regulation, it must be considered that the system is a new one, having been in operation only a few months in some of the counties studied; that the character of the problem presented varies greatly from county to county, making regulation much more difficult in some counties than in others; that public opinion on the

32 T. R. Adam, *Motion Pictures in Adult Education* (New York, 1940), pp. 67 ff.

subject has been more active and better organized in some counties than in others; and that even in those counties where there are the most serious conditions in dance halls, it is necessary to judge whether conditions were not still worse before the present ordinances went into effect. In some counties officials complain of lack of public support; in others civic organizations complain of lack of earnest coöperation from the officials concerned in the enforcement of the dance hall law. In counties where the regulation seems to be effective and conditions have been improved, it appears that public sentiment is strongly and generally in favor of enforcement. In one county where enforcement is lax and conditions bad such sentiments were expressed by officials and citizens as: "Everyone is doing it. We are in the drift of the times and what can you do?" "So many of the so-called best people are involved that it is hard to propose a remedy." "Inspectors turn their backs and see nothing. If I were acting as inspector I should do the same thing because one cannot get any backing." "The county dance hall situation is impossible. It is useless to try to regulate drinking and sex immorality among older people. Public sentiment is all with those who want a good time and a drink." [33]

Constant modifications of the patterns approved by the group are made by insurgents. That is to say, the patterns of any society are constantly changing by reason of the ideas and attitudes of inventive or revolting individuals. New facts in science are discovered. They become common mental property. Those who possess them first change their own attitude toward an established form of behavior and then become centers of influence for their modification. A new philosophy arises. Again, certain individuals are affected by it and lead the way in modifying certain standards of group behavior. Illustrative of these two facts is the enormous change in forms of conduct due to the new science and new philosophy of the last fifty years. A new world of ideas has come into being. This new world of ideas has generated new attitudes for individuals by providing a rational realization of the wishes in new behavior frames. Whether or not the new tendency is socially good, we have here an explanation of why problems of social adjustment exist, and how maladjustments are brought about. Without a question, however, this new world of ideas has generated a different attitude on many of the relationships of life in individuals affected by it. The old and approved forms have been very seriously modified as more and more of the members of any given group have been affected by these ideas.

Let us take another example. The proper attitude toward the beggar approved by the group of a former day was "Give to him lest you pass by a worthy person." New values in philanthropy generated by careful

[33] *Journal of Social Hygiene*, pp. 4, 5 (January, 1927).

observation of the results of indiscriminate giving have created in observant individuals a new attitude toward the beggar. With the growing number of such individuals a new form of behavior for the group has begun to make itself manifest, *viz.*, that before giving to the beggar one should know about his past history and then treat him in a way that will restore him to independence.

Another example of the shift of social attitudes is the change in the treatment of the criminal by society. The approved attitude that grew out of the old classical penology, based upon the theory that everyone is free to do good or evil, and that therefore all who commit a certain crime should be treated in the same way, is being very greatly modified. As the result of the work of Lombroso in Italy and of those who have studied the matter more carefully since, it is coming to be seen that no matter what our theory of free will and determinism may be, the experiences through which one goes in early life have a very definite effect upon his conduct. It has also been observed that uniform treatment for the same offense does not produce uniform results. Here and there individuals have had their attitudes changed by this new knowledge, and gradually a new pattern of social attitudes toward the delinquent has been developing. That pattern now includes careful investigation of all facts of the case and the endeavor to adjust social treatment to the delinquent so that if possible he may be reformed, or if not, he may be segregated from society for its protection.

Nevertheless, established behavior patterns resist the new attitude for a long time with resulting conflict between the attitudes of individuals and the established conduct norms of the group. Illustrations of this may be seen in many fields of human behavior. In the course of American history, owing to causes that it is not necessary to go into, a protective-tariff system has come to be looked upon as the cause of American prosperity. On the other hand, in England just the reverse is true; the free-trade policy was looked upon as the cause of its prosperity. Consequently, both in England and in the United States, individuals who have been moved to take an attitude contrary to the established tariff doctrine have had a terrific battle on their hands. In the South the theory has prevailed that "the Negro should keep his place." The consequence has been that the behavior pattern for the white man was dominance of the Negro, an attitude of superiority, and at the same time kindly consideration for the Negro's welfare. In the North, on the other hand, growing out of the War Between the States and the long discussion of the race problem, the proper behavior for a white man toward colored men was to concede equality of opportunity, at least in the industrial and educational world. Consequently, a Northern man in a Southern community was likely to find himself in conflict with the dominant pattern of the group, and likewise the Southern man in the North.

Again, from the old patriarchal family came the theory that "children should be seen and not heard." The resulting behavior pattern is the subordination and obedience of children, whether the request of the parent be reasonable or not. Recent times, however, have seen a very great change in the attitude of some of our leading people toward children. They have felt that children should not be subordinated and repressed in this way, but should be developed. Gradually their attitudes have modified the old ways, and a new pattern is rapidly coming to take their place. In certain religious circles in the last century, dancing was looked upon as indecent and immoral. However, owing to the attitudes of certain leading people in many communities, in our day dancing is not looked upon as either. Consequently, the accepted standard is changing. However, a person coming from a community in which dancing is looked upon as disreputable finds his attitudes in conflict with the mores of, let us say, a university town.

The tenacity of established behavior patterns in the face of social change also is illustrated in the field of industry. Not more than fifty years ago in America it was said that any man who is not lazy can make a living. With the change in our industrial organization, experience has shown that there are many men out of employment who really desire work and cannot find it at certain seasons of the year or in different periods of industrial activity. The consequence is that in different groups at the present time two different behavior patterns with respect to the workman are in conflict. Similarly, in the individualistic stage of our industrial development it was believed that the employer had a right to discharge any man whenever he pleased. Labor, however, as it has become organized, has taken a different attitude. Its leaders have urged that the working-man has a stake in his job as much as the employer. These two patterns are in conflict at the present time. Whether the one will modify the other remains to be seen.

Finally, we may observe that the conflict of new fashions in behavior with the established *mores* of a group often leads to social problems. An example is provided by the new ideals of behavior with respect to the opposite sex, which conflict with the established sex mores. The so-called "revolt of youth" manifests itself sometimes in a clash with what have long been considered the proprieties in sex conduct. Here the trouble is made by the coming in of ideas and standards of conduct at variance with those long held by the older generation. Those accustomed to the patterns acceptable to their generation are disturbed by the new attitudes of youth. Again, the Italians coming to this country have standards of chaperonage of daughters that are quite at variance with American customs. The Italian girls find the girls with whom they associate at school and in the neighborhoods in which they live going out in the evening, associating freely with young men, and sometimes wonder why their "old folks" are so strict with them. Often this leads to a conflict between the young Italian girls and their parents and raises problems of adjustment not easily solved.

From what has been said it is apparent that attitudes are partly the product of the acceptance of behavior patterns by the individual on the basis of his hereditary characteristics, his experiences, and the treatment of the individual by the group. It is also apparent that the attitudes of forceful individuals ultimately determine the behavior pattern held by a group. These behavior patterns set the standard of each individual's conduct so long as the patterns are not challenged by a large and influential number of people. It is also apparent that the maladjustment between the individual's attitude and the pattern laid upon him by the group, and also the awkwardness with which the group endeavors to make him conform, provide us with our chief social problems. These conflicts between individual attitudes and accepted patterns of behavior give us the types of social problems arising from the clash of new attitudes and established patterns that we have surveyed in the previous chapters. Without an understanding of this fundamental relationship between attitudes and patterns of behavior, we are likely to make many mistakes in attempts at social adjustment. How often reforms are advocated that leave these fundamental psychosocial facts out of consideration! And how important that society, especially all those who have to deal with growing children—parents, teachers, recreation leaders, neighbors, religious leaders, and industrial managers—should have some understanding of the social importance of wise treatment!

REFERENCES

DAVIS, J., BARNES, H. E., and others, *An Introduction to Sociology* (Boston, 1931), pp. 453–466.

DORSEY, G. A., *Why We Behave Like Human Beings* (New York, 1925).

ELLIOTT, Mabel A., and MERRILL, Francis E., *Social Disorganization* (New York, 1941), Chs. I, II.

GABRIEL, Ralph H., *The Course of American Democratic Thought* (New York, 1940).

GROVES, E. R., *Personality and Social Adjustment* (New York, 1924).

LINTON, Ralph, *The Study of Man* (New York, 1936), Chs. 25, 26.

PATTEN, Simon, *The Social Basis of Religion* (New York, 1911).

REUTER, E. B., and HART, C. W., *Introduction to Sociology* (New York, 1933), Chs. 15, 16.

SMITH, Charles W., *Public Opinion in a Democracy* (New York, 1939).

VAN WATERS, Miriam, *Youth in Conflict* (New York, 1925).

YOUNG, K., *et al.*, *Social Attitudes* (New York, 1931), especially Chs. I–III.

QUESTIONS AND EXERCISES

1. What are social attitudes? How do they express themselves? How are they formed?
2. List some of the behavior patterns required by the groups with which you are associated, relative to some commonly accepted standard or institution such as church-going, divorce, or women in industry.
3. What light does the discussion in the text throw upon the fact that the children of immigrants are more delinquent than the children of native born? Upon the failure of some parents to control their children?
4. Cite examples from your own observation to show how personal contact between individuals may shape the social attitudes of those individuals either favorably or unfavorably.
5. The text cites the need of "great ideals" in controlling the social conduct of groups. What ideals do you consider dominant in American life to-day, and what sort of conduct does each call forth from the individual?
6. Name an outstanding American whom you regard as a leader and analyze (a) the bases of his leadership, and (b) the methods he has used in acquiring and holding his position of leadership.
7. List the agencies in the formation of attitudes in what you consider the order of decreasing effectiveness and give reasons for your arrangement.
8. What problems are presented by the cultural lag of *mores* controlling attitudes relative to social and material change?
9. Is change always rapid and spontaneous, or is it continually in process?
10. Which is more to be feared as a disruptive force in social organization —uncontrolled material changes, or the influence of individual leaders (either radical or conservative)? Explain your position.

Chapter 19

FACTORS AFFECTING SOCIAL ADJUSTMENT

SOCIAL REFORM concerns itself with the vast social maladjustments that are the aftermath of the great and rapid changes of our time. But why is the achievement of social reform so slow? What is it that seems to block the road to a speedy and sound social adjustment to the requirements of the new social conditions? As individuals we may be brought quickly to a clear recognition of our problems, and may as quickly respond to practical plans for adjustment. But when we are dealing with groups, and especially when we are dealing with a whole nation or with groups of nations, our problem of obtaining adjustments is complicated by a number of factors that offer stubborn resistance to speedy reform. *The larger the body, the slower it moves*—this is as true in the social sciences as it is in physics. The social scientist must concern himself with these elements which resist movement and adjustments in society, just as the physicist and engineer concern themselves with the friction and resistances that retard the movements and lessen the power of their huge dynamos and giant machines. We must be able to discern the difference between the forces that serve as a balance-wheel of social action and those which resist progress and thwart social adjustment.

At least nine major factors affecting social adjustments should be carefully considered in developing programs and policies for social reform: (1) custom and tradition, (2) geographic and physical conditions, (3) economic factors and conditions, (4) biological factors, (5) educational forces and conditions, (6) governmental and political influences and forces, (7) significance of group action, (8) the stability or mobility of the population, and (9) the status of the spiritual life of the people.

CUSTOM AND TRADITION

One of the most important sets of factors affecting social adjustment is concerned with the *cultural background* of the people who are in process of adjustment—their *customs* and *traditions,* or their "folkways" and "mores," as some writers have called them.[1]

Custom results from the handing down, from one generation to another, of *ways of doing.* Most of our habits of life, especially habits of

[1] W. G. Sumner, *Folkways* (1913).

consumption, our "standard of living," our manners and social conduct, are governed largely by custom.[2] The difference between the American-born man and his foreign-born neighbor is largely the difference in their social habits or customs. It is more difficult to teach grown-ups new modes of doing things, because the older they get the more fixed become their old habits, and the more difficult it is to form any new habits that conflict with the old ones. So it is with persuading groups of people to adopt new ways of doing things: the old ways seem so much more comfortable, though they may be less efficient, slower, or perhaps even injurious.

Tradition results from the handing down from one generation to another of loyalties and of *ways of thinking and believing*.[3] Strangely enough, as we come to think of it, most of our concepts of morality, our concepts of ethics, our standards of value, our standards of propriety, and our "guiding principles" are determined by the past. From our birth to our burial, our lives are to a very large degree circumscribed, controlled, and directed by the forces of tradition.

We might liken our present-day culture to an ever-widening river flowing out of the past and on into the future (see Fig. 17). The various twists and turns of this river represent the important turning-points in history. At times its current has been sluggish, shallow, and quiet; at other times, swift, troubled, and noisy—as it is to-day. At various points in its course it has been joined by tributaries flowing from strange sources, some very ancient and some new. Many of the strange and new culture elements of the tributaries quickly fused with the culture content of the main stream; others, it seems, refused to mix with the culture of the main stream, but flowed with the main current like oil and water, or like a substance held in suspension but not dissolving.

Thus custom and tradition form the social foundation upon which group life is based, and constitute a firm cement that binds the present to the past. When we come to a careful examination of the beliefs, the ideals, the social standards, the institutions, and the modes of conduct of the various groups that make up the population of the United States, we find that in varying degrees they reflect the cultural contributions from all the great civilizations that have influenced the history of the Western world—the ancient Greeks, the Jews, the Romans, the Nordics, and the more recent culture of South and East Europe.[4]

[2] E. A. Ross, *Social Psychology* (1908), p. 196.
[3] Ross, *loc. cit.*
[4] Charles Ellwood, *The Social Problem* (1919); E. A. Ross, *The Old World in the New* (1914).

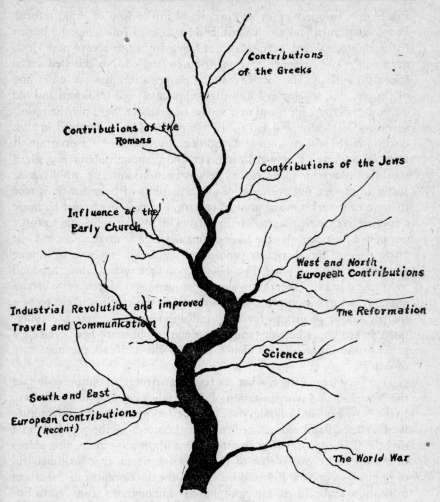

Contributions of the Greeks

Contributions of the Romans

Contributions of the Jews

Influence of the Early Church

West and North European Contributions

The Reformation

Industrial Revolution and improved Travel and Communication

Science

South and East European Contributions (Recent)

The World War

FIG. 17.—SOME OF THE MAIN CONTRIBUTIONS TO THE STREAM OF PRESENT-DAY CULTURE—OUR SOCIAL INHERITANCE

All of the ideals and elements that go to shape and direct the social mind must be taken into account in facing the problems of social adjustment.

The older and the more settled and static a community becomes, the more it is bound by the influences of custom and tradition. But even in a relatively new, mobile, and dynamic society, such as characterizes the major portion of the United States, custom and tradition are tremendous forces that, in one way or another, stand in the way of rapid reform. People as groups feel much more comfortable in following the beaten paths; they are vexed, even pained, at being forced to accept new views or abandon old habits to take up the newfangled. No initiated social scientist overlooks the fact that social progress requires the unsettling of people, and, at least in a measure, supplanting old traditions and old customs with new ideas and new modes of conduct. Yet only the unseasoned social idealist will fail to recognize the *danger* involved in thus disturbing the old customs and traditions by too radical a program. It must be admitted that we do not yet know enough about our social world to blueprint plans for its reconstruction and cast wholly new forms to replace outworn and obsolete patterns of behavior. It is true that we can work toward gradual reform; but the effort must be made a coöperative enterprise, each individual in his own way helping to forge out new adjustments on the basis of our heritage from the past and our knowledge of the particular problem at hand. Any attempt to impose completely new and untried proposals upon society as a whole is bound to arouse a healthy skepticism among its members. Moreover, when an attempt to force such proposals is successful, the result is likely to be a sharp cleavage of groups favoring and opposing it, because the consequences are unpredictable; and in the confusion, there may even be a general dissolution of confidence in *both* the old and the new way of doing.

To a very large extent, what we regard as American culture is in fact the New England reorganization of the English customs and traditions. In the New England colonies the Puritan concepts of the English culture were reshaped and reorganized to meet the needs of the pioneer and a slightly different form of government. One of the most interesting phases of American history is that of the influence which that little handful of population in New England has had on the development of American institutions and culture. Though millions of immigrants from North Europe have had a large share in the settling and development of the States west of the Alleghenies, they did not entirely cling to the customs and traditions of their native countries, but instead absorbed and carried the New England pattern, somewhat modified, westward with them, and, at least in major outlines, have developed almost a uniform national tradition and culture.

However, with the disappearance of the frontier and the increase of immigration from South Europe, these newly formed American traditions and customs began to be threatened. The new immigrants did not scatter, but settled in compact colonies in the large industrial centers. There they tended to cling to the old customs and traditions of their native countries, instead of adopting, as did the earlier immigrants, the pattern that had evolved from the New England traditions.

This tendency to perpetuate customs and traditions that are not in harmony with "American ideals" is the chief basis for our objections to the new immigration. We are not inclined to accept "foreigners of this class" as our neighbors or to associate with them unless they are willing to think and act as we do. Consequently we not only close the door to their coming to America, but we turn our attention to the serious job of making of them "respectable" Americans. Just what we mean by *Americanization* has not been satisfactorily defined, but perhaps the central idea of it was expressed by Abraham Lincoln as "government of the people, by the people, for the people." To be sure, this expression has to be interpreted as applying not only to the State but also to the family, the church, the school, and our industrial and community life.[5] The South European follows the old tradition of his native land of being the head of the house. His wife and children are regarded as his servants, and he feels it his duty to see that they are employed and that he collects and uses their income as he sees fit. The American, on the other hand, takes the point of view that has been expressed in granting woman suffrage and the passage of child-labor laws.

When we undertake to persuade the foreigner to give up his old traditions and customs, we find that it is a slow and ofttimes discouraging task. We want him to live in a house that is painted and fronted by a grass-plot; we insist that he must have floor coverings, curtains at the windows, table-cloth on the dining-room table, and enough bedrooms to permit a reasonable privacy for the various members of the family. All this seems like gross extravagance to many a foreigner, and he hesitates to demand the wage that is necessary to maintain these "luxuries." To be sure, these outward expressions are but a few of the changes that we expect the foreigner to make in his habits of living, but they are perhaps the ones that we stress the most.

But it is not only in Americanization that we see custom and tradition retarding the possibilities of rapid adjustment. Many of our own native customs and traditions have to be considered. The rapid progress of science and invention has disturbed not a few of our most time-honored habits and beliefs. For example, a few years ago tuberculosis took a large toll of life each year, and it was discovered that the best way to prevent

5 J. R. Commons, *Races and Immigrants in America* (1920), p. 213.

and cure this "white plague" was to correct our old habit of sleeping with closed windows and in heated or poorly ventilated rooms. Somehow we had developed the idea that night air was to be shut out, that it was poisonous, and it has taken more than a decade to persuade the American people to change their habits and thus reduce the annual toll of deaths caused by tuberculosis. Then, too, medical science has shown us that frequent bathing is essential to good health and vitality. But the habit of bathing was indeed hard to establish. The first bathtub installed in the United States (1842) was exhibited as a curiosity at a party; and in 1850 Virginia placed a tax on all bathtubs on the basis that they were an extravagant luxury. And even sophisticated Boston required that a doctor's permission be given to those who desired to take a bath in the wintertime, as winter bathing was regarded as injurious to the health. Now we regard bathing as one of the essentials to decent living and a bathroom is almost as essential to the American family as the kitchen. But this new custom was not easily nor quickly established. On the other hand, we must not forget that "old fashioned" ideas often have understandable bases, even in their tendency to persist. In our first example, closed windows keep out health-giving fresh air; yet they also performed functions now done by screening—keeping out malarial and other disease-carrying mosquitoes and insects. In the case of bathtubs, it must be admitted that frequent bathing would have been a Spartan habit in the days of poor heating and virtually non-existent plumbing facilities; and such primitive conditions still prevail in many sections of our country.

In matters of education the forces of custom and tradition are perhaps the most serious handicaps to the improvement of our schools. The old traditional concept of education was that it was a means of distinguishing the gentleman and the lady from the common folks. Consequently the curricula of the schools were composed of such subjects as Latin, literature, mathematics, astronomy, and other subjects that had no direct bearing on the means of getting a living. During the past third of a century, however, there has grown a different idea or ideal of education: "the transmission of experience that will make for more complete and efficient living." Vocational schools have sprung up alongside the regular school system, and some inroads have been made in the traditional curriculum permitting the teaching of applied arts and industries. However, the conflict between the traditional and the new forms of education constitutes one of the main issues in community life.

In religion, likewise, tradition and custom have played and still play a most important rôle. In many communities the church has been looked upon merely as an institution to be used for Sunday worship and for funerals. Thus religion came to be regarded as a Sunday affair and of more importance for those who were reaching the last milestone of life rather than as a seven-day-a-week influence for the benefit and strengthening of the lives of all. We now see a new movement aiming to make the church serve the social needs of the community and to interpret the daily spiritual problems that are exerting an increasing pressure in these days of intensive living. But here, too, we see the old resisting the new with every theological tenet at its disposal.

To our Puritan forefathers recreation, and especially Sunday recreation, was regarded as a sure sign of utter depravity. Many of our States still have on their statute books numerous "blue laws" that were designed to keep the "unregenerate sinner" in the paths of "righteousness." Dancing and even the "fiddle" were not allowed in the home, and to play cards was to invite open condemnation of the pious. There are many communities that still cling to these ideas of play and recreation. In many communities, not even the public school—much less the parish house of the church—can be opened for dances or even for social festivities. Obviously the modern programs for community recreation must move with caution and be content with slow progress where people still cling to these old customs and traditions. To ignore or defy these traditions merely leads to community conflict, which retards progress instead of advancing it.

Thus we might multiply our illustrations of the influence of custom and tradition as factors affecting adjustment. What we have just said should suffice to make clear the need of considering these forces in developing our plans and policies for meeting the major social problems. Needless to say, no two communities are quite alike in regard to the play of these forces on the various social problems. Consequently the social reformer must carefully consider each community's "peculiarities" before undertaking his program of social adjustment.

GEOGRAPHIC AND PHYSICAL CONDITIONS

It is easy enough to see how geographic and physical conditions affect the social problems in the different parts of the world. Thus the people living at the foot of a volcano will naturally face problems and develop an outlook different from those of the people who live on the fertile inland plains of a great continent.[6] People living in the tropics may be expected to develop altogether different customs and traditions from those

[6] R. Mukerjee, *Regional Sociology* (1926).

of people who live in the regions visited by winter, and the problems of the former greatly differ from those which harass the people who must provide for shelter and comfort in the lands of snow and ice.[7]

However, even in the United States, geographic and physical conditions must be taken into account in the making of social adjustments. Thus the people pocketed in the isolated valleys of the Appalachians have been shut off from the main highways and currents of social progress. They are still governed by the social customs and habits of the first pioneers who crossed the Alleghenies. The development of schools, of ample public health facilities, and of progressive community life is dependent upon the development of improved highways, and means of communication that will eliminate barriers and bring the people into closer contact with the forces of social progress.

Taking the map of the United States and the records of the Weather Bureau, we are able to chart the zones over which there are frequent cyclones and hurricanes. Yet when we come to observe the communities in these regions, we notice that they build the same sort of farm buildings and live in the same sort of houses that are to be found in the regions less frequently visited by devastating storms. Furthermore, the people in these regions as a rule carry no more insurance against the storms than do the people of the regions where storms are less frequent. Thus every year we read of whole communities being wiped out, schools being destroyed, and thousands of lives being lost. Appeals go up to all of the people of the United States to assist the Red Cross in aiding the sufferers and rebuilding their homes. It would seem, therefore, that due recognition of the geographic conditions would greatly assist in the making of more permanent adjustments in these communities.

Similarly, the thousands who live in the lowlands where, repeatedly, floods sweep away millions of dollars' worth of property and hundreds of lives, still cling to the hope that floods will cease to recur. Not until these peoples are willing to recognize the geographic factors will they be able to make any permanent adjustments that will protect them against future disaster.

A less obvious, but nevertheless significant, influence of climatic conditions is to be observed in the adaptation of the Northern population moving into the Southern States. Invariably we hear the complaint that the Southern climate "makes folks lazy." This may be true to a certain extent, but in a large measure it is due to a failure to recognize the influence of climate on habits of living. People from the North invariably

[7] J. R. Smith, *North America* (1926), Ch. I.

take with them their habits of diet and housing. A heavy protein and meat diet, which is necessary to furnish the heat and energy for comfortable and efficient living in the North, becomes a drug to the vitality and efficiency of the individual living in a warm climate. Then, too, the snug cottages with small rooms and low ceilings and with little ventilation provided for above the ceiling may be perfectly satisfactory and comfortable in Wisconsin, but are stuffy and close when located in Mississippi. Thus, healthy and efficient living in the warm climate requires that we regulate our habits and living conditions in accordance with the demands of the climatic conditions.

Failure to take into account the influence of the geographic condition in social adjustment has been responsible for more waste and delay in the working out of sound policies for community well-being than has generally been recognized.

ECONOMIC FACTORS IN SOCIAL ADJUSTMENT

Another set of factors that we must recognize in making social adjustments, whether for individuals or for communities, is the *economic*, that is, the ability of an individual or of the community to pay for the requirements of health, education, and other social advantages prescribed by the American standard of living.[8] Even in as wealthy a nation as ours, there are many communities in which the income is too small to provide the families with the necessities for physical comfort, to say nothing of providing the children with good schools, or supporting a public health nurse or a director of public playgrounds. This is especially true in many of the old agricultural communities where the soil has been depleted and the old population has moved off, leaving the land to less thrifty and poorer tenant-farmers; or in the cut-over lands that were developed during the period of high prices of farm products, but which fail to produce even a meager living since the great decline of prices; or during long periods of industrial depression and unemployment.

There are other groups and communities in which the annual income would seem to be sufficient to maintain a fairly high standard of living, but in which the forces of commercialization and exploitation absorb so much of that income that the people are unable to provide themselves with the means of progress. Thus many mining communities remain dingy, unhealthy, and backward not from poverty, but because the wealth is not expended in a way that secures to the working population the elements of a high standard of living. For example, the miner may

[8] Scott Nearing, *Financing a Wage Earner's Family* (1913).

earn $7 or $8 a day and work on an average of 150 to 200 days in the year, or even more, but he must pay for sharpening his picks, he must pay for his explosives, and he is taxed for weighing the coal that he mines. When these discounts are taken from his wage, the remainder must be spent for groceries and goods purchased at the "company store" and rent paid to the "company" landlord. The company has no competitor, nor will it tolerate competition. Consequently the laborer is in no position to remedy his unfavorable conditions without moving and changing his occupation, and, as a general rule, he is in debt to the company and unable to find a way of moving his family into a better community. Improvement in the conditions in such communities is largely initiated by organized effort outside of them.

THE BIOLOGICAL FACTORS AFFECTING ADJUSTMENT

Another set of factors that we must take into account in attempting to formulate programs of social adjustment are those which relate to the character and temperament of the human stock of which our population is composed.[9] There are, of course, the normal differences in temperament to be noted among the various racial groups, and even these differences reflect widely different responses to the social requirements of community life. Professor Ross, in analyzing the nature of the crimes that have been committed by prisoners, describes in a most interesting way the difference between the crimes committed by the Swedes, the Jews, the Italians, and the other national groups.[10] Thus, for example, as a general rule the Swede who is in prison is there for committing a crime over which he brooded for a long time and seems not to regret, while the condemned Italian is in prison generally for a crime that he committed on the spur of the moment while in a rage, and he was penitent and sorry for the deed within perhaps a few minutes after he had committed it. Social settlement workers, in working with foreign groups, have noticed these differences in temperament and have found it necessary to adapt their programs to them.

An interesting difference in temperament is to be noted between the white and the Negro. As a general rule the Negro works best in a gang, and sings while he works. Some time ago an enterprising superintendent who had engaged several hundred Negroes to work on repairing a strip

[9] Charles Ellwood, *The Social Problem* (1919), Ch. III.
[10] E. A. Ross, *The Old World in the New* (1914).

of levee along the Mississippi employed also a jazz band. The chief concern of the superintendent was to keep the band playing fast rag-time pieces that were familiar to his laborers. The Negroes worked to the time of the music, wheeling the heavy bags of sand and cement at a pace that was much faster than they would have worked had it not been for the music. To the average American the suggestion of speeding up labor by the use of a band would seem amusing if not absurd, and most certainly we would not attempt to employ this method to speed up a group of Scandinavian workers!

Efficiency engineers have called attention to the great difference in the various racial stocks as to their ability to withstand the effects of monotony in industry. It appears that the South European is able to bear up under a strain of monotonous machine operation much longer than the English or the Irish workers. This fact has led to the development of schedules of relief that take into account difference in temperament. Thus, these natural differences should be considered in practically every aspect of our programs for social adjustment.[11]

There are to be noted in almost every community and in different sections of the country abnormal biological conditions that are matters of more serious concern than mere differences of temperament. Perhaps we should divide the abnormal elements of the population into two general groups, both of which have been considered more in detail in earlier chapters: first, the depleted or drained-out stock that we find in many of the older communities; and second, the feeble-minded, epileptic, and degenerate stock, which is, for the most part, scattered through the population in every locality, and constitutes an increasing burden on our charitable and correctional agencies.

In attempting to develop a program of social adjustment in many of the old communities, we find that the response of the people is slow and weak. Undoubtedly there is a definite biological basis for this lethargy and indifference. For years such communities have been continually drained of their vigorous and ambitious elements, and only the easily satisfied remained behind to intermarry and perpetuate their traits.[12]

The chief consideration in regard to the effect of the feeble-minded, epileptic, and degenerate elements of the community upon the problem of social adjustment consists in the increasing attention that this hopeless group requires. Invariably this class of people constitute the most serious

[11] E. B. Gowin, *The Executive and his Control of Men* (1916), pp. 49, 139.
[12] E. A. Ross, *The Social Trend* (1922), Ch. III.

menace to health, morals, and security when they are allowed to remain at large in the community. Consequently, any sound program must necessarily consider the ways and means of safeguarding community life against these unfortunate and undependable groups.

EDUCATIONAL FACTORS

As our social life becomes more and more complex, education becomes an increasingly important factor in accomplishing social adjustment. As we have previously noted, our New England forefathers established traditions that have given to us our public schools; and these traditions had their beginnings as early as the middle of the seventeenth century. But the gigantic task of settling and taming the frontier and the incidental scattering of the population, to say nothing of the continual influx of new immigration, made it difficult for the schools to accomplish the task of education. Even as late as 1870, 20 per cent of the population of the United States of ten years of age and over were unable to read and write. By 1910 this percentage had been reduced to 7.7, and by 1940 illiteracy had been reduced to 3.7 per cent of the population ten years of age and over.

Illiteracy, however, is not equally distributed either as to classes of people, or as to divisions of the United States. Thus, in 1940, among the population twenty-five years of age and over, some 2,800,000 had no schooling at all, while more than 7,300,000 had less than five years of educational training. Together these groups were largest in the South Atlantic and East South Central States, ranging from 12 per cent in Delaware to as high as 34.7 per cent in South Carolina. New Mexico and Arizona illiteracy likewise was high, 27.3 and 19.4 per cent respectively of their population having had no more than four years of education. The high rate of illiteracy in these States results from the large proportion of Mexican laborers in their population.

In the other Southern States, it was largely due to the illiteracy of the Negroes and the isolated whites in the mountainous sections and in the bayou regions along the Gulf. It is also interesting to note that the native whites of native parentage have a higher percentage of illiteracy than do the native whites of foreign and mixed parentage. The census explains this difference on the ground that the native whites of native parentage are more scattered throughout the rural and isolated regions where schooling facilities are less available, while the native whites of foreign and mixed parentage constitute a large part of our urban population, for

TABLE 29

EXTENT OF ILLITERACY AMONG UNITED STATES POPULATION
25 YEARS OF AGE AND OVER, 1940 *
(All Expressed in Per Cents)

Group	Education	All Classes	Native White	Foreign-born Whites	Negroes	Others
United States	No schooling	3.7	1.3	12.2	10.0	18.8
	Less than 5 years	9.8	6.1	16.1	31.3	17.1
Urban	No schooling	3.6	0.8	12.5	6.6	12.5
	Less than 5 years	7.7	3.7	15.6	23.7	14.3
Rural, non-farm	No schooling	3.4	1.7	10.9	12.7	17.9
	Less than 5 years	10.2	7.3	17.2	35.5	17.6
Rural, farm	No schooling	4.7	2.5	10.5	15.0	26.1
	Less than 5 years	15.7	11.1	19.0	44.1	19.7

* Bureau of the Census Releases, 1941.

which educational opportunities are abundant.[13] The Negro population in 1920 was 22.9 per cent illiterate. In the years since then almost phenomenal progress was made in educational advancement by the Negroes; illiteracy among them now being no more than half the 1920 figure.

The cities, in spite of their large foreign-born element, show less illiteracy than the agricultural population. These wide differences constitute only a part of the story of the difference between educational opportunities in the rural communities and those in the city.[14] The "little red

[13] "The census defines as *illiterate* any person 10 years of age and over who is unable to read and write. The classification is based upon the answers given to the enumerators in response to the question 'Whether able to read and write.' No specific test of ability to read and write was prescribed, but the enumerators were instructed not to return the answer 'Yes' (which would classify the person as literate) simply because a person was able to write his or her name. A person able to read and write in his native language was not counted as illiterate, even though he could not read or write English." Explanation and data from tentative report, *Fifteenth Census of the United States* (Released July 1, 1931).

[14] Census figures on illiteracy must not be taken wholly without question, however. While the 1920 Census reported but 6 per cent of the population illiterate, it was revealed that 24 per cent of the World War draft recruits were unable to write letters.

school-house," so dear to the traditions of America, has proven more of a drawback than an aid to the educational progress of many of our rural communities. So long as this time-honored institution controls the sentiments of the school district to the extent that the inhabitants refuse to abandon it and consolidate with other school districts to provide better equipped schools, the rural communities will lag far behind the urban communities in educational progress. The movement toward consolidated rural schools is one that has developed in recognition of the needs of the rural districts, and it should do much to wipe out the differences in educational opportunity between rural and urban communities.

It is not merely the *amount* of education that must be considered in social adjustment, but also the *kind* of education and training. Here, there must be a difference between the rural and the urban schools if the country boy is to receive the type of education that will lay the foundation for scientific agriculture and for a clear vision of his economic opportunities on the farm. Undoubtedly one of the most significant influences causing the migration of the country boy to the city lies in the nature of his schooling, which tends to make the economic opportunities of industry and business more clear to him than the opportunities in agriculture and farm life. But it is not merely in the matter of economic activity that education plays an important rôle; it is one of the most vital essentials for achieving progress in every other phase of social life.

However, the educational factors affecting social adjustment cannot be considered apart from the extent to which the people of the community are *educable*. It has been estimated that the number of feeble-minded ranges from 2 to 5 per 1,000 in the population as a whole. In some sections and regions the ratio is much higher. In addition to the definitely feeble-minded, there are many other persons incapable of learning even to read and write. Inevitably there will continue to be a considerable number of persons, especially in the older communities, whose inability to comprehend the requirements of complex social and economic society will present a stubborn problem for social reform.

GOVERNMENT AND POLITICS AS FACTORS IN SOCIAL ADJUSTMENT

To an increasing degree Americans are depending upon governmental action as a means of making social adjustments. Yet forward-looking people frequently are discouraged and disheartened by the slowness and inefficiency with which the government moves in matters of social reform. For example, with the development of our improved methods of transportation and travel, our State laws relative to marriage and divorce no longer offer the necessary safeguards to stable family life. Moreover, what one State may attempt to accomplish in regulating marriages and divorces may be defeated by the laxity of other States. Unquestionably the whole problem would be greatly simplified if the Federal Government were charged with the regulation of marriage and divorce. A similar situation is illustrated in the efforts to obtain a federal child-labor law, which was declared unconstitutional and left for the States to work out as they saw fit.

Governmental policies also are twisted and perverted by the pressure of various groups seeking to control the policies or even the processes of government for their own purposes. Such groups are apt to profess their concern for the public welfare even while they further their own interests; yet the net result often is an increase in the complex problems of balancing group interests for the welfare of all concerned. Thus the revenues derived from one section or group have often been distributed in a way that has provided disproportionate services. For example, as late as 1929 the United States paid out $143,594,000 for pensions for the War Between the States.[15] It is estimated that 98 per cent of this pension fund was expended in the Northern States, while the eleven Southern States, which are not included in the federal pension system, paid approximately one-fifth of the revenue that went into this fund. Consequently approximately $30,000,000 was drained out of the Southern States and expended to build up the prosperity and to take care of the dependents of the North. Similarly we have farm blocs perennially seeking approval of various crop subsidy or farm credit proposals, manufacturers clamoring for high tariffs, employers and workers each seeking laws to protect themselves or to restrain their rivals.

The problems of advancing the public welfare also are complicated in some ways by the very processes of democratic government itself. The framers of our Constitution were careful to preserve a maximum of power in the hands of the individual States, with the result that to-day many functions that formerly were carried on within the States now concern whole regions if not the entire country. For example, the State child-labor laws, which we mentioned a moment ago, are grossly inadequate when the products of the States are sold in competition with other States of the nation. Moreover, we have the general system of functional "checks and balances" in the machinery of government: the tri-partite balance of responsibility between the legislative, judicial, and

---

[15] *Statistical Abstract of the United States, 1930*, p. 160.

administrative agencies, each body a check upon the others. This device was formulated to prevent the perversion of power by any one group; yet it often results in inefficiency or even minority control, because any one of the three can vitiate even the most reasonable activities of the other two.

However, to acknowledge the limitations and handicaps of our type of government is by no means equivalent to denouncing the democratic technique as a way of getting our mutual affairs accomplished. Rather, the characteristic feature of our governmental structure is to be accepted and taken into account in every program of social adjustment. The alternative to the democratic way is that of oligarchic collectivism; and the world experience of recent years has taught us nothing if not that we cannot depend on the mystic leader for benevolent administration of governmental agencies. On the other hand, our own tremendous strides in social welfare legislation and government administration in the midst of world confusion suggests most emphatically that our democratic forms have vitality and resiliency.

Perhaps one of the best indications of the importance of the government in matters of social adjustment is to be noted in the way the States spend the taxpayer's dollar. (See Table 30.) While increasing demands are made on the various units of government—federal, State, and local— the mounting cost of government has been a growing source of dissatisfaction. Yet slow and clumsy though governmental action may seem, it must be increasingly depended upon to secure those regulations which will obtain protection and service for the population in matters of health, education, occupational adjustment, industrial relations, and social welfare, as well as in the administration of justice.

GROUP ACTION AS A FACTOR IN SOCIAL ADJUSTMENT

When our forefathers framed our government, they based their hope for the future upon the action of the individual voter. Hence, patriots look with dire misgiving upon the fact that our modern elections fail to "get out all the voters" and attribute this failure to vote to indifference and disloyalty. Whatever the reasons for the failure of large portions of our adult population to vote, it is true that their absence from the polls makes it much easier for minorities to impose their candidates and philosophies upon the majority of the citizenry. It has been estimated that in local and State elections, as many as half to two-thirds of the voters do not register their wishes. Thus, a "majority" may be as little as a sixth or a quarter of the total of qualified voters; and especially in local, ward

TABLE 30

EXPENDITURES OF STATE GOVERNMENTS, 1915 AND 1938 *

Type of Service	1915			1938		
	Amount	Percentage	Per Capita	Amount	Percentage	Per Capita
All purposes	$379,039,094	100.0	$3.85	$3,182,162,000	100.0	$24.72
General government	44,508,417	11.7	0.45	154,008,000	4.8	1.20
Protection to person and property	26,294,691	6.9	0.27	123,412,000	3.9	0.96
Health and sanitation	9,453,673	2.5	0.10	45,001,000	1.4	0.35
Development and conservation of natural resources	16,558,685	4.4	0.17	89,099,000	2.8	0.70
Highways	22,767,766	6.0	0.23	466,105,000	14.7	3.62
Charities, hospitals, and corrections	89,189,400	23.5	0.91	1,059,800,000	33.3	8.23
Schools	145,832,324	38.5	1.48	889,485,000	27.9	6.90
Libraries	1,331,923	0.4	0.01	2,492,000	0.1	0.02
Recreation	878,646	0.2	0.01	8,279,000	0.3	0.06
Compensation and employment service			—	249,413,000	7.8	1.94
Miscellaneous	22,214,569	5.9	0.22	95,068,000	3.0	0.74

* *Financial Statistics of States* (1928) (United States Bureau of the Census, 1931); *Statistical Abstract of the United States, 1941,* p. 239.

politics it is easy to see that a "machine" controlling as few as fifty active votes often can exert a formidable show of strength. This matter is of special importance, since so much of life to-day is controlled by government, either directly or by laws affecting the activities of other agencies like industry and commerce.

Whether inside the governmental framework or in the realm of private enterprise, it is increasingly true that we are dependent, for better or worse, upon the activities of organized groups in shaping social attitudes and policies. Whether it be public welfare organization to handle the problems of charity, the promotion of business interests by associations of commerce, the industrial clashes between labor-unions and employers' associations, or any one of the hundreds of other organized activities, these same groups are having tremendous influence in determining what sort of adjustments or working relations we shall have with one another. The individual to-day makes his power felt, as a rule, only by pooling his efforts with those of other individuals in a mutual, common enterprise. Much depends upon the relative strength of the competing forces and upon the quality of leadership they have. Of equal importance socially, however, are the principles and motivating forces *underlying* the activities of these many groups, since it is the objectives of the successful competing groups that will determine, in the end, the sort of social adjustments that will emerge. A certain amount of "self-interest" must always be assumed. It is unsound to expect that organizations, or even individuals in large numbers, will ever exert themselves wholly for idealistic reasons. A more practical approach to the matter is to try to keep the struggle within the limits of socially acceptable behavior and goals.

STABILITY OF POPULATION AS A FACTOR IN SOCIAL ADJUSTMENT

As we have already noted, one of the features that distinguishes the United States from Europe is the mobility and shifting of population that is constantly altering the structure of the community. This incessant movement of the population seriously impedes social adjustment. As we ripen into national maturity, this tendency seems to become more pronounced. The nature of these shifts of population has been discussed elsewhere, and here we need only mention those phases which affect adjustment.

As our agricultural communities become more settled, the value of farm land and the amount of capital required for stocking a farm make it increasingly difficult for a young man to become a farm-owner. Consequently, tenancy has been increasing and will doubtless continue to increase. In 1880 approximately one-quarter of the farms of the United States were operated by tenants. In 1940, 38.7 per cent of the farms, or 29.4 per cent of farm lands, were in the hands of tenants.[16] In the twelve States of the North Central divisions, 35 per cent of the farms were operated by tenants, including 742,742 farms containing 145,699,-000 acres. Migration from farm to farm is very high among tenant farmers, and their primary aim is to get out of the soil as much as they can without putting anything back into it. Thus, for example, in all the States of the "deep South" except Florida, 20 per cent or more of the farmers were reported in 1935 to have lived on their farms less than a year.[17] The increase of tenancy commonly means also the growth of a landlord class which is likely to be as little interested in paying taxes for the benefit of the tenant class as the tenants are in maintaining the fertility of the soil and supporting the social institutions of the community. As the proportion of tenant population increases, the difficulties of maintaining social adjustments increase.

Many of the professional or paid leaders of social life in the agricultural communities are transients, like the tenants. Seldom do the school-teachers remain in the same community for more than three years, and the tenure of the rural preachers is even less. The rural church has faced and still faces the serious problem of maintaining a grip upon the spiritual life of the community, chiefly because the rural minister is either a young man whose ambition is to secure a church in a larger center as early as possible, or, what is worse, an old man who has given his best years to the city. Hence the rural institutions have not only lagged behind those of the city but, in a large proportion of the rural communities, have actually degenerated.

Mobility of population is not only characteristic of the rural community but is becoming even more accentuated in the larger cities. The boarding-house and apartment population is hardly more interested in community development than is the tenant-farmer. Thus we find a constant turnover in the population of the various residential zones of our cities, and community institutions have found it necessary to change the character of their work to fit the needs of the constantly changing population.[18]

[16] *Statistical Abstract of the United States, 1941,* p. 685.

[17] J. H. Kolb, and E. deS. Brunner, *A Study of Rural Society* (Boston, 1940), p. 231.

[18] LeRoy E. Bowman, "Population Mobility and Community Organization," *American Journal of Sociology,* XXXII: 133–137 (1926).

SPIRITUAL LIFE AS A FACTOR IN SOCIAL ADJUSTMENT

Finally, a factor that must be taken into account and which to no small extent determines the rate of social adjustment, is the spiritual life of the community. By the spiritual life we mean here *the attitude that people take toward themselves, toward others, and toward their ideals and religion.* Clearly, the lives of nations and communities alike necessarily are influenced very fundamentally by the sort of self-esteem they possess. A people that thinks itself "chosen" or especially privileged is likely to be aggressive in its dealings with others, nay, even ruthless! If the society is highly stratified, its dealings among its own members are apt to be similar to the conditions just cited, with the bonds of sympathy and mutual respect limited to members of one's own economic class or social group. On the other hand, a society that is highly democratic and respects the rights of the individual—*any* individual—is much more likely to coöperate wholeheartedly with each other, and with other cultures and nations.

Naturally enough, we associate religion with the spiritual life of peoples. But many of us do not realize fully how important and how varied its influence is upon the particular people involved. For instance, Tawney and Weber have analyzed ingeniously the relation between the individualism and free enterprise which are at the heart of both Protestantism and capitalism.[19] The Protestant emphasis upon "works" (or work) as a means of "salvation" seemed to give religious sanction to the long hours of hard toil so characteristic of early capitalism, while the projection of the individual conscience as law-giver tended to break down the medieval governmental and religious restraints upon industry and trade.

The prevailing religious belief regarding the relation between the present and the future life also shapes the popular attitude toward social problems. If the present is considered only an interlude preceding a future life for the individual soul, then existing evils will be endured without much protest. On the other hand, if people are convinced that future "salvation" depends upon striving for a world more perfect than the one which exists, improvements in social relationships will be hastened. However, the experience and interests of *special groups* of people also are a factor which influence the character of their religious beliefs and practices. For example, a church in a prosperous area is apt

---

[19] Max Weber, *The Protestant Ethic and the Spirit of Capitalism* (1930); R. H. Tawney, *Religion and the Rise of Capitalism* (1926).

to reflect the conservatism of its members, while one in a locality in which acute social problems exist is likely to have more militant policies. And the fact of *organization*, in either case, will itself tend to give force to the attitudes of the people in matters pertaining to social adjustment.

REFERENCES

ADAM, T. R., *Motion Pictures in Adult Education* (American Association for Adult Education, 1940).

BUSHEE, F. A., *Social Organization* (New York, 1930), Ch. XV.

FURNAS, C. C., *The Next Hundred Years* (New York, 1936).

GILLIN, J. L., and BLACKMAR, F. W., *Outlines of Sociology* (New York, 1930, 3rd Edition), Chs. V, VI.

HILL, Frank E., *Listen and Learn* (American Association for Adult Education, 1937).

LUMLEY, F. E., *Means of Social Control* (New York, 1925), Ch. I.

MUKERJEE, R., *Regional Sociology* (New York, 1926).

SMITH, J. R., *North America, Its People and Resources* (New York, 1925).

THOMAS, Franklin, *Environmental Basis of Society* (New York, 1924).

WISSLER, Clark, *Man and Culture* (New York, 1923), Ch. XII.

QUESTIONS AND EXERCISES

1. List three or four worn-out customs and show how they impede the process of social adjustment.
2. List three or four customs which you consider still of merit and show how they facilitate the process of social adjustment.
3. Is the inertia of custom and tradition of value at times in the process of social adjustment, or are custom and tradition simply forces that stand in the way of reform? Discuss.
4. What part have geographic and physical conditions had in the development of social life in the United States? To what extent have we overcome the influences of topography and climate? What geographic and climatic conditions still affect our problems of social adjustment?
5. Show how economic factors affect the problem of social adjustment. How does poverty affect the possibility of keeping pace with the progress demanded by social change? Give an illustration that relates to the situation of a single family. Give another illustration that relates to a whole group or section.
6. In how far would you say that apparent inherent differences may be produced by environmental differences, and by differences in custom and tradition, between one nationality and another?
7. Show how the continual migration of the progressive and discontented inhabitants of a community to other communities may in time affect the social life of the old community.
8. Show the influence of the natural and social environment upon the frequency of illiteracy.

9. Outline a program for the reduction of illiteracy in your State.
10. Give three illustrations of your own to show how government and politics affect the problem of social adjustment.
11. Give an illustration of your own, obtained either from your personal observation or from your general reading, to show how the mobility of the population affects the process of meeting community problems.
12. After considering carefully the social life of your community answer the following: (*a*) To what extent and in what particulars does *laissez-faire* ("hands off") express the attitude of the community toward social maladjustments? (*b*) To what extent and in what particulars are co-operation and mutual service coming to be recognized as the proper attitude? (*c*) What groups or agencies of the community are the chief exponents of each of these policies?

Chapter 20

PROPOSED WAYS OUT

ALL SOCIAL PROBLEMS grow out of *the* social problem—the problem of
the adjustment of man to his universe, and of the social universe to man.
The maladjustments in these relationships give us all our social problems
—disease, poverty, family disorganization, race and group conflicts,
crime, mental defect and disease, individual failure, and the breakdown
of our social institutions.

It must be clear at the outset, of course, that these maladjustments are
not static or unchanging. The character of poverty, for example, has
changed immensely since the days of ancient Egypt, or even since the
reign of Queen Elizabeth in England. The *problem* of poverty has
changed, because the conditions producing it, and the ideas of mankind concerning it, have changed. Slavery was the answer to the problem of poverty till fairly recent times. But as social attitudes began to
change, it was seen that slavery itself was a "social problem"—a far from
satisfactory adjustment in man's relations with his fellow-man or with
his universe. The same is true of all our social problems. They change,
just as surely as society itself changes; and maladjustments do not turn
into problems till they become generally recognized as such. So the
many proposals we shall discuss in this chapter reveal not only a wide
variety of social thinking but also something of the kaleidoscopic nature
of social change and the problem it produces.

HISTORICAL SOLUTIONS OF THE SOCIAL PROBLEM

Attempts to solve the problem of man's relationship to his physical
and social environment are not new. Ever since he has reflected on the
tangles of life, man has been guessing at the causes of the difficulty he
experiences in adjusting his social world to the demands of daily living,
and he has been devising methods to deal with those causes. In philosophy and theology it has become known as "the problem of evil." When
political philosophy arose, it involved the problem of the relationship
of the individual to the political organization. When economics was born
discussion centered around the relationship of the State to the economic
activities of the individual, theory swinging from the *Nazionalökonomie*

of the Physiocrats to the *laissez-faire* of the Classical Economists and back to limitation of the self-seeking of the individual by the State for the welfare of all. The problem became the center of discussion by religious philosophers and Utopians, giving rise to dreams of social organization as widely different as St. Augustine's *City of God* and Edward Bellamy's *Looking Backward*. As the scientific method developed diagnoses and solutions as widely different as those of the economic materialism of Karl Marx and the hereditary determinism of the eugenists took the place of these Utopian dreams. All these different theories of the origin of the social problem and plans for its solution are alike in one respect—they rest upon *one* explanation of the difficulty, and provide *one* solution of the problem. That each of them contains truth we may admit—but not the whole truth. Life is not so simple that its maladjustments can be understood by one theory, and solved by a panacea. Only modern knowledge with its deeper probing into the nature of man and into the complex nature of his surroundings could make that apparent. Man himself is anatomically a much more complicated machine than any one but a modern scientist could fully realize. Similarly, only rather recently has man begun to understand how very complex is his social being resulting from the tangled growth of traditions, customs, beliefs, and social organizations produced by the effort of mankind through millennia of endeavors to order its life in this little-understood world. The human mind confronted by the problems of adjustment and self-preservation and without modern scientific knowledge and inventions often sought a short and simple way out. Most of the historic analyses and "solutions" of these problems are the result of the demand of man's mind for clarity and guidance. Let us look at some of these theories.

Religious Solutions. The problem of evil is to be found at the base of every religion. It is probable that religion arose out of man's attempts to solve the maladjustments between his purposes and his environment and from his attempt to explain these maladjustments. What else is the meaning of the rites and ceremonies designed to ward off disease, to promote the growth of crops and the fertility of flocks? How else explain the widespread concept of what we call "sin," however varied may be the content of that concept, whether it be conceived of as "folly" (as in Buddhism), as failure to come up to the demands of an ideal (as among the Greeks), or as alienation from God (as with St. Paul). Evil is there. Everywhere it is lack of consonance between personal ideals and circumstance, whether the personal ideals be those of physical welfare or of spiritual communion with God. The conception of the origin of evil may vary widely. It may be due to *karma* among the Buddhists, to *Fate* among the Greeks, or to the *sin of Adam* among the Hebrews. The solution of the problem also differs from religion to religion. Among the philosophical Buddhists the problem is solved by a denial of the natural appetites and the social aspirations, and by absorption in contemplation of Deity until the individual attains Nirvana. In most religions, however, the problem leads to active efforts either to affect an adjustment of the individual to the will of God, or to bend God's will to the need of the individual, or both. In Judaism and primitive Christianity the solution lay in the expiation of the sin that had created the maladjustment. However, as the theory that misery is the fruit of sin was put to the acid test of experience, questions were raised that were difficult to answer on this simple explanation. So far as we can tell from the Old Testament, the first great challenge to the theory came when the Hebrew kingdoms were destroyed by nations that were less "righteous" than the Hebrews. The problem of the individual righteous man, who in spite of his righteousness suffers greatly, is the theme of the profound Book of Job. How can it be that a man who has adjusted his conduct to the will of God, as had Job, must suffer as he suffered? What is the matter with the theory? A similar question arose to plague the Christian apologists over the suffering of the sinless Jesus. They answered it on the basis of vicarious suffering. So far as Jesus himself is revealed in the Gospels He had no complete answer to the question. The conflict between His wish as a young man to live, and His desire to maintain His individual integrity comes out in that cry on the cross, "My God, my God, why hast thou forsaken me?" The puzzling question still remains to vex us when we send millions of youth to death on the field of battle, or when we see millions die of disease, or when we see the honest toiler come down to an old age of want. The answer of religion is still "sin," but the content of the term has vastly widened to take in the selfishness and ignorance of men in organized society. That the answer of the historic religions has truth, but not the whole truth, is plain in the light of modern knowledge. The conception of religion must be widened to take in the wide reach of what psychology and biology have told us about the nature of man, what the social sciences are just beginning to tell us about the nature of the social complex in the midst of which man lives. Then perhaps religion may be geared up with the social machinery to resolve the conflict between man and his human environment, by supplying the motives and ideals that can modify both in the direction of better adjustment between man and his social milieu. Thus far, organized religion generally has been too one-sided to serve the larger social purpose, although it has not failed any more completely than most of the other proposed solutions. To the contrary, it can be argued effectively that in so far as it has been honestly and correctly applied, religion has contributed its full share toward creating and advancing those elements in our modern life we cherish most.

Utopian Solutions. Another type of solution is that of the Utopians, who feel that society as now constituted contains the germs of its own failure. And for this reason they would throw our ill-functioning social forms and institutions upon the scrap-heap and replace them with a new social order, a system as perfect as the mind of man can make it. Thus, a Utopia is an imaginary society built on the lines of what is held to be perfection. It may be brought forth for various purposes: social reform, as in the case of the Hebrew prophets; emphasis on certain ethical principles, as with Jesus; concrete statement of a great social philosopher's theories, as with Plato; satirization of contemporary social life by comparison, as with More; expression of longings, as with Bacon; or argument for the establishment of a strong centralized church, as with St. Augustine. Whatever the purpose to be served, a Utopia is always the, joint product, in varying proportions, of the imagination and the intellect, and its realization can only be approached in accordance with the practicability of the ideal that it sets forth.

First in historical sequence come the *religious Utopias*. That a Utopia should be the next step following the attempt of the early Hebrew prophets on the basis of a reformed Hebrew State in the solution of the social problem is not surprising. The concept of a reformed Hebrew State gave way, on the destruction of the Hebrew kingdoms, to a Messianic dream. If the concept of sin and its undesirable consequences was not sufficient to change men's ways, perhaps the painting of the blissful state attainable by the following of religious precepts would be of some avail. The first among the religious Utopians were the later of the so-called "literary prophets" of Israel. With Isaiah (740–700 B.C.) came the dawn of the Messianic hope. Here was social reconstruction to be effected by religious faith through the efficacy of ethical and spiritual forces. His perfect kingdom included a just king, absence of physical ailments, moral and intellectual improvement, abundance in nature, and universal peace. Jeremiah (626–586 B.C.) emphasized the importance of individual religion in attaining social perfection. Ezekiel carried this idea of individual responsibility further, and prophesied the ideal State absorbed in the church. In that part of the book of Isaiah known as the work of Deutero-Isaiah, another Utopia is set forth, depending upon the complete spiritualization of its citizens, including all races, and everlasting. Among all the prophets we are aware of a divine optimism that implies a change in human nature and a recognition of a Supreme Being. Utopia for them was the natural culmination of right living.

Following the prophets we have the apocalyptists who flourished from 210 B.C. to 1300 A.D. They are on the whole fantastic where the prophets had been concrete, imitative rather than creative, and pseudepigraphic, whereas their predecessors for the most part had written under their own names. They deal only with the remote future and their Utopias are attainable only by supernatural convulsions and catastrophes that shall completely wreck the old order and institute a millennium. Their works were written for the most part to steady the faith of the people under oppression. Daniel (166 B.C.) taught that it was the duty of the faithful to wait in resignation for the divinely ordained collapse of earthly affairs, after which Israel would be delivered by supernatural help and have glory forever. The Utopias of Enoch, Ezra, and Peter paint pictures of heaven and hell with assorted fantastic millenniums calculated to cheer the heart of the lowliest Jewish captive in the clutches of Babylon, Assyria, Macedonia, or Rome, as the case might be at different periods. The Revelation of John, the last book of the New Testament, depicts a Utopia preceded by a millennium during which there would be resurrection for the righteous and judgment for the wicked. The New Jerusalem that he described was symbolic of pure spiritual bliss. The apocalyptists are of small value because they wrote only for their own time, gave free rein to uninstructed imagination, and glowingly described an end without offering a means of attainment.

The utopianism of Jesus is embodied in his conception of the Kingdom of God, which is the ideal state of perfect social and spiritual adjustment. He emphasized that its founding was dependent upon love of God and man, and that the practice of this essential prerequisite, and hence the attainment of the Kingdom, was the responsibility of each individual. The Kingdom was both present and future, and aimed at the social redemption of the earth. Love, penitence, obedience to God, humility, freedom from hypocrisy and deceit, freedom from mammonism, devotion, service, and cosmopolitanism are among the essential principles laid down for the realization of this Utopia, which as an ideal at least we may safely say has had more influence in human life than any other.

Faith in God, freedom from lusts, and the practice of Christian ethics are the keystones of Augustine's *City of God*. This militant treatise, however, is of little social value, being on the whole rather a poor restatement of the ideas of its predecessors, and concerned less with the ideal society than with the establishment of a hierarchical church.

The only important attempt actually to establish a religious Utopia on earth is that of Savonarola's (1452–98) Florentine theocracy. Coming into control of the government of Florence, Savonarola effected startling reforms through his rigid and Puritanical application of Christian precepts. It was a remarkable testimonial to the results achievable through applied Christianity, but it fell in the end because of its rigidity and intolerance.

Plato (427–347 B.C.) with his *Republic* stands as the model for all *philosophical Utopians*. The *Republic* represents the concrete statement of a great social philosopher's theories. The search for justice was the keynote, and to effect this much-to-be-desired consummation the Republic was constructed. The Republic was a city-state, an association of ethically minded individuals who accepted the supremacy of the State on ethical grounds. The basic principle underlying the entire organization was the Idea of Good; and in accordance with this principle Plato felt that the individual welfare should be submerged in the social welfare, since the former depends upon the latter. The two fundamental means of attaining the social good, he believed, are: (1) communism, which involved the renunciation of family and property and the submersion of the individual in the group, and (2) ethical education with a view to the selection of leaders and the physical and mental welfare of the citizens. Plato was thus more practical than the Hebrew prophets and, while his Utopia is humanly unattainable because of the fundamental characteristics of human nature, he nevertheless set up an ideal that has affected social thinking ever since.

About the time of what is rather vaguely termed the end of the Middle Ages a remarkable series of circumstances combined to give impetus to a reawakened expression of utopianism in what is known as the *early modern Utopias*. These circumstances were (1) the Crusades, (2) the journeys of Marco Polo, (3) the Black Death with its consequent labor shortage, and the growth of class-consciousness, (4) the rise of the new learning with the entrance of Greek manuscripts into the Western world after the fall of Constantinople, (5) the spread of knowledge, due to the invention of the printing-press, (6) the discovery of the American continents, and (7) the introduction of gun powder. These novel occurrences changed considerably the aspect of European life. The spirit of freedom was awakened, the desire to start afresh and create a new mode of life free from the imperfections of the old. In the religious field this found expression in the Protestant Reformation, and in the social field in a Utopian plea for simplicity in civilization.

The *Utopia* of Sir Thomas More, written in 1516 as a satire on the corrupt condition into which England had fallen under the Tudors, because of its realism and constructiveness has given its name to all idealistic solutions of the social problems and has had a wide-reaching influence on social thought. It was based on several principles: (1) The community of property would result in the abolition of class and the equality of all citizens before the law. There would thus be a disdain of material wants, no use for money, no distinction of dress, and elimination of all the attendant evils of selfishness. (2) A ruling prince, elected from an intellectual aristocracy by representatives of the people, would provide wise and at the same time centralized government. Utopia had the city-state form of organization. Equal social opportunity for all was the goal, not an absurd ideal of the absolute equality of all citizens. (3) The family would be State-controlled and supervised, thus insuring the eugenic soundness of offspring. (4) Universal and lifelong education would provide for the mental and physical happiness of all. There was to be a six-hour workday in which everyone participated. (5) Religion was pantheistic, reasonable, tolerant, and based on social service.

Francis Bacon with his *New Atlantis* (1623) sought social perfection through science, and attempted to show that knowledge, properly applied, could do away with all the major social maladjustments. For this reason he felt that there must be a communism of knowledge effected through a great endowed city-state college called Solomon's House, which would be an educational, research, and governmental institution in one. Bacon failed to see, however, that science must be responsive to ethical principles; otherwise it tends toward the chaos that our own scientifically inspired civilization is attaining in some places. Note, for example, how Germany subjected all science to the power-mad dictator and his war aims.

Italian utopianism was represented at this period by Campanella with his *City of the Sun* (1623), the principal features of which are: (1) centralized government by an enlightened ruler assisted by Power, Wisdom, and Love; (2) universal coeducation by the visualization method from the third year, with particular emphasis on natural science; (3) communism of wealth and family; and (4) astrology and the Christian religion for its guidance in matters supernatural.

James Harrington's *Oceana* appeared in England at the time of the rise of Puritanism (1656), and is really a magnified written constitution for the purpose of solving the many perplexing problems facing his country at that time. He plead for: (1) the sovereignty of the people through a perfected political government with definite written laws; (2) balance of property through proper economic distribution; (3) governmental devices of (*a*) secret ballot, (*b*) indirect election of officials, (*c*) rotation of officers, (*d*) two-chamber legislative system; (4) religious toleration limited by an established church but allowing liberty of private conscience; and (5) general education of boys for the purpose of perpetuating the principles of government and directing the energies of the citizens.

These are perhaps the most important of the Utopians. Their service has been mainly that of setting an ideal, the value of which has in all cases depended upon their adaptation to social conditions and human nature. The Utopians were all critics of their times, men filled with a "divine discontent" and a desire for social betterment, and men of broad and constructive imagination. If they have been dismissed as "dreamers" it is because they tended to fly too far from reality. Their flight may reflect a frank confession that the affairs of the world were too much for them and may be a deliberate turning to a "dream world" by way of escape from reality. It must be remembered, too, that direct and open criticism is a rare privilege—and one more often denied than granted; so that criticism in many cases had to be veiled in the obscurity of allegory and fanciful reference to avoid drastic retaliation by established powers. And in every case the author has labored under the handicap of the limit on existing knowledge and on the means of securing that knowledge.

Evolutionary Solutions. The scientific movement, which had slowly been developing during the first half of the nineteenth century, had not only introduced new scientific techniques in the shape of quantitative analysis and the inductive method, but also had witnessed the growth of a new attitude among scientists; namely, an increasing consideration of nature as a dynamic process rather than a static group of phenomena. Thus it was that the mutability of organisms had been realized for some time before Darwin's *Origin of Species* (1859). In the social field this principle had been sensed in a general way by Adam Smith, who held that the common human desire for self-improvement leads to social well-being and prosperity, a theory he developed in his treatise on *The Wealth of Nations* (1776). Smith's influence was instrumental in transforming economics from a philosophy into a science at a time when social thinkers were becoming decidedly concerned over the economic maladjustment incident to the Industrial Revolution. Godwin, in his *Political Justice* (1793), philosophically explained poverty as the result of exploitation of labor for profit under government protection. The freeing of reason from political interference and the spirit of gain was in his opinion the panacea for social ills. Condorcet, in his *Historical Sketch of the Progress of the Human Mind* (1793), had taken the similar view that improvement in social welfare would accompany human perfectibility. Malthus, with the first really scientific sociological study on *The Principle of Population* (1798), established a precedent in technique and offered startling conclusions that afforded a decided impetus to all subsequent activity in the field. By demonstrating the disparity between the rates of population growth and of the increase of food supply, he launched two fundamental concepts, *the law of diminishing returns* in economics, and *the struggle for existence* in biology.

We mention these writers and their works thus briefly in order to show the change in attitude toward the solution of these social problems. They represent a groping toward a scientific principle that it remained for Charles Darwin to formulate and set forth in the shape of the "evolutionary concept." The essential fact for us here is that Darwin showed that man as well as the whole of nature is governed throughout by the same laws. It was made clear that man, as an organism at least, has developed from lower stages to his present form by the fundamental processes of natural and sexual selection in the struggle for existence.

That this view should be carried over from organic life to social life was only natural. It was Walter Bagehot who, in his *Physics and Politics* (*circa* 1868), first attempted to show that society is also an evolutionary development. John Fiske pointed out, in his *Outlines of Cosmic Philosophy* (1874), that psychic changes have superseded physical in this development. Benjamin Kidd emphasized, in his *Social Evolution* (1894), the influence of religious faith in psychic evolution.

Karl Marx, whose theories are sketched more completely later in this chapter, must be classed among the evolutionary thinkers on the social problem, even though his doctrines do logically and eventually lead to revolution. He advanced the doctrine of *economic determinism* as the basis of social evolution and argued that the solution of the social problem would work itself out only through successive economic stages.

It remained for Spencer to tell the story of society and elucidate the solution of the social problem most completely from the evolutionary standpoint. His theory of the universe is based on evolution. Spencer went to great lengths, both scholastically and in the quantity of his writings, to show that this process goes on in every corner of creation. He argued that, in accordance with all existing forms, social forms and processes also develop according to natural selection and the survival of the fittest. He recognized the social problem as the poor adaptation of man to his surroundings. This is the cause of all unhappiness and friction. The problem is to establish *equilibrium*. Spencer argued that this is possible because human nature is modifiable. Through reaction to external conditions equilibrium is established first with animals, then with man, and finally with society, and this is secured through natural selection by the elimination of non-adapted individuals and social forms. Progress for this reason he regarded as natural and inevitable. The goal is *the ultimate happiness* which means the perfect reconciliation of the individual with social solidarity. Spencer's solution, then, in common with those of all the members of the evolutionary school of which he is the capstone and synthesizer, is to "let nature take its course." Evolution is the law of the universe, and since it is a process of change from indefinite, incoherent homogeneity to definite, coherent heterogeneity, *i.e.*, from disorganization to integrated efficiency, improvement is bound to come.

It is obvious that implicit belief in the evolutionary philosophy as represented by the foregoing writers is at least comforting, if not constructive. Remedial measures are for them merely gestures in the face of fate, which in its own good time will accomplish the desired changes through evolution. This means, as a logical corollary, a placid attitude of "hands off"—*laissez-faire*. But the great criticism of all *laissez-faire* philosophy is simply that it is not true to experience—social life is much too complex to be so easily explained by one principle. There are too many factors in social maladjustment to allow its eradication solely by the survival of the fittest.

We shall do well, also, to scrutinize the doctrine of "the survival of the fittest," if only because it has been used so often to condone socially ruthless policies or activities by exploitive individuals and groups. Its true meaning and implication should be clearly understood. Standing alone, the idea implies the presence of an absolute and final measure of fitness, which obviously does not exist in fact. It acquires validity only with reference to specific circumstances: a given form of life or adjustment can be "fittest" only at a given time and place and with regard to the special conditions prevailing then and there. The same form may be quite *unfit* in other times and places. It often happens, too, that further development of the very qualities that made for survival under certain conditions leads to unfitting the group or species for survival as times and conditions change. Indeed, this is the basic reason for the "extinction" of many species and social patterns alike.

Socialistic Solutions. There are two types of socialism at present that have considerable vitality. What has been called *Fabian socialism,* sometimes *guild socialism,* has to-day a wide following in many European countries and to a lesser extent in the United States, although strictly speaking it is British in origin. In theory it is State socialism, *i.e.,* it proposes that the State or municipality take over certain services and agencies of production, such as municipal utilities, coal-mines, railroads, and other monopolies. In that respect it is not very different from socialism on the Continent before the Russian revolution. On the Continent this kind of socialism is known as *opportunist* or *possibilist socialism.* These terms indicate its method—not by violent measures, but by waiting until the opportunity arrives when State ownership seems to the people to be the only promising way out of a difficulty. It uses the ordinary political machinery to put its principles into operation.

In contrast as to method, not as to aims and purposes, stands the *scientific socialism* of Karl Marx and his followers. Marx himself held the opinion that the capitalistic system holds in its nature the seeds of its own destruction. He believed that monopolistic control of the agencies of production is economically inevitable. But monopolies under capitalistic control operating for profit lead as inevitably to the exploitation of the workers, who alone produce, and result in the end in the overthrow by the workers of the capitalistic régime and in their control of the agencies of production. That is why this type of socialism is sometimes called *revolutionary socialism.* In Marx's mind it was *evolutionary.* The Russian Soviet Republic is the first actual experiment in this type of socialism.

In both these types of socialism it is clear that the fundamental basis of the solution is a change in the economic system. The socialists of both types believe that economic maladjustment is fundamental to all other adjustments. They are hard put to it to explain how their proposed change in the economic system will cure such maladjustments as come about from the biological inferiority of certain stocks. This comes out, for example, in Bonger's treatment of the matter in his *Criminality and Economic Conditions.* While he devotes a chapter to pathological criminals, he says that they are not really criminals and subjects for criminology: criminals are made only by economic conditions. Nothing could better exemplify the one-sided diagnosis and solution of the social problem. It should be said, however, that such Fabian socialists as the Webbs, while stressing the importance of the economic factors in social maladjustment, have a place in their scheme of reform for biological inferiority, for medicine, for psychology, and for sociology. While economic reorganization is fundamental, they do not ignore the other factors.

"Practical" Solutions of Social Problems. Those who insist that any solution must be "practical" are likely to reject all such idealistic schemes. By "practical" they mean that in order to solve social maladjustments we must face facts as they are and adopt means that are not too far removed from those with which people are familiar. They insist that "common sense" must dominate those who endeavor to correct evils in our social relationships. They hold that "Rome was not built in a day" and that a new social order cannot be created by any radical change that runs counter to the accepted beliefs, traditions, wonted ways of organization, and customs which are embedded in the everyday life of large numbers of people. One small change after another must be introduced, and thus gradually the whole maladjustment must be remedied. These people are not likely to become enamoured of any idealistic scheme, such as the Utopias we have just discussed, and are not sufficiently engulfed in any science to believe that the application of that science may alter the whole pattern of social life. Often they subscribe to some popular stereotype like that of "democracy," "education," "religion," "equality," "justice," "individual rights," or "natural law," or any number of them in combination. Certain ones believe that the tariff will solve our problems. Others take just the opposite stand, that free trade will solve our ills. Some may be persuaded that the income tax, or federal old-age pensions, or government sale of alcoholic liquors will solve the social evils. They, like the idealists, are disposed to think that the root of our social problems is the thing in which they have become most intensely interested. They have made no careful study of all the facts in the complex situation. What facts they have are often twisted to bolster up their beliefs. In many cases, too, "practical" solutions are supported by groups or individuals for basically *selfish* reasons; by promoting a particular program, they aspire to further their own social prestige, economic interests, or political power, as the case may be. It is true that *some* social good might come of adopting the proposals; but the benefits are likely to be distributed on a one-for-you-and-two-for-me basis, with society as a whole on the "short end" of the contract. This is especially

well illustrated by the legislative programs of the various "blocs" in Congress.

Others seem to believe that there is some magic potency in legislation and that anything can be brought to pass by having a law passed. In many situations the passage of a well-considered law with the proper sanctions does help. But how often laws are passed containing provisions that are at cross-purposes with the lines intended by the lawmaker or that run counter to the fundamental social and economic patterns of the time and that therefore become valueless! In the Middle Ages laws forbade the taking of interest on money lent. With the growth of commerce based upon a growing money economy rather than upon barter, the tendency was all against such a law. As a result it was circumvented by such devices as "bottomry" and a dozen others, and finally the law had to be changed. Laws on marriage and divorce illustrate the same situation. With changing conditions, old customs and laws give way to those better adapted to the new situation. On the other hand, sometimes laws are too far ahead of the changes in sentiments and customs of the people. If not too far ahead, they may be one means of hastening the process of social change.

Often these "practical" schemes, whether in the economic, the political, or the social field, are hit-or-miss experiments. People have not taken the trouble to ascertain the facts before they tried the experiment. Frequently those very experiments already have been tried elsewhere. If only the promoters had taken counsel of those who had already tested the proposal!

Too often these "practical" solutions simply are not founded upon a thorough study of the situation with which they are intended to deal. They are attempts to remedy a maladjustment by crude rule-of-thumb methods. In the absence of facts that would throw light upon the causes of the problem they are justifiable. When we cannot know what we should do, we are entitled to experiment. However, so great is the accumulation of knowledge both as to past experiments and as to the factors in a given maladjustment that it is no longer necessary to follow these wasteful, inadequate, and antiquated methods of solving our difficulties. As an example, consider how much more efficient is the legislation enacted in a State that has a Legislative Reference Bureau to provide information regarding the results of similar experiments elsewhere than that of those States where no such agency exists. In a great many fields sufficient facts have been accumulated to throw light upon the working of many proposed pieces of legislation and upon various methods of solving economic, political, and social maladjustment.

Furthermore, scientific analysis of many of our social problems has now developed to the place where even a new problem can be attacked to ascertain the underlying factors in the maladjustment. A careful investigation of the whole situation would often provide guidance as to the way to solve a difficulty had we the good sense to apply such a method rather than the costly one of rule-of-thumb experiment. Even in our census figures, inadequate as they are for many of our purposes, there lies a great mass of information at the present time too little used. Engineering and medicine illustrate the possibilities of the application of scientific methods to their problems, which methods have saved enormous sums of money and have given results that no amount of the old-fashioned crude experimenting would provide. Without the use of such methods the present-day sky-scraper, if possible at all, would be built at very much greater expense and with much less safety. Modern medicine and surgery would be quite impossible without modern science. Similar methods must be introduced for the solution of our social problems.

MODERN ONE-SIDED SCIENTIFIC APPROACHES TO THE SOLUTION OF SOCIAL PROBLEMS

Again and again in recorded human history there occurs a climax in the culture of a people that marks an epoch. Familiar instances are the Age of Pericles in Greece, the Golden Age of Augustus in Rome, the Italian Renaissance, the Elizabethan Age, and the Industrial Revolution in England. The advance in scientific knowledge began early in the latter half of the nineteenth century and is still "going strong." During these nine decades man has learned more about the universe in which he lives than had ever been discovered before. With indefatigable industry scientists have unlocked the mysteries of nature hitherto hidden. They have devised scientific methods that have affected every phase of human thought.

A number of the modern sciences touch the problem of social maladjustment. Among these are biology, physiological chemistry, medicine, psychology, psychiatry, economics, education, politics, and sociology.

Biology with its theories of heredity throws at least some light on why certain families produce leaders and inventors, great thinkers, and captains of industry, while other families give us generation after generation our paupers, insane, mental defectives, ne'er-do-wells, loafers, "cumberers of the ground." It has called attention to the importance of the human stock in the origin and the solution of social problems.

Physiological chemistry has studied the function of the secretion of the various glands of the human body. In recent years, it has been giving attention to the function of the secretions of the ductless glands in regulating the physiological balance of the bodily organism. Certain enthusiasts in this field have held that conduct is the result of the way in which these various glands function. The more conservative scholars, however, judge that much careful study must yet be made before confident statements as to the bearing of gland-functioning on conduct can be decided. Likewise they have made great strides in giving us a better understanding of nutrition and food problems, poisons, allergies, vitamins, and kindred matters.

The psychologists since the turn of the present century have analyzed the working of the human mind as never before. As a result we now have new insight into how the human mind works, the nature of the emotions, what intelligence is, and how intelligence, emotion, and action are determined. Especially the students of abnormal psychology, the psychiatrists have uncovered the genesis and development of those abnormal mental states which lead so inevitably to social maladjustment. Here again there has been a tendency among some of the more enthusiastic to claim that psychology can furnish the solution of all social difficulties. They point out the large number of mentally defective or mentally disordered persons among the social failures. They leave one with the impression that psychology and psychiatry have said the last word on the solution of the social problem. They agree in part with the geneticists that control of the human stock is one answer to social ills. They point out, however, that mental and emotional disorders may arise in cases where there is no known hereditary defect. They also place much more emphasis than the eugenists on the part played in mental disorder by one's experience.

There is a certain school of economic determinists, the Marxian socialists, who believe that all social maladjustment is due to the economic organization. Their panacea is the reorganization of the economic life of society. The present capitalistic organization of society, in their view, accounts for poverty, crime, sexual irregularity, and even mental defect and disorder. With our economic arrangements based upon State ownership of the instruments of production, they contend, all these evils and many others would automatically disappear. The greed and selfishness of men, now generated and emphasized by our capitalistic system with its stress upon profits, would disappear, and in their stead would appear unselfishness and mutual aid, kindness and coöperation. Here again we have a lopsided explanation of social maladjustment, and a unilateral solution.

Again, there is a class of sociologists who hold that the social circumstances of an individual account for his behavior, making him a good citizen or a social parasite. They tend to belittle the influence of heredity, the importance of psychology, the economic organization of society, and the chemistry of the human body. Their diagnosis of the problem is based upon a one-sided study of social organization in its influence upon the individual. They are as off-center as any of these other special pleaders.

To one acquainted with the progress of the various sciences bearing upon the understanding of human conduct, all of these special approaches are inadequate. Man in organized society is a much more complex being than any of these advocates would have us believe. His conduct is the result of a large number of factors. First, he is an animal. As a biological organism he operates in much the same way as other biological organisms of the same general order of mammals. Like all others he has two great hungers—food and sex. But he is a more complex biological organism than any other by reason of his much more highly developed brain. In a much greater degree than other animals, his conduct is determined not only by instincts but also by reason and social sanctions, such as shame, approval and disapproval, tradition, custom, and prestige among his fellows. Many of these other factors in his conduct conflict with aboriginal instincts and tendencies. Consider the infinitely complex nature of his brain as compared with that of lower animals. How delicate must be the adjustments between the millions of brain cells to insure the coördinated activities necessary to successful human conduct in a highly complex social order like that of the twentieth century! How easily upset is that delicate balance between body and brain one sees among the inmates of a hospital for the insane! How necessary it is that the quality of the brain be of a high order in modern society is revealed by the conduct of imbeciles and morons—and it may be added, by the failures of those who are just above the level of the mental defective. Moreover, how upon this delicate organism beat those social contrivances, the product of man's social experiments—the ambitions, the ideals, aspirations, standards, customs, traditions, of the group! If the individual quits his group with its wonted complex of social arrangements, as happens in the vast migration movements of the present, there arises a situation that calls for adjustments of the most radical nature, for a high degree of mental plasticity and originality on the part of the individual. Only the well-integrated personality can meet that situation satisfactorily. The others fail—fail when they probably would not, had they remained in a situation to which they were adjusted.

Consider also the situation in a highly dynamic society, as compared with one in which the situation is changing only slowly, or not at all. Every swift change in social life demands adjustments requiring a high level of mental ability. Many fail to make those adjustments or else make the adjustments after the manner of parasites.

These considerations make it apparent that scientific approach to social maladjustment must be many-sided. The social scientist must take into consideration *all* the facts of the social situation. He must know the nature of the individual as the psychologist and the psychiatrist, as the biologist and the physiological chemist, know him. He cannot ignore economics and politics. He must understand social psychology. He must know his sociology—how human aggregates come together, spread, develop social institutions, organize for various purposes, and control their members. Even then with the synthesis of all the knowledge available he will have difficulty. But only that way lies hope of success.

"PLANNED" SOLUTIONS

Inspired to some extent by the example of the Union of Social Soviet Republics of Russia during the 1920's, and driven by the persistent and increasing economic difficulties of the 1930's, all the major powers of the world have in the past score of years resorted to "social planning" for the solution of their social and economic problems. The main outlines of social planning are everywhere the same. It entails a more or less complete organization of the economic and social life of a nation, the control being exercised by the political machinery of the country. The government becomes the focal point or medium through which the activities of the citizenry are organized to execute as efficiently as possible general plans looking toward a strong nation. As social planning has developed, the life of every individual within the nation has become minutely controlled in the attempt to create national power and unity. And it is precisely at this point that the dangers of social planning arise. Clearly, modern life has grown so complex and the processes of economic production and social contact so huge, that there are many individuals who cannot possibly make effective decisions for themselves. Authority to-day must be delegated and centralized in order that the social group may function with any degree of success; yet that very fact makes for enormous power in the hands of the leaders and a virtually complete submission by everyone to the will of those leaders. How the common people will fare under such conditions depend upon both the nature of the professed plan to be followed by the nation and the motives and integrity of the leaders, but mainly upon the amount of veto power retained by the voters.

Social planning has been practiced under "communistic" (Soviet Russia), fascistic (Nazi Germany and Fascistic Italy), and democratic types of government in our times. "Communism" and fascism are similar in that the dictator has been the supreme authority, and all other individuals are expected to submit almost completely to the will of the dictator. The individual as such is of value only as an agent of the State, and everyone has a very definite job and status in the service of the State. But beyond this, the two systems are quite different. Under "communism" all productive wealth is owned by the State, and the government itself directs the productive efforts of the people. Fascism preserves at least the semblance of private ownership of productive wealth, even though the governmental control, to all practical purposes, is as complete as under "communism." Russian "communism" has retained a larger degree of popular control over basic policies that has been accomplished in any of the fascist countries; and the objectives of "social planning" are more directly those of public welfare than are those of the fascists. Fascism has been intensely nationalistic, and its dictators have proven ruthlessly aggressive in their quest for power, both in their internal and foreign policies, while the communists have not been characterized by any extensive plans for conquest.

We in the democratic countries have turned to social planning more recently than the totalitarian nations. Especially here in the United States, our *laissez-faire* tradition in economic affairs has made the idea of social planning seem quite foreign to us. Yet we ourselves have resorted to it now and again in emergency, ever since the days when colonists occasionally were driven to rigid organization and discipline as a hard matter of sheer survival amidst the rigors of primitive life. Nevertheless, the social planning of democracy is distinctive in comparison with that of fascism or "communism," mainly as to its purposes and the degree to which the citizenry retains its basic control over the planners. Motives of planning are more clearly those of public welfare, while the delegation of authority has been qualified, for specific periods of time, and is subject to ratification by legislative or direct popular ballot. Moreover, the means of re-capturing that authority and power still remain effective, so long as the secret and free ballot and the rights of free speech and assembly are retained. Thus abuses of power or perversion of purposes by the leaders can be more easily noted and corrected in a democracy than in either of the other major systems of government.

THE SCIENTIFIC ATTACK UPON SOCIAL PROBLEMS

It is not likely that we know enough at present to solve the problem of how to adjust man to his surroundings or how to adapt the social machinery to each individual so as to give each one a chance to develop whatever capacity he has. Do we know enough of heredity to enable even the most enthusiastic eugenist to say just what stocks should be selected for elimination, just what matings should be made in the interest of race betterment and social welfare? He will insist that hereditary imbeciles should not reproduce, and perhaps indicate a few types of the hereditary insane that should not propagate. But even if the most radical elimination of the "unfit" were practiced, are we sure that social conditions might not be producing more weaklings and psychotics? Do we know enough of the interrelation of social stress and conduct to enable us to say just what strains should be permitted to different people? The First World War showed us that certain persons can with safety be subjected to much more severe strain than others. How can we pick each kind out beforehand and adjust social circumstance to their capacities? In a general way we know that under certain conditions immigrants have a tendency to be social failures, but we see others who under the same circumstances suceed. It seems that illegitimate children and orphans have a higher expectancy of criminality than the legitimate and non-orphans. Yet there are enough cases to the contrary to lead us to suspect that our knowledge is not yet of that exactitude and certainty to enable us to predict what will happen under a given set of circumstances. Many other examples might be given to show the necessity of further and more exact knowledge before we can expect to do as good a job of social engineering as the bridge-builder does in mechanical engineering. *Research and experiment, then, are the first steps in a scientific attempt to solve social problems.*

Nevertheless, in spite of the great gaps in our knowledge, we know enough to make a beginning. Since we must attempt in the interests of society to solve this problem of the adjustment of man to the world in which he lives, is it not good sense to use all the knowledge we have, rather than some highly speculative guesses? If we must experiment, will it not be wise to be guided in our experiments by all that science at present can afford us—*all* the sciences?

Does it not seem reasonable that one who attempts to make suggestions should take into account, for example, what biology has discovered as to the hereditary transmission of capacity and defect? So with the other sciences that throw light on the nature of man and of his world. We would not be so foolish as to attempt to build a house without reference to the law of gravitation, or to what is known about the stresses that building material will stand. The builder takes into account pertinent facts from every science. So in the solution of social problems—the adjustment of man to his world—all sciences must share.

It is clear enough that in general terms the social problems we have discussed grow out of maladjustment of the individual and his circumstances. Either he is by nature and training not adapted to the world in which he lives and is expected to function, or else the universe in which he finds himself is not adjusted to his capacities. One of the great contributions of Darwin to our understanding of the infinite variety of life on our planet was the theory that the production of beings adapted to a given situation came about by a rigid natural selection for death of those not adaptable. Curiously, however, adaptation to the circumstances of life gradually becomes artificial. The birds learn to build nests and to migrate from cold to warm climates. Some of the animals burrow in the ground and lay up stores of food. Indeed, as Kropotkin long ago pointed out, animals learn to coöperate through what he called "mutual aid" and thus circumvent a rigid natural selection. Thus wolves hunt in packs, cattle graze in herds and on being attacked by enemies gather together with horns out and with the calves on the inside of the circle. Cattle, horses, and sheep in a storm gather together in a body, apparently both for bodily warmth and to prevent straying. Moreover, certain animals attach themselves to others as parasites and thus prevent destruction of themselves. In these and other ways the lower animals to a certain extent bend nature to their purposes.

Man has carried the process of mutual aid and the adaptation of nature to his purposes to a higher point than that of any of the lower animals. The story of mankind from prehistory to modern civilization has been an account of the progressive development of mutual aid and the conquest of the material universe in a unique degree. The former has given him his sentiments of mercy and kindness, concern for the helpless, the aged, the child, the weak—and tolerance for the socially worthless. The latter has enabled him to spread to all parts of the globe and contrive living conditions and luxuries impossible to any other being. His very success in the control of nature has produced some of his social problems. His exploitation of nature's resources has made it possible for him to live and multiply in regions of the earth naturally hostile to man as a mere animal. Millions can be supported where it was possible without his modern control of nature for only hundreds to exist.

Organization of economic life, while making possible the production of undreamed-of quantities of consumption goods, and while permitting the multiplication of population to an unheard-of degree, has not proceeded with equal pace in the distribution of goods in accordance with economic need, and has given little attention to the adjustment of population to economic production and distribution. Man has not progressed in the adjustment of means to social ends as he has in the adjustment of means to economic production. He has not given the same attention to the improvement of the racial stock as he has to the conquest of physical Nature. His sympathetic toleration and aid of the unfit has not been guided by scientific considerations. While he has applied all he can learn from science to the control of nature for his purposes, he has neglected what science has to tell him about the control of the human element. While man long ago abandoned the doctrine of *laissez-faire* in his struggle with physical Nature, he has continued to deal with human nature largely on that basis. The consequence is that much of human nature is not adapted to the complex conditions of modern life, and man's social organization is not adjusted to secure a race adapted to modern life, and is only partially adjusted to train human beings for successful struggle with its conditions.

On the basis of modern knowledge what is needed, then, to solve these social problems is: (1) measures calculated to produce individuals of such native capacity as can under the proper conditions adjust themselves to the complex conditions of modern life; (2) such adjustment of our social organization as will provide for each individual the opportunities to develop himself to his utmost capacity and to direct his efforts to the highest social purposes.

Implicit in these two suggestions are a number of things: (1) Negative eugenics, *i.e.*, by sterilization, segregation, or education to limit the propagation of stock innately unfit to cope with modern conditions of life. (2) Positive eugenics, *i.e.*, promotion of such selection of mates as modern biological knowledge indicates will produce capable children. (3) The perfection of our educational system in the direction of preparing every individual to make the most of his capacities in modern society. Such an educational system probably will have to utilize all agencies that mold public opinion, including not only the school, but also the press, the platform, the screen, the stage, and the radio. Such education must endeavor to reach not only the students in the schools but also the workers and leaders in the active conduct of affairs. It must be depended on so to modify the social ideals, customs, and attitudes established in the mores of the people as to meet the changed conditions of society growing out of new inventions, new knowledge, and new industrial processes. (4) The modification of our political machinery, such as the legal and administrative agencies, to keep pace with new knowledge and to put into effect the changes made necessary by scientific investigation. (5) Research agencies to explore the fields of human action, motivation, and organization. Much more study must be given to human heredity before we shall know just how to control population. We have just begun the probing into psychology, especially social psychology. How little we know about how social ideals are produced, how customs are established, how traditions form, and how the individual is affected by the play of social influences upon his developing personality! We have only guesses as to the results of our present institutions—such as orphanages, almshouses, prisons, factories, and even schools, churches, and homes—upon the persons who are under their influence. Great social experiments are going on all about us, but there is very little attempt to learn how they affect the human beings they touch. In short, we do not know enough yet to enable us to say with confidence just what changes ought to be made to solve social problems. (6) Finally, we need to devise methods whereby the results of scientific research may be made the property of the people. Tuberculosis is yielding not to the doctor's knowledge of its nature and how to prevent it, but to the dissemination of that knowledge among the people generally. While we know enough now about insanity to prevent much of it, mental disorder still occurs partly because the knowledge of how to prevent it is not widely disseminated among the people. Some of us are certain that jails are a social menace, but the people as a whole are quite unaware that there is anything wrong with them. We know enough about sterilization now to enable us to say that some mental defectives can be sterilized with great benefit to society, but the people—and many judges—do not. So with a great many other matters. What we do not yet know we must learn. What we learn must become common property.

These suggestions are not such as will appeal to panacea-hunters.

There is no short-cut to a solution, in spite of the number and the vociferousness of the short-cut prophets. If it has taken the long and patient research and experimentation of hundreds of physicists and chemists to solve certain problems of our physical universe, why suppose that the vastly more complicated problem of human relationships can be solved in a day? In that quarter only, however, lies hope. The long and tedious way ahead should appeal to those spirits who yearn for a more perfect social order—the followers of Utopia, those dreamers of the Kingdom of God who can with patience possess their souls. For the rest—those who look for instant remedies, who must find a short-cut to the Kingdom of God—one can only hope that their tribe will not increase.

REFERENCES

BEARD, Charles A., and BEARD, Mary R., *America in Midpassage* (New York, 1939), Chs. 16, 17.

DAVIS, Jerome, *Contemporary Social Movements* (New York, 1930).

EDWARDS, Lyford P., *The Natural History of Revolution* (Chicago, 1927), Ch. X.

GABRIEL, Ralph H., *The Course of American Democratic Thought* (New York, 1940).

KASTLER, N. M., *Modern Human Relations* (Boston, 1940), Chs. 27, 29.

LICHTENBERGER, J. P., *Development of Social Theory* (New York, 1925).

MACKENZIE, Findlay, *Planned Society, Yesterday, Today, Tomorrow* (New York, 1937).

PERRY, Ralph B., *Shall Not Perish From the Earth* (New York, 1939).

RUSSELL, Bertrand, *Proposed Roads To Freedom* (New York, 1933).

SMALL, Albion W., *The Meaning of Social Science* (Chicago, 1910).

THOMAS, Norman, *The Choice Before Us* (New York, 1934).

QUESTIONS AND EXERCISES

1. What is meant in the text by "*the* social problem"? In what sense do social problems grow out of the social problem?
2. How do you account for the one-sidedness of the Utopias described in the text? Why are they so generally impractical?
3. Why are the one-sided explanations of the social problem inadequate?
4. Utopias thrive best in times of depression. What Utopias developed out of the hard times prior to the Second World War?
5. How far would you agree with the statement that "economic maladjustment is the root of all social evils"?
6. Can vital social reform ignore economic inequalities? Discuss.
7. Why should we distrust the "practical" solutions of our social problems?
8. Of what value were the various Utopias if we cannot accept their various solutions of the social problem?

9. What is the nature of modern social planning? What fundamental dangers are inherent in the development of social planning?
10. Show the differences in the methods and objectives of social planning under (a) communism; (b) fascism; (c) democracy.
11. What are some of the problems involved in any effective action proposed to solve a given set of social problems?
12. Why is research so important a step at this time in any attempt to solve our social problems?

INDEX OF NAMES

INDEX OF SUBJECTS

(15)

DATE DUE

DEMCO 38-297